Oxford Handbook of Endocrinology and Diabetes

Oxford Handbook of Endocrinology and Diabetes

Helen E Turner
and
John A H Wass

OXFORD
UNIVERSITY PRESS

OXFORD
UNIVERSITY PRESS

Great Clarendon Street, Oxford OX2 6DP

Oxford University Press is a department of the University of Oxford. It furthers the University's objective of excellence in research, scholarship, and education by publishing worldwide in

Oxford New York

Auckland Cape Town Dar es Salaam Hong Kong Karachi Kuala Lumpur Madrid Melbourne Mexico City Nairobi New Delhi Shanghai Taipei Toronto

With offices in

Argentina Austria Brazil Chile Czech Republic France Greece Guatemala Hungary Italy Japan Poland Portugal Singapore South Korea Switzerland Thailand Turkey Ukraine Vietnam

Oxford is a registered trade mark of Oxford University Press in the UK and in certain other countries

Published in the United States by Oxford University Press Inc., New York

First published 2002
GSK edition printed 2007

British Library Cataloguing in Publication Data
Data available

Library of Congress Cataloging in Publication Data
Oxford handbook of endocrinology and diabetes / edited by Helen E. Turner and John A.H. Wass.

1. Endocrinology–Handbooks, mauals, etc. 2. Diabetes–Handbooks, manuals, etc. I. Turner, Helen, 1967– II. Wass, John.

RC649. O96 2001 616.4–dc21 2001052102

Typeset by EXPO Holdings, Malaysia
Printed in Italy
on acid-free paper by LegoPrint S.p.A.

ISBN 978–0–19–922854–6

10 9 8 7 6 5 4 3 2 1

Preface

Our aim with this handbook is to provide a readily assimilable 'white coat pocket' book in endocrinology and diabetes, which is complementary to the *Oxford Textbook of Endocrinology and Diabetes.* Our target audience is trainees and also the trained who may have the occasional mental blank.

We are grateful to our contributors for their excellent and timely efforts and we are particularly grateful to Richard Sheaves for his considerable help in planning the book.

We have necessarily been didactic, but in order to minimize the effects of personal idiosyncrasies, we have sent each chapter to two external referees. Their names are recorded elsewhere. We are very grateful indeed to this panel of experts and for the enormous trouble that they have taken in going through the manuscript with the utmost care.

We regard this volume as the start of an evolutionary process and the first of many editions. We encourage readers to write with constructive comments and suggestions.

Helen Turner
John Wass
Department of Endocrinology
Oxford Centre for Diabetes, Endocrinology and Metabolism
Radcliffe Infirmary
Oxford
UK

March 2002

Acknowledgements

We would like to record our sincere thanks to the following friends and colleagues for their review and advice on various sections:

Professor A B Atkinson, Metabolic Unit, Royal Victoria Hospital, Belfast
Dr JS Bevan, Department of Endocrinology, Aberdeen Royal Infirmary, Aberdeen
Dr P M Bouloux, Department of Endocrinology, Royal Free Hospital, London
Dr P E Clayton, Department of Child Health, Royal Manchester Children's Hospital, Manchester
Dr G S Conway, Cobbold Laboratories, Middlesex Hospital, London
Dr N Finer, Department of Endocrinology, Luton and Dunstable Hospital, Luton
Professor J A Franklyn, Department of Medicine, Queen Elizabeth Hospital, Birmingham
Professor S Franks, Department of Endocrinology, St Mary's Hospital Medical School, London
Professor AB Grossman, Department of Endocrinology, St Bartholomew's Hospital, London
Professor R R Holman, Diabetes Trials Unit, Oxford Centre for Diabetes, Endocrinology and Metabolism, Radcliffe Infirmary, Oxford
Professor D Hosking, Division of Mineral Medicine, City Hospital, Nottingham
Dr D R Matthews, Oxford Centre for Diabetes, Endocrinology and Metabolism, Radcliffe Infirmary, Oxford
Dr A Neil, Oxford Centre for Diabetes, Endocrinology and Metabolism, Radcliffe Infirmary, Oxford
Professor CWG Redman, Nuffield Department of Obstetrics and Gynaecology, John Radcliffe Hospital, Oxford
Professor M O Savage, Department of Paediatric Endocrinology, St Bartholomew's Hospital, London
Dr B Shine, Department of Biochemistry, John Radcliffe Hospital, Oxford
Professor PM Stewart, Department of Medicine, Queen Elizabeth Hospital, Edgbaston, Birmingham
Professor R Thakker, Nuffield Department of Medicine, John Radcliffe Hospital, Oxford and Oxford Centre for Diabetes, Endocrinology and Metabolism, Radcliffe Infirmary, Oxford
Professor A P Weetman, Clinical Science Centre, Northern General Hospital, Sheffield
Professor F Wu, Department of Endocrinology, Manchester Royal Infirmary, Manchester.

Contents

Part VIII
Neuroendocrine tumours of the gastrointestinal tract

Part IX
Inherited endocrine syndromes and multiple endocrine neoplasia

Part X
Miscellaneous endocrinology

Part XI
Diabetes

Foreword

In this day and age of the internet, multimedia materials, and interactive CDs it is easy to forget that old-fashioned method of learning and education – the book. I suspect that many like myself still prefer to look things up in a book rather than wrestle with a computer. There are two main types of book – the reference book and the handy manual. The former is useful when you wish to review a topic in depth or look up an uncommon condition or presentation, but often one wants to check a simple detail, for example a reference range or diagnostic criterion. Handbooks are ideal for this as they can be carried around or kept easily available. The current work is an ideal example. It is packed with useful information and is very up to date – something not shared by most major textbooks. It is ideally suited for the specialist registrar in endocrinology and diabetes – and even more so for the ageing consultant. It will also be useful in general practice with specific regard to the diabetes and thyroid sections. This is extremely important with the development of primary care diabetes clinics and the explosive rise in prevalence of diabetes, particularly in non-Europeans. It contains many helpful practical nuggets and will, I am sure, be required briefcase or pocket content. It fills a gap in an important area of clinical practice. The authors and publishers are to be commended – I just hope that the next edition has already been planned.

Professor Sir George Alberti
President
Royal College of Physicians
London, UK

Contributors

David B Dunger Department of Paediatrics, University of Cambridge, Cambridge, UK

Mohgah Elsheikh Department of Diabetes and Endocrinology, Royal Berkshire Hospital, Reading, Berkshire, UK

Ken Ong Department of Paediatrics, University of Cambridge, Cambridge, UK

Mahesh Sathiavageeswaran Department of Endocrinology, Oxford Centre for Diabetes, Endocrinology and Metabolism, Radcliffe Infirmary, Oxford OX2 6HE, UK

Barry M Seemungal Department of Endocrinology, Oxford Centre for Diabetes, Endocrinology and Metabolism, Radcliffe Infirmary, Oxford OX2 6HE, UK

Peter Selby Department of Medicine, Manchester Royal Infirmary, Oxford Road, Manchester M13 9WL, UK

Richard Sheaves Division of Medicine, Jersey Hospital, Jersey, Channel Islands

Kevin P Shotliff Department of Medicine, Kingston Hospital, Kingston upon Thames, Surrey KT2 7QB, UK

Garry D Tan Oxford Centre for Diabetes, Endocrinology and Metabolism, Radcliffe Infirmary, Oxford OX2 6HE, UK

Helen E Turner Department of Endocrinology, Oxford Centre for Diabetes, Endocrinology and Metabolism, Radcliffe Infirmary, Oxford OX2 6HE, UK

John A H Wass Department of Endocrinology, Oxford Centre for Diabetes, Endocrinology and Metabolism, Radcliffe Infirmary, Oxford OX2 6HE, UK

H John Wong Department of Clinical Biochemistry, Kingston Hospital, Kingston upon Thames, Surrey KT2 7QB, UK

Abbreviations

ACE	angiotensin converting enzyme
ACEI	angiotensin converting enzyme inhibitor
AD	autosomal dominant
ADA	American Diabetes Association
ADH	antidiuretic hormone
AGE	advanced glycation end-products
AIH	amiodarone-induced hypothyroidism
AIT	amiodarone-induced thyrotoxicosis
ALT	alanine transaminase
ANP	atrial natriuretic peptide
ART	assisted reproductive techniques
AST	aspartate transaminase
ATD	antithyroid drug
BMD	bone mineral density
BP	blood pressure
CaE	calcium excretion
CAH	congenital adrenal hyperplasia
CBG	cortisol binding globulin
CHD	coronary heart disease
CMV	cytomegalovirus
CPA	cyproterone acetate
CRF	chronic renal failure
CRH	corticotrophin releasing hormone
CSF	cerebrospinal fluid
CSII	continuous subcutaneous insulin infusion
CSW	cerebral salt wasting syndrome
CT	computed tomography
CVP	central venous pressure
DCCT	Diabetes Control and Complications Trial
DCT	distal convolutued tubule
DHEA	dihydroepiandrostenedione

DHT	dihydrotestosterone
DI	diabetes insipidus
DIDMOAD	*d*iabetes *i*nsipidus, *DM*, *o*ptic *a*trophy + sensorineural *d*eafness (Wolfram's syndrome)
DVLA	Driver and Vehicle Licensing Agency
DVT	deep vein thrombosis
DXA	dual energy X-ray absorptiometry
EE2	ethinyl oestradiol
ESR	erythrocyte sedimentation rate
ESRF	end-stage renal failure
ETDRS	Early Treatment of Diabetic Retinopathy Study
FBC	full blood count
FCHL	familial combined hyperlipidaemia
FDB	familial defective apolipoprotein B-100
FH	familial hypercholesterolaemia
FHH	familial hypocalciuric hypercalcaemia
FNAC	fine needle aspiration cytology
FSH	follicle stimulating hormone
FTC	follicular carcinoma
GAD	glutamic acid decarboxylase
GFR	glomerular filtation rate
GH	growth hormone
GHD	growth hormone deficiency
GI	gastrointestinal
GIFT	gamete intrafallopian transfer
GIP	gastric inhibitory peptide
GRTH	generalized resistance to thyroid hormone
hCG	human chorionic gonadotrophin
HDL	high-density lipoprotein
5HIAA	5-hydroxyindole acetic acid
HLA	human leukocyte antigens
HMG CoA	3-hydroxy-3-methylglutaryl coenzyme A
HNF	hepatic nuclear factor
HPA	hypothalmic–pituitary–adrenal (axis)
HSG	hysterosalpingography
HZV	herpes zoster virus
ICSI	intracytoplasmic sperm injection

IDDM	insulin dependent diabetes mellitus (type 1)
IDL	intermediate-density lipoprotein
IFG	impaired fasting hyperglycaemia
IGF-I	insulin-like growth factor-1
IGT	impaired glucose tolerance
IHH	idiopathic hypogonadotrophic hypogonadism
IPSS	inferior petrosal sinus sampling
IRMA	intraretinal microvascular abnormalities
ITT	insulin tolerance test
IU	international units
IUGR	intrauterine growth retardation
IUI	intrauterine insemination
IVF	*in vitro* fertilization
KS	Kaposi sarcoma
LCAT	lecithin : cholesterol acyltransferase
LDL	low-density lipoprotein
LFT	liver function test
LH	luteinizing hormone
MAI	Mycobacterium aviium intracellulare
MC	mineralocorticoid
MEN	multiple endocrine neoplasia
MHC	major histocompatibility complex
MI	myocardial infarct
MIBG	^{123}Iodine-metaiodobenzylguanidine
MIS	mullerian inhibitory substance
MODY	maturity onset diabetes of the young
MPH	mid-parental height
MRSA	methicillin-resistant *Staphylococcus aureus*
MTC	medullary thyroid cancer
NF	neurofibromatosis
NFA	non-functioning pituitary adenoma
NGF	nerve growth factor
NICH	non-islet cell hypoglycaemia
NIDDM	non-insulin dependent diabetes mellitus (type 2)
NVD	new vessels on the disc (diabetic retinopathy)
NVE	new vessels elsewhere (diabetic retinopathy)
OCP	oral contraceptive pill

OGTT	oral glucose tolerance test
25OHD	25-hydroxy vitamin D
17OHP	17-hydroxyprogesterone
OHSS	ovarian hyperstimulation syndrome
PAI	platelet activator inhibitor
PCOS	polycystic ovary syndrome
PCT	postcoital test
PET	positron emission spectrography
PID	pelvic inflammatory disease
PIH	pregnancy-induced hypertension
PMC	papillary microcarcinoma of the thyroid
PNMT	phenylethanolamine-*N*-methyl transferase
POF	premature ovarian failure
POMC	pro-opiomelanocortin
PP	pancreatic polypeptide
PPAR	peroxisome proliferator activated receptor
PRL	prolactin
PRTH	pituitary resistance to thyroid hormones
PSA	prostatic specific antigen
PTH	parathyroid hormone
PTHrP	parathyroid hormone related peptide
QALY	Quality Adjusted Life Year
QCT	quantitative computed tomography
QUS	quantitative ultrasound
SHBG	sex hormone binding globulin
T_3	tri-iodothyronine
T_4	thyroxine
TB	tuberculosis
TBG	T_4-binding globulin
TBPA	T_4-binding prealbumin
TFT	thyroid function test
TG	triglycerides
TGF	transforming growth factor
TNF	tumour necrosis factor
TPO	thyroid peroxidase
TRH	thyrotropin releasing hormone
TSAb	TSH stimulating antibodies

TSG	tumour suppressor genes
TSH	thyroid stimulating hormone
TSH-RAB	TSH receptor antibodies
TTR	transthyretin
U&Es	urea and electolytes
UFC	urinary free cortisol
UKPDS	UK Prospective Diabetes Study
VEGF	vascular endothelial growth factor
VHL	Von Hippel–Lindau disease
VIP	vasoactive intestinal peptide
VLDL	very high-density lipoprotein
WDHA	watery diarrhoea, hypokalaemia, and achlorhydria
WHO	World Health Organization
ZE	Zollinger Ellison syndrome

Part I
Thyroid

Chapter 1

Anatomy and physiology of the thyroid

Anatomy

The thyroid gland comprises

- a midline isthmus lying horizontally just below the cricoid cartilage
- two lateral lobes that extend upward over the lower half of the thyroid cartilage.

The gland lies deep to the strap muscles of the neck, enclosed in the pre-tracheal fascia, which anchors it to the trachea, so that the thyroid moves up on swallowing.

Histology

- Fibrous septa divide the gland into pseudolobules.
- Pseudolobules are composed of vesicles called follicles or acini, surrounded by a capillary network.
- The follicle walls are lined by cuboidal epithelium.
- The lumen is filled with a proteinaceous colloid, which contains the unique protein thyroglobulin. The peptide sequences of T_4 and T_3 are synthesized and stored as a component of thyroglobulin.

Development

- Develops from the endoderm of the floor of the pharynx with some contribution from the lateral pharyngeal pouches.
- Descent of the midline thyroid anlage gives rise to the thyroglossal duct, which extends from the foramen caecum near the base of the tongue to the isthmus of the thyroid.
- During development the posterior aspect of the thyroid becomes associated with the parathyroid gland and the parafollicular C cells, derived from the ultimo-branchial body, which become incorporated into its substance.
- The C cells are the source of calcitonin and give rise to medullary thyroid carcinoma when they undergo malignant transformation.
- The foetal thyroid begins to concentrate and organify iodine at about 10–12 weeks gestation.
- Maternal TRH readily crosses the placenta, maternal TSH and T_4 do not.
- T_4 from the foetal thyroid is the major thyroid hormone available to the foetus. The foetal pituitary–thyroid axis is a functional unit distinct from that of the mother.

Thyroid examination

Inspection

- Look at the neck from the front. If a goitre (enlarged thyroid gland of whatever cause) is present, the patient should be asked to swallow. Goitre moves up with swallowing.
- Watch for appearance of any nodule not visible before swallowing, e.g. retrosternal goitre in the elderly.

Palpation

- Is the thyroid gland tender to touch?
- With index and middle finger feel below thyroid cartilage where the isthmus of the thyroid gland lies over the trachea.
- Palpate the two lobes of the thyroid, which extend laterally behind the sternomastoid muscle.
- Ask the patient to swallow again while you continue to palpate the thyroid.
- Assess *size,* whether it is *soft,* firm *or hard,* it is *nodular* or *diffusely* enlarged and whether it *moves* readily on swallowing.
- Palpate along the medial edge of the sternomastoid muscle on either side to look for a pyramidal lobe.
- Palpate for lymph nodes

Percussion

- Percuss upper mediastinum for retrosternal goitre.

Auscultation

- Auscultate to identify bruits, consistent with Graves' disease.
- Occasionally inspiratory stridor can be heard with a large or retrosternal goitre causing tracheal compression.

Assess thyroid status

- Observe for signs of thyroid disease – exophthalmos, proptosis, thyroid acropachy, pretibial myxoedema, hyperactivity, restlessness, or whether immobile and uninterested.
- Take pulse; note presence or absence of tachycardia, bradycardia or atrial fibrillation.
- Feel palms – whether warm and sweaty or cold.
- Look for tremor in outstretched arms.
- Examine eyes:
  exophthalmos (sclera visible above lower lid); lid retraction: sclera visible above cornea; lid lag; conjuctivitis; periorbital oedema; loss of full-range movement

Physiology

- Thyroid hormone contains iodine. Iodine enters the thyroid in the form of inorganic or ionic iodide, which is oxidized by a peroxidase enzyme at the cell–colloid interface. Subsequent reactions result in the formation of iodothyronines.
- The thyroid is the only source of T_4.
- The thyroid secretes 20% of T_3; the remainder is generated in extraglandular tissues by the conversion of T_4 to T_3.

Synthesis of the thyroid hormones can be inhibited by a variety of agents termed *goitrogens.*

- Perchlorate and thiocyanate inhibit iodide transport
- Thioureas and mercaptoimidazole inhibit the initial oxidation of iodide and coupling of iodothyronines.
- In large doses iodine itself blocks organic binding and coupling reactions.
- Lithium has several inhibitory effects on intrathyroidal iodine metabolism.

In the blood, T_4 and T_3 are almost entirely bound to plasma proteins. T_4 is bound in decreasing order of intensity to T_4 binding globulin (TBG), transthyretin (TTR), and albumin. T_3 is bound 10–20 times less firmly by TBG and not significantly by TTR. Only the free or unbound hormone is available to tissues. The metabolic state correlates more closely with the free than the total hormone concentration in the plasma. The relatively weak binding of T_3 accounts for its more rapid onset and offset of action. Table 1.1 summarizes those states associated with primary alterations in the concentration of TBG. When there is primarily an alteration in the concentration of thyroid hormones, the concentration of TBG changes little (Table 1.2).

Concentration of free hormones does not vary directly with that of the total hormones; e.g. while the total T_4 level rises in pregnancy, the free T_4 level remains normal.

The levels of thyroid hormone in the blood are tightly controlled by feedback mechanisms involved in the hypothalamo–pituitary–thyroid axis (Fig. 1.1).

- TSH secreted by the pituitary stimulates the thyroid to secrete principally T_4 and also T_3. TRH stimulates the synthesis and secretion of TSH. T_4 and T_3 inhibit TSH synthesis and secretion directly.

Table 1.1 Disordered thyroid hormone–protein interactions

	Serum total T_4 and T_3	Free T_4 and T_3
Primary abnormality in TBG		
▲Concentration	↑	Normal
▼Concentration	↓	Normal
Primary disorder of thyroid function		
Hyperthyroidism	↑	↑
Hypothyroidism	↓	↓

- T_4 and T_3 are bound to TBG, TTR, and albumin. The remaining free hormones inhibit synthesis and release of TRH to influence growth and metabolism.

Table 1.2 Circumstances associated with altered concentration of TBG

Increased TBG	Decreased TBG
Pregnancy	Androgens
Newborn state	Large doses of glucocorticoids; Cushings' syndrome
OCP and other sources of oestrogens	Chronic liver disease
Tamoxifen	Severe systemic illness
Hepatitis A; chronic active hepatitis	Active acromegaly
Biliary cirrhosis	Nephrotic syndrome
Acute intermittent porphyria	Genetically determined
Genetically determined	Drugs, e.g. phenytoin

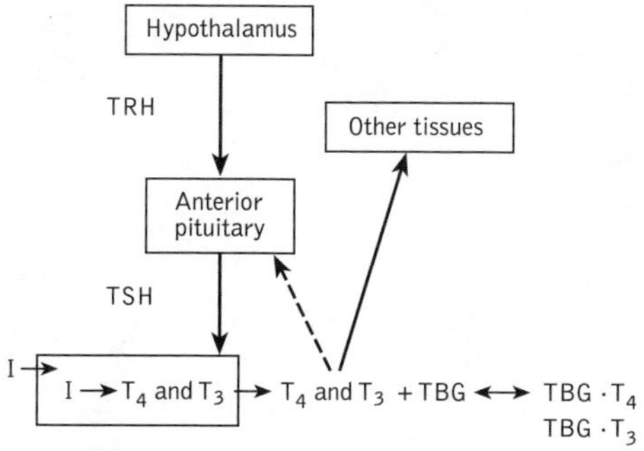

Fig. 1.1 Regulation of thyroid function. Solid arrows indicate stimulation, broken arrow indicates inhibitory influence. TRH, thyrotropin releasing hormone; TSH, thyroid stimulating hormone; T_4, thyroxine; T_3, tri-iodothyronine; I, iodine; TBG, thyroid binding globulin.

- T_4 is converted peripherally to the metabolically active T_3 or the inactive reverse T_3 (rT_3).
- T_4 and T_3 are metabolized in the liver by conjugation with glucuronate and sulfate. Enzyme inducers such as phenobarbital, carbamazepine, and phenytoin increase the metabolic clearance of the hormones without decreasing the proportion of free hormone in the blood.

Abnormalities of development

- Remnants of the thyroglossal duct may be found in any position along the course of the tract of its descent:
  - in the tongue, it is referred to as '*lingual thyroid*'
  - *thyroglossal cysts* may be visible as midline swellings in the neck
  - *thyroglossal fistula* develops an opening in the middle of the neck.
  - *thyroglossal nodules* or
  - the '*pyramidal lobe*', a structure contiguous with the thyroid isthmus which extends upwards.
- The gland can descend too far down to reach the anterior mediastinum.
- Congenital hypothyroidism results from failure of the thyroid to develop.

Chapter 2
Thyroid investigations

Tests of hormone concentration

(Table 2.1)

Highly specific and sensitive radioimmunoassays are used to measure serum T4 and T3 concentrations. Free hormone concentrations usually correlate better with the metabolic state than do total hormone concentrations because they are unaffected by changes in binding protein concentration or affinity.

Tests of homeostatic control

- Serum TSH concentration is used as first line in the diagnosis of primary hypothyroidism and hyperthyroidism. The test is misleading in patients with secondary thyroid dysfunction.
- The TRH stimulation test, which can be used to assess the functional state of the TSH secretory mechanism, is now rarely used to diagnose primary thyroid disease since it has been superseded by sensitive TSH assays. It is of limited use; its main use is in the differential diagnosis of elevated TSH in the setting of elevated thyroid hormone levels.

In interpreting results of TFTs, the effects of drugs that the patient might be on should be borne in mind. Table 2.2 lists the influence of drugs on TFTs.

Table 2.1 Thyroid hormone concentrations in various thyroid abnormalities

Condition	TSH	Free T_4	Free T_3
Primary hyperthyroidism	Undetectable	↑↑	↑
T_3 toxicosis	Undetectable	Normal	↑↑
Subclinical hyperthyroidism	↓	Normal	Normal
Secondary hyperthyroidism (TSHoma)	↑ or normal	↑	↑
Thyroid hormone resistance	↑ or normal	↑	↑
Primary hypothyroidism	↑	↓	↓ or normal
Secondary hypothyroidism	↓ or normal	↓	↓ or normal

Thyroid hormone resistance (RTH)

- Syndrome characterized by reduced responsiveness to elevated circulating levels of free T_4 and free T_3, non-suppressed serum TSH and intact TSH responsiveness to TRH. Clinical features may be absent but may include short stature, hyperactivity, attention deficits with mental deficiency or learning disability, and goitre.
- Differential diagnosis includes TSH-secreting pituitary tumour.
- Treatment depending on clinical features is to supplement thyroid hormone, depending on parameters of tissue responses to thyroid hormone. See page 47.

Table 2.2 Influence of drugs on thyroid function tests

Metabolic process	Increased	Decreased
TSH secretion	Amiodarone (transiently: becomes normal after 2–3 months)	Glucocorticoids, dopamine agonists, phenytoin, dopamine
T_4 synthesis/ release	Iodide	Iodide, lithium
Binding proteins	Oestrogen, clofibrate, heroin	Glucocorticoids, androgens, phenytoin, carbamazepine
T_4 metabolism	Anticonvulsants; rifampicin	
T_4/T_3 binding in serum		Salicylates, frusemide, mefenamic acid, amiodarone, ß-blockers, glucocorticoids

Table 2.3 Atypical thyroid function tests

Test	Possible cause
Suppressed TSH and normal free T_4	T_3 toxicosis (approximately 5% of thyrotoxicosis)
Suppressed TSH and normal free T_4 and free T_3	Early subclinical thyrotoxicosis Recovery from thyrotoxicosis Excess thyroxine replacement Sick euthyroidism
Detectable TSH and elevated free T_4 and free T_3	TSH secreting pituitary tumour Thyroid hormone resistance Heterophile antibodies
Elevated free T_4 and low free T_3	Amiodarone

Antibody screen (Table 2.4)

High titres of antithyroid peroxidase (Anti TPO) antibodies or antithyroglobulin antibodies are found in patients with autoimmune thyroid disease (Hashimoto's thyroiditis; Graves' disease)

Table 2.4 Antithyroid antibodies and thyroid disease

Condition	Anti-TPO	Anti-thyroglobulin	TSH receptor antibody
Graves' disease	70–80%	30–50%	70–100% (stimulating)
Autoimmune hypothyroidism	Majority	Majority	10–20% (blocking)

Note: TSH receptor antibodies may be stimulatory or inhibitory.

Screening for thyroid disease

The following categories of patients should be screened for thyroid disease:

- patients with atrial fibrillation or hyperlipidaemia
- periodic (6 monthly) assessments in patients receiving amiodarone and lithium
- annual check of thyroid function in the annual review of diabetic patients
- women with type 1 diabetes in the first trimester of pregnancy and post delivery (because of the threefold rise in incidence of postpartum thyroid dysfunction in such patients)
- women with past history of postpartum thyroiditis
- annual check of thyroid function in people with Down's syndrome, Turner's syndrome and Addison's disease, in view of the high prevalence of hypothyroidism in such patients.

(WM Tunbridge and MP Vanderpump; *Endocrinology and Metabolism Clinics of North America* 2000; 29(2): 239–253)

Scintiscanning

Permits localization of sites of accumulation of radioiodine or sodium pertechnetate [^{99m}Tc], which gives information about the activity of the iodine trap (Table 2.5). This is useful:

- to define areas of increased or decreased function within the thyroid (Table 2.6) which occasionally helps in cases of uncertainty as to the cause of the thyrotoxicosis
- to detect retrosternal goitre
- to detect ectopic thyroid tissue
- to detect functioning metastases of thyroid carcinoma.

Agents which influence thyroid uptake, including

- intake of high-iodine foods, such as kelp (seaweed)
- drugs containing iodine, such as amiodarone
- recent use of radiographic contrast dyes

can potentially interfere with the interpretation of the scan.

Table 2.5 Radioisotope scans

	^{123}Iodine	^{99}Technitium pertechnetate
Half-life	Short	Short
Advantage	Low emission of radiation Have higher energy photons. Hence useful for imaging a toxic goitre with a substernal component	Maximum thyroid uptake within 30 min of administration. Can be used in breast-feeding women (discontinue feeding for 24 h)
Disadvantage		Technetium is only trapped by the thyroid without being organified
Use	Functional assessment of the thyroid	Rapid scanning

Table 2.6 Radionuclide scanning (scintigram) in thyroid disease

Condition	Scan appearance
Graves' hyperthyroidism	Enlarged gland Increased homogeneous radionucleotide uptake
Thyroiditis (e.g. de Quervains)	Low or absent uptake
Toxic nodule	A solitary area of high uptake
Thyrotoxicosis factitia	Depressed thyroid uptake
Thyroid cancer	Successful ^{131}I uptake by tumour tissue requires an adequate level of TSH, achieved by stopping T_3 replacement 10 days before scanning or giving recombinant TSH injection

Ultrasound scanning

Provides an accurate indication of size and is useful for differentiating cystic nodules from solid ones, but cannot be used to distinguish between benign and malignant disease.

- Microcalcification within nodules favours the diagnosis of malignancy; micro-calcifications smaller than 2 mm in diameter are observed in ~60% of malignant nodules, but in <2% of benign lesions.
- Calcification is a prominent feature of medullary carcinoma of the thyroid.
- It can detect whether a nodule is solitary or part of a multinodular process.
- Sequential scanning can be employed to assess changes in size of thyroid over time.

Note Neither scintigraphy or ultrasound is routinely indicated in a patient with goitre.

Fine needle aspiration cytology

- FNAC is now considered the most accurate test for diagnosis of thyroid nodules. It is performed in an outpatient setting. 2–4 aspirations are carried out at different sites for each nodule. Cytologic findings are *satisfactory* or *diagnostic* in approximately 85% of specimens and *non-diagnostic* in the remainder.
- In experienced hands FNAC is an excellent diagnostic technique, as shown in the table below.
- Repeat FNAC after 3–6 months further reduces the proportion of false negatives.
- It is impossible to differentiate between benign and malignant follicular neoplasm using FNAC. Therefore surgical excision of a follicular neoplasm is always indicated.

Feature	Range (%)	Mean Value(%)
Accuracy	85–100	95
Specificity	72–100	92
Sensitivity	65–98	83
False negative	1–11	5

Computed tomography (CT)

- CT is useful in the evaluation of retrosternal and retrotracheal extension of an enlarged thyroid.
- Compression of the trachea and displacement of the major vessels can be identified with CT of the superior mediastinum.
- It can demonstrate the extent of intrathoracic extension of thyroid malignancy and infiltration of adjacent structures such as the carotid artery, internal jugular vein, trachea, oesophagus and regional lymph nodes.

Additional laboratory investigations

Haematological tests

- Long-standing thyrotoxicosis may be associated with a *normochromic anaemia* and occasionally a *mild neutropenia, lymphocytosis* and rarely a *thrombocytopenia.*
- In hypothyroidism a *macrocytosis* is typical, although concurrent vitamin B_{12} deficiency should be considered.
- There may also be a *microcytic anaemia* due to menorrhagia and impaired iron utilization.

Biochemical tests

- *Alkaline phosphatase* may be elevated.
- Mild *hypercalcaemia* occasionally occurs in thyrotoxicosis and reflects increased bone resorption. *Hypercalcuria* is more common.
- In a hypothyroid patient, *hyponatraemia* may be due to reduced renal tubular loss or less commonly due to co-existing cortisol deficiency.
- In hypothyroidism *creatinine kinase* is often raised and the lipid profile altered with *increased LDL cholesterol.*

Endocrine tests

- In hypothyroidism, serum *prolactin* may be elevated because increased TRH leads to increased prolactin secretion.
- In thyrotoxicosis there is an increase in *sex hormone binding globulin (SHBG),* and a complex interaction with sex steroid hormone metabolism, resulting in changes in the levels of androgens and oestrogens. The net physiological result is an increase in *oestrogenic* activity, with *gynaecomastia* and a decrease in libido in men presenting with thyrotoxicosis.

Sick euthyroid syndrome (Non thyroidal illness syndrome)

- Biochemistry – Low T4 and T3
  – Inappropriately normal/suppressed TSH
- Tissue thyroid hormone concentrations are very low
- Context – Starvation
  – Severe illness eg ITU, severe infections, renal failure, cardiac failure, liver failure, end-stage malignancy
- Whether replacement thyroxine treatment provides benefit is unclear.

Atypical clinical situations

- *Thyrotoxicosis factitia*
  – no thyroid enlargement
  – elevated free T_4 and suppressed TSH
  – depressed thyroid uptake on scintigraphy
  – low thyroglobulin differentiates from thyroiditis (which shows depressed uptake on scintigraphy but increased thyroglobulin) and all other causes of elevated thyroid hormones.
- *Struma ovarii* (ovarian teratoma containing hyperfunctioning thyroid tissue):
  – no thyroid enlargement
  – depressed thyroid uptake on scintigraphy
  – body scan after radioiodine confirms diagnosis.
- *Trophoblast tumours* hCG has structural homology with TSH and leads to thyroid gland stimulation, and usually mild thyrotoxicosis.
- *Hyperemesis gravidarum* Thyroid function tests may be abnormal with a suppressed TSH (See Chapter 70 on thyroid disorders and pregnancy).
- *Choriocarcinoma of the testes* may be associated with gynaecomastia and thyrotoxicosis – measure hCG.

Chapter 3
Thyrotoxicosis

Aetiology

Epidemiology

- 10 times more common in women than in men in the UK.
- Prevalence is approximately 2% of the female population.
- Annual incidence is 3 cases per 1000 women.

Definition of thyrotoxicosis and hyperthyroidism

- The term *thyrotoxicosis* denotes the clinical, physiological, and biochemical findings that result when the tissues are exposed to excess thyroid hormone. It can arise in a variety of ways (Table 3.1). It is essential to establish a specific diagnosis as this determines therapy choices and provides important information for the patient regarding prognosis.
- The term *hyperthyroidism* should be used to denote only those conditions in which hyperfunction of the thyroid leads to thyrotoxicosis.

Genetics of Graves' disease

- Graves' disease is a complex autoimmune disorder. Genes make only a moderate contribution to susceptibility.
- Several genetic susceptibility loci and environmental factors are likely to contribute to the development of the disease
- HLA-DR3, HLA-DQA1*0501, and the *CTLA-4* (cytotoxic T lymphocyte associated-4) gene region have been established as susceptibility loci; HLA-DQA1*0701 protects against Graves' disease.
- Additional loci are likely to be identified via a combination of genome-wide linkage analysis and allelic association analysis of candidate genes.

Table 3.1 Classification of the aetiology of thyrotoxicosis

Associated with hyperthyroidism	
Excessive thyroid stimulation	Graves' disease, Hashitoxicosis
	Pituitary thyrotroph adenoma
	Pituitary thyroid hormone resistance syndrome (excess TSH)
	Trophoblastic tumours producing hCG with thyrotrophic activity
Thyroid nodules with autonomous function	Toxic solitary nodule, toxic multinodular goiter
	Very rarely, thyroid cancer
Not associated with hyperthyroidism	
Thyroid inflammation	Silent and postpartum thyroiditis, subacute (de Quervain's) thyroiditis
	Drug-induced thyroiditis (amiodarone)
Exogenous thyroid hormones	Overtreatment with thyroid hormone
	Thyrotoxicosis factitia (thyroxine use in non-thyroidal disease)
Ectopic thyroid tissue	Metastatic thyroid carcinoma
	Struma ovarii (teratoma containing functional thyroid tissue)

Manifestations of hyperthyroidism

Manifestations of hyperthyroidism (all forms)

Symptoms

- hyperactivity, irritability, altered mood, insomnia
- heat intolerance, increased sweating
- palpitations
- fatigue, weakness
- dyspnoea
- weight loss with increased appetite (weight gain in 10% of patients)
- pruritus
- increased stool frequency
- thirst and polyuria
- oligomenorrhoea or amenorrhoea, loss of libido

Signs

- sinus tachycardia, atrial fibrillation
- fine tremor, hyperkinesia, hyperreflexia
- warm, moist skin
- palmar erythema, onycholysis
- hair loss
- muscle weakness and wasting
- congestive (high output) heart failure, chorea, periodic paralysis (primarily in Asian men), psychosis (rare)

Investigation of thyrotoxicosis

- *Thyroid function tests* raised free T_4 and suppressed TSH (raised free T_3 in T_3 toxicosis)
- *Thyroid antibodies* see Table 2.4 (page 13).
- *Radionucleotide thyroid scan* if diagnosis uncertain (page 18).
- Thyrotoxic hypokalaemic periodic paralysis
  - Thyrotoxicosis
  - Potassium low
  - Intermittent muscle weakness + CPK ↑
  - Precipitated by heavy exertion or CHO load
  - Common in Asians

Manifestations of Graves' disease (in addition to the above)

- diffuse goitre
- ophthalmopathy (see p. 50)
  - a feeling of grittiness and discomfort in the eye
  - retrobulbar pressure or pain, eyelid lag or retraction
  - periorbital oedema, chemosis*, scleral injection*
  - exophthalmos (proptosis)*
  - extraocular muscle dysfunction*
  - exposure keratitis*
  - optic neuropathy*
- localized dermopathy (pretibial myxoedema p. 53)
- lymphoid hyperplasia
- thyroid acropachy (p. 53)

*Combination of these suggests congestive ophthalmopathy.

Urgent action necessary: if corneal ulceration, congestive ophthalmopathy, or optic neuropathy (p. 50).

Conditions associated with Graves' disease

- type 1 diabetes mellitus
- Addison's disease
- vitiligo
- pernicious anaemia
- alopecia areata
- myasthenia gravis
- coeliac disease
- other autoimmune disorders associated with the HLA-DR3 haplotype

Treatment

Medical treatment

In general, the standard policy in Europe is to offer a course of antithyroid drugs (ATD) first. In the USA, radioiodine is more likely to be offered as first-line treatment.

Aims and principles of medical treatment

- To induce remission in Graves' disease
- Monitor for relapse off treatment initially 6–8 weekly for 6 months, then 6 monthly for 2 years, and then annually thereafter or sooner if symptoms return.
- For relapse, consider definitive treatment such as radioiodine or surgery. A second course of ATD almost never results in remission.

Choice of drugs

- *Carbimazole*, which can be given as a single dose, is usually the drug of first choice in the UK.
- During pregnancy and lactation *propylthiouracil* is the drug of choice because of its lower concentration in breast milk and the possible association of carbimazole with aplasia cutis.
- 5 mg of carbimazole is roughly equivalent to 50 mg of propylthiouracil. Propylthiouracil has a theoretical advantage of inhibiting the conversion of T_4 to T_3, and T_3 levels decline more rapidly after starting the drug.
- 30–40 % of patients treated with an ATD remain euthyroid 10 years after discontinuation of therapy. If hyperthyroidism recurs after treatment with an ATD, there is little chance that a second course of treatment will result in permanent remission. Young patients, those with large goitres, ophthalmopathy, or high serum concentrations of thyrotropin receptor antibody at the time of diagnosis are unlikely to have a permanent remission.
- *β-Adrenergic antagonists* Propranolol 20–80 mg 3× daily. Considerable relief from such symptoms as anxiety, tremor, and palpitations may be gained in the initial 4–8 weeks of treatment.

Side-effects

- ATDs are generally well tolerated. Uncommonly, patients may complain of gastrointestinal symptoms or an alteration in their sense of taste and smell.

Treatment regimes

Two alternative regimes are practised: dose titration and block and replace.

Dose titration regime

- The primary aim is to achieve euthyroid state with high drug doses and then to maintain euthyroidism with a low stable dose. The dose of carbimazole or propylthiouracil is titrated according to the thyroid function tests performed every 4–8 weeks, aiming for a detectable TSH in the normal range. If free T_3 is >6 pmol/L carbimazole is started at 40 mg and if free T_3 is <6 pmol/L it is started at 30 mg.
- The treatment is continued for 18 months, as this appears to represent the length of therapy which is generally optimal in producing the remission rate of 40% at 5 years after discontinuing therapy.
- Relapses are most likely to occur within the first year and may be more likely in the presence of a large goitre and high T_3 level at the time of diagnosis.

Block and replace regime

- After achieving an euthyroid state on carbimazole alone, carbimazole at a dose of 40 mg daily together with T_4 at a dose of 100 μg can be prescribed. This is usually continued for 6 months.
- The main advantages are fewer hospital visits for checks of thyroid function and shorter duration of treatment.
- The originally reported higher remission rate was not confirmed in a large prospective multicentre European trial when combination treatment was compared to carbimazole alone.
- Relapses are most likely to occur within the first year and may be more likely in the presence of a large goitre and high T_3 level at the time of diagnosis.

- Much more common are the allergic type reactions of fever, rash, urticaria, and arthralgia, which occur in 1–5% of patients taking these drugs. These side-effects are often mild and do not usually necessitate drug withdrawal, although one ATD may be substituted for another in the expectation that the second agent may be taken without side-effects.
- Agranulocytosis represents a serious but rare side-effect of ATD occurring in 0.1–0.5% of patients. It occurs with equal frequency with carbimazole and propylthiouracil and because cross reactivity of this reaction has been reported, one drug should never be substituted for the other after this reaction has been diagnosed. Agranulocytosis usually occurs within the first 3 months after initiation of therapy but it is important to be aware of the documented cases, which have occurred (less frequently) a long time after starting treatment.
- As agranulocytosis occurs very suddenly, routine monitoring of full blood count is thought to be of little use. Patients typically present with fever and evidence of infection, usually in the oropharynx, and **each patient should therefore receive written instructions to discontinue the medication and contact their doctor for a blood count should the situation arise.**

Radioiodine therapy

Indications

- definitive treatment of multinodular goitre or adenoma
- relapsed Graves' disease.

Contra-indications

- young children, because of the potential risk of thyroid carcinogenesis.
- pregnant and lactating women.
- situations where it is clear that the safety of other people cannot be guaranteed
- *Graves' ophthalmopathy*: There is some evidence that Graves' ophthalmopathy may worsen after the administration of radioactive iodine, especially in smokers. In cases of moderate to severe ophthalmopathy radioiodine may be avoided. Alternatively steroid cover in a dose of 40 mg prednisolone should be administered on the day of administering radioiodine, 30 mg daily for the next 2 weeks, 20 mg daily for the following 2 weeks, reducing to zero over subsequent 3 weeks.

Radioiodine treatment

Clinical guidelines

The recommendation is to administer enough radioiodine to achieve euthyroidism with the acceptance of a moderate rate of hypothyroidism, e.g. 15–20% at 2 years and 1–3% per annum thereafter.

Instructions to patients

- Discontinue ATDs 2 days before radioiodine administration since their effects last for 24 h or more, though propylthiouracil has a prolonged radioprotective effect. ATDs may be recommenced 3 days or more after radioiodine administration without significantly affecting the delivered radiation dose.
- Patients should not have close contact (<1 m) with children under the age of 11 years for about 2 weeks after treatment.

Administration of radioiodine

- Radioactive iodine-131 is administered orally as a capsule or a drink.
- There is no universal agreement regarding the optimal dose. Dosing according to size alone is not successful in 90% of cases.
- A dose of 400–800 MBq should be sufficient to cure thyrotoxicosis in 90%. This would also render 50% of patients hypothyroid within 10 years.

Outcomes of radioiodine treatment

- In general 50–70% of patients have restored normal thyroid function and shrinkage of goitre within 6–8 weeks of receiving radioiodine.
- Persistent hyperthyroidism is treated by a further one or two administrations, at least 6 months apart.

(Reference: *The use of radioiodine in the management of hyperthyroidism.* Royal College of Physicians of London, November 1995)

Caveats

- The control of disease may not occur for a period of weeks or a few months.
- More than one treatment may be needed in some patients, depending on the dose given; 15% require a second dose and a few patients require a third dose. The second dose should be considered only at least 6 months after the first dose.
- Compounds that contain iodine, such as amiodarone, block iodine uptake for a period of several months following cessation of therapy; iodine uptake measurements may be helpful in this instance in determining the activity required and the timing of radioiodine therapy.
- Women of childbearing age should avoid pregnancy for a minimum of 4 months following radioactive iodine ablation.
- The incidence of hypothyroidism is about 50% at 10 years, and continues to occur thereafter.

Side-effects

- nausea and anterior neck pain caused by radiation-induced thyroiditis
- transient rise in thyroid hormone levels which may exacerbate heart failure if present.

Hypothyroidism after radioiodine

- After radioiodine administration, ATDs may be recommenced. The ATDs should be withdrawn gradually guided by a 6–8 weekly thyroid function test. Early post-radioiodine hypothyroidism may be transient. TSH should be monitored every 6 months after radioiodine to determine late hypothyroidism.
- In patients treated for autonomous toxic nodules the incidence of hypothyroidism is much lower since the toxic nodule takes up the radioactive iodine while the surrounding tissue will recover normal function once the hyperthyroidism is controlled, though this is disputed by some experts.

Cancer risk after radioiodine therapy

- In a recent large series, no overall excess risk of cancer was found. It is unclear whether the risk of thyroid cancer is slightly increased.

Table 3.3 Recommended activity of radioiodine

Aetiology	Comments	Guide dose (MBq)
Graves' disease	First presentation; no significant eye disease Moderate goitre (40–50 g)	400–550
Toxic multinodular goitre in older person	Mild heart failure; atrial fibrillation or other concomitant disease, e.g. cancer	At least 550
Toxic adenoma	Usually mild hyperthyroidism	300–500
Severe Graves' disease with thyroid eye disease	Postpone radioiodine till eye disease stable. Prednisolone 40 mg to be administered at same time as radioiodine and for further 4–6 weeks (p. 29)	400–550
Ablation therapy	Severe accompanying medical condition such as heart failure; atrial fibrillation or other concurrent medical disorders (e.g. psychosis)	800

Reference: *The use of radioiodine in the management of hyperthyroidism.* Royal College of Physicians of London, November 1995.

Surgery

Indications

- Documented suspicious or malignant thyroid nodule by FNAC.
- Pregnant mothers who are not adequately controlled by ATDs or in whom serious allergic reactions develop while being treated medically. Thyroidectomy is usually performed in the second trimester.
- Patients:
  - who reject or fear exposure to radiation
  - with poor compliance to medical treatment
  - in whom a rapid control of symptoms is desired
  - with severe manifestations of Graves' ophthalmopathy, as total or near total thyroidectomy does not worsen eye manifestations
  - with relapsed Graves' disease.
  - with local compressive symptoms which may not improve rapidly with radioiodine, whereas operation removes these symptoms in most patients
  - with large thyroid glands and relatively low radioiodine uptake.

Preparation of patients for surgery

- ATDs should be used preoperatively to achieve euthyroidism.
- Propranolol may be added to achieve ß-blockade especially in those patients where surgery must be performed sooner than achieving euthyroid state.
- Occasionally, potassium iodide, 60 mg 3xdaily can be used during the preoperative period to prevent an unwanted liberation of thyroid hormones during surgery. Preoperatively it should be given for 10 days. Operating later than this can be associated with exacerbation of thyrotoxicosis as the thyroid escapes from the inhibitory effect of the iodide. In practice it is rarely needed as good control of thyrotoxicosis can be achieved with ATDs in the majority of patients. Lugol's iodine should not be used because of its variable iodine content.

Hypothyroidism after surgery

- Reported incidence of hypothyroidism following subtotal thyroidectomy is around 10–20% at 10 years and continues to rise inexorably.
- A small remnant size(<4 g) results in a high incidence(>50%) of hypothyroidism
- Thyroid antibody activity and infiltration of the gland by lymphocytes cause destruction of the gland and hypothyroidism.

- If the thyroid remnant is 8 g or larger, there is an increase in the incidence of persistent or recurrent disease (approximately 15%).
- The best centres achieve less than 4% recurrence. Cure (i.e. low recurrence) inevitably means a high rate of long-term hypothyroidism.

Table 3.4 Complications of thyroidectomy

Immediate	Late
Recurrent laryngeal nerve damage	Hypothyroidism
Hypoparathyroidism	Keloid formation
Thyroid crisis	
Local haemorrhage, causing laryngeal oedema	
Wound infection	

Thyroid storm (crisis)

Thyroid crisis represents a rare but life threatening exacerbation of the manifestations of thyrotoxicosis. It should be promptly recognized since the condition is associated with a significant mortality (30–50% depending on series). Thyroid crisis develops in hyperthyroid patients who

- have an acute infection
- undergo thyroidal or non thyroidal surgery or radioiodine treatment
- are postpartum
- receive radiographic contrast agents
- have had ATDs withdrawn.

Thyroid crisis should be considered in a very sick patient if there is:

- recent past history suggestive of thyrotoxicosis
- acute stressful precipitating factor such as surgery
- history of previous thyroid treatment
- family history of a thyroid disorder.

Treatment

General supportive therapy

- The patient is best managed in an intensive care unit where close attention can be paid to the cardiorespiratory status, fluid balance, and cooling.
- Standard anti-arrhythmic drugs can be used, including digoxin (usually in higher than normal dose) after correction for hypokalaemia. If anticoagulation is indicated because of atrial fibrillation then it must be remembered that thyrotoxic patients are very sensitive to warfarin.
- Chlorpromazine (50–100 mg i/m) can be used to treat agitation and because of its effect in inhibiting central thermoregulation it may be useful in treating the hyperpyrexia.
- Broad-spectrum antibiotics should be given if infection is suspected.

Specific treatment

- Aim: to inhibit thyroid hormone synthesis completely.
- Propylthiouracil 200–300 mg 6 hourly via nasogastric tube. Propylthiouracil is preferred because of its ability to block T_4 to T_3 conver-

Thyroid storm

Clinical signs suggestive of a thyroid storm

- alteration in mental status
- high fever
- tachycardia or tachyarrhythmias
- severe clinical hyperthyroid signs
- vomiting, jaundice, and diarrhoea
- multisystem decompensation: cardiac failure, respiratory distress, congestive hepatomegaly, dehydration, and prerenal failure.

Laboratory investigation

- Routine haematology may indicate a leukocytosis, which is well-recognized in thyrotoxicosis even in the absence of infection.
- The biochemical screen may reveal a raised alkaline phosphatase and mild hypercalcaemia.
- Thyroid function tests and thyroid antibodies should be requested although treatment should not be delayed while awaiting the results
- The levels of thyroid hormones will be raised but may not be grossly elevated and are usually within the range of uncomplicated thyrotoxicosis

sion in peripheral tissues. There are no clinical data comparing propylthiouracil and carbimazole in this situation

- Potassium iodide 60 mg via nasogastric tube, 6 hourly, 6 h *after* starting propylthiouracil will inhibit thyroid hormone release.
- β-Adrenergic blocking agents are essential in the management to control tachycardia, tremor, and other adrenergic manifestations: Propranolol 160–480 mg/day in divided doses or as an infusion at a rate of 2–5 mg/h.
- Calcium channel blockers can be tried in patients with known bronchospastic disease where ß-blockade is contraindicated.
- High doses of glucocorticoids may help to stabilize the vascular bed and are capable of blocking T_4 to T_3 conversion: Prednisolone 60 mg daily or hydrocortisone 40 mg i/m, 4× daily.
- Plasmapheresis and peritoneal dialysis may be effective in cases resistant to the usual pharmacological measures.

Subclinical hyperthyroidism

- Subclinical hyperthyroidism is defined as undectectable thyrotropin (TSH) concentration in patients with normal levels of T_4 and T_3. Subtle symptoms and signs of thyrotoxicosis may be present.
- May be classified as endogenous in patients with thyroid hormone production associated with nodular thyroid disease or underlying Graves' disease; and as exogenous in those with undectectable serum thyrotropin concentrations as a result of treatment with levothyroxine.
- The evidence that subclinical hyperthyroidism is a risk factor for the development of atrial fibrillation or osteoporosis is not definitive.
  - There is only limited evidence that established atrial fibrillation in patients with subclinical hyperthyroidism reverts spontaneously or after cardioversion once the serum thyrotropin concentration has been normalized with antithyroid therapy. Available evidence suggest that among patients with atrial fibrillation that is unrelated to rheumatic heart disease, those with thyrotoxicosis have a higher rate of embolism than do patients without the condition.
  - The increased risk of fracture reported in older women taking thyroid hormone disappears when those with a history of hyperthyroidism are excluded.
- The natural history of subclinical hyperthyroidism remains unclear. In statements issued in 1996 and 1998 respectively, the Royal College of Physicians of London and the American College of Physicians concluded that there is no agreement about the benefits of detecting and treating endogenous subclinical hyperthyroidism or about whether it causes excess morbidity. However an expert panel of the American Thyroid Association has recommended routine screening of adults for thyroid disease by measurement of serum thyrotropin.
- In many patients with endogeneous subclinical hyperthyroidism who do not have nodular thyroid disease or complications of excess thyroid hormone, treatment is unnecessary, but thyroid-function tests should be performed every six months. In older patients with atrial fibrillation or osteoporosis that could have been caused or exacerbated by the mild excess of thyroid hormone, ablative therapy with ^{131}I is the best initial option.

- In patients with exogeneous subclinical hyperthyroidism, the dose of thyroxine should be reduced, excluding those with prior thyroid cancer in whom thyrotropin suppression may be required. Dose of thyroxine used for treating hypothyroidism may be reduced if the patient develops
  - new atrial fibrillation, angina or cardiac failure
  - accelerated bone loss
  - borderline high serum triiodothyronine concentration

Thyrotoxic hypokalaemic periodic paralysis

- Thyrotoxic
- Potassium loss
- Intermittent muscle weakness + CPK ↑
- Precipitated by heavy exertion or CHO load
- More common in Asians

Thyrotoxicosis in pregnancy (See p. 501)

- Thyrotoxicosis occurs in about 0.2% of pregnancies
- Graves' disease accounts for 90% of cases
- Less common causes include toxic adenoma and multinodular goitre
- Other causes are hyperemesis gravidarum and trophoblastic neoplasia

Diagnosis of thyrotoxicosis during pregnancy may be difficult or delayed.

- Physiological changes of pregnancy are similar to those of hyperthyroidism.
- Total T_4 and T_3 are elevated in pregnancy because of an elevated level of TBG but, with free hormone assays available, this is no longer a problem.
- Physiological features of normal pregnancy include an increase in basal metabolic rate, cardiac stroke volume, palpitations, and heat intolerance.
- Serum free T_3 concentrations remain within the normal range in most pregnant women; serum TSH concentration decreases during the first trimester.

Symptoms

- Hyperemesis gravidarum is the classic presentation. Tiredness, palpitations, insomnia, heat intolerance, proximal muscle weakness, shortness of breath, and irritability may be other presenting symptoms.
- Thyrotoxicosis may occasionally be diagnosed when the patient presents with pregnancy-induced hypertension or congestive heart failure.

Signs

- failure to gain weight despite a good appetite
- persistent tachycardia with a pulse rate >90 beats/min at rest
- other signs of thyrotoxicosis as described previously

Natural history of Graves' disease in pregnancy

- There is aggravation of symptoms in the first half of the pregnancy; amelioration of symptoms in the second half of the pregnancy, and often recurrence of symptoms in the postpartum period.

Transient hyperthyroidism of hyperemesis gravidarum

- The likely mechanism is a raised β-hCG level.
- βHCG, LH, FSH, and TSH are glycoprotein hormones that contain a common α-subunit and a hormone-specific β-subunit. There is an inverse relationship between the serum levels of TSH and hCG, best seen in early pregnancy. There is also structural homology of the TSH and hCG receptors.
- Serum free T_4 concentration may be increased and the TSH levels suppressed in women with hyperemesis gravidarum.
- Thyroid function tests recover after the resolution of hyperemesis.
- Pregnant women with hyperemesis gravidarum should not be given ATD treatment but managed supportively with fluids, antiemetics, and nutritional support.
- There is no increased risk of thyrotoxicosis in subsequent pregnancies.
- Can be differentiated from Graves' disease by the presence of antithyroid antibodies, or family history of Graves' disease, a history of other autoimmune phenomena and a previous history of ophthalmic Graves'
- The dosage of ATDs is frequently adjusted during the course of the pregnancy; therefore thyroid tests should be done at 2–4 week intervals, with the goal of keeping free thyroid hormone levels in the upper one-third of the reference range.

Management of Graves' disease in the mother

- Aim of treatment is alleviation of thyroid symptoms and normalization of tests in the shortest time. Patients should be seen every 4–8 weeks and TFTs performed. Serum free T_4 is the best test to follow the response to ATDs. Block and replace regime should not be used as this will result in fetal hypothyroidism.
- Both PTU (150 mg b.d.) and carbimazole (10–20 mg once daily) are effective in controlling the disease in pregnancy. As propylthiouracil is more bound to plasma proteins, theoretically less drug would be transferred to the foetus. Compliance with carbimazole might be better. A β-blocker (propranolol 20–40 mg 6–8 hourly) is effective in controlling the hypermetabolic symptoms but should be used only for a few weeks until symptoms abate.
- Thyroid tests may normalize spontaneously with the progression of a normal pregnancy as a result of immunological changes.
- The use of iodides and radioiodine is contraindicated in pregnancy.
- Surgery is rarely performed in pregnancy. It is reserved for patients not responding to ATDs. It is preferable to perform surgery in the second trimester.
- Breast-feeding mothers should be treated with the lowest possible dose of propylthiouracil.

Prepregnancy counselling

- Hyperthyroid women who want to conceive should attain euthyroidism before conception, as stillbirth due to cranial synostosis is the most serious complication.
- There is no evidence that radioactive iodine treatment given to the mother 4 months or more before pregnancy has an adverse effect on the foetus or on an offspring in later life.
- Antithyroid medication requirements decrease during gestation; in about 50–60% of women the dose may be discontinued in the last few weeks of gestation.
- The risk of postpartum thyroiditis or recurrent hyperthyroidism should be discussed with the patient
- The rare occurrence of foetal and neonatal hyperthyroidism should be included during counselling sessions.

Management of the foetus

- The hypothalamopituitary thyroid axis is well developed at 12 weeks gestation but remains inactive until 18–20 weeks. Circulating TSH receptor antibodies (TSH-RAB) in the mother can cross the placenta. The risk of hyperthyroidism to the neonate can be assessed by measuring TSH-RAB in the maternal circulation at the beginning of the third trimester. Antithyroglobulin antibody and thyroid peroxidase antibodies have no effect on the foetus.
- Long-term follow-up studies of children whose mothers received either carbimazole or propylthiouracil have not shown an increased incidence of any physical or psychological defects. The block and replace regime using relatively high doses of carbimazole is contraindicated because the ATDs cross the placenta, but replacement T_4 does not, thus potentially rendering the foetus hypothyroid.
- Monitoring the foetal heart rate and growth rates are the standard means whereby foetal thyrotoxicosis may be detected. A rate above 160 beats/min is suspicious of foetal thyrotoxicosis in the third trimester. Foetal thyrotoxicosis may complicate the latter part of the pregnancy of women with Graves' disease even if they have previously been treated with radioiodine or surgery. If there is evidence of foetal thyrotoxicosis, the dose of the ATD should be increased. If this causes maternal hypothyroidism a small dose of T_4 can be added since, unlike carbimazole, T_4 does not cross the placenta. A paediatrician should be involved to monitor neonatal thyroid function and detect thyrotoxicosis.
- Hypothyroidism in the mother should be avoided because of the potential adverse effect on subsequent cognitive function of the neonate.
- If the mother has been treated with carbimazole, the post-delivery levels of T_4 may be low and neonatal levels of T_4 may only rise to the thyrotoxic range after a few days. In addition, TSH is usually absent in neonates who subsequently develop thyrotoxicosis. Clinical indicators of neonatal thyrotoxicosis include low birth weight, poor weight gain, tachycardia, and irritability. Carbimazole can be given at a dose of 0.5 mg/kg per day and withdrawn after a few weeks after the level of TSH-RAB declines.

Thyrotoxicosis presenting in the postpartum period

- Defined as a syndrome of postpartum thyrotoxicosis or hypothyroidism in women who were euthyroid during pregnancy.
- Postpartum thyroid dysfunction, which occurs in women with autoimmune thyroid disease, is characterized in a third by a thyrotoxic phase occurring in the first 3 months postpartum, followed by a hypothyroid phase that occurs 3–6 months after delivery, followed by spontaneous recovery. In the remaining two-thirds, single-phase pattern or the reverse occurs.
- 5–7 % percent of women develop biochemical evidence of thyroid dysfunction after delivery. An increased risk is seen in patients with type I diabetes mellitus (25%), other autoimmune diseases, in the presence of anti-TPO antibodies and in the presence of a family history of thyroid disease.
- Hyperthyroidism due to Graves' disease accounts for 10–15% of all cases of postpartum thyrotoxicosis. In the majority of cases, hyperthyroidism occurs later in the postpartum period (>3–6 months) and persists.
- Providing the patient is not breast-feeding, a radioiodine uptake scan can differentiate the two principal causes of autoimmune thyrotoxicosis by demonstrating increased uptake in Graves' disease and low uptake in postpartum thyroiditis. In fact, ^{99m}Tc can be usefully employed in breast-feeding which need be discontinued for 24 h only.
- Graves' hyperthyroidism should be treated with ATDs. Propylthiouracil is preferable if the patient is breast-feeding. Thyrotoxic symptoms due to postpartum thyrotoxicosis are managed symptomatically using propranolol.
- One-third of affected women develop symptoms of hypothyroidism and may require T_4 for 6–12 months. There is a suggestion of an increased risk of postpartum depression in those with hypothyroidism.
- Histology of the thyroid in the case of postpartum thyroiditis shows lymphocytic infiltration with destructive thyroiditis and predominantly occurs at 16 weeks in women with positive antimicrosomal antibodies.
- There is an increased chance of subsequent permanent hypothyroidism in 25–30%. Patients should be followed up with annual TSH measurements.

Table 3.6 Potential maternal and foetal complications in uncontrolled hyperthyroidism in pregnancy

Maternal	Foetal
Pregnancy induced hypertension	Hyperthyroidism
Preterm delivery	Neonatal hyperthyroidism
Congestive heart failure	Intrauterine growth retardation
Thyroid storm	Small-for-gestation age
Miscarriage	Prematurity
Abruptio placentae	Stillbirth: cranial synostosis is the most serious complication

Hyperthyroidism in children

Epidemiology

Thyrotoxicosis is rare before the age of 5 years. Although there is a progressive increase in incidence throughout childhood it is still rare and accounts for less than 5% of all cases of Graves' disease.

Clinical features

- Behavioural abnormalities, hyperactivity, declining school performance may bring the child to medical attention. Features of hyperthyroidism as described previously.
- Acceleration of linear growth is common in patients increasing in height percentiles on the growth charts. The disease may be part of McCune–Albright syndrome and café-au-lait pigmentation, precocious puberty, and bony abnormalities should be considered during clinical examination.

Investigations

The cause of thyrotoxicosis in children is nearly always Graves' disease (with positive antibodies to thyroglobulin, thyroid peroxidase, or both) although thyroiditis and toxic nodules have been described and a radioiodine scan may be useful if the diagnosis is not clear. Hereditary thyroid-resistant syndromes often misdiagnosed as Graves' disease are now being increasingly recognized in children.

Treatment

ATDs represent the treatment of choice for thyrotoxic children. Therapy is generally started with Propylthiouracil 2–4 mg/kg (Initial dose 100–150 mg/day) or carbimazole 0.2–0.4 mg/kg (initial dose 10–15 mg/day).

Secondary hyperthyroidism

- Thyrotoxicosis resulting from primary TSH overproduction by the pituitary gland with secondary thyroid enlargement and hyperfunction.
- Causes:
  - TSH-producing pituitary tumours (TSHomas)
  - syndrome of resistance to thyroid hormones.
- There are characteristically *elevated* serum free T_4 and T_3 concentrations and *non-suppressed* (inappropriately normal or frankly elevated) serum TSH levels.
- Among the 280 TSHomas reported in the literature (till 1998), 72% secreted TSH alone; the remainder co-secreted growth hormone (16%), prolactin (11%), or rarely gonadotrophins. Approximately 90% were macroadenomas (>1 cm in diameter) and 71% exhibited suprasellar extension, invasion, or both into adjacent tissues (see p. 219).
- Patients with pure TSHomas present with typical symptoms and signs of thyrotoxicosis and the presence of a diffuse goitre. Unilateral exophthalmos from tumour invasion of the orbit and bilateral exophthalmos have been reported. Patients may exhibit features of over secretion of the other pituitary hormones, e.g. prolactin or growth hormone. Headaches, visual field defects, menstrual irregularities, amenorrhoea, delayed puberty, and hypogonadotrophic hypogonadism have also been reported. Careful establishment of the diagnosis is the key to treatment. Inappropriate treatment of such patients with subtotal thyroidectomy or radioiodine administration not only fails to cure the underlying disorder but also seems to be associated with subsequent pituitary tumour enlargement and an increased risk of invasiveness into adjacent tissues.
- Treatment options are
  - transphenoidal surgery
  - pituitary radiotherapy if surgical results are unsatisfactory, or surgery is contraindicated or not desired
  - medical therapy with somatostatin analogues such as octreotide or lanreotide may be useful preoperatively and suppresses TSH secretion in 80% of the cases.

Resistance to thyroid hormones

- Patients with generalized resistance to thyroid hormone (GRTH) may present with mild hypothyroidism, deaf mutism, delayed bone maturation, raised circulating thyroid hormone concentrations, non-suppressed TSH, and failure of TSH to decrease normally upon administration of supraphysiological doses of thyroid hormones. Most patients present with goitre or incidentally abnormal TFTs. Treatment is determined by thyroid status.
- In selective pituitary resistance to thyroid hormones (PRTH) the thyroid hormone resistance is more pronounced in the pituitary; thus the patient exhibits definite clinical manifestations of thyrotoxicosis.
- About 90% of thyroid hormone resistance syndromes result from mutations in the gene encoding *TR* β. Mutant receptors have a reduced affinity for T_3 and are functionally deficient. It is usually inherited in an autosomal dominant pattern with the affected individuals being heterozygous for the mutation.
- A subset of RTH receptors has been identified that are capable of inhibiting wild type receptor action. When co-expressed, the mutant proteins are able to inhibit the function of their wild type counterparts in a dominant negative manner.
- Common features of patients with the thyroid hormones resistance syndromes include goitre, tachycardia, hyperkinetic behaviour, emotional disturbances, ear nose and throat infections, language disabilities, auditory disorders, low body weight, cardiac abnormalities, and subnormal intelligence quotients.
- Treatment options after carefully establishing the diagnosis in PRTH include:
  - Chronic suppression of TSH secretion with D T4, triiodothyroacetic acid, octreotide, or bromocriptine
  - If above ineffective, thyroid ablation with radioiodine or surgery with subsequent close monitoring of thyroid hormone status and pituitary gland size.

Table 3.5 Tests useful in the differential diagnosis of TSHomas, PRTH, and GRTH

Test	TSHomas	PRTH	GRTH
Clinical thyrotoxicosis	Present	Present	Absent
Family history	Absent	Present	Present
TSH response to TRH	No change	Increase	Increase
TSH response to low dose T_3	No change	Decrease	Decrease
SHBG	Elevated[a]	Normal[b]	Normal
Pituitary MRI	Tumour[c]	Normal	Normal

[a] Not raised in mixed GH/TSH tumour.

[b] Peripheral markers of toxicosis sometimes affected.

[c] The best biochemical test is α-subunit

Chapter 4

Graves' ophthalmopathy, dermopathy, and acropachy

Graves' ophthalmopathy

- An organ-specific autoimmune disorder characterized by swelling of the extra-ocular muscles, lymphocytic infiltration, late fibrosis, muscle tethering, and proliferation of orbital fat and connective tissue.
- There are two stages in the development of the disease, which can be recognized as an active inflammatory (dynamic) stage and a relatively quiescent static stage. 5% of patients with Graves' ophthalmopathy have hypothyroidism and 5% are euthyroid. 75% of patients develop Graves' disease within a year either side of Graves' ophthalmopathy developing. The lesions are due to localized accumulation of glycosaminoglycans.
- The appearance of eye disease follows a different time course to thyroid dysfunction and in a minority there is a lag period between the presentation of hyperthyroidism and the appearance of eye signs.
- Smoking and hypothyroidism moderately worsen Graves' ophthalmopathy.
- The role of an endocrinologist during a routine review of Graves' patients is to record accurately the clinical features of Graves' eye disease and to identify ocular emergencies, such as corneal ulceration, congestive ophthalmopathy, and optic neuropathy, which should be referred urgently to an ophthalmologist.

Clinical features

- Retraction of eyelids is extremely common in thyroid eye disease. The margin of the upper eyelid normally rests about 2 mm below the limbus and retraction can be suspected if the lid margin is either level or above the superior limbus allowing the sclera to be visible. The lower lid normally rests at the inferior limbus and retraction is suspected when the sclera shows above the lid.
- Proptosis can result in failure of lid closure, increasing the likelihood of exposure keratitis and the common symptom of gritty eyes. This can be confirmed with a fluorescein or Rose Bengal stain. As papilloedema can occur, fundoscopy should be performed. Proptosis may result in periorbital oedema and chemosis because the displaced orbit results in less efficient lachrymal drainage.
- Persistent visual blurring may indicate an optic neuropathy and requires urgent treatment.
- Severe conjunctival pain may indicate corneal ulceration requiring urgent referral.

Investigation of proptosis

- *Documentation using a Hertel exophthalmometer* The feet of the apparatus are placed against the lateral orbital margin as defined by the zygomatic bones. The marker on the body of the exophthalmometer is then superimposed on the reflection of the contralateral one by adjusting the scale. The position of each cornea can be read off against the reflections on a millimetre scale as seen on the mirror of the apparatus. A normal result is generally taken as being <20 mm. A reading of 21 mm or more is abnormal and a difference of 2 mm between the eyes is suspicious.
- *Soft tissue involvement* Soft tissue signs and symptoms include conjunctival hyperaemia, chemosis, tearing, and foreign body sensation. The soft tissue changes can be secondary to exposure and lagophthalmos but are often seen in the absence of these aetiological factors.
- *CT or MRI scan of the orbit* demonstrates enlargement of the extra-ocular muscles and this can be useful in cases of diagnostic difficulty. This is also more accurate for demonstration of proptosis.

Table 4.1 Treatment of Graves' ophthalmopathy

Problem	Treatment
Grittiness	Artificial tears and simple eye ointment
Eyelid retraction	Tape eyelids at night to avoid corneal damage. Surgery if risk of exposure keratopathy
Proptosis	Head elevation during sleep Diuretics Systemic steroids Radiotherapy Orbital decompression
Optic neuropathy	Systemic steroids Radiotherapy Orbital decompression
Ophthalmoplegia	Prisms in the acute phase Orbital decompression Orbital muscle surgery

Examining for possible optic neuropathy

- History of *poor vision*, a recent or *rapid change in vision*, or *poor colour vision* are reasons for prompt referral.
- *A visual acuity* of less than 6/18 warrants referral to an ophthalmologist. For *colour vision*, each eye should be evaluated by using a simple 15-plate Ishihara colour vision test. Decreased colour vision is a subtle indicator of optic nerve function. Failure to identify more than 2 of the plates with either eye is an indication for referral. This is unhelpful in the 8% of men who may be colour blind.
- *Marcus Gunn pupil* The 'swinging flashlight' test detects the presence of an *afferent pupillary defect.*

Ophthalmoplegia

- Patients may complain of diplopia due to ocular muscle dysfunction caused by either oedema during the early active phase or fibrosis during the later phase. Assessment using a Hess chart may be helpful. Intra-optic pressure may increase on upgaze and result in compression of the globe by a fibrotic inferior rectus muscle. Ocular mobility may be restricted by oedema during the active inflammatory phase or by fibrosis during the fibrotic stage.
- The two most common findings are defective elevation caused by fibrotic contraction of the inferior rectus muscle and a convergence defect caused by fibrotic contraction of the medial rectus. Disorders of the medial rectus, superior rectus, and lateral rectus muscle produce typical signs of defective adduction, depression and abduction respectively.

Treatment

Eyelid retraction

- Most patients do not require any treatment, since clinical signs usually improve with treatment of hyperthyroidism or spontaneously with time (27%). In patients with significant lid retraction and exposure keratopathy, surgery to reduce the vertical lid fissures can be considered.
- Orbital decompression and strabismus surgery, if required, should be considered before eyelid surgery because the outcome of these influences the eyelid position.
- Surgery to correct lid-lag retraction, soft tissue abnormalities including periorbital laxity, and ophthalmoplegia, may be performed once the active phase has resolved and the patient is euthyroid

Graves' dermopathy

- This is a rare complication of Graves' thyrotoxicosis. It is usually pre-tibial in location and hence called *pre-tibial myxoedema.*
- It typically appears as raised, discoloured, and indurated lesions on the front or back of the legs, or on the dorsum of the feet, and has occasionally been described in other areas, including the hands and the face.
- The lesions are due to localized accumulation of *glycosaminoglycans.* It is now recognized that there is a lymphocytic infiltrate. Lesions are characteristically asymptomatic but they can also be pruritic and tender. They can be very disfiguring.
- *Treatment* Usually not treated. Potent topical fluorinated steroids such as fluocinolone acetonide are effective, not only in the treatment of localized pain and tenderness but also in some resolution of the visible skin signs. Severe pre-tibial myxoedema may require systemic steroids in conjunction with compression bandages. Surgery may worsen the condition.

Thyroid acropachy

- This is the rarest manifestation of Graves' disease.
- It presents as clubbing of the digits and sub-periosteal new bone formation. The soft tissue swelling is similar to that seen in localized myxoedema and consists of glycosaminoglycan accumulation.
- Patients almost inevitably have Graves' ophthalmopathy or pretibial myxoedema. If not, an alternative cause of clubbing should be looked for.
- It is typically painless and there is no effective treatment.

Soft tissue involvement

- Artificial tears and liquid paraffin eye ointment (Lacri-Lube) may give symptom relief. Head elevation during sleep or diuretics may reduce morning orbital oedema.

Proptosis

- Severe proptosis prevents adequate lid closure and may lead to exposure keratopathy and corneal ulceration. Systemic steroids, orbital radiotherapy. or surgery may be considered in those patients with very active disease. Intravenous methyl prednisolone, 500 mg daily, repeated on three consecutive days may produce a rapid response, which can be continued with a course of oral prednisolone. Oral prednisolone can be tried from the outset although high doses of at least 60 mg daily are usually required and adverse affects may be a disadvantage. The dose of prednisolone should be reduced over the subsequent few weeks, depending on the clinical response.
- Orbital radiotherapy may also be considered early in the course of active inflammatory eye disease.
- Orbital surgical decompression.

Optic neuropathy

- Oral corticosteroids, orbital decompression, and radiotherapy have been used extensively.
- Oral prednisolone, 80 mg/day, in divided doses should be given for 2 weeks and then tapered gradually to zero. Lack of improvement or recurrence should prompt surgical intervention.
- Orbital decompression surgery aims to release pressure on the optic nerve in the posterior orbit where the muscles are tremendously enlarged. The medial wall or lamina papyracea and orbital floor are removed.
- Radiotherapy works slowly and is usually a method of last resort. Corticosteroids are given at the same time to avoid the initial worsening of symptoms. Complications include radiation keratitis and retinitis, which occur rarely.

Ophthalmoplegia

- Temporary measures such as occluding one eyeglass lens, or the use of a Fresnel prism on one or both lenses, are beneficial.
- Complex surgery on several ocular muscles is often indicated. Multiple operations may be necessary.

Further reading

Brix TH, Kyvik KO, Hegedus L. What is the evidence of genetic factors in the etiology of Graves' disease? A brief review. *Thyroid* 1998; 8: 727–34.

Fatourechi V, Pajouhi M, Fransway AF. Dermopathy of Graves disease (pretibial myxedema). Review of 150 cases. *Medicine* (Baltimore) 1994; 73: 1–7.

Franklyn JA. The management of hyperthyroidism *N Engl J Med* 1994; 330: 1731–1738 [Erratum *N Engl J Med* 1994; 331:559].

Franklyn JA, Maisonneuve P, Sheppard MC, Betteridge J, Boyle P. Mortality after the treatment of hyperthyroidism with radioactive iodine *N Engl J Med* 1998; 338: 172–718.

Franklyn JA, Maisonneuve P, Sheppard MC, Betteridge J, Boyle P. Cancer incidence and mortality after radioiodine treatment for hyperthyroidism: a population-based cohort study *Lancet* 1999; 353: 2111–2115.

Gunji K, Kubota S, Swanson J *et al.* Role of the eye muscles in thyroid eye disease: identification of the principal autoantigens. *Thyroid* 1998; 8:553–556 [Erratum *Thyroid* 1998; 8: 1079].

Heufelder AE. Pathogenesis of Graves' ophthalmopathy: recent controversies and progress *Eur J of Endocrinol* 1995; 132: 532–541.

Heward JM, Allahabadis A, Daykin J *et al.* Linkage disequilibrium between the human leukocyte antigen class II region of the major histocompatibility complex and Graves' disease: replication using a population case control and family-based study. *J of Clin Endocrinol Metab* 1998; 83: 3394–3397.

Laurberg P, Nygaard B, Glinoer D *et al.* Guidelines for TSH-receptor antibody measurements in pregnancy: results of an evidence-based symposium organized by the European Thyroid Association. *Eur J Endocrinol* 1998;139: 584–586.

Lazarus JH, Hall R, Ottman S, Barks AB *et al.* The clinical spectrum of postpartum thyroid disease *QJM* 1996; 89: 429–435.

Mandel SJ, Brent GA, Larsen PR. Review of antithyroid drug use during pregnancy and report of a case of aplasia cutis. *Thyroid* 1994; 4:129–133.

Mestman JH. Hyperthyroidism in pregnancy. *Endocrinol Metab Clin N America* 1998; 27(1): 127–149.

Perros P, Crombie AL, Matthews JNS, Kendall-Taylor P. Age and gender influence the severity of thyroid-associated ophthalmopathy: a study of 101 patients attending a combined thyroid-eye clinic. *Clin Endocrinol* (Oxf)1993; 38: 367–372.

Risk of agranulocytosis and aplastic anaemia in relation to use of antithyroid drugs. International Agranulocytosis and Aplastic Anaemia Study. *BMJ* 1988; 297: 262–265.

Rivkees SA, Sklar C, Freemark M. The management of Graves's disease in children, with special emphasis on radioiodine treatment. *J Clin Endocrinol Metab* 1998; 83: 3767–3776.

Ron E, Doody MM, Becker DV *et al.* Cancer mortality following treatment for adult hyperthyroidism. Cooperative Thyrotoxicosis Therapy Follow-up Study Group. *JAMA* 1998; 280: 347–355.

Tellez M, Cooper J, Edmonds C. Graves' ophthalmopathy in relation to cigarette smoking and ethnic origin. *Clin Endocrinol* (Oxf) 1992; 36: 291–294.

Toft AD. Clinical practice. Subclinical hyperthyroidism *New Engl J Med* 2001; 345(7): 512–516.

Toft AD, Weetman AP. Screening for agranulocytosis in patients treated with antithyroid drugs. *Clin Endocrinol* (Oxf) 1998; 49: 271.

Wartofsky L, Sherman SI, Gopal J, Schlumberger M, Hay ID. The use of radioactive iodine in patients with papillary and follicular thyroid cancer. *J Clin Endocrinol Metab* 1998; 83: 4195 –4203.

Weetman AP. Graves's disease *N Engl J Med* 2000; 343(17): 1236–1248.

Weetman AP, Pickerill AP, Watson P, Chatterjee VK, Edwarda OM. Treatment of Graves' disease with the block-replace regimen of antithyroid drugs: the effect of treatment duration and immunogenetic susceptibility on relapse. *QJM* 1994; 87: 337–341.

Chapter 5

Multinodular goitre and solitary adenomas

Background

Nodular thyroid disease denotes the presence of single or multiple palpable or non-palpable nodules within the thyroid gland.

- Prevalence rates range from 5–50% depending on population studied and sensitivity of detection methods. Prevalence increases linearly with age, exposure to ionizing radiation and iodine deficiency.
- Clinically apparent thyroid nodules are evident in ~10% of the UK population.
- Incidence of thyroid nodules is about 4 times more in women.
- Thyroid nodules always raise the concern of cancer, but <5% are cancerous.

Clinical evaluation

- An asymptomatic thyroid mass may be discovered either by a clinician on routine neck palpation or by the patient during self-examination.
- History should concentrate on
  - an enlarging thyroid mass
  - a previous history of radiation, especially childhood head and neck irradiation
  - a family history of thyroid cancer
  - the development of hoarseness or dysphagia.
- Nodules are more likely to be malignant in patients <20 or >60 years.
- Thyroid nodules are more common in women but more likely to be malignant in men.
- Physical findings suggestive of malignancy include a firm or hard non-tender nodule; a recent history of enlargement, fixation to adjacent tissue, and the presence of regional lymphadenopathy.
- A hot nodule on a radioisotope scan makes malignancy less likely.

Table 5.1 Aetiology of thyroid nodules

Common causes	Uncommon causes
Colloid nodule	Granulomatous thyroiditis
Cyst	Infections
Lymphocytic thyroiditis	Malignancy
Benign neoplasms	Medullary
Hurthle cell	Anaplastic
Follicular	Metastatic
Malignancy	Lymphoma
Papillary	
Follicular	

Clinical features raising the suspicion of thyroid malignancy

- age (childhood or elderly)
- short history of enlarging nodule
- local symptoms including dysphagia, stridor, or hoarseness
- previous exposure to radiation
- positive family history of thyroid cancer or MEN syndrome
- Gardner's syndrome (familial large intestinal polyposis)
- familial polyposis coli
- Cowden's syndrome (autosomal dominantly inherited hamartoma syndrome)
- lymphadenopathy
- history of Hashimoto's disease (increased incidence of lymphoma)

Investigations

- fine needle aspiration cytology (see p. 13)
- TSH
- pulmonary function tests especially for a large goitre causing tracheal obstruction
- CT scan if there are concerns about retrosternal goitre.

Treatment

Toxic multinodular goitre or nodule

The patient should initially be rendered euthyroid with medical treatment.

ATDs

- ATD are effective in controlling the hyperthyroidism but are not curative. As the hot nodules are autonomous the condition will recur after stopping the drugs. Carbimazole is useful treatment to gain control of the disease in preparation for surgery or as long-term treatment in those patients unwilling to accept radioiodine or surgery.

Radioiodine

- This form of treatment is often considered as first choice for definitive treatment. ^{131}I is preferentially accumulated in hot follicles but not in normal thyroid tissue which, because of the thyrotoxic state, is non-functioning.
- Radioiodine treatment commonly induces a euthyroid state as the hot follicles are destroyed and the previously non-functioning follicles gradually resume normal function.

Surgery

- The aim of surgery is to remove as much of the nodular tissue as possible and if the goitre is large to relieve local symptoms. Postoperative follow-up should involve checks of thyroid function.
- Goitre recurrence, although rare, does occasionally occur.

Non-toxic multinodular goitre

Surgery

Is the preferred treatment for patients with:

- local compression symptoms
- cosmetic disfigurement
- solitary nodule with FNAC suspicious of malignancy.

Radioiodine

- Radioiodine may be particularly indicated in elderly patients in whom surgery is not appropriate. Up to 50% shrinkage of goitre mass has been reported in recent studies.

- Hypothyroidism following radioiodine is low but is still recognized and seems to be related to the degree of TSH suppression and reduction in radioiodine uptake by the extranodular tissue.

Medical treatment

- Use of T_4 to suppress TSH is associated with risk of cardiac arrhythmias and bone loss. T_4 is useful only if TSH is detectable. It is less useful in nodular goitre.

Aetiology of goitre

- autoimmune thyroid disease
- sporadic
- endemic (iodine deficiency, dietary origins)
- pregnancy
- drug-induced (ATDs, lithium, amiodarone)
- thyroiditis syndromes.

Pathology

Thyroid nodules may be described as *adenomas* if the follicular cell differentiation is enclosed within a capsule; *adenomatous* when the lesions are circumscribed but not encapsulated.

Further reading

Gharib H. Changing concepts in the diagnosis and management of thyroid nodules. *Endocrinology and Metabolism Clinics of North America* 1997; 26(4): 777–800.

Chapter 6
Thyroiditis

Background

Inflammation of the thyroid gland often leads to a transient thyrotoxicosis followed by hypothyroidism. Overt hypothyroidism caused by autoimmunity has two main forms: *Hashimoto's (goitrous) thyroiditis* and *atrophic thyroiditis (myxoedema)*

Table 6.1 Causes and characteristics of thyroiditis

Cause	Characteristic features
Pyogenic	*Staph. aureus*, streptococci, *E. coli*, tuberculosis, fungal
Sub-acute (de Quervain) (p. 67)	Thought to be viral in origin, multinuclear giant cells
Autoimmune thyroiditis (Hashimoto's)	Grossly lymphocytic and fibrotic thyrotoxicosis or hypothyroidism
Postpartum thyroiditis	Chronic lymphocytic thyroiditis, transient thyrotoxicosis or hypothyroidism
Riedel thyroiditis	Extensive fibrosis of the thyroid (p. 66)
Radiation thyroiditis	Radiation injury, transient thyrotoxicosis
Drug induced	Particularly with amiodarone

Table 6.2 Clinical presentation of thyroiditis

Form of thyroiditis	Clinical presentation	Thyroid function
Suppurative (acute)	Painful, tender thyroid, fever	Usually normal
Subacute (de Quervain)	Painful anterior neck, arthralgia, antecedent upper respiratory tract infection; generalized malaise.	Early thyrotoxicosis, occasionally late hypothyroidism
Autoimmune	Hashimoto's : goitre Atrophic: no goitre	Usually hypothyroid Sometimes euthyroid Rarely early thyrotoxicosis
Riedel	Hard woody consistency of thyroid	Usually normal

Chronic autoimmune (atrophic or Hashimoto's) thyroiditis

- *Subclinical autoimmune thyroiditis* Denotes the early stage of chronic thyroiditis. The thyroid gland is soft or firm and is usually normal in size or slightly enlarged. Thyroid function tests are normal.
- *Hashimoto's thyroiditis* Characterized by a painless, variably sized goitre with rubbery consistency and an irregular surface. The normal follicular structure of the gland is extensively replaced by lymphocytic and plasma cell infiltrates with formation of lymphoid germinal centres. The patient may have normal thyroid function or subclinical or overt hypothyroidism. Occasional patients present with thyrotoxicosis in association with a thyroid gland that is unusually firm and with high titres of circulating antithyroid antibodies.
- *Atrophic thyroiditis* Probably indicates endstage thyroid disease. These patients do not have goitre and are antibody positive. Biochemically, the picture is that of frank hypothyroidism.

Investigations

Investigations which are useful in establishing a diagnosis of Hashimoto's thyroiditis include:

- testing of thyroid function,
- thyroid antibodies (antithyroglobulin antibodies and antithyroperoxidase antibodies)
- occasionally a thyroid biopsy to exclude malignancy in patients who present with a goitre and dominant nodule.

Prognosis

The long-term prognosis of patients with chronic thyroiditis is good because hypothyroidism can easily be corrected with T_4 and the goitre is not usually of sufficient size to cause local symptoms. In the atypical situation where Hashimoto's thyroiditis presents with rapidly enlarging goitre and pain a short dose of prednisolone at a dose of 40 mg daily may prove helpful.

Any unusual increase in size of the thyroid in patients known to suffer from Hashimoto's thyroiditis should be investigated with FNAC since there is an association between this condition and thyroid lymphoma.

Other types of thyroiditis

Silent thyroiditis

Associated with transient thyrotoxicosis or hypothyroidism. A significant percentage of patients have personal or family history of autoimmune thyroid disease. It may progress to permanent hypothyroidism.

Postpartum thyroiditis (p. 506)

Thyroid dysfunction occurring within the first 6 months postpartum. Prevalence ranges from 5% to 7%. Postpartum thyroiditis develops in 30–52% of women who have positive thyroid peroxidase (TPO) antibodies. Most patients have a complete remission but some may progress to permanent hypothyroidism. It is twice as common in patients with Type I diabetes mellitus.

Chronic fibrosing (Riedel's) thyroiditis

A rare disorder characterized by intense fibrosis of the thyroid gland and surrounding structures leading to induration of the tissues of the neck. May be associated with mediastinal and retroperitoneal fibrosis, salivary gland fibrosis, sclerosing cholangitis, lachrymal gland fibrosis, and parathyroid gland fibrosis leading to hypoparathyroidism. Patients are usually euthyroid. Main differential diagnosis is thyroid neoplasia.

Management

Corticosteroids are usually ineffective. Tamoxifen is now the first line of treatment. Surgery may be required to relieve obstruction and to exclude malignancy.

Pyogenic thyroiditis

- Rare. Usually anteceded by a pyogenic infection elsewhere. Characterized by tenderness and swelling of the thyroid gland, redness and warmth of the overlying skin, and constitutional signs of infection.
- Piriform sinus should be excluded. Excision of tract is preferable to incision and drainage
- Treatment consists of antibiotic therapy and incision and drainage if a fluctuant area within the thyroid should occur.

Sub-acute thyroiditis (granulomatous, giant cell or de Quervain's thyroiditis)

- Viral in origin.Symptoms include pronounced asthenia, malaise, pain over the thyroid or pain referred to lower jaw, ear, or occiput. Less commonly the onset is acute with fever, pain over the thyroid, and symptoms of thyrotoxicosis. Characteristically signs include exquisite tenderness and nodularity of the thyroid gland. There is characteristically an elevated ESR and a depressed radionuclide (^{99m}Tc can be used) uptake. Biochemically, the patient may be initially thyrotoxic though later the patient may become hypothyroid.
- In mild cases, non-steroidal anti-inflammatory agents offer symptom relief. In severe cases glucocorticoids (prednisolone 20–40 mg/day) are effective. Propranolol can be used to control associated thyrotoxicosis. Treatment can be withdrawn when T_4 returns to normal. T_4 replacement is required if the patient becomes hypothyroid. Treatment with carbimazole or propylthiouracil is not indicated.

Further reading

Lazarus JH, Hall R, Othman S, Parkes AB, Richards CJ, McCulloch B, Harris B. The clinical spectrum of postpartum thyroid disease. *QJM* 1996; 89: 429–435.

Muller AF, Drexhage HA, Berghout A. Postpartum thyroiditis and autoimmune thyroiditis in women of child bearing age: recent insights and consequences for antenatal and postnatal care. *Endocrine Reviews* 2001; 22: 605–30.

Weetman AP. Autoimmune thyroid disease in *Endocrinology* ed DeGroot LJ and Jameson JL Vol. 2. WB Saunders & Co, Philadelphia, 2000.

Chapter 7
Hypothyroidism

Background

Hypothyroidism results from a variety of abnormalities that cause insufficient secretion of thyroid hormones. The commonest cause is autoimmune thyroid disease. *Myxoedema* is severe hypothyroidism in which there is accumulation of hydrophilic mucopolysaccharides in the ground substance of the dermis and other tissues leading to thickening of the facial features and doughy induration of the skin.

Table 7.1 Classification of the causes of hypothyroidism

	TSH	Free T_4
Non-goitrous	↑	↓
Postablative (radioiodine, surgery)		
Congenital development defect		
Atrophic thyroiditis		
Postradiation (e.g. for lymphoma)		
Goitrous	↑	↓
Chronic thyroiditis (Hashimoto's thyroiditis)		
Iodine deficiency		
Drug elicited (amiodarone, aminosalicylic acid, iodides, phenylbutazone, lithium)		
Heritable biosynthetic defects		
Maternally transmitted (antithyroid agents, iodides)		
Pituitary	↓	↓
Panhypopituitarism		
Isolated TSH deficiency		
Hypothalamic	↓	↓
Neoplasm		
Infiltrative (sarcoidosis)		
Congenital defects		
Infection (encephalitis)		
Self-limiting		
Following withdrawal of suppressive thyroid therapy		
Subacute thyroiditis and chronic thyroiditis with transient hypothyroidism		
Postpartum thyroiditis		

Clinical picture

Adult

- insidious non-specific onset
- fatigue, lethargy, constipation, cold intolerance, muscle stiffness, cramps, carpal tunnel syndrome, menorrhagia, later oligo- or amenorrhoea
- slowing of intellectual and motor activities
- decreasing appetite and weight gain
- dry skin; hair loss
- deep hoarse voice, decreasing visual acuity
- obstructive sleep apnoea

Myxoedema

- dull expressionless face, sparse hair, periorbital puffiness, macroglossia
- pale, cool skin that feels rough and doughy
- enlarged heart (dilation and pericardial effusion)
- megacolon/ intestinal obstruction
- cerebellar ataxia; psychiatric symptoms e.g. depression, psychosis
- prolonged relaxation phase of deep tendon reflexes
- peripheral neuropathy
- encephalopathy

Myxedema coma

- predisposed to by cold exposure, trauma, infection, administration of central nervous system depressants
- marked respiratory depression with increasing arterial P_{CO2}
- hyponatraemia from impaired water excretion and disordered regulation of vasopressin secretion/

Subclinical hypothyroidism

- This term is used to denote raised TSH levels in the presence of normal concentrations of free thyroid hormones. Treatment is indicated in patients with a past history of radioiodine treatment for thyrotoxicosis or positive thyroid antibodies as in these situations progression to overt hypothyroidism is almost inevitable (at least 5% per year of those with positive antithyroid peroxidase antibodies).
- There is controversy over the advantages of T_4 treatment in patients with negative thyroid antibodies and no previous radioiodine treatment.
- Some symptom scores have been shown to improve with T_4 treatment.
- There are concerns regarding the possible adverse effects in the form of reduced bone mineral density and increased risk of atrial fibrillation.
- Follow up with annual thyroid function tests is important.

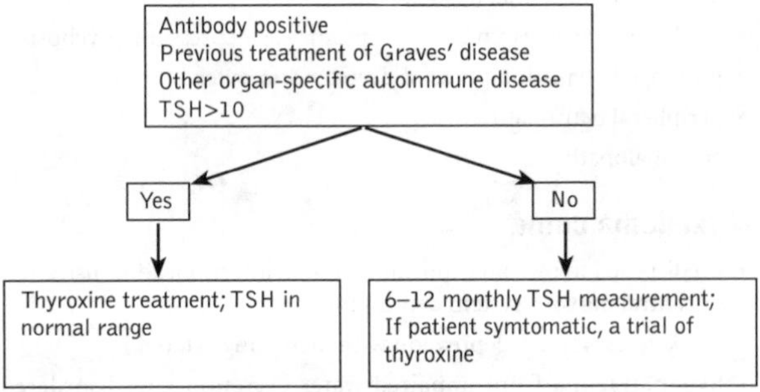

Fig. 7.1 Algorithm for management of subclinical hypothyroidism Modified from Lindsay and Toft 1997; 349: 413–7.

Treatment of hypothyroidism

- Normal metabolic state should be restored gradually as rapid increase in metabolic rate may precipitate cardiac arrhythmias
- In the younger patients, start thyroxine at 100 μg. In the elderly, with a history of ischaemic heart disease, an initial dose of thyroxine 25–50 μg can be increased by 25 μg increments at 4 week intervals until normal metabolic state is attained.
- Optimum dose determined by clinical criteria and TSH measurements
- TSH should be checked only 2 months after any dose change. Once stabilized TSH should be checked on an annual basis.
- In patients with secondary hypothyroidism, free T_4 is the most useful parameter to follow.

Management of myxoedema coma

- Identify and treat concurrent precipitating illness.
- Antibiotic therapy after blood cultures.
- Management of hypothermia by passive external rewarming.
- Manage in intensive treatment unit if comatose. If not, nurse in a warm side room.
- Give warm humidified oxygen by facemask. Mechanical ventilation needed if hypoventilating.
- Aim for slow rise in core temperature (0.5° C/h).
- Cardiac monitor for supraventricular arrhythmias.
- Correct hyponatraemia (mild fluid restriction), hypotension (cautious volume expansion with crystalloid or whole blood), and hypoglycaemia (glucose administration).
- Monitor rectal temperature, oxygen saturation, BP, CVP, and urine output hourly.
- Take blood samples for thyroid hormones, TSH and cortisol before starting treatment. If hypocortisolaemic, administer glucocorticoids.
- Thyroid hormone replacement: no consensus has been reached. The following is an accepted regimen:
  - T_4 300–500 μg i/v or by nasogastric tube as a starting dose followed by 50–100 μg daily until oral medication can be taken
  - if no improvement within 24–48 h, T_3 10 μg i/v 8 hourly or 25 μg i/v 8 hourly can be given in addition to above.
- Give hydrocortisone 50–100 mg 6–8 hourly in case of cortisol deficiency.

Congenital hypothyroidism

Incidence: About 1 in 5000 neonates. All neonates should be screened.

Thyroid agenesis

Occurs 1 in 1800 births. In 80% cases the left lobe is affected. The remaining lobe is hypertrophied. There is no palpable tissue over the agenetic lobe

Thyroid hormone dysgenesis

- Caused by inborn errors of thyroid metabolism. The disorders are mostly autosomal recessive, indicating single protein defects.
- Can be caused by inactivation of the TSH receptor, abnormalities of the thyroid transcription factors TTF1, TTF2, and PAX8, or due to defects in iodide transport, organification (peroxidase), coupling, deiodinase, or thyroglobulin synthesis.
- In a large proportion of patients with congenital hypothyroidism, the molecular background is unknown.

Pendred's syndrome

Characterized by overt or subclinical hypothyroidism, goitre, and moderate to severe sensorineural hearing impairment. The prevalence varies between 1 in 15 000 and 1 in 100 000. There is a partial iodide organification defect detected by increased perchlorate discharge. Thyroid hormone synthesis is only mildly impaired and so may not be detected by neonatal thyroid screening.

Clinical features

The following features are late sequelae of congenital hypothyroidism and, with routine screening now available, should never be seen nowadays.

- physiological jaundice
- goitre
- hoarse cry, feeding problems, constipation, somnolence
- delay in reaching normal milestones of development; short stature
- coarse features with protruding tongue, broad flat nose, widely set eyes
- sparse hair and dry skin, protuberant abdomen with umbilical hernia
- impaired mental development, retarded bone age
- epiphyseal dysgenesis, delayed dentition.

Laboratory tests

- neonatal screening
- imaging procedure: ultrasonography or ^{123}I scintigraphy
- measurement of serum thyroglobulin and low molecular weight iodopeptides in urine to discriminate between the various types of defects.
- measurement of total urinary iodine excretion to differentiate inborn errors of metabolism from acquired transient forms of hypothyroidism due to iodine deficiency or iodine excess.

Treatment

Irrespective of the cause of congenital hypothyroidism, early treatment is essential to prevent cerebral damage. Sufficient T_4 should be given to maintain the TSH in the normal range.

Further reading

de Vijlder JJM, Vulsma T. In DeGroot LJ and Jameson JL (ed.) *Endocrinology*, Vol. 2, WB Saunders & Co, Philadelphia, 2000.

Chapter 8

Amiodarone and thyroid function

Background

- Amiodarone has a high concentration of iodine (39% by weight). It is a benzofuranic derivative and its structural formula closely resembles that of thyroxine. On a dose of Amiodarone between 200–600 mg daily, 7–21 mg iodine is made available each day. The optimal daily iodine intake is 150–200 μg. Amiodarone is distributed in several tissues from where it is slowly released. In one study terminal elimination half-life of amiodarone averaged 52.6 days with a standard deviation of 23.7 days.
- Abnormalities of thyroid function occur in up to 50% of patients (Table 8.2).
- In the UK and USA, 2% of patients on Amiodarone develop thyrotoxicosis and about 13% develop hypothyroidism.
- Patients residing in areas with high iodine intake develop amiodarone induced hypothyroidism (AIH) more often than amiodarone induced thyrotoxicosis (AIT), but AIT occurs more frequently in regions with low iodine intake.
- AIT can present several months after discontinuing the drug because of its long half-life.
- Hypothyroidism is commoner in women and in patients with thyroid autoantibodies.
- Thyroid function tests should be monitored every 6 months in patients taking amiodarone.

Pathogenesis

- The high iodine content of amiodarone may inhibit thyroid hormone synthesis and release causing AIH or leading to iodine-induced thyrotoxicosis.
- Thyrotoxicosis resulting from iodine excess and therefore increased hormone synthesis is referred to as *AIT type I*. Thyrotoxicosis due to a direct toxic effect of amiodarone is referred to as *AIT type II*. (Table 8.1)
- Drug-induced destructive thyroiditis results in leakage of thyroid hormones from damaged follicles into the circulation and like subacute thyroiditis can be followed by a transient hypothyroid state before euthyroidism is restored.

Table 8.1 Characteristics of AIT

	AIT type I	AIT type II
Aetiology	Iodine toxicity	Thyroiditis
Signs of clinical thyroid disease	Yes	No
Goitre	Frequent	Infrequent
Thyroid antibodies	Positive	Negative
Radioiodine uptake	Normal	Decreased
Thyroglobulin	Normal or slightly elevated	Very elevated
Serum IL6	Normal	Very elevated
Late hypothyroidism	No	Possible
Vascularity (Doppler)	Increased/normal	Reduced

Table 8.2 Thyroid function tests in clinically euthyroid patients after administration of amiodarone

Tests	1–3 months	>3 months
Free T_3	Decreased	Remains slightly decreased, but within normal range
TSH	Transient increase	Normal
Free T_4	Modest increase	Slightly increased compared to pre-treatment values, may be in normal range or slightly increased.
Reverse T_3	Increased	Increased

Table 8.3 Side effects and complications of amiodarone therapy

Side effect	Incidence (%)
Corneal microdeposits	100
Anorexia and nausea	80
Photosensitivity; Blue/grey skin discolouration	55–75
Ataxia, tremors, peripheral neuropathy	48
Deranged liver function tests	25
Abnormal thyroid function tests	14–18
Interstitial pneumonitis	10–13
Cardiac arrhythmias	2–3

Table 8.4 Treatment of amiodarone induced thyrotoxicosis

	Type 1 AIT	Type 2 AIT
Step 1 Aim: Restore euthyroidism	Carbimazole 30–40 mg/d or Propylthiouracil 300–400 mg/d in combination with potassium perchlorate 1 g/day for 16–40 days If possible discontinue amiodarone*	Discontinue amidarone if possible* Prednisolone 40 mg/day. In mixed forms add Carbimazole or propylthiouracil as in Type 1 AIT
Step 2: Definitive treatment	Radioiodine treatment or thyroidectomy	Follow up for possible spontaneous progression to hypothyroidism
*	If amiodarone cannot be withdrawn and medical therapy is unsuccessful, consider total thyroidectomy	If amiodarone cannot be withdrawn and medical therapy is unsuccessful, consider total thyroidectomy

Table 8.5 Treatment of amiodarone induced hypothyroidism

Underlying thyroid abnormality (Usually Hashimoto's thyroiditis)	Apparently normal thyroid
Amiodarone therapy can be continued. Add thyroxine replacement therapy.	• Discontinue amiodarone if possible and follow up for restoration of euthyroidism. Potassium perchlorate 1 g/day for 30 days to accelerate return to euthyroidism • If amiodarone cannot be withdrawn, start thyroxine replacement therapy

Treatment

- Discontinuation of amiodarone does not always control the thyrotoxic state because of its long half-life (particularly in the obese).
- The first line of treatment is ATDs (carbimazole or propylthiouracil).
- Radioiodine is not usually effective because of reduced uptake by the thyroid gland.
- Surgery remains a very successful form of treatment, with euthyroidism being restored within a matter of days. Achieving preoperative euthyroidism may be difficult, however.
- Cardiac function may be compromised by propranolol used in combination with amiodarone, since this may produce bradycardia and sinus arrest.
- A combination of corticosteroids and ATDs may be effective in AIT type II. A high dose of prednisolone, 40–60 mg daily, may be required for 8–12 weeks; studies where steroids have been discontinued after 2–3 weeks have been associated with a high relapse rate.
- Potassium perchlorate inhibits iodide uptake by the thyroid gland, reduces intrathyroidal iodine, and renders thionomides more effective. It can be given as a 1 g daily dose together with carbimazole, a regime shown to restore euthyroidism in a large percentage of patients with both type I and type II AIT. In small case studies a combination of potassium perchlorate and carbimazole has been effective while treatment with amiodarone was continued.
- After chronic administration a steady state is achieved. Thus in clinically euthyroid patients on amiodarone a slightly elevated T_4 is not indicative of hyperthyroidism, nor is a low T_3 indicative of hypothyroidism.

Further reading

Wiersinga WM (1997) Amiodarone and the thyroid. In Weetman AP, Grossman A (ed.) *Pharmacotherapeutics of Thyroid Gland*, Berlin: Springer-Verlag, pp. 225–287.

L Bartalena, S Brogioni, L Grasso, F Bogazzi, A Burelli, and E Martino. Treatment of amiodarone-induced thyrotoxicosis, a difficult challenge: results of a prospective study *J Clin Endocrinol Metab.* 1996; 81: 2930–2933.

Martino E, Bartalena L, Bogazzi F, Braverman LE. The Effects of Amiodarone on the Thyroid. *Endocrine Reviews* 2001; 22(2): 240–254.

Newman CM, Price A, Davies DW, Cray TA, Weetman AP. Amiodarone and the thyroid. *Heart* 1998; 79: 121–127.

Chapter 9

Thyroid cancer

Epidemiology

- Clinically detectable thyroid cancer is rare. It accounts for <1% of all cancer and <0.5% of cancer deaths.
- Thyroid microcarcinoma (diameter <1 cm) may be found in multinodular goitres.
- Thyroid cancers are commonest in adults aged 40–50, and rare in children and adolescents.
- Women are affected more frequently than men.

Table 9.1 Classification of thyroid cancer

Cell of origin	Tumour type	Frequency (%)
Papillary	Differentiated	
	Papillary	70–80
	Follicular	15
	Undifferentiated (anaplastic)	6
C-cells	Medullary	5–10
Lymphocytes	Lymphoma	5–10

Table 9.2 Comparison of papillary, follicular and anaplastic carcinomas of the thyroid

Characteristic	Papillary Ca	Follicular Ca	Anaplastic Ca
Age at presentation	30–50 (mean 44)	40–50	60–80
Spread	Lymphatic	Haematogenous	Haematogenous
Prognosis	Good	Good	Poor
Treatment	Initially: near total thyroid-ectomy Postoperative TSH suppression High-risk patient: ^{131}I remnant ablation Postoperative total body radioiodine scan	Initially: near total thyroidectomy Postoperative TSH suppression ^{131}I remnant ablation Postoperative total body radioiodine scan	Total thyroidectomy with lymph node clearance Chemotherapy with adriamycin and cisplatin External beam irradiation

Aetiology

Irradiation

- There does not appear to be a threshold dose of external irradiation for thyroid carcinogenesis; doses of 200–500 cGy seem to produce thyroid cancer at a rate of about 0.5%/year.
- There is no evidence that therapeutic or diagnostic ^{131}I administration can induce thyroid cancer, although there is a small increase in death rates from thyroid cancer after ^{131}I. At present it is unclear whether this is due to an effect of ^{131}I or part of the natural history of the underlying thyroid disease.
- External irradiation at an age <20 years is associated with an increased risk of thyroid nodule development and thyroid cancer (most commonly papillary). The radioactive fallout from the Chernobyl nuclear explosion in 1986, resulted in a 4.7-fold increase in thyroid cancer in the regions of Belarus from 1985 to 1993, including a 34-fold increase in children. Most of these were papillary carcinomas.
- The risk is greater for women and when irradiation occurs at an younger age.
- There is a latency of at least 5 years with maximum risk at 20 years following exposure, though this was not seen following the Chernobyl disaster.

Other environmental factors

- Most investigators agree that iodine supplementation has resulted in a decrease in the incidence of follicular carcinoma.

Genetic syndromes and oncogenes

- *RET/PTC1* proto-oncogene abnormalities in the long arm of chromosome 10 are associated with some papillary tumours (5–30%), especially after irradiation (60–80%). It is similar to the abnormality associated with medullary thyroid carcinoma in MEN2A.
- 2 new protooncogenes have been have been identified: *RET/PTC2* and *RET/PTC3* TRK (less common).
- The tumour suppressor gene *p53* has been found to be mutated in dedifferentiated cancers.
- Overexpression of the *ras* oncogenes is found in papillary thyroid cancers and was found to be a marker for adverse prognosis in one study.

- c-*myc* mRNA expression has been correlated with histologic markers of papillary cancer aggression.
- PAX8-PPARγ1 may be useful in the diagnosis and treatment of thyroid carcinoma.

Papillary microcarcinoma of the thyroid (PMC)

- PMC is defined by WHO as a tumour focus of 1.0 cm or less in diameter. It is detected coincidentally on histopathological examination of the thyroid following resection of multinodular goitre.
- Autopsy studies show:
  - prevalence ranges from 1 to 35.6%
  - no significant difference in the prevalence rates of papillary microcarcinoma has been demonstrated between the sexes
  - PMC rarely progresses to clinically apparent thyroid cancer with advancing age
  - PMC can be multifocal
  - cervical lymphnode metastasis from PMC ranges from 4.3 to 18.2%
  - lymph node metastasis was most often associated with multifocal tumours.
- Although exposure to irradiation increases the likelihood of developing papillary thyroid cancer, the tumours will usually be >1.0 cm in diameter and thus not PMC.
- Follow-up studies suggest that PMC is a slow growing lesion which rarely spreads to distant sites and which carries a good prognosis.
- The recommendations for treatment of PMC vary widely:
  - The low morbidity and long survival mean that collection of randomized prospective data has never been performed and comparisons of therapies are based on retrospective studies.
  - The treatment of PMC should not cause more morbidity than the disease process itself.
  - Surgical treatment recommendations range from simple excision to ipsilateral lobectomy.
  - With adjuvant therapy the consensus is routine use of T_4 to suppress TSH, but not the use of radioiodine as there is no difference in the recurrence rate.

Papillary thyroid carcinoma

- constitutes almost 70% of all thyroid cancers
- commoner in women (3 : 1)
- rare in childhood, peaks occur in second and third decades and again in later life (bimodal frequency)
- incidence: 3–5 per 100 000 population.

Pathology

- Slow growing, usually non-encapsulated, may spread through the thyroid capsule to structures in the surrounding neck, especially regional lymph nodes. Multifocal in 30% of cases.
- Recognized variants are follicular, papillary, dorsal, columnar cell, tall cell, and diffuse sclerosing.
- *Histology* the tumour contains complex branching papillae that have a fibrovascular core covered by a single layer of tumour cells.
- Nuclear features include:
  - large size with pale staining, 'ground-glass' appearance (*orphan Annie-eye nucleus*).
  - deep nuclear grooves.
- The characteristic and pathognomic cytoplasmic feature is the 'psammoma body' which is a calcified, laminated, basophilic, stromal structure.
- It is confined to the neck in over 95% of cases, although 15–20% have local extra thyroidal invasion. Metastases (1–2% of patients) occur via lymphatics to local lymph nodes and more distantly to lungs.
- Several prognostic scoring systems are in use, none of which permits definitive decisions to be made for individual patients.

Management

Primary treatment: surgery

- Should be performed by an experienced thyroid surgeon at a centre with adequate case load to maintain surgical skills.
- In general, as near total thyroidectomy as possible should be performed.
- Clinically evident cervical lymph node metastasis is best treated with radical modified neck dissection with preservation of stern-

Adverse prognostic factors in papillary carcinoma (high-risk patients)

Thyroglobulin

- A very sensitive marker of recurrence of thyroid cancer
- Secreted by the thyroid tissue
- After total thyroidectomy and radioactive iodine ablation, the levels of thyroglobulin should be <2 ng/L.
- Measurement of thyroglobulin levels could be made difficult in the presence of antithyroglobulin antibodies.
- There is controversy over whether the patient should come off T_4 or T_3 or be started on recombinant TSH before checking the thyroglobulin levels. Coming off thyroid hormones or giving TSH increases the sentivity of thyroglobulin to detect recurrence, but this may not effect survival rates.

Recurrent disease/distant metastases

- In the case of recurrence, treatment employs all methods used in primary and adjuvant therapy.
- Surgery for local metastases.
- External radiotherapy is indicated in tumours that do not take up ^{131}I.
- Bony and pulmonary metastases (usually osteolytic) may be treated with ^{131}I.
- Unfortunately only 50% of metastases concentrate ^{131}I and bony metastases are often very difficult to irradiate.
- Some advocate use of external beam radiation.
- Response to chemotherapy is usually poor.

ocleidomastoid muscle, spinal accessory nerve, and internal jugular vein.

Adjuvant therapy: radioiodine therapy

- Postoperative radioiodine therapy is advised in the high-risk patient with differentiated thyroid cancer. After surgery in a low risk group, some thyroidologists argue that ^{131}I is not required. A dose of 3.1 GBq is used for thyroid ablation. A whole body scan done 4–6 months after administration of 150 MBq ^{131}I helps determine the presence of any residual disease. In the presence of metastasis a dose of approximately 5.5–7.4 GBq radioiodine is used. Liothyronine should be administered for 4–6 weeks in place of thyroxine. It is then omitted for 10 days prior to the scan, allowing TSH to rise. A low-iodine diet for 2 weeks increases the effective specific activity of the administered iodine.
- The patient should be isolated until residual dose meter readings indicate <30 MBq.
- Chronic suppression of serum TSH levels to <0.10 mU/l is standard practice in patients with differentiated thyroid carcinoma. Inhibition of TSH secretion reduces recurrence rate as TSH stimulates growth of the majority of thyroid cancer cells.
- Patients are followed up with thyroglobulin levels. After effective treatment thyroglobulin levels are undetectable. A trend of increasing thyroglobulin values should be investigated with a radioiodine uptake scan. Liothyronine (T_3) is substituted for T_4 4–6 weeks before the scan, and omitted for 10 days immediately beforehand.

Recombinant TSH

- Avoids morbidity of hypothyroidism during T_4 withdrawal.
- Useful for patients with TSH deficiency (hypopituitarism).
- Comparable thyroglobulin rise but reduced ^{131}I scan sensitivity compared to T_4 withdrawal.

Follicular carcinoma (FTC)

- constitutes 15% of all thyroid cancers
- mean patient age in most studies is 50 years
- commoner in women (2 : 1).
- relatively more common in endemic goitre areas.

Pathology

- Follicular carcinoma is a neoplasm of the thyroid epithelium that exhibits follicular differentiation and shows capsular or vascular invasion.
- Differentiation of benign follicular adenoma from encapsulated low-grade or minimally invasive tumours can be impossible to diagnose, particularly for the cytopathologist, and surgery is usually necessary for a follicular adenoma.
- FTC may be minimally invasive or widely invasive.
- Metastases (15–20% cases) are more likely to be spread by haematogenesis to the lung and bones and less likely to local lymph nodes.
- Hurthle cell carcinoma is an aggressive type of follicular tumour with a poor prognosis because it fails to concentrate ^{131}I.

Treatment

As for papillary thyroid carcinoma.

Follow-up of papillary and follicular thyroid carcinoma

- Follow-up usually involves an annual clinical review, with clinical examination for presence of suspicious lymph nodes and measurements of serum TSH (to ensure adequate TSH suppression to <0.1 mU/L) and thyroglobulin.
- Serum thyroglobulin should be undetectable in patients with total thyroid ablation. However, detectable levels may be seen for up to 6 months after thyroid ablation. A trend of increasing thyroglobulin level requires investigations with ^{131}I uptake scan (of thyroid hormones or with TSH stimulation) or any specific imaging modalities, such as CT scan of the lungs, or bone scans. Thyroglobulin antibodies must be checked, as there may be interactions with the thyroglobulin assays.
- Radioiodine scans are done annually for the first 3 years and if negative, not repeated unless there are clinical indications, like an increasing thyroglobulin level.
- Isolated lymph node metastases can occasionally be associated with normal thyroglobulin. Stopping thyroid hormone replacement before the measurement of thyroglobulin can increase sensitivity of detecting persistent recurrent disease.
- Detectable thyroglobulin and absent uptake on radioiodine uptake scan may be due to dedifferentiation of the tumour and failure to take up iodine. A PET scan may be useful in this situation. If a PET scan is not available, an iodine uptake scan following 150 MBq ^{131}I can be useful.

Thyroid cancer in children

- Uncommon, with an incidence of 0.2–5 per million per year.
- >85% are papillary, but with more aggressive behaviour than in adults (local invasion and distant metastases are commoner).
- Recently an increased incidence in children in Belarus and Ukraine has been reported following the Chernobyl nuclear accident in 1986. RET oncogene rearrangements are common in these tumours.
- Management is similar to adults, with a similar controversy as to the extent of initial surgery.
- Various studies report an overall recurrence rate of 0–39%; disease-free survival of 80–93%, and disease-specific mortality of 0–10%.
- Evidence is currently lacking on the independent risks or benefits of radioactive iodine or extensive surgery.
- Many investigators recommend lifelong follow-up with a combination of thyroglobulin and radionuclide scanning.

Thyroid cancer and pregnancy

- The natural course of thyroid cancer developing during pregnancy may be different from that in non-pregnant women.
- Any woman presenting with a thyroid nodule in pregnancy appears to have an increased risk for thyroid cancer.
- Evaluation should be undertaken with FNAC. Radioiodine scan is contraindicated.
- Lesions <2 cm diameter or any lesion appearing after 24 weeks gestation should be treated with TSH suppression and further evaluations carried out postpartum.
- If FNAC is suspicious or diagnostic, operation should be performed at the earliest safe opportunity – generally the second trimester or immediately postpartum.
- ^{131}I ablation should be scheduled for the postpartum period and the mother advised to stop breast-feeding.
- Avoid pregnancy for 6 months after any ^{131}I ablation.

Medullary thyroid carcinoma (MTC)

See section on MEN (Chapters 96 and page 717).

Anaplastic (undifferentiated) thyroid cancer

- Rare.
- Peak incidence: 7th decade. F : M = 1 : 1.5.
- Characterized by rapid growth of a firm/hard fixed tumour.
- Often infiltrates local tissue such as larynx and great vessels and so does not move on swallowing. Stridor and obstructive respiratory symptoms are common.
- Aggressive, with poor long term prognosis – 7% 5 year survival rate and a mean survival of 6 months from diagnosis.
- Optimal results occur following total thyroidectomy. This is usually not possible and external irradiation is used, sometimes in association with chemotherapy.

Lymphoma

- Uncommon
- Almost always associated with autoimmune thyroid disease (Hashimoto's thyroiditis). Occurs more commonly in women and in patients aged >40 years.
- Characterized by rapid enlargement of the thyroid gland.
- May be limited to thyroid gland or part of a more extensive systemic lymphoma (usually non-Hodgkin's lymphoma). Trucut biopsy may be required.
- Treatment with radiotherapy alone or chemotherapy if more extensive often produces good results.

Further reading

Ain KB. Papillary thyroid carcinoma: Aetiology, Assessment and therapy; *Endocrinology and Metabolism Clinics of North America* 1995; 24(4): 711–760.

Grebe SK, Hay ID. Follicular thyroid cancer. *Endocrinology and Metabolism Clinics of North America* 1995; 24(4): 761–802.

Kroll TG, Sarraf P, Pecciarini L, Chen CJ, Mueller E, Spiegelman BM, Fletcher JA. PAX8-PPAR gamma1 fusion oncogene in human thyroid carcinoma *Science* 2000; 289(5483): 1357–1360.

Mazzaferri EL, Jhiang SM. Long term impact of initial surgery and medical therapy on follicular and papillary cancer. *American Journal of Medicine* 1998

Wartofsky L, Sherman SI, Gopal J, Schlumberger M, Hay ID. The use of radioactive iodine in patients with papillary and follicular thyroid cancer. *Journal of Clinical Endocrinology Metabolism* 1998; 83: 4195–420.

Part II
Pituitary

Chapter 10
Anatomy and physiology of anterior pituitary gland

Anatomy

The pituitary gland is situated in the pituitary fossa. Below is the sphenoid air sinus, on either side the internal carotid artery and cavernous sinus, and above the posterior pituitary is continuous with the pituitary stalk of the basal hypothalamus, which with the pituitary portal vessels passes down through the dura mater which roofs the pituitary fossa.

The posterior pituitary gland is supplied by the inferior hypophyseal branches of the internal carotid artery, and the anterior pituitary gland by the hypothalamohypophyseal portal veins.

Physiology

Prolactin (PRL) secretion*

Pulsatile secretion in a circadian rhythm with around 14 pulses/24 h, and a superimposed bimodal 24 h pattern of secretion, with a nocturnal peak during sleep and a lesser peak in the evening.

Growth hormone (GH) secretion*

Pulsatile – GH is usually undetectable in the serum apart from 5–6 90 min pulses/24 h that occur more commonly at night.

LH/FSH secretion

Glycoprotein hormone, with a chain common to LH, FSH (also TSH and hCG), but ß chain specific for each hormone. Pulsatile secretion.

Thyroid stimulating hormone (TSH) secretion

Pulsatile, with 9 ± 3 pulses/24 h, and increased amplitude of pulses at night.

Adrenocorticotrophic hormone (ACTH)*

- Single-chain polypeptide cleaved from pro-opiomelanocortin (POMC).
- Circadian rhythm of secretion, beginning to rise from 3 a.m. to a peak before waking in the morning, and falling thereafter.

*Concentrations increased with stress: NB venepuncture.

Chapter 11
Imaging

Background

- Magnetic resonance imaging (MRI) currently provides the optimal imaging of the pituitary gland.
- Computed tomography (CT) scans may still be useful in demonstrating calcification in tumours (e.g. craniopharyngiomas) and hyperostosis in association with meningiomas, or evidence of bone destruction.
- Plain skull radiography may show evidence of pituitary fossa enlargement but has been superseded by MRI.

MRI appearances

- T1 weighted images demonstrate cerebrospinal fluid (CSF) as dark grey, and brain as much whiter. This imaging is useful for demonstrating anatomy clearly. The normal posterior pituitary gland appears bright white (due to neurosecretory granules and phospholipids) on T1 weighted images, in contrast to the anterior gland which is of the same signal as white matter. The bony landmarks have low signal intensity on MRI, and air in the sphenoid sinus below the fossa shows no signal. Fat in the dorsum sellae may shine white. T2 weighted images may sometimes be used to characterize haemisoderin and fluid contents of a cyst.
- Intravenous gadolinium compounds are used for contrast enhancement. Because the pituitary and pituitary stalk have no blood–brain barrier, in contrast to the rest of the brain, the normal pituitary gland enhances brightly following gadolinium injection. Particular uses are the demonstration of cavernous sinus involvement and microadenomas.
- The normal pituitary gland has a flat or slightly concave upper surface. In adolescence or pregnancy, the surface may become slightly convex.

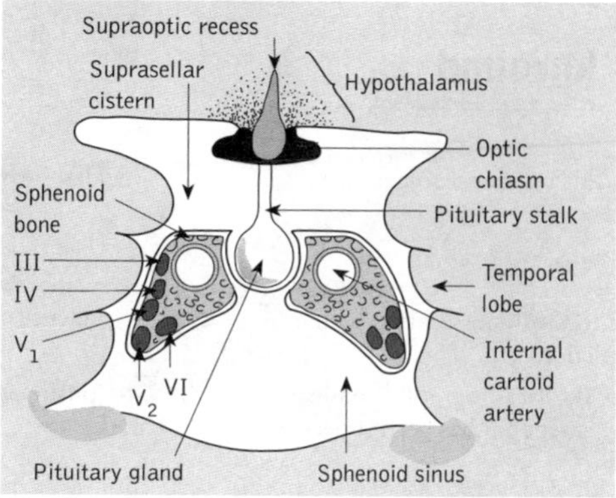

Reproduced from *Oxford Textbook of Medicine*, 3rd edn. With permission.

Pituitary adenomas

On T1 weighted images, pituitary adenomas are of lower signal intensity than the remainder of the normal gland. The size and extent of the pituitary adenomas are noted in addition to the involvement of other structures such as invasion of the cavernous sinus, erosion of the fossa, and relations to the optic chiasm. Larger tumours may show low intensity areas compatible with necrosis or cystic change, or higher intensity signal due to haemorrhage. The presence of microadenomas may be difficult to demonstrate. Contrast enhancement may assist, as may asymmetry of the gland or stalk position.

Craniopharyngiomas

These appear as suprasellar (occasionally intrasellar) masses with cystic and/or calcified portions.

Further reading

Naidich MJ, Russell EJ. Current approaches to imaging of the sellar region and pituitary. *Endocrinology and Metabolism Clinics of N America* 1999; 28: 45.

Chapter 12
Pituitary function: dynamic tests

Insulin tolerance test (ITT)

Indications

- assessment of ACTH reserve
- assessment of GH reserve.

Physiology

Intravenous insulin is used to induce hypoglycaemia (glucose <2.2 mmol/L with signs of glycopenia) which produces a standard stress causing ACTH and GH secretion.

Contraindications

- basal cortisol <100 nmol/L
- untreated hypothyroidism
- abnormal ECG
- ischaemic heart disease
- seizures
- NB Patients should discontinue oestrogen replacement for 6 weeks before the test as increased CBG will make the cortisol results difficult to interpret.

Procedure

- Continued medical surveillance is essential throughout.
- Patient is fasted overnight. Weight is checked.
- Insert cannula. Check basal (time 0) glucose, cortisol, and GH.
- Administer intravenous soluble insulin 0.15 U/kg (occasionally 0.3 U/kg needed in untreated Cushing's syndrome and acromegaly because of increased insulin resistance).
- Measure glucose, GH, and cortisol at 30, 45, 60, 90 and 120 min. Repeat insulin dose if a stick test for glucose does not show hypoglycaemia at 45 min.
- Test is terminated if prolonged hypoglycaemia – may need to administer 25 mL of 25% dextrose and i/v 100 mg hydrocortisone after sampling for cortisol and GH.
- Ensure patient eats lunch and has normal glucose before discharge.

Response

- The normal response is for glucose to fall to <2.2 mmol/L, and for cortisol to rise to >580 nmol/L and GH to >20 mU/L.

- In the presence of inadequate hypoglycaemia, the test cannot be interpreted.
- A normal cortisol response demonstrates ability to withstand stress (including major surgery) without requiring glucocorticoid cover.
- A subnormal response in an asymptomatic patient (e.g. peak cortisol 450–580 nmol/L) may be managed by administration of glucocorticoids at time of stress only.
- Other patients with subnormal responses require glucocorticoid replacement treatment (see p. 121).
- A GH response less than 10 mU/L is indicative of severe GH deficiency and in the appropriate clinical situation (see p. 124) GH replacement therapy may be recommended. Values between 10 and 20 are borderline.

Glucagon test

Indications

- assessment of ACTH reserve
- assessment of GH reserve.

Physiology

Glucagon leads to release of insulin which then leads to GH and ACTH release. The response may be secondary to the drop in glucose seen after the initial rise following glucagon injection, or may relate to the nausea induced by glucagon.

Contraindications

- Often unreliable in patients with diabetes mellitus.
- NB Patients should discontinue oestrogen replacement for 6 weeks before the test as increased CBG will make the cortisol results difficult to interpret.

Procedure

The test is performed at 9 a.m. following an overnight fast. Basal GH and cortisol are measured then 1 mg (1.5 mg if patient weighs >90 kg) glucagon is administered s/c. Samples for GH, cortisol, and glucose are checked from 90 min every 30 min till 240 min.

Response

- The normal response is a rise in glucose to a maximum at 90 min. Cortisol rises to >580 nmol/L and GH rises to >20 mU/L.
- This is a less reliable test than the ITT as 20% normal individuals may fail to respond.

ACTH stimulation test

Short synacthen test.

Indication

- assessment of adrenal cortical function
- assessment of ACTH reserve

Physiology

Low cortisol that does not rise following administration of ACTH demonstrates adrenal cortical disease. Prolonged ACTH administration will lead to cortisol secretion in ACTH deficiency but not in primary adrenal disease. It *can* be used to assess ACTH reserve, as in ACTH deficiency the adrenal cortex is unable to respond to a stimulatory signal within 30 minutes. (See p. 117)

Procedure

- The test can be done at any time of the day; the response is not time dependent.
- Synacthen is administered 250 μg i/m, and cortisol measured at 0, 30, and 60 min. When this test is used to measure ACTH reserve, only the 0 and 30 min values are required. The dose may also be given i/v with identical results.
- NB Patients should discontinue oestrogen replacement for 6 weeks before the test as increased CBG will make the cortisol results difficult to interpret.

Response

The post-stimulation cortisol should rise to >580 nmol/L at 30 min. This is an unreliable test of ACTH reserve within 6 weeks of an insult e.g. surgery to the pituitary.
Note Since 250 mcg synacthen is a supra-physiological stimulus, some investigators recommend the use of 1 mcg (low dose short synacthen)

Arginine test

Indication

Second line test for assessment of GH reserve.

Physiology

Arginine leads to GH release.

Contraindications

None

Procedure

- Fast from midnight, and administer 0.5 g/kg (max 30 g) arginine i/v in 100 mL normal saline over 30 min from time 0 (9 a.m.).
- Sample glucose and GH at 0, 30, 60, 90, and 120 min.

Response

A normal response is a rise in GH to >15–20 mU/L.

Clomiphene test

Indications

Assessment of gonadotrophin deficiency (e.g. Kallmann's syndrome).

Physiology

Clomiphene has mixed oestrogen and antioestrogenic effects. The basis of the test is competitive inhibition of oestrogen binding at the hypothalamus and pituitary gland, leading to increased LH and FSH after 3 days.

Contraindications

- Avoid in those with liver disease.
- May transiently worsen depression.

Procedure

- Advise patient of possible side-effects – visual disturbance (peripheral flickering of vision), and also of possible ovulation in women (contraceptive advice).
- Measure LH and FSH on days 0, 4, 7, and 10. In women measure day 21 progesterone to detect whether ovulation has occurred.
- Administer clomiphene 3 mg/kg (max 200 mg/day) in divided doses for 7 days.

Response

- The normal response is a doubling of gonadotrophins by day 10, usually rising beyond the normal range.
- In hypothalamic disease no gonadotropin rise is seen. Pre-pubertal patients may show a fall in gonadotrophins.
- Ovulation is presumed if day 21 progesterone is >30 nmol/L.

hCG test

Indications

To examine Leydig cell function, see p. 437.

GnRH test

Indication

Assessment of LH/FSH reserve

Physiology

Synthetic GnRH leads to pituitary gland release of FSH and LH.

Contraindications

None

Procedure

- Because of variations through the menstrual cycle, this is usually performed in women during the follicular phase if patients are cycling.
- Sample LH and FSH 0, 20, and 60 min after administration of GnRH.

Response

- LH levels rise quickly to peak at 20 min whereas FSH levels are maximal at 60 min.
- This test does not diagnose gonadotrophin deficiency, as subnormal, normal, or exaggerated responses may be seen. It demonstrates the amount of pituitary reserve of LH/FSH secretion. It is now rarely used.
- Occasional patients with acromegaly have a GH response

TRH test

This is rarely required with currently available sensitive TSH assays.

Indications

- Differentiation of pituitary TSH and hypothalamic TRH deficiency.
- Differentiation of TSH-secreting tumour from thyroid hormone resistance (Table 3.5, p. 48).
- Diagnosis of hyperthyroidism (largely superseded by sensitive TSH assay).

Procedure

- Administer TRH 200 μg i/v to supine patient.
- Measure T_4 and TSH at time 0, and TSH at 20 and 60 min.
- Note occasional reports of pituitary tumour haemorrhage. TRH induces a rise in blood pressure.

Response

- Normal response is rise in TSH by more than 2 mU/L to >3.4 mU/L, with a maximum at 20 min and lower values at 60 min.
- A delayed peak (60 min rather than 20 min) is typically found in hypothalamic disease.
- In hyperthyroidism there is no TSH response to TRH.
- The TRH test is also used rarely in investigation of hyperprolactinaemia and acromegaly (see pp. 140 and 149)

Chapter 13

Hypopituitarism

Definition

Hypopituitarism refers to either partial or complete deficiency of anterior and/or posterior pituitary hormones, and may be due to primary pituitary disease or to hypothalamic pathology which interferes with the hypothalamic control of the pituitary.

Causes

- pituitary tumours
- parapituitary tumours (craniopharyngiomas, meningiomas, secondary deposits (breast, lung), chordomas, gliomas)
- radiotherapy (pituitary, cranial, nasopharyngeal)
- pituitary infarction (apoplexy), Sheehan's syndrome
- infiltration of the pituitary gland (sarcoidosis, lymphocytic hypophysitis, haemochromatosis, Langerhans cell histiocytosis)
- empty sella
- infection (tuberculosis, pituitary abscess)
- trauma
- isolated hypothalamic releasing hormone deficiency (e.g. Kallmann's syndrome due to GnRH deficiency).

Apoplexy

Apoplexy refers to infarction of the pituitary gland due to either haemorrhage or ischaemia. It occurs most commonly in patients with pituitary adenomas, usually macroadenomas, but other predisposing conditions include postpartum (Sheehan's syndrome), radiation therapy, diabetes mellitus, anticoagulant treatment, reduction in intracranial pressure.

It may present with a syndrome which is difficult to differentiate from any other intracranial haemorrhage with sudden onset headache, vomiting, meningism, and visual disturbance and cranial nerve palsy. The diagnosis is based on the clinical features and pituitary imaging which shows high signal on T1 and T2 weighted images (see the section on imaging). It has been suggested that early surgery (within 8 days) provides the optimal chance for neurological recovery. However, some patients may be managed conservatively if the patient has no significant visual or other neurological loss.

Empty sella syndrome

An enlarged pituitary fossa, which may be primary (due to arachnoid herniation through a congenital diaphragmatic defect) or secondary to surgery, radiotherapy, or pituitary infarction. The majority of patients have normal pituitary function. Hypopituitarism (and or hyperprolactinaemia) is found in <10%. A radiologically empty sella may rarely be associated with a functioning pituitary tumour.

Sheehan's syndrome

Haemorrhagic infarction of the enlarged postpartum pituitary gland following severe hypotension usually due to blood loss, e.g. postpartum haemorrhage. Improvement in obstetric care has made this a rare occurrence in the developed world.

Features

- The clinical features depend on the severity of pituitary hormone deficiency and the rate of development, in addition to whether there is intercurrent illness. In the majority of cases, the development of hypopituitarism follows a characteristic order, with secretion of GH, then gonadotrophins being affected first followed by TSH and ACTH secretion at a later stage. PRL deficiency is rare, except in Sheehan's syndrome associated with failure of lactation. ADH deficiency is virtually unheard of with pituitary adenomas, but may be seen rarely with infiltrative disorders and trauma.
- The majority of the clinical features are similar to those occurring when there is target gland insufficiency. There are important differences – e.g. lack of pigmentation and normokalaemia in ACTH deficiency in contrast to increased pigmentation and hyperkalaemia (due to aldosterone deficiency) in Addison's disease.
- NB *Houssay phenomenon* amelioration of diabetes mellitus in patients with hypopituitarism due to reduction in counter-regulatory hormones.

Table 13.1 Summary of clinical features of hypopituitarism

Hormone deficiency	Clinical features
GH	Adult GHD (see p. 123)
	Reduced exercise capacity, reduced lean body mass, impaired psychological well-being, increased cardiovascular risk
LH/FSH	Anovulatory cycles, oligo/amenorrhoea, dyspareunia in women
	Erectile dysfunction and testicular atrophy in males
	Reduced libido, infertility and loss of secondary sexual hair (often after many years) in both sexes
ACTH	As in Addison's disease, except lack of hyperpigmentation, absence of hyperkalaemia (p. 312)
TSH	As in primary hypothyroidism (see p. 71)
PRL	Failure of lactation
ADH	Polyuria and polydipsia

Investigation

The aims of investigation of hypopituitarism are to biochemically assess the extent of pituitary hormone deficiency and also to elucidate the cause.

Basal hormone levels

Basal concentrations of the anterior pituitary hormone as well as the target organ hormone should be measured, as the pituitary hormones may remain within the normal range despite low levels of target hormone. Measurement of the pituitary hormone alone does not demonstrate that the level is inappropriately low, and the diagnosis may be missed.

- LH and FSH, and testosterone (9 a.m.) or oestradiol
- TSH and thyroxine
- 9 a.m. cortisol
- PRL
- IGF-1 (NB May be normal in up to half of GHD depending on age).

Dynamic tests

- Dynamic tests, such as the insulin tolerance test (ITT) (p. 104) or glucagon test (p. 106) if the ITT is contraindicated, are used to assess cortisol and GH reserve.
- Some centres use the short synacthen test to assess ACTH reserve using the 0 and 30 min values of cortisol (p. 107). There are few false negatives using this investigation, and it is simpler to perform than the former tests but gives no measure of GH reserve. It is important to note that falsely normal results occur when hypopituitarism is of recent onset because the test relies on the fact that ACTH deficiency causes atrophy of the adrenal cortex and therefore a delayed response to synacthen. Less than 6 weeks of ACTH deficiency may allow a 'normal' adrenal response.

Posterior pituitary function

- It is important to assess and replace corticotroph function before assessing posterior pituitary hormone production because ACTH deficiency leads to reduced GFR and the inability to excrete a water load, which may therefore mask diabetes insipidus (DI).

- Plasma and urine osmolality are often adequate as baseline measures. However, in patients suspected to have DI, a formal water deprivation test should usually be performed (see p. 235).

Investigation of the cause

- Pituitary imaging – MRI ± contrast
- Investigation of hormonal hypersecretion if a pituitary tumour is demonstrated.
- Investigation of infiltrative disorders as discussed in Chapter 27, e.g. serum and CSF ACE, ferritin, hCG.
- Occasionally biopsy of the lesion is required.

Treatment

Treatment involves adequate and appropriate hormone replacement (see chapters 14, 15 and 33), and management of the underlying cause.

Isolated defects of pituitary hormone secretion

Rarely, patients have isolated insufficiency of only one anterior pituitary hormone. The aetiology of these disorders is largely unknown, although loss of hypothalamic control may play a role; an autoimmune pathology has been suggested in some and genetic mutations in others

- GnRH deficiency (Kallman's syndrome – congenital GnRH deficiency ± anosmia)
- isolated ACTH deficiency
- Pit-1 gene mutation (leads to isolated GH, PRL, and TSH deficiency)
- Prop-1 gene mutation (leads to isolated GH, PRL, TSH and gonadotrophin deficiency).

Chapter 14

Anterior pituitary hormone replacement

Background

Anterior pituitary hormone replacement therapy is usually performed by replacing the target hormone rather than the pituitary or hypothalamic hormone that is actually deficient. The exceptions to this are GH replacement (discussed on p. 123) and when fertility is desired (p. 474).

Table 14.1 Usual doses of hormone replacement therapy

Hydrocortisone	10 mg on waking, 5 mg at lunch time, and 5 mg early evening or twice daily regimens with a total dose of 15–30 mg/d
or	
Prednisolone	4 mg on waking and 2 mg early evening (total dose 5–7.5 mg/d)
Thyroxine	100–150 μg/d
GH	0.2–0.6 mg/d (0.4–1.5 IU)
Oestrogens/testosterone	Depends on formulation

Thyroid hormone replacement

This is discussed in the section on primary hypothyroidism (p. 79).

Monitoring of therapy

In contrast to replacement in primary hypothyroidism, the measurement of TSH cannot be used to assess adequacy of replacement in TSH deficiency due to hypothalamopituitary disease. Therefore, monitoring of treatment in order to avoid under- and over-replacement should be via both clinical assessment and by measuring Free thyroid hormone concentrations.

Sex hormone replacement

See pp. 405 and 439. Oestrogen/testosterone administration is the usual method of replacement, but gonadotrophin therapy is required if fertility is desired (see p. 480).

Glucocorticoids

Replacement therapy

Patients with ACTH deficiency usually need glucocorticoid replacement only and do not require mineralocorticoids, in contrast to patients with Addison's disease (p. 318).

The glucocorticoid most commonly used for replacement therapy is *hydrocortisone*. It is rapidly absorbed with a short half-life (90–120 min). *Prednisolone* and *dexamethasone* can occasionally be used for glucocorticoid replacement. The longer half-lives of these two drugs makes them useful where sustained ACTH suppression is required in, for example, congenital adrenal hyperplasia (CAH). Dexamethasone is useful when monitoring endogenous production as it is not detected in most cortisol assays. Cortisol acetate was previously used for glucocorticoid replacement therapy but requires hepatic conversion to the active cortisol.

Monitoring of replacement

This is important to avoid over-replacement which is associated with increased blood pressure, elevated glucose and insulin, and reduced bone mineral density (BMD). Under-replacement leads to the non-specific symptoms as seen in Addison's disease (p. 314). A clinical assessment is important but biochemical monitoring using plasma and urine cortisol (UFC) measurements are used by most endocrinologists. The aim is to keep the UFC within the reference range (<220 nmol/24 h). Many centres use plasma cortisol measurements on a hydrocortisone day curve. The aim is to keep the plasma cortisol between 150 and 300 nmol/L, avoiding nadirs of <50 nmol/L pre-doses.

Safety

Patients should be encouraged to wear a Medic-Alert indicating that they are cortisol deficient, to carry a steroid card, and to keep a vial of parenteral hydrocortisone at home to be administered in emergency situations.

Equivalent oral glucocorticoid doses

Prednisolone 5 mg is approximately equivalent to

- hydrocortisone 20 mg
- dexamethasone 0.75 mg
- methylprednisolone 4 mg.

Acute/severe intercurrent illness

- *Mild disease without fever* No change in glucocorticoid replacement.
- *Pyrexial illness* Double replacement dose (e.g. hydrocortisone 20, 10, 10 mg) for duration of fever.
- *Vomiting or diarrhoea* Parenteral therapy 100 mg i/m (from GP/trained relative; useful for patient to have vial of hydrocortisone at home with instruction sheet for emergency administration by suitable trained personnel).
- *Severe illness/operation* Parenteral therapy with i/m hydrocortisone 50–100 mg 6 hourly (e.g. 72 h for major surgery, 24 h for minor surgery).

Hydrocortisone day curve

There are various protocols for this test ranging from a three-point curve to detect under-replacement (used with 24 h UFC to detect over-replacement) – serum cortisol checked at 9. a.m., 12.30 p.m. (before the lunch time dose), and 5 p.m. (pre evening dose), to more frequent sampling to detect over and under-replacement. This involves serum cortisol at time 0, then administration of the morning dose of hydrocortisone. Plasma cortisol is then checked at 30 min, 1 h, 2, 3, and 5 h (prelunchtime dose specimen), and 7 and 9 h (pre evening dose) followed by samples at 10 and 11 h.

- Oral oestrogen therapy should be stopped 6 weeks before the test as increased CBG leading to higher cortisol values will make the test uninterpretable.
- This test is only valid for hydrocortisone replacement. Prednisolone or dexamethasone replacement can only be monitored clinically.

Chapter 15
Growth hormone replacement therapy in adults

Background

There is now a considerable amount of evidence that there are significant and specific consequences of GH deficiency (GHD) in adults, and that many of these features improve with GH replacement therapy. GH replacement for adults has now been approved in many countries.

Definition

It is important to differentiate between adult and childhood onset GHD.

- Although *childhood onset* GHD occurs secondary to structural lesions such as craniopharyngiomas and germinomas, and following treatment such as cranial irradiation, the commonest cause in childhood is an isolated variable deficiency of GH releasing hormone (GHRH) which may resolve in adult life because of maturation of the hypothalamo-somatotroph axis. It is therefore important to retest patients with childhood onset GHD when linear growth is completed (50% recovery of this group).
- *Adult onset* GHD usually occurs secondary to a structural pituitary or parapituitary condition or due to the effects of surgical treatment or radiotherapy.

Prevalence

- adult onset GHD 1/10 000
- adult GHD due to adult and childhood onset GHD 3/10 000.

Benefits of GH replacement

- Improved quality of life and psychological well-being.
- Improved exercise capacity.
- Increased lean body mass and reduced fat mass.
- Prolonged GH replacement therapy (more than 12–24 months) has been shown to increase BMD, which would be expected to reduce fracture rate.
- There are as yet no outcome studies in terms of cardiovascular mortality. However, GH replacement does lead to a reduction (approximately 15%) in cholesterol. GH replacement also leads to improved ventricular function and increased left ventricular mass.

Diagnosis

The diagnosis of GHD depends on appropriate biochemical testing in the presence of an appropriate clinical context. The latter is important, because distinguishing 'partial GHD' from physiological causes of reduced GH secretion such as obesity or ageing and pathological causes, e.g. hypercortisolaemia in Cushing's syndrome, can be problematic. In these situations GHD can be diagnosed when there is supportive evidence such as pituitary disease and other anterior pituitary hormone deficiencies.

Who should be tested?

As the features of GHD may be non-specific, and biochemical tests can be misleading in certain clinical situations such as obesity, investigation of GHD should only be performed in the following groups of patients:

- Patients with hypothalamo-pituitary disease (GHD occurs early in hypopituitarism, and is almost invariable in patients with other anterior pituitary hormone deficiencies).
- Patients who had childhood onset GHD.
- Patients who have received cranial irradiation.

Investigation of GH deficiency

Dynamic tests of GH secretion

- ITT most widely used test. Peak GH <10 mU/L(3 μg/L) are diagnostic of GHD. GH values of 10–20 mU/L indicate partial GHD.
- Alternative tests if the ITT is contraindicated include a combination of GHRH and GH releasing peptide-6 (GHRP-6), glucagon, arginine stimulation tests, or arginine in combination with GHRH. The clonidine test, although useful in paediatric practice, is not helpful in the diagnosis of adult GHD. The recently described natural ligand for the GHRH receptor GHrelin may prove useful in the future. Further validation of these newer tests and determination of cut-off values is required.
- A second confirmatory dynamic biochemical test is recommended, particularly in patients who have suspected isolated GH deficiency. A single GH dynamic test is sufficient to diagnose GHD in patients with two or three pituitary hormonal defects.

IGF-1

IGF-1 concentrations may remain within the age-matched reference range despite severe GHD in up to 50% of patients, and therefore does not exclude the diagnosis, and reduced IGF-1 is seen in a number of conditions.

Investigations in adult GH deficiency

- stimulated GH below 10 mU/L (3 μg/L)
- low or low–normal IGF-1 (IGF-1 may be normal in up to 50%, depending on age)
- decreased BMD
- increased insulin resistance
- hyperlipidaemia (increased LDL)
- impaired cardiac function.

Causes of lowered IGF-1 levels

- GHD
- malnutrition
- poorly controlled diabetes mellitus
- hepatic disease
- renal disease
- severe intercurrent illness.

Clinical features of GH deficiency

- impaired well-being
- reduced energy and vitality (depressed mood, increased social isolation, increased anxiety)
- reduced muscle mass and impaired exercise capacity
- increased central adiposity (increased waist : hip ratio) and increased total body fat
- decreased sweating and impaired thermogenesis
- increased cardiovascular risk
- increased fracture risk (osteoporosis).

Treatment of GH deficiency

All patients with GHD should be considered for GH replacement therapy. In particular, patients with impaired quality of life, reduced mineral density, an adverse cardiovascular risk profile, and reduced exercise capacity should be considered for treatment.

Dose

- Unlike paediatric practice, where GH doses are determined by body weight and surface area, most adult endocrinologists use dose titration using serial IGF-1 measurements to increase the dose of GH until the IGF-1 approaches the middle to upper end of the age-matched IGF-1 reference range. This reduces the likelihood of side-effects, mainly related to fluid retention, which were frequently observed in the early studies of GH replacement in adults when doses equivalent to those used in paediatric practice were used.
- The normal production of GH is 0.2–0.5 mg/day in an adult. Current recommendations are a starting dose of 0.1–0.4 mg/d. The maintenance dose is usually 0.2–0.6 mg/d. The dose in women is often higher than for age-matched men.

Monitoring of treatment

- A clinical examination, looking for reduction in overall body weight (a good response is loss of 3–5 kg in 12 months), and reduced waist to hip ratio. Blood pressure may fall in hypertensive patients because of reduction in peripheral systemic vascular resistance.
- IGF-1 is monitored to avoid over-replacement, aiming to keep values within the age-matched reference range. During dose titration, IGF-1 should be measured every 1–2 months. Once a stable dose is reached, IGF-1 should be checked at least once a year.
- The adverse effects experienced with GH replacement usually resolve with dose reduction, and tend to be less frequent with the lower starting doses used in current practice.
- GH treatment may be associated with impairment of insulin sensitivity, and therefore markers of glycaemia should be monitored.
- Lipids should be monitored annually. Bone mineral density should be monitored every 2 years, particularly in those with reduced BMD.
- It may be helpful to monitor quality of life using a questionnaire such as the AGHDA (adult GHD assessment) questionnaire.

GH therapy in special situations

- *Pregnancy* There are currently no data on GH replacement in pregnancy. There are occasional reports of continued GH replacement throughout pregnancy with no adverse effect.
- *Critical illness* There is no good evidence for a beneficial effect of GH replacement during critical illness. Patients should continue GH replacement during non-severe illness, but many endocrinologists would suggest that GH should be discontinued in patients who are severely ill: for example, receiving major surgery or on ITU.
- *Cardiac failure* GH treatment has recently been suggested as a potential therapy in dilated cardiomyopathy. Longer term data are required in this group of patients.

Adverse effects of GH replacement

- Sodium and water retention.
  - weight gain
  - carpal tunnel syndrome
- Hyperinsulinaemia.
- Arthralgia (possibly due to intra-articular cartilage swelling).
- Myalgia.
- Benign intracranial hypertension (resolves on stopping treatment).
- There are no data to suggest that GH therapy affects tumour development. (No evidence from long-term studies in children of increased risk of recurrence with GH treatment. Insufficient long-term data in adults.)

Contraindications to GH replacement

- active malignancy
- benign intracranial hypertension
- pre-proliferative/proliferative retinopathy in diabetes mellitus.

- As the long-term safety and efficacy of GH replacement in adults is as yet unknown, it is recommended that patients receiving GH therapy should remain under the care of an endocrinologist. There are large databases of patients receiving GH in order to monitor and determine these questions regarding long-term benefits and safety, particularly with regard to cardiovascular risk.

Further reading

Carroll PV, Christ ER, Bengtsson BA *et al.*, GH deficiency in adulthood and the effects of GH replacement: a review. *Journal of Clinical Endocrinology and Metabolism* 1998;83: 382–395.

Consensus Guidelines for the Diagnosis and Treatment of Adults with GH deficiency: Summary Statement of the GH Research Society Workshop on adult GH deficiency. *Journal of Clinical Endocrinology and Metabolism* 1998;83: 379–381.

Chapter 16
Pituitary tumours

Pathogenesis

The mechanism of pituitary tumourogenesis remains largely unclear. Pituitary adenomas are monoclonal, supporting the theory that there are intrinsic molecular events leading to pituitary tumourogenesis. However, the mutations (e.g. p53) found in other tumour types are only rarely found. A role for hormonal factors and in particular the hypothalamic hormones in tumour progression is likely.

Table 16.1 Approximate relative frequencies of pituitary tumours

Tumour type	Prevalence	Annual incidence
Incidental pituitary microadenomas	10–25% autopsies	
Clinically overt pituitary adenomas		1–2/100 000
Acromegaly	60 cases/million	4 cases/million
Cushing's syndrome		2 cases/million
Non-functioning adenoma		6 cases/million
Prolactinomas		10 cases/million (if hyperprolactinaemia is considered, then higher incidence)

NB Good epidemiological data are lacking except in acromegaly. Many of these figures derive from the pre-MRI era.

Molecular mechanisms of pituitary tumour pathogenesis

Activation of oncogenes

- *Gsα mutation* found in up to 40% GH-secreting tumours (less in non-Caucasians), and also described in a minority of NFAs and ACTH-secreting tumours.
- *Ras mutation* found in aggressive tumours and mainly pituitary carcinomas. ?Role in malignant transformation.
- *PTTG (pituitary tumour transforming gene)* has recently been described and found to be over-expressed in pituitary tumours. Its role in tumour pathogenesis is as yet uncertain.

Inactivation of tumour suppressor genes (TSG)

- *MEN-1 gene* LOH at 11q13 had been previously demonstrated in up to 20% sporadic pituitary tumours; however, the expression of the MEN-1 gene product, menin, is not down-regulated in the majority of sporadic pituitary tumours.
- *Rb gene* Mutations in mice lead to intermediate lobe corticotroph adenomas; however, no mutations have been demonstrated in human pituitary adenomas.

Cyclins and modulators of cyclin activity

- Mutations of the cyclin-dependent kinases *p27 and p18* are rare in human pituitary tumours (unlike studies in mice). p27 may be translationally down-regulated and p16 may be transcriptionally silenced by methylation of its gene. Cyclin D1 over-expression may be an early step in pituitary tumourogenesis as it is commonly found in different tumour types.
- *p53* Mutations are rare in pituitary tumours.

Alterations in receptor and growth factor expression (e.g. TGF, activin, bFGF)

No consistent patterns have emerged.

Further reading

Asa SL, Ezzat S. The cytogenesis and pathogenesis of pituitary adenomas. *Endocrine Reviews* 1998;19: 798–827.

Chapter 17
Prolactinomas

Epidemiology

- Prolactinomas are the commonest functioning pituitary tumour.
- Post-mortem studies show microprolactinomas in 10% the population.
- During life, microprolactinomas are commoner than macroprolactinomas, and there is a female preponderance of microprolactinomas.

Pathogenesis

Unknown. Occur in 20% of patients with MEN-1. (Prolactinomas are commonest pituitary tumour in MEN-1 and may be more aggressive than sporadic prolactinomas.) Malignant prolactinomas are very rare and may harbour *ras* mutations.

Causes of hyperprolactinaemia

- *Physiological*
  - pregnancy
  - sexual intercourse
  - nipple stimulation/suckling
  - neonatal
  - stress
- *Pituitary tumour*
  - prolactinomas
  - mixed GH/PRL secreting tumour
  - macroadenoma compressing stalk
  - empty sella
- *Hypothalamic disease* mass compressing stalk (craniopharyngioma, meningioma, neurofibromatosis)
- *Infiltration* sarcoidosis, Langerhans cell histiocytosis
- *Stalk section* head injury, surgery
- *Cranial irradiation*
- *Drug treatment*
  - dopamine receptor antagonists (metoclopramide, domperidone)
  - neuroleptics* (thioridazine, chlorpromazine, haloperidol, sulpiride, fluphenazine, flupenthixol)
  - antidepressants (tricyclics, selective serotonin reuptake inhibitors, monoamine oxidase inhibitors)
  - cardiovascular drugs (verapamil, methyldopa)
  - opiates
  - protease inhibitors (e.g. ritonavir, indinavir, zidovudine)
  - others (bezafibrate, omeprazole, H2 antagonists)
- *Metabolic*
  - hypothyroidism (TRH increases PRL)
  - chronic renal failure (reduced PRL clearance)
  - severe liver disease (disordered hypothalamic regulation)
- *Other*
  - PCOS (can make differential diagnosis of menstrual problems difficult)
  - chest wall lesions – zoster, burns, trauma (stimulation of suckling reflex).

* clozapine, quetiapine and olanzapine are antipsychotics with little or no effect on prolactin.

Clinical features

Hyperprolactinaemia (microadenomas and macroadenomas)

- Galactorrhoea (up to 90% women, 10–20% men).
- Disturbed gonadal function in women presents with menstrual disturbance (up to 95%) – amenorrhoea, oligomenorrhoea, or with infertility, and reduced libido.
- Disturbed gonadal function in men presents with loss of libido and/or erectile dysfunction. Presentation with reduced fertility and oligospermia or gynaecomastia is unusual.
- Hyperprolactinaemia is associated with a long-term risk of reduced BMD.
- Hyperprolactinaemia inhibits GnRH release, leading to reduced LH secretion. There may be a direct action of PRL on the ovary to interfere with LH and FSH signalling which inhibits oestradiol and progesterone secretion and also follicle maturation.

Mass effects (macroadenomas only)

- Headaches and visual field defects (uni- or bitemporal field defects).
- Hypopituitarism.
- Invasion of the cavernous sinus may lead to cranial nerve palsies.
- Occasionally very invasive tumours may erode bone and present with a CSF leak or secondary meningitis.

Investigation

Serum PRL

- The differential diagnosis of elevated PRL is shown on p. 137. Note that the stress of venepuncture may cause mild hyperprolactinaemia, so 2–3 levels should be checked, preferably through an indwelling cannula after 30 min.
- Serum PRL >3000 mU/L is suggestive of a tumour – either a microprolactinoma or a macroadenoma compressing the pituitary stalk with loss of dopamine inhibitory tone to the lactotroph and subsequent hyperprolactinaemia.
- Serum PRL >6000 mU/L is diagnostic of a macroprolactinoma.
- Serum PRL 3000–6000 mU/L in association with a macroadenoma may be due to disconnection or due to a macroprolactinoma. Since the serum PRL falls with dopamine agonist treatment in either situation, but tumour shrinkage occurs only with macroprolactinomas, these patients should be carefully followed if treated with dopamine agonists and rescanned at 6 weeks. Lack of tumour shrinkage suggests a macroadenoma with stalk effect and surgery is advisable.
- *Hook effect* This occurs where the assay utilizes antibodies recognizing two ends of the molecule. One is used to capture the molecule, and one to label it. If PRL levels are very high, it may be bound by one antibody but not by the other. Thus above a certain concentration, the signal will reduce rather than increase and very high PRL levels will be spuriously reported as normal.

Thyroid function and renal function

Hypothyroidism and chronic renal failure are causes of hyperprolactinaemia.

Dynamic tests

These tests are used by some groups to attempt to differentiate between true idiopathic hyperprolactinaemia and hyperprolactinaemia due to an undetectable microprolactinoma.

Dopamine antagonist test

- I/v metoclopramide (10 mg).
- *Normal/hyperprolactinaemia due to other causes* At least twofold rise in PRL. No change in TSH.
- *Prolactinomas* Blunted PRL response and/or exaggerated TSH response

TRH test (p. 111)

- 200 μg TRH i/v
- Serum PRL at 0, 20 and 60 min.
- *Prolactinomas* blunted rise in PRL.

Imaging

- *MRI* Microadenomas usually appear as hypointense lesions within the pituitary on T1 weighted images. Negative imaging is an indication for contrast enhancement with gadolinium. Stalk deviation or gland asymmetry may also suggest microadenoma.
- Macroadenomas are space-occupying tumours often associated with bony erosion and/or cavernous sinus invasion

'Big' PRL

Occasionally, larger forms of PRL are detected in the circulation. Although these are measurable in the prolactin assay, they do not interfere with reproductive function. The most common is 'macroprolactin'. Typically there is hyperproctinaemia with regular ovulatory menstrual cycles. Assays for macroprolactin are available.

Hyperprolactinaemia and drugs

Antipsychotic agents are the most likely psychotropic agents to cause hyperprolactinaemia. If dose reduction is not possible or not effective, then an MRI to exclude a prolactinoma, and treatment of hypogonadism may be indicated. Where dopamine antagonism is the mechanism of action of the drug, then dopamine agonists may reduce efficacy. Drug-induced increases in PRL are usually <5000 mU/L.

'Idiopathic' hyperprolactinaemia

When no cause is found following evaluation as above, the hyperprolactinaemia is designated idiopathic, but in many cases is likely to be due to a tiny microprolactinoma which is not demonstrable on current imaging techniques. In other cases it may be due to alterations in hypothalamic regulation. Follow-up of these patients shows that in 1/3, PRL levels return to normal, in 10–15% there is a further increase in PRL, and in the remainder PRL levels remain stable.

Treatment

Aims of therapy

- *Microprolactinomas* restoration of gonadal function.
- *Macroprolactinomas*
  - reduction in tumour size and prevention of tumour expansion
  - restoration of gonadal function.
- Although microprolactinomas may expand in size without treatment, the majority do not (<7%). Therefore although restoration of gonadal function is usually achieved by lowering PRL levels. Ensuring adequate sex hormone replacement is an alternative if the tumour is monitored in size.
- Macroprolactinomas, however, will continue to expand and lead to pressure effects. Definitive treatment of the tumour is therefore necessary.

Drug therapy – dopamine agonists

- Dopamine agonist treatment (see p. 224) leads to suppression of PRL in most patients, with secondary effects of normalization of gonadal function and termination of galactorrhoea. Tumour shrinkage occurs at a variable rate and extent, and must be carefully monitored.
- *Cabergoline* is more effective in normalization of PRL in microprolactinoma (83% compared with 59% on bromocriptine) with fewer side-effects than *bromocriptine*.
- In patients with macroadenomas and PRL 3000–5000 mU/L a trial of dopamine agonist therapy is reasonable provided that surgical intervention occurs if there is visual deterioration or failure to shrink significantly at 6–12 weeks. Approximately 60% of patients will show normalization of PRL and tumour shrinkage with bromocriptine or cabergoline.
- Dopamine agonist resistance may occur when there are reduced numbers of D2 receptors.

Surgery (see p. 212)

- Since the introduction of dopamine agonist treatment, transsphenoidal surgery is indicated only for patients who are resistant to or intolerant of dopamine agonist treatment. The cure rate for macroprolactinomas treated with surgery is poor (30%), and therefore drug treatment is first-line in tumours of all size. Occasionally surgery may be required for patients with CSF leak secondary to an invasive macroprolactinoma. Cure rates for microprolactinomas treated with surgery are >80%, but the risk of hypopituitarism (GH deficient in 25%) and recurrence (4% at 5 yrs) makes this a second-line option.

- The surgical management of a CSF leak can be very difficult in patients with very invasive tumours. Tumour shrinkage with dopamine agonists will either precipitate or worsen the leak, with the subsequent risk of meningitis. There is no evidence for the long-term use of prophylactic antibiotics in this group, but patients at risk should be informed of the warning symptoms and advised to seek expert medical attention urgently.

Radiotherapy (see p. 218)

- Standard pituitary irradiation leads to slow reduction (over years) of PRL in the majority of patients. While waiting for radiotherapy to be effective, dopamine agonist therapy is continued, but should be withdrawn on a biannual basis at least to assess if it is still required.
- Radiotherapy is rarely indicated in the management of patients with microprolactinomas. It is useful in the treatment of macroprolactinomas once the tumour has been shrunk away from the chiasm.

Prognosis

- The natural history of microprolactinomas is difficult to assess. However, they are a common post-mortem incidental finding, and <17% show any increase in tumour size. It has been demonstrated that hyperprolactinaemia in approximately 1/3 of women will resolve particularly after the menopause or pregnancy. This shows that patients receiving dopamine agonist treatment for microprolactinoma should have treatment withdrawn intermittently to assess the continued requirement for it, and certainly the dose may be titrated downwards over time.
- There are few data on dopamine agonist withdrawal in macroprolactinomas in the absence of definitive treatment (radiotherapy or surgery). There are data suggesting that cautious attempts at dose reduction could be considered after 2–5 years. These patients would need close monitoring and scans. In the absence of definitive management of the tumour, complete withdrawal of drug treatment is likely to be associated with tumour enlargement.

Management of prolactinomas in pregnancy

See p. 512.

Further reading

Bevan JS, Webster J, Burke CW, Scanlon MF. Dopamine agonists and pituitary tumour shrinkage. *Endocrinology Reviews* 1992; 13: 220–240.

Molitch ME. Pregnancy and the hyperprolactinaemic woman. *New England Journal of Medicine* 1985; 312: 1364–1370.

Molitch ME. Pathologic hyperprolactinaemia. *Endocrinology and Metabolism Clinics of North America* 1992; 21: 877–910.

Tsagarakis S, Grossman A, Plowman PN, Jones AE, Touzel R, Rees LH, Wass JAH, Besser GM. Megavoltage pituitary irradiation in the management of prolactinomas: long-term follow-up. *Clinical Endocrinology* 1991; 34: 399–406.

Chapter 18
Acromegaly

Definition

Acromegaly is the clinical condition resulting from prolonged excessive GH and hence, IGF-1 secretion in adults. GH secretion is characterized by blunting of pulsatile secretion and failure of GH to become undetectable during the 24 h day, unlike normal controls.

Epidemiology

- Rare. Equal sex distribution.
- Prevalence 40–60 cases/million population. Annual incidence of new cases in the UK is 4/million population.
- Onset is insidious, and there is therefore often a considerable delay between onset of clinical features and diagnosis. Most cases are diagnosed at 40–60 years. Typically acromegaly occurring in an older patient is a milder disease with lower GH levels and a smaller tumour.

Pituitary gigantism

The clinical syndrome resulting from excess GH secretion in children prior to fusion of the epiphyses.

- Rare.
- Increased growth velocity without premature pubertal manifestations should arouse suspicion of pituitary gigantism.
- *Differential diagnosis* Marfan's syndrome, neurofibromatosis, pubertal disorders, cerebral gigantism (large at birth with accelerated linear growth, and disproportionately large extremities – associated normal IGF-1 and GH).
- Arm span > standing height is compatible with eunochoid features, and suggests onset of disease before epiphyseal fusion (pituitary gigantism).

Causes

- *Pituitary adenoma* (>99% of cases) Macroadenomas > microadenomas. Local invasion is common, but frank carcinomas are very rare.
- *GHRH secretion*
  - hypothalamic secretion
  - ectopic GHRH e.g. carcinoid tumour (pancreas, lung) or other neuroendocrine tumours
- *Ectopic GH secretion* Very rare. One report of a pancreatic islet cell tumour secreting GH and one of a lymphoreticulosis.
- There has been some progress on the molecular pathogenesis of the GH secreting pituitary adenomas – as mutations of the Gsα are found in up to 40% of tumours. This leads to an abnormality of the G protein that usually inhibits GTPase activity in the somatotroph.

Associations

- *MEN-1* less common than prolactinomas (p. 718).
- *Carney complex* AD, spotty cutaneous pigmentation, cardiac and other myxomas, and endocrine overactivity, particularly Cushing's syndrome due to nodular adrenal cortical hyperplasia and GH secreting pituitary tumours in less than 10% of cases. Mainly due to activating mutations of protein kinase A (p. 732).
- *Isolated familial somatotrophinomas* existence of two or more cases of acromegaly or gigantism in a family that does not exhibit MEN-1 or Carney complex. (Possibly linked to chromosome 11q13.)

Clinical features

The clinical features arise from the effects of excess GH/IGF-1, excess PRL in some (as there is co-secretion of PRL in a minority (30%) of tumours, or rarely stalk compression), and the tumour mass.

Symptoms

- increased sweating (>80% of patients)
- headaches (independent of tumour effect)
- tiredness and lethargy
- joint pains
- change in ring or shoe size.

Signs

- *Facial appearance* Coarse features, oily skin, frontal bossing, enlarged nose, deep nasolabial furrows, prognathism and increased interdental separation.
- *Deep voice* (laryngeal thickening).
- *Tongue enlargement* (macroglossia).
- *Musculoskeletal changes* enlargement of hands and feet, degenerative changes in joints lead to osteoarthritis. Generalized myopathy.
- *Soft tissue swelling* may lead to entrapment neuropathies such as carpal tunnel syndrome (40% of patients).
- *Goitre and other organomegaly* (liver, heart, kidney).

Complications

- hypertension (40%)
- insulin resistance and impaired glucose tolerance (40%)/ diabetes mellitus (20%)
- obstructive sleep apnoea (due to soft tissue swelling in nasopharyngeal region)
- increased risk of colonic polyps and colonic carcinoma (extent currently considered controversial)
- ischaemic heart disease and cerebrovascular disease
- congestive cardiac failure.

Effects of tumour

- visual field defects
- hypopituitarism.

Investigations

Oral glucose tolerance test

- In acromegaly, there is failure to suppress GH to <2 mU/L in response to a 75 g oral glucose load. In contrast, the normal response is GH suppression to undetectable levels.
- *False positives* chronic renal and liver failure, malnutrition, diabetes mellitus, heroin addiction, adolescence (due to high pubertal GH surges).

Random GH

Not useful in the diagnosis of acromegaly as although normal healthy subjects have undetectable GH levels throughout the day, there are pulses of GH which are impossible to differentiate from the levels seen in acromegaly. However, a random GH <1 mU/L excludes the diagnosis.

IGF-1

Useful in addition to the OGTT in differentiating patients with acromegaly from normals, as it is almost invariably elevated in acromegaly except in severe intercurrent illness. It has a long half-life as it is bound to binding proteins, and reflects the effect of GH on tissues. However, abnormalities of GH secretion may remain while IGF-1 is normal.

IGFBP3

IGFBP3 concentrations correlate with IGF-1, and the use of this assay in both the diagnosis and monitoring of acromegaly has been advocated. It does not give such clear differentiation in the diagnosis as IGF.

TRH test (p. 111)

The normal GH response at 20 and 60 min following 200 g TRH i/v is GH suppression; however, 80% of patients with acromegaly show an increase (by 50% of basal). This test is usually not required as the OGTT and IGF-1 usually provide the diagnosis. It may be helpful in patients with equivocal results.

MRI

MRI usually demonstrates the tumour, and whether there is extrasellar extension either suprasellar or into the cavernous sinus. In addition, plain radiographs may demonstrate enlargement of the pituitary fossa and frontal sinuses, although these are usually not performed routinely.

Pituitary function testing (see p. 104)

Serum PRL should be measured as some tumours co-secrete both GH and PRL.

Serum calcium

Some patients are hypercalcaemic due to increased 1,25-DHCC as GH stimulates renal 1α-hydroxylase. There may be an increased likelihood of renal stones due to hypercalcaemia as well as hypercalciuria (which occurs in 80%). Rarely hypercalcaemia may be due to associated MEN-1 and hyperparathyroidism.

GHRH

Occasionally it is not possible to demonstrate a pituitary tumour, or pituitary histology reveals hyperplasia. A serum GHRH in addition to radiology of the chest and abdomen may then be indicated to identify the cause, usually a GHRH carcinoid of lung or pancreas.

GHDC

- GH taken at 4–5 time points during the day.
- This is used to assess response to treatment following surgery or radiotherapy, and also to assess GH suppression on somatostatin analogues, in order to determine whether an increase in dose is required.
- It does not have a role in the diagnosis of acromegaly, but in acromegaly GH is detectable in all samples in contrast to normal. The degree of elevation of GH is relevant to the response to all forms of treatment; the higher the GH the less frequent is treatment by surgery, drugs, or radiotherapy effective.

Differential diagnosis of elevated GH

- pain
- pregnancy
- puberty
- adolescence if tall
- stress
- chronic renal failure
- chronic liver failure
- heart failure
- diabetes mellitus
- malnutrition
- prolonged fast.
- severe illness
- heroin addiction

Note on units for GH assay

- GH concentrations may be measured in mU/L or μg/L. The equivalent ratio of mU/L to μg/L was previously considered to be 2 and now 3.
- To improve standardization, it is recommended that the GH reference preparation should be a recombinant 22 kDa hGH; presently 88/624.
- There is currently no acceptable IGF-1 reference preparation.

Management

The management strategy depends on the individual patient, and also on the tumour size. A tumour causing compressive effects requires definitive management, whereas microadenomas do not necessarily need tumour removal. Lowering of GH is essential in all situations.

Trans-sphenoidal surgery (see p. 212)

- This is usually the first line for treatment in most centres.
- Reported cure rates vary: 40–91% for microadenomas and 10–48% for macroadenomas, depending on surgical expertise.
- A GHDC should be performed following surgery to assess whether 'safe' levels of GH and IGF-1 have been attained. If the mean GH is < 5 mU/L then the patient can be followed up with annual IGF-1 and/or GH assessment. If safe levels of GH have not been achieved, then medical treatment and or radiotherapy is indicated.

Role of preoperative octreotide treatment

This leads to some tumour shrinkage in at least 40% of cases, and it has been suggested that it may lead to reduced operative morbidity, and possibly improve surgical results.

Tumour recurrence following surgery

This is defined as tumour regrowth and increase in GH levels leading to active acromegaly following postoperative normalization of GH levels. Using the definition of postoperative cure as mean GH <5 mU/L, the reported recurrence rate is low (6% at 5 years).

Radiotherapy (see p. 218)

- This is usually reserved for patients following unsuccessful trans-sphenoidal surgery, only occasionally is it used as primary therapy. The largest fall in GH occurs during the first 2 years, but GH continues to fall after this. However, normalization of mean GH may take several years and during this time adjunctive medical treatment (usually with somatostatin analogues) is required. With a starting mean GH >50 mU/L, it takes on average 6 years to achieve mean GH <5 mU/L compared with 4 years with starting mean GH <50 mU/L.
- After radiotherapy, somatostatin analogues should be withdrawn on an annual basis to perform a GHDC to assess progress and identify when mean GH <5 mU/L and therefore radiotherapy has been effective and somatostatin analogue treatment is no longer required.

Definition of cure

- Epidemiological data suggest that a mean GH <5 mU/L should be the aim of treatment, as this is associated with reduction of the increased mortality associated with acromegaly to that of the normal population. More recently normalization of IGF-1 has also been shown in one study to be associated with reduction of increased mortality to normal.
- For this reason, patients are monitored during treatment using a GH day curve aiming for a mean of <5 mU/L over 5 points throughout the day. Others use suppression to <2 mU/L on an OGTT as this has been shown to correlate well with mean GH. It is likely that normalization of IGF-1 may also be used, but there are limited epidemiological data on this approach.

Colonic polyps and acromegaly

- Increased incidence of *colonic polyps and colonic carcinoma* has been reported by many groups. Both retrospective and prospective studies have demonstrated that 9–39% of acromegalic patients studied have colonic polyps and 0–20% have been shown to have colonic carcinoma.
- *Mechanism* IGF-1 and/or GH are implicated as both may stimulate colonic mucosal turnover. However, some studies have failed to demonstrate a direct relationship between serum levels and polyps/carcinoma.
- *Importance* Patients with acromegaly are at increased risk and therefore need screening for polyps. It has been proposed that all patients aged >40 years should have 3 yearly routine colonoscopy, and those with polyps should receive annual colonoscopy. Agreement has not been reached on the frequency of follow up colonoscopy.

Drug treatment

Somatostatin analogues (see p. 226)

- Somatostatin analogues lead to suppression of GH secretion in 60% of patients with acromegaly. At least 40% of patients are complete responders and somatostatin analogues will lead to normalization of mGH (<5 mU/L) and IGF-1. However, some patients are partial responders and although somatostatin analogues will lead to lowering of mean GH, they do not suppress to normal despite dose escalation.
- Acute response to these drugs is assessed by measuring GH at hourly intervals for 6 h following the injection of 50–100 μg octreotide s/c. This predicts long-term response.
- The usual dose required is 50–200 μg s/c 3xdaily. More recently the depot preparations lanreotide SR, lanreotide autogel, and octreotide LR have become available. Lanreotide SR is administered at 30 mg i/m every 14 days with dose escalations up to every 7 days if adequate GH suppression does not occur. Octreotide LAR 20 mg i/m is administered every 4 weeks, with dose alterations either down or up to 10–30 mg every 3 months. Lanreotide autogel 90 μg i/m is administered every 4 weeks with dose alteration either down to 60 mg or up to 120 mg every 3 months.
- These drugs may be used as primary therapy where the tumour does not cause mass effects, or in patients who have received surgery and or radiotherapy who have elevated mean GH.

Dopamine agonists (see p. 224)

These drugs do lead to lowering of GH levels, but very rarely lead to normalization of mGH or IGF-1 (<10%). They may be helpful particularly if there is coexistent secretion of PRL, and in these cases there may be significant tumour shrinkage. Cabergoline has recently been shown to be more effective than bromocriptine and may lead to IGF-1 normalization in up to 30%. Doses of 10–60 mg bromocriptine daily or cabergoline 1.5–3 mg weekly are used.

GH receptor antagonists (pegvisomant)

A new GH receptor antagonist has been developed and early data suggest normalization of IGF-1 in more than 90% of patients. More data on the effect on tumour size are required.

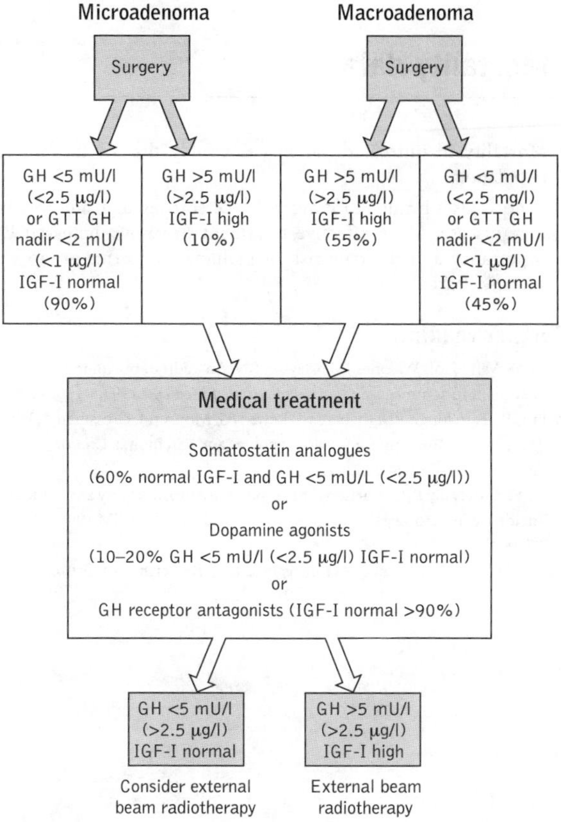

Fig. 18.1 Treatment paradigms in acromegaly. Reproduced with permission of BioScientifica Ltd.

Mortality data

- Mortality in untreated patients is double that of the normal population.
- Major causes include cardiovascular, cerebrovascular, and respiratory disease. More effective treatment has now increased life expectancy and the true risk of malignancy in this group will become clearer.

Further reading

Bates AS, Van't Hoff W, Jones JM, Clayton RN. An audit of outcome of treatment in acromegaly. *Quarterly Journal of Medicine* 1993;86: 293–299.

Jenkins PJ, Fairclough PD, Richards T, Lowe DG, Monson J, Grossman A, Wass JAH, Besser M. Acromegaly, colonic polyps and carcinoma. *Clinical Endocrinology* 1997;47: 17–22.

Orme SM, McNally RJQ, Cartwright RA, Belcheltz PE. Mortality and Cancer Incidence in Acromegaly: A retrospective cohort study JCEM 1998; 83: 2730–2734.

Wass JAH (ed.) Handbook of Acromegaly (2001). BioScientifica, Bristol.

Chapter 19
Cushing's disease

Definition

Cushing's syndrome is an illness resulting from excess cortisol secretion which has a high mortality if left untreated. There are several causes of hypercortisolaemia which must be differentiated, and the commonest cause is iatrogenic (inhaled or topical steroids). It is important to decide whether the patient has true Cushing's syndrome rather than pseudo-Cushing's associated with depression or alcoholism. Secondly, ACTH-dependent Cushing's must be differentiated from ACTH-independent disease (usually due to an adrenal adenoma or rarely carcinoma – see page 290). Once a diagnosis of ACTH-dependent disease has been established, it is important to differentiate between pituitary dependent (Cushing's disease) and ectopic secretion (see page 774).

Epidemiology of Cushing's disease

- rare, annual incidence approximately 2/million.
- commoner in women (3–15 : 1, F : M).
- age – most commonly 20–40 years.

Pathophysiology

- The vast majority of Cushing's syndrome is due to a pituitary ACTH-secreting corticotroph microadenoma. The underlying aetiology is ill-understood.
- Occasionally corticotroph adenomas reach larger sizes (macroadenomas) and rarely become invasive or malignant. The tumours typically maintain some responsiveness to the usual feedback control factors that influence the normal corticotoph (e.g. high doses of glucocorticoids, and CRH). However, this may be lost and the tumours become fully autonomous, particularly in Nelson's syndrome.
- NB Crooke's hyaline change is a fibrillary appearance seen in the non-tumorous corticotroph associated with elevated cortisol levels from any cause.

Causes of Cushing's syndrome

- pseudo-Cushing's syndrome
  - alcoholism <1%
  - severe depression 1%
- ACTH-dependent
  - pituitary adenoma 68% (Cushing's disease)
  - ectopic ACTH syndrome 12%
  - ectopic CRH secretion <1%
- ACTH-independent
  - adrenal adenoma 10%
  - adrenal carcinoma 8%
  - nodular hyperplasia 1%

Clinical features

See facing page.

The features of Cushing's syndrome are progressive and may be present for several years prior to diagnosis. A particular difficulty may occur in a patients with cyclical Cushing's, where the features and biochemical manifestations appear and disappear with a variable periodicity.

Clinical features

- *Facial appearance* round plethoric complexion, acne and hirsutism, thinning of scalp hair
- *Weight gain* truncal obesity, buffalo hump, supraclavicular fat pads.
- *Skin* thin and fragile due to loss of s/c tissue, purple striae on abdomen, breasts, thighs, axillae (in contrast to silver healed postpartum striae), easy bruising, tinea versicolor, occasionally pigmentation due to ACTH.
- Proximal *muscle weakness.*
- *Mood disturbance* labile, depression, insomnia, psychosis.
- *Menstrual disturbance.*
- *Low libido and impotence.*
- *Growth arrest* in children.

Associated features

- Hypertension (>50%) due to mineralocorticoid effects of cortisol. (Cortisol overwhelms the renal 11β-hydroxysteroid dehydrogenase enzyme protecting the mineralocorticoid receptor from cortisol). Cortisol may also increase angiotensinogen levels.
- Impaired glucose tolerance/diabetes mellitus (30%).
- Osteopenia and osteoporosis (leading to fractures of spine and ribs).
- Vascular disease.
- Susceptibility to infections.

Investigation

Does the patient have Cushing's syndrome?

Outpatient tests

- *24 h urinary free cortisol* This test can be useful for outpatient screening – however the false negative rate of 5–10% means that it should not be used alone.
- *Overnight dexamethasone suppression test* Administration of 1 mg dexamethasone at midnight is followed by a serum cortisol measurement at 9 a.m. The false negative value is 2% of normal individuals but rises to <20% in obese or hospitalized patients.
- If both the above tests are normal, Cushing's syndrome is unlikely.

Inpatient tests

- *Midnight cortisol* Loss of circadian rhythm of cortisol secretion is seen in Cushing's syndrome and this is demonstrated by measuring a serum cortisol at midnight (patient must be asleep for this test to be valid). In normal subjects the cortisol at this time is at a nadir (<50 nmol/L), but in patients with Cushing's syndrome it is elevated.
- *Low dose dexamethasone suppression test* Administration of 0.5 mg dexamethasone 6 hourly for 48 h at 9 a.m., 3 p.m., 9 p.m. and 3 a.m. should lead to complete suppression of cortisol to <50 nmol/L in normal subjects. Serum cortisol is measured at time 0 and 48 h (day 2).
- NB Oestrogen effect on CBG. False positive results may also occur if dexamethasone metabolism is increased by drugs that induce liver enzyme activity such as rifampicin and phenytoin.
- Patients with pseudo-Cushing's syndrome will also show loss of diurnal rhythm and lack of low dose suppressibility. However, alcoholics return to normal cortisol secretory dynamics after a few days' abstinence in hospital. Severe depression can be more difficult to differentiate, particularly since this may be a feature of Cushing's syndrome itself. Typically patients with pseudo-Cushing's show a normal cortisol rise with hypoglycaemia (tested using insulin tolerance test), whereas patients with true Cushing's syndrome show a blunted rise. However, this is not 100% reliable, as up to 20% of patients with Cushing's syndrome (especially those with cyclical disease) show a normal cortisol rise with hypoglycaemia.

Cyclical Cushing's

A small group of patients with Cushing's syndrome have alternating normal and abnormal cortisol levels on an irregular basis. All causes of Cushing's syndrome may be associated with cyclical secretion of cortisol. Clearly the results of dynamic testing can only be interpreted when the disease is shown to be active (elevated urinary cortisol secretion and loss of normal circadian rhythm and suppressability on dexamethasone).

Table 19.1 Screening tests for Cushing's syndrome

Test	False positives	False negatives	Sensitivity
24 h urinary free cortisol	1%	5–10%	95%
Overnight 1 mg dexamethasone suppression test	2% normal 13% obese 23% hospital inpatients	2%	
Midnight cortisol	?	0	100%
Low-dose dexamethasone suppression test	<2%	2%	98%

What is the underlying cause?

ACTH

- Once the presence of Cushing's syndrome has been confirmed, a serum basal ACTH should be measured to differentiate between ACTH dependent and ACTH independent aetiologies (Fig. 19.1).
- The basal ACTH is, however, of very little value in differentiating between pituitary dependent Cushing's syndrome and ectopic Cushing's syndrome as there is considerable overlap between the two groups although patients with ectopic disease tend to have higher ACTH levels (Fig. 19.1).

Serum potassium

A rapidly spun potassium is a useful discriminatory test as hypokalaemia <3.2 mmol/L is found in almost 100% of patients with ectopic secretion of ACTH but less than 10% of patients with pituitary dependent disease.

High dose dexamethasone suppression test

The high dose dexamethasone suppression test is performed in an identical way to the low dose test but with 2 mg doses of dexamethasone. In Cushing's disease the cortisol falls by >50% of the basal value. In ectopic disease, there is no suppression. However, approximately 10% of cases of ectopic disease – particularly those due to carcinoid tumours show >50% suppression, and 10% of patients with Cushing's disease do not suppress.

Corticotrophin releasing hormone test (Fig. 19.2)

- The administration of 100 μg of CRH i/v leads to an exaggerated rise in cortisol and ACTH in 95% of patients with pituitary-dependent Cushing's syndrome. There are occasional reports of patients with ectopic disease who show a similar response.
- Because of the spontaneous fluctuation of cortisol levels in patients with Cushing's syndrome – a response to CRH is defined as a rise in peak cortisol of 20% above basal and of 50% in ACTH.

Inferior petrosal sinus sampling (Fig. 19.3)

- Bilateral simultaneous inferior petrosal sinus sampling with measurement of ACTH centrally and in the periphery in the basal state and following stimulation with intravenous CRH (100 μg) allows differentiation between pituitary dependent and ectopic disease. A central to peripheral ratio of >2 prior to CRH is very suggestive of pituitary dependent disease, and >3 following CRH gives a diagnostic accuracy of approaching 100% for pituitary dependent disease.

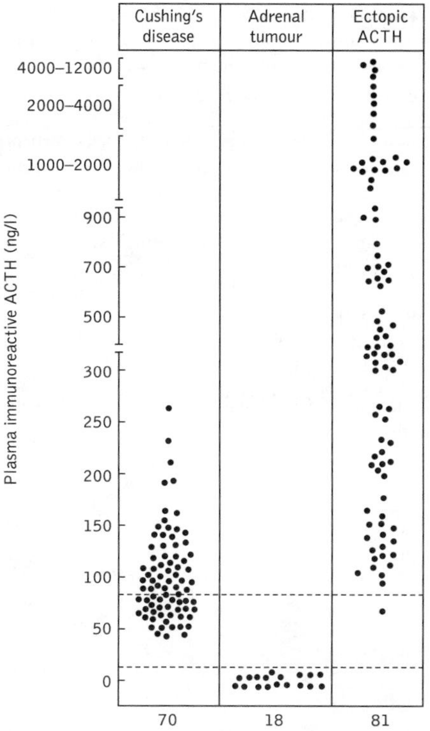

Fig. 19.1 Plasma ACTH levels (9 a.m.) in patients with pituitary dependent Cushing's disease, adrenal tumours and ectopic ACTH secretion. © Reprinted from Besser & Thorner *Clinical endocrinology*, by permission of the publisher Mosby.

Table 19.2 Investigation of ACTH-dependent Cushing's syndrome

Test	Pituitary dependent disease (% with this finding)	Ectopic disease (% with this finding)
Serum potassium <3.2 mmol/L	10	100
Suppression of basal cortisol to over 50% on high dose dexamethasone suppression test	90	10
Exaggerated rise in cortisol on CRH test	95	<1

- The accurate lateralization of a tumour using the results from inferior petrosal sinus sampling (IPSS) is difficult as differences in blood flow and catheter placement, etc. will affect the results.

Pituitary imaging

MRI following gadolinium enhancement localizes corticotroph adenomas in up to 80% of cases. However, it should be remembered that at least 10% of the normal population harbour microadenomas and therefore the biochemical investigation of these patients is essential as a patient with an ectopic source to Cushing's syndrome may have a pituitary 'incidentaloma'.

Other pituitary function

Hypercortisolism suppresses the thyroidal, gonadal, and GH axes leading to lowered levels of TSH and thyroid hormones as well as reduced gonadotrophins, gonadal steroids and GH.

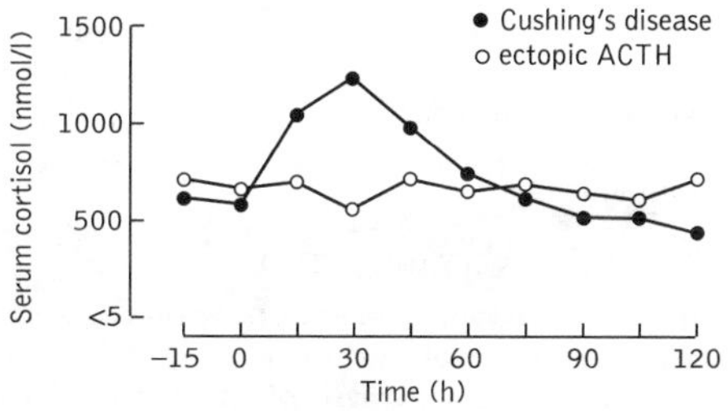

Fig. 19.2 CRH test in pituitary-dependent and ectopic disease. In the patient with pituitary-dependent disease, the characteristic marked plasma cortisol rise after an i/v bolus of 100 μg of CRH is seen. Serum cortisol levels are unaltered in the patient with ectopic ACTH secretion. © Reprinted from Besser & Thorner *Clinical endocrinology*, by permission of the publisher Mosby.

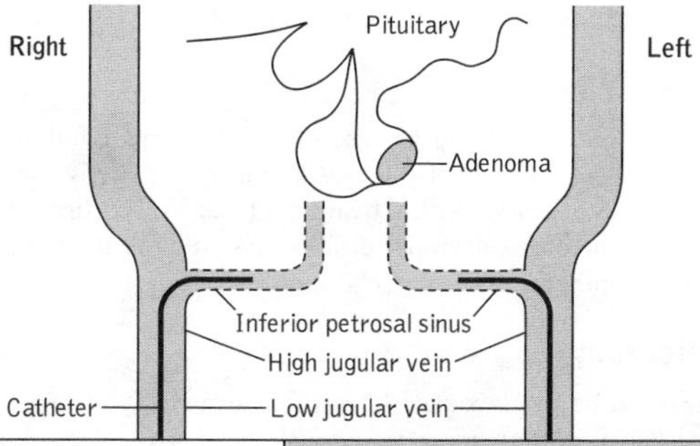

	Plasma ACTH (ng/l)			
		After i/v CRH 100 mg		
	0 min	5 min	10 min	15 min
Left inferior petrosal sinus	14	477	280	123
Right inferior petrosal sinus	16	23	28	54
Simultaneous peripheral vein	17	19	25	32

Fig. 19.3 Simultaneous bilateral inferior petrosal sinus and peripheral vein sampling for ACTH. The ratio of >3 between the left central and peripheral vein confirm a diagnosis of Cushing' disease. © Reprinted from Besser & Thorner *Clinical endocrinology*, by permission of the publisher Mosby.

Treatment

Trans-sphenoidal surgery (see p. 212)

- This is the first line option in most cases. Selective adenomectomy gives the greatest chance of cure with a reported remission rate of up to 90%. However, strict criteria of a postoperative cortisol of <50 nmol/L lead to lower cure rates, but much lower recurrence rates (<10% compared with up to 50% in those with detectable postoperative cortisols). This should be the current definition of successful surgery as the long-term outcome is significantly better in this group of patients.
- Complications of surgery may be higher in these patients as their preoperative general status and the condition of the tissues is poorer than other patients who are referred for surgery. It is often useful to administer medical treatment for at least 6 weeks prior to surgery to allow improvement in wound healing and reduce anaesthetic risk in those with severe metabolic problems.

Pituitary radiotherapy (see p. 218)

This is usually administered as second-line treatment following unsuccessful trans-sphenoidal surgery. As control of cortisol levels may take months to years, medical treatment to control cortisol levels while waiting for cortisol levels to fall is essential. A more rapid response to radiotherapy is seen in childhood.

Adrenalectomy

- This used to be the favoured form of treatment. It successfully controls cortisol hypersecretion in the majority of patients. Occasionally a remnant is left and leads to recurrent hypercortisolaemia.
- Nelson's syndrome may occur in up to 30% of patients. The administration of prophylactic radiotherapy reduces the liklihood of this complication. Careful follow-up of these patients is therefore essential to allow prompt treatment of the tumour. These tumours are associated with marked increase in ACTH, and associated pigmentation is common. Loss of normal responsiveness to glucocorticoids is characteristic and therefore biochemical monitoring should be performed at least annually by measuring a basal ACTH and re-checking it 1 and 2 h after the morning dose of glucocorticoid (ACTH curve).

Peri- and postoperative management following trans-sphenoidal surgery for Cushing's disease

- Perioperative hydrocortisone replacement is given in the standard way as it is assumed that the patient will become cortisol deficient after successful removal of the tumour.
- After 3–4 days, the evening steroid replacement is omitted, and 9 a.m. cortisol and ACTH checked the following day, and 24 h later after withholding steroids. Undetectable cortisol (<50 nmol/L) is suggestive of cure and glucocorticoid replacement is commenced. Cortisol 50–300 nmol/L is compatible with resolution of symptoms and a day curve should be performed. Patients with levels higher than 300 nmol/L should be considered for re-exploration and/or radiotherapy.

Nelson's syndrome

- Occurs in patients with Cushing's disease following adrenalectomy.
- Hyperpigmentation and an enlarging (often invasive) pituitary tumour associated with markedly elevated ACTH levels.
- Usually within 2 years of adrenalectomy.

- Bilateral adrenalectomy may still be indicated when pituitary surgery, radiotherapy and medical treatment have failed to control the disease. It is also helpful in Cushing's syndrome due to ectopic disease, when the ectopic source remains elusive or inoperable. Laparoscopic surgery minimalizes morbidity and complications.

Medical treatment

- This is indicated during the preoperative preparation of patients, or while awaiting radiotherapy to be effective or if surgery or radiotherapy are contra-indicated. *Metyrapone* is usually used first line, but *ketoconazole* should be used as first line in children as it is unassociated with increased adrenal metabolites. There is also a suggestion that ketoconazole may have a direct action on the corticotroph as well as lowering cortisol secretion.
- The dose of these drugs needs to be titrated against the cortisol results from a day curve (cortisol taken at 9 a.m., 12 noon, 3 p.m., 6 p.m.) aiming for a mean cortisol of 150–300 nmol/L as this approximates the normal production rate.
- Successful treatment (surgery or radiotherapy) of Cushing's disease leads to cortisol deficiency, and therefore glucocorticoid replacement therapy is essential. In addition patients who have undergone bilateral adrenalectomy require fludrocortisone. These patients should all receive instructions for intercurrent illness and carry a Medic-Alert bracelet and steroid card.

Table 19.3 Drug treatment of Cushing's syndrome

Drug	Dose	Action	Side-effects
Metyrapone	1–4 g/d (usually given in 4 divided doses)	11ß-hydroxylase inhibitor	Nausea Increased androgenic and mineralocorticoid precursors lead to hirsutism and hypertension
Ketoconazole	200–400 mg tds First line in children NB Avoid if taking H2 antagonists as acid required to metabolize active compound.	Direct inhibitor of P450 enzymes at several different sites	Abnormalities of liver function (usually reversible) Gynaecomastia
Mitotane (*o-p-* DDD)	4–12 g/d (begin at 0.5–1 g/d and gradually increase dose)	Inhibits steroidogenesis at the side-chain cleavage, 11 and 18-hydroxylase and 3ß-hydroxysteroid dehydrogenase Adrenolytic	Nausea and vomiting Cerebellar disturbance Somnolence Hypercholesterolaemia NB May increase clearance of steroids – replacement dosage may need to be increased NB May be teratogenic. Avoid if fertility desired.
Etomidate	Useful when parenteral treatment is required.	Inhibits side-chain cleavage and 11ß-hydroxylase.	

Definition of cure

Successful treatment for Cushing's disease leads to a cortisol that is undetectable (<50 nmol/L) following surgery. (This is due to the total suppression of cortisol production from the normal corticotroph in Cushing's disease). An undetectable postoperative cortisol leads to a significantly higher chance of long-term cure compared to the patients who had postoperative cortisols between 50 and 300 nmol/L.

Follow-up

- The aim of follow-up is
  - to detect recurrent Cushing's, and also
  - to recognize when recovery of the pituitary adrenal axis occurs.
- Therefore patients need to have regular assessment of cortisol production off glucocorticoid replacement. When cortisol is detectable following surgery, recurrent disease must be excluded (UFC and low dose dexamethasone suppression). If recurrence is excluded, it is then important to document the adequacy of the stress response once weaned off glucocorticoid replacement (insulin tolerance test).

Cushing's syndrome in children

In a series of 59 patients aged 4–20 years:

Causes

- pituitary dependent disease 85%
- adrenal disease 10%
- ectopic ACTH secretion 5%.

Initial presentation

- excessive weight gain 90%
- growth retardation 83%.

Below the age of 5 years, adrenal causes are common. In neonates and young children the McCune–Albright syndrome should be considered, whereas in late childhood and early adolescence, ACTH independence may suggest Carney's syndrome.

Treatment

- Trans-sphenoidal surgery is used as first line therapy in pituitary dependent Cushing's in children as in adults and is usually successful. Radiotherapy cures up to 85% children and this may be considered first line in some patients. Ketoconazole is the preferred medical therapy in this age group as it is not associated with increased adrenal androgens.
- The long-term management of children with Cushing's syndrome requires careful attention to growth as growth failure is a very common presentation of this condition. Postoperatively or after radiotherapy, GH therapy may restore growth and final height to normal.

Prognosis

- Untreated disease leads to an approximately 30–50% mortality at 5 years owing to vascular disease and increased susceptibility to infections.
- Treated Cushing's syndrome has a good prognosis. Patients who have an undetectable postoperative cortisol are very unlikely to recur (0–20%), whereas 50–75% recur if the postoperative cortisol is detectable.
- Although the physical features and severe psychological disorders associated with Cushing's improve or resolve within weeks or months of successful treatment, more subtle mood disturbance may persist for longer. In addition, it is likely that there is an increased cardiovascular risk.
- Osteoporosis will usually resolve in children, but may not improve significantly in older patients. Bone mineral density therefore requires monitoring and may need specific treatment. *Alendronate* has been shown to be effective therapy leading to improved bone mineral density in patients with Cushing's syndrome and osteoporosis. Hypertension has been shown to resolve in 80% and diabetes mellitus in up to 70%.

Further reading

Estrada J, Boronat M, Mielgo M, Magallon R, Millan I, Diez S, Lucas T, Barcelo B. The long-term outcome of pituitary irradiation after unsuccessful transsphenoidal surgery in Cushing's syndrome. *New England Journal of Medicine* 1997; 336: 172–177.

Howlett TA, Drury PL, Perry L, Doniach I, Rees LH, Besser GM. Diagnosis and management of ACTH-dependent Cushing's syndrome: comparison of the features in ectopic and pituitary ACTH production. *Clinical Endocrinology* 1986; 24: 699–713.

Magiakou MA, Mastorakos G, Oldfield EH, Gomez MT, Doppman JL, Cutler GB, Niemann LK, Chrousos GP. Cushing's syndrome in children and adolescents. *New England Journal of Medicine* 1994; 331: 629–636.

Newell-Price J, Trainer P, Besser M, Grossman A. The diagnosis and differential diagnosis of Cushing's syndrome and pseudo-Cushing's states. *Endocrinology Reviews* 1998; 19(5): 647–672.

Oldfield EH, Doppman JL, Nieman LK, Chrousos GP, Miller DL, Katz DA, Cutler GB, Loriauz DL. Petrosal sinus sampling with and without corticotrophin-releasing hormone for the differential diagnosis of Cushing's syndrome. *New England Journal of Medicine* 1991; 325: 897–905.

Orth DN. Cushing's syndrome *New England Journal of Medicine* 1995; 332: 791–803.

Chapter 20

Non-functioning pituitary tumours

Background

These pituitary tumours are unassociated with clinical syndromes of anterior pituitary hormone excess.

Epidemiology

- Non-functioning pituitary tumours (NFA) are the commonest pituitary macroadenoma. They represent 25% of all pituitary tumours.
- There is an equal sex distribution and the majority of cases present in patients aged >50 years.

Pathology

- Despite the fact that NFAs are unassociated with hormone production, they may immunostain for:
  - glycoprotein hormones (most commonly gonadotrophins) – LH, FSH, the α or β subunits or TSH
  - ACTH (silent corticotroph adenomas), or
  - be negative on immunostaining – either null cell tumours or oncocytomas (characteristically contain multiple mitochondria on electron microscopy).
- Tumour behaviour is variable, with some tumours behaving in a very indolent slow-growing manner and others invading the sphenoid and cavernous sinus.

Clinical features

Mass effects

- visual field defects (uni or bitemporal quadrantanopia or hemianopia)
- headache
- ophthalmoplegia (III, IV, and VI cranial nerves – rarely)
- optic atrophy (rarely, following long-term optic nerve compression)
- apoplexy (rarely).

Hypopituitarism

See page 113.

- At diagnosis, approximately 50% are gonadotrophin deficient.

Incidental finding

A NFA may be detected on the basis of imaging performed for other reasons.

Investigation

- *Pituitary imaging* MRI/CT demonstrates the tumour and/or invasion into the cavernous sinus or supraoptic recess.
- *Visual fields assessment* Abnormal in up to 2/3 of cases.
- *PRL* Essential to exclude a PRL secreting macroadenoma (see p. 139).
  - mild elevation (<3 000 mU/L) may occur secondary to stalk compression
  - borderline PRL 3000–6000 mU/L may warrant a trial of dopamine agonist treatment (see p. 224).
- *Pituitary function* Assessment for hypopituitarism (see p. 103).

Management

Surgery

- The initial definitive management in virtually every case is surgical. This removes mass effects and may lead to some recovery of pituitary function in around 10%. The majority of patients can be operated on successfully via the trans-sphenoidal route.
- Close follow-up is necessary after surgery as tumour regrowth can only be detected using pituitary imaging and visual field assessment, as there is no reliable consistent biochemical marker in the majority of cases.

Radiotherapy

- The use of postoperative radiotherapy remains controversial. Some centres advocate its use for every patient following surgery; others reserve its use for those patients who have had particularly invasive or aggressive tumours removed or those with a significant amount of residual tumour remaining (e.g. in the cavernous sinus).
- The regrowth rate at 10 years without radiotherapy approaches 45% and there are no good predictive factors for determining which tumours will regrow. However, administration of postoperative radiotherapy reduces this regrowth rate to less than 10%. As discussed in p. 220, however, there are sequelae to radiotherapy – with a significant long-term risk of hypopituitarism and a possible increased risk of visual deterioration and malignancy in the field of radiation.

Medical treatment

- Unlike the case for GH and PRL-secreting tumours, medical therapy for NFAs is usually unhelpful, although there have been reports of the somatostatin agonist octreotide leading to tumour shrinkage and/or visual field improvement in some cases.
- Hormone replacement therapy is required to treat any hypopituitarism (see p. 120).

Biochemical markers for NFAs?

- The majority of patients lack a hormone marker – despite approximately half immunostain positively for gonadotrophins and contain secretory granules at the EM level.
- A minority of patients have elevated circulating FSH/LH levels, see section on gonadotrophinomas (p. 182).
- The use of the response of α subunit or LH/FSH as a tumour marker has been suggested. Small series have shown that up to 70% of patients with functionless tumours show a 50% rise in serum gonadotrophin/subunit after 200 μg i/v TRH. As this response disappears after tumour resection it may be a useful tumour marker, although this is not widely practised.

Follow-up

- Patients who have not received postoperative irradiation require careful long-term follow-up with serial pituitary imaging and visual field assessment. The optimal protocol is still not known but an accepted practice is to image in the first 3 months following surgery and then re-image annually for 5 years and then biannually thereafter. Tumour recurrence has been reported at up to 15 years following surgery and therefore follow-up needs to be long-term.
- In patients who have received postoperative radiotherapy, follow-up with annual visual field assessment and imaging only if a deterioration is noted.

Prognosis

- Patients with NFAs have a good prognosis once the diagnosis and appropriate treatment including replacement of hormone deficiency is performed. The main concern is the risk of tumour regrowth with subsequent visual failure. As mentioned above, the administration of radiotherapy, although not without potential complications itself significantly reduces this risk. Unirradiated patients require very close follow-up in order to detect regrowth and perform repeat surgery or administer radiotherapy.

- Visual field defects at diagnosis may improve following surgery in the majority and improvement may continue for a year following tumour debulking.

Chapter 21
Gonadotrophinomas

Background

These are tumours that arise from the gonadotroph cells of the pituitary gland and produce FSH, LH, or the α subunit. They are often indistinguishable from other non-functioning pituitary adenomas as they are usually silent and unassociated with excess detectable secretion of LH and FSH, although studies demonstrate gonadotrophin/α subunit secretion *in vitro*. Occasionally however, these tumours do produce detectable excess hormone *in vivo*.

Clinical Features

Gonadotrophinomas present in the same manner as other non-functioning pituitary tumours with mass effects and hypopituitarism (see p. 177).

The rare FSH-secreting gonadotrophinomas may lead to macro-orchidism in men.

Investigation

The secretion of FSH and LH from these tumours is usually undetectable in the plasma. Occasionally elevated FSH and more rarely LH is measured. This finding is often ignored, particularly in post-menopausal women, although elevated gonadotrophins together with ACTH and/or TSH deficiency in the presence of a macroadenomas should raise the suspicion of a functioning gonadotrophinoma.

Management

These tumours are managed as non-functioning tumours. The potential advantage of FSH/LH secretion from a functioning gonadotrophinoma is that it provides a biochemical marker of presence of tumour for follow-up.

Chapter 22

Thyrotrophinomas

Epidemiology

These are rare tumours comprising approximately 1% of all pituitary tumours. The diagnosis may be delayed, because the significance of an unsuppressed TSH in the presence of elevated free thyroid hormone concentrations may be missed. Approximately 1/3 of cases in the literature have received treatment directed at the thyroid in the form of radioiodine treatment or surgery, before diagnosis.

Unlike primary hyperthyroidism, thyrotrophinomas are equally common in men and women.

Tumour biology and behaviour

- The majority are macroadenomas (90%) and secrete only TSH (72%), often with α-subunit in addition, but some co-secrete GH and/or PRL.
- The pathogenesis of thyrotoxicosis in the presence of normal TSH levels is poorly understood, but there are reports of secretion of TSH with increased bioactivity possibly due to changes in post-translational hormone glycosylation.
- The observation that prior thyroid ablation is associated with deleterious effects on the size of the tumour suggests some feedback control, and is similar to the aggressive tumours seen in Nelson's syndrome after bilateral adrenalectomy has been performed for Cushing's syndrome. Thyrotropin-secreting pituitary carcinoma has been very rarely reported.

Clinical features (see p. 46)

- Clinical features of *hyperthyroidism* are usually present, but often milder than expected given the level of thyroid hormones. In mixed tumours, hyperthyroidism may be overshadowed by features of *acromegaly*.
- *Mass effects* visual field defects and hypopituitarism

Investigation

- *TSH is inappropriately normal or elevated* The range of TSH that has been described is <1–568 mU/L, and 1/3 untreated patients had TSH in the normal range. There is no correlation between TSH and T_4.
- *Free thyroid hormones* elevated.
- *α-Subunit* Typically patients have an increased α-subunit : TSH molar ratio(>1).
- *Other anterior pituitary hormone levels* PRL and/or GH may be elevated in mixed tumours (an oral glucose tolerance test may be indicated to exclude acromegaly).
- *SHBG* elevated into the hyperthyroid range
- *TRH test* absent TSH response to stimulation with TRH (useful to differentiate TSH-secreting tumours from thyroid hormone resistance where the TSH response is normal or exaggerated).
- *Thyroid antibodies* In contrast to Graves' disease, the incidence of thyroid antibodies is similar to that in the general population.
- *Pituitary imaging* MRI scan will demonstrate a pituitary tumour (macroadenoma) in the majority of cases.

Causes of an elevated fT4 in the presence of an inappropriately unsuppressed TSH (see p. 46)

- TSH-secreting tumour
- thyroid hormone resistance
- amiodarone therapy
- inherited abnormalities of thyroid-binding proteins.

Management

Surgery

Surgery leads to cure in approximately 1/3 of patients as judged by apparent complete removal of tumour mass and normalization of thyroid hormone levels, with another 1/3 improved with normal thyroid hormone levels but incomplete removal of the adenoma.

Radiotherapy

Radiotherapy is useful following unsuccessful surgery, and leads to gradual (over years) reduction in TSH.

Medical treatment

Somatostatin analogues

- Medical treatment with the somatostatin agonists octreotide and lanreotide is successful in the majority of patients in suppressing TSH secretion and leading to tumour shrinkage. In one study, octreotide reduced TSH secretion in almost all patients treated, and normalized thyroid hormone levels in 73% of patients. There was partial tumour shrinkage in 40%.
- Drug therapy is useful in the preoperative preparation of these patients to ensure that they are fit for general anaesthetic and also while waiting for radiotherapy to be effective.

Anti-thyroid medication

- Treatment with antithyroid drugs has been associated with increased TSH in approximately 60% of patients reported. It should be avoided if possible and the more appropriate somatostatin agonist therapy utilized.

Further reading

Beck-Peccoz P, Brucker-Davis F Persani L, Smallridge RC, Weintraub BD. Thyrotropin-secreting pituitary tumours. *Endocrine Reviews* 1996;17: 610–638.

Chanson P, Weintraub BD, Harris AG. Octreotide therapy for thyroid stimulating hormone-secreting pituitary adenomas. *Annals of Internal Medicine* 1993;119: 236–240.

Chapter 23
Pituitary incidentalomas

Definition

The term incidentaloma refers to an incidentally detected lesion that is unassociated with hormonal hyper or hyposecretion and has a benign natural history.

The increasingly frequent detection of these lesions with technological improvements and more widespread use of sophisticated imaging has led to a management challenge – which, if any lesions need investigation and/or treatment, and what is the optimal follow-up strategy (if required at all)?

Epidemiology

- Autopsy studies have shown that 10–20% of pituitary glands unsuspected of having pituitary disease harbour pituitary adenomas. Approximately half the tumours stain for PRL and the remainder are negative on immunostaining.
- Imaging studies using MRI demonstrate pituitary microadenomas in approximately 10% of normal volunteers.
- Incidentally detected macroadenomas have been reported when imaging has been performed for other reasons. However, these are not true incidentalomas as they are often associated with visual field defects, and/or hypopituitarism.

Natural history

Incidentally detected microadenomas are very unlikely to increase in size (<10%) whereas larger incidentally detected meso- and macroadenomas are more likely to enlarge (30%).

Clinical features

By definition, a patient with an incidentaloma should be asymptomatic. Any patient who has an incidentally detected tumour should have visual field assessment and a clinical review to ensure that this is not the initial presentation of Cushing's syndrome or acromegaly.

Investigation

- Aims:
  - exclude any hormone hypersecretion from the tumour
  - detect hypopituitarism.
- Investigation of hypersecretion of hormones should include measurement of PRL, IGF-1, and an oral glucose tolerance test if acromegaly is suspected, 24 h urinary free cortisol and overnight dexamethasone suppression test and thyroid function tests (unsuppressed TSH in the presence of elevated T_4).
- Others suggest that this approach is unnecessary, but with limited data most endocrinologists would perform investigations as above.

Management

- All extra-sellar macroadenomas (incidentally detected but by definition not true incidentalomas) require definitive treatment.
- Tumours with excess hormone secretion require definitive treatment.
- Mass <1 cm repeat MRI at 1, 2, and 5 years.
- Mass >1 cm diameter – repeat MRI at 6 months, 1, 2, and 5 years.

Further reading

Turner HE, Moore NR, Byrne JV, Wass JAH. Pituitary, adrenal and thyroid incidentalomas. *Endocrine-related Cancer* 1998; 5: 131–150.

Chapter 24
Pituitary carcinoma

Definition

Pituitary carcinoma is defined as a primary adenohypophyseal neoplasm with craniospinal and/or distant systemic metastases.

Epidemiology

These are extremely rare tumours, and only approximately 60 cases have been reported in the world literature.

Pathology and pathogenesis

- The initial tumours and subsequent carcinomas show higher proliferation indices than the majority of pituitary adenomas. They are also likely to demonstrate p53 positivity and have an increased mitotic index.
- The aetiology of these tumours is unknown, but the adenoma–carcinoma sequence is followed in ACTH-secreting tumours:- pituitary adenoma causing Cushing's disease, followed by locally invasive adenoma (Nelson's syndrome) leading to pituitary carcinoma.

Features

Virtually all pituitary carcinomas initially present as invasive pituitary macroadenomas. After a variable interval of time (mean 6.5 years) the majority present with local recurrence. There is a tendency to systemic (liver, lymph nodes, lungs, and bones) rather than craniospinal metastases but metastases do not usually predominate in the clinical picture.

Table 24.1 Types of pituitary carcinoma

Type	Proportion of reported cases
PRL	30%
ACTH	28%
GH	2%
Non-functioning	30%

NB Many 'non-functioning' carcinomas were reported prior to routine measurement of PRL or routine immunostaining, and therefore the true incidence of PRL-producing carcinomas may be higher.

Treatment

Radiotherapy or medical treatment provide palliation only.

Further reading

Pernicone PJ, Scheithauer BW, Sebo TJ, Kovacs KT, Horvath E, Young WF, LLoyd RV, Davis DH, Guthrie BL, Schoene WC. Pituitary carcinoma. *Cancer* 1997;79: 804–812.

Chapter 25
Craniopharyngiomas and perisellar cysts

Incidence

1–2/million/year

Epidemiology

Any age, only 50% present in childhood (<16 years).

Pathology

Tumour arising from squamous epithelial remnants of Rathke's pouch. Histology may be either adamantinous epithelial, with cyst formation and calcification, or squamous papillary (generally associated with a better prognosis). Cyst formation and calcification is common. Benign tumour, although infiltrates surrounding structures. hCG is present in cyst fluid.

Rathke's cleft cysts

Pathology

Derived from the remnants of Rathke's pouch, lined by epithelial cells and filled with fluid. (Ciliated cuboidal/columnar epithelium, compared with squamous for craniopharyngiomas.)

Features

Usually asymptomatic, although may present with headache and amenorrhoea, and rarely hypopituitarism and hydrocephalus.

Investigation

CT/MRI – variable enhancement.

Management

- Decompression if symptomatic.
- Recurrence is rare.

Other perisellar cysts

- Arachnoid
- Epidermoid
- Dermoid

Features

- raised intracranial pressure
- visual disturbance
- hypothalamopituitary disturbance
  - growth failure in children
  - precocious puberty and tall stature are less common
  - anterior and posterior pituitary failure, including DI.

Investigation

- MRI/CT (CT may be helpful to evaluate boney erosion)
- visual field assessment
- anterior and posterior pituitary assessment (p. 113).

Management

Surgery is the primary treatment for the majority, usually trans-cranial, occasionally trans-sphenoidal.

The extent of surgery is variable – high risk of recurrence leads some to recommend radical surgery, but high postoperative morbidity, e.g. hypothalamic syndrome, has led many neurosurgeons to recommend subtotal removal and postoperative radiotherapy.

Chapter 26
Parasellar tumours

Meningiomas

- Suprasellar meningiomas arise from the tuberculum sellae or the chiasmal sulcus.
- Usually present with a chiasmal syndrome where loss of visual acuity occurs in one eye followed by reduced acuity in the other eye.
- Differentiation from a primary pituitary tumour can be difficult where there is downward extension into the sella.
- MRI is the imaging of choice. T1 weighted images demonstrate meningiomas as isodense with grey matter and hypointense with respect to pituitary tissue, with marked enhancement after gadolinium.
- Cerebral angiography also demonstrates a tumour blush.
- Management is surgical and may also be complicated by haemorrhage as these are often very vascular tumours. They are relatively radioresistant but inoperable or partially removed tumours may respond. As they are slow-growing, a conservative approach with regular imaging may be appropriate.
- Associations include type 2 neurofibromatosis.

Clivus chordomas

- Rare. Arise from embryonic rest cells of the notochord.
- May present with cranial nerve palsies (III, VI, IX, X) or pyramidal tract dysfunction.
- Anterior and posterior pituitary hypofunction is reported.
- Often invasive and relentlessly progressive.
- Treatment is surgical followed by radiotherapy in some cases, although they are relatively radioresistant. Data on radiosurgery are not yet available, but this may be considered.

Hamartomas

- Non-neoplastic overgrowth of neurones and glial cells.
- Rare. May present with seizures – typically gelastic (laughing).
- May release GnRH leading to precocious puberty or very rarely GHRH leading to disorders of growth or acromegaly.
- Appear as homogeneous isointense with grey matter, pedunculated or sessile non-enhancing tumours on T1 weighted MRI scans.

Management

Tumours do not enlarge, and therefore treatment is of endocrine consequences – most commonly precocious puberty.

Ependymomas

- Intracranial ependymomas typically affect children and adolescents.
- Pituitary insufficiency may follow craniospinal irradiation.
- Occasionally third ventricle tumours may interfere with hypothalamic function.

Secondary neoplasm

- Patients particularly with breast or bronchial carcinoma may present with secondaries usually in the hypothalamus or in the pituitary itself.
  DI is common.

Chapter 27
Parasellar inflammatory conditions

Neurosarcoidosis

Pituitary and hypothalamus may be affected by meningeal disease. Most patients with hypothalamic sarcoidosis also have involvement outside the CNS.

Features

Hypopituitarism and DI, in addition to hypothalamic syndrome of absent thirst, somnolescence, and hyperphagia.

Investigations

- Serum and CSF ACE may be raised.
- CSF examination may reveal a pleocytosis, oligoclonal bands, and low glucose.
- MRI may demonstrate additional enhancement, e.g. meningeal.
- Gallium scan may reveal increased uptake in lacrimal and salivary glands.

Management

- High doses of glucocorticoids (60–80 mg prednisolone) for initial treatment. Subsequent treatment with 40 mg/day is often required for several months. Pulsed methylprednisolone may also be useful. Steroid sparing agents such as azathioprine may be helpful.
- Management of hormonal deficiency can be very difficult particularly in the context of absent thirst and poor memory.

Langerhans' cell histiocytosis

- Over 50% of cases occur in children.
- Most frequent endocrine abnormalities are DI and growth retardation due to hypothalamic infiltration by Langerhans' cells or involvement of the meninges adjacent to the pituitary. Rarely hyperprolactinaemia and panhypopituitarism develop. In adults, DI may precede the bone and soft tissue abnormalities making diagnosis difficult.

Management

The role of radiotherapy is controversial, with some workers reporting improvement, and others questioning the efficacy. If radiotherapy is used, rapid institution of treatment appears to be important (within 10 days of diagnosis). High dose glucocorticoids can lead to transient improvement, but chemotherapy does not alter the course of DI although it may lead to temporary regression of lesions.

Tuberculosis

TB may present as a tuberculoma which may compromise hypothalamic or pituitary function. DI is common. Most patients have signs of TB elsewhere, but not invariably so. Trans-sphenoidal biopsy is therefore sometimes required. An alternative strategy is antituberculous treatment with empirical glucocorticoid treatment.

Further reading

Freda PU, Post KD. Differential diagnosis of sellar masses. *Endocrinology and Metabolism Clinics of North America* 1999; 28: 81.

Chapter 28
Lymphocytic hypophysitis

Background

This is a rare inflammatory condition of the pituitary.

Epidemiology

Lymphocytic hypophysitis occurs more commonly in women, and usually presents during late pregnancy or the first year thereafter.

Pathogenesis

Ill-understood – probably autoimmune. Approximately 25% of cases of lymphocytic hypophysitis have been associated with other autoimmune conditions – Hashimoto's thyroiditis in the majority, but also pernicious anaemia

Pathology

- Somatotroph and gonadotroph function are more likely to be preserved than corticotroph or thyrotroph function, unlike the findings in hypopituitarism due to a pituitary tumour. The posterior pituitary is characteristically spared so that DI is not part of the picture, but there are occasional reports of coexistent or isolated DI, presumably because of different antigens.
- Lymphocytic hypophysitis has occasionally involved the cavernous sinus and extra-ocular muscles.
- Light microscopy typically reveals a lymphoplasmacytic infiltrate, occasionally forming lymphoid follicles, with variable destruction of parenchyma and fibrosis.

Clinical features

- Mass effects leading to headache and visual field defects.
- Often a temporal association with pregnancy.
- Hypopituitarism (ACTH and TSH deficiency, less commonly gonadotrophin and GH deficiency).
- Posterior pituitary involvement and cavernous sinus involvement occur less commonly.

Investigations

- Investigation of hypopituitarism is essential, and may not be thought of because gonadotrophin secretion often remains intact, leaving the potentially life-threatening ACTH deficiency unsuspected.
- MRI shows an enhancing mass, with variably loss of hyperintense bright spot of neurohypophysis, thickening of pituitary stalk, enlargement of the neurohypophysis. Suprasellar extension often appears tongue-like along the pituitary stalk. There may be central necrosis but no calcification.
- Biopsy of the lesion is often required, but may be avoided in the presence of typical features.
- The presence of antipituitary antibodies has been investigated by some groups and shown to be variably present. This is, however, a research tool and an unreliable marker.

Table 28.1 Classification of hypophysitis

Acute	Bacterial infections
Chronic	Lymphocytic hypophysitis
	Xanthomatous (characterized by lipid-laden macrophages)
Granulomatous	Tuberculosis
	Sarcoidosis
	Syphilis
	Giant cell (? variant of lymphocytic hypophysitis)

Treatment

- Treatment of hypopituitarism.
- Most often, no specific treatment is necessary. There is anecdotal evidence only of the effectiveness of immunosupressive doses of glucocorticoids – for example prednisolone 60 mg /day for 3 months and progressive reduction for 6 months. This has been reported to be associated with reduction in the mass and gradual recovery of pituitary function. However, relapse after discontinuing therapy is also reported.
- Spontaneous recovery may also occur.
- Surgery has also been used to improve visual field abnormalities

Natural history

Variable – some progress rapidly to life-threatening hypopituitarism, while others spontaneously regress.

Relationship to other conditions

Lymphocytic hypophysitis remains an ill-understood condition but has been suggested to be the underlying cause of other conditions such as isolated ACTH deficiency and the empty sella syndrome.

Further reading

Thodou *et al. Journal of Clinical Endocrinology and Metabolism* 1995; 80: 2302–2311.

Thodoy E, Asa SL, Kontogeorgos G, Kovacs K, Harvath E, Ezzat S Clinical case seminar: lymphocytic hypophysitis: clinicopathological findings.

Chapter 29

Surgical treatment of pituitary tumours

Trans-sphenoidal surgery

This is now the favoured technique for pituitary surgery, and is first line for virtually every case. It is preferred to the previously used technique of craniotomy because there is minimal associated morbidity as a result of the fact that the cranial fossa is not opened and there are therefore no immediate sequelae due to direct cerebral damage (particularly frontal lobe) and no long-term risk of epilepsy. There is reduced duration of hospital stay and improved cure rates as there is better visualization of small tumours. Unfortunately the technique may be inadequate to deal with very large tumours with extensive suprasellar extension. In these situations craniotomy is required if adequate debulking is not possible following the trans-sphenoidal approach.

Preparation for trans-sphenoidal surgery

Pretreatment before surgery

- Pretreatment with *metyrapone* or *ketoconazole* to improve the condition of patients with Cushing's syndrome is often given for at least 6 weeks. This allows some improvement in healing and also improves the general state of the patient.
- Patients with macroprolactinomas will in the majority of cases have received treatment with dopamine agonists in any case, and surgery is usually indicated for resistance of intolerance. There is a risk of tumour fibrosis, with long-term (>6/12) dopamine agonist therapy.

Immediately preoperative

- Immediate preoperative treatment requires appropriate anterior pituitary hormone replacement. In particular, a decision as to whether perioperative glucocorticoid treatment is required. The majority of microprolactinomas will not require perioperative hydrocortisone, but patients with Cushing's syndrome will require peri-and postoperative glucocorticoid treatment (see p. 784). Patients with macroadenomas and an intact preoperative pituitary–adrenal axis do not usually require perioperative steroids, but those who are deficient or whose reserve has not been tested need to be given perioperative glucocorticoids. TSH deficiency should be corrected with thyroxine.
- Prophylactic antibiotics are started in some centres the night before surgery to reduce the chances of meningitis.

Complications

See table on p. 214.

- Patients should be counselled about the possible complications of trans-sphenoidal surgery prior to consent. The commonest complications are DI which may be transient or permanent (5% and 0.1% respectively; often higher in Cushing's disease and prolactinoma) and the development of new anterior pituitary hormonal deficiencies (uncommon with microadenomas, approximately 10% of TSA for macroadenomas).
- The risk of meningitis can be reduced by preoperative and perioperative prophylactic antibiotic administration. In Oxford our practice is to give 5 days of oral antibiotics (*amoxycillin* and *flucloxacillin*, or *erythromycin* if penicillin allergic) starting the night before surgery. Other complications include CSF leak, visual deterioration, haemorrhage (rare), and transient hyponatraemia usually 7 days postoperatively.

Indications

- non-functioning pituitary adenoma
- GH-secreting adenoma
- ACTH secreting tumour
- Nelson's syndrome
- prolactinoma (if patient dopamine agonist resistant or intolerant)
- recurrent pituitary tumour

Less common

- gonadotrophin-secreting tumours
- TSH-secreting adenoma
- craniopharyngioma
- pituitary biopsy to define diagnosis e.g. hypophysitis, pituitary metastases
- chordoma
- Rathke's cleft cyst
- arachnoid cyst

Table 29.1 Complications of trans-spenoidal surgery

Complications of any surgical procedure	Anaesthetic related
	Venous thrombosis and pulmonary embolism
Immediate	Haemorrhage
	Hypothalamic damage
	Meningitis
Permanent	Visual deterioration or loss
	Cranial nerve damage (e.g. oculomotor nerve palsies)
	Hypopituitarism
	DI
	SIADH
Transient	DI
	CSF rhinorrhoea
	Visual deterioration
	Cerebral salt wasting

Cerebral salt wasting

A rare but important complication of trans-sphenoidal surgery, that is more commonly seen after subarachnoid haemorrhage is cerebral salt wasting syndrome (CSW). This typically occurs at day 5–10 postoperatively and is associated with often massive urinary salt loss, and hypovolaemia. It needs to be differentiated from SIADH which may also occur at this stage (often using central venous pressure measurement to demonstrate hypovolaemia in CSW compared with euvolaemia in SIADH). The management of CSW involves administration of saline, whereas fluid restriction is indicated for SIADH.

Trans-frontal craniotomy

Indications

- Pituitary tumours with major suprasellar and lateral invasion where trans-sphenoidal surgery is unlikely to remove a significant proportion of the tumour.
- Craniopharyngiomas.
- Parasellar tumours, e.g. meningioma.

Complications

- In addition to the complications of trans-sphenoidal surgery, brain retraction leads to cerebral oedema or haemorrhage.
- Manipulation of the optic chiasm may lead to visual deterioration.
- Vascular damage.
- Damage to the olfactory nerve.

Perioperative management

Similar to that for patients undergoing trans-sphenoidal surgery.

Postoperative management

- Recovery is typically slower than after trans-sphenoidal surgery.
- Prophylactic anticonvulsants are administered for up to 1 year.
- The DVLC must be advised of surgery, and driving is allowed following adequate visual recovery, but drivers of group 2 vehicles (HGV) cannot drive for 6 months.

Further reading

Laws ER, Thapar K. Pituitary surgery. *Endocrinology and Metabolism Clinics of North America* 1999; 28: 119.

Chapter 30
Pituitary radiotherapy

Indications

See table on facing page.

- Pituitary radiotherapy is an effective treatment used to reduce the liklihood of tumour regrowth, to further shrink a tumour, and to treat persistent hormone hypersecretion following surgical resection.
- Occasionally it is used as a primary therapeutic option, but its usual role is following non-curative surgery or following macroprolactinoma shrinkage with dopamine agonists.
- Pituitary radiotherapy is usually only administrable once in a lifetime.

Technique

- Conventional external beam three-field radiotherapy is able to deliver a beam of ionizing irradiation accurately to the pituitary fossa.
- Accurate targeting requires head fixation in a moulded plastic shell to keep the head immobilized. The fields of irradiation are based on simulation using MRI or CT scanning and the volume is usually the tumour margins plus 0.5 cm in all planes. The preoperative tumour volume is used for planning, whereas the post-drug (dopamine agonist) shrinkage films are used for prolactinomas. There are three portals, two temporal and one anterior.
- The standard dose is 4500 cGy in 25 fractions over 35 days, but 5000 cGy may be used for relatively 'radioresistant' tumours such as craniopharyngiomas.

Efficacy

Radiotherapy is effective in reducing the chances of pituitary tumour regrowth. For example, in a large series of 400 patients who received pituitary radiotherapy over a period of 20 years, the progression-free survival rate was 97% at 10 years and 92% at 20 years. Comparison of functionless tumour recurrence following surgery and radiotherapy compared with surgery alone, shows that radiotherapy is effective in reducing the liklihood of regrowth (Figure 30.1).

Table 30.1 Indications for pituitary radiotherapy

Tumour	Aim of treatment
Non-functioning pituitary adenoma	To shrink residual mass or reduce liklihood of regrowth
GH/PRL/ACTH secreting tumour	To reduce persistent hormonal hypersecretion and shrink residual mass
Craniopharyngioma	To reduce likelihood of regrowth
Recurrent tumour	

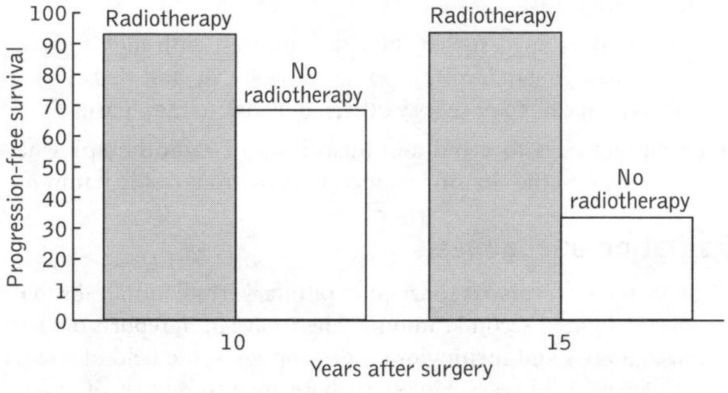

Fig. 30.1 Recurrence rates following radiotherapy. (Modified from Gittoes NJL, Bates AS, Tse W *et al.* Radiotherapy for non-functioning pituitary tumours. *Clinical Endocrinology* 1998; 48: 331–7).

Complications

Short term

- nausea
- headache
- temporary hair loss at radiotherapy portals of entry.

Hypopituitarism

- Anterior pituitary hormone deficiency occurs due to the effect of irradiation on the hypothalamus leading to reduced hypothalamic releasing hormone secretion. The total dose of irradiation determines the speed, incidence and extent of hypopituitarism. In addition the presence of pre-existing hormonal deficiency increases the chances of post-radiotherapy hypopituitarism (Table 30.2).
- The onset of hypopituitarism is gradual, and the order of development of deficiency is as for any other cause of developing hypopituitarism – namely GH first followed by gonadotrophin and ACTH followed finally by TSH. Posterior pituitary deficiencies are very rare, but secondary temporary mild hyperprolactinaemia may be seen after about 2 years which gradually returns to normal.

Visual impairment

- The optic chiasm is particularly radioresistant, but may undergo damage thought to be due to vascular damage to the blood supply. Visual deterioration typically occurs within 3 years of irradiation, and is progressive.
- The literature suggest that the risk is greatest with high total and daily doses. A standard total dose of 4500 cGy and daily dose of 180 cGy appears to pose very little, if any, risk to the chiasm.
- Our practice is to avoid administration of radiotherapy where possible when the chiasm is under pressure from residual tumour.

Radiation oncogenesis

- There is controversy as to whether pituitary irradiation leads to the development of second tumours. There have been reports of sarcomas, gliomas and meningiomas developing in the field of irradiation after 10–20 years. However, there are also reports of gliomas and meningioma occurring in unirradiated patients with pituitary adenomas. A retrospective review of a large series of patients given pituitary irradiation suggested a risk of second tumour of 1.9% by

20 years after irradiation when compared to the normal population (but not patients with pituitary tumours).

- More subtle changes in neurocognition have been suggested.

Table 30.2 Development of new hypopituitarism at 10 years following pituitary radiotherapy

	No previous surgery	Surgery
Gonadotrophin deficiency	47%	70%
ACTH deficiency	30%	54%
Thyrotrophin deficiency	16%	38%

Focal forms of radiotherapy

Stereotactic radiosurgery uses focused radiation to deliver a precise dose of radiation:

- Gamma knife 'radiosurgery' – ionizing radiation from a cobalt 60 source delivered by convergent collimated beams
- Linear accelerator focal radiotherapy – photons focused on a stationary point from a moving gantry
- Potential advantages are that a single high dose of irradiation is given which can be sharply focused on the tumour with minimal surrounding tissue damage.
- Long-term data are required to demonstrate endocrine efficacy, but it may have a particular role in recurrent or persistent tumours which are well-demarcated and surgically inaccessible e.g. in the cavernous sinus.
- Potential limitations include proximity to the optic chiasm.

Further reading

Brada M, Ford D, Ashley S *et al.* Risk of second brain tumour after conservative surgery and radiotherapy for pituitary adenoma. *BMJ* 1992; 304: 1343–1346.

Jackson IMD, Noren G. Role of gamma knife therapy in the management of pituitary tumours. *Endocrinology and Metabolism Clinics of North America* 1999; 28: 133.

Jones A. Radiation oncogenesis in relation to treatment of pituitary tumours. *Clinical Endocrinology* 1991; 35: 379

Plowman PN. Pituitary adenoma radiotherapy. *Clinical Endocrinology* 1999; 51: 265–271.

Chapter 31
Drug treatment of pituitary tumours

Dopamine agonists

Types

- *Bromocriptine* The first ergot alkaloid to be used, short acting, taken daily. Usually administered orally, although vaginal and i/m formulations can be used and may reduce gastrointestinal intolerance.
- *Quinagolide* Non-ergot, longer acting, taken daily.
- *Cabergoline* Ergot derivative. Long acting – taken once or twice a week.
- *Less commonly used* pergolide and lisuride.

Mechanism of action

Activation of D2 receptors.

Side-effects

Commonly at initiation of treatment

- nausea
- postural hypotension

Less common

- Headache, fatigue, nasal stuffiness, constipation, abdominal cramps, and a Raynaud like phenomenon in hands.
- Very rarely patients have developed hallucinations and psychosis (usually at higher doses).
- Side-effects may be minimized by slow initiation of therapy (e.g. 1.25 mg bromocriptine or 0.25 mg cabergoline), taking medication before going to bed, and taking the tablets with food.

Uses

Hyperprolactinaemia (see p. 136)

- D2 receptor stimulation leads to inhibition of PRL secretion and reduction in cell size leading to tumour shrinkage. The PRL often falls before significant tumour shrinkage is seen.
- Problems may arise when patients are either intolerant of the medication or resistant. Cabergoline appears to be better tolerated than bromocriptine and it is often worth trying an alternative in the case of intolerance, although true intolerance is probably a class effect. Dopamine agonist resistance (10–25% patients) may be due to dif-

ferences in receptor subtype (e.g. loss of D2 receptors) or possibly altered intracellular signalling.

GH-secreting tumours

- Although administration of L-dopa to normal individuals leads to acute increase in GH due to hypothalamic dopamine and noradrenaline synthesis and inhibition of somatostatin secretion, over half of patients with GH-secreting tumours given dopamine agonists have a fall in GH. Dopamine acts directly on somatotroph tumours to inhibit GH release.
- Patients with acromegaly often need larger doses of dopamine agonist than patients with prolactinomas. Tumour shrinkage is most likely if there is concomitant secretion of PRL from the tumour. Dopamine agonists are currently usually reserved for second line drug therapy in patients who are somatostatin agonist resistant or as a co-prescription with somatostatin agonists in patients with mixed GH-and PRL-secreting tumours.

Pregnancy

Bromocriptine is licensed for use in pregnancy, but cabergoline is not licensed in the UK, although it has not thus far been associated with any increased teratogeneicity.

Somatostatin analogues

Mechanism of action

- Since the half-life of somatostatin is very short, a longer acting analogue was synthesized – octreotide. This has a half-life of 110 min in the circulation, inhibits GH secretion 45 times more actively than native somatostatin, with none of the rebound hypersecretion that occurs with somatostatin.
- The somatostatin analogues act predominantly on the somatostatin receptors 2 and 5. Unlike dopamine agonists, somatostatin analogues do not lead to dramatic tumour shrinkage, but some shrinkage is still seen in the majority of tumours.

Types

- S/c octreotide (50–200 μg) administered 3× daily
- Lanreotide SR (30 mg i/m) administered every 7–14 days
- Octreotide LAR (10–30 mg i/m) administered every 4–6 weeks.
- Lanreotide autogel (60–120 mg i/m) administered every 4 weeks.

Side-effects

- Gallstones At least 20–30% of patients develop gallstones or sludge on octreotide (thought by most to antedate stone formation), but only 1%/year develop symptoms. The incidence is unknown on octreotide LAR or Lanreotide.
- Gastrointestinal due to inhibition of motor activity and secretion leading to nausea, abdominal cramps, and mild steatorrhoea. These usually settle with time.
- Injection site pain Obviated by allowing vial to warm to room temperature before injecting.

Uses (see relevant section)

- acromegaly
- carcinoid tumours
- pancreatic neuroendocrine tumours
- TSH-secreting pituitary tumours
- non-functioning pituitary tumours.

Chapter 32
Posterior pituitary

Physiology and pathology

The posterior lobe of the pituitary gland arises from the forebrain, and comprises up to 25% of the normal adult pituitary gland. It produces arginine vasopressin and oxytocin. Both hormones are synthesized in the hypothalamic neurons of the supra-optic and paraventricular nuclei and migrate as neurosecretory granules to the posterior pituitary before release into the circulation. The hormones are unbound in the circulation and their half-life is short.

Oxytocin

- Oxytocin has no known role in men. It may aid contraction of the seminal vesicles.
- In women, oxytocin contracts the pregnant uterus and also causes breast duct smooth muscle contraction leading to breast-milk ejection during breast-feeding. Oxytocin is released in response to suckling and also to cervical dilatation during parturition. However, oxytocin deficiency has no known adverse effect on parturition or breast-feeding.
- There are several as yet ill-understood features of oxytocin physiology. For example, osmotic stimulation may also lead to oxytocin secretion. Oxytocin may play a role in the ovary and testis, as ovarian luteal cells and testicular cells have both been shown to synthesize it, although its subsequent role is not known.

Vasopressin and neurophysin

- Arginine vasopressin is the major determinant of renal water excretion and therefore fluid balance. Its main action is to reduce free water clearance.
- Vasopressin is a nonapeptide, and derives from a large precursor – with a signal peptide, and a neurophysin. The vasopressin gene is located on chromosome 20, and is closely linked to the oxytocin gene. Vasopressin travels to the posterior pituitary at about 2 mm/h, and undergoes cleavage as it travels. Neurophysin is released with vasopressin but has no further role after acting as a carrier protein in the neurons.
- Release of vasopressin occurs in response to changes in osmolality detected by osmoreceptors in the hypothalamus. Large changes in blood volume (5–10%) also influence vasopressin secretion. Many substances modulate vasopressin secretion including the catecholamines and opioids.
- The main site of action of vasopressin is in the collecting duct and the thick ascending loop of Henle where it increases water permeability so that solute free water may pass along an osmotic gradient to the interstitial medulla. Vasopressin in higher concentrations has a pressor effect. It also acts as an ACTH secretagogue synergistically with CRH.

Chapter 33
Diabetes insipidus

Definition

DI is defined as the passage of large volumes (>3 litre/24 h) of dilute urine (osmolality <300 mOsmol/kg).

Classification

Cranial

Due to deficiency of circulating arginine vasopressin (anti-diuretic hormone)

Nephrogenic

Due to renal resistance to vasopressin.

Primary polydipsia

- Polyuria due to excessive drinking.
- In addition to suppressed levels of vasopressin due to low plasma osmolality, there may be impaired renal effectiveness because of wash out of solute and therefore reduced urine-concentrating ability.

Features

- *Adults* polyuria, nocturia, and thirst
- *Children* polyuria, enuresis, and failure to thrive
- NB Clinical syndrome of cranial DI may be masked by cortisol deficiency as this results in failure to excrete a water load.
- Syndrome may worsen in pregnancy due to placental breakdown (vasopressinase) of circulating vasopressin.

Causes of DI

Cranial

10% vasopressin cells should be sufficient to keep the urine volume <4l/day.

Familial

- autosomal dominant (vasopressin gene)
- DIDMOAD syndrome (DI, diabetes mellitus, optic atrophy, deafness).

Acquired

- trauma (head injury, neurosurgery)
- tumours (craniopharyngiomas, pituitary infiltration by metastases)
- inflammatory conditions (sarcoidosis, tuberculosis, Langerhans cell histiocytosis, lymphocytic hypophysitis)
- infections (meningitis, encephalitis)
- vascular (Sheehan's syndrome, sickle cell disease)
- idiopathic.

Nephrogenic

Familial

- X-linked recessive (vasopressin receptor gene)
- autosomal recessive (aquaporin-2 gene).

Acquired

- drugs (lithium, demeclocycline)
- metabolic (hypercalcaemia, hypokalaemia, hyperglycaemia)
- chronic renal disease
- post-obstructive uropathy.

Primary polydipsia

- psychological.

Investigation

Diagnosis of type of DI

- Confirm large urine output (> 3000 mL/day).
- Exclude diabetes mellitus and renal failure (osmotic diuresis).
- Check electrolytes. Hypokalaemia and hypercalcaemia (nephrogenic DI).
- Fluid deprivation test (see p. 235) and assessment of response to vasopressin.
- Occasionally further investigations are required, particularly when only partial forms of the condition are present;
- Measurement of plasma vasopressin, osmolality, and thirst threshold:
  - in response to infusion of 0.05 mL/kg per min 5% hypertonic saline for 2 h for cranial DI (no increased vasopressin)
  - in response to fluid deprivation for nephrogenic DI (vasopressin levels rise with no increased urine osmolality).
- An alternative is a therapeutic trial of desmopressin with monitoring of sodium and osmolality.

Investigation of the cause

- MRI head
  - looking for tumours – hypothalamic, pineal, or infiltration
  - often demonstrates loss of bright spot of posterior pituitary gland.
- Serum ACE (sarcoidosis) and tumour markers, e.g. βHCG (pineal germinoma).

Fluid deprivation test

1 Patient is allowed fluids overnight. If psychogenic polydipsia suspected, consider overnight fluid deprivation to avoid morning overhydration).

2 Patient is then deprived of fluids for 8 h or until 5% loss of body weight if earlier. Weigh patient hourly.

3 Plasma osmolality is measured 4 hourly and urine volume and osmolality every 2 h.

4 The patient is then given 2 μg i/m desmopressin with urine volume, and urine and serum osmolality measured over the next 4 h.

Results

If serum osmolality >305 mOsm/kg – patient has DI and test is stopped.

Urine osmolality (Osm/kg)

Diagnosis	After fluid deprivation	After desmopressin
Cranial DI	<300	>800
Nephrogenic DI	<300	<300
Primary polydipsia	>800	>800
Partial DI or polydipsia	300–800	<800

Treatment

Maintenance of adequate fluid input

In patients with partial DI, and an intact thirst mechanism, then drug therapy may not be necessary if the polyuria is mild (<4l/24 h).

Drug therapy

Desmopressin

- Vasopressin analogue, acting predominantly on the V2 receptors in the kidney, with little action on the V1 receptors of blood vessels. It thus has reduced pressor activity and increased antidiuretic efficacy, in addition to a longer half-life than the native hormone.
- Drug may be administered in divided doses, orally (100–1000 μg/day), intranasally (10–40 μg/day) or parenterally (s/c, i/v, im) (0.1–2 μg/day). There is wide variation in the dose required by an individual patient.
- Monitoring of serum sodium and osmolality is essential as hyponatraemia or hypo-osmolality may develop.

Lysine vasopressin

- The antidiuretic hormone of the pig family.
- Not used very often as its effects are short lived (1–3 h) and it may retain pressor activity. Intranasal administration. Dose 5–20 U/day.

Chlorpropamide (100–500 mg/day) and carbamazepine enhance the action of vasopressin on the collecting duct.

Nephrogenic DI

- Correction of underlying cause (metabolic or drugs).
- High doses of desmopressin (e.g. up to 5 μg i/m) can be effective.
- Maintenance of adequate fluid input.
- Thiazide diuretics and prostaglandin synthase inhibitors (decrease the action of prostaglandins which locally inhibit the action of vasopressin in the kidney), e.g. indomethacin, can be helpful.

Polydipsic polyuria

Management is difficult. Treatment of any underlying psychiatric disorder is important.

Chapter 34
Hyponatraemia

Causes

Excess water (dilutional)

- excess water intake
- increased water reabsorption (cirrhosis, congestive cardiac failure, nephrotic syndrome)
- reduced renal excretion of a water load (SIADH, glucocorticoid deficiency)

Salt deficiency

- Renal loss (salt wasting nephropathy – tubulointerstitial nephritis, polycystic kidney disease, analgesic nephropathy, recovery phase of acute tubular necrosis, relief of bilateral ureteric obstruction).
- Non-renal loss (skin, gastrointestinal tract [bowel sequestration, high fistulae]).
- Renal sodium conservation of sodium is efficient and therefore low salt intake alone never causes sodium deficiency.

Pseudohyponatraemia

- Lipids, proteins (e.g. paraproteinaemia)
- Sodium only in aqueous phase of plasma, therefore, depending on assay, total sodium concentration may be spuriously low if concentrations of lipid or protein are high.

Solute

- Glucose, mannitol, ethanol.
- Addition of solute confined to the ECF causes water to shift from the ICF lowering ECF sodium concentration.

Sick cell syndrome

- Symptomless hyponatraemia at 120–130 mmol/L
- True clinically apparent hyponatraemia is associated with either excess water or salt deficiency. The other causes can usually be easily excluded.

Table 34.1 Hyponatraemia

Hypovolaemic		Euvolaemic		Hypervolaemic	
NaU <20 mmol/L	NaU >20 mmol/L	NaU <20 mmol/L	NaU >20 mmol/L Serum osmolality <270 mOsm/kg	NaU <20 mmol/L	NaU >20 mmol/L Serum osmolality <270 mOsm/kg
			Urine osmolality >100 mOsm/kg		Urine osmolality >100 mOsm/kg
Non-renal sodium loss	Renal sodium loss	Depletional ECF loss with inappropriate fluid replacement	Distal dilution	Excess water	
?GIT loss	?Salt losing nephropathy		SIADH	Cirrhosis	SIADH
?Skin loss	?Mineralocorticoid deficiency		GC deficiency	Nephrotic syndrome	
				CCF	

GC = glucocorticoid

Features

- The clinical features are dependent both on the underlying cause and also on the rate of development of hyponatraemia. They may develop once the sodium reaches 115 mmol/L or may occur earlier if the fall is rapid. Values of 100 mmol/L or less are life threatening.
- The features of excess water are mainly neurological because of brain injury, and depend on the age of the patient and rate of development. They include confusion and headache, progressing to seizures and coma. In addition, in the hypervolaemic forms of excess water (where the fluid is confined to the ECF e.g. cardiac failure, nephrotic syndrome, and cirrhosis) oedema and fluid overload is apparent. In contrast, in the syndromes of excess water associated with SIADH the fluid is distributed throughout the ECF and ICF and there is no apparent fluid overload. In contrast, salt deficiency presents with features of hypovolaemia with tachycardia and postural hypotension.

Investigation

- Urinary sodium is very helpful in differentiating the underlying cause (Table 34.1).
- Assess volume status
- Other investigations as indicated e.g. serum and urine osmolality, cortisol, thyroid function, liver biochemistry.

Treatment

Salt deficiency (renal or non-renal)

- Increase dietary salt.
- May need intravenous normal saline if dehydrated

Excess water (cirrhosis, nephrotic syndrome, CCF)

- Fluid restriction to 500–1000 mL/24 h.
- Occasionally hypertonic (3%) saline (513 mmol/L) may be required in patients with acute symptomatic hyponatraemia. The appropriate infusion rate can be calculated from the formula:

  rate of sodium replacement (mmol/hour) = total body water (60% of body weight) × desired correction rate (0.5–1 mmol/h).

  E.g. for a 70 kg man:

  $Na^+ = 60\% \times 70\text{ kg} \times 1\text{ mmol/hr} = 42\text{ mmol/hr}$

  $= 42 \times \frac{1000}{513} \qquad = 82\text{ ml/hr of 3\% saline}$
- Rapid normalization (faster than 0.5 mmol/h) of sodium may be associated with central pontine myelinolysis.

SIADH

See following chapter.

Chapter 35
Syndrome of inappropriate ADH

SIADH is a common cause of hyponatraemia. It is clinically normovolaemic hyponatraemia, since the increased water is distributed through all compartments.

Criteria for diagnosis

- Hyponatraemia and hypotonic plasma (osmolality <270 mOsm/kg).
- Inappropriate urine osmolality >100 mOsm/kg.
- Excessive renal sodium loss (>20 mmol/L, often >50 mmol/L).
- Absence of clinical evidence of hypovolaemia or of volume overload.
- Normal renal, adrenal, and thyroid function.
- NB Fluid restriction may reduce sodium loss
- Exclude adrenal or thyroid dysfunction.

Types of SIADH

Type 1

- erratic excess ADH secretion, unrelated to plasma osmolality commonest (40%) associated (not exclusively) with tumours.

Type 2

- 'reset osmostat': patients autoregulate around a lower serum osmolality
- chest and CNS disease.

Type 3

- 'leaky osmostat' normal osmoregulation until plasma hypotonicity develops when vasopressin secretion continues.

Type 4

- normal osmoregulated vasopressin secretion, possible receptor defect or alternative antidiuretic hormone.

Table 35.1 Causes of SIADH

Tumours	Small cell lung carcinoma, thymoma, lymphoma, leukaemia, sarcoma, mesothelioma
Chest disease	Infections (pneumonia, tuberculosis, empyema)
	Pneumothorax
	Asthma
	Positive pressure ventilation
CNS disorders	Infections (meningitis, encephalitis, abscess)
	Head injury
	Guillain Barré
	Vascular disorders (subarachnoid haemorrhage, cerebral thrombosis)
	Psychosis
Drugs	Chemotherapy (vincristine, vinblastine, cyclophosphamide)
	Psychiatric drugs (phenothiazines, MAOI)
	Carbamazepine
	Clofibrate
	Chlorpropamide
Metabolic	Hypothyroidism
	Glucocorticoid deficiency
	Acute intermittent porphyria
Idiopathic	

Treatment

- Treatment of the underlying cause.
- Fluid restriction to 500–1000 mL/24 h.
- If the problem is not temporary and fluid restriction long-term can be difficult for the patient, drug treatment may be tried. *Demeclocycline* may be effective by inducing partial nephrogenic DI. New specific vasopressin antagonists are under trial.
- In an emergency, saline infusion may be required – great care is required as rapid overcorrection of hyponatraemia may cause central pontine myelinolysis (demyelination). This can be avoided if the rate of correction does not exceed 0.5 mmol/L per hour (see p. 241).

Chapter 36
Hypothalamus

Pathophysiology

- The hypothalamus releases hormones that act as releasing hormones at the anterior pituitary gland. It also produces dopamine that inhibits PRL release from the anterior pituitary gland. It also synthesizes arginine vasopressin and oxytocin (see p. 228).
- The commonest syndrome to be associated with the hypothalamus is abnormal GnRH secretion leading to reduced gonadotrophin secretion and hypogonadism. Common causes are stress, weight loss, and excessive exercise. Management involves treatment of the cause if possible. Administration of pulsatile GnRH is usually effective at reversing the abnormality but rarely undertaken.

Hypothalamic syndrome

Uncommon but may occur due to a large tumour, following surgery for a craniopharyngioma, or due to infiltration from e.g. Langerhans cell histiocytosis. The typical features are hyperphagia and weight gain, loss of thirst sensation, DI, somnolence and behaviour change. Management can be challenging. E.g. DI with the loss of thirst sensation may require the prescription of regular fluid in addition to desmopressin, and monitoring with daily weights and fluid balance as a routine.

Metabolic effects of hypothalamic mass lesions

- appetite
  - hyperphagia and obesity
  - anorexia
- thirst
  - adipsia
  - compulsive drinking
- temperature
  - hyperthermia
  - hypothermia
- somnolence and coma.

Chapter 37
Eating disorders

Anorexia nervosa

Features

- Typical presentation is a woman aged <25 with weight loss, amenorrhoea, and behavioural changes.
- There is a long-term risk of severe osteoporosis associated with >6 months amenorrhoea. There is loss of bone mineral content and bone density with little or no recovery after resolution of the amenorrhoea.

Endocrine abnormalities

- Deficiency of GnRH, low LH and FSH, normal PRL, and low oestrogen in women or testosterone in men.
- Elevated circulating cortisol (usually non-suppressible with dexamethasone).
- Low normal thyroxine, reduced T_3, and normal TSH.
- Elevated resting GH levels.
- In addition, it is common to find various metabolic abnormalities such as reduced magnesium, zinc, phosphorus, and calcium levels in addition to hyponatraemia and hypokalaemia.
- Weight gain leads to a reversion of the prepubertal LH secretory pattern to the adult-like secretion. Administration of GnRH in a pulsatile pattern leads to normalization of the pituitary–gonadal axis, demonstrating that the primary abnormality is hypothalamic.

Management

The long-term treatment of these patients involves treatment of the underlying condition and then management of osteoporosis, although many patients will refuse oestrogen replacement.

Bulimia

Features

- Typically occurs in women who are slightly older than the group with anorexia nervosa. Weight may be normal and patients often deny the abnormal eating behaviour. Patients gorge themselves, using artificial means of avoiding excessive weight gain (laxatives, diuretic abuse, vomiting). This may be a cause of 'occult' hypokalaemia.
- These patients may or may not have menstrual irregularity. If menstrual irregularity is present, this is often associated with inadequate oestrogen secretion and anovulation.

Chapter 38
Pineal gland

Physiology

- The pineal gland lies behind the third ventricle, is highly vascular, and produces melatonin and other peptides.
- During daylight, light-induced hyperpolarization of the retinal photoreceptors inhibits signalling and the pineal gland is quiescent.
- Darkness stimulates the gland, and there is synthesis and release of melatonin.
- Melatonin levels are usually low during the day, rise during the evening, peak at midnight and then decline independent of sleep.
- Exposure to darkness during the day does not increase melatonin secretion.

Jet lag

- It is claimed that pharmacological doses of melatonin can reset the body clock.
- Studies have suggested that melatonin may reduce the severity or duration of jet lag. There are few safety data, and currently melatonin does not have a product licence in the UK.

Pineal and intracranial germ cell tumours

- *Incidence* 0.5%–3% intracranial neoplasms.
- *Epidemiology* M > F. All ages. 2/3 present between age 10 and 21 years.
- Germ cell tumours are now classified as germinomas or non-germinomatous germ cell tumours (choriocarcinoma, teratoma). The latter term includes the tumours previously called 'true' pinealomas.

Features

- raised intracranial pressure (compression of cerebral aqueduct), headache, and lethargy
- visual disturbance (pressure on quadrigeminal plate)
- Parinaud's syndrome (paralysis of upward gaze, convergent nystagmus, Argyll–Robertson pupils)
- ataxia
- pyramidal signs
- hypopituitarism
- DI
- sexual precocity in boys (excess hCG secretion mimics LH leading to Leydig cell testosterone secretion, or related to space-occupying mass).

Investigations

- imaging of craniospinal axis MRI/CT (may detect second tumour/metastases)
- CSF examination
- tumour markers (hCG, α-fetoprotein)
- cytology
- biopsy if tumour markers unhelpful
- pituitary function assessment.

Management

- External beam radiotherapy – standard therapy is to irradiate the whole craniospinal axis
- Germinomas are exquisitely radiosensitive.
- Chemotherapy may be indicated, e.g. vincristine, etopside, carboplatin.
- Recent work suggests that a combination of radiotherapy and chemotherapy can considerably increase long-term cure rates.

Prognosis

Excellent for germinomas (70–85% 5 year survival), but non-germinomatous germ cell tumours have a worse prognosis (15–40% 5 year survival).

Part III
Adrenal glands

Chapter 39
Anatomy and physiology

Anatomy

The normal adrenal glands weigh 4–5 g. The cortex represents 90% of the normal gland and surrounds the medulla. The arterial blood supply arises from the renal arteries, aorta, and inferior phrenic artery. Venous drainage occurs via the central vein into the inferior vena cava on the right, and into the left renal vein on the left.

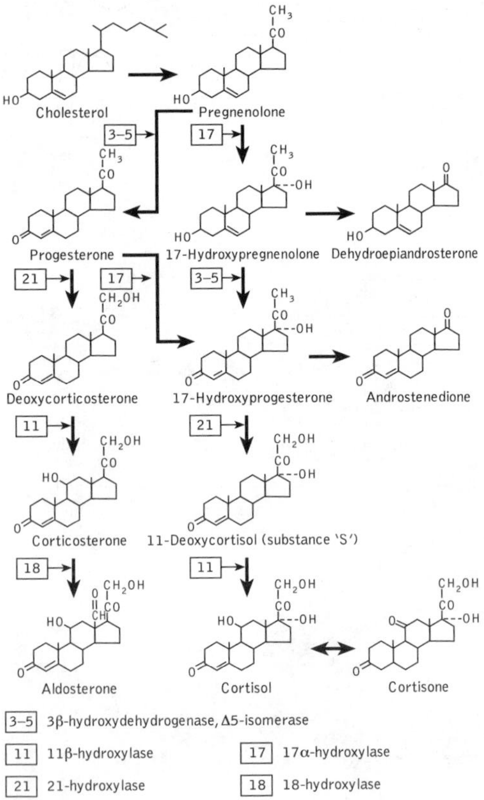

Fig 39.1 Pathways and enzymes involved in synthesis of glucocorticoids, mineralocorticoids, and adrenal androgens from a cholesterol precursor. © Reprinted from Besser & Thorner: *Clinical endocrinology*, by permission of the publisher Mosby.

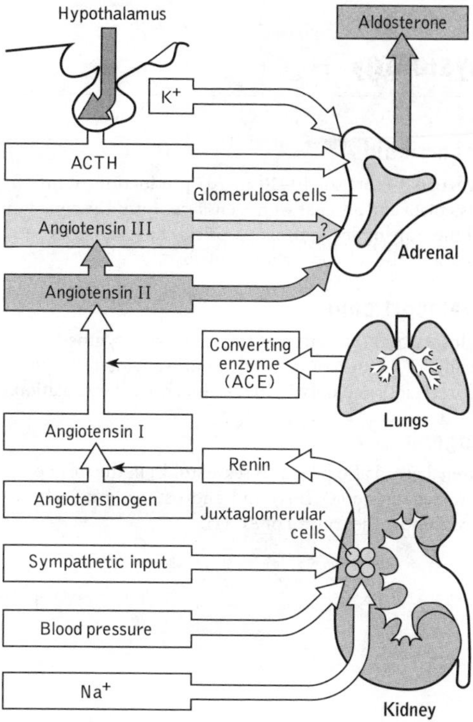

Fig. 39.2 Physiological mechanisms governing the production and secretion of aldosterone. © Reprinted from Besser & Thorner: *Clinical endocrinology*, by permission of the publisher Mosby.

Physiology

Glucocorticoids

Glucocorticoid (cortisol 10–20 mg/d) production occurs from the zona fasiculata and adrenal androgens arise form the zona reticularis. Both of these are under control of ACTH, which regulates both steroid synthesis, and also adrenocortical growth.

Mineralocorticoids

Mineralocorticoid (aldosterone 100–150 μg/d) synthesis occurs predominantly under the control of the renin–angiotensin system, in the zona glomerulosa and only 5–10% is under ACTH regulation.

Androgens

The adrenal gland also produces sex steroids, in the form of dehydroepiandrostenedione (DHEA) and androstenedione. The synthetic pathway is under the control of ACTH.

Chapter 40
Imaging

Computed tomography scanning

CT is the most widely used modality for imaging the adrenal glands. It is able to detect masses >5 mm in diameter, and is currently the optimal means of differentiating between different adrenal cortical pathologies.

Magnetic resonance imaging

MRI can also reliably detect adrenal masses >5–10 mm in diameter, and in some circumstances provides additional information to CT, e.g. differentiation of cortical from medullary tumours

Ultrasound imaging

Ultrasound detects masses >20 mm in diameter, but normal adrenal glands are not usually visible except in children. Body morphology and bowel gas can provide technical difficulties.

Further reading

Peppercorn PD, Grossman AB, Reznek RH. Imaging of incidentally discovered adrenal masses *Clinical Endocrinology* 1998; 48: 379–388.

Reznek RH, Armstrong P. The adrenal gland. *Clinical Endocrinology* 1994; 40: 561–576.

Normal adrenal

Normal adrenal cortex is assessed by measuring limb thickness, and is considered enlarged at >5 mm approximately the thickness of the diaphragmatic crus nearby.

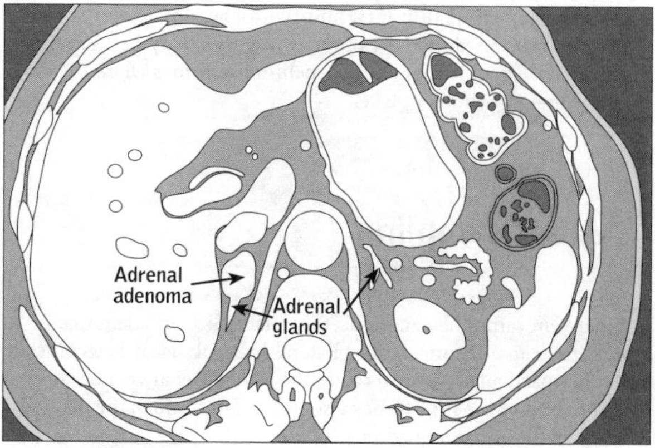

Fig. 40.1 Typical appearance of adrenal adenoma on CT scan.

Radionucleotide imaging

- *^{75}Se 6β-selenomethyl-19-norcholesterol* This isotope is concentrated in functioning steroid synthesizing tissue, and is used to image the adrenal cortex. It is particularly useful in determining whether a nodule is functioning or not. In addition it can be helpful in localizing residual adrenal tissue following failed bilateral adrenalectomy.
- *^{123}Iodine-metaiodobenzylguanidine* (MIBG) is a guanethidine analogue, concentrated in some phaeochromocytomas, paragangliomas, carcinoid tumours, and neuroblastomas, and is useful diagnostically. A different isotope, ^{131}I-MIBG, may be used therapeutically, e.g. in malignant phaeochromocytomas when the diagnostic imaging shows uptake.

Venous sampling

Adrenal vein sampling can be useful to lateralize an adenoma, or to differentiate an adenoma from bilateral hyperplasia. It is technically difficult – particularly catheterizing the right adrenal vein because of its drainage into the IVC. It may also be used to confirm the diagnosis of bilateral phaeochromocytoma.

Chapter 41
Mineralocorticoid excess

Definitions

The majority of cases of mineralocorticoid excess are due to excess aldosterone production which may be primary or secondary and are typically associated with hypertension and hypokalaemia.

- *Primary hyperaldosteronism* is a disorder of autonomous aldosterone hypersecretion with suppressed renin levels.
- *Secondary hyperaldosteronism* occurs when aldosterone hypersecretion occurs secondary to elevated circulating renin levels, due to renal artery stenosis, or renal hypoperfusion, and occasionally a very rare renin-producing tumour (reninoma).
- Other mineralocorticoids may occasionally be the cause of this syndrome (see opposite).

Causes of mineralocorticoid excess

Primary hyperaldosteronism

- Conn's syndrome (aldosterone-producing adrenal adenoma)
- bilateral adrenal hyperplasia
- glucocorticoid suppressible hyperaldosteronism
- aldosterone-producing adrenal carcinoma.

Secondary hyperaldosteronism

- renal artery stenosis
- renal hypoperfusion
- cirrhosis
- congestive cardiac failure
- nephrotic syndrome
- renin-secreting tumour.

Other mineralocorticoid excess syndromes

- apparent mineralocorticoid excess
- liquorice ingestion
- deoxycorticosterone and corticosterone
- ectopic ACTH secretion
- congenital adrenal hyperplasia
- exogenous mineralocorticoids.

'Pseudoaldosteronism' due to abnormal renal tubular transport

- Bartter's syndrome (p. 301)
- Gitelman's syndrome (p. 302)
- Liddle's syndrome (p. 300)

Chapter 42
Primary aldosteronism

Epidemiology

Primary hyperaldosteronism accounts for at least 2% (and possibly up to 10%) of hypertensive patients. The most common cause is a unilateral adrenal adenoma (see Table 42.1).

Pathophysiology

Aldosterone causes renal sodium retention and potassium loss. This results in expansion of body sodium content, resulting in suppression of renal renin synthesis. The direct action of aldosterone on the distal nephron causes sodium retention and loss of hydrogen and potassium ions, resulting in a hypokalaemic alkalosis, although serum potassium may not be significantly reduced and may be normal in up to 50% of cases.

Clinical features

- Moderately severe hypertension, which is often resistant to conventional therapy.
- Hypokalaemia is usually asymptomatic. Occasionally patients may present with tetany, myopathy, polyuria and nocturia (hypokalaemic nephrogenic diabetes insipidus) due to severe hypokalaemia.

Table 42.1 Causes of primary hyperaldosteronism

Condition	Relative frequency	Age	Sex	Pathology
Aldosteronoma (Conn's adenoma)	70%	3rd–6th decade	Predominant in females	Benign, adenoma, <2.5 cm diameter, yellow because of high cholesterol content
Idiopathic aldosteronism/ adrenal hyperplasia	Common	Older than Conn's	No sex difference	Macronodular or micronodular hyperplasia
Adrenal carcinoma	Rare	5th–7th decade (occasionally young)	More common in females	Tumour >4 cm in diameter – often larger, may be evidence of local invasion
Glucocorticoid suppressible hyperaldosteronism	Rare	Childhood	No sex difference	Bilateral hyperplasia of zona glomerulosa

Conn's syndrome – aldosterone-producing adenoma

Very high levels of aldosterone synthase are expressed, and greater amounts of aldosterone are usually produced than in other causes. Although aldosterone production is autonomous, ACTH has a greater stimulatory effect than angiotensin II, although a subtype that remain more responsive to angiotensin II has been described (implications for postural testing – see later).

Bilateral adrenal hyperplasia (bilateral idiopathic hyperaldosteronism)

This is the second most common form of primary hyperaldosteronism in adults. Hyperplasia is more commonly bilateral than unilateral, and may be associated with micronodular or macronodular hyperplasia. The pathophysiology is not known although aldosterone secretion is very sensitive to circulating angiotensin II, and not ACTH. Hypokalaemia tends to be milder.

Glucocorticoid-suppressible hyperaldosteronism (GSH)

A rare autosomal dominantly inherited condition due to the presence of a chimeric gene (8q22) containing the 5′ sequence which determines regulation of the 11β-hydroxylase gene (*CYP11B1*) coding for the enzyme catalysing the last step in cortisol synthesis, and the 3′ sequence from the aldosterone synthase gene (*CYP11B2*) coding for the enzyme catalysing the last step in aldosterone synthesis. This results in expression of aldosterone synthase in the zona fasiculata as well as the zona glomerulosa and aldosterone secretion becomes under ACTH control. Glucocorticoids lead to suppression of ACTH and suppression of aldosterone production.

Early haemorrhagic strokes are characteristic in GSH pedigrees.

Aldosterone-producing carcinoma

Rare, and usually associated with excessive secretion of other corticosteroids (cortisol, androgen, oestrogen). Hypokalaemia may be profound, and aldosterone levels very high.

Investigation

- NB If serum potassium is <3 mmol/L, this should be normalized before measuring aldosterone.
- Many antihypertensive drugs interfere with testing (see Table 2). α-Blockers, e.g. doxazosin may be used if continued treatment is required.

Screening

Who?

- Patients resistant to conventional antihypertensive medication
- Hypertension associated with hypokalaemia
- Hypertension developing before age of 40 years.

How?

- *Serum potassium* Hypokalaemic alkalosis is highly suggestive of primary hyperaldosteronism, but 20–40% patients may be normokalaemic. A low salt diet will often mask hypokalaemia.
- *Urinary potassium* excretion>30 mmol/24 h following discontinuation of diuretics, in the presence of hypokalaemia, is suggestive of hyperaldosteronism.
- *Plasma renin* Suppressed in patients with primary hyperaldosteronism, but also suppressed in a third of patients with essential hypertension. Sodium intake and antihypertensive medication may alter plasma renin levels (see Table 42.3).
- *Aldosterone: renin ratio* A high ratio is suggestive of primary hyperaldosteronism (aldosterone [pmol/L]/plasma renin activity [ng/mL/h] >750 or aldosterone [ng/dl]/plasma renin activity [ng/mL/h] >30–50). The greater the ratio, the more likely the diagnosis of primary aldosteronism. The timing (morning), posture (upright), potassium (normal) and concomitant medication (avoid antihypertensive agents in particular β-blockers and diuretics) interfering with renin and aldosterone (Table 2), should be standardized. A false negative is found in patients with chronic renal failure.

Table 42.2 Drugs and investigation of renin–angiotensin II axis

Drug	Effect	Duration of washout required (weeks)
ACE inhibitors and angiotensin II antagonists	↑ PRA	2
Diuretics	↑ PRA	2
Spironolactone	↑ PRA	6
β-blockers	↓ PRA	2
Calcium channel blockers	↓ Aldosterone	2

Confirmation of hyperaldosteronism and differentiation of underlying cause

- *Oral salt loading* A high sodium diet (120 mmol sodium/day) for 3 days may precipitate hypokalaemia in a patients with normokalaemia on a low salt diet. In addition, since the normal response to a salt load is aldosterone suppression, the lack of suppression in primary hyperaldosteronism can be used to confirm the diagnosis. Correct hypokalaemia before measuring aldosterone levels, as low potassium levels will tend to suppress aldosterone *per se.*
- *Postural test* Plasma aldosterone, renin, and cortisol are measured after the patient has been lying down overnight, and repeated after an upright posture has been maintained for 4 h. This test relies on the fact that aldosterone production from the majority of adenomas is dependent on ACTH secretion, but independent of posture, whereas in adrenal hyperplasia, aldosterone production is stimulated by angiotensin II in response to an upright posture. Failure of aldosterone to rise to more than a third above baseline is suggestive of an adenoma.
- *Serum cortisol* is measured to confirm the circadian pattern of ACTH secretion with a fall in cortisol after 4 h. A rise in the post-ambulatory cortisol invalidates the test.
- *Urinary 18 hydroxycortisol* Elevated levels of this precursor are found in primary aldosteronism due to a Conn's adenoma or glucocorticoid suppressible hyperaldosteronism. (GSH >> Conn's > adrenal hyperplasia)
- *Dexamethasone suppression test* Treatment with dexamethasone (0.5 mg 6 hourly) for >3 days leads to lowering of aldosterone and blood pressure in glucocorticoid suppressible hyperaldosteronism.
- *Genetic analysis* Can be used to confirm the diagnosis of glucocorticoid suppressible hypertension.
- *Other dynamic tests* which may be helpful include the response to an ACEI which may help differentiate adenomas from hyperplasia. Plasma aldosterone is measured in the sitting position, basally and 60 min after captopril. Inhibition of angiotensin II leads to a fall in aldosterone in patients with idiopathic hyperaldosteronism but not in Conn's syndrome. Another test which is rarely used is the fludro-

cortisone suppression test where fludrocortisone 400 μg/d for 4 days leads to no suppression of aldosterone in Conn's syndrome.

Table 42.3 Differential diagnosis of primary hyperaldosteronism

Test		Upright posture and time	ACE inhibitor	Dexamethasone suppression
Normal	PRA	↑	↑	→
	Aldosterone	↑	↓	→
Aldosterone-producing adenoma	PRA	→	→	→
	Aldosterone	↓	→	→
Angiotensin-responsive adenoma (?~20% adenomas)	PRA	↑	↑	→
	Aldosterone	↑	↓	→
Idiopathic adrenal hyperplasia	PRA	↑	↑	→
	Aldosterone	↑	↓	→
Glucocorticoid-suppressible hyperaldosteronism	PRA	→	→	↑
	Aldosterone	↓	→	↓

Localization

CT/MRI scan

- Identifies most adenomas >5 mm diameter. Bilateral abnormalities or tumours <1 cm in diameter require further localization procedures.
- In idiopathic aldosteronism, both glands appear enlarged or normal in size.
- Macronodular hyperplasia may result in identifiable nodules on imaging.
- A mass >4 cm in size is suspicious of carcinoma but is unusual in Conn's syndrome.
- NB. In essential hypertension nodules are described.

Adrenal vein sampling

Aldosterone measurements from both adrenal veins allow a gradient between the two sides to be identified in the case of unilateral disease. It is the gold standard for differentiation between uni- and bilateral aldosterone production, but cannulating the right adrenal vein is technically difficult. Cortisol measurements should also be taken concomitantly with aldosterone, to confirm successful positioning within the adrenal veins.

Radiolabelled iodocholesterol scanning

Unilateral increase uptake indicates the presence of an adenoma. Prior administration of dexamethasone (e.g. 1 mg 4× daily for 3 days before isotope administration and for 1 week afterwards) to suppress cortisol production increases accuracy. Normal adrenal is not visualized before the 5th day using the dexamethasone protocol, and adenomas are seen before this.

Treatment

Surgery

Adrenalectomy is the treatment of choice for aldosterone secreting adenomas. Hypertension is cured in about 70%. If it persists (more likely in those with long-standing hypertension and old people) it is more amenable to medical treatment. The blood pressure response to treatment with spironolactone (200–400 mg/d) before surgery can be used to predict the response to surgery of patients with adenomas. (NB Spironolactone has a long half-life and may need to be stopped for 2 days before surgery to avoid postoperative mineralocorticoid deficiency). Overall 50% become normotensive in 1 month and 70% within 1 year.

Laparoscopic adrenalectomy is increasingly being successfully performed and is associated with lower morbidity and promising results. Presurgical spironolactone treatment may be used to correct potassium stores before surgery.

Angiotensin II responsive adenomas can be successfully treated with surgery, but may also respond to ACEI.

Surgery is contra-indicated in patients with idiopathic hyperaldosteronism as even bilateral adrenalectomy does not cure the hypertension.

Medical treatment

The aldosterone antagonist *spironolactone* (200–400 mg/day) has been used successfully for many years to treat the hypertension and hypokalaemia associated with bilateral adrenal hyperplasia and idiopathic hyperaldosteronism. There may be a delay in response of hypertension of 4–8 weeks. However, combination with other antihypertensive agents (ACEI and calcium channel blockers) is usually required. Side-effects are common – particularly gynaecomastia and impotence in men, menstrual irregularities in women, and gastrointestinal effects.

Alternative drugs include the potassium-sparing diuretics *amiloride* and *triamterene*. Calcium channel antagonists may also be helpful.

Glucocorticoid-suppressible hyperaldosteronism can be treated with low dose *dexamethasone* (0.5 mg on going to bed and 0.25 mg on waking). Side-effects often limit therapy, and spironolactone treatment is often preferred. In addition, spironolactone may reduce the poorly understood increased risk of stroke in this group.

Adrenal carcinoma

Surgery and postoperative adrenolytic therapy with *ortho-para*-DDD (*mitotane*) is usually required, but the prognosis is usually poor (see p. 292).

Further reading

Ganguly A. Primary aldosteronism. *New England Journal of Medicine* 1998; 339: 1828–1833.

Chapter 43
Excess other mineralocorticoids

Epidemiology

Occasionally, the clinical syndrome of hyperaldosteronism is not associated with excess aldosterone, and a process due to another mineralocorticoid is suspected. These conditions are rare.

When to suspect it?

Hypertension and hypokalaemic alkalosis in association with low plasma renin activity and the absence of elevated aldosterone.

Apparent mineralocorticoid excess

This is due to deficiency of the 11β-hydroxysteroid dehydrogenase (HSD) enzyme type 2, which usually protects the distal nephron mineralocorticoid receptor from stimulation by cortisol. The mineralocorticoid receptor has an equal affinity for cortisol and aldosterone, but there is a 100-fold excess of circulating cortisol over aldosterone. Cortisol is metabolized to the relatively inactive cortisone by 11βHSD at the mineralocorticoid receptor.

Congenital absence of the enzyme or inhibition of its activity (e.g. following liquorice ingestion) allows cortisol to stimulate the receptor and leads to severe hypertension. This condition is seen predominantly in children, presenting with failure to thrive, thirst, polyuria, and severe hypertension. Patients are not cushingoid as there is intact negative feedback.

Biochemistry

- Suppression of PRA and aldosterone
- Elevated ratio of urinary tetrahydrocortisol and *allo*-tetrahydrocortisol to tetrahydrocortisone (>10 in AME; normal = 1).

Treatment

Dexamethasone leads to suppression of ACTH secretion, reduced cortisol concentrations, and lowered blood pressure. It has a much lower affinity for the mineralocorticoid receptor.

Deoxycorticosterone and corticosterone

Two forms of congenital adrenal hyperplasia (see p. 368) are associated with this syndrome:

- 17α-hydroxylase deficiency (deoxycorticosterone and corticosterone)
- 11β-hydroxylase (deoxycorticosterone)

Glucocorticoid replacement to inhibit ACTH is effective treatment for these conditions.

Adrenal tumours rarely secrete excessive amounts of deoxycorticosterone or corticosterone. Usually this is concomitant with excessive aldosterone production, but occasionally it may occur in an isolated fashion.

Ectopic ACTH syndrome

The aldosterone receptor has equal affinity for cortisol and aldosterone, and is usually protected from the effects of stimulation by cortisol by the 11β-hydroxysteroid type 2 dehydrogenase enzyme which converts cortisol to cortisone to protect the receptor. In the syndrome of ectopic ACTH, this protection is overcome because of high cortisol secretion rates which saturate the enzyme, leading to impaired conversion of cortisol to cortisone, and thus hypokalaemia and hypertension.

Further reading

Chidiac RM, Aron DC. Incidentalomas. *Endocrinology and Metabolism Clinics of North America* 1997;26: 233–253.

Kloos RT, Gross MD, Francis IR, Korobkin M, Shapiro B. Incidentally discovered adrenal masses. *Endocrine Reviews* 1995;16: 460–484.

Newell-Price J, Grossman A. Adrenal incidentaloma. *Postgraduate Medical Journal* 1996;72: 207–210.

Turner HE, Moore NR, Byrne JV, Wass JAH. Pituitary, adrenal and thyroid incidentalomas *Endocrin Related Cancer* 1998;5: 131–150.

Chapter 44
Adrenal Cushing's syndrome

Definition and epidemiology

- Cushing's syndrome results from chronic excess cortisol, and is described on page 158.
- The causes may be classified as ACTH dependent and ACTH independent. This section describes ACTH-independent Cushing's syndrome, which is due to adrenal tumours (benign and malignant), and is responsible for 10–20% cases of Cushing's syndrome.
- Adrenal tumours causing Cushing's syndrome are commoner in women. The peak incidence is in the fourth and fifth decade.
- Causes and relative frequencies of adrenal Cushing's syndrome in adults:

– adrenal adenoma	10%
– adrenal carcinoma	8%
– bilateral micronodular adrenal hyperplasia	1%
– bilateral macronodular hyperplasia	1%

Pathophysiology

- Benign adenomas are usually encapsulated, and <6 cm in diameter. They are usually associated with pure glucocorticoid excess.
- Adrenal carcinomas are usually >6 cm in diameter, although they may be smaller, and are often associated with local invasion and metastases at the time of diagnosis. They may be associated with secretion of excess androgen production in addition to cortisol. Occasionally they may be associated with mineralocorticoid or oestrogen secretion.
- Adrenal hyperplasia may be micronodular (<1 cm diameter) or macronodular (>1 cm). A rare cause of adrenal hyperplasia causing Cushing's syndrome due to inappropriate adrenal responsiveness to gastric inhibitory peptide (GIP) has been reported, resulting in food-induced glucocorticoid excess.
- *Carney complex* (see p. 731) is an autosomal dominant condition characterized by atrial myxomas, spotty skin pigmentation, peripheral nerve tumours, and endocrine disorders e.g. Cushing's syndrome due to pigmented adrenal nodular hyperplasia.

Clinical features

- The clinical features of ACTH independent Cushing's syndrome are as described on p. 161 in the section on ACTH-dependent disease.
- It is important to note that in patients with adrenal carcinoma, there may also be features related to excessive androgen production in women, and also a relatively more rapid time course of development of the syndrome.

Investigation

- Once the presence of Cushing's syndrome is confirmed (page 162), subsequent investigation of the cause depends on whether ACTH is suppressed (ACTH independent) or measurable/elevated (ACTH dependent) – see page 164.
- Patients with ACTH-independent Cushing's syndrome do not suppress cortisol to <50% basal on high dose dexamethasone testing, and fail to show a rise in cortisol and ACTH following administration of CRH. (The latter test is often important when patients have borderline/low ACTH to differentiate pituitary dependent disease from adrenal.)
- ACTH-independent causes are adrenal in origin, and the mainstay of further investigation is adrenal imaging.
- CT scan allows excellent visualization of the adrenal glands and their anatomy.
- Adenomas are usually small and homogeneous, and usually associated with contralateral gland atrophy.
- Adrenal carcinomas are usually >6 cm in diameter, heterogeneous with calcification and necrosis, and evidence of local invasion.

Treatment (see also p. 168)

Adrenal adenoma

- Unilateral adrenalectomy (laparoscopic or open) is curative.
- Postoperative temporary adrenal insufficiency ensues because of long-term suppression of ACTH and the contralateral adrenal gland, requiring glucocorticoid replacement for up to 2 years.

Adrenal carcinoma

- Surgery is useful to debulk tumour mass, and occasionally adrenalectomy and local clearance leads to cure. However, most patients have distant metastases at the time of diagnosis.
- Postoperative drug treatment with the adrenolytic agent *mitotane* (*ortho-para* DDD) 3–12 g daily is usually used. This may lead to adrenal insufficiency and glucocorticoid replacement may be required. Side-effects may limit therapy – nausea and vomiting, dizziness, and diarrhoea. Monitoring of drug levels can be helpful to ensure concentrations within the therapeutic range (14–20 μg/mL), and so limit unwanted side-effects.
- Other drugs may be required to control cortisol hypersecretion (*metyrapone*, *aminoglutethamide*).
- Newer treatments such as *suramin*, *5-fluorouracil*, and *gossypol* have also been tried.

Bilateral adrenal hyperplasia

Bilateral adrenalectomy is curative. Lifelong glucocorticoid and mineralocorticoid treatment is required.

Prognosis

- Adrenal adenomas which are successfully treated with surgery have a good prognosis, and recurrence is unlikely. The prognosis depends on the long-term effects of excess cortisol before treatment – in particular atherosclerosis and osteoporosis.
- The prognosis for adrenal carcinoma is very poor, despite surgery. Reports suggest a 5 year survival of 22%, and median survival time of 14 months. Age >40 years and distant metastases are associated with a worse prognosis.

Subclinical Cushing's syndrome

- Describes the subset of patients with apparently silent adrenal cortical adenomas that possess some features of autonomous function.
- Cortisol secretion may be sufficient to suppress ACTH and suppress contralateral adrenal function.
- There may be subtle changes in cortisol secretion with loss of normal diurnal rhythm of cortisol secretion and failure of dexamethasone suppressibility despite apparently normal cortisol levels.
- At present it is not clear whether these changes are associated with clinically relevant symptomatology. There have been suggestions that these patients may have a higher prevalence of diabetes, hypertension, and osteoporosis.
- The natural history of this condition remains to be determined.

Chapter 45
Adrenal surgery

Adrenalectomy

Open adrenalectomy has been the standard approach for all adrenal pathology. More recently the advent of the laparoscopic approach has led to open surgery being reserved in many centres for either larger lesions (>6 cm), or suspected malignancy.

Laparoscopic adrenalectomy

First performed in 1992, this procedure has become the procedure of choice in many centres for removal of most adrenal tumours. There have been to date, no prospective randomized clinical trials, but retrospective comparisons with open approaches suggest reduced hospital stay, reduced analgesic requirements and lower postoperative morbidity. However, there are few long-term outcome data on this technique. Cure rate and recurrence/regrowth due to incomplete excision or spillage will need to be assessed.

Currently it appears to be most useful in the management of small (<6 cm) benign adenomas. Larger tumours may be malignant and therefore should be operated on via an open incision, and bilateral adrenalectomy may be problematic because of longer operating times.

Further reading

Dudley NE, Harrison BJ. Comparison of open posterior versus transperitoneal laparoscopic adrenalectomy. *British Journal of Surgery* 1999; 86: 656–660.

Wells SA, Merke DP, Cutler GB, Norton JA, Lacroix A. The role of laparoscopic surgery in adrenal disease. *Journal of Clinical Endocrinology and Metabolism* 1998; 83: 3041–3049.

Preoperative preparation of patients

- Cushing's – metyrapone or ketoconazole (see p. 170)
- Phaeochromocytoma – α- and β-blockade (see p. 340).

Perioperative management of patients undergoing adrenalectomy

Adrenal cortical tumours (benign and malignant)/bilateral adrenalectomy for Cushing's syndrome

- Perioperative glucocorticoid cover is required, as even 'silent' adenomas may be associated with subclinical excess cortisol secretion and hence suppression of the contralateral adrenal gland.
- Hydrocortisone is given as for pituitary surgery – 100 mg i/m with the premedication, and then continued every 6 h for 24–48 h, until the patient can take oral medication and is eating and drinking.
- This is changed to oral hydrocortisone at double replacement dose – 20 mg on waking, 10 mg at lunchtime and 10 mg at 5 p.m., and mineralocorticoid replacement commenced if bilateral adrenalectomy has been performed (100 μg fludrocortisone daily). Electrolytes and blood pressure guide adequacy of treatment. Normal replacement hydrocortisone (10, 5, 5 mg) can be commenced when the patient is recovered and may be omitted altogether if the patient did not have preoperative evidence of Cushing's syndrome/suppression of the contralateral gland/bilateral adrenalectomy. Mineralocorticoid replacement is only required in patients who have had bilateral adrenalectomy.
- A short synacthen test (off hydrocortisone for at least 24 h) is performed after at least 2 weeks to demonstrate adequate function of the contralateral adrenal. However, in patients with ACTH-independent Cushing's syndrome, it may take up to 2 years for full recovery of the contralateral adrenal gland to recover.
- The exception is patients undergoing adrenalectomy for mineralocorticoid-secreting tumour. These patients do not usually require peroperative glucocorticoid replacement, but preoperative amiloride or spironolactone allows recovery of potassium stores and control of hypertension prior to surgery.

Chapter 46
Renal tubular abnormalities

Background

Bartter's syndrome and Gitelman's syndrome are both associated with hypokalaemic alkalosis and activation of the renin–angiotensin system, but in the absence of hypertension. In contrast, Liddle's syndrome is associated with hypokalaemic alkalosis and hypertension but low renin and aldosterone levels.

Liddle's syndrome

A rare autosomal dominant (AD) condition with variable penetrance. Mutations have been localized to genes on chromosome 16.

Cause

A mutation in the gene encoding the ß or γ subunit of the highly selective epithelial sodium channel in the distal nephron. This leads to constitutive activation of sodium/potassium exchange independent of circulating mineralocorticoid.

Features

Hypokalaemia and hypertension

Investigation

- hypokalaemic alkalosis
- suppressed renin and aldosterone levels

Treatment

Hypertension responds to amiloride but not spironolactone, because amiloride acts on the sodium channel directly whereas spironolactone acts on the mineralocorticoid receptor.

Bartter's syndrome

Cause

Loss of function of the bumetanide-sensitive Na–K–2Cl co-transporter in the thick ascending limb of the loop of Henle. Linkage of the disease has been shown to 15q15–q21. Inactivation of the co-transporter leads to salt wasting, activation of the renin–angiotensin system, and increased aldosterone which leads to increased sodium reabsorption at the distal nephron and causes hypokalaemic alkalosis. Reabsorption of calcium also occurs in the thick ascending loop and thus inactivation leads to hypercalciuria. Mutations in the rat outer medullary K channel (*ROMK*) gene have also been shown in some families, leading to the same clinical syndrome. The lack of associated hypertension is thought to be due to increased prostaglandin production from the renal medullary interstitial tissue in response to hypokalaemia.

- Rare (~1/million) autosomal recessive hypokalaemic metabolic alkalosis associated with salt wasting and normal or reduced blood pressure
- Usually present at an early age (<5 years).

Features

- intravascular volume depletion
- seizures
- tetany
- muscle weakness.

There is also an antenatal variant which is a life-threatening disorder of renal tubular hypokalaemic alkalosis and hypercalciuria.

Investigation

- hypokalaemic alkalosis
- increased PRA and aldosterone
- hypercalciuria

Treatment

- *Potassium replacement* Potassium sparing diuretics may be helpful. However, they are usually inadequate in correcting hypokalaemia. Prostaglandin synthase inhibitors (NSAIDS) e.g. indomethacin 2–5 mg/kg per day or ibuprofen may be required.
- ACEI in adults may be useful.

Gitelman's syndrome

Cause

- Loss of function in the thiazide-sensitive Na–Cl transporter of the distal convoluted tubule (DCT). Linkage to 16q13 has been shown. This leads to salt wasting, hypovolaemia, and metabolic alkalosis. Hypovolaemia leads to activation of the renin–angiotensin system, and increased aldosterone levels.
- Hypokalaemic alkalosis in conjunction with hypocalciuria and hypomagnaesaemia.
- Present at older ages without overt hypovolaemia (essentially a less severe phenotype of Bartter's syndrome).

Investigation

- hypokalaemic alkalosis, in association with increased renin and aldosterone
- hypomagnaesaemia
- hypocalciuria.

Treatment

- potassium and magnesium replacement.
- potassium sparing diuretics may be required.

Further reading

Amirlak I, Dawson KP. Bartter syndrome. *Quarterly Journal of Medicine* 2000; 93: 207–215.

Chapter 47
Mineralocorticoid deficiency

Epidemiology

Rare apart from the hyporeninaemic hypoaldosteronism associated with diabetes mellitus.

Causes

Congenital

- *Adrenal hypoplasia* (X-linked failure of development of the adrenal gland. Presents in infancy with salt losing state. Differentiated form CAH by normal external genitalia and steroid levels).
- *CAH* (certain types – most commonly 21-hydroxylase deficiency – are associated with MC deficiency; see p. 364).
- Rare *inherited disorders* of aldosterone biosynthesis.
- *Adrenoleukodystrophy* (X-linked affecting 1/20 000 males, where very long chain fatty acids cannot be oxidized in peroxisomes and accumulate in tissues.
- *Pseudohypoaldosteronism* (inherited resistance to the action of aldosterone, see p. 794). Autosomal dominant and recessive forms are described. Usually presents in infancy. Treated with sodium chloride.

Acquired

- *Adrenal insufficiency* (see p. 306).
- *Drugs* Heparin, cyclosporin (heparin for >5 days, may cause severe hyperkalaemia due to a toxic effect on the zona glomerulosa).
- *Hyporeninaemic hypoaldosteronism* Interference with the renin–angiotensin system leads to mineralocorticoid deficiency and hyperkalaemic acidosis (type IV renal tubular acidosis). e.g. diabetic nephropathy. Treatment is fludrocortisone and potassium restriction. ACEI may produce a similar biochemical picture, but here the PRA will be elevated as there is no angiotensin II feedback on renin.

Treatment

Fludrocortisone.

Chapter 48
Adrenal insufficiency

Definition

Adrenal insufficiency results from inadequate adrenocortical function, and may be due to destruction of the adrenal cortex (primary or Addison's disease), or due to disordered pitutary and hypothalamic function (secondary).

Epidemiology

- The incidence of Addison's disease is approximately 40–60/million adults.
- Secondary adrenal insufficiency is most commonly due to suppression of pituitary–hypothalamic function by exogenous glucocorticoid administration.

Causes of secondary adrenal insufficiency

Lesions of the hypothalamus and/or pituitary gland

- *tumours* pituitary tumour, metastases, craniopharyngioma
- *infection* tuberculosis
- *inflammation* sarcoidosis, histiocytosis X, haemochromatosis, lymphocytic hypophysitis
- *iatrogenic* surgery, radiotherapy
- *other* isolated ACTH deficiency, trauma.

Suppression of the hypothalamo–pituitary–adrenal axis

- glucocorticoid administration
- Cushing's disease (after pituitary tumour removal).

Features of secondary adrenal insufficiency

As primary (p. 312), except:

- absence of pigmentation – skin is pale
- absence of mineralocoticoid deficiency
- associated features of underlying cause, e.g. visual field defects if pituitary tumour
- other endocrine deficiencies may manifest due to pituitary failure (p. 116, Chapter 13))
- acute onset may occur due to pituitary apoplexy.

Isolated ACTH deficiency

- rare.
- pathogenesis unclear – may be autoimmune (associated with other autoimmune conditions, and antipituitary antibodies described in some patients).
- absent ACTH response to CRH.
- POMC mutations and POMC processing abnormalities (e.g. proconvertase PC1).

Pathophysiology

Primary

- Adrenal gland destruction or dysfunction occurs due to a disease process which usually involves all three zones of the adrenal cortex, resulting in inadequate glucocorticoid, mineralocorticoid, and androgen secretion. The manifestations of insufficiency do not usually appear till at least 90% of the gland has been destroyed, and are usually gradual in onset, with partial adrenal insufficiency leading to an impaired cortisol response to stress, and the features of complete insufficiency occurring later. Acute adrenal insufficiency may occur in the context of acute septicaemia (e.g. meningococcal or haemorrhage).
- Mineralocortcoid deficiency leads to reduced sodium retention and hypotension with reduced intravascular volume, in addition to hyperkalaemia due to reduced renal potassium and hydrogen ion excretion.
- Androgen deficiency presents in women with reduced axillary and pubic hair and reduced libido. (Testicular production of androgens is more important in males.)
- Lack of cortisol negative feedback increases CRH and ACTH secretion. An increase in other POMC-related peptides leads to skin pigmentation and other mucous membranes.

Secondary

- Inadequate ACTH results in deficient cortisol production (and reduced androgens in women).
- There is no pigmentation because ACTH and POMC secretion is reduced. Mineralocorticoid secretion remains normal as it is mainly regulated by the renin–angiotensin system.
- The onset is usually gradual with partial ACTH deficiency resulting in reduced response to stress. Prolonged ACTH deficiency leads to atrophy of the zona fasiculata and reduced ability to respond acutely to ACTH.

Investigation

See p. 117 for pituitary/hypothalamic disease and p. 324 for long-term endogenous or exogenous glucocorticoids.

Chapter 49
Addison's disease

Causes of primary adrenal insufficiency

- *Autoimmune* Commonest cause in developed world (approximately 70% cases)
- Autoimmune polyglandular deficiency type 1 or 2 (p. 313).
- *Malignancy* Metastatic (lung, breast, kidney – adrenal metastases found in ~50% of patients, but symptomatic adrenal insufficiency much less common), lymphoma.
- *Infiltration* amyloid, haemochromatosis.
- *Infection*
  - tuberculosis (medulla more frequently destroyed than cortex)
  - fungal e.g. histoplasmosis, cryptococcosis
  - opportunistic infections in e.g. AIDS – CMV, mycobacterium intracellulare, cryptococcus (up to 5% patients with AIDS develop primary adrenal insufficiency in the late stages).
- *Vascular* haemorrhage e.g. anticoagulants, Waterhouse–Friedrichson syndrome in meningococcal septicaemia.
- *Infarction* (e.g. secondary to thrombosis in antiphospholipid syndrome)
- *Adrenomyeloneuropathy* (X-linked recessive disorder of metabolism of fatty acids, leading to spastic paralysis and adrenal insufficiency. Onset early adulthood)
- *Adrenoleucodystrophy* (inherited disorder of fatty acid metabolism, presenting in childhood, and progressing to quadraparesis and dementia in association with adrenal failure)
- *CAH* (see p. 364).
- *Congenital adrenal hypoplasia* (rare familial failure of adrenal cortical development due to mutations/deletion of *DAX 1* gene)
- *Iatrogenic*
  - adrenalectomy
  - drugs: ketoconazole and fluconazole (inhibit cortisol synthesis), phenytoin, rifampicin (increases cortisol metabolism), etomidate, aminoglutethamide (usually do not cause hypoadrenalism unless reduced adrenal or pituitary reserve)

Autoimmune adrenalitis

- Mediated by humoral and cell-mediated immune mechanisms. Autoimmune insufficiency associated with polyglandular autoimmune syndrome is more common in females (70%).
- Adrenal cortex antibodies are present in the majority of patients at diagnosis, and although titres decline and eventually disappear, they are still found in approximately 70% of patients 10 years later. Up to 20% patients/year with positive adrenal antibodies develop adrenal insufficiency. Antibodies to 21-hydroxylase are commonly found, although the exact nature of other antibodies that block the effect of ACTH for example are yet to be elucidated.
- Antiadrenal antibodies are found in <2% of patients with other autoimmune endocrine disease (Hashimoto's thyroiditis, diabetes mellitus, autoimmune hypothyroidism, hypoparathyroidism, pernicious anaemia). In addition, antibodies to other endocrine glands are commonly found in patients with autoimmune adrenal insufficiency (thyroid microsomal in 50%, gastric parietal cell, parathyroid, and ovary and testis).
- Polyglandular autoimmune conditions (see p. 313). The presence of 17-hydroxylase antibodies in association with 21-hydroxylase antibodies is a good marker of patients at risk of developing premature ovarian failure in association with primary adrenal failure.
- Patients with type 1 diabetes mellitus and autoimmune thyroid disease only rarely develop autoimmune adrenal insufficiency. Approximately 50% of patients with Addison's disease have other autoimmune, or endocrine disorders.

Clinical features

Chronic

- anorexia and weight loss (>90%)
- tiredness
- weakness (generalized – no particular muscle groups)
- pigmentation (generalized, but most common in light exposed areas, and areas exposed to pressure (elbows and knees, and under bras and belts), mucosae and scars acquired after onset of adrenal insufficiency). Look at palmar creases in Caucasians.
- dizziness and postural hypotension
- gastrointestinal symptoms (nausea and vomiting, abdominal pain, diarrhoea)
- arthralgia and myalgia
- symptomatic hypoglycaemia (rare in adults)
- decreased axillary and pubic hair and reduced libido in women
- pyrexia of unknown origin (rarely)

Associated conditions

- vitiligo
- features of other autoimmune endocrinopathies.

Laboratory investigations

- hyponatraemia
- hyperkalaemia
- elevated urea
- anaemia (normocytic normochromic)
- elevated ESR
- eosinophilia
- mild hypercalcaemia.

Autoimmune polyglandular syndrome type 1

- autosomal recessive
- hypoparathyroidism (90%)
- chronic mucocutaneous candidiasis
- primary adrenal insufficiency (60%)
- primary gonadal failure
- primary hypothyroidism
- rarely hypopituitarism, diabetes insipidus
- associated malabsorption, pernicious anaemia, chronic active hepatitis, vitiligo.

Autoimmune polyglandular syndrome type 2

- autosomal recessive, autosomal dominant, polygenic
- adrenal insufficiency (100%)
- primary hypothyroidism
- type 1 diabetes mellitus
- primary gonadal failure
- rarely diabetes insipidus
- associated vitiligo, myasthenia gravis, alopecia, pernicious anaemia, immune thrombocytopenic purpura.

Investigation of primary adrenal insufficiency

Electrolytes

- hyponatraemia is present in 90% and hyperkalaemia in 65%
- elevated urea.

Serum cortisol and ACTH

- Undetectable serum cortisol is diagnostic of adrenal insufficiency, but the basal cortisol is usually in the normal range. A cortisol >580 nmol/L precludes the diagnosis. At times of acute stress, an inappropriately low cortisol is very suggestive of the diagnosis.
- Simultaneous 9 a.m. cortisol and ACTH will show an elevated ACTH for the level of cortisol. This is a very sensitive means of detecting Addison's disease.
- NB. Drugs causing increased cortisol-binding globulin (e.g. oestrogens) will result in higher total cortisol concentration measurements.

Response to ACTH

Short synacthen test

- Following basal cortisol measurement, 250 μg synacthen is administered i/m and serum cortisol checked at 30 and 60 min.
- Serum cortisol should rise to a peak of 580 nmol/L.
- Failure to respond suggests adrenal failure.
- A long synacthen test may be required to confirm secondary adrenal failure if ACTH is equivocal.
- Recent onset secondary adrenal failure (2 weeks) may produce a normal response to a short synacthen test.
- (There is recent interest in the low dose (1 μg ACTH) synacthen test as a more physiological assessment of adrenal reserve).

Long synacthen test

- Following basal cortisol level, depot synacthen 1 mg i/m is administered, and serum cortisol measured at 30, 60, 120 min, 4, 8, 12 and 24 h. A normal response is an elevation in serum cortisol to >1000 nmol/L.

Emergency management of acute adrenal insufficiency

- This is a life-threatening emergency, and should be treated if there is strong clinical suspicion rather than waiting for confirmatory test results.
- Blood should be taken for urgent analysis of electrolytes and glucose, in addition to cortisol and ACTH.

Fluids

Large volumes of 0.9% saline are required to reverse the volume depletion and sodium deficiency. Several litres may be required in the first 24–48 h.

Hydrocortisone

- A bolus dose of 100 mg hydrocortisone is administered intravenously. Hydrocortisone 100 mg i/m is then continued 6 hourly for 24–48 h, or until the patient can take oral therapy. Double replacement dose hydrocortisone (20, 10 and 10 mg orally) can then be instituted until well.
- Specific mineralocorticoid replacement is not required as the high dose glucocorticoid has sufficient mineralocorticoid effects. Once the dose of glucocorticoid is reduced after a couple of days, and the patient is taking food and fluids by mouth, fludrocortisone 0.1 mg/day can be commenced.

Glucose supplementation

Occasionally required because of risk of hypoglycaemia (low glycogen stores in the liver as a result of glucocorticoid deficiency).

Investigate and treat precipitant

This is often infection.

Monitoring treatment

Electrolytes, glucose, and urea.

- Differentiation of secondary from primary adrenal failure can be made more reliably following 3 days i/m ACTH 1 mg. This is because the test relies on the ability of the atrophic adrenal glands to respond to ACTH in secondary adrenocortical failure, whereas in primary adrenal failure, the diseased gland is already maximally stimulated by elevated endogenous levels of ACTH and therefore unable to respond to further stimulation.
- Serum cortisol responses within the first 60 min are superimposable with the short synacthen test.
- There is a progressive rise in cortisol secretion in secondary adrenal insufficiency, but little or no response on primary adrenal insufficiency.

Increased plasma renin activity (assessment of mineralocorticoid sufficiency)

This is one of the earliest abnormalities in developing primary adrenal insufficiency.

Thyroid function tests

Reduced thyroid hormone levels and elevated TSH may be due to a direct effect of glucocorticoid deficiency or due to associated autoimmune hypothyroidism. Re-evaluation is therefore required after adrenal insufficiency has been rectified.

Establish cause of adrenal insufficiency

- *Adrenal autoantibodies* (detect antibodies to adrenal cortex, and more recently specific antibodies to 21-hydroxylase, side-chain-cleavage enzyme, and 17-hydroxylase). 21-Hydroxylase antibodies are the major component of adrenal cortex antibodies. Adrenal cortex antibodies are not detectable in non-autoimmune primary adrenal failure.
- *Imaging*
  - Adrenal enlargement with or without calcification may be seen on CT of the abdomen, suggesting tuberculosis, infiltration or metastatic disease. The adrenals are small and atrophic in autoimmune adrenalitis.
  - Percutaneous CT guided adrenal biopsy is occasionally required.
- *Specific tests*, e.g. serological, or microbiological investigations directed at particular infections, very long chain fatty acids (adrenoleucodystrophy)

Acute adrenal insufficiency

Clinical features

- shock
- hypotension (often not responding to measures such as inotropic support)
- abdominal pain (may present as 'acute abdomen')
- unexplained fever
- often precipitated by major stress such as severe bacterial infection, major surgery, unabsorbed glucocorticoid medication due to vomiting
- occasionally occurs due to bilateral adrenal infarction.

Investigation

- As chronic.
- In the acute situation if the diagnosis is suspected, an inappropriately low cortisol (i.e. <600 nmol/L) is often sufficient to make the diagnosis.
- If the diagnosis is suspected, glucocorticoid therapy with dexamethasone will not interfere with subsequent testing.

Investigation of other associated endocrinopathies

Patients with autoimmune adrenal failure should be investigated for thyroid disease, diabetes mellitus, pernicious anaemia gonadal failure, and parathyroid dysfunction.

Treatment

Maintenance therapy

Glucocorticoid replacement

- Hydrocortisone is the treatment of choice for replacement therapy, as it is reliably and predictably absorbed and allows biochemical monitoring of levels.
- It is administered 3xdaily 10 mg on waking, 5 mg at midday, and 5 mg at 6 p.m.
- An alternative is prednisolone 3 mg on waking and 1–2 mg at 6 p.m. This has the disadvantage that levels cannot be biochemically monitored, but its longer half-life may lead to better suppression of ACTH if pigmentation and markedly elevated morning ACTH levels are a problem. Occasionally dexamethasone is required for this purpose.

Mineralocorticoid replacement

Fludrocortisone (9-flurohydrocortisone) is given at a dose of 0.1 mg daily. Occasionally lower (0.05 mg) or higher (0.2 mg) doses are required.

Monitoring of therapy

Clinical

- For signs of glucocorticoid excess e.g increasing weight
- Blood pressure (including postural change)
- Hypertension and oedema suggest excessive mineralocorticoid replacement, whereas postural hypotension and salt craving suggest insufficient treatment.

Biochemical

- Serum electrolytes
- Plasma renin activity (elevated if insufficient fludrocortisone replacement)
- Cortisol day curve to assess adequacy of treatment (see page 122)
- ACTH levels prior to and following morning glucocorticoids replacement if patient develops increasing pigmentation. If elevated or rising with little suppression following glucocorticoid, MRI scan to exclude rare possibility of pituitary hyperplasia or very rarely the development of a corticotroph adenoma.

Intercurrent illness

- Cortisol requirements increase during severe illness or surgery.
- For moderate elective procedures or investigations, e.g. endoscopy or angiography, patients should receive a single dose of 100 mg hydrocortisone before the procedure.
- For major surgery, patients should take 20 mg hydrocortisone orally or 100 mg intramuscularly with the premedication, and receive 100 mg i/m hydrocortisone 6 hourly for the first 3 days, before reverting rapidly to a maintenance dose.
- To cover severe illness, e.g. pneumonia, patients should receive 50–100 mg hydrocortisone 6 hourly until resolution of the illness.

Pregnancy (see p. 520)

The usual glucocorticoid and mineralocorticoid replacement is continued during pregnancy. Severe hyperemesis gravidarum during the first trimester may require temporary parenteral therapy and patients should be warned about this to avoid precipitation of a crisis. During labour, parenteral glucocorticoid therapy is administered (100 mg i/m every 6 h). Fluid replacement with intravenous 0.9% saline may be required

Education of the patient

- Patient education is the key to successful management. Patients must be taught never to miss a dose. They should be encouraged to wear a MedicAlert bracelet or necklace and always to carry a steroid card.
- Every patient should know how to double the dose of glucocorticoid during febrile ilness, and to get medical attention if unable to take the tablets because of vomiting. They should have a vial of 100 mg hydrocortisone with syringe, diluent, and needle for times when parenteral treatment may be required.

Further reading

Oelkers W. Adrenal insufficiency. *New England Journal of Medicine* 1996; 335: 1206–1212.

Chapter 50
Long-term glucocorticoid administration

Both exogenous glucocorticoid administration and endogenous excess glucocorticoids (Cushing's syndrome) lead to a negative feedback effect on the hypothalamo–pituitary axis (HPA), leading to suppression of both CRH and ACTH secretion and atrophy of the zonae fasiculata and reticularis of the adrenal cortex.

Short-term steroids

- Any patient who has received glucocorticoid treatment for <3 weeks is unlikely to have clinically significant adrenal suppression, and if the medical condition allows it, glucocorticoid treatment can be stopped acutely. A major stress within a week of stopping steroids should, however, be covered with glucocorticoids.
- Exceptions to this are patients who have other possible reasons for adrenocortical insufficiency, who have received more than 40 mg prednisolone (or equivalent), where a short course has been prescribed within 1 year of cessation of long-term therapy, or evening doses (increased HPA axis suppression).

Steroid cover

While receiving glucocorticoid treatment and within 1 year of steroid withdrawal, patients should receive standard steroid supplementation at times of stress, e.g. major trauma, surgery and infection (page 319).

Dehydroepiandrosterone

- DHEA is an abundant circulating adrenal androgen, with a production rate of 25–30 mg/day. Its levels undergo a progressive decline with increasing age, and there has been interest in its physiological role.
- Epidemiological data suggest a link between changes in DHEA and age-related changes including an inverse relationship between DHEA and cardiovascular disease, Alzheimer's disease, and malignancy. Although animal studies have suggested potential therapeutic benefit of DHEA therapy, small studies in humans have so far failed to demonstrate convincing benefit apart from short-term improvement in well-being. Recent evidence suggests that DHEA replacement in patients with Addison's disease may have beneficial effects on well-being.

Long-term steroids

- When patients are receiving supraphysiological doses (>7.5 mg prednisolone, or equivalent) of glucocorticoid, dose reduction depends on disease activity.
- Once a daily equivalent of 7.5 mg prednisolone is reached, the rate of reduction should be slower to allow recovery of the HPA axis.
- If concerned about disease resolution, then the rate of reduction of glucocorticoids is determined by the disease process until 7.5 mg equivalent is reached.
- If the disease has resolved, the dose can be rapidly reduced to 7.5 mg prednisolone by a reduction of 2.5 mg every 3–5 days.
- Once the patient is established on 7.5 mg prednisolone, consider changing to hydrocortisone (20 mg in the morning), as this has a shorter half-life and will therefore lead to less prolonged suppression of ACTH.
- Daily hydrocortisone dose should be reduced by 2.5 mg every 1–2 weeks, or as tolerated until a dose of 10 mg is reached. After 2–3 months a 9 a.m. cortisol is checked 24 h after last dose of hydrocortisone. If it is >300 nmol/L, then hydrocortisone can be stopped and a short synacthen test performed. If the 9 a.m. cortisol is <300 nmol/L, then continue hydrocortisone 10 mg for another 2–3 months and repeat the 9 a.m. cortisol. When basal cortisol is >400 nmol/L, we usually stop regular hydrocortisone and administer in emergency only. Once a short synacthen test demonstrates a normal response, it is helpful to perform an ITT to confirm full recovery of the HPA axis.

Cushing's syndrome

Patients with Cushing's syndrome, whatever the cause, also have HPA axis suppression and may therefore need steroid replacement at times of stress.

Further reading

Baulieu E. DHEA: A fountain of youth? *Journal of Clincal Endocrinology and Metabolism* 1996; 81: 3147–3151.

Nippoldt TB, Nair KS. Is there a case for DHEA replacement? *Ballière's Clinical Endocrinology and Metabolism* 1998; 12: 507–520.

Chapter 51
Adrenal incidentalomas

Definition and epidemiology

- A true incidentaloma, is an incidentally detected lesion with no pathophysiological significance, and needs to be differentiated from incidentally detected but clinically relevant masses.
- The incidental detection of an adrenal mass is becoming more common, as increased numbers of imaging procedures are performed, and with technological improvements in imaging.
- Autopsy studies suggest an incidence of adrenal adenomas of 1–9%.
- Imaging studies suggest an incidence of approximately 3.5%.

Importance

It is important to determine whether the incidentally discovered adrenal mass is

- malignant
- functioning and associated with excess hormonal secretion.

Differential diagnosis of an incidentally detected adrenal nodule

- cortisol-secreting adrenal adenoma causing Cushing's syndrome or subclinical Cushing's syndrome
- CAH
- mineralocorticoid-secreting adrenal adenoma
- androgen-secreting adenoma
- phaeochromocytoma
- adrenal carcinoma
- metastasis
- adrenal cysts
- lipoma
- myelolipoma
- haematoma

Investigation

- Clinical assessment for symptoms and signs of excess hormone secretion and signs of extra-adrenal carcinoma.
- Urinary free cortisol and overnight dexamethasone suppression test, urinary free catecholamines, potassium on 120 mmol sodium day (aldosterone and renin if hypertensive).
- Short synacthen test for 17-hydroxyprogesterone (CAH), and cortisol (for adrenal insufficiency).

Management

- Surgery if evidence of syndrome of hormonal excess attributable to tumour.
- Surgery if diameter of mass >4 cm (increased likelihood of malignancy and definitely if >6 cm in diameter), or imaging features suggestive of malignancy (e.g. lack of clearly circumscribed margin, vascular invasion).
- If size <4 cm, and no sign of excess hormone production, repeat MRI adrenals at 3, 6, 12 and 24 months looking for increase in size.

Chapter 52
Phaeochromocytomas and paragangliomas

Definition

- *Phaeochromocytomas* are adrenomedullary catecholamine-secreting tumours
- *Paragangliomas* are tumours arising from extra-adrenal medullary neural crest derivatives, e.g. organ of Zuckerkandl (sympathetic) or carotid body, aorticopulmonary, intravagal, or jugulotympanic (parasymapthetic).

Incidence

Rare tumours, accounting for <0.1% of causes of hypertension. However, it is a very important diagnosis not to be missed as it can be fatal if undiagnosed.

Epidemiology

- Equal sex distribution, and most commonly present in the 3rd and 4th decades. Up to 50% may be diagnosed post-mortem.
- Although the majority (90%) are sporadic, 10% are inherited (Table 52.1).

Table 52.1 Syndromes associated with phaeochromocytomas

Familial phaeochromocytomas	Isolated autosomal dominant trait
MEN-IIa and b p. 731	Mutation in RET proto-oncogene (chromosome 10)
	Hyperparathyroidism and medullary thyroid carcinoma associated with phaeochromocytoma
	MEN IIb also associated with marfanoid phenotype (p. 1132)
Von Hippel–Lindau syndrome p. 711	Mutation of VHL tumour suppressor gene (chromosome 3)
	Renal cell carcinoma, cerebellar haemangioblastoma, retinal angioma, renal and pancreatic cysts
	Phaeochromocytomas in 25%
Neurofibromatosis p. 707	Autosomal dominant condition caused by mutations of NF1 gene on chromosome 17
	Phaechromocytomas in 0.5–1.0%

Pathophysiology

Sporadic tumours are usually unilateral, and <10 cm in diameter. Tumours associated with familial syndromes are more likely to be bilateral, and associated with pre-existing medullary hyperplasia.

Malignancy

- Approximately 15–20% are malignant (less in familial syndromes) and these are characterized by local invasion or distant metastsis rather than capsular invasion. Chromosomal ploidy has been suggested as useful in differentiating benign and malignant tumours.
- Paragangliomas are more likely to be malignant, and to recur.
- Typical sites for metastases are retroperitoneum, lymph nodes, bone, liver, and mediastinum.

Secretory products

- Catecholamine secretion is usually adrenaline or noradrenaline and may be constant or episodic.
- Phenylethanolamine-*N*-methyl transferase (PNMT) is necessary for methylation of noradrenaline to adrenaline, and is cortisol dependent. Small adrenal tumours tend to produce more adrenaline, whereas larger adrenal tumours produce more noradrenaline as a proportion of their blood supply is direct rather than corticomedullary, and therefore lower in cortisol concentrations.
- Paragangliomas (exception – organ of Zuckerkandl) secerete noradrenaline only, as they lack PNMT.
- Pure dopamine secretion is rare, and may be associated with hypotension.
- Other non-catecholamine secretory products may also be produced, including VIP, neuropeptide Y, ACTH (associated with Cushing's syndrome), PTH, and PTHrP.

Clinical features

- Sustained or episodic *hypertension* often resistant to conventional therapy.
- *General*
  - sweating and heat intolerance >80%
  - pallor or flushing
  - feeling of apprehension
  - pyrexia.
- *Neurological* headache (throbbing or constant) (65%), paraesthesiae, visual disturbance, seizures.
- *Cardiovascular* palpitations (65%), chest pain, dyspnoea, postural hypotension.
- *Gastrointestinal* abdominal pain, constipation, nausea.

Complications

- *Cardiovascular* left ventricular failure, dilated cardiomyopathy (reversible), dysrhythmias.
- *Respiratory* pulmonary oedema.
- *Metabolic* carbohydrate intolerance, hypercalcaemia.
- *Neurological* cerebrovascular, hypertensive encephalopathy.

Who should be screened for the presence of a phaeochromocytoma?

- patients with a family history of MEN, VHL, neurofibromatosis
- patients with paroxysmal symptoms
- young patients with hypertension
- patient developing hypertensive crisis during general anaesthesia/surgery
- patients with unexplained heart failure.

Factors precipitating a crisis

- straining
- exercise
- pressure on abdomen – tumour palpation, bending over
- surgery
- drugs
  - anaesthetics
  - unopposed β-blockade
  - intravenous contrast agents
  - opiates
  - tricyclic antidepressants
  - phenothiazines
  - metoclopramide
  - glucagon

Investigations

Demonstrate catecholamine hypersecretion

24 h urine collection for catecholamines (see opposite)

- Urine is collected into bottles containing acid (warn patient).
- Because of the episodic nature of catecholamine secretion, at least two 24 h collections should be performed. It is useful to perform a collection while a patient is having symptoms, if episodic secretion is suspected.
- The sensitivity of urinary metanephrines and VMAs is less than free catecholamines, and also influenced by dietary intake.
- NB Tricyclic antidepressants and labetalol intefere with adrenaline measurements and should be stopped for 4 days.

Plasma catecholamine measurement

- Intermittent secretion, and the short half-life of catecholamines, makes this test of limited use in screening.
- It can be helpful if drawn while a patient is having a crisis, as normal levels in these circumstances are against the diagnosis. In patients with overt symptoms and signs, plasma catecholamines are usually >2000 pg/mL. However, patients with overt clinical features and plasma catecholamines <1000 pg/mL are unlikely to have a phaeochromocytoma.
- Routine measurement requires controlled conditions – supine and cannulated for 30 min, 10 mL blood drawn into a lithium heparin tube and cold spun.
- NB Plasma catecholamines are elevated by caffeine, nicotine, exercise, and some drugs.

Suppression tests (p. 341)

These tests are useful to differentiate patients who have borderline catecholamine levels.

- *Pentolinium 2.5 mg i/v* Elevated plasma catecholamines at 10 min are seen in phaeochromocytomas, whereas the normal response is suppression into the normal range.
- *Clonidine 300 μg orally* Failure of suppression of plasma catecholamines into the normal range at 120 and 180 min is suggestive of a tumour.

Table 52.2 Substances interfering with urinary catecholamine levels

Increased catecholamines	Decreased catecholamines	Variable effect
α-Blockers	Mono-amine oxidase inhibitors	Levodopa
β-Blockers	Clonidine	Tricyclic antidepressants
Levodopa	Guanethidine and other adrenergic neurone blockers	Phenothiazines
Drugs containing catecholamines, e.g. decongestants		Calcium channel inhibitors
Metoclopramide		ACE inhibitors
Domperidone		Bromocriptine
Hydralazine		
Diazocide		
Nitroglycerine		
Sodium nitroprusside		
Nicotine		
Theophylline		
Caffeine		
Amphetamine		

Table 52.3 Sensitivity and specificity of tests

Test	Sensitivity	Specificity
2 × 24 h urinary free catecholamines	100%	95%
Urinary metanephrines	80%	86%
Urinary VMA	65%	88%
Clonidine suppression test	97%	
MRI	98%	70%
CT	93%	70%
MIBG	80%	95%

Provocative tests (p. 341)

- These are not used routinely as they do not enhance diagnostic accuracy and are potentially dangerous. They should therefore be performed in a specialist unit, under carefully controlled conditions, and covered with calcium channel antagonists.
- Occasionally it may be helpful to perform a glucagon provocation test when negative testing has been associated with high levels of suspicion for the presence of a tumour. A positive glucagon test requires an ×2.5 increase in catecholamines. It is most safely performed with prior α- and β-blockade.

Localization of tumour

Imaging

- These are large tumours, in contrast to Conn's syndrome, and not easily missed with good quality imaging to the bifurcation of the aorta. Approximately 90% will be detected in the abdomen.
- Adrenal imaging should be performed initially, then body imaging (ideally MRI) if tumour not localized in adrenal.
- *MRI* bright hyperintense image on T2.
- *CT* less sensitive and specific – less good at distinguishing between different types of adrenal tumours

^{123}I-MIBG scan

- *meta*-Iodobenzylguanidine is a chromaffin-seeking analogue. Imaging using MIBG is positive in 60–80% phaeochromocytomas, and may locate tumours not visualized on MRI – e.g. multiple and extra-adrenal tumours.
- Performed preoperatively to exclude multiple tumours
- NB Phenoxybenzamine may lead to false negative MIBG imaging, so these scans should be preformed before commencing this drug.

Venous sampling

- Used to localize a phaeochromocytoma/paraganglioma if imaging is unhelpful.
- Caution: α- and β-blockade should be administered before the procedure.
- Reversal of the ratio of noradrenaline : adrenaline ratio (N <1) in the adrenal vein is suggestive of a phaeochromocytoma.

Screening for associated conditions

Up to 23% patients with apparently sporadic phaeochromocytomas may have familial disorders and all patients should therefore be screened for the presence of associated conditons, even if asymptomatic.

MEN

- serum calcium
- serum calcitonin (phaeochromocytomas precede medullary thyroid carcinoma in 10%).

VHL

- opthalmoscopy (retinal angiomas are usually the first manifestation)
- MRI posterior fossa
- ultrasound of kidneys (if not adequately imaged on MRI of adrenals).

Management

Medical

- It is essential that any patient is fully prepared with α- and β-blockade before receiving intravenous contrast, or undergoing a procedure such as venous sampling, or surgery.
- α-Blockade must be commenced before β-blockade to avoid precipitating a hypertensive crisis due to unopposed α-adrenergic stimulation.
- *α-Blockade* commence phenoxybenzamine, as soon as diagnosis made. Start at 10 mg 2× day by mouth, and increase up to 20 mg 4× day.
- *β-Blockade* Commence propanolol 40 mg 8 hourly by mouth 48–72 h after starting phenoxybenzamine.
- Treatment is commenced in hospital. Monitor blood pressure, pulse, and haematocrit. Reversal of α-mediated vasoconstriction may lead to haemodilution. (Check Hb preoperatively).
- To ensure complete blockade before surgery, intravenous *phenoxybenzamine* (0.5 mg/kg over 4 h in 100 mL 5% dextrose) is administered on the 3 days before surgery. There is less experience with competetive α-adrenergic blockade such as prazosin.

Surgical

- Surgical resection is curative in the majority of patients, leading to normotension in at least 75%.
- Mortality from elective surgery is <2%.
- Surgery may be open adrenalectomy, or laparoscopic if the tumour is small and apparently benign. Careful perioperative anaesthetic management is essential as tumour handling may lead to major changes in blood pressure and also occasionally cardiac arrythmias. *Phentolamine* or *nitroprusside* is useful to treat perioperative hypertension, and *esmolol* or *propanolol* for perioperative arrythmias. Hypotension (e.g. after tumour devascularization) usually responds to volume replacement, but occasionally requires inotropic support.

Follow-up

- Cure is assessed by 24 h urine free catecholamine measurement, but since catecholamines may remain elevated for up to 10 days follow-

Test procedures

Clonidine suppression test

- patient supine and cannulated for 30 min
- clonidine 300 μg orally
- plasma catecholamines measured at time 0, 120, and 180 min
- failure to suppress into the normal range is suggestive of a tumour
- 1.5% false positive rate in patients with essential hypertension

Pentolinium suppression test

- patient supine and cannulated for 30 min
- pentolinium 2.5 mg i/v
- plasma catecholamines measured at time 0 and 10 min
- failure to suppress into the normal range is suggestive of a tumour

Glucagon provocation test

- caution – may provoke a crisis
- patients should have received full α- and β-blockade before the test is performed
- patient supine and canulated for 30 min
- glucagon 1 mg i/v at time 0
- plasma catecholamines measured at 0, 2, 4, 6, 8, and 10 min
- catecholamine levels rise in patients with phaeochromocyotomas

ing surgery, these should not be performed until 2 weeks postoperatively.

- Lifelong follow-up is essential to detect recurrence of a benign tumour, or metastasis from a malignant tumour, as it is impossible to exclude malignancy on a histological specimen.

Malignancy

- Malignant tumours require long-term α- and β-blockade. The tyrosine kinase inhibitor α-*methylparatyrosine* may help control symptoms.
- High dose ^{131}I MIBG can be used to treat metastatic disease, although results can be disappointing.
- Chemotherapy using *cyclophosphamide*, *vincristine*, *adriamycin*, and *dacarbazine* has been associated with symptomatic improvement.
- Radiotherapy can be useful palliation in patients with bony metastases.

Prognosis

- Hypertension may persist in 25% patients who have undergone successful tumour removal.
- 5 year survival for 'benign' tumours is 96%, and the recurrence rate is <10%.
- 5 year survival for malignant tumours is 44%.

Further reading

Bouloux PMG, Fakeeh M. Investigation of phaeochormocytoma. *Clinical Endocrinology* 1995; 43: 657–664.

Neumann HPH, Berger DP, Sigmund G, Blum U, Schmidt D, Parmer RJ, Volk B, Kirste G. Phaeochromocytomas, multiple endocrine neoplasia type 2 and Von Hippel–Lindau disease *New England Journal of Medicine* 1993; 329: 1531–1538.

Young WF. Phaeochromocytoma and primary aldosteronism: diagnostic approaches. *Endocrinology and Metabolism Clinics of North America* 1997; 26: 801–827.

Part IV
Reproductive endocrinology

Chapter 53
Hirsutism

Definition

Hirsutism (not a diagnosis in itself) is the presence of excess hair growth in women as a result of increased androgen production and increased skin sensitivity to androgens.

Physiology of hair growth

Before puberty the body is covered by fine unpigmented hairs, or vellus hairs. These, in addition to eyebrows and eyelashes, are not dependent on androgens for growth. During adolescence, androgens convert vellus hairs into coarse, pigmented terminal hairs in androgen-dependent areas. The extent of terminal hair growth depends on the concentration and duration of androgen exposure as well as on the sensitivity of the individual hair follicle. The reason different body regions respond differently to the same androgen concentration is unknown but may be related to the number of androgen receptors in the hair follicle. Genetic factors play an important role in the individual susceptibility to circulating androgens, as evidenced by racial differences in hair growth.

Androgen production in women

In females, testosterone is secreted primarily by the ovaries and adrenal glands although a significant amount is produced by the peripheral conversion of androstenedione and dehydroepiandrostenedione (DHEA). Ovarian androgen production is regulated by luteneizing hormone, whereas adrenal production is ACTH dependent. The predominant androgens produced by the ovaries are testosterone and androstenedione, and the adrenal glands are the main source of dehydroepiandrostenedione. Circulating testosterone is mainly bound to sex hormone binding globulin (SHBG) and it is the free testosterone which is biologically active. To be active, testosterone is converted to the more potent dihydrotestosterone in the skin by the enzyme 5α-reductase. Androstenedione and DHEA are not significantly protein-bound.

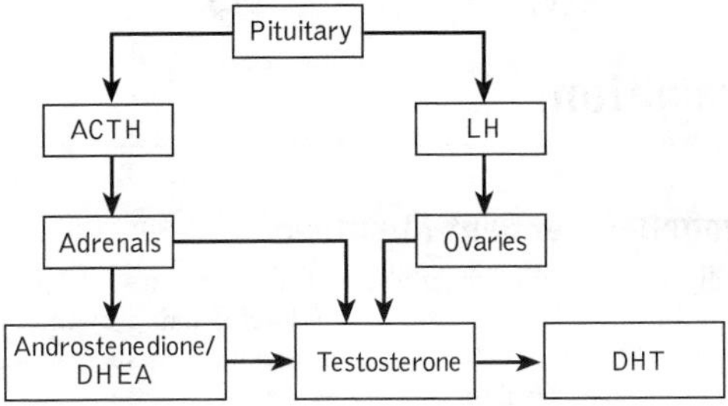

Fig. 53.1 Regulation of andogen production in women.

Signs of virilization

- frontal balding
- deepening of voice
- increased muscle size
- clitoromegaly

Causes of androgen-independent hair growth

- drugs, e.g. phenytoin, cyclosporin, glucocorticoids
- anorexia nervosa
- hypothyroidism
- familial

Table 53.1 Causes of hirsutism

Ovarian	Polycystic ovary syndrome	95%
	Androgen-secreting tumours	<1%
Adrenal	Congenital adrenal hyperplasia	<1%
	Cushing's syndrome	<1%
	Androgen-secreting tumours	<1%
	Acromegaly	1%

Evaluation

Androgen-dependent hirsutism

Normally develops following puberty. Hairs are coarse and pigmented and typically grow in areas where men develop hair growth. It is often accompanied by other evidence of androgen excess such as acne, oily skin and male pattern alopecia.

Androgen-independent hair growth

Excess vellus hairs over face and trunk including forehead. It does not respond to anti-androgen treatment.

History

- *Age and rate of onset of hirsutism* Slowly progressive hirsutism following puberty suggests a benign cause, whereas rapidly progressive hirsutism of recent onset requires further immediate investigation to rule out an androgen-secreting neoplasm.
- *Menstrual history* ?oligomenorrhoeic.
- Presence of other evidence of *hyperandrogenism*, e.g. acne or bitemporal alopecia.
- *Drug history* Some progestins used in oral contraceptive preparations may be androgenic (e.g. norethisterone).

Physical examination

- Distinguish beween *androgen-dependent* and *androgen-independent* hair growth.
- Assess the *extent and severity* of hirsutism. The Ferriman–Gallwey score (see table) assesses the degree of hair growth in 11 regions of the body. This provides a semi-objective method of monitoring disease progression and treatment outcome.
- *Virilization* should be looked for, as this indicates severe hyperandrogenism and should be further investigated.
- *Acanthosis nigricans* is indicative of insulin resistance and probable polycystic ovary syndrome.
- *Rare causes* of hyperandrogenism such as Cushing's syndrome and acromegaly should be ruled out.

Table 53.2 Assessment of hirsutism (from Ferriman-Gallwey, 1961)

Site	Grade	Definition
Upper lip	1	A few hairs at outer margin
	2	A small moustache at outer margin
	3	A moustache extending halfway from outer margin
	4	A moustache extending to midline
Chin	1	A few scattered hairs
	2	Scattered hairs with small concentrations
	3	Complete cover, light
	4	Complete cover, heavy
Chest	1	Circumareolar hairs
	2	With midline hair
	3	Fusion of these areas
	4	Complete cover
Upper back	1	A few scattered hairs
	2	More, but still scattered
	3	Complete cover, light
	4	Complete cover, heavy
Lower back	1	Sacral tuft of hair
	2	Some lateral extension
	3	Three-quarter cover
	4	Complete cover
Upper abdomen	1	A few midline hairs
	2	Rather more, still midline
	3	Half cover
	4	Full cover
Lower abdomen	1	A few midline hairs
	2	A midline streak of hair
	3	A midline band of hair
	4	An inverted V-shaped growth
Arm	1	Sparse growth affecting not more than a quarter of the limb surface
	2	More than this, cover still incomplete
	3	Complete cover, light
	4	Complete cover, heavy
Forearm	1,2,3,4	Complete cover of dorsal surface, 2 grades of light and 2 grades of heavy growth
Thigh	1,2,3,4	As for arm
Leg	1,2,3,4	As for arm
Total score		

Laboratory investigation

Serum testosterone should be measured in all women. If this is <5 nmol/L then the risk of a sinister cause for her hirsutism is minimal. Further investigations and management of the individual disorders will be discussed in the following chapters.

Further reading

Ferriman DG, *Journal of Clinical Endocrinology and Metabolism* 1961; 21(11): 1440–1447.

Chapter 54
Polycystic ovary syndrome

Definition

- A heterogenous clinical syndrome characterized by hyperandrogenism and ovulatory dysfunction in which other causes of androgen excess have been excluded.
- The diagnosis is further supported by the presence of characteristic ovarian morphology on ultrasound.

Epidemiology

PCOS is the most common endocrinopathy in women of reproductive age. 95% of women presenting to outpatients with hirsutism have polycystic ovary syndrome. The estimated prevalence of PCOS ranges from 8% on clinical criteria alone, to 22% on ultrasonic diagnosis.

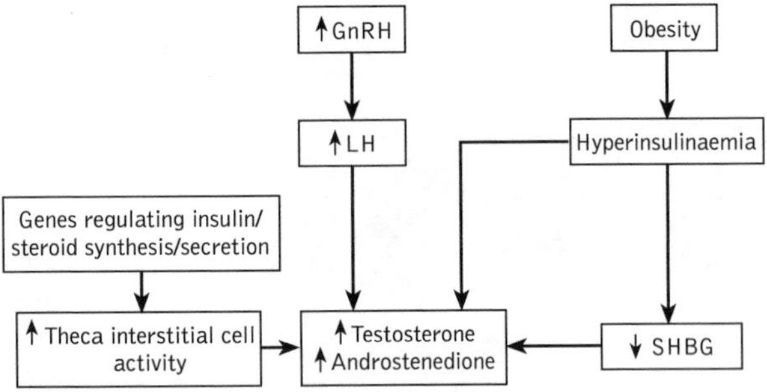

Fig. 54.1 Pathogenesis of PCOS.

Pathogenesis

Genetic

- PCOS is an oligogenic or polygenic disorder.
- Insulin synthesis genes and steroid enzyme biosynthesis gene are likely candidates, e.g. *INS*, *VNTR*, and *CYP11* genes.

Hyperandrogenism

- The main source of hyperandrogenaemia is the ovaries although there may also be adrenal androgen hypersecretion.
- The biochemical basis of ovarian dysfunction is unclear. Studies suggest an abnormality of cytochrome P-450c17α activity but this is unlikely to be the primary event but rather an index of increased steroidogenesis by ovarian theca cells.
- There is also an increase in the frequency and amplitude of GnRH pulses, resulting in the increase in LH concentration which is characteristic of the syndrome. This is probably secondary to anovulation and low progesterone levels.

Hyperinsulinaemia

- Insulin and IGF-1 receptors are found in abundance in the ovarian stroma and it has been shown that insulin, in the presence of LH, stimulates ovarian production of androgens. This is exaggerated in PCOS.
- Insulin also diminishes SHBG levels with a consequent rise in free androgen levels.

Features

- *Onset of symptoms* Symptoms often begin around puberty, after weight gain or after stopping the oral contraceptive pill but can present at any time.
- *Oligo/amenorrhoea* (70%) Due to anovulation. These women are well-oestrogenized so there is no risk of osteoporosis, unlike other causes of amenorrhoea.
- *Hirsutism* (60%)
  - 25% of women also suffer from acne or male pattern alopecia. Virilization is not a feature of PCOS.
  - There is often a family history of hirsutism or irregular periods. Hirsutism secondary to adrenal or ovarian tumours is usually rapidly progressive, associated with virilization and higher testosterone concentrations.
  - 1% of hirsute women have non-classical congenital adrenal hyperplasia(see p. 366) and this should be excluded particularly in women with significantly raised serum testosterone levels.
- *Obesity* (35%) Symptoms worsen with obesity as it is accompanied by increased testosterone concentrations as a result of the associated hyperinsulinaemia.
- *Infertility* (30%) Due to anovulation.

Rule out an androgen-secreting tumour

If there is:

- evidence of virilization
- testosterone >5 nmol/L (or >3 nmol/L in postmenopausal women)
- rapidly progressive hirsutism
- *MRI of adrenals and ovaries* will detect adrenal or ovarian tumours >1 cm.
- *Selective venous sampling*:
  - Occasionally necessary to locate virilizing tumours undetected by imaging.
  - Blood samples are taken from both adrenal and ovarian veins and from the peripheral circulation.
  - A virilizing tumour is likely if an androgen concentration gradient is detected

Table 54.1 Pharmacological treatment of hirsutism

Ovarian androgen suppression	Oral contraceptive pill
	GnRH analogues
Adrenal androgen suppression	Glucocorticoids
Androgen receptor blockers	Cyproterone acetate
	Spironolactone
	Flutamide
5α-reductase inhibitors	Finasteride

Investigations

The aims of investigations are threefold: to confirm the diagnosis, to exclude serious underlying disorders, and to screen for complications.

Confirmation of diagnosis

- *Testosterone concentration*
  - Performed primarily as a screen for the presence of other causes of hyperandrogenism.
  - Women with PCOS may have normal serum testosterone levels and serum androgen concentrations do not necessarily reflect the degree of hirsutism.
- *LH concentration*
  - Raised in 50–70% of anovulatory patients with reversal of the FSH/LH ratio.
  - The higher the LH level the more likely the risk of anovulation and infertility. Cannot be used alone to diagnose PCOS since it is normal in half the patients.
- *SHBG*
  - Low in 50% of women with PCOS owing to the hyperinsulinaemic state, with a consequent increase in circulating free androgens.
- *Pelvic ultrasound of ovaries and endometrium*
  - 91% sensitivity in experienced hands, with transvaginal ultrasounds giving the highest yield.
  - Ultrasonic diagnosis of PCOS is made by the presence of >8 follicular cysts of <10 mm and increased ovarian stroma.
  - Measurement of endometrial thickness is also useful in the diagnosis of endometrial hyperplasia in the presence of anovulation. Endometrial hyperplasia is diagnosed if the endometrial thickness is >10 mm.
  - Transvaginal ultrasound will also identify 90% of ovarian virilizing tumours.

Exclusion of serious underlying disease

- *Serum prolactin*
  - In the presence of infertility or oligoamenorrhoea.
  - Mild hyperprolactinaemia (up to 2000 mU/L) is present in up to 30% of women with PCOS, and dopamine agonist treatment of this may be necessary if pregnancy is desired.

- *17 OH (17OHP) progesterone level*
  - Used to exclude late onset congenital adrenal hyperplasia.
  - Indicated in those with testosterone concentrations in excess of 5 nmol/L or with evidence of virilization.
  - May also perform a synacthen test looking for an exaggerated rise in 17 OHP in response to ACTH in the presence of non-classic 21-hydroxylase deficiency (see p. 366).
  - If the patient is ovulating then all 17OHP measurements should be performed during the follicular phase of the cycle to avoid false positives.
- *DHEAS and androstenedione concentrations*
  - Both can be moderately raised in PCOS. DHEAS is a useful adrenal marker of hyperandrogenism. In cases of suspected tumours levels are usually in excess of 20 μmol/L.
- *Other*
  - Depending on clinical suspicion, e.g urinary free cortisol or overnight dexamethasone suppression test if Cushing's syndrome is suspected, but not routinely.

Screening for complications

- *Serum lipids and blood glucose*
  - Insulin resistance increases the risk of type 2 diabetes mellitus and hypertriglyceridaemia.
  - Up to 40% of women with PCOS have impaired glucose tolerance and up to 10% have frank diabetes mellitus.

Management

Weight loss

Weight loss in obese patients will reduce insulin resistance and thus hyperandrogenaemia. Obese women are less likely to respond to antiandrogens and infertility treatment. With a loss of 5% of their starting weight, women with PCOS show a 40% improvement in their hirsutism. Restoration of menstrual regularity and fertility can be acheived by weight loss alone.

Insulin sensitizers

In obese and lean women with PCOS and insulin resistance, metformin (500 mg 3x daily) may improve insulin sensitivity with a corresponding reduction in serum androgen and LH concentrations and an increase in SHBG levels. It may also regulate menstruation by improving ovulatory function and thus inducing fertility. No long-term studies have been done on its effect on hirsutism. Its effects seem to be independent of weight reduction, although the benefits are greatest when weight reduction occurs in obese women. However, there have been very few controlled trials using metformin in PCOS and all trials have been limited by small numbers of subjects. Women should be warned of its gastrointestinal side-effects. In order to minimize these, they should be started on a low dose (500 mg once daily) which may be increased gradually to a therapeutic dose over a number of weeks.

Troglitazone is a thiazolidinedione, another insulin sensitizer which has shown encouraging effects on menstruation and fertility in women with PCOS. However, it has been withdrawn from both the UK and US markets because of liver problems. Other thiazolidinediones may in the future be used in the treatment of PCOS.

Hirsutism

Pharmacological treatment of hirsutism is directed at slowing the growth of new hair but has little impact on established hair. It should be combined with mechanical methods of hair removal such as electrolysis and laser therapy. Therapy is most effective when started early. There is slow improvement over the first 6–12 months of treatment. Patients should be warned that facial hair is slow to respond, treatment is prolonged, and symptoms may recur after discontinuation of drugs. Adequate contraception is mandatory during pharmacological treatment of hirsutism because of possible teratogenicity.

Ovarian androgen suppression

- *Oral contraceptive pill (OCP)*
  - The oestrogen component increases SHBG levels and thus reduces free androgen concentrations; the progestogen component inhibits LH secretion and thus ovarian androgen production.
  - Dianette, which contains cyproterone acetate (2 mg), is preferred.
  - The effect of the OCP alone on hair growth is modest at best, so it may be combined with an antiandrogen (see below). Avoid OCP with androgenic progestagen.
- *GnRH analogues*
  - Suppress gonadotrophin secretion and thus ovarian androgen production.
  - Rarely used. They cause oestrogen deficiency so have to be combined with 'add-back' oestrogen treatment. Also, they are expensive and need to be given parenterally.
  - Use is confined to women with severe hyperandrogenism in whom antiandrogens have been ineffective or not tolerated.

Adrenal androgen suppression

- *Glucocorticoids* Suppress adrenal androgen production. However, the effect on hirsutism is minimal and there is the risk of hypothalamic-pituitary-adrenal suppression. Steroids may worsen hyperinsulinaemia, thus exacerbating ovarian androgen excess.

Androgen receptor blockers

These are most effective when combined with oral contraceptives. All are contraindicated in pregnancy. They act by competitively inhibiting the binding of testosterone and dihydrotestosterone to the androgen receptor.

- *Cyproterone acetate (CPA)*
  - A progestagen which also increases *hepatic androgen clearance.*
  - *Dose* 25–100 mg for last 10 days of the menstrual cycle in combination with the OCP.
  - *Side-effects* Amenorrhoea if given alone for prolonged periods or in higher doses. *Progesterone side-effects* Hepatic toxicity rare, but monitoring of liver function 6 monthly is recommended.
  - A *washout period* of 3–4 months is recommended prior to attempting conception.
- *Spironolactone*
  - weak antiandrogen
  - *Dose* 50–200 mg a day.

  - *Side-effects* polymenorrhoea if not combined with the OCP. A fifth of women complain of GI symptoms when on high doses of spironolactone. Potassium levels should be monitored and other potassium-sparing drugs should be avoided.
- *Flutamide*
  - A potent antiandrogen.
  - *Dose* 125 mg a day.
  - *Side-effects* Dry skin, nausea in 10%. However, there is a 0.4% risk of hepatic toxicity and it should therefore be used with extreme caution.

5α-reductase inhibitors

Block the conversion of testosterone to the more potent androgen, dihydrotestosterone.

- *Finasteride*
  - *Dose* 5 mg a day. Is at least as effective as CPA.
  - *Side-effects* no significant adverse effects.
  - Can be used as monotherapy and is therefore of value if the OCP is contraindicated. However, adequate contraceptive measures are mandatory because of its teratogenicity. In addition, pregnancy should not be attempted until at least 3 months after drug cessation.
  - Further experience is required before recommending it as first line therapy.

Amenorrhoea

- Associated with endometrial hyperplasia.
- Threefold increased risk of endometrial carcinoma.
- A minimum of a withdrawal bleed every 3 months minimizes the risk of endometrial neoplasia
- *Treatment*
  - OCP
  - Metformin (500 mg 3× daily)
  - *Alternatives* A progestogen may be added for the latter half of the cycle. However, there is the risk of exacerbating hirsutism. Less androgenic progestogens include *dydrogesterone* (Duphaston) and *medroxyprogesterone e.g.* Medroxyprogesterone 20 mg last 14/7 of 3 mth cycle (Provera). Norethisterone should be avoided.

Infertility

Ovulation induction regimens are indicated. Obesity adversely affects fertility outcome with poorer pregnancy rates and higher rates of spontaneous abortions so weight reduction should be strongly encouraged.

- *Clomiphene citrate*
  - Inhibits oestrogen negative feedback, increasing FSH secretion and thus stimulating ovarian follicular growth.
  - *Dose* 25–150 mg a day from day 5 of menstrual cycle for 5 days.
  - *Response rates* 80% of women with PCOS will ovulate, although the pregnancy rate is only 67%. Recent studies have shown that treatment with metformin may improve response to clomphene in resistant cases.
  - *Complications* Risk of ovarian neoplasia following prolonged clomiphene treatment remains unclear, so limit treatment to a maximum of 6 cycles.
- *Gonadotrophin preparations (hMG or FSH)*
  - Used in those unresponsive to clomiphene. Low dose regimes show better response rates and less complications., e.g. 75 IU/day for 2 weeks then increase by 37.5 IU/day every 7 days as required.
  - 94% ovulation rate and 40% conception rate after 4 cycles.
  - *Complications* hyperstimulation, multiple pregnancies.
  - Close ultrasonic monitoring is essential.
- *Surgery*
  - Laparoscopic ovarian diathermy or laser drilling may restore ovulation in up to 90% of women with cumulative pregnancy rates of 80% within 8 months of treatment.
  - *Complications* surgical adhesions, although usually mild.
- *In vitro fertilization*
  - In the minority of women who fail to respond to ovulation induction.
  - 60–80% conception rate after 6 cycles.

Prognosis and follow up

- The natural history of untreated hirsutism is that of a gradual progression up until the time of the menopause, following which there is gradual improvement apart from facial hair, which continues to progress.
- Follow-up studies of postmenopausal women with histological evidence of PCOS show a 15% prevalence of type 2 diabetes mellitus, compared with <2% in the general population. These studies also revealed a significantly increased prevalence of hypertension in

women with PCOS. It therefore seems prudent to monitor blood pressure on a regular basis and have a baseline fasting blood glucose and serum lipid profile.

- Long term follow-up of women with PCOS has revealed that they are apparently not at increased risk of developing ischaemic heart disease despite the presence of multiple risk factors.

Further reading

Barnes RB. Diagnosis and therapy of hyperandrogenism. *Baillière's Clinical Obstretric Gynaecology* 1997; 11(2): 369–396.

Conn JJ, Jacobs HS. The clinical management of hirsutism. *European Journal of Endocrinology* 1997; 136: 339–348.

Dahlgren E, Johansson S, Lindstedt G *et al.* Women with polycystic ovary syndrome wedge resected in 1956 to 1965: a long term follow up focusing on natural history and circulating hormones. *Fertility and Sterility* 1992; 57(3): 505–513.

Dunaif A. Insulin resistance and polycystic ovary syndrome: mechanism and implications for pathogenesis. *Endocrine Review* 1997; 18(6): 774–800.

Ehrmann DA. Insulin lowering therapeutic modalities for polycystic ovary syndrome. *Endocrinology and Metabolism Clinics of North America* 1999; 28(2):423–438.

Franks S, Gharani N, Waterworth D *et al.* The genetic basis of polycystic ovary syndrome. *Human Reproduction* 1997; 12(12): 2641–2648.

Pierpoint T, McKeigue PM, Isaacs AJ, Wild SH, Jacobs HS. Mortality of women with polycystic ovary syndrome at long term follow up. *Journal of Clinical Epidemiology* 1998; 51(7): 581–586.

Chapter 55

Congenital adrenal hyperplasia in adults

Definition

CAH is an inherited group of disorders characterized by a deficiency of one of the enzymes necessary for cortisol biosynthesis.

- >90% of cases are due to 21α-hydroxylase deficiency.
- Wide clinical spectrum, from presentation in neonatal period with salt wasting and virilization to non-classic CAH in adulthood.
- Inherited in an autosomal recessive manner.

Epidemiology

- Wide racial variations, most common in those of Jewish origin.
- Carrier frequency of classic CAH 1 : 60 in white people.
- Carrier frequency of non-classic CAH 19% in Ashkenazi Jews, 13.5% in Hispanics, 6% in Italians and 3% in other white people.

Pathogenesis

Genetics

- *CYP21* encodes for the 21α-hydroxylase enzyme, located on the short arm of chromosome 6 (chromosome 6p21.3). In close proximity is the *CYP21* pseudogene, with 90% homology but no functional activity.
- 21α-hydroxylase deficiency results from gene mutations, partial gene deletions or gene conversions in which sequences from the pseudogene are transferred to the active gene, rendering it inactive. There is a correlation between the severity of the molecular defect and the clinical severity of the disorder. Non-classic CAH is usually due to a point mutation (single base change) whereas a gene conversion or partial deletion usually results in presentation in infancy with salt wasting or severe virilization.

Biochemistry

See Fig. 55.1.

21α-hydroxylase deficiency results in aldosterone and cortisol deficiency. There is ACTH oversecretion because of the loss of negative feedback, and this causes adrenocortical hyperplasia and excessive accumulation of 17-hydroxy progesterone (17OHP) and other steroid precursors. These are then shunted into androgen synthesis pathways resulting in testosterone and androstenedione excess.

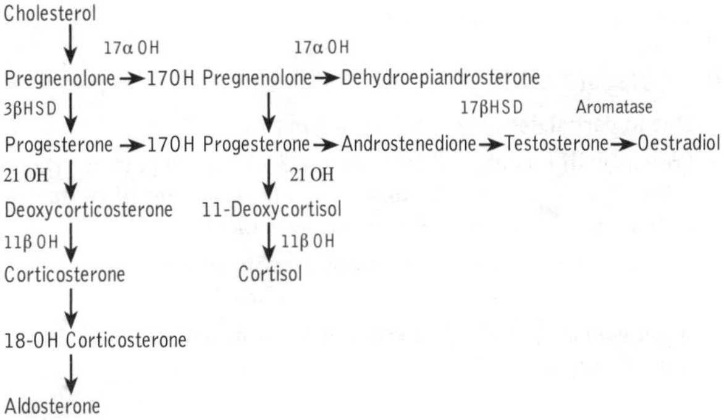

Fig 55.1 Adrenal steroid biosynthesis pathway. 3βHSD, 3β-hydroxysteroid dehydrogenase; 21 OH, 21-hydroxylase; 11β OH, 11β-hydroxylase; 17α OH, 17α-hydroxylase; 17β HSD, 17β-hydroxysteroid dehydrogenase.

Clinical presentation

Classic CAH

- Most patients are diagnosed in infancy, and their clinical presentation is discussed elsewhere (see p. 654).
- *Problems persisting into adulthood* sexual dysfunction and subfertility in females, particularly in salt wasters. Reconstructive genital surgery is required in the majority of women who were virilized at birth to create an adequate vaginal introitus. With improvement of medical and surgical care, pregnancy rates have improved. Fertility rates of 60% have been reported in women with classic CAH.
- In males, high levels of adrenal androgens suppress gonadotrophins and thus testicular function. Spermatogenesis may therefore be affected if CAH is poorly controlled.

Non-classic CAH

- Due to partial deficiency of 21α-hydroxylase.
- Present with hirsutism (82%), acne (25%), and oligomenorrhoea (50%), often around the onset of puberty. Subfertility due to anovulation occurs in 50% of untreated patients.
- A third of women have polycystic ovaries on ultrasound and adrenal incidentalomas or hyperplasia are seen in 40%.
- *Asymptomatic in males* The effect of non-classic CAH on male fertility is unknown.

Investigations

Because of the diurnal variation in adrenal hormonal secretion, all investigations should be performed at 9 a.m.

Diagnosis of non-classic CAH – 17OHP measurement

Timing of measurement

- Screen in the follicular phase of the menstrual cycle. 17OHP is produced by the corpus luteum, so false positive results may occur if measured in the luteal phase of the cycle.
- Must be measured at 9 a.m. to avoid false negative results as 17OHP has a diurnal variation similar to that of ACTH.

Interpretation of result

<5 nmol/Lnormal

>15 nmol/L CAH

5–15 nmol/L proceed to ACTH stimulation test. A fifth will have non-classic CAH.

ACTH stimulation test

- Measure 17OHP 60 min after ACTH administration.
- An exaggerated rise in 17OHP is seen in non-classic CAH.
- 17OHP level <30 nmol/L post-ACTH excludes the diagnosis.
- Most patients have levels >45 nmol/L.
- Levels of 30–45 nmol/L suggest heterozygosity.
- Cortisol response to ACTH stimulation is usually low-normal.

Other investigations

Androgens

- In poorly controlled classic CAH in women, testosterone and androstenedione levels may be in the adult male range. Dehydroepiandrosterone sulphate levels are usually only mildly, and not consistently, elevated in CAH.
- Circulating testosterone and, particularly androstenedione, are elevated in non-classic CAH, but there is a large overlap with levels seen in PCOS so serum androgen concentrations cannot be used to distinguish between the disorders.

Renin

- Plasma renin levels are markedly elevated in 75% of patients with inadequately treated classic CAH, reflecting deficient aldosterone production.
- A proportion of women with non-classic CAH may also have mildly elevated renin concentrations.

ACTH

- Greatly elevated in poorly controlled classic CAH.
- Usually normal levels in non-classic CAH.

Table 55.1 Enzyme deficiencies in CAH

Enzyme deficiency	Incidence (per births)	Clinical features
Classic 21α-hydroxylase	1 : 10 000–1 : 15 000	Salt wasting, ambiguous genitalia in females, precocious pubarche in males
Non-classic 21α-hydroxylase (partial deficiency)	1 : 27–1 : 1000	Hirsutism, oligomenorrhoea in pubertal girls, asymptomatic in boys
11ß-hydroxylase	1 : 100 000	Ambiguous genitalia, virilization, hypertension
3ß-hydroxylase	Rare	Mild virilization, salt wasting in severe cases
17α-hydroxylase	Rare	Delayed puberty in females, pseudohermaphroditism in males, hypertension, hypokalaemia

Management

The aims of treatment of CAH in adulthood are:

- to maintain normal energy levels and weight and avoid adrenal crises in all patients
- to minimize hyperandrogenism and to restore regular menses and fertility in women
- to avoid glucocorticoid over-replacement.

Classic CAH

- *Prednisolone*, total dose 5–7.5 mg/day. Given in two divided doses, with a third of the total dose given on waking (about 7 a.m.) and two-thirds of the dose on retiring. The aim is to suppress the early morning peak of ACTH and thus androgen secretion. Occasional patients who are not controlled on prednisolone may be optimally treated with nocturnal dexamethasone instead (0.5 mg).
- As with other forms of adrenal insufficiency, glucocorticoid doses should be doubled during illness. This is discussed in detail elsewhere (p. 319).
- 75% of patients are salt wasters and thus require mineralocorticoid replacement therapy. Fludrocortisone in a dose of 50–200 μg/day is given as a single daily dose. The aim is to keep plasma renin levels in the mid-normal range.
- Bilateral adrenalectomy may very occasionally be considered in patients with severe virilization.

Non-classic CAH

- *Oligo/amenorrhoea* Glucocorticoid therapy, e.g. noctural dexamethasone 0.25–0.5 mg or prednisolone 2.5–5 mg/day, may be used. Slightly higher doses may be required to normalize ovulatory function.
- *Hirsutism and acne* May alternatively, and more effectively, be treated using antiandrogens, e.g. cyproterone acetate combined with oral oestrogens (see management of PCOS, p. 359). Spironolactone should be avoided because of the potential risk of salt wasting and thus hyperreninaemia.
- If plasma renin level is elevated then fludrocortisone given in a dose sufficient to normalize renin concentrations may improve adrenal hyperandrogenism.
- Males do not usually require treatment.

Management of pregnancy in CAH

Indications for prenatal treatment

- *Maternal classic CAH* Screen partner using basal ± ACTH-stimulated 17OHP levels (see investigations above). If levels elevated, proceed to genotyping. If heterozygote, then prenatal treatment of foetus recommended.
- Previous child from same partner with CAH

Aims of prenatal treatment (p. 372)

- Prevention of virilization of an affected female foetus.

Treatment (commenced before 10 weeks gestation)

- Dexamethasone (20 μg/kg) crosses the placenta to reduce foetal adrenal hyperandrogenism.

Outcome

- 50% of affected females do not require reconstructive surgery.

Complications

- No known foetal congenital malformations from dexamethasone treatment.
- Subtle effects of glucocorticoids on neuropsychological function unknown.
- Maternal complications of glucocorticoid excess in 1%, e.g. mood swings and weight gain. Some suggest reducing the dose of dexamethasone in the third trimester of pregnancy in order to reduce the risk of maternal complications. However, the efficacy of this regime in preventing neonatal virilization has not been proven.

There is debate about whether women with non-classic CAH should be offered prenatal treatment with dexamethasone. There have been no cases of women with non-classic CAH giving birth to a virilized female. Additionally, the estimated risk of conceiving an infant with classic CAH is 1 : 1000. As the risk of foetal virilization is therefore low, dexamethasone treatment of this group of women seems unwarranted. However, these infants should be screened in the neonatal period by measuring 17OHP levels.

Monitoring of treatment

Annual follow up is usually adequate in adults.

- *Clinical assessment* Look for evidence of hyperandrogenism and glucocorticoid excess. Amenorrhoea in females usually suggests inadequate therapy.
- *17OHP* Aim for a mildly elevated level (about 2× normal). Normalizing 17OHP will result in complications from supraphysiological doses of glucocorticoids.
- *Plasma renin* Aim for renin in mid-normal range. Hyperandrogenism will be difficult to control if patient is mildly salt-depleted (ACTH production stimulated by hypovolaemia).
- *Androgens* Aim to normalize serum androstenedione taken before a.m. steroids.

Prenatal treatment protocol

Start dexamethasone 20μg/kg per day (prepregnancy weight)
Best results if started at 4–6 weeks, certainly before week 9 of gestation

↓

Chorionic villus sampling at 10–12 weeks for
fetal karyotype
DNA analysis

↓	↓	↓
46XX, unaffected	46XY	46XX, affected (1 in 8)
↓	↓	↓
Discontinue treatment		Continue treatment to term

Fig 55.2 Prenatal treatment protocol.

Prognosis

Adults with treated CAH have a normal life expectancy. Improvement in medical and surgical care has also improved quality of life for most sufferers. However, there are a few unresolved issues:

- *Height* Despite optimal treatment in childhood, patients with CAH are, on average, significantly shorter than their predicted genetic height. Studies suggest that this may be due to overtreatment with glucocorticoids during infancy.
- *Fertility* Remains reduced in females with CAH, particularly in salt wasters, due to factors including inadequate vaginal introitus and anovulation secondary to both hyperandrogenism and high 17OHP levels. Fertility may also be affected in males with poorly controlled classic CAH.
- *Adrenal incidentalomas and testicular adrenal rest tumours* Benign adrenal adenomas have been reported in up to 50% of patients with classic CAH. Males with classic CAH may develop gonadal adrenocortical rests which may be misdiagnosed as testicular tumours. These are ACTH-responsive and should be treated by optimizing glucocorticoid therapy.
- *Psychosexual issues* There is an increased propensity for gender identity disorders. In animal studies, prenatal exposure of genetic females to testosterone during critical periods of development enhances masculine behaviour. Females with classic CAH also show an increased tendency to male pattern behaviour. A significant number of women with classic CAH, despite adequacy of vaginal reconstruction, are not sexually active.

Further reading

Azziz R, Dewailly D, Owerbach D. Non-classic adrenal hyperplasia: current concepts. *Journal of Clinical Endocrinology and Metabolism* 1994; 78(4): 810–815.

Hunt PJ, Inder WJ. Diagnosis, monitoring and management of congenital adrenal hyperplasia. *Current Opinions in Endocrinology and Diabetes* 1995; 2: 231–238.

Premawaradhana LDKE, Hughes IA, Read GF, Scanlon MF. Longer term outcome in females with congenital adrenal hyperplasia: the Cardiff experience. *Clinical Endocrinology* 1997; 46: 327–332.

Van Wyk JJ, Gunther DF, Ritzen EM, Wedell A, Cutler GB, Migeon CJ. The use of adrenalectomy as treatment for congenital adrenal hyperplasia. *Journal of Clinical Endocrinology and Metabolism* 1996; 81(9): 3180–3190.

Chapter 56
Androgen-secreting tumours

Definition

Rare tumours of the ovary or adrenal gland which may be benign or malignant, which cause virilization in women through androgen production.

Epidemiology and pathology

Androgen secreting ovarian tumours

- 75% develop before the age of 40 years.
- Account for 0.4% of all ovarian tumours. 20% are malignant.
- Tumours are 5–25 cm in size. The larger they are, the more likely they are to be malignant. They are rarely bilateral.
- Two major types:
  - sex cord stromal cell tumours: often contain testicular cell types
  - adrenal-like tumours: often contain adrenocortical or Leydig cells.
- Other tumours, e.g. gonadoblastomas and teratomas, may also on occasion present with virilization.

Androgen secreting adrenal tumours

- 50% develop before the age of 50 years.
- Larger tumours, particularly >6 cm, are more likely to be malignant.

Clinical features

- *Onset of symptoms* Usually recent onset of rapidly progressive symptoms.
- *Hyperandrogenism*
  - hirsutism of varying degree, often severe (Ferriman–Gallwey score) (p. 346); male pattern balding and acne are also common.
  - usually oligo-amenorrhoea
  - infertility may be a presenting feature.
- *Virilization* (p. 347) indicates severe hyperandrogenism is associated with clitoromegaly and is present in 98% of women with androgen-producing tumours. Not usually a feature of PCOS.
- *Other*
  - abdominal pain
  - palpable abdominal mass
  - ascites
  - symptoms and signs of Cushing's syndrome are present in 50% of women with adrenal tumours.

Investigations

See Fig. 56.1 on facing page.

Management

Surgery

- Adrenalectomy or ovarian cystectomy/oophorectomy.
- Curative in benign lesions.

Adjunctive therapy

- Malignant ovarian and adrenal androgen-secreting tumours are usually resistant to chemotherapy and radiotherapy.

Prognosis

Benign tumours

- Prognosis excellent.
- Hirsutism improves postoperatively, but clitoromegaly, male pattern balding, and deep voice may persist.

Malignant tumours

- *Adrenal tumours* 20% 5 year survival. Most have metastatic disease at the time of surgery.
- *Ovarian tumours* 30% disease-free survival and 40% overall survival at 5 years.

Further reading

Hamilton-Fairley D, Franks S Androgen secreting tumours. In Sheaves R, Jenkins PJ, Wass JAH (ed), *Clinical Endocrine Oncology*. 1997. Oxford: Blackwell Science, pp. 323–329.

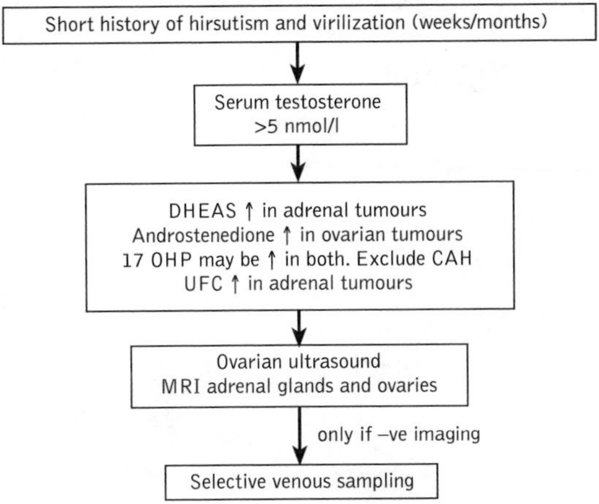

Fig. 56.1 Investigation of androgen-secreting tumours.

Chapter 57
Menstrual disorders – assessment and investigation

Definitions

- *Oligomenorrhoea* is defined as the reduction in the frequency of menses to less than 9 periods a year.
- *Primary amenorrhoea* is the failure of menarche by the age of 16 years.
- *Secondary amenorrhoea* refers to the cessation of menses for >6 months in women who had previously menstruated.

However, the common causes may present with either primary or secondary amenorrhoea.

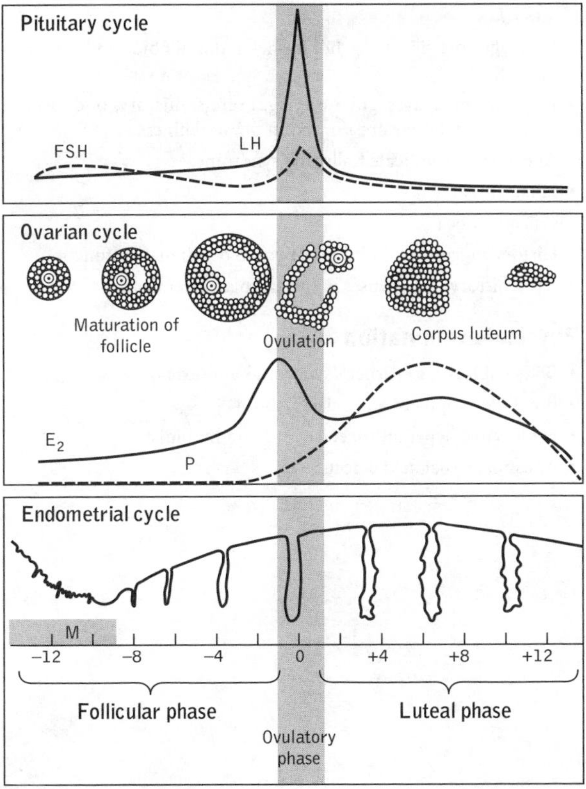

Fig. 57.1 The normal menstrual cycle. Reproduced with permission.

Clinical evaluation

History

- Oestrogen deficiency, e.g. hot flushes, reduced libido and dyspareunia
- Hypothalamic dysregulation, e.g. exercise history, body weight changes, emotional stress or recent physical illness
- Anosmia may indicate Kallman's syndrome
- Hirsutism or acne
- Galactorrhoea
- History suggestive of pituitary, thyroid or adrenal dysfunction
- Drug history – e.g. causes of hyperprolactinaemia.

Physical examination

- Body habitus, e.g. Turner's syndrome, anorexia nervosa
- Breast development and galactorrhoea
- Evidence of hyperandrogenism or hypothyroidism
- Anosmia, visual field defects.

Causes of amenorrhoea

Physiological

- pregnancy and lactation
- postmenopause

Pathological

Primary

- androgen insensitivity syndrome
- congenital absence of uterus
- Turner's syndrome
- Kallman's syndrome

Secondary

- ovarian
  - polycystic ovary syndrome
  - premature ovarian failure
- uterine
  - intrauterine adhesions
- pituitary
  - hyperprolactinaemia
  - hypopituitarism
- hypothalamic
  - weight loss
  - excessive exercise
  - physical or psychological stress
  - craniopharyngioma
  - infiltrative lesions of the hypothalamus.

Investigations

See Fig. 57.2 on facing page.

- Is it primary or secondary ovarian dysfunction?
  - FSH, LH, oestradiol, and prolactin.
- Pelvic ultrasound
  - ovarian and uterine morphology – exclude anatomical abnormalities, polycystic ovary syndrome and Turner's syndrome
  - endometrial thickness – to assess oestrogen status.
- Other tests depending on clinical suspicion
  - serum testosterone in the presence of hyperandrogenism
  - karyotype in primary amenorrhoea or if Turner's syndrome suspected
  - MRI of the pituitary fossa.

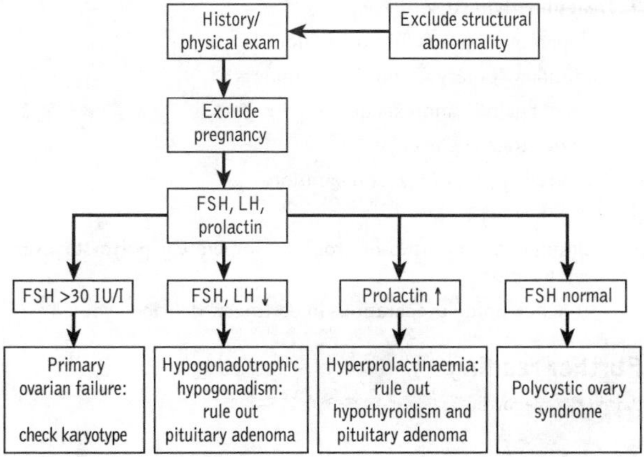

Fig. 57.2 Investigation of amenorrhea.

Management

- Treat underlying disorder, e.g.
  - dopamine agonists for prolactinomas
  - pituitary surgery for pituitary tumours
  - weight gain in anorexia nervosa
- Treat oestrogen deficiency
  - oestrogen/progestogen preparations
- Treat infertility
  - clomiphene in normo-oestrogenic women (e.g. polycystic ovary syndrome)
  - gonadotrophin preparations in oestrogen-deficient women

Further reading

Baird DT Amenorrhoea. *Lancet* 1997; 350: 275–279.

Chapter 58
Premature ovarian failure

Definition

Premature ovarian failure (POF) is a disorder characterized by amenorrhoea, oestrogen deficiency and elevated gonadotropins developing in women <40 years, as a result of loss of ovarian follicular function.

Epidemiology

- Incidence – 0.1% of women <30 years and 1% of those <40 years.
- Accounts for 10% of all cases of secondary amenorrhoea.

Causes of POF

- Chromosomal abnormalities (60%)
  - Turner's syndrome
  - fragile X syndrome
  - other X chromosomal abnormalities
- Gene mutations
  - β subunit of FSH
  - FSH receptor
  - LH receptor
- Autoimmune disease (20%)
- Iatrogenic
  - chemotherapy
  - radiotherapy
- Other
  - galactosaemia
  - enzyme deficiencies, e.g. 17α-hydroxylase deficiency
  - infections, e.g. mumps, HIV, shigella
  - posthysterectomy.

Turner's syndrome (page 631)

- Most common X-chromosome abnormality in females, affecting 1 : 2500 live female births
- Result of complete or partial absence of one X chromosome
- *Clinical features* short stature and gonadal dysgenesis. 90% of affected women have POF.
- *Characteristic phenotype* webbed neck, micrognathia, low-set ears, high arched palate, widely spaced nipples, and cubitus valgus
- *Other associated abnormalities* aortic coarctation and other left sided congenital heart defects, hypothyroidism, osteoporosis, skeletal abnormalities, lymphoedema, congenital renal abnormalities and ENT abnormalities.
- *Diagnosis* lymphocyte karyotype
- *Management in adults:*
  - sex hormone replacement therapy
  - treat complications
- *Follow-up:*
  - baseline renal ultrasound, thyroid autoantibodies
  - annual blood pressure, TFT, lipids, fasting blood glucose
  - 3–5 yearly echocardiogram and bone densitometry.

Pathogenesis

Failure of normal ovarian follicular response to gonadotrophins with consequent failure of ovarian steroidogenesis. POF is the result of either ovarian follicle depletion or failure of the follicles to function (resistant ovary syndrome). May be distinguished by ovarian ultrasound or histologically by ovarian biopsy. Treatment options are the same so invasive techniques looking for the presence of follicles are not indicated.

POF is usually permanent, although women with transient disease have been described. Additionally, <50% of karyotypically normal women with established disease produce oestrogen intermittently and up to a fifth of women may ovulate despite high gonadotrophin levels. Spontaneous pregnancy has been reported in 5%.

Clinical presentation

- *Amenorrhoea*
  - may be primary, particularly in patients with chromosomal abnormalities
- Symptoms of *oestrogen deficiency*
  - not present in those with primary amenorrhoea
  - 75% of women who develop secondary amenorrhoea report hot flushes, night sweats, mood changes, fatigue or dyspareunia; symptoms may precede the onset of menstrual disturbances
- *Autoimmune disease*
  - screen for symptoms and signs of associated autoimmune disorders.
- *Other*
  - past history of radiotherapy, chemotherapy, or pelvic surgery
  - positive family history in a few patients.

Autoimmune diseases and POF

- Responsible for 20% of all cases of POF.
- A second autoimmune disorder is present in 10–40% of women with autoimmune POF:
  - Addison's disease 10%
  - autoimmune thyroid disease 25%
  - type 1 diabetes mellitus 2%
  - myaesthenia gravis 2%
  - SLE also more common.
- POF is present in:
  - 60% of women with autoimmune polyglandular syndrome type 1 (p. 317)
  - 25% of women with autoimmune polyglandular syndrome type 2 (p. 317).
- Steroid cell antibodies are positive in 60–100% of patients with Addison's disease in combination with POF. The presence of positive steroid cell antibodies in women with Addison's disease confers a 40% risk of ultimately developing POF. Other ovarian antibodies have no predictive value.

Investigation

- *Serum gonadotropins*
  - diagnosis is confirmed by serum FSH >40 mIU/L on at least 2 occasions at least 1 month apart
  - disease may have a fluctuating course with high FSH levels returning to normal and later regain of ovulatory function
  - LH also elevated, but FSH usually disproportionately higher than LH.
- *Serum oestradiol* levels are low.
- *Karyotype*
  - all women presenting with primary (hypergonadotropic) amenorrhoea should be karyotyped
  - women with Y chromosomal material should be referred for bilateral gonadectomy to prevent the development of gonadoblastoma. (Testicular feminization, complete androgen resistance.)
- *Pelvic ultrasound* To identify normal ovarian and uterine morphology in women with primary amenorrhoea.
- *Screen for autoimmune disease*
  - thyroid and adrenal cortex autoantibodies; if positive, increases the risk of progression to overt adrenal or thyroid insufficiency
  - ovarian antibodies are of no proven clinical value
  - TSH and fasting blood glucose
  - synacthen test only if adrenal insufficiency is suspected clinically
  - other tests as clinically indicated.
- *Ovarian biopsy* Not indicated.

Annual assessment of women with POF

- Assess adequacy of sex hormone replacement therapy:
  - tolerance and compliance
  - side-effects and complications
  - persistent symptoms of sex hormone deficiency
- Address fertility issues
- Screen for other autoimmune disease (in autoimmune POF):
  - clinical evaluation
  - TSH and fasting blood glucose
  - synacthen test if clinically indicated
- Screen for complications:
  - osteoporosis
  - cardiovascular and cerebrovascular disease.

Management

Sex hormone replacement therapy

- Exogenous oestrogens (HRT) are required to alleviate symptoms and prevent the long-term complications of oestrogen deficiency – osteoporosis and cardiovascular disease. Initial doses depend on the duration of amenorrhoea – if oestrogen deficient for at least 12 months, then start on lowest doses of oestradiol available, to prevent side-effects, but titrate up to full dose within 6 months. If recently amenorrhoeic then full dose may be commenced immediately (see Table 58.1). Doses used in HRT are not contraceptive and do not suppress spontaneous ovarian follicular activity. HRT should be continued at least until the age of 50 years, the mean age of the natural menopause.
- In non-hysterectomized women, a progestagen should be added for 12–14 days a month to prevent endometrial hyperplasia.
- It has been suggested that low-dose androgen replacement therapy may improve persistent fatigue and poor libido despite adequate oestrogen replacement.

Fertility

- A minority of women with POF and a normal karyotype will recover spontaneously. 5% spontaneous fertility rate.
- Oocyte donation and *in vitro* fertilization offer these women their best chance of fertility. Results are promising, with a pregnancy rate of 35% per patient. Results are less good in women with chemotherapy-induced gonadal damage.
- Ovulation induction therapy has been tried but the results have been poor.
- Glucocorticoid therapy has been used in autoimmune POF but efficacy is as yet unknown.

Table 58.1 Hormone replacement therapy in POF

Hormone replacement	Dose
Oestrogen	
Conjugated oestrogen	0.625–1.25 mg daily
Oestradiol valerate	2–4 mg daily
Transdermal oestradiol	100 μg twice a week
Progestagen	12–14 days a month:
Norethisterone	1 mg
Medroxyprogesterone	10 mg
Testosterone	
Intramuscular	50–100 mg every 6–8 months mg/month
Subcutaneous implants	

See section on the menopause (page 405) for full review of hormone replacement therapy.

Prognosis

- Mortality of women with POF is increased twofold.
- Oestrogen deficiency leads to:
  - increased risk of cardiovascular and cerebrovascular disease
  - increased risk of osteoporosis. Up to two-thirds of women with POF and a normal karyotype have reduced BMD, with a z score of –1 or less despite at least intermittent hormone replacement therapy. This may be due to a combination of factors including an initial delay in initiating ERT, poor compliance with ERT and oestrogen 'underdosing'.

Further reading

Barlow DH. Premature ovarian failure. *Baillière's Clinical Obstetrics and Gynaecology* 1996; 10(3): 361–384.

Kalantaridou SN, Davis SR, Nelson LM. Premature ovarian failure. *Endocrinology and Metabolism Clinics of North America* 1998; 27(4): 989–1006.

Chapter 59
Menopause

Definition

- The *menopause* is the permanent cessation of menstruation as a result of ovarian failure and is a retrospective diagnosis made after 12 months of amenorrhoea. The average age of women at the time of the menopause is ~50 years, although smokers reach the menopause ~2 years earlier.
- The *perimenopause* encompasses the menopause transition and the first year following the last menstrual period.

Long-term consequences

- *Osteoporosis* During the perimenopausal period there is an accelerated loss of bone mineral density (BMD), rendering postmenopausal women more susceptible to osteoporotic fractures.
- *Ischaemic heart disease (IHD)* Postmenopausal women are 2–3 times more likely to develop IHD than are premenopausal women, even after age adjustments. The menopause is associated with an increase in risk factors for atherosclerosis, including less favourable lipid profile, decreased insulin sensitivity, and an increased thrombotic tendency.
- *Dementia* Women are 2–3 times more likely to develop Alzheimer's disease than men. It is suggested that oestrogen deficiency may play a role in the development of dementia.

Physiology

The physiology of the menopause remains poorly understood. Ovaries have a finite number of germ cells, with maximal numbers at 20 weeks of intrauterine life. Thereafter, there is a reduction in the number of oocytes until the store is depleted at the time of the menopause. Table 59.1 summarizes hormonal changes during the menopausal transition.

Inhibin B, a peptide produced by the ovarian follicles in response to FSH stimulation, is believed to play a crucial role in the neuroendocrinology of the perimenopause. It is a sensitive indicator of ovarian follicular number and is the earliest marker of ovarian ageing, levels beginning to fall ~12 years before the menopause. Inhibin B acts by suppressing FSH, particularly in the follicular phase of the menstrual cycle. A fall in inhibin B production by failing ovarian follicular cells results in the rise of FSH so characteristic of the menopause. In the early perimenopausal period, FSH levels fluctuate, but the gradual rise in FSH levels maintains oestradiol production by the ovarian follicles. So, contrary to previous belief, average serum oestradiol levels may be high at the onset of the menopause transition, falling only towards the end as the follicles are depleted.

Clinical presentation

There are marked cultural differences in the frequency of symptoms related to the menopause; in particular, vasomotor symptoms and mood disturbances are more commonly reported in western countries.

- *Menstrual disturbances* (90%) Cycles gradually become increasingly anovulatory, and variable in length from about 4 years prior to the menopause. Oligomenorrhoea often precedes permanent amenorrhoea. In 10% of women, menses cease abruptly with no preceding transitional period.
- *Hot flushes* (40%) Often associated with sweats and skin flushing. Highly variable and are thought to be related to fluctuations in oestrogen concentrations. Tend to resolve spontaneously within 5 years of the menopause.
- *Urinary symptoms* (50%) Atrophy of urethral and bladder mucosa after the menopause and decreased sensitivity of a-adrenergic receptors of the bladder neck in the perimenopausal period. This may result in urinary incontinence and an increased risk of urinary tract infections.
- *Sexual dysfunction* (40%) Vaginal atrophy may result in dyspareunia and vaginal dryness. Additionally, falling androgen levels may reduce sexual arousal and libido.
- *Mood changes* (25–50%) Anxiety, forgetfulness, difficulty in concentration and irritability have all been attributed to the menopause. Women with a history of affective disorders are at increased risk of mood disturbances in the perimenopausal period.

Table 59.1 Hormonal changes during the menopausal transition

	Premenopause (from age 36 years)	Early perimenopause	Advanced perimenopause	Menopause
Menstrual cycle	Regular, ovulatory	Irregular, often short cycles, increasingly anovulatory	Oligomenorrhoea	Amenorrhoea
FSH	Rising but within normal range	Intermittently raised, especially in follicular phase	Persistently ↑	↑ ↑
Inhibin B	Declining	Low	Low	Very low
E_2	Normal	Normal	Normal/low	Low

Evaluation (e.g. if HRT is being considered)

- *History:*
  - perimenopausal symptoms and their severity
  - assess risk factors for cardiovascular disease and osteoporosis
  - assess risk factors for breast cancer and thromboembolic disease
  - history of active liver disease
- *Examination:*
  - blood pressure
  - breasts
  - pelvic examination, including cervical smear
- *Investigations:*
  - *FSH* levels fluctuate markedly in perimenopausal period and correlate poorly with symptoms. Remember, a raised FSH in the perimenopausal period may not necessarily indicate infertility, so contraception, if desired, should continue until the menopause
  - *mammography* indicated prior to starting oestrogen replacement therapy only in high risk women; otherwise, mammography should be offered as per national screening programme
  - *endometrial biopsy* does not need to be performed routinely, but is essential in women with abnormal uterine bleeding.

Hormone replacement therapy

The aims of treatment of perimenopausal women are twofold:

- alleviation of menopausal symptoms
- preventing the long-term consequences of oestrogen deficiency.

Alleviation of symptoms

- *Hot flushes* Respond very well to oestrogen therapy in a dose-dependent manner. High doses may be required initially (up to the equivalent of 2.5 mg conjugated oestrogens), particularly in younger women or in those whose symptoms develop abruptly. Reduce dose gradually.

Alternative treatment (e.g. in those with a contraindication to HRT, or intolerant of it): megestrol acetate in a dose of 20 mg 2× daily reduces hot flushes by up to 70%. Main side-effect is weight gain. Clonidine is less effective, reducing the occurrence of flushes by 20%, and its use is limited by side-effects. Venlataxine may be useful.

- *Urinary symptoms* A trial of HRT, local or systemic, may improve stress and urge incontinence as well as the frequency of cystitis.
- *Vaginal atrophy* Systemic or local oestrogen therapy improves vaginal dryness and dyspareunia. A maximum of 6 months' use is recommended unless combined with a progestagen as systemic absorption may increase the risk of endometrial hyperplasia. If oestrogens are contraindicated, then vaginal moisturizers, e.g. Replens, may help.
- *Mood disturbances* HRT may improve psychological well-being and mood.

Prevention of long-term consequences of oestrogen deficiency

Cardiovascular disease

HRT users have a lower age-adjusted all-cause mortality compared with non-users, primarily as a result of the reduction in IHD risk. Studies have shown that the risk of IHD is reduced by up to 50% in women receiving HRT.

HRT reduces risk factors for IHD (see Table 59.2). However, recent evidence suggests that HRT may not be beneficial for secondary prevention of IHD and may actually increase morbidity in the year following a myocardial infarction.

Osteoporosis

HRT has been shown to increase bone mineral density in the lumbar spine by 3–5% and at the femoral neck by about 2%, by inhibiting bone resorption. There is an associated 50% reduction in fracture risk, protection being highest in women on HRT for at least 10 years. Timing of initiation of treatment in order to achieve maximal bone protection remains controversial. Evidence suggests that initiation of HRT soon after the menopause is associated with the lowest hip fracture risk, but discontinuation of HRT results in bone loss to pretreatment levels.

Women at increased risk of osteoporosis may therefore be offered HRT to prevent bone loss and osteoporotic fractures. This may be initiated at the time of the menopause or alternatively deferred until the time when fracture risk is greatest, i.e. age 65 years and over.

Alzheimer's disease

Recent evidence suggests that the risk of developing Alzheimer's disease is reduced by up to 50% in women receiving HRT. In women with established Alzheimer's disease, cognitive function may improve if HRT is started and disease progression is delayed by up to 2 years. Protection is maximal with higher doses of oestrogen and longer durations of treatment. In postmenopausal women without dementia, HRT may also improve cognitive function. Mechanisms are unknown but it is thought that oestrogens may improve cerebral perfusion and afford neuronal protection.

Further research is required but it may be prudent to recommend HRT in women at risk of dementia, e.g. family history of Alzheimer's disease. Additionally, a trial of HRT may help women with established disease.

Colorectal cancer

Preliminary research suggests that the rates of colorectal cancer are 50% lower in current users of HRT. However, more research is required before recommending HRT to prevent this disease.

Risks of HRT

Table 59.3 summarizes contraindications to HRT.

Breast cancer

- *No personal or family history of breast cancer* 30% increased risk of breast cancer after 10 years of HRT. Risk is not related to HRT type, only to duration of use. The risk is increased by 2.3% per year of use. Risk is reduced to that of general population 5 years after discontinuing HRT. Mortality is not increased in breast cancer developing in women on HRT.

Side-effects commonly associated with HRT

- *Breast tenderness* usually subsides within 4–6 months of use. If troublesome, use lower oestrogen dose and increase gradually.
- *Mood changes* commonly associated with progestin therapy; manage by changing dose or preparation of progestin.
- *Irregular vaginal bleeding* may be a problem in women on a continuous combined preparation; usually subsides after 6–12 months of treatment. Spotting persists in 10% – may change to a cyclic preparation.

Table 59.2 Effects of HRT on IHD risk factors

Risk factor	Effect of HRT
Lipids	
HDL	↑
LDL	↓
Triglycerides	↑ (transdermal oestrogens have no effect on triglycerides)
Fasting glucose and insulin	↓ (postprandial levels are unchanged)
Fibrinogen	↓
Arterial blood pressure	Unchanged
Obesity	HRT does not cause weight gain
Endothelial function	Endothelial-dependent vasodilatation is enhanced, possibly by increasing nitric oxide production

Current recommendations for the institution of HRT in women for IHD prevention

- *women at high risk of IHD but no clinical disease*
  HRT recommended
- *women with a history of a coronary event*
  initiation of HRT probably not recommended, but may be continued in women already receiving it.

Table 59.3 Contraindications to HRT

Absolute	Relative – seek advice
Undiagnosed vaginal bleeding	Past history of endometrial cancer
Pregnancy	Family or past history of thromboembolism
Active DVT	Active liver disease
Active endometrial cancer	Hypertriglyceridaemia
Breast cancer	

- *Family history of breast cancer* Risk of breast cancer may be increased fourfold as a result of the family history, but there is little evidence that the risk is increased further by the use of HRT. May use HRT in these women if strong indications exist after explaining above risks.
- *Past history of breast cancer* Avoid HRT. If patient is very troubled with vasomotor symptoms and the breast cancer is cured with good prognostic factors, then short-term HRT may be considered as long as patient understands risks. Studies are underway looking at the use of HRT in women with history of breast cancer.
- *Benign breast disease* HRT does not increase the risk of breast cancer.

Venous thromboembolism

- *Low-risk women* Up to fourfold increased risk of deep vein thrombosis (DVT) in HRT users. Absolute risk remains small – 30/100 000 women.
- *Family history of DVT* Do thrombophilia screen. If positive, then avoid HRT. Women with a positive family history of thromboembolism are still at a slightly increased risk themselves even if the results of the thrombophilia screen are negative.
- *Past history of DVT/PE* Risk of recurrence is 5% per year so avoid HRT unless on long-term warfarin therapy.

Endometrial cancer

No increased risk in women taking combined oestrogen/progestin preparations. Women with cured stage I tumours may safely take HRT.

Gallstones

Risk of gallstones is increased twofold in HRT users.

Migraine

Migraines may increase in severity and frequency in HRT users. A trial of HRT is still worthwhile if indications are present. Modification in the dose of oestrogen or its preparation may improve symptoms. Avoid conjugated oestrogens as these are most commonly associated with an increase in the frequency of migraines.

Endometriosis and uterine fibroids

The risk of recurrence of endometriosis or of growth of uterine fibroids is low on HRT.

Liver disease

Use parenteral oestrogens to avoid hepatic metabolism and monitor liver function

Phytoestrogens

Phytoestrogens have not been shown to improve menopausal symptoms. Some data suggest a cardioprotective effect and protection against bone loss, although further work is required. The effect on breast cancer is unclear.

HRT regimens

Oestrogen preparations

In younger, symptomatic, often perimenopausal women, higher doses of oestrogen are often required initially, which can be reduced gradually to the recommended bone-conserving doses shown in Table 59.4.

Older women who have been amenorrhoeic for over a year often do not tolerate the introduction of the recommended dose of oestrogen. The lowest possible dose of oestrogen should therefore be used initially and the dose gradually built up over 6 months.

Route of administration

- *Oral route* is the most popular. Disadvantages:
  - first pass hepatic metabolism means that plasma oestrogen levels are variable, so symptoms do not always respond
  - may be associated with nausea and may exacerbate liver disease
  - must be taken daily so there is no breakthrough of symptoms
- *Transdermal patches* avoid first pass effect and are thus ideal in women with liver disease or hypertriglyceridaemia. Additionally, patches provide constant systemic hormone levels. However, 10% of women develop skin reactions. Try to avoid moisture and to rotate patch sites to prevent this.
- *Gels* have the advantages of patches but skin irritation is less common.
- *Subcutaneous implants* have the advantage of good compliance. However, if side-effects develop, implants are difficult to remove. Additionally, may release oestradiol for up to 3 years after insertion and cyclical progestagens must be given until oestrogen levels are not detectable.

Progestagen preparations

See Table 59.5 Must be added in non-hysterectomized women to avoid endometrial hyperplasia and subsequent carcinoma.

Sequential cyclical regimen

Give progestagen for a minimum of 10 days a month. Usually given for the first 12 days of each calendar month. Quarterly regimen available – progestagen given for 14 days four times a year. However, the risk of endometrial hyperplasia on such a regimen is unknown.

90% of women have a monthly withdrawal bleed. 10% may be amenorrhoeic with no harmful consequences. Bleeding should start after the 9th day of progestagen therapy.

Continuous combined regimen

Lower doses of progestagen are given on a daily basis. Uterine bleeding is usually light in amount but timing is unpredictable. Bleeding

Table 59.4 Oestrogen presparations

Preparation	Dose
Conjugated oestrogens (PO)	0.625–1.25 mg daily
Oestradiol valerate (PO)	2 mg daily
Oestradiol transdermal patch	100 μg twice a week. New patch twice a week
Oestradiol gel	1–1.5 mg daily
Oestradiol subcutaneous implant	25–100 mg every 4–8 months. Check serum E_2 prior to implant

Table 59.5 Dosage of progestagen presparations

Progestin	Cyclical dose (d1–12)	Continuous daily dose
Medroxyprogesterone acetate (least androgenic)	10 mg	2.5–5 mg (higher dose reduces bleeding)
Dydrogesterone	10 mg	Unknown
Norgestrel	150 μg	Unknown
Norethisterone (most androgenic)	0.7–1 mg	0.35–1 mg

Who and how to investigate for irregular uterine bleeding

- *Sequential cyclical HRT* 3 or more cycles of: bleeding before the 9th day of progestagen therapy or change in the duration or intensity of uterine bleeding.
- *Continuous combined HRT* In first 12 months if bleeding is heavy or extended, if it continues after 12 months of use, or if it starts after a period of amenorrhoea.
- *Endometrial assessment* Essential in women with irregular uterine bleeding. Vaginal ultrasound, looking at endometrial thickness, is a sensitive method of detecting endometrial disease. Endometrial thickness of <5 mm excludes disease in 96–99% of cases, a sensitivity similar to that of endometrial biopsy. However, specificity is poor so if the endometrium is >5 mm (as it will be in 50% of postmenopausal women on HRT) endometrial biopsy will be required to rule out carcinoma.

should stop in 90% of women within 12 months, the majority in 6 months.

Ideal for older women who do not want monthly withdrawal bleeds. Contraindicated in perimenopausal women, as irregular uterine bleeding is more likely and difficult to assess.

Tibolone (2.5 mg a day)

A synthetic steroid with mixed oestrogenic, progestogenic and weak androgenic activities. An alternative form of HRT which does not induce uterine bleeding. It is protective against osteoporosis but its effects on the cardiovascular system are unknown.

Androgen replacement therapy

- *Indications* Poor well-being and libido despite HRT. Studies suggest that low dose testosterone replacement therapy may enhance libido in addition to improving mood.
- *Mode of administration* Subcutaneous testosterone implants 50–100 mg every 6–8 months. No other androgen preparation currently available in the UK in doses suitable for women.
- *Side-effects and possible complications* Virilization has been reported in over a third of women. Adverse changes to lipid profile commonly occur.

Further reading

Greendale GA, Lee NP, Arriola ER. The menopause. *Lancet* 1999; 353: 571–580.

Johnson SR. The clinical decision regarding hormone replacement therapy. *Endocrinology and Metabolism Clinics of North America* 1997; 26(2): 413–434.

Prior JC. Perimenopause: the complex endocrinology of the menopausal transition. *Endocrine Reviews* 1998; 19(4): 397–428.

Chapter 60
Combined oral contraceptive pill

- *Ethinyl oestradiol (EE2)*
  - standard dose is 30 μg, but in older women or those with possible cardiovascular risk factors, 20 μg EE2 may be appropriate
  - 50 μg of EE2 may be indicated in patients on antiepileptic medication.
- *Progestagen* Commonly used oral contraceptive pills (OCPs) contain second-generation progestagens such as *levonorgestrel* (0.15–0.25 mg) and *norethisterone* (1 mg). OCPs containing third-generation progestagens (e.g. *gestodene* and *desogestrel*) are now less commonly used because of the increased risk of thromboembolism.

OCP side-effects

- low mood
- nausea
- fluid retention and weight gain
- breast tenderness and enlargement
- headache
- reduced libido
- chloasma

OCP preparation

- *1st generation*
  - Norynyl-1
  - Ovran
- *2nd generation*
  - Bi Novum
  - Brevinor
  - Cilest
  - Eugynon 30
  - Loestrin 20/30
  - Logynon
  - Microgynon 30/30 ED
  - Norimin
  - Ovran 30
  - Ovranette
  - Ovysmen
  - Synphase
  - Trinordiol
  - Tri Novum
- *3rd generation*
  - Femodene/ED
  - Femodette
  - Marvelon
  - Marvelon
  - Mercilon
  - Triadene
  - Tri Minulet

Risks

Venous thromboembolism

- The risk of venous thromboembolism in non-pregnant women (5 per 100 000 women/year) is increased threefold in women on the OCP, particularly in obese women.
- Women with a family history of thromboembolism should undergo a thrombophilia screen before starting the OCP.

Arterial thrombosis

- There is an increased risk of developing IHD in women over the age of 35 years who are on the OCP. The risk is further increased tenfold in smokers.
- The relative risk of ischaemic or haemorrhagic stroke is only slightly increased in women over the age of 35 years, but not in younger women.
- Risk of either arterial or venous thrombosis returns to normal within 3 months of discontinuing the OCP.

Hypertension

May be caused by the OCP, and if already present, may be more resistant to treatment.

Hepatic disease

Raised hepatic enzymes may be seen in women on the OCP.
The incidence of benign hepatic tumours is also increased.

Gallstones

The risk of developing gallstones is slightly increased by taking the OCP (RR = 1.2).

Breast cancer

- There is a slightly increased risk of breast cancer developing before the age of 36 years in women using the OCP (RR = 1.3), particularly in those who began taking the OCP in their teens.
- The risk does not seem to be related to the duration of exposure to the OCP nor to the EE2 dose.
- The relative risk of developing breast cancer returns to normal 10 years after discontinuing the OCP.

Thrombophilia screen

antithrombin III
protein C
protein S
factor V Leiden

Table 60.1 OCP contraindications

Absolute	Relative
History of heart disease – ischaemic or valvular	Migraine
Pulmonary hypertension	Sickle-cell disease
History of arterial or venous thrombosis	Gallstones
History of cerebrovascular disease	Inflammatory bowel disease
High risk of thrombosis, e.g. factor V Leiden, antiphospholipid antibodies	Hypertension
Liver disease	Hyperlipidaemia
Migraine if severe or associated with focal aura	Diabetes mellitus
Breast or genital tract cancer	Obesity
Pregnancy	Smokers
Presence of two or more relative contraindications	
Age over 35 years	Otosclerosis
	Family history of thrombosis
	Family history of breast cancer

Consider using a progesterone-only pill in women with contraindications to the combined OCP.

Practical issues

Age and the OCP

- Women with no risk factors for arterial or venous thrombosis may continue to use the combined OCP until the age of 50 years.
- Those with risk factors for thromboembolism and IHD should avoid the OCP after the age of 35 years.
- All women on the OCP after the age of 35 years should be on the lowest effective oestrogen dose (e.g. 20 μg EE2).
- Contraception after the menopause: assume fertile for the first year after last menstrual period if >50 years.

Breakthrough bleeding

Causes include:

- genital tract disease
- insufficient oestrogen dose
- inappropriate progestagen
- missed pill
- taking two packets continuously
- gastroenteritis
- drug interactions, e.g. antibiotics, hepatic enzyme inducers

Antibiotics and the OCP

Broad-spectrum antibiotics interfere with intestinal flora, thereby reducing bioavailability of the OCP. Additional methods of contraception should be used.

OCP and surgery

- Stop OCP at least 4 weeks before major surgery and any surgery to the legs. Do not restart until fully mobile for at least 2 weeks.
- If emergency surgery, then stop OCP and start antithrombotic prophylaxis.

Chapter 61

Testicular physiology

Anatomy

- Normal adult male testicular volume 15–30 ml.
- Testicular temperature 2°C lower than rest of body because of scrotal location. This is necessary for normal spermatogenesis.
- Two main units with differing functions:
  - *Interstitial cells* Comprised of Leydig cells which are found in between the seminiferous tubules and close to the blood vessels. Produce testosterone.
  - *Seminiferous tubules* Make up 90% of testicular volume. Spermatogenesis occurs here, in the presence of high intratesticular concentrations of testosterone. Made up of *germ cells* and *Sertoli cells.* Sertoli cells support spermatogenesis and secrete various hormones, including inhibin and in the embryo, Mullerian inhibitory factor. The former inhibits FSH secretion from the pituitary gland and the latter is responsible for suppressing female sex organ development during sexual differentiation *in utero.*

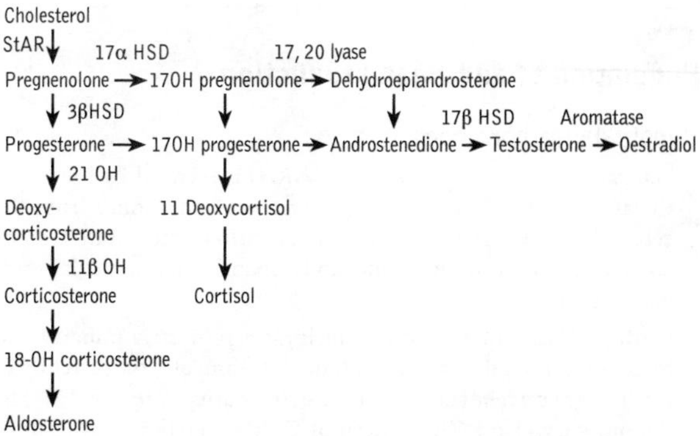

Fig. 61.1 Testosterone biosynthesis pathway. StAR, steroidogenic autoregulatory protein; 3βHSD, 3β-hydroxydehydrogenase; 21 OH, 21-hydroxylase; 17α OH, 17α-hydroxylase; 11β OH, 11β-hydroxylase.

Regulation of testicular function

Regulation of androgen production

Hypothalamic hormones

- *Gonadotropin releasing hormone (GnRH)* is secreted by the hypothalamus in a pulsatile manner in response to stimuli from the cerebral cortex and limbic system via various neurotransmitters, e.g. endorphins, catecholamines and dopamine and testicular feedback systems.
- GnRH release initially occurs during sleep in early puberty and then throughout the day in adulthood. It stimulates the secretion of *luteinizing hormone* (LH) and *follicle stimulating hormone* (FSH) by the pituitary gland. The pattern of GnRH secretion is crucial for normal gonadotrophin secretion. Faster pulse frequencies are essential for LH secretion whereas slower frequences favour FSH secretion. Continuous administration of GnRH abolishes both LH and FSH secretion.

Pituitary hormones

- LH binds to Leydig cell receptors and stimulates the synthesis and secretion of testosterone.
- FSH binds to Sertoli cell receptors and stimulates the production of seminiferous tubule fluid as well as a number of substances thought to be important for spermatogenesis.
- Their secretion is regulated by GnRH pulses and through negative feedback from testicular hormones and peptides.

Testis

- Testosterone is the main androgen produced by the Leydig cells of the testis. Small amounts of androstenedione, dehydroepiandrostenedione (DHEA), and dihydrotestosterone (DHT) are also produced. Testosterone has a circadian rhythm with maximum secretion at around 8 a.m. and minimum around 9 p.m.
- Small amounts of oestradiol are also produced in the testis, by the conversion from testosterone. However, most of the circulating oestradiol in males occurs as a result of aromatization of androgens in adipose tissue.
- FSH, in the presence of adequate testosterone levels, stimulates the secretion of inhibin by Sertoli cells. This in turn acts as a potent inhibitor of FSH secretion.

- The secretion of pituitary gonadotrophins is tightly regulated by testicular function. LH secretion is inhibited by testosterone and its metabolites whereas FSH secretion is controlled by both inhibin and testosterone. High concentrations of testosterone or of inhibin results in a negative feedback inhibition of FSH secretion (see Fig. 61.2).
- Testicular function is also under paracrine control. Inhibin and insulin-like growth factor-1 (IGF-1) act with LH to enhance testosterone production, whereas cytokines inhibit Leydig cell function.

Regulation of spermatogenesis

See Fig. 61.2.

- Both FSH and LH are required for the initiation of spermatogenesis at puberty. LH, by stimulating Leydig cell activity, plays an important part in the early phases of sperm production, when high intratesticular concentrations of testosterone are essential. FSH through its action on the Sertoli cells, is vital for sperm maturation.
- The whole process of spermatogenesis takes approximately 74 days, followed by another 12–21 days for sperm transport through the epididymis. This means that events which may affect spermatogenesis may not be apparent for up to 3 months.

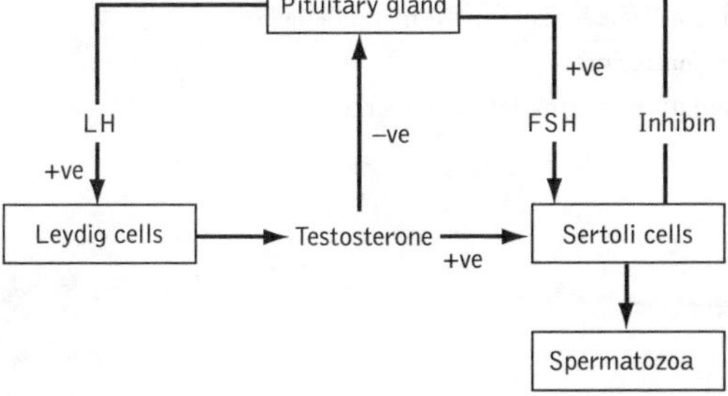

Fig. 61.2 Regulation of spematogenesis.

Physiology

Testosterone transport

- 2–4% of circulating testosterone is free and therefore biologically active. The rest is bound to proteins, particularly albumin and sex hormone binding globulin (SHBG).

Testosterone metabolism

- Testosterone is converted in target tissues to the more potent androgen DHT in the presence of the enzyme 5α reductase. There are multiple 5α-reductase isoenzymes; type 2 is the isoenzyme responsible for DHT synthesis in the genitalia, genital skin and hair follicles. It is therefore essential for normal male virilization and sexual development.
- Both testosterone and DHT exert their activity by binding to androgen receptors, the latter more avidly than testosterone. The androgen receptor is encoded by a gene found on the long arm of the X chromosome (Xq).
- Testosterone may alternatively be converted into oestradiol through the action of the aromatase enzyme, found in greatest quantities in adipose tissue.
- Testosterone and its metabolites are inactivated in the liver and excreted in the urine.

Androgen action

- male sexual differentiation during embryogenesis
- development and maintenance of male secondary sex characteristics after puberty
- normal male sexual function and behaviour
- spermatogenesis
- regulation of gonadotropin secretion.

Chapter 62
Male hypogonadism

Definition

Failure of testes to produce adequate amounts of testosterone, spermatozoa, or both.

Epidemiology

- Klinefelter's syndrome is the most common congenital cause and is thought to occur with an incidence of 1 : 500 live births.
- Acquired hypogonadism is even more common, affecting up to 20% of males.

Evaluation of male hypogonadism

Presentation

- failure to progress through puberty
- erectile dysfunction
- infertility.

The clinical presentation depends on:

- the age of onset (congenital vs acquired)
- the severity (complete vs partial)
- the duration (functional vs permanent).

Secondary hypogonadism

Definition

Hypogonadism as a result of hypothalamic or pituitary dysfunction.

Diagnosis

- low 9 a.m. serum testosterone
- normal/low LH and FSH.

Causes

Kallmann's syndrome

A genetic disorder characterized by failure of episodic GnRH secretion ± anosmia. Results from disordered migration of GnRH-producing neurons into the hypothalamus.

Epidemiology

- incidence of 1 in 10 000 males
- male : female ratio = 4 :1.

Diagnosis

- anosmia in 75%
- increased risk of cleft lip and palate, sensorineural deafness, cerebellar ataxia, and renal agenesis.
- low testosterone, LH, and FSH levels
- normal rest of pituitary function
- normal MRI pituitary gland and hypothalamus; absent olfactory bulbs may be seen on MRI
- normalization of pituitary and gonadal function in response to physiological GnRH replacement.

Genetics

- most commonly a result of an isolated gene mutation
- may be inherited in an X-linked, autosomal dominant, or recessive trait
- *KAL* gene defect responsible for some cases of Kallmann's syndrome is located on Xp22.3
- 12–15% incidence of delayed puberty in families of subjects with Kallmann's syndrome compared with 1% general population.

Causes of secondary hypogonadism

- Idiopathic
  - Kallmann's
  - idiopathic hypogonadotrophic hypogonadism (IHH)
  - fertile eunuch syndrome
  - congenital adrenal hypoplasia
- Functional
  - exercise
  - weight changes
  - anabolic steroids
  - stress – physical/psychological
  - systemic illness
  - medication and recreational drugs
  - infiltrative disorders, e.g. sarcoidosis, haemochromatosis
  - head trauma
  - radiotherapy
  - surgery to the pituitary gland or hypothalamus
- Miscellaneous
  - haemochromatosis
  - Prader–Willi syndrome (p. 431)
  - Laurence–Moon–Biedl syndrome (p. 431)

Management

- androgen replacement therapy.
- when fertility is desired, testosterone is stopped and exogenous gonadotropins are administered (see p. 477).

Idiopathic hypogonadotrophic hypogonadism (IHH)

- Congenital form is indistinguishable from Kallmann's syndrome apart from the absence of anosmia. Over 90% of patients are male.
- GnRH receptor gene mutation is an uncommon cause of IHH.
- Men with acquired IHH may go through normal puberty and have normal testicular size, but present with infertility or poor libido and potency. May be temporary, with normalization of gonadal function after stopping GnRH or testosterone therapy.

Fertile eunuch syndrome

- Incomplete GnRH deficiency. Enough to maintain normal spermatogenesis and testicular growth but insufficient for adequate virilization.
- May require testosterone/hCG for fertility.

Congenital adrenal hypoplasia

- Rare X-linked or autosomal recessive disease caused by a mutation of the *DAX* gene, which is located on the X chromosome.
- Presents with primary adrenal failure in infancy.
- Hypothalamic hypogonadism is also present.

Structural

- Usually associated with other pituitary hormonal deficiencies.
- In children, craniopharyngiomas are the most common cause. Cranial irradiation for leukaemia or brain tumours may also result in secondary hypogonadism.
- The commonest lesions in adulthood are prolactinomas.

Systemic illness

- Severe illness of any kind may cause hypogonadotropic hypogonadism (see table).

Drugs

- Anabolic steroids, cocaine and narcotic drugs may all result in secondary hypogonadism
- All drugs causing hyperprolactinaemia (see p. 137) will also cause hypogonadism.

Systemic illness resulting in hypogonadism

- Secondary hypogonadism
  - any acute illness (e.g. myocardial infarction, sepsis, head injury)
  - severe stress
  - haemochromatosis
  - endocrine disease (Cushing's syndrome, hyperprolactinaemia)
- Primary hypogonadism
  - liver cirrhosis
  - chronic renal failure
  - chronic anaemia (thalassaemia major, sickle cell disease)
  - gastrointestinal disease (coeliac disease, Crohn's disease)
  - AIDS
  - rheumatological disease (rheumatoid arthritis)
  - respiratory disease (e.g. chronic obstructive airways disease, cystic fibrosis)
  - cardiac disease (e.g. congestive cardiac failure)

Prader–Willi syndrome

- A congenital syndrome caused by deletion of part of paternally derived chromosome 15q which is characterized by severe obesity, mental retardation, and hypogonadotropic hypogonadism.

Laurence–Moon–Biedl syndrome

- Congenital syndrome characterized by severe obesity, gonadotropin deficiency, retinitis pigmentosa, polydactyly, and mental retardation.

Primary hypogonadism

Due to testicular failure

Diagnosis

- low 9 a.m. serum testosterone
- elevated LH and FSH.

Causes

Genetic

Klinefelter's syndrome

The most common congenital form of primary hypogonadism, affecting approximately 1 : 500 men.

- Clinical manifestations
  - reduced testicular volume
  - gynaecomastia
  - eunuchoidism
  - intellectual dysfunction in 40%
  - NB 20 times increased risk of breast carcinoma.
- Diagnosis
  - karyotyping – 47,XXY or 46,XY/47,XXY mosaicism
  - low testosterone, elevated LH and FSH
  - elevated SHBG and oestradiol
  - azoospermia.
- Management
  - androgen replacement
  - NB Unlikely to normalize gonadotrophins.

Other chromosomal disorders

XX males

- Due to an X to Y translocation with only a part of the Y present in one of the X chromosomes.
- Incidence 1 : 10 000 births.
- Similar clinical and biochemical features to Klinefelter's syndrome. In addition, short stature and hypospadias may be present.

XX/X0 (mixed gonadal dysgenesis)

- Occasionally phenotypically male with hypospadias and intra-abdominal dysgenetic gonads.
- Bilateral gonadectomy is essential because of the risk of neoplasia, followed by androgen replacement therapy.

XYY syndrome

- Taller than average, but often have primary gonadal failure with impaired spermatogenesis.

Y chromosome deletions

- Causes oligo/azoospermia. Testosterone levels are not usually affected.

Noonan's syndrome

- 46,XY karyotype and male external genitalia. However, several stigmata of Turner's syndrome (short stature, webbed neck, ptosis, low set ears, lymphoedema) and increased risk of right-sided cardiac anomalies. Most have cryptorchidism and primary testicular failure.

Cryptorchidism

- 10% of male neonates have undescended testes, but most of these will descend into the scrotum eventually, so that the incidence of postpubertal cryptorchidism is less than 0.5%.
- 15% of cases have bilateral cryptorchidism.

Consequences

- 75% of males with bilateral cryptorchidism are infertile.
- 10% risk of testicular malignancy, highest risk in those with intra-abdominal testes.
- Low testosterone and raised gonadotropins in bilateral cryptorchidism.

Treatment

- *Orchidopexy* Best performed before 18 months, certainly before age 5 years.
- *Gonadectomy* In patients with intra-abdominal testes, followed by androgen replacement.

Orchitis

- 25% of males who develop mumps after puberty have associated orchitis and 25–50% of these will develop primary testicular failure.
- HIV infection may also be associated with orchitis.
- Primary testicular failure may occur as part of an autoimmune disease.

Chemotherapy and radiotherapy

- Cytotoxic drugs, particularly alkylating agents, are gonadotoxic. Infertility occurs in 50% of patients following chemotherapy for most malignancies, and a significant number of men require androgen replacement therapy because of low testosterone levels.
- The testes are radiosensitive so hypogonadism can occur as a result of scattered radiation during the treatment of Hodgkin's dosease, for example.
- If fertility is desired, sperm should be cryopreserved prior to cancer therapy.

Other drugs

- Sulfasalazine, colchicine and statins may all affect testicular function.
- Alcohol excess will also cause primary testicular failure.

Chronic illness

- Any chronic illness may affect testicular function, in particular chronic renal failure, liver cirrhosis, and haemochromatosis.

Varicocoele

- A debatable cause of primary hypogonadism.

Testicular trauma

- Testicular torsion is another common cause of loss of a testis, and it may also affect the function of the remaining testis.

Testicular dysfunction: clinical characteristics of male hypogonadism

Testicular failure occurring before onset of puberty

- testicular volume <5 ml
- penis <5 cm long
- lack of scrotal pigmentation and rugae
- gynaecomastia
- high-pitched voice
- central fat distribution
- eunuchoidism:
  - arm span 1 cm greater than height
  - lower segment > upper segment
- delayed bone age
- no male escutcheon
- decreased body and facial hair.

Testicular failure occurring after puberty

- testes soft, volume <15 ml
- normal penile length
- normal skeletal proportions
- gynaecomastia
- normal male hair distribution but reduced amount
- osteoporosis.

Clinical assessment

History

- *Developmental history* congenital urinary tract abnormalities, e.g. hypospadias, late testicular descent or cryptorchidism
- *Delayed or incomplete puberty*
- *Infections* e.g. mumps, orchitis
- *Abdominal/genital trauma*
- *Testicular torsion*
- *Anosmia*
- *Drug history* e.g. sulfasalazine, antihypertensives, chemotherapy, cimetidine, radiotherapy; alcohol and recreational drugs also important.
- *General medical history* Chronic illness, particularly respiratory, neurological and cardiac.
- *Gynaecomastia* Common (see p. 446) during adolescence. Recent onset gynaecomastia in adulthood – must rule out oestrogen-producing tumour.
- *Family history* Young's syndrome (p. 472), cystic fibrosis, Kallman's syndrome.
- *Sexual history* Erectile function, frequency of intercourse, sexual techniques. Absence of morning erections suggests an organic cause of erectile dysfunction.

Physical examination

- body hair distribution
- muscle mass and fat distribution
- eunuchoidism
- gynaecomastia
- genital examination:
  - *pubic hair* normal male escutcheon
  - *phallus* normal >5 cm length and >3 cm width
  - *testes* size and consistency (normal >15 ml and firm)
    - look for nodules or areas of tenderness
- general examination
  - look for evidence of systemic disease
  - assess sense of smell and visual fields.

Hormonal evaluation of testicular function

Serum testosterone

Diurnal variation in circulating testosterone, peak levels occurring in the early morning. 30% variation between highest and lowest testosterone levels, so 9 a.m. plasma testosterone essential. If level is low, this should be repeated.

Sex hormone binding globulin (SHBG)

- Only 2–4% of circulating testosterone is unbound. 50% is bound to SHBG and the rest to albumin.
- Concentrations of SHBG should be taken into account when interpreting a serum testosterone result. SHBG levels may be affected by a variety of conditions (see table 62.1).

Gonadotrophins

Raised FSH and LH in primary testicular failure and inappropriately low in pituitary or hypothalamic hypogonadism. Should always exclude hyperprolactinaemia in secondary hypogonadism.

Oestradiol

Results from the conversion of testosterone and androstenedione by aromatase. See table 62.2 for causes of an elevated oestradiol. Request serum oestradiol level if gynaecomastia is present or a testicular tumour is suspected.

hCG stimulation test

- Diagnostic test for examining Leydig cell function.
- hCG 2000 iu i/m given on days 0 and 2; testosterone measured on days 0,2, and 4.
- In prepubertal boys with absent scrotal testes, a response to hCG indicates intra-abdominal testes. Failure of testosterone to rise after hCG suggests absence of functioning testicular tissue. An exagerated response to hCG is seen in secondary hypogonadism.

Clomiphene stimulation test

- Used to assess the integrity of the hypothalamo–pituitary testicular axis.
- A normal response to 3 mg/kg (max 200 mg) clomiphene daily for 7 days is a twofold increase in LH and FSH measured on days 0,4,7, and 10.
- Subnormal response indicates hypothalamic or pituitary hypogonadism but does not differentiate between the two.

Table 62.1 Factors affecting SHBG concentrations

Raised SHBG	Low SHBG
Androgen deficiency	Hyperinsulinaemia
GH deficiency	Obesity
Ageing	Acromegaly
Thyrotoxicosis	Androgen treatment
Oestrogens	Hypothyroidism
Liver cirrhosis	Cushing's syndrome/glucocorticoid therapy
	Nephrotic syndrome

Table 62.2 Causes of raised oestogens in men

Neoplasia testicular adrenal hepatoma
Primary testicular failure
Liver disease
Thyrotoxicosis
Obesity
Androgen resistance syndromes
Antiandrogen therapy.

Chapter 63
Androgen replacement therapy

Treatment aims

- *Improve libido and sexual function* Testosterone replacement therapy will induce virilization in the hypogonadal male and restores libido and erectile function.
- *Improve mood and well-being* Most studies show an improvement in mood and well-being following testosterone replacement therapy.
- *Improve muscle mass and strength* Testosterone has direct anabolic effects on skeletal muscle and has been shown to increase muscle mass and strength when given to hypogonadal men. Lean body mass is also increased with a reduction in fat mass.
- *Prevent osteoporosis* Hypogonadism is a risk factor for osteoporosis. Testosterone inhibits bone resorption, thereby reducing bone turnover. Its administration to hypogonadal men has been shown to improve bone mineral density and reduce the risk of developing osteoporosis.
- NB *Fertility* is not restored by androgen replacement therapy. Men with secondary hypogonadism who desire fertility may be treated with gonadotropins to initiate and maintain spermatogenesis (see p. 477). Prior testosterone therapy will not affect fertility prospects but should be stopped before initiating gonadotropin treatment. Men with primary hypogonadism will not respond to gonadotropin or GnRH therapy.

Indications for treatment

Male hypogonadism of any cause

Table 63.1 Contraindications to andogen replacement therapy

Absolute	Relative
Prostate cancer	Benign prostate hyperplasia
Breast cancer	Polycythaemia
	Sleep apnoea

Pretreatment evaluation

Clinical evaluation

History or symptoms of:

- prostatic hypertrophy
- breast or prostate cancer
- cardiovascular disease
- sleep apnoea.

Examination

- rectal examination of prostate
- breasts

Laboratory evaluation

- prostatic specific antigen (PSA) (NB PSA is often low in hypogonadal men, rising to normal age-matched levels with androgen replacement.)
- haemoglobin and haematocrit
- serum lipids

Monitoring of therapy

3 months after initiating therapy and then 6–12 monthly:

- clinical evaluation
- serum testosterone
- rectal examination of the prostate
- PSA (if>45 years)
- haemoglobin and haematocrit
- serum lipids.

Risks and side-effects

Prostatic disease

- Androgens stimulate prostatic growth, and testosterone replacement therapy may therefore induce symptoms of bladder outflow obstruction in men with prostatic hypertrophy.
- It is unlikely that testosterone increases the risk of developing prostate cancer but it may promote the growth of an existing cancer.

Polycythaemia

- Testosterone stimulates erythropoiesis. Androgen replacement therapy may increase haemoglobin levels, particularly in older men. It may be necessary to reduce the dose of testosterone in men with clinically significant polycythaemia.

Cardiovascular disease

- Testosterone replacement therapy may cause a fall in both LDL and HDL cholesterol levels, the significance of which remains unclear. The effect of androgen replacement therapy on the risk of developing coronary heart disease is unknown.

Other

- *Acne*
- *Gynaecomastia* is occasionally enhanced by testosterone therapy, particularly in peripubertal boys. This is the result of the conversion of testosterone to oestrogens.
- *Fluid retention* may result in worsening symptoms in those with underlying congestive cardiac failure or hepatic cirrhosis.
- *Obstructive sleep apnoea* may be exacerbated by testosterone therapy.
- *Hepatotoxicity* may be induced by oral androgens, particularly the 17α alkylated testosterones.
- *Mood swings.*

Further reading

Matsumoto AM. Hormonal therapy of male hypogonadism. *Endocrinology and Metabolism Clinics of North America* 1994; 23(4): 857–874.

Tenover JL. Male hormone replacement therapy. *Endocrinology and Metabolism Clinics of North America* 1998; 27(4):969–987.

Table 63.2 Testosterone preparations

Preparation	Dose	Advantage	Problems
Intramuscular testosterone esters	250 mg every 2–3 weeks Monitor pre-dose serum testosterone (should be above the lower limit of normal)	2–3 weekly dosage Effective	I/m injection Wide variations in serum testosterone levels between injections which may be associated with symptoms
Testosterone implants	200–600 mg every 3–6 months Monitor predose serum testosterone	Physiological testosterone levels achieved 3–6 monthly dosing	Minor surgical procedure Risk of infection and pellet extrusion Must remove pellet surgically if complications develop
Transdermal non-scrotal	2.5–7.5 mg daily Monitor testosterone 8 hours after application	Physiological testosterone levels achieved	Skin reactions common
Oral, e.g. testosterone undecanoate and mesterolone (analogue of DHT)	40 mg 3x daily 25 mg 3x daily	Oral preparation	Highly variable efficacy and bioavailability Rarely achieves therapeutic efficacy Multiple daily dosing 17α-alkylated testosterones are not used because of the risk of hepatotoxicity
Transdermal scrotal	4–6 mg daily	Physiological testosterone levels achieved	Supraphysiological levels of DHT may be associated with BPH Unacceptibility of wearing scrotal patch Testosterone levels depend on skin preparation

Chapter 64
Gynaecomastia

Definition

Enlargement of the male breast as a result of hyperplasia of the glandular tissue to a diameter of >2 cm. Common, present in up to 1/3 of men <30 years and in up to 50% of men >45 years.

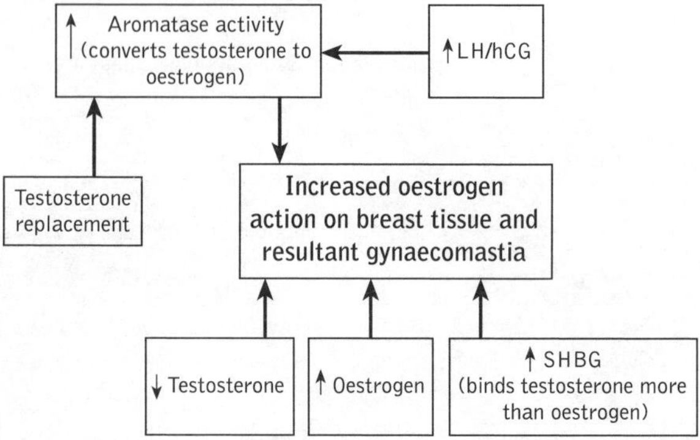

Fig. 64.1 Hormonal influences on gynaecomastia.

Table 64.1 Causes of gynaecomastia

Physiological	Neonatal
	Puberty
	Familial
	Idiopathic
Drugs[a]	Oestrogens, anti-androgens, testosterone
	Spironolactone, ACE inhibitors, calcium antagonists, digoxin
	Alkylating agents
	Alcohol, marijuana, heroin, methadone
	Cimetidine
	Ketoconazole, metronidazole, antituberculous agents
	Tricyclic antidepressants, dopamine antagonists, opiates, benzodiazepines
Hypogonadism	Primary (p. 432)
	Secondary (p. 428)
Tumours	Oestrogen- or androgen-producing testicular or adrenal tumours
	hCG-producing tumours, usually testicular, e.g. germinoma; occasionally ectopic, e.g. lung
	Aromatase-producing testicular tumours
Endocrine	Thyrotoxicosis
	Cushing's syndrome
	Acromegaly
	Androgen insensitivity syndromes
Systemic illness	Liver cirrhosis
	Chronic renal failure
	HIV infection
Other	Chest wall trauma
	Herpes zoster of the chest wall
	Obesity

[a] Possible mechanisms: oestrogen containing, androgen receptor blockers, inhibiting androgen production.

Evaluation

History

- Duration and progression of gynaecomastia.
- Further investigation warranted if:
  - rapidly enlarging gynaecomastia
  - recent onset gynaecomastia in a lean postpubertal man
  - painful gynaecomastia.
- *Exclude underlying tumour*, e.g. testicular cancer.

Symptoms of hypogonadism reduced libido, erectile dysfunction, infertility.

Symptoms of systemic disease e.g. hepatic, renal, and endocrine disease.

Drug history including recreational drugs, e.g. alcohol.

Physical examination

- *Breasts*:
  - Pinch breast tissue between thumb and forefinger – distinguish from fat.
  - Measure glandular tissue diameter. Gynaecomastia if >2 cm.
  - If >5 cm, hard, or irregular, investigate further.
  - Look for galactorrhoea.
- *Testicular palpation:*
  - exclude tumour
  - assess testicular size – ?atrophy.
- *Secondary sex characteristics*
- Look for evidence of *systemic disease* e.g. chronic liver or renal disease, thyrotoxicosis, Cushing's syndrome, chronic cardiac or pulmonary disease

Investigations

Baseline investigations

- serum testosterone
- serum oestradiol
- LH and FSH
- prolactin
- SHBG
- hCG
- liver function tests

Additional investigations

- If testicular tumour is suspected, e.g. raised oestradiol/hCG: testicular ultrasound
- If adrenal tumour is suspected, e.g. markedly raised oestradiol: dehydroepiandrosterone sulfate; abdominal CT or MRI scan.
- If breast malignancy is suspected: mammography; FNAC/tissue biopsy
- If lung cancer is suspected, e.g. raised hCG: chest radiograph

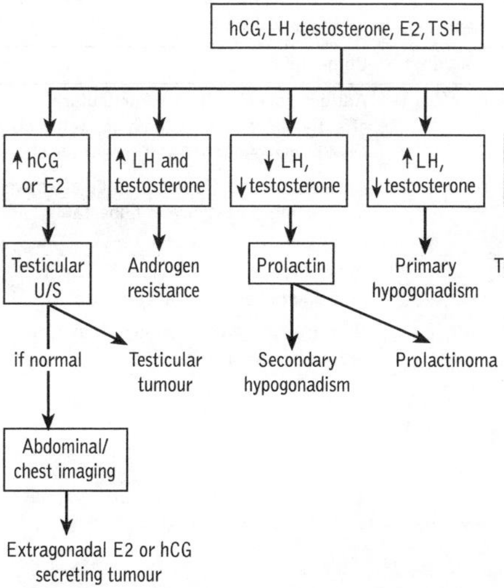

Fig. 64.2 Investigation of gynaecomastia.

Management

- Treat underlying disorder when present. Withdraw offending drugs where possible.
- Reassurance in the majority of idiopathic cases. Often resolves spontaneously.
- Treatment may be required for cosmetic reasons or to alleviate pain.
- Drug treatment rarely effective

Medical

See Table 64.2.

Surgical

Reduction mammoplasty may be required in men with severe and persistent gynaecomastia.

Table 64.2 Medical treatment of gynaecomastia

Drug	Dose (mg/day)	Comments
Tamoxifen	10–30	Antioestrogenic effects. Particularly effective in reducing pain and swelling if used in gynaecomastia of recent onset
Clomiphene	50–100	Antioestrogenic. Reported to be effective in reducing breast size in pubertal gynaecomastia
Testolactone	450	Aromatase inhibitor. Also effective in reducing pubertal gynaecomastia
Danazol	300–600	Non-aromatizable androgen. May also reduce breast size in adults

Chapter 65
Erectile dysfunction

Definition

The consistent inability to acheive or maintain an erect penis sufficient for satisfactory sexual intercourse. Common, present in approximately 10% of males and in >50% of men >70 years.

Physiology of male sexual function

- The erectile response is the result of the coordinated interaction of nerves, smooth muscle of the corpora cavernosa, pelvic muscles and blood vessels.
- It is initiated by psychogenic stimuli from the brain or physical stimulation of the genitalia, which are modulated in the limbic system, transmitted down the spinal cord to the sympathetic and parasympathetic outflows of the penile tissue.
- Penile erectile tissue consists of paired corpora cavernosa on the dorsum of the penis and the corpus spongiosum. These are surrounded by fibrous tissue known as the tunica albuginea.
- In the flaccid state, the corporeal smooth muscle is contracted, minimizing corporeal blood flow and enhancing venous drainage.
- Activation of the erectile pathway results in penile smooth muscle relaxation and cavernosal arterial vasodilatation. As the corporeal sinuses fill with blood, the draining venules are compressed against the tunica albuginea so venous outflow is impaired. This results in penile rigidity and an erection.
- Corporeal vasodilatation is mediated by parasympathetic neuronal activation, which induces nitric oxide release by the cavernosal nerves. This activates guanyl cyclase, thereby increasing cGMP, and causing smooth muscle relaxation.
- Detumescence occurs after the inactivation of cGMP by the enzyme phosphodiesterase, resulting in smooth muscle contraction and vasoconstriction.
- Ejaculation is mediated by the sympathetic nervous system.

Pathophysiology

Erectile dysfunction may thus occur as a result of several mechanisms:

- neurological damage
- arterial insufficiency
- venous incompetence
- androgen deficiency
- penile abnormalities.

Evaluation

History

Sexual history

- Extent of the dysfunction, its duration and progression.
- Presence of nocturnal or morning erections.
- Abrupt onset of erectile dysfunction which is intermittent is often psychogenic in origin.
- Progressive and persistent dysfunction indicates an organic cause.

Symptoms of hypogonadism

- Reduced libido, muscle strength and sense of well-being

Full medical history

- E.g. diabetes mellitus, liver cirrhosis, neurological, cardiovascular or endocrine disease.
- Intermittent claudication suggests a vascular cause.
- A history of genitourinary trauma or surgery is also important.
- Recent change in bladder or bowel function may indicate neurological cause.
- Psychological history.

Drug history

- Onset of impotence in relation to commencing a new medication

Social history

- Stress
- Relationship history
- Recreational drugs including alcohol.

Physical examination

- Evidence of primary or secondary hypogonadism
- Evidence of endocrine disorders
  - hyperprolactinaemia, thyroid dysfunction, hypopituitarism
  - other complications of diabetes mellitus, if present

Table 65.1 Causes of erectile dysfunction

Psychological (20%)	Stress, anxiety
	Psychiatric illness
Drugs (25%)	Alcohol
	Antihypertensives, e.g.diuretics, ß-blockers, methyldopa
	Cimetidine
	Marijuana, heroin, methadone
	Major tranquillizers
	Tricyclic antidepressants, benzodiazepines
	Digoxin
	Glucocorticoids, anabolic steroids
	Oestrogens, antiandrogens
Endocrine (20%)	Hypogonadism (primary or secondary)
	Hyperprolactinaemia
	Diabetes mellitus (30–50% of men with DM >6 years)
	Thyroid dysfunction
Neurological	Spinal cord disorders
	Peripheral and autonomic neuropathies
	Multiple sclerosis
Vascular	Peripheral vascular disease
	Trauma
	Diabetes mellitus
	Venous incompetence
Other	Haemochromatosis
	Debilitating diseases
	Penile abnormalities, e.g. priapism, Peyronie's disease
	Prostatectomy

- Evidence of neurological disease
  - autonomic or peripheral neuropathy
  - spinal cord lesions
- Evidence of systemic disease, e.g.:
  - chronic liver disease
  - chronic cardiac disease
  - peripheral vascular disease
- Genital examination
  - assess testicular size – ?atrophy
  - penile abnormalities, e.g. Peyronie's disease.

Investigation of erectile dysfunction

Baseline investigations

- serum testosterone
- prolactin
- fasting blood glucose
- LH and FSH
- thyroid function tests
- liver function tests
- renal function
- serum lipids
- serum ferritin.

Additional investigations

Rarely required. To assess vascular causes of impotence if corrective surgery is contemplated:

- *Intracavernosal injection* of a vasodilator, e.g. prostaglandin E1 or papaverine. A sustained erection excludes significant vascular insufficiency.
- *Penile doppler ultrasonography* Cavernous arterial flow and venous insufficiency are assessed.

Management

Treat underlying disorder or withdraw offending drugs where possible.

Medical

Androgens

This should be first line therapy in men with hypogonadism (see page 440). Hyperprolactinaemia, when present, should be treated with dopamine agonists and the underlying cause of hypogonadism treated.

Sildenafil (see table 65.2)

Oral phosphodiesterase inhibitor. Acts by enhancing cGMP activity in erectile tissue, thereby amplifying the vasodilatory action of nitric oxide and thus the normal erectile response to sexual stimulation. Only effective following sexual arousal.

- Trials indicate a 70–80% success rate.
- *Dose* 50–100 mg 1 h before sexual activity and no more than once a day. In elderly men and those with renal or hepatic impairment, use 25 mg.

Intracavernous injection

- 70–100% success rate, highest in men with non-vasculogenic impotence.
- Prostaglandin E1 is a potent vasodilator. The dose should be titrated in 1 μg increments until the desired effect is achieved in order to minimize side-effects.
- Papaverine, a phosphodiesterase inhibitor, induces cavernosal vasodilatation and penile rigidity but causes more side-effects.
- *Side-effects*
  - Priapism in 1–5%. Patients must seek urgent medical advice if an erection lasts >4 h.
  - Fibrosis in the injection site in up to 5% of patients. Minimize risk by alternating sides of the penis for injection and injecting a maximum of twice a week.
  - Infection at injection site is rare.
- *Contraindication* Sickle cell disease
- *Injection technique* Avoid the midline so as to avoid urethral and neurovascular damage. Clean the injection site, hold the penis under slight tension and introduce the needle at 90°. Inject after the

Table 65.2 Sildenafil (Viagra), 50 mg

Selective inhibitor of phosphodiesterase type 5	
→ prolonged cyclic GMP activity	
↑ vasodilatory actions of NO on cavernosal smooth muscle	
Contraindications	Recent MI/stroke
	Unstable angina
	Current nitrate use, including isosorbide mononitrate/GTN
	Hypotension (<90/60 mmHg)
	Severe heart failure
	Severe hepatic impairment
	Retinitis pigmentosa
Caution	Hypertension
	Heart disease
	Peyronie's disease
	Sickle cell anaemia
	Leukaemia
	Multiple myeloma
	Bleeding disorders, e.g. active peptic ulcer disease
Ketoconazole HIV protease inhibitors	Indinavir, nelfinavir, saquinavir – start with 25 mg sildenafil (inhibit cytochrome enzyme to give ↑ levels)
Adverse effects	Headaches (16%)
	Facial flushing (19%)
	Dyspepsia (7%)
	Nasal congestion
	Prolonged erection and priapism
	Eye disorders – temporary loss of vision, ↑ ocular pressure, green/blue vision, photosensitivity, blurred vision
	MI
	Ventricular arrhythmia
	Sudden death – mostly in men with pre-existing cardiovascular risk factors

characteristic 'give' of piercing the fibrous capsule. Apply pressure to injection site after removing the needle to prevent bruising.

Vacuum device

- Results are good, with 90% of men achieving a satisfactory erection. The flaccid penis is put into the device and air is withdrawn, creating a vacuum which then allows blood to flow into the penis. A constriction band is then placed on to the base of the penis so that the erection is maintained. This should be removed within 30 min.
- *Side-effects* pain, haematoma.

Penile prosthesis

- Is usually tried in men either reluctant to try other forms of therapy or when other treatments have failed. They may be semi-rigid or inflatable.
- *Complications* infection, mechanical failure.

Psychosexual counselling

- Particularly for men with psychogenic impotence and in men who fail to improve with the above therapies.

Surgical

- Rarely indicated as results are generally disappointing.
- Revascularization techniques may be available in specialist centres.
- Ligation of dorsal veins may restore erectile function temporarily in men with venous insufficiency, although rarely permanently.

Further reading

Cohan P and Korenman SG (2001). Erectile dysfunction. *Journal of Clinical Endocrinology and Metabolism* 86: 2391–2394.

Korenman SG (1998) Sexual function and dysfunction. In Wilson JD, Foster DW, Kronenberg HM, Larson PR (ed.), *William's Textbook of Endocrinology*, 9th edn, pp. 927–938. WB Saunders, Philadelphia.

Sildenafil for erectile dysfunction. *Drugs and Therapeutics Bulletin* 1998; 36(11): 81–83.

Chapter 66
Testicular tumours

Epidemiology

Incidence rising. Currently 6/100 000 men per year.

Risk factors

- cryptorchidism
- gonadal dysgenesis
- infertility/reduced spermatogenesis.

Table 66.1 Classification of testicular tumours

Tumours		Tumour markers
Germ cell tumours (95%)	Seminoma	None
	Non-seminoma	hCG, α-fetoprotein, CEA
	Mixed	
Stromal tumours (2%)	Leydig cell	
	Sertoli cell	
Gonadoblastoma (2%)		
Other (1%)	Lymphoma	
	Carcinoid	

Prognosis

Seminomas

- 95% cure for early disease. 80% cure for stages II/IV.
- Increased incidence of second tumours and leukaemias 20 years after therapy.

Non-seminoma germ cell tumours

- 90% cure in early disease, falling to 60% in metastatic disease.
- Increased incidence of second tumours and leukaemias 20 years after therapy.

Stromal tumours

- Excellent prognosis for benign tumours.
- Malignant tumours are aggressive and are poorly responsive to treatment.

Further reading

Griffin JE, Wilson JD (1998) Disorders of the testes and male reproductive tract. In Wilson JD, Foster DW, Kronenberg HM, Larson PR (ed.), *William's Textbook of Endocrinology*, 9th edn, pp. 819–876. WB Saunders, Philadelphia.

Matsumoto AM (1992) The testis and male sexual function. In Wyngaarden JB, Smith LH, Bennett JC (ed.) *Cecil's Textbook of Medicine*, 19th edn., pp. 1333–1350. WB Saunders, Philadelphia.

Chapter 67
Infertility

Definition

Infertility is defined as failure of pregnancy after 1 year of unprotected regular (2× week) sexual intercourse. It affects 10–15% of all couples.

Causes

- female factors (eg PCOS, tubal damage) 35%
- male factors (idiopathic gonadal failure in 60%) 30%
- combined factors 20%
- unexplained infertility 15%.

Causes of female infertility

- Anovulation
  - PCOS
  - secondary hypogonadism
  - hyperprolactinaemia
  - hypothalamic disease
  - pituitary disease
  - systemic illness
  - drugs, e.g. anabolic steroids
  - POF
- Tubal disorders
  - infective, e.g. chlamydia
  - endometriosis
  - surgery
- Cervical mucus defects
  - Autoimmune
- Uterine abnormalities
  - congenital
  - intrauterine adhesions
  - uterine fibroids.

Causes of male infertility

- Primary gonadal failure
  - genetic Klinefelter's syndrome, Y chromosome deletions, others, e.g. immotile cilia, cystic fibrosis
  - congenital cryptorchidism
  - orchitis
  - torsion or trauma
  - chemotherapy and radiotherapy
  - other toxins, e.g. alcohol, anabolic steroids
  - varicocoele
  - idiopathic
- Secondary gonadal failure
  - Kallman's syndrome (p. 428)
  - IHH
  - structural hypothalamic/pituitary disease
- Genital tract abnormalities
  - obstructive congenital, infective, postsurgical
  - sperm autoimmunity
- Erectile dysfunction
- drugs e.g. spironolactone, corticosteroids, sulfasalazine
- systemic disease e.g. cystic fibrosis, Crohn's disease, and other chronic debilitating diseases.

Evaluation

Sexual history

- *Frequency of intercourse* Infrequent intercourse may reduce sperm quality.
- *Timing of intercourse* Ideal timing is 1–2 days before or after ovulation.
- *Use of lubricants* Should be avoided because of the detrimental effect on semen quality.

Female factors

History

- *Age* Fertility declines rapidly after the age of 36 years.
- *Menstrual history*
  - age at menarche
  - length of menstrual cycle and its predictability (e.g. oligo/amenorrhoea)
  - presence or absence of intermenstrual spotting.
- *Hot flushes* may be indicative of oestrogen deficiency.
- *Spontaneous galactorrhoea* may be caused by hyperprolactinaemia
- *Hypothalamic hypogonadism* suggested by excessive physical exercise (e.g. running >4 miles/day) or weight loss in excess of 10% in 1 year.
- *Drug history*
  - drugs which may cause hyperprolactinaemia (see p. 137), including cocaine and marijuana
  - the use of anabolic steroids may cause secondary hypogonadism
  - cytotoxic chemotherapy or radiotherapy may cause ovarian failure.
- *Medical history* diabetes mellitus, thyroid or pituitary dysfunction, and other systemic illnesses.
- Exclude *tubal disease*
  - recurrent vaginal or urinary tract infections may predispose to pelvic inflammatory disease (PID)
  - dyspareunia and dysmenorrhoea are often present
  - sexually transmitted disease and previous abdominal or gynaecological surgery all predispose to fallopian tube obstruction.

- *Secondary infertility* Details of previous pregnancies including abortions (spontaneous and therapeutic) and ectopic pregnancies should be ascertained.

Physical examination

- *Body mass index* (BMI) The ideal BMI for fertility is 19–24.
- *Secondary sexual characteristics* If absent, look for evidence of Turner's syndrome.
- *Hyperandrogenism* PCOS
- *Galactorrhoea* hyperprolactinaemia
- *External genitalia and pelvic examination.*

Investigations

See Fig. 67.1.

- *Assess ovulatory function*
  - In women with regular menstrual cycles – basal body temperature chart for 2–3 months. A sustained 0.5°C rise in body temperature in the luteal phase (latter half of the menstrual cycle) suggests ovulation. A midluteal (day 21) progesterone (day 1 = first day of menses) should also be measured for confirmation.
  - In women with oligomenorrhoea, check serum FSH, LH, oestradiol, and prolactin.
- *Karyotype* If primary ovarian failure is present (FSH, LH)
- *Serum testosterone, androstenedione and 17α hydroxyprogesterone* if there is clinical evidence of hyperandrogenism.
- *MRI of the pituitary fossa* in hyperprolactinaemia and hypogonadotropic hypogonadism.
- *TSH, free T_4* to exclude thyroid disorders
- *Exclude cervical infection* send vaginal discharge for bacteriology and do chlamydia trachomatis serology
- *Pelvic ultrasound* assess uterine and ovarian anatomy
- *Assess tubal patency*
  - hysterosalpingography (HSG) or laparoscopy (do in the early follicular phase of cycle to avoid doing during pregnancy)
  - should be performed in ovulatory women with a partner who has a normal semen analysis.
- *Further investigations* to be performed if anovulation, male and tubal factors have been excluded as a cause of infertility.
  - *Postcoital test (PCT)* is used to assess cervical mucus receptivity to sperm penetration. Should be performed when mucus is of acceptable quality and quantity (i.e. just before ovulation), and infection and sperm disorders should be excluded prior to

interpretation of results. If PCT is abnormal, then test cervical secretion for antisperm antibodies. Rarely done.

– If there is a past history of recurrent spontaneous abortions, then the presence of *anticardiolipin antibody* should be looked for.

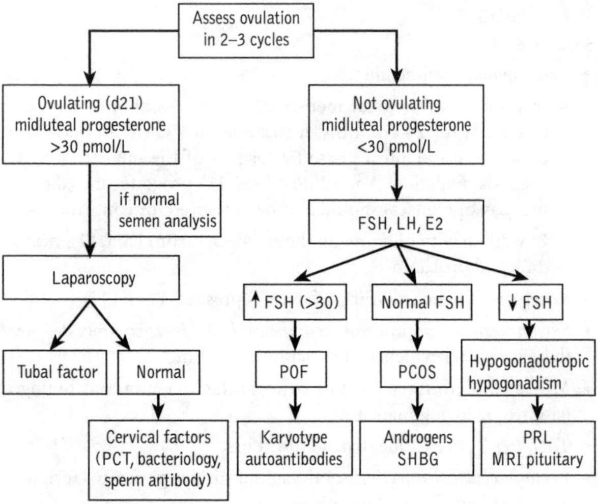

Fig. 67.1 Investigation of female infertility

Male factors

History and physical examination

- *Symptoms of androgen deficiency*
  - reduced libido and potency
  - reduced frequency of shaving
  - may be asymptomatic.
- *Drug history*
  - drug or alcohol abuse and the use of anabolic steroids may all contribute to hypogonadism
  - cytotoxic chemotherapy may cause primary testicular failure.
- *History of infection* e.g. mumps, orchitis, sexually transmitted disease or epididymitis.
- *Bronchiectasis* may be associated with epididymal obstruction (Young's syndrome) or severe aesthenospermia (immotile cilia syndrome).
- *Testicular injury or surgery* may cause disordered spermatogenesis.
- *Secondary sex characteristics* may be absent in congenital hypogonadism.
- *Anosmia* Kallmann's syndrome
- *Eunuchoid habitus* (see p. 435) suggestive of prepubertal hypogonadism.
- *Gynaecomastia* may suggest hypogonadism.
- *Testicular size* (using orchidometer)
  - normal 15–25 ml
  - reduced to <15 ml in hypogonadism
  - in Klinefelter's syndrome, they are often <5 ml.
  - in patients with normal testicular size, suspect genital tract obstruction, e.g. congenital absence of vas deferens.
- Examine rest of *external genitalia* look for penile/urethral abnormalities and epididymal thickening.

Investigations

Semen analysis

Essential in the diagnostic work up of any infertile couple.

- If *normal* (see table 67.1) then a male cause is excluded and the test does not have to be repeated.
- If *abnormal*, then repeat semen analysis 6–12 weeks later.
- Semen collection should be performed after 3 days of sexual abstinence. See Table 67.1 for interpretation of results.
- If *azoospermia* is present, then obstruction is ruled out by normal FSH and testosterone concentrations.
- *Asthenospermia*, or immotile sperm, is usually due to immunological infertility or infection, e.g. of the prostate (high semen viscosity and pH, and leukocytospermia)

FSH, LH, and testosterone levels

- FSH may be elevated in the presence of normal LH and testosterone levels and oligospermia. This may be seen in men who are normally virilized but infertile as a result of disordered spermatogenesis.
- Low FSH, LH and testosterone concentrations suggest secondary hypogonadism. An MRI of the pituitary gland and hypothalamus is necessary to exclude organic disease.

Further investigations

- *Urinary bacteriology* should be performed in men with leukocytospermia.
- *Sperm antibodies* in blood and semen should also be measured in most infertile men.
- *Scrotal ultrasound* may help in the diagnosis of chronic epididymitis. Men being investigated for infertility are at increased risk of testicular tumours.
- *Karyotyping* may be helpful in men with primary testicular failure. Klinefelter's syndrome (47,XXY) is a common cause of infertility, and deletions on the long arm of the Y chromosome have been found in a significant proportion of azoospermic males.
- *Testicular biopsy* is rarely diagnostic, but may be used to retrieve sperm for assisted reproduction techniques in men with obstructive azoospermia.
- *Sperm function tests* are rarely required, but may be used to predict ability of sperm to fertilize human oocytes.

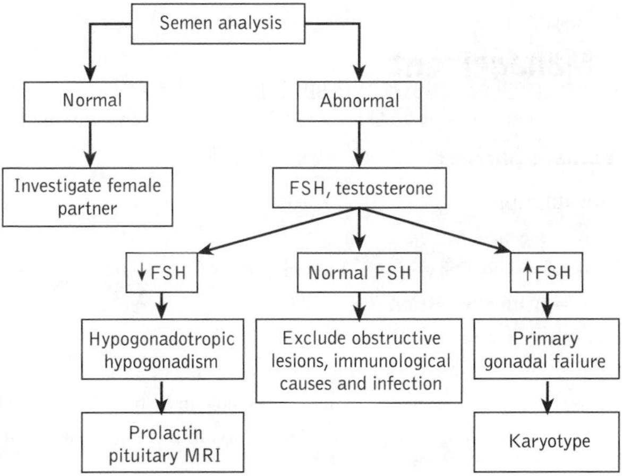

Fig. 67.2 Investigation of male infertility.

Table 67.1 WHO criteria for normal semen analysis

Test	Normal values	Nomenclature for abnormal values
Volume	2–6 ml	Aspermia (no ejaculate)
pH	7.2–8	
Sperm concentration	$>20 \times 10^6$/ml	Oligozoospermia
Total sperm count	$>40 \times 10^6$/ejaculate	Azoospermia (no sperm in ejaculate)
Motility	>50%	Asthenospermia
Morphology	>30% normal forms	Teratospermia
Live sperm	>70%	Necrospermia
Leukocytes	$<1 \times 10^6$/ml	Leukocytospermia
Immunobead test (for sperm antibodies)	<20% spermatozoa with adherent particles	

(from Guzick *et al. NEJM*, 2001, 345: 1388–93.)

Management

Female partner

Anovulation

- *Normogonadotrophic*
  - usually PCOS: weight reduction if obese
  - ovulation induction (see p. 479).
- *Hypergonadotrophic*
  - *POF* ovum donation followed by IVF is only option.
  - spontaneous transient remission possible in early POF
  - if still cycling and FSH 15–25IU/L, ovarian hyperstimulation and IVF may be attempted, but poor results.
- *Hypogonadotrophic*
  - if hyperprolactinaemic then dopamine agonists are usually effective
  - lifestyle changes if underweight/excessive exercise
  - otherwise, ovulation induction (see p. 479).

Tubal infertility

- Surgical tubal reconstruction may be attempted.
- 50–60% 2 year cumulative pregnancy rate in patients with mild disease, but only 10% in more severe disease and high risk of ectopic pregnancy, so IVF better in most cases.
- Cumulative pregnancy rate at least 50% following IVF (20–25% per cycle) unless hydrosalpinx is present, in which case the pregnancy rate is halved.

Endometriosis

- *Minimal/mild*
  - GnRH agonists, danazol, and progestagens are ineffective
  - laparoscopic destruction of superficial disease improves pregnancy chances slightly.
  - assisted reproductive techniques (ART) (p. 475) give pregnancy rate of 25–35% per cycle.
- *Severe* (tubal obstruction ovarian involvement) Surgery. However, ART often necessary.

Table 67.2 Assisted reproduction techniques (ART)

Technique	Indications	Pregnancy rates	Notes
Intrauterine insemination (IUI)	Unexplained infertility Mild oligozoospermia ($>2 \times 10^6$ motile sperm) Immunological factors	50% after 3 cycles	hMG and hCG are used to induce superovulation. Prepared spermatozoa are then injected into the uterine cavity through a catheter 12 h after ovulation Ineffective if severe male factor, endometriosis, or tubal damage
In vitro fertilization (IVF)	Most forms of infertility unless severe male factor	25% pregnancy rate per cycle 80–90% delivery rate after 6 cycles in women under the age of 35 years Success rates markedly reduced >40 years of age	After superovulation, ovarian follicles are aspirated under ultrasonic guidance and are fertilized with prepared sperm in vitro. The embryos are then transferred back into the uterine cavity, usually 48 h after aspiration May adopt a similar technique in women with premature ovarian failure, using donated ova which are then fertilized in vitro with partner's sperm. Hormonal support will be required following embryo transfer. Cumulative pregnancy rate of 50–60%

Table 67.2 *contid.*

Technique	Indications	Pregnancy rates	Notes
Gamete intrafallopian transfer (GIFT)	Most forms of infertility unless severe male factor Do not use in women with tubal disease	Similar to IVF	Similar to IVF except that retrieved follicles and sperm are injected laparoscopically into a fallopian tube to fertilize naturally
Intracytoplasmic sperm injection (ICSI)	Male infertility	20% per cycle if female partner <40 years of age	Spermatozoa injected directly into oocytes retrieved following superovulation. Embryos are then implanted into the uterus. Spermatozoa may be concentrated from an ejaculate or be aspirated from the epididymis or testis in men with obstructive azoospermia Small risk of sex chromosome abnormalities in males (1%) conceived following ICSI

Vaginal/cervical factors

- *Infection* Each episode of acute PID causes infertility in 10–15% of cases. Chlamydia trachomatis is responsible for half the cases of PID in the developed countries. Treat both partners with antibiotics.
- *Immunological* Intruterine insemination (IUI) ± superovulation. If this fails, then ART.

Male partner

Hypogonadotrophic hypogonadism

- Gonadotrophins: hCG 1000–2000 IU i/m 2–3x week. Most also require FSH/hMG 75–150 IU i/m 3x week. Main side-effect: gynaecomastia.

or

- Pulsatile GnRH using a subcutaneous infusion pump (see p. 481). Dose varies from 25–600 ng/kg every 90–120 min. Titrate to normalize LH, FSH, and testosterone. Will not work in pituitary disease.
- Once testes are >8 ml, semen analysis every 6 months. Takes at least 2 years to maximize spermatogenesis. 30% of couples will achieve pregnancy.

Obstructive azoospermia

Microsurgery possible, but better results with ICSI.

Varicocoele

Controversial association with male subfertility. Treat in adolescents if affected testis reduced by 3 ml compared with other testes, and in young infertile couples (<30 years) of <3 years infertility if subnormal semen analysis.

Unexplained infertility

Definition

Infertility despite normal sexual intercourse occurring at least twice weekly, normal semen analysis, documentation of ovulation in several cycles, and normal laparoscopy.

Management

30% will become pregnant within 3 years of expectant management. If not pregnant by then, chances that spontaneous pregnancy will occur are greatly reduced and ART should be considered. In women >30 years of age then expectant management is not an option and superovulation + IUI or IVF should be considered.

Results

- IUI can acheive a pregnancy rate of 15% per cycle and cumulative delivery rate after several cycles = 50%.
- IVF offers a pregnancy rate of 25% per cycle and a cumulative delivery rate approaching 80%. Significant risk of multiple pregnancy with any form of ART.

Ovulation induction

Indications

- Anovulation due to:
  - polycystic ovary syndrome
  - hypopituitarism
  - hypogonadotrophic hypogonadism
- Controlled ovarian hyperstimulation for ART.

Pretreatment assessment

- Exclude thyroid dysfunction and hyperprolactinaemia.
- Check rubella serology.
- Confirm normal semen analysis.
- Confirm tubal patency (laparoscopy) prior to gonadotrophin use and/or after failed clomiphene use.
- Optimize lifestyle: maintain satisfactory BMI, exercise in moderation, reduce alcohol intake and stop smoking.
- Baseline pelvic ultrasound is essential to exclude ovarian masses and uterine abnormalities prior to treatment.

Clomiphene citrate

- *Mode of action*
  - binds to oestrogen receptors in hypothalamus, blocking normal –ve feedback thereby increasing pulse frequency of GnRH. This stimulates FSH and LH release
  - antioestrogen effect on endometrium, cervix, and vagina.
- *Indications* eugonadotropic anovulation, e.g. PCOS. Requires normal hypothalamo–pituitary–ovarian axis to work therefore ineffective in hypogonadotrophic hypogonadism.
- *Contraindications* hepatic dysfunction
- *Administration* Start on days 2–5 of menstrual cycle (may have to induce bleed by giving a progestagen for 10 days) and take for a total of 5 days.
- *Dose*
  - start on 25–50 mg/day and increase by 50 mg every month until midluteal progesterone is >30 nmol/L
  - spontaneous ovulation should occur 5–10 days after last day of medication

- remain on optimum dose for 3–6 months
- most require 50–100 mg/day
- Some centres advocate regular vaginal ultrasound to monitor follicle growth.

- *Efficacy*
  - 80–90% ovulate, with conception rates of 50–60% in first 6 ovulatory cycles. May enhance chances of ovulation in non-responders by the administration of 10 000 IU of hCG midcycle (use ultrasound guidance; administer hCG when leading follicle is at least 20 mm).
  - In hyperandrogenic women, particularly adult onset CAH, addition of dexamethasone 0.5 mg at night may improve success rates.
- *Side-effects*
  - hot flushes in 10%, mood swings, depression and headaches in 1%, pelvic pain in 5%, nausea in 2%, breast tenderness in 5%, hair loss in 0.3%, visual disturbances in 1.5%
  - mild OHSS in 5%
  - multiple pregnancies in 10%.
- *Risk of ovarian cancer* Unknown. Infertility is associated with an increased risk of ovarian cancer. Additionally, one study suggests a twofold increased risk of low grade ovarian cancer following long-term clomiphene use. Further studies necessary but currently recommended maximum treatment duration is 6 months.

Gonadotrophins

- *Indications*
  - hypogonadotrophic hypogonadism
  - women with PCOS who are clomiphene resistant.
  - in combination with IUI in unexplained infertility
  - for superovulation as part of ART.
- *Dose and administration* Several regimes available, all require close monitoring with twice weekly oestradiol (E2) measurements and vaginal ultrasounds. One suggested regime (low dose step-up approach):
  - Start at 50–75IU/day hMG (or FSH) on day 2–4 of the menstrual cycle. On day 7 of treatment measure serum E2 and perform a vaginal ultrasound. If E2 <200 pmol/L and there has been no change in follicle development then increase hMG (or FSH) to 75–112 IU/day.
  - If >3 mature follicles (>14 mm) develop or E2 >3000 pmol/L then abandon cycle and restart on half-dose hMG/FSH because of risk of OHSS.

  - Otherwise, give hCG at a dose of 5000 IU to trigger ovulation when follicle >18 mm diameter. May increase to 10 000 IU in subsequent cycle if ovulation doesn't occur.
  - May use gonadotrophins for a total of 6 cycles. If unsuccessful then consider ART.
- *Efficacy* 80–85% pregnancy rate after 6 cycles.
- *Side-effects*
  - multiple pregnancy (20%)
  - OHSS.
- *Ovarian hyperstimulation syndrome* (OHSS)
- A syndrome of ovarian enlargement and increased vascular permeability with accumulation of fluid in the peritoneal, pleural and pericardial cavities. Occurs during the luteal phase of the cycle, i.e. after hCG stimulation and is more severe if pregnancy occurs due to endogenous hCG production.
- Mild OHSS occurs in up to 25% of stimulated cycles and results in abdominal bloating and nausea. It resolves with bed rest and fluid replacement. Severe OHSS, associated with hypotension, markedly enlarged ovaries, ascites, and pleural and pericardial effusions, occurs in <0.1%. Women need to be hospitalized and resuscitated as there is an increased mortality from disseminated intravascular coagulation and pulmonary emboli.
- OHSS is best prevented by witholding hCG during at-risk cycles.

GnRH treatment

- *Indications* Hypothalamic hypogonadism with normal pituitary function.
- *Dose and administration* Pulsatile GnRH using an infusion pump which is worn continuously. This delivers a dose of GnRH every 90–120 min. The dose may be administered either intravenously (5 μg/90 min) or subcutaneously (20 μg/90 min).
- *Monitoring*
  - monitor E2 levels because risk of hypo-oestrogenaemia if GnRH is given too frequently.
  - no risk of OHSS or multiple pregnancies so ultrasonic monitoring is unnecessary.
- *Side-effects* allergic reaction
- *Efficacy* cumulative pregnancy rate of 80–90%.

Further reading

Forti G, Krausz C. Evaluation and treatment of the infertile couple. *Journal of Clinical Endocrinology and Metabolism* 1998; 83(12): 4177–4188.

Hargreave T, Ghosh C. Male fertility disorders. *Endocrinology and Metabolism Clinics of North America* 1998; 27(4): 765–782.

Hull MGR, Cahill DJ. Female infertility. *Endocrinology and Metabolism Clinics of North America* 1998; 27(4): 851–876.

Chapter 68
Disorders of sexual differentiation

Clinical presentation

- *Infancy* ambiguous genitalia (evaluation is discussed p. 650)
- *Puberty*
  - failure to progress through puberty (male or female phenotype)
  - primary amenorrhoea in a female phenotype
  - virilization of a female phenotype
- *Adulthood*
  - hypogonadism
  - infertility

Evaluation

- *Karyotype* 46,XX vs 46,XY male or female
- Imaging
  - look for presence of testes or ovaries and uterus
  - most easily performed using pelvic ultrasound but MRI may be more sensitive in identifying internal genitalia.

Hormonal evaluation

- LH/FSH
- Testosterone, androstenedione, SHBG
- 17-hydroxyprogesterone ± ACTH stimulation (p. 367)
- hCG stimulation test (p. 437) – to assess the presence of functioning testicular material. Measure testosterone, androstenedione, DHT and SHBG post-stimulation
- Others depending on clinical suspicion, e.g. 5α-reductase deficiency – check DHT levels before and after hCG stimulation.

Causes (see also p. 650)

46,XY – undervirilized male

- Gonadal differentiation abnormalities, e.g. gonadal dysgenesis
  - cause unknown in the majority
  - may result from 45,X/46,XY mosaicism or SRY gene mutation.
- Leydig cell abnormalities
  - autosomal recessive
  - due to inactivating LH receptor gene mutation
- CAH, e.g.
  - 3β-HSD, 17α-hydroxylase/17,20-desmolase or 17β-HSD deficiencies
  - congenital lipoid adrenal hyperplasia (due to StAR gene mutation).
- Androgen receptor defects
  - androgen insensitivity syndrome
- 5α-reductase deficiency
  - mutation of 5α-reductase type 2 gene
  - autosomal recessive inheritance
  - results in high testosterone but low DHT concentrations
- Persistent mullerian duct syndrome
  - mullerian inhibitory substance (MIS) or MIS receptor gene mutation
- True hermaphrodite

46,XX – virilized female

- Excess foetal androgens – CAH
  - 21-OH deficiency (commonest cause)
  - 11β-OH deficiency.
- Excess maternal androgens
  - drugs
  - virilizing tumours
- Placental aromatase deficiency

46,XX males

- due to a Y to X translocation so that the *SRY* gene is present
- phenotype similar to Klinefelter's syndrome

- True hermaphrodite

Androgen insensitivity syndrome

Pathogenesis

- Results from a defect in androgen receptor number or function. This may be complete or partial. The androgen receptor is on chromosome Xq. Several mutations may occur, inherited in an X-linked recessive fashion. Poor correlation between genotype and phenotype.
- Rare – 1 : 20 000–1 : 64 000 males.

Clinical features

- *Complete androgen insensitivity (testicular feminization)* results in normal female external genitalia. No male external sex organs present, but remnants of mullerian structures are occasionally present. Testes abdominal or in the inguinal canal. Vagina often shorter than normal.
- Often present during puberty with primary amenorrhoea. Height above female average, breast development normal. Little or no pubic and axillary hair. Gender identity is female.
- *Partial androgen insensitivity* has a wide phenotypic spectrum, ranging from ambiguous genitalia to a normal male phenotype presenting with infertility.
- 9% risk of seminoma.

Hormonal evaluation

- Testosterone and androstenedione levels are often above normal. hCG stimulation results in a further rise in testosterone, with little increase in SHBG.
- Oestradiol levels are higher than in normal males, but lower than the female average. Oestrogen is produced from the aromatization of testosterone.
- LH levels are usually markedly elevated, but FSH is normal.
- Genetic testing is possible in some centres.

Management

- Orchidectomy in adolescence after attaining puberty
- Oestrogen replacement therapy to induce puberty and continue thereafter

True hermaphroditism

Pathogenesis

- Unknown. May be familial.
- Affected individuals have both ovarian and testicular tissue, either in the same gonad (ovotestis), or an ovary on one side and a testis on the other. A uterus and a fallopian tube are usually present, the latter on the side of the ovary or ovotestis. Wolffian structures may be present in a third of individuals on the side of the testis. The testicular tissue is usually dysgenetic although the ovarian tissue may be normal.

Clinical features

- Most individuals have ambiguous genitalia and are raised as males, but just under 10% have normal female external genitalia.
- At puberty, 50% of individuals menstruate, which may present as cyclic haematuria in males and most develop breasts.
- Feminization and virilization vary widely. Most are infertile, but fertility has been reported.
- 2% risk of gonadal malignancy, higher in 46,XY individuals.

Hormonal evaluation

- 46,XX in 70%, 46,XX/46,XY in 20% and 46,XY in 10%.
- Hypergonadotropic hypogonadism is usual.
- Diagnosis can only be made on gonadal biopsy.

General principles of management

Assignment of gender and reconstructive surgery

Female pseudohermaphroditism

- As these girls are potentially fertile, they should be brought up as female.
- Clitoromegaly is usually corrected in infancy by clitoroplasty. Vaginoplasty is usually deferred until late adolescence. Results of feminizing genitoplasty with regard to sexual activity are promising, albeit variable.

Male pseudohermaphroditism

- The decision regarding gender reassignment is more complex and depends on the degree of sexual ambiguity in addition to the cause of the disorder and the potential for normal sexual function and fertility.
- Individuals with complete androgen insensitivity are assigned a female sex as they are resistant to testosterone therapy, develop female sexual characteristics, and have a female gender identity. They may require vaginaplasty in adolescence.
- Individuals with 5α-reductase deficiency should be raised as males where possible because of subsequent virilization and attainment of male gender identity at puberty.
- Sex assignment of other forms of male pseudohermaphroditism depends on phallic size. If the stretched penile length is >2.5 cm then it is likely that reconstructive surgery will be successful and therefore a male sex may be assigned. A trial of 3 months of testosterone may be used to enhance phallic growth prior to surgery (25–50 mg depot testosterone/month).
- Penile reconstruction and orchidopexy is best performed at about 1 year of age. However, multiple surgery is often required. Testicular prostheses inserted in adolescence may be required if orchidopexy is not possible. Results for sexual function are encouraging, with centres reporting an average of 70% success.

Gonadectomy

- Increased risk of gonadoblastoma in most individuals with abdominal testes. Risk is highest in those with dysgenetic gonads and

Y chromosome material. Bilateral gonadectomy should therefore be performed.

- Optimal timing of the gonadectomy is unknown. In androgen insensitivity, the risk of gonadoblastoma appears to rise only after the age of 20 years so orchidectomy is recommended in adolescence after attaining puberty. In most other disorders, gonadectomy prior to puberty is recommended.
- Early bilateral orchidectomy should also be performed in 46,XY subjects with 5α-reductase deficiency or 17ß HSD deficiency who are being raised as females to prevent virilization at puberty.

Hormone replacement therapy

- Patients with disorders of adrenal biosynthesis, e.g. CAH, require lifelong glucocorticoid and usually mineralocorticoid replacement therapy.
- Most male pseudohermaphrodites and hermaphrodites being raised as male require long-term testosterone replacement therapy.
- Individuals with 5α-reductase deficiency usually receive supra-physiological doses of testosterone in order to achieve satisfactory DHT levels.
- Subjects with androgen insensitivity and male pseudohermaphrodites being raised as female should receive oestrogen replacement therapy to induce puberty and this should be continued thereafter.

Psychological support

- Disorders relating to sexual identity and function often require experienced counselling.
- Patient support groups are often helpful.

Further reading

Simpson JL. Disorders of sexual differentiation. *Current Opinion in Endocrinology and Diabetes* 1996;3: 452–462.

Vogiatzi MG, New MI. Differential diagnosis and therapeutic options for ambiguous genitalia. *Current Opinion in Endocrinology and Diabetes* 1998;5: 3–10.

Warne GL, Zajac JD. Disorders of sexual differentiation. *Endocrinology and Metabolism Clinics of North America* 1998;27(4): 945–967.

Chapter 69
Transsexualism

Definition

A condition in which an anatomically and genetically normal person feels that he or she is a member of the opposite sex. There is an irreversible discomfort with the anatomical gender, which may be severe, often developing in childhood.

Epidemiology

- More common in males.
- Estimated incidence of 1 : 12 000 men and 1 : 30 000 women.

Management

Principles

- Multidisciplinary approach between psychiatrists, endocrinologists and surgeons.
- Endocrine disorders should be excluded prior to entry into the gender reassignment programme – i.e. ensure normal internal and external genitalia, karyotype, gonadotrophins, and testosterone/ oestradiol.
- Psychological assessment is essential before definitive therapy. This should take place over at least 2 years to ensure a permanent diagnosis.
- Following this period, the subject is encouraged to cross-gender dress under the supervision of a psychiatrist. This should continue for at least 1 year before hormonal manipulation.
- Psychological follow-up should continue throughout the programme, including after surgery.

Hormonal manipulation

Male to female transsexuals

- Suppress male secondary sex characteristics: cyproterone acetate (CPA) (100 mg/day)
- Induce female secondary sex characteristics: EE2 (100 μg/day)
- *Aims:*
  - breast development – maximum after 1–2 years of treatment
  - development of female fat distribution
  - decreased body hair and smoother skin
  - decreased muscle bulk and strength
  - reduction in testicular size
  - ?effect on behaviour.
- Gradually reduce dose of CPA as testosterone levels fall. May stop CPA following gender reassignment surgery.
- The dose of EE2 may be reduced when there is little further progression in female secondary sex characteristics, usually after 1 year of treatment.
- May then substitute EE2 for conjugated oestrogens or oestradiol valerate, both of which are associated with a lower complication rate.

Gender reassignment surgery

- Performed at least 6–9 months after starting sex hormone therapy
- Usually performed in several stages.

Male to female transsexuals

- bilateral orchidectomy and resection of the penis
- construction of a vagina and labia minora
- clitoroplasty
- breast augmentation.

Female to male transsexuals

- bilateral mastectomy
- hysterectomy and salpingo-oophorectomy
- phalloplasty and testicular prostheses.

Table 69.1 Maintenance doses of oestrogens used in male to female transsexuals

Oestrogen	Daily dose
Ethinyl oestradiol	30–50 μg
Oestradiol valerate (oral)	2–4 mg
Oestradiol valerate (transdermal)	50–100 μg
Conjugated oestrogen	1.25 mg

- Adjust oestrogen dose depending on plasma LH and oestradiol levels (see table 69.1).
- *Side-effects* (particularly while on high dose EE2+CPA therapy):
  - hyperprolactinaemia (EE2 stimulates prolactin synthesis and secretion in addition to inducing proliferation of pituitary lactotrophs)
  - thromboembolism, both arterial and venous
  - abnormal liver enzymes
  - depression
  - ? increased risk of breast cancer.

Female to male transsexuals

- Induce male secondary sex characteristics and suppress female secondary sex characteristics: parenteral testosterone (e.g. Sustanon 250 mg) every 2 weeks.
- *Aims:*
  - cessation of menstrual bleeding
  - atrophy of uterus and breasts
  - increase muscle bulk and strength
  - deepenening of voice
  - hirsutism
  - male body fat distribution
  - increase in libido.
- Once sexual characteristics are stable (after approximately 1 year of treatment), reduce testosterone injection frequency according to serum testosterone levels.
- *Side-effects:*
  - acne
  - weight gain
  - abnormal liver function
  - adverse lipid profile.

Monitoring of therapy

- Every 3 months for first year then every 6 months
- Hormonal therapy is lifelong and so patients should be followed up indefinitely:
  - physical examination
  - liver function tests
  - serum lipids
  - hormonal status (LH, FSH, prolactin, oestradiol, testosterone).

Prognosis

- No increased mortality.
- Increased morbidity in male to female transsexuals from thromboembolism.
- No increased morbidity in female to male transsexuals.
- Hyperprolactinaemia and elevation in liver enzymes are self-limiting in the majority of cases.
- The risk of osteoporosis is not increased in transsexuals.
- There may be a slightly increased risk of breast cancer in male to female transsexuals.
- Results from reconstructive surgery, particularly in female to male transsexuals, remain suboptimal.

Further reading

Schlatterer K, von Werder K, Stalla GK. Multistep treatment concept of transsexual patients. *Experimental and Clinical Endocrinology and Diabetes* 1996; 104: 413–419.

Part V
Endocrine disorders of pregnancy

Chapter 70
Thyroid disorders

Normal physiology

Effect of pregnancy on thyroid function

- *Iodide stores* Fall due to increased renal clearance and transplacental transfer to foetus.
- *Thyroid size* Increase in thyroid volume by 10–20% due to hCG stimulation and relative iodide deficiency.
- *Thyroglobulin* Rise corresponds to rise in thyroid size.
- *Thyroid binding globulin (TBG)* Twofold increase in concentration as a result of reduced hepatic clearance and increased synthesis stimulated by oestrogen. Concentration plateaus at 20 weeks gestation, and falls again postpartally.
- *Total T_4 and T_3* Increased concentrations, corresponding to rise in TBG.
- *Free T_4 and T_3* Small rise in concentration in first trimester due to hCG stimulation then fall into normal range.
- *Thyroid stimulating hormone (TSH)* Within normal limits in pregnancy. However, suppressed in 13.5% in 1st trimester, 4.5% in 2nd trimester and 1.2% in 3rd trimester due to hCG thyrotropic effect. +ve correlation between free T_4 and hCG levels and –ve correlation between TSH and hCG levels in first half of pregnancy.
- *Thyrotropin releasing hormone (TRH)* Normal
- *TSH receptor antibodies* When present in high concentrations in maternal serum may cross the placenta. Antibody titre decreases with progression of pregnancy.

Foetal thyroid function

- TRH and TSH synthesis occurs by 8–10 weeks gestation and thyroid hormone synthesis occurs by 10–12 weeks gestation. In intrauterine life, T_4 is mainly converted to reverse T_3, but there is a marked increase of T_4 to T_3 conversion at the time of labour.
- TSH, total and freeT_4 and T_3 and TBG concentrations increase progressively throughout gestation.
- Maternal TSH does not cross the placenta and although TRH crosses the placenta it does not regulate foetal thyroid function. Iodide crosses the placenta and excessive quantities may induce foetal hypothyroidism. Maternal T_4 and T_3 cross the placenta in small quantities and are important for foetal growth early in pregnancy.

Maternal hyperthyroidism (see p. 39)

Incidence

- 0.2% of pregnant women.
- Most are diagnosed before pregnancy or in the first trimester of pregnancy.
- In women with Graves' disease in remission, exacerbation may occur in 1st trimester of pregnancy.

Hyperemesis gravidarum

- Characterized by severe vomiting and weight loss. Cause unknown.
- Begins in early pregnancy (week 6–9 of gestation) and tends to resolve spontaneously by week 20 of gestation.
- Biochemical hyperthyroidism in two-thirds of affected women but T_3 is less commonly elevated. Mechanism: hCG has TSH-like effect, thus stimulating the thyroid gland and suppressing TSH secretion.
- Degree of thyroid stimulation correlates with severity of vomiting.
- No other evidence of thyroid disease, i.e. no goitre, no history of thyroid disease, no ophthalmopathy and negative thyroid autoantibodies.
- Antithyroid drugs not required and do not improve symptoms of hyperemesis.

Graves' disease

- The commonest scenario is pregnancy in a patient with pre-existing Graves' disease on treatment as fertility is low in patients with untreated thyrotoxicosis. Newly diagnosed Graves' disease in pregnancy is rare.
- Aggravation of disease in 1st trimester with amelioration in 2nd half of pregnancy because of a decrease in maternal immunological activity at that time.
- Symptoms of thyrotoxicosis are difficult to differentiate from normal pregnancy. The most sensitive symptoms are weight loss and tachycardia. Goitre is found in most patients.

Management

- Antithyroid drugs (ATDs) are the treatment of choice but cross the placenta.
- Either *carbimazole* or *propylthiouracil* may be used. Risk of aplasia cutis, which is reversible, with carbimazole is negligible.

- Most patients will be on a maintenance dose of ATD which may need increasing. A high dose of ATD may be necessary initially to achieve euthyroidism as quickly as possible (carbimazole 20–40 mg/day or propylthiouracil 200–400 mg/day) in newly diagnosed patients, then use the minimal dose of ATD to maintain euthyroidism. Do not use block-replace regime as higher doses of ATDs required and there is minimal transplacental transfer of T_4, thereby risking foetal hypothyroidism.
- Monitor TFTs every 4–6 weeks.
- Aim to keep FT_4 at upper limit of normal.
- In approximately 30% of women ATD may be discontinued at 32–36 weeks gestation. Consider if euthyroid for at least 4 weeks on lowest dose of propylthiouracil, but continue to monitor TFTs frequently. The presence of a large goitre or ophthalmopathy suggests severe disease and the chances of remission are low so do not stop ATD.
- Risk of neonatal hypothyroidism is avoided if woman on 200 mg propylthiouracil or less (or carbimazole 20 mg) in last few weeks of gestation.
- Propylthiouracil is secreted in negligible amounts in breast milk. Carbimazole is secreted in higher amounts. Breast feeding is not contraindicated if mother is on 150 mg propylthiouracil or 10 mg carbimazole. Give in divided doses after the feeds and monitor neonatal thyroid function.
- Surgical management of thyrotoxicosis is rarely necessary in pregnancy. Only indication: serious ATD complication (e.g. agranulocytosis) or drug resistance. Radioiodine therapy is contraindicated in pregnancy and for 4 months beforehand.

Infants born to mothers with Graves' disease

- Risks to foetus of uncontrolled thyrotoxicosis:
  - increased risk of spontaneous abortion and stillbirth
  - intrauterine growth retardation (IUGR)
  - prematurity
  - foetal or neonatal hyperthyroidism.
- Follow-up of babies born to mothers on ATDs show normal weight, height, and intellectual function.
- *Foetal hypothyroidism* May occur following treatment of mother with high doses of ATDs, particularly in the latter half of pregnancy. This is rare and may be diagnosed by demonstrating a large foetal goitre on foetal ultrasound in the presence of foetal bradycardia. May treat with intra-amniotic T_4 injection.

- *Foetal exposure to radioiodine* After 12–14 weeks gestation causes hypothyroidism and mental impairments should not occur.
- *Foetal hyperthyroidism* May occur after week 25 of gestation. It results in IUGR, foetal goitre and tachycardia (foetal heart rate >160 bpm). It may develop if the mother has high titres of TSH stimulating antibodies (TSAb). Treat by giving mother ATD and monitor foetal heart rate (aim <140 bpm), growth and goitre size. May need to supplement mother with thyroxine if she becomes hypothyroid.
- *Neonatal thyrotoxicosis* Develops in 1% of infants born to thyrotoxic mothers. Due to placental transfer of TSAb. Transient, usually subsides by 6 months, but up to 30% mortality if untreated. Treat with ATD and β-blockers.

Causes of maternal hyperthyroidism

- Graves' disease (85% of cases)
- toxic nodule
- toxic multinodular goitre
- hydatidiform mole
- hyperemesis gravidarum.

Maternal hypothyroidism

Incidence

- 2.5% subclinical hypothyroidism
- 0.3% overt hypothyroidism.

Risks

- *Spontaneous abortion* Twofold increased risk even in euthyroid women with positive thyroid antibodies.
- *Pre-eclampsia* 21% of suboptimally treated mothers have pregnancy-induced hypertension (PIH).
- Also, increased risk of anaemia during pregnancy and postpartal haemorrhage.
- Risks to foetus are those associated with PIH (IUGR, premature delivery, etc). Slight decrease in IQ.
- No increased risk of congenital malformations.

Management

- Spontaneous pregnancy in overtly hypothyroid women is unusual as hypothyroid women are likely to have anovulatory menstrual cycles.
- *Thyroxine therapy* Start on 150 μg. Measure TSH 4 weeks later. Aim to normalize TSH and fT_4.
- If already on T_4 before pregnancy, assess TFT at 6–8 weeks gestation, then between weeks 16–20, then again between weeks 28–32 of gestation.
- Increased T_4 dose likely (by an average of 25–50 μg) as pregnancy progresses. After delivery, thyroid requirements decrease immediately.
- NB Do not give $FeSO_4$ simultaneously with T_4 – reduces its efficacy. Separate times for drug ingestion by at least 2 h.

Causes of maternal hypothyroidism

- Hashimoto's thyroiditis (most common cause)
- previous radioiodine therapy or thyroidectomy
- previous postpartum thyroiditis
- hypopituitarism.

+ve thyroid antibodies but euthyroid

- Higher risk of spontaneous abortions.
- No other complications.
- No risk of neonatal hypothyroidism
- Risk of PIH not increased
- The occasional mother will develop hypothyroidism at the end of the pregnancy, so check TSH between weeks 28–32 then at 3 months postpartum.

Postpartum thyroid dysfunction

Incidence

5–10% of women within 1 year of delivery.

Clinical manifestation

- Stages:
  - *Hyperthyroidism* Within 4 months of delivery. The most common symptom is fatigue which may go unnoticed. It may be associated with an enlarging goitre.
  - *Hypothyroidism* Develops 3–7 months after delivery. Symptoms are mild and non-specific. There may be an increased risk of postpartum depression.
  - *Spontaneous recovery* Within 6–12 months of delivery.
- Not all women go through the three stages – in some, hyperthyroidism or hypothyroidism is the only manifestation.

Differential diagnosis

- Graves' disease may relapse in the postpartum period. This is differentiated from postpartum thyroiditis by a high uptake on radioiodine scanning.
- Lymphocytic hypophysitis may cause hypothyroidism. However, serum TSH concentrations are inappropriately low and other pituitary hormones may also be deficient.

Management

- Treat only if symptomatic.
- β-blockers if thyrotoxic.
- Low dose T_4 (e.g. 50 μg) if hypothyroid (to allow spontaneous recovery of thyroid gland). This should be withdrawn at about 6 months to detect recovery.

Prognosis

- Recurrence in future pregnancies common.
- Permanent hypothyroidism eventually develops in 40%.

Cause of postpartum thyroid dysfunction

- Due to chronic thyroiditis (p. 66)
- Thyroid autoantibodies are usually positive, but there is low uptake on radioiodine scan.

Thyroid cancer in pregnancy (see p. 92)

Further reading

Lazarus JH, Kokandi A. Thyroid disease in relation to pregnancy: a decade of change. *Clinical Endocrinology* 2000; 53: 265–278.

Mestman JH, Goodwin TM, Montoro MM. Thyroid disorders of pregnancy. *Endocrinology and Metabolism Clinics of North America* 1995; 24(1): 41–71.

Roti E, Minelli R, Salvi M. Management of hyperthyroidism and hypothyroidism in the pregnant woman. *Journal of Clinical Endocrinology and Metabolism* 1996; 81(5): 1679–1683.

Chapter 71

Pituitary disorders

Normal anatomical changes during pregnancy

- *Prolactin (PRL)-secreting cells* Marked lactotroph hyperplasia during pregnancy.
- *Gonadotropin-secreting cells* Marked reduction in size and number.
- *TSH and ACTH-secreting cells* No change in size or number.
- *Anterior pituitary* Size increases by up to 70% during pregnancy. May take 1 year to shrink to near pre-pregnancy size in non-lactating women. Gradual slight increase in size with each pregnancy.
- *MRI* Enlarged anterior pituitary gland, but stalk is midline. Posterior pituitary gland may not be seen in late pregnancy.

Normal physiology during pregnancy

- *Serum PRL* Concentrations increase markedly during pregnancy and fall again to pre-pregnancy levels approximately 2 weeks post-partum in non-lactating women. However, normal response to TRH and dopamine antagonists.
- *Serum LH and FSH* Undetectable levels in pregnancy and blunted response to GnRH because of negative feedback inhibition from high levels of sex hormones and PRL.
- *Serum TSH, T_4, and T_3* Normal TSH but elevated total T_4 and T_3 because of increased TBG levels. Free thyroid hormones usually within the normal range.
- *Growth hormone (GH) and IGF-I* Low basal GH levels and blunted response to hypoglycaemia due to placental production of GH-like substance. IGF-I levels are normal or high in pregnancy.
- *ACTH and cortisol* CRH, ACTH and cortisol levels are high in pregnancy. CRH and ACTH are produced by the placenta. In addition, oestrogen-induced increase in cortisol binding globulin (CBG) synthesis during pregnancy will further increase maternal plasma cortisol concentrations. Incomplete suppression of cortisol following dexamethasone suppression test and exagerrated response of cortisol to CRH stimulation. However, normal diurnal variation persists.

Prolactinoma in pregnancy

Effect of pregnancy on tumour size

Risk of significant tumour enlargement (i.e. resulting in visual field disturbances or headaches):

- microadenoma 1.5–5.5%
- macroadenoma 15–36%
- macroadenoma treated with surgery and/or radiotherapy before pregnancy 4–7%

Effect of dopamine agonists on the foetus

- *Bromocriptine* Over 6000 pregnancies have occurred in women receiving bromocriptine in early pregnancy and the incidence of complications in these pregnancies with regards foetal outcome is similar to that of the normal population, indicating that bromocriptine is probably safe in early pregnancy. Data are available on approximately 100 children whose mothers received bromocriptine throughout pregnancy and again the incidence of congenital abnormalities is negligible.
- *Cabergoline* Also probably safe in early pregnancy, with no increased risk of foetal loss or congenital abnormalities but data is only available on approximately 300 pregnancies. It is thus recommended that women with prolactinomas seeking fertility should receive bromocriptine to induce ovulation until more data is accrued on the safety of cabergoline.

Management

Microprolactinoma

- Initiate bromocriptine therapy to induce normal ovulatory cycles and fertility.
- Stop bromocriptine as soon as pregnancy is confirmed.
- No formal monitoring is required as the risk of complications is low. Serum PRL levels are difficult to interpret during pregnancy as they are normally elevated.
- Visual field testing and MRI indicated only in the occasional patient who becomes symptomatic.
- In the postparum period, re-check serum PRL level after cessation of breast-feeding. Reassess size of microprolactinoma by MRI only if serum PRL level higher than pre-pregnancy concentrations.

Macroprolactinoma

Management is controversial and must therefore be individualized. Three possible approaches:

- May use bromocriptine to induce ovulation and then stop it after conception. However, patient must be monitored very carefully during pregnancy with monthly visual field testing. If symptoms of tumour enlargement develop or there is a deterioration in visual fields then MRI should be performed to assess tumour growth.
- Alternatively, the patient may undergo surgical debulking of the tumour and/or radiotherapy before seeking fertility. This will reduce but not eliminate the risk of complications associated with tumour growth. These patients should again be monitored using monthly visual fields.
- If significant tumour enlargement develops then bromocriptine therapy is the treatment of choice. Surgical treatment in pregnancy is associated with a significant risk of foetal loss.
- Finally, bromocriptine may be used throughout pregnancy to reduce the risk of tumour growth. The patient is again monitored by monthly visual fields. This is probably the safest approach.
- The effect of breast-feeding on prolactinoma growth is unknown but is probably less than that of pregnancy. Thus it is not contra-indicated in most women with a macroprolactinoma, but may not be advisable.
- MRI should be performed in the postpartum period in women with macroprolactinomas to look for tumour growth.

Cushing's syndrome

- Pregnancy is rare in women with untreated Cushing's syndrome as 75% of women will experience oligo- or amenorrhoea.
- The diagnosis of Cushing's syndrome is difficult to establish during pregnancy as fatigue, hypertension and glucose intolerance may be features of a normal pregnancy. However, the presence of red striae and proximal myopathy should alert the physician to the diagnosis of Cushing's syndrome.
- If suspected, the investigation of Cushing's syndrome should be carried out as in the non-pregnant state. However, high urinary free cortisols and non-suppression of cortisol production on a low dose dexamethasone suppression test may be features of a normal pregnancy. The diurnal variation of cortisol secretion is, however, preserved in normal pregnancy.
- Diagnosis is important, as pregnancy in Cushing's syndrome is associated with a high risk of maternal and foetal complications (see Table 71.1).
- Adrenal disease seems to be the most common cause of Cushing's syndrome in pregnancy, responsible for over 50% of reported cases.

Management

Mild Cushing's syndrome

- Supportive management.
- Medical treatment may be hazardous to the foetus and mother so avoid during pregnancy.
- Surgical management has not been shown to improve maternal or foetal outcome.

Severe Cushing's syndrome

- *1st trimester* Terminate pregnancy and instigate treatment. Alternatively, surgical treatment early in the second trimester.
- *2nd trimester* Surgery, e.g. adrenalectomy or pituitary adenomectomy. Minimal risk to foetus.
- *3rd trimester* Deliver baby as soon as possible and instigate treatment.

Table 71.1 Complications of Cushing's syndrome in pregnancy

Maternal complications	Incidence (%)	Foetal complications	Incidence (%)
Hypertension	70	Spontaneous abortion	12
Diabetes mellitus	27	Perinatal death	18
Congestive cardiac failure	7	Prematurity	60%
Poor wound healing	6	Congenital malformations	Low risk; no risk of virilization
Death	4		

Acromegaly

- Fertility in acromegaly is reduced, partly due to hyperprolactinaemia in addition to secondary hypogonadism. However, there have been several reported cases of pregnancy in acromegaly.
- Acromegaly increases the risk of gestational diabetes and hypertension. However, growth hormone excess does not seem to have any deleterious effects on foetal development.
- Significant tumour enlargement occasionally occurs together with enlargement of the normal pituitary lactotrophs, so monthly visual field testing is recommended. It may be treated with bromocriptine until there are more safety data on other forms of treatment. However, treatment may be deferred until after delivery in the majority of patients.
- Few data are available on the use of somatostatin analogues during pregnancy so their routine use is currently not recommended. However, there have been a couple of reports of uneventful pregnancies developing in patients treated with *octreotide*.

Hypopituitarism in pregnancy

Pre-existing hypopituitarism

- Most commonly due to surgical treatment of and/or radiotherapy for a pituitary adenoma.
- May induce ovulation and thus conception by gonadotrophin stimulation.

Lymphocytic hypophysitis (see p. 208)

- Rare disorder thought to be autoimmune in origin.
- Characterized by pituitary enlargement on imaging and variable loss of pituitary function.
- Most commonly seen in women in late pregnancy or in the first year postpartum.
- Symptoms are due to pressure effects, e.g. visual field defects and headaches, or due to hormonal deficiency.
- Most common hormonal deficiencies:
  - ACTH and vasopressin deficiency
  - TSH deficiency may also exist
  - gonadotrophins and GH levels are usually normal.
  - PRL levels may be mildly elevated in a third, normal in a third or low in a third.
- Diagnosis is only made definitively by pituitary biopsy but anti-pituitary antibodies may obviate the need for this in the future. Presumptive diagnoses based on clinical and biochemical findings are increasingly being made.
- There is an association with other autoimmune diseases, particularly Hashimoto's thyroiditis.
- Course variable. Pituitary function may deteriorate or improve with time.

Management

- Surgical decompression if pressure symptoms are present.
- Hormone replacement therapy as required
- The use of high dose steroid therapy is controversial, with mixed results.

Causes of hypopituitarism during pregnancy

- pre-existing hypopituitarism
- pituitary adenoma
- lymphocytic hypophysitis
- Sheehan's syndrome.

Management of pre-existing hypopituitarism during pregnancy

- *Steroids* Parenteral *hydrocortisone*in a dose of 100 mg i/m every 6 h should be given during labour and the dose reduced back to maintenance levels in the postpartum period (24–72 hours). No other dose adjustments are usually necessary.
- *Thyroxine* Requirements usually increase as pregnancy progresses. Monitor free T_4 each trimester and increase T_4 dose accordingly.
- *GH* There is little data on the effects of GH on pregnancy, but case reports do not suggest a detrimental effect on foetal outcome. However, until more data accrue, GH should be stopped prior to pregnancy. Moreover, as the placenta synthesizes a GH variant, GH therapy is unnecessary.
- *Vasopressin* The placenta synthesizes vasopressinase, which breaks down vasopressin but not DDAVP. Women with partial diabetes insipidus may therefore require DDAVP treatment during pregnancy. Those already receiving DDAVP may require a dose increment during pregnancy. Vasopressinase levels fall rapidly after delivery.

Sheehan's syndrome

- Postpartum pituitary infarction resulting in hypopituitarism. Increasingly uncommon in developed countries with improvements in obstetric care.
- *Pathogenesis* The enlarged pituitary gland of pregnancy is susceptible to any compromise to its blood supply.
- Investigations will confirm hypopituitarism.
- *Management* Pituitary hormone replacement therapy (see p. 120).

Sheehan's syndrome

Risk factors

- postpartum haemorrhage
- type 1 diabetes mellitus
- sickle cell disease

Clinical features

- failure of lactation
- involution of breasts
- fatigue, lethargy and dizziness
- amenorrhoea
- loss of axillary and pubic hair
- symptoms of hypothyroidism
- diabetes insipidus is rare

Further reading

Molitch M. Medical treatment of prolactinomas. *Endocrinology and Metabolism Clinics of North America* 1999; 28(1): 143–169.

Prager D, Braunstein GD. Pituitary disorders in pregnancy. *Endocrinology and Metabolism Clinics of North America* 1995; 24(1): 1–14.

Sheeler LR. Cushing's syndrome and pregnancy. *Endocrinology and Metabolism Clinics of North America* 1994; 23(3): 619–626.

Chapter 72
Adrenal disorders during pregnancy

Normal changes during pregnancy

Changes in maternal adrenocortical function

Markedly increased concentrations of all adrenal steroids due to increased synthesis and decreased catabolism.

Foeto-placental unit

- *Foetal adrenal gland* DHEAS is produced in vast quantities by the foetal adrenal gland. This is the major precursor for oestrogen synthesis by the placenta. The foetal adrenal gland has a large capacity for steroidogenesis. Stimulus for foetal adrenal gland unknown – possibly hCG or PRL.
- *Placenta* Maternal glucocorticoids are inactivated in the placenta by 11βHSD. Maternal androgens are converted to oestrogens by placental aromatase, thus protecting female foetus from virilization.

Table 72.1 Management of adrenal insufficiency during pregnancy

Hydrocortisone 20–30 mg p/o in divided doses, as per prepregnancy dose
Fludrocortisone 50–200 μg p/o, as per prepregnancy dose
During uncomplicated labour:
Hydrocortisone 100 mg i/m 6 hourly for 24 h, then reduce to maintenance dose over 72 h
Keep well hydrated
Fludrocortisone may be discontinued while on high doses of hydrocortisone

Addison's disease in pregnancy

- No associated foetal morbidity in women who have pre-existing primary adrenal insufficiency as foetus produces and regulates its own adrenal steroids.
- Management of Addison's disease does not differ in pregnancy.
- Glucocorticoids which are metabolized by placental 11βHSD preferred (i.e. prednisolone or hydrocortisone) to avoid foetal adrenal suppression.
- No increase in glucocorticoid dose is required throughout pregnancy.
- However, high dose intramuscular hydrocortisone should be given at the time of delivery to cover the stress of labour.
- Doses may be tapered to normal maintenance doses in the post-partum period (see Table 72.1).
- Addison's disease developing in pregnancy may result in an adrenal crisis, particularly at the time of delivery, because of a delay in diagnosis.
- In early pregnancy vomiting, fatigue and hyperpigmentation and low BP may be wrongly attributed to pregnancy. However, persisting symptoms should alert the clinician.
- If supected, the diagnosis is confirmed by the presence of low serum cortisol concentrations with failure to rise following ACTH stimulation, and high ACTH levels. However, the normal ranges for serum ACTH and cortisol concentrations have not been established in pregnancy.
- Chronic maternal adrenal insufficiency may be associated with intrauterine foetal growth retardation.
- There is no increased risk of developing Addison's disease in the immediate postpartum period.

Congenital adrenal hyperplasia

- Fertility is reduced, particularly women with the salt-wasting form of CAH.
- Reasons:
  - inadequate vaginal introitus despite reconstructive surgery
  - anovulation as a result of hyperandrogenaemia
- 30–60% of women with CAH and an adequate vaginal introitus are fertile.
- Fertility may be maximized by optimal suppression of hyperandrogenism by glucocorticoid therapy (see p. 369).
- No major complications in pregnancy are known in women with CAH.
- However, women are more likely to require caesarian section for cephalopelvic disproportion.
- Management is the same as in the non-pregnant woman and steroids are increased at the time of delivery as for Addison's disease.
- Monitor serum testosterone and electrolytes every 6–8 weeks
- Risk to foetus:
  - no risk of virilization from maternal hyperandrogenism as placenta will aromatize androgens to oestrogens
  - glucocorticoids do not increase the risk of congenital abnormalities
  - if partner is a hetereozygote or homozygote for CAH then the foetus has a 50% risk of CAH. Prenatal treatment with dexamethasone will then be necessary to avoid virilization of a female foetus (see p. 370).

Phaeochromocytoma

- Rare but potentially lethal in pregnancy. Maternal mortality may still be as high as 17%, and 30% foetal mortality if not treated promptly. Highest risk of hypertensive crisis and death is during labour.
- Suspect in women with hypertension, persistent or intermittent, especially in the absence of proteinuria or oedema.
- Suspect if paroxysmal symptoms are present: palpitations, sweating, headache.
- Prenantal screening in high-risk women eg those with a history or family history of MEN-2 or von Hippel–Lindau syndrome.
- Diagnose by 24 hurinary catecholamine collection.
- Tumour localization is important – MRI is the imaging of choice in pregnancy.
- Localization:
  - right adrenal 25%
  - left adrenal 17%
  - bilateral adrenal 17%
  - intra-abdominal extra-adrenal 32%

Management of phaeochromocytoma

- *α-blockade: phenoxybenzamine* Safe in pregnancy. The starting dose is 10 mg 12 hourly and is built up gradually to a maximum of 20 mg every 8 h.
- *β-blockade: propranolol* Only after adequate α-blockade. May increase the risk of intrauterine foetal growth retardation. Give in a dose of 40 mg 8 hourly.
- *Surgery* Before 24 weeks gestation, surgical removal of phaeochromocytoma is relatively safe following α- and β-blockade. After 24 weeks gestation, defer surgery until foetal maturity, then combine caesarian section with removal of tumour. Ensure adequate adrenergic blockade before surgery.

Further reading

Hadden DR. Adrenal disorders of pregnancy. *Endocrinology and Metabolism Clinics of North America* 1995; 24(1): 139–151.

Part VI
Calcium and bone metabolism

Chapter 73

Calcium and bone physiology

Bone turnover

In order to ensure that bone can undertake its mechanical and metabolic functions it is in a constant state of turnover (see Figure 73.1).

- *osteoclasts* derived from the monocytic series, resorb bone
- *osteoblasts* derived from the fibroblast like cells, make bone
- *osteocytes* buried osteoblasts, sense mechanical strain in bone.

Bone mass during life

See Fig. 73.2.

Bone is laid down rapidly during skeletal growth at puberty. Following this there is a period of stabilization of bone mass in early adult life. After the age of ~40 there is a gradual loss of bone in both sexes. This occurs at the rate of approximately 0.5% annually. However, in women after the menopause there is a period of rapid bone loss. The accelerated loss is maximal immediately after the cessation of ovarian function and then gradually declines over about 10 years until the previous gradual rate of loss is once again established. The excess bone loss associated with the menopause is of the order of 10% of skeletal mass. This menopause-associated loss coupled with higher peak bone mass in men explains why osteoporosis and its associated fractures are more common in women.

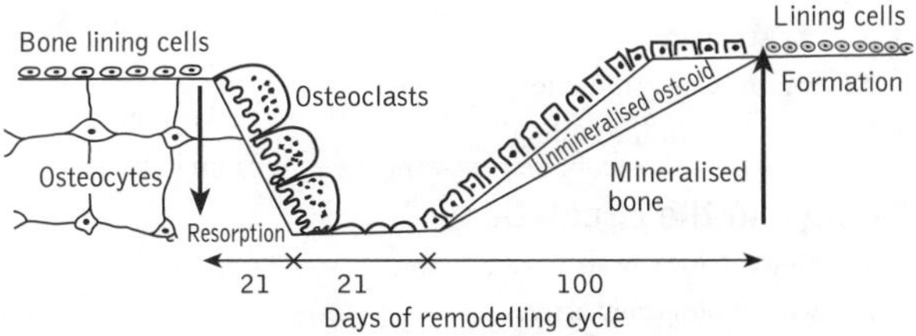

Fig. 73.1 Bone turnover during remodelling cycle.

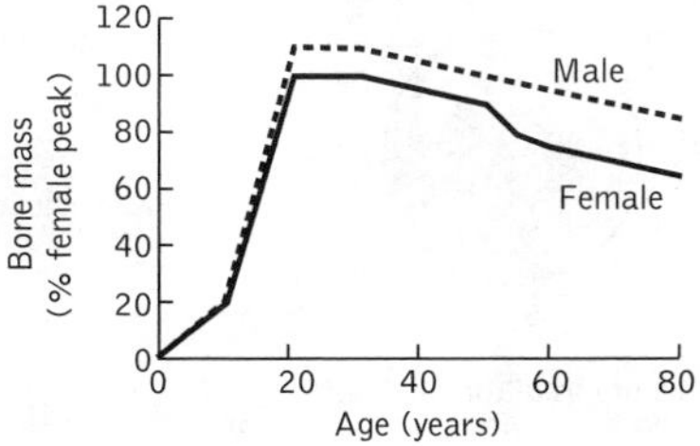

Fig. 73.2 Bone mass and age.

Calcium

Roles of calcium

- Skeletal strength
- Neuromuscular conduction
- Stimulus secretion coupling

Calcium in the circulation

Circulating calcium exists in several forms (see Fig. 73.3).

- ionized – biologically active
- complexed to citrate, phosphate etc – biologically active
- bound to protein, mainly albumin – inactive.

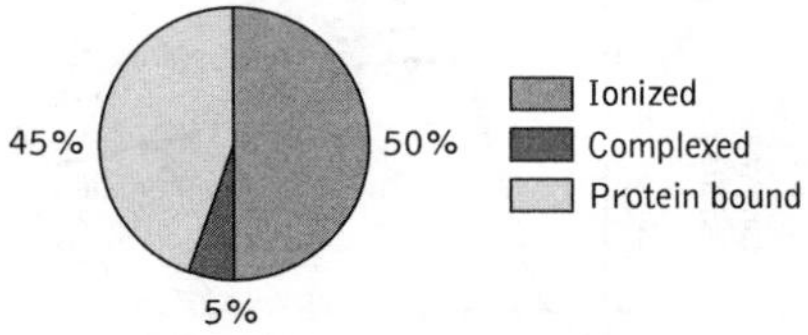

Fig. 73.3 Forms of circulating calcium.

Chapter 74
Investigation of bone

Bone turnover markers

May be useful in:
- assessing overall risk of osteoporotic fracture
- judging response to treatments for osteoporosis.

Resorption markers

- *Collagen crosslinks* These make use of the fact that when collagen is laid down in bone the fibres are held in trimers by covalent links. These links are chemically very stable and are specific to the type of collagen. The excretion of fragments containing these crosslinks is a much better indicator of bone turnover. It can be measured either as the excretion of the linking molecules themselves, known as deoxypyridinoline crosslinks or as small fragments of the ends of the collagen molecule including these crosslinks, known as *telopeptides.* These latter markers can be derived from either the N- or the C-terminal of the collagen molecule and separate assays are available for each.
- *Urinary hydroxyproline* relies on the fact that hydroxyproline is unique to collagen and so any hydroxyproline in urine must come from collagen breakdown. Unfortunately, this is not specific to bone (type 1) collagen; furthermore, hydroxyproline is variably metabolized before excretion and so its urinary levels are not a true index of collagen destruction. It has accordingly been superseded.

Formation markers

- *Total alkaline phosphatase* not specific also found in the liver, intestine, and placenta. It is also relatively insensitive to small changes in bone turnover and has only found general use in the monitoring of the activity of Paget's disease.
- *Bone-specific alkaline phosphatase* is more specific but its clinical utility is not yet clear.
- *Osteocalcin* a vitamin K dependent protein that accounts for about 1% of bone matrix. The serum level of osteocalcin appears to reflect osteoblast activity. However, the results obtained with bone specific alkaline phosphatase and osteocalcin do not always correlate. This is particularly true in Paget's disease where the osteocalcin is frequently scarcely elevated despite the marked increase in bone turnover.

Bone imaging

Skeletal radiology

- useful for:
  - diagnosis of fracture
  - diagnosis of specific diseases (e.g. Paget's disease and osteomalacia)
  - identification of bone dysplasia
- not useful for assessing bone density.

Isotope bone scanning

Bone seeking isotopes, particularly ^{99m}technetium-labelled bisphosphonates, are concentrated in areas of localized increased bone cell activity. They are useful for identifying localized areas of bone disease such as fracture, metastasis, or Paget's disease. However, isotope uptake is not selective and so increased activity on a scan does not indicate the nature of the underlying bone disease. Hence, subsequent radiology of affected regions is frequently needed to establish the diagnosis. Isotope bone scans are particularly useful in Paget's disease to establish the extent of skeletal involvement and the underlying disease activity

Bone mass measurements

See Table 74.1.

Interpretation of results

- The differences in normal ranges between the machines of different manufacturers has led to the practice of quoting bone mass measurements in terms of the number of standard deviations they lie from an expected mean. This can be done in two ways, T score and Z score: see Table 74.2.
- It is generally accepted a reduction of 1 SD in bone density will double the risk of fracture
- WHO has developed guidelines for the diagnosis of osteoporosis in postmenopausal women (see Table 74.3).
- No similar criteria have been set in men, but the same thresholds are gaining general acceptance.
- For some secondary causes of osteoporosis, particularly corticosteroid use, it has been suggested that the less stringent criterion of T score <–1.5 be used.

Bone biopsy

Bone biopsy is occasionally necessary for the diagnosis of difficult patients with metabolic bone disease. This is usually in the context of suspected osteomalacia. Bone biopsy is not indicated for the routine diagnosis of osteoporosis. It is best undertaken in specialist centres.

Table 74.1 Measurement of bone density

Technique	Site	Measures	Radiation	Reproducibility
Dual energy absoptiometry (DXA)	Spine* Femur* Whole body Forearm Calcaneus	Bone mineral per unit area (g/cm^2)	~1 μSv per site	<1% at spine <2% at femur
Quantitative computed tomography (QCT)	Spine Forearm	True bone mineral density (BMD) (g/cm^3)	~50 μSv at spine	~1%
Quantitative ultrasound (QUS)	Calcaneus Tibia Fingers	Speed of sound or broadband ultrasound attenuation	Nil	Poor

* Accepted as 'gold standard' measurement.

Table 74.2 T score and Z score

	T score	Z score
Definition	Number of SDs bone density lies from peak mean density for that sex	Number of SDs bone density lies from mean density expected for that sex and age
Significance		Age-independent effect on BMD i.e. secondary osteoporosis
Normal range	Not applicable	–2 – +2

Table 74.3 WHO proposals for diagnosis of postmenopausal osteoporosis

T score	Fragility fracture	Diagnosis
≥–1		Normal
<–1 but ≥–2.5		Low bone mass (osteopenia)
<–2.5	No	Osteoporosis
<–2.5	Yes	Established (severe) osteoporosis

Chapter 75
Investigation of calcium, phosphate, and magnesium

Blood concentration

Calcium

The importance of obtaining blood for calcium measurement in the fasting state with little venous stasis has been overstated. It is, however, important to collect blood for the estimation of parathyroid hormone (PTH) and phosphate levels after an overnight fast.

In most clinical situations direct measurement of the ionized calcium concentration is not necessary. However, it is important to correct the measured calcium concentration for the prevailing level of albumin (see below).

Phosphate and magnesium

Measurements of plasma phosphate and magnesium do not normally require to be corrected for plasma proteins. However, phosphate should be measured after an overnight fast.

Correction of measured calcium concentration

corrected Ca = measured Ca + 0.02 × (40 – albumin)
where calcium is in mmol/L and albumin in g/L.

Urine excretion

Calcium

A measurment of 24 h excretion of calcium is useful for the assessment of the risk of renal stone formation or calcification in states of chronic hypercalcaemia. In other circumstances, particularly the assessment of the cause of hypercalcaemia (primary hyperparathyroidism versus familial hypocalciuric hypercalcaemia) an estimate of the renal handling of calcium is more useful. This is best estimate using the fasting urine calcium excretion (CaE). This is calculated from simultaneous measurement of urine and plasma calcium and creatinine concentrations (see below). If all the concentrations are in mmol/L the normal range is <0.05mmol/L in glomerular filtrate (<0.01 in FHH).

Phosphate

A 24 h measurement of phosphate excretion largely reflects dietary phosphate intake and has little clinical utility.

Calculation of calcium excretion (CaE)

CaE = [urine calcium]/[urine creatinine] × [plasma creatinine]

Calcium-regulating hormones

Parathyroid hormone

Reliable immunoassays for PTH are now available. In general, these are two-site assays aimed at estimating the concentration of the intact PTH molecule. PTH is relatively labile and specimens require careful handling including early separation from the cells and speedy freezing for storage if the assay is not performed immediately. Since PTH secretion is suppressed by calcium ingestion, it should be measured in the fasting state. The normal range depends on the precise assay employed but typical values are 10–60 pg/mL (1–6 pmol/L).

Vitamin D and its metabolites

25OH vitamin D (25OHD)

This is the main storage form of vitamin D and the best measure of vitamin D status. It is relatively stable and samples do not require as speedy handling as PTH. In clinical terms, it is the total vitamin D concentration that is important. The conventionally accepted normal range is in the region of 5–30 ng/mL (roughly 12.5–75 nmol/L). However, this normal range was set with the idea of avoiding frank osteomalacia. If the 25OHD is 5–15 ng/mL there is likely to be a state of vitamin D insufficiency with elevated PTH concentration and increased bone turnover. This can be associated with increased risk of fracture, particularly in the old people. Low levels of 25OHD can result from a variety of causes (see table on p. 574). Likewise, it is unlikely that serious intoxication will occur unless the 25OHD is >100 ng/mL. A more pragmatic reference range might be in the region of 20–80 ng/mL (50–200 nmol/L). (For conversion from ng/mL to nmol/L, multiply by 2.46).

1,25$(OH)_2$ vitamin D (1,25$(OH)_2$D)

Although this is the active form of vitamin D, measurement of its concentration is less often clinically useful than measurement of 25OHD or PTH. It is sometimes useful as a marker of PTH activity and in diseases such as sarcoidosis where there is increased extrarenal synthesis of 1,25$(OH)_2$D. The normal range is generally accepted as 20–50 pg/mL (50–125 pmol/L).

Parathyroid hormone related peptide (PTHrP)

It is possible to measure the level of this oncofoetoprotein in serum. Although it is raised in many cases of humoural hypercalcaemia of malignancy the diagnosis is usually readily made from other sources (i.e. Ca with suppressed PTH) and this measurement is non-contributory. PTHrP is highly labile and specimens need to be collected into special preservative (trasylol) and separated and stored rapidly after venepuncture.

Calcitonin

Calcitonin assays are available but their utility is confined to the diagnosis and monitoring of medullary carcinoma of the thyroid. There is no role for calcitonin measurements in the routine investigation of calcium and bone metabolism.

Chapter 7

Chapter 76
Hypercalcaemia

Epidemiology

Hypercalcaemia is found in 5% of hospital patients but in only one-tenth that proportion of the general population.

Causes

Many different disease states can lead to hypercalcaemia. These are listed by order of importance in hospital practice on p. 545. In asymptomatic community-dwelling subjects the vast majority of hypercalcaemia is the result of hyperparathyroidism.

Causes of hypercalcaemia

Common

- hyperparathyroidism
  - primary
  - tertiary
- malignancy
  - humoral hypercalcaemia
  - multiple myeloma
  - bony metastases

Less common

- vitamin D intoxication
- familial hypocalciuric hypercalcaemia
- sarcoidosis and other granulomatous diseases

Uncommon

- thiazide diuretics
- immobilization
- hyperthyroidism
- renal failure
- Addison's disease
- vitamin A intoxication

Clinical features

Notwithstanding the underlying cause of hypercalcaemia, the clinical features are similar. With corrected calcium levels <3.0 mmol/L it is unlikely that any symptoms will be related to the hypercalcaemia itself. With progressive increases in calcium concentration the likelihood of symptoms increases.

The clinical features of hypercalcaemia are well recognized (see below): unfortunately, they are non-specific and may equally relate to underlying illness.

Clinical signs of hypercalcaemia are rare. With the exception of band keratopathy, these are not specific. It is important to seek clinical evidence of underlying causes of hypercalcaemia, particularly malignant disease.

In addition to these specific symptoms of hypercalcaemia, symptoms of the long-term consequences of hypercalcaemia should be sought. These include the presence of bone pain or fracture and renal stones. These tend to indicate the presence of chronic hypercalcaemia.

Symptoms of hypercalcaemia

Symptoms of hypercalcaemia

- renal
  - polyuria
  - polydipsia
- gastrointestinal
  - anorexia
  - vomiting
  - constipation
  - abdominal pain
- central nervous system
  - confusion
  - lethargy
  - depression
- other
  - pruritus
  - sore eyes

Investigation of hypercalcaemia

Confirm the diagnosis

- plasma calcium (corrected for albumin)

Determine the mechanism

- *increased PTH* parathyroid overactivity (primary or tertiary hyperparathyroidism)
- *decreased PTH* non-parathyroid cause
- *normal PTH:*
  - may imply parathyroid overactivity – incomplete suppression
  - may imply altered calcium sensor – familial hypocalciuric hypercalcaemia – CaE will be low
- CaE

Seek underlying illness (where indicated)

- history and examination
- chest radiograph
- FBC and ESR
- biochemical profile (renal and liver function)
- thyroid function tests (exclude thyrotoxicosis)
- 25OHD and $1,25(OH)_2D$
- plasma and urine protein electrophoresis (exclude myeloma)
- serum cortisol (short synacthen test (exclude Addison's disease))

To determine end organ damage

- 24 h urine calcium (± urine creatinine for reproducibility)
- renal tract ultrasound (exclude calculi, nephrocalcinosis)
- skeletal radiographs (lateral thoracolumbar spine, hands, knees)
- BMD
- bone turnover markers

Hyperparathyroidism

Present in up to 1 in 500 of the general population where it is predominantly a disease of postmenopausal women.

The normal physiological response to hypocalcaemia is an increase in PTH secretion. This is termed *secondary hyperparathyroidism* and is not pathological inasmuch as the PTH secretion remains under feedback control. Continued stimulation of the parathyroid glands can lead to autonomous production of PTH. This in turn causes hypercalcaemia which is termed *tertiary hyperparathyroidism*. This is usually seen in the context of renal disease but can occur in any state of chronic hypocalcaemia such as vitamin D deficiency or malabsorption.

Pathology

- 85% single adenoma
- 14% hyperplasia
- often associated with other endocrine abnormalities, particularly multiple endocrine neoplasia (MEN) types I and II (p. 717).
- <1% carcinoma

Clinical features

- Majority of patients are asymptomatic
- Features of hypercalcaemia
- End organ damage see box on p. 549.

Investigation

Potential diagnostic pitfalls:

- FHH – differentiate with CaE (p. 555) (<0.01 in FHH).
- Long-standing vitamin D deficiency where the concomitant osteomalacia and calcium malabsorption can mask hypercalcaemia which becomes apparent only after vitamin D repletion.

Investigation is, therefore, primarily aimed at determining the presence of end organ damage from the hypercalcaemia in order to determine whether operative intervention is indicated.

Localization of abnormal parathyroid glands

This should only form part of a preoperative assessment and is not indicated in the initial diagnosis of hyperparathyroidism.

- Neck exploration by experienced surgeon is optimal in first instance.
- After failed neck exploration may need other techniques, which include:
  - ^{99m}Tc-sestamibi
  - thallium/technetium subtraction scanning (less sensitive)
  - CT
  - ultrasound.
- Following failed neck exploration it is often useful to undertake angiography with selective venous sampling – this should be confined to specialist centres.

End organ damage in hyperparathyroidism

Bone

- osteoporosis
  - common
  - affects all sites but predominant loss is in peripheral cortical bone
- radiographic changes
  - uncommon
  - include subperiosteal resorption, abnormal skull vault, eroded lamina dura (around teeth), and bone cysts
- osteitis fibrosa cystica
  - rare
  - usually with tertiary hyperparathyroidism

Kidneys

- renal calculi
- nephrocalcinosis
- renal impairment

Joints

- chondrocalcinosis
- pseudogout

Pancreatitis

Treatment

Surgery

- for indications see box on facing page.
- only by experienced surgeon (>20 procedures per year)
  - *adenoma* remove affected gland
  - *hyperplasia* either
    - partial parathyroidectomy (perhaps with reimplantation of tissue in more accessible site), or
    - total parathyroidectomy with medical treatment for hypoparathyroidism

Observation

- suitable for patients with mild disease with no evidence of end organ damage
- such patients can continue for many years without deterioration
- they require follow up:
  - *annual* plasma calcium, renal function, blood pressure
  - *every 2–3 years* BMD, renal ultrasound
- any significant deterioration is an indication for surgery.

Medical management

Only indicated if patient not suitable for surgery.

- hormone replacement therapy
  - reduces plasma and urine calcium
  - preserves bone mass
- bisphosphonates
  - only transient effect on plasma and urine calcium
  - preserve bone mass
- oral phosphate
  - sustained reduction in plasma calcium
  - increased ectopic calcification (particularly kidney)
  - increased PTH
  - cannot be recommended.

Indications for surgery in primary hyperparathyroidism (American NIH consensus)*

Definite

- markedly elevated serum calcium (>3 mmol/L)
- previous disequilibrium hypercalcaemia
- impaired renal function
- renal stones (symptomatic or on radiograph)
- nephrocalcinosis
- substantially elevated urinary calcium excretion (>10 mmol/24 h)
- reduced BMD

Relative

- concomitant illness
- difficulty of follow up
- younger (<50) patients
- patient preference.

* These guidelines (1990) will shortly be updated.

Complications of parathyroidectomy

Mechanical

- vocal cord paresis
  - usually transient
  - may be permanent with extensive exploration, particularly repeated surgery
  - may require teflon injection of vocal cord
- tracheal compression from haematoma

Metabolic (hypocalcaemia)

- transient
  - due to suppression of remaining glands
  - usually causes little problem
  - may sometimes require oral therapy with calcium ± vitamin D metabolites (see below)
- severe
  - due to hungry bones (calcitriol 1 μg/day and oral calcium, e.g. Sandocal-400 3× daily may be required for several weeks)
  - occurs in patients with pre-existing bone disease
  - prevent by pretreatment with calcium and vitamin D (1 g and 20 μg (800 I.U.) respectively daily) for several weeks – rarely required in practice nowadays
  - may settle with oral therapy but often requires intravenous calcium (see below).

Outcome after surgery

- <10% fail to become normocalcaemic; of these half will respond to a second operation
- Relapse occurs in 1/20 patients with adenoma but 1/6 with hyperplasia.
- All patients with parathyroid hyperplasia (including MEN) need indefinite follow-up.
- If the patient is rendered hypoparathyroid by surgery they will need lifelong supplements of calcium ± active metabolites of vitamin D. This can lead to hypercalciuria and the risk of stone formation may still be present in these patients.

Other causes of hypercalcaemia

Hypercalcaemia of malignancy

Mechanism

See Table 76.1.

Clinical features

Hypercalcaemia is usually a late manifestation of malignant disease and frequently indicates the presence of an untreatable tumour load. One exception to this is is in small endocrine tumours such as carcinoids and islet cell tumours which can produce humoural mediators of hypercalcaemia (PTHrP) in the absence of significant spread. Hypercalcaemic symptoms are non-specific and frequently difficult to distinguish from those of the underlying disease.

Investigation

See investigation of hypercalcaemia (p. 547).

Factors suggesting hypercalcaemia of malignancy include:

- ↑calcium
- ↓PTH
- other features of malignant disease
- ↑PTHrP – not usually measured in clinical practice

Steroid suppression test is not usually needed now that modern hormone assays are available. Even when used its sensitivity and specificity are poor.

Treatment

Frequently patients requiring treatment will have severe symptomatic hypercalcaemia. Often emergency treatment is necessary to stabilize the patient before confirmation of the diagnosis of the underlying malignant state can be confirmed. In such circumstances the principles of management are the same as those of severe hypercalcaemia from any cause (see p. 556).

Table 76.1 Mechanism of hypercalcaemia of malignancy

Mechanism	Tumour type
	Direct invasion Haematological
	Extensive metastases, e.g. breast
	Direct release of calcium from bone
	Cytokine mediated, e.g. IL-1, IL-6, TNF
Humoral hypercalcaemia	Due to production of PTHrP
	Specific tumour types:
	– squamous carcinomas from any site
	– some breast carcinomas
	– lymphoma due to HTLV-1
	Effect on PTH receptor
	– increased renal reabsorption of calcium – increased bone resorption
True ectopic PTH production	Very rare

Familial hypocalciuric hypercalcaemia

FHH: also known as familial benign hypercalcaemia.

- 2% of all asymptomatic hypercalcaemia.
- Autosomal dominant with virtually complete penetrance.
- Mutation in the calcium sensing receptor which reduces its sensitivity such that the body behaves as if it were experiencing normocalcaemia even though the plasma calcium level is elevated.
- generally benign and is not usually associated with symptoms or adverse effects such as renal stones or bone disease
- Does not show any sustained benefit from parathyroidectomy.
- A few adults with FHH have had recurrent pancreatitis. In such cases parathyroidectomy may reduce the frequency of attacks.
- The homozygous state produces severe life-threatening hypercalcaemia soon after birth (neonatal severe hyperparathyroidism). In such cases total parathyroidectomy is life saving.
- Patients have low 24 hr urine calcium excretion (CaE), see p. 539.

Management of severe hypercalcaemia

1 Stabilize the level of hypercalcaemia and prevent any further decline in renal function. This requires the intravenous infusion of large quantities of 0.9% saline, frequently 3–6 L over the first 24 h. If there is a danger of salt and water retention a loop diuretic should be added. This is the only role of diuretics in the management of hypercalcaemia. There is no evidence that they lead to sustained reduction in plasma calcium. As they cause intravascular volume depletion they can worsen the situation and so should otherwise be avoided. In very severe renal impairment dialysis might help both stabilize the fluid balance and also assist in the removal of calcium from the plasma.

2 Once the patient is volume replete it is necessary to treat the cause of the hypercalcaemia. The most effective therapy available for this is intravenous bisphosphonate. Although these agents are specific inhibitors of bone resorption they are frequently beneficial when hypercalcaemia is the result of increased tubular reabsorption of calcium brought about by PTHrP production. Two bisphosphonates are currently available in the UK for this use. *Pamidronate* is given as a single intravenous infusion of between 15 and 90 mg, depending on the level of hypercalcaemia. The infusion should be made up in a concentration no greater than 60 mg in 250 mL 0.9% saline and given at 20 mg/h. *Clodronate* is given as a single infusion of 1500 mg in 500 mL of 0.9% saline over 4 h. Plasma calcium will usually fall by about 72 h with a nadir at 5 days. Clodronate can be given orally to prolong the duration of effect although it is more usual to retreat with intravenous bisphosphonate as the calcium rises. I/v bisphosphonate therapy is generally well tolerated but a minority of patient may develop increased bone pain or a transient pyrexia and flu-like symptoms. Rarer complications include rashes and iritis. Bisphosphonates have been associated with deterioration in renal function. For this reason, they should not be given to patients until adequate rehydration has been administered. In addition, consideration of dose reduction should be made in patients with GFR less than 30 mL/min.

3 Although the majority of patients will respond to intravenous bisphosphonates not all will do so. In such cases treatment with calcitonin may be helpful. This is usually given as *salmon calcitonin* and may need to be given as high doses of up to 400 IU by i/m injection every 6 h. In addition to the large volume of injection required this is frequently poorly tolerated with side-effects such as flushing and nausea. Some cases of resistant hypercalcaemia will respond to corticosteroid therapy which needs to be given in high doses such as prednisolone 40 mg daily.

Vitamin D intoxication

- The diagnosis is established by the presence of greatly elevated concentrations of 25OHD (>100 ng/mL) and $1,25(OH)_2D$ together with suppressed PTH. If calcitriol or alfacalcidol is the offending compound then 25OHD levels will not be elevated.
- In mild cases, particularly when the active vitamin D metabolites are involved, the only treatment necessary is to withdraw the offending treatment and let the calcium levels settle. If the longer-acting vitamin D metabolites are involved then active treatment may be necessary. Patients should first be stabilized with a saline infusion (see p. 556). Following this the traditional management has been to give high dose oral corticosteroids such as prednisolone 40 mg daily. This reduces the vitamin D-stimulated calcium absorption and may have beneficial effects on vitamin D metabolism following intoxication. However, there is now emerging evidence to suggest that bisphosphonates given as for hypercalcaemia of malignancy are equally effective.

Sarcoidosis

- Together with other granulomatous disorders sarcoidosis causes hypercalcaemia by extrarenal production of $1,25(OH)_2D$ in granulomata. This process is not under feedback inhibition, but is substrate regulated. The hypercalcaemia is therefore dependent on vitamin D supply. Patients frequently present with hypercalcaemia in summer or following foreign holidays when the endogenous production of vitamin D is maximal.
- The biochemical picture is of normal 25OHD, raised $1,25(OH)_2D$ and suppressed PTH. In addition, other markers of sarcoid activity such as raised angiotensin converting enzyme (ACE) activity are frequently present.
- Treatment with high-dose corticosteroids as in vitamin D intoxication is generally recommended to control sarcoid activity and to minimize the gastrointestinal effects of the excess $1,25(OH)_2D$. The antifungal *ketaconazole*, and the antimalarial *chloroquine* (or its derivative, hydroxychloroquine) modulate vitamin D metabolism and have been reported to reduce hypercalcaemia in patients with sarcoidosis. If the calcium levels do not respond to these, there is evidence that bisphosphonates might be useful in this situation.

Chapter 77
Hypocalcaemia

Causes

Although hypocalcaemia can result from failure of any of the mechanisms by which plasma calcium concentration is maintained, it is usually the result of either failure of PTH secretion or because of the inability to release calcium from bone. These causes are summarized in the box on the facing page.

Causes of hypocalcaemia

Hypoparathyroidism

- destruction of parathyroid glands
  - autoimmune
  - surgical
  - radiation
  - infiltration
- failure of parathyroid development
  - isolated, e.g. X-linked
  - with other abnormalities, e.g. DiGeorge syndrome (with thymic aplasia, immunodeficiency. and cardiac anomolies)
- failure of PTH secretion
  - magnesium deficiency
  - overactivity of calcium sensing receptor
- Failure of PTH action
  - pseudohypoparathyroidism – due to G protein abnormality

Failure of $1,25(OH)_2D$ levels

- drugs, e.g. ketaconazole
- acute pancreatitis
- acute systemic illness

Failure of release of calcium from bone

- osteomalacia
  - vitamin D deficiency
  - vitamin D resistance
  - renal failure
- inhibition of bone resorption
  - hypocalcaemic drugs e.g. cisplatin, calcitonin, oral phosphate
- increased uptake of calcium into bone
  - osteoblastic metastases
  - hungry bone syndrome

Complexing of calcium from the circulation

- increased albumin binding in alkalosis
- acute pancreatitis
  - formation of calcium soaps from autodigestion of fat
  - abnormal PTH and vitamin D metabolism
  - phosphate infusion
- multiple blood transfusion – complexing by citrate

Clinical features

The clinical features of hypocalcaemia are largely as a result of increased neuromuscular excitability. In order of increasing severity these include:

- tingling, especially of fingers, toes, or lips
- numbness, especially of fingers, toes, or lips
- cramps
- carpopedal spasm
- stridor due to laryngospam
- seizures.

The symptoms of hypocalcaemia tend to reflect the severity and rapidity of onset of the metabolic abnormality.

Clinical signs of hypocalcaemia depend upon the demonstration of neuromuscular irritability before this necessarily causes symptoms:

- *Chvostek's sign* is elicited by tapping the facial nerve in front of the ear. A positive result is indicated by twitching of the corner of the mouth. Slight twitching is seen in up to 15% of normal women but more major involvement of the facial muscles is indicative of hypocalcaemia or hypomagnesaemia.
- *Trousseau's sign* is produced by occlusion of the blood supply to the arm by inflation of a sphygmomanometer cuff above arterial pressure for 3 min. If positive, there will be carpo-pedal spasm which may be accompanied by painful paraesthesiae.

In addition, there may be clinical signs and symptoms associated with the underlying condition:

- *Vitamin D deficiency* may be associated with bone pain, fractures, or proximal myopathy (see below).
- *Hypoparathyroidism* can be accompanied by mental retardation and personality disturbances as well as extrapyramidal signs, cataracts, and papilloedema.
- If *hypocalcaemia* is present during the development of the permanent teeth, these may show areas of enamel hypoplasia. This can be a useful physical sign indicating that the hypocalcaemia is longstanding.

Albright's hereditary osteodystrophy

Patients with the most common type of pseudohypoparathyroidism (type Ia) have a characteristic set of skeletal abnormalities known as Albright's hereditary osteodystrophy. This comprises:

- short stature
- obesity
- round face
- short metacarpals.

Some individuals with Albright's hereditary osteodystrophy do not appear to have a disorder of calcium metabolism. In the past the term *pseudopseudohypoparathyroidism* has been used to describe these. However, it is now clear that these reflect different manifestations of the same underlying genetic defect. This leads to a deficiency of the Gsα protein. In the light of the same underlying cellular abnormality, there has been a tendency to avoid the more cumbersome designations and refer to all such patients as having Albright's hereditary osteodystrophy.

Investigation

- Plasma calcium
- PTH The presence of a low, or even normal, PTH concentration implies failure of PTH secretion
- Vitamin D
- Magnesium may be needed if patient fails to respond
- Ellsworth–Howard test if pseudohypoparathyroidism suspected (see p. 565)
- In chronic hypocalcaemia skull radiographs will frequently demonstrate calcification of the basal ganglia. As this is of no clinical consequence it is debatable whether the investigation can be justified.

Modified Ellsworth–Howard test

Method

1 Fast overnight

2 Give 200 mL water every 30 min from 6 a.m. to 11 a.m.

3 From 8:30 a.m. collect timed 30 min urine samples for phosphate, creatinine, and cAMP.

4 At 8:45 a.m., 10:15 a.m., and 10:45 a.m. collect blood for creatinine and phosphate.

5 At 10:00 a.m. commence 10 min infusion of synthetic PTH 1–34, 5 units/kg to a maximum of 200 units.

6 Calculate urinary cAMP excretion as

cAMPE=[urine cAMP] × [plasma creatinine]/[urine creatinine]

7 Calculate tubular maximum for phosphate reabsorption:

$TmP/GFR = ([plasma\ PO_4] - P_E)/(1 - 0.01 \times \log_e([plasma\ PO_4]/P_E)$

where $P_E = [urine\ PO_4] \times [plasma\ creatinine]/[urine\ creatinine]$ and all measurements are in mmol/L

or using the nomogram of Walton and Bijvoet (*Lancet* 1975; 2: 309).

Interpretation

- Patients with a normal response to PTH will demonstrate a brisk increase in cAMP excretion and a decrease in TmP.
- Patients with pseudohypoparathyroidism type I show neither response.
- There is a rarer condition, pseudohypoparathyroidism type II, in which there is a normal cAMP response but a blunted phosphaturic response.
- A similar pattern can be seen in some patients with profound hypocalcaemia due to vitamin D deficiency. It is therefore important to ensure that patients are vitamin D replete before undertaking a PTH infusion test.

Treatment

- *Acute symptomatic hypocalcaemia* is a medical emergency and demands urgent treatment whatever the cause (see p. 567).
- Treatment of *chronic hypocalcaemia* is more dependent on the cause.

Chronic hypocalcaemia

Hypoparathyroidism

- In hypoparathyroidism the aim is not to achieve normalization of the plasma calcium, rather to render them asymptomatic with a plasma calcium at, or just below, the normal lower limit. The reason for this is that the renal retention of calcium brought about by PTH has been lost. Thus, any attempt to raise the plasma calcium well into the normal range is likely to result in unacceptable hypercalciuria with the risk of nephrocalcinosis and renal stones.
- In patients with mild parathyroid dysfunction it may be possible to achieve acceptable calcium concentrations by using calcium supplements alone. If used in this way these need to be given in large doses, perhaps as much as 1 g elemental calcium 3x daily.
- The majority of patients will not achieve adequate control with such treatment. In those cases it is necessary to use vitamin D or its metabolites in pharmacological doses to maintain plasma calcium. The more potent analogues of vitamin D such as *calcitriol* or *alfacalcidol* have the advantage over high-dose calciferol that it is easier to make changes in therapy in response to plasma calcium levels. If hypercalcaemia does occur it settles much more quickly following withdrawal of these compounds than calciferol. The dose of vitamin D is determined by the clinical response but usually lies in the range of 0.5 – 2 μg of the potent analogues daily. Hypercalcaemia is the main hazard of such therapy. Plasma calcium levels must be checked frequently after any change in therapy and no less than three monthly whilst on maintenance.
- It is essential to ensure an adequate intake of calcium as well as vitamin D analogues. In some patients it is necessary to give calcium supplementation, particularly in the young. It is very rarely needed in patients aged >60 years.

Pseudohypoparathyroidism

- The principles underlying the treatment of pseudohypoparathyroidism are the same as those underlying hypoparathyroidism.

- Patients with the most common form of pseudohypoparathyroidism may have resistance to the action of other hormones which rely on G protein signalling. They therefore need to be assessed for thyroid and gonadal dysfunction (because of defective TSH or gonadotrophin action). If these deficiencies are present they need to be treated in the conventional manner.

Vitamin D deficiency

Treatment of osteomalacia and vitamin D deficiency is dealt with on p. 574.

Treatment of acute hypocalcaemia

- Patients with tetany or seizures require urgent intravenous treatment with calcium gluconate (less irritant than the chloride).
  - This is a 10% w/v solution (10 mL + 2.25 mmol elemental calcium).
  - The solution should always be further diluted to minimize the risk of phlebitis or tissue damage if extravasation occurs.
- Initially, 20 mL of 10% calcium gluconate should be diluted in 100–200 mL of 0.9% saline or 5% glucose and infused over about 10 min.
- Repeat, if symptoms not resolved.
- Care must be taken if the patient has heart disease, especially if taking digoxin, as too rapid elevation of the plasma calcium can cause arrhythmias. In such patients it is advisable to monitor the cardiac rhythm during calcium infusion.
- In order to maintain the plasma calcium give a continuous calcium infusion. 100 mL of 10% calcium gluconate should be added to 1 L of saline or glucose solution and infused over 24 h.
- The plasma calcium should be checked regularly (not less than 6 hourly) and the infusion rate adjusted in response to the change in concentration.
- Failure of the plasma calcium to respond to infused calcium should raise the possibility of hypomagnesaemia. This can be rapidly ascertained by plasma magnesium estimation and, if appropriate, a magnesium infusion commenced (see p. 581).

Chapter 78
Rickets and osteomalacia

Definitions

Osteomalacia occurs when there is inadequate mineralization of mature bone. *Rickets* is a disorder of the growing skeleton where there is inadequate mineralization of bone as it is laid down at the epiphysis. In most instances osteomalacia leads to build up of excessive unmineralized osteoid within the skeleton. In rickets there is build up of unmineralized osteoid in the growth plate. This leads to the characteristic radiological appearance of rickets with widening of the growth plate and loss of definition of the ossification centres. These two related conditions may coexist.

Table 78.1 Biochemical findings and causes of rickets and osteomalacia

	Ca	PO_4	Alkaline phosphatase	25OHD	$1,25(OH)_2D$	PTH	Other
Vitamin D deficiency	↓	↓	↑	↓	↓	↑	
Renal failure	↓	↑	↑	N	↓	↑	↓ GFR
VDDR type I (deficient 1a-hydroxylase)	↓	↓	↑	N	↓	↑	
VDDR type II (deficient vitamin D receptor)	↓	↓	↑	N	↑	↑	
X-linked hypophosphataemia (vitamin D resistant rickets)	N	↓	↑	N	N	N or ↑	
Oncogenic	N or ↓	↓	↑	N	↓	N	May have aminoaciduria, proteinuria
Phosphate depletion	N	↓	↑	N	[illegible]	N	↑ urine Ca
Fanconi syndrome	↓ or N	↓	↑	N	↓	N	acidosis, aminoaciduria, glycosuria
Renal tubular acidosis	↓ or N	↓	↑	N	N or ↓	N	Acidosis
Toxic (etidronate, fluoride, aluminium)	N	N	N	N	N	N	Diagnosed on biopsy

Clinical features

Osteomalacia

- bone pain
- deformity
- fracture
- proximal myopathy (depending on the underlying cause)
- hypocalcaemia (in vitamin D deficiency)

Rickets

- growth retardation
- bone pain and fracture
- skeletal deformity
  - bowing of the long bones
  - widening of the growth plates widening of the wrists, 'rickety rosary' (costochondral junctions enlarged)

Diagnosis

- The diagnosis of osteomalacia is usually based on the appropriate biochemical findings (see table 78.1).
- The majority of patients with osteomalacia will show no specific radiological abnormalities.
- The most characteristic abnormality is the *Looser's zone* or pseudofracture. If these are present they are virtually pathognomonic of osteomalacia.
- If the diagnosis of osteomalacia remains in doubt then bone biopsy may be necessary. This is often the only way of establishing the diagnosis in low turnover conditions such as the toxic osteomalacias.

Vitamin D resistance

Several different kindreds have been shown to have a defective vitamin D receptor. This is inherited as an autosomal recessive condition. It produces hypocalcaemia and osteomalacia with elevated serum levels of $1,25(OH)_2D$. Approximately two thirds of affected individuals have total alopecia. This condition is known as vitamin D-dependent rickets type II. If alopecia is present it is often termed type IIA in contrast to type IIB where hair growth is normal.

Treatment usually requires administration of large doses of active vitamin D metabolites, sometimes reaching doses of 60 μg of calcitriol daily.

Abnormal vitamin D metabolism

Although liver disease could, in theory, lead to deficient 25-hydroxylation of vitamin D there is so much functional reserve that this is seldom a clinical problem. Two cases of rickets due to hereditary defects of 25-hydroxylase have been reported.

The most common cause of failure of 1α-hydroxylase is renal failure. Congenital absence of this enzyme leads to a condition known as vitamin D-dependent rickets type I. This is inherited in an autosomal recessive fashion. It leads to profound rickets with myopathy and enamel hypoplasia. Very large doses of calciferol are needed to heal the bone lesions which, in contrast, will respond to physiological doses of alfacalcidol or calcitriol.

Vitamin D deficiency

Causes

- poor sunlight exposure
  - elderly housebound
  - Asian women who cover their bodies with clothing
- poor diet (especially vegetarians)
  - malabsorption
  - increased catabolism of vitamin D
- secondary hyperparathyroidism
  - malabsorption
  - post gastrectomy
  - enzyme-inducing drugs e.g. phenytoin.

Investigation

The diagnosis of vitamin D deficiency is based on the characteristic biochemical abnormalities (see table 78.1). Frank osteomalacia is usually associated with very low levels of 25OHD (<5 ng/mL) but the associated secondary hyperparathyroidism frequently results in normal or even elevated concentrations of $1,25(OH)_2D$.

Treatment

- Treatment is best given in the form of calciferol which will restore the biochemistry to normal and heal the bony abnormalities. Although the use of the active metabolites of vitamin D will heal the bony abnormalities it will not correct the underlying biochemical problem and is associated with increased risk of hypercalcaemia.
- In adults treatment can be given as a daily dose of calciferol of 20–25 μg (800–1000 IU) which is often most easily administered in combination with a calcium supplement. An alternative, which is particularly helpful if poor compliance is suspected, is to give a single large dose of 3.75–7.5 mg (150 000–300 000 IU). This is most effectively given as a single oral dose (3–6 × 1.25 mg tablets of calciferol) which can be supervised in clinic. It is possible to give a similar dose by i/m injection but the absorption from this route is variable.
- Following treatment there usually is a rapid improvement of myopathy and symptoms of hypocalcaemia. Bone pain frequently

X linked hypophosphataemia

- X-linked dominant genetic disorder
- severe rickets and osteomalacia
- mutation of an endopeptidase gene but its function not known.

Clinical features

- The abnormal phosphate levels are often detected early in infancy but skeletal deformities are not apparent until walking commences.
- Typical severe rickets, with short stature and bony deformity.
- Continues into adult life with bone pain, deformity, and fracture in the absence of treatment.
- Proximal myopathy is absent.
- Adults suffer from excessive new bone growth particularly affecting entheses and the longitudinal ligaments of the spinal canal. This can cause spinal cord compression which may need surgical decompression.

Oncogenic osteomalacia

Certain tumours appear to be able to produce a phosphaturic substance. This is rare and usually occurs with mesenchymal tumours (such as haemangiopericytomas, haemangiomata, or osteoid tumours) but has also been reported with a variety of adenocarcinomas (particularly prostatic cancer) and haematological malignancies (eg myeloma and chronic lymphocytic leukaemia). A similar picture can also be seen in some cases of neurofibromatosis. Clinically such patients usually present with profound myopathy as well as bone pain and fracture. Biochemically, the major abnormality is hypophosphataemia but this is usually accompanied by marked reduction in $1,25(OH)_2D$ concentrations. In some patients, other abnormalities of renal tubular function such as glycosuria or aminoaciduria are also present.

Complete removal of the tumour results in resolution of the biochemical and skeletal abnormalities. If this is not possible, or if a causal tumour is not identified, treatment with vitamin D metabolites and phosphate supplements (as for X-linked hypophosphataemia) may help the skeletal symptoms.

persists longer and biochemical abnormalities may not settle for several months. Indeed, following the onset of therapy markers of bone turnover such as alkaline phosphatase might even show a transient increase as the osteoid is mineralized and remodelled. Beware hypercalcaemia once the osteomalacia is healed. Calcium concentrations should be monitored and the dose of vitamin D should be reduced if necessary.

Fanconi syndrome

The Fanconi syndrome is a combination of renal tubular defects which can result from several different pathologies. In particular there is renal wasting of phosphate, bicarbonate, glucose, and amino acids. The combination of hypophosphataemia with renal tubular acidosis means that osteomalacia is a frequent accompaniment. This can be exacerbated by defective 1α-hydroxylation of vitamin D to its active form. The osteomalacia is treated by correction of the relevant abnormalities. This might involve the administration of phosphate, alkali or 1,25$(OH)_2$D depending on the precise circumstances.

Causes of hypophosphataemia

- decreased intestinal absorption
  - phosphate binding antacids
  - malabsorption
  - starvation/malnutrition
- increased renal losses
- hyperparathyroidism
  - primary
  - secondary, e.g. in vitamin D deficiency
- renal tubular defects
  - Fanconi syndrome
  - X-linked hypophosphataemia
  - oncogenic osteomalacia
- alcohol abuse
- poorly controlled diabetes
- acidosis
- drugs
  - diuretics
  - corticosteroids
  - calcitonin
- shift into cells
  - septicaemia
  - insulin treatment
  - glucose administration
  - salicylate poisoning.

Hypophosphataemia

Phosphate is important for normal mineralization of bone. In the absence of sufficient phosphate osteomalacia results. Clinically the osteomalacia is often indistinguishable from other that due to other causes, although there may be features that will help distinguish the underlying cause of hypophosphataemia. In addition, phosphate is important in its own right for neuromuscular function and profound hypophosphataemia can be accompanied by encephalopathy, muscle weakness and cardiomyopathy. It must be remembered that, as phosphate is primarily an intracellular anion, a low plasma phosphate does not necessarily represent actual phosphate depletion. Several different causes of hypophosphataemia are recognized (see p. 577).

Treatment

- Mainstay is phosphate replacement, usually Phosphate-Sandoz, each tablet of which provides 500 mg of elemental phosphate.
- Ideally, patients should receive 2–3 g of phosphate daily between meals but this is not easy to achieve. All phosphate preparations are unpalatable and act as osmotic purgatives causing diarrhoea.
- Long-term administration of phosphate supplements stimulates parathyroid activity. This can lead to hypercalcaemia, a further fall in phosphate, with worsening of the bone disease due to the development of hyperparathyroid bone disease which may necessitate parathyroidectomy.
- To minimize parathyroid stimulation it is usual to give one of the active metabolites of vitamin D in conjunction with phosphate. Typically, alfacalcidol or calcitriol in a dose of 1–3 μg daily is used.
- Patients receiving such supraphysiological doses of vitamin D metabolites are at continued risk of hypercalcaemia and require regular monitoring of plasma calcium, preferably at least every 3 months. The adequacy of calcitriol replacement can be assessed by maintaining 24 h urinary calcium excretion >4–6 mmol/day.
- In adults the role of treatment for X-linked hypophosphataemia is probably confined to symptomatic bone disease.
  - There is little evidence that it will improve the long term outcome
  - There has even been some evidence that treatment might accelerated new bone formation.
- In children treatment is usually given in the hope of improving final height and minimising skeletal abnormality.
  - The evidence that it is possible to achieve these goals is conflicting.

Chapter 79
Hypomagnesaemia

- Low plasma magnesium levels are common in acutely ill patients. Clinical manifestations of this are less common. The most common clinical feature of magnesium deficiency is neuromuscular excitability which is virtually indistinguishable from that associated with hypocalcaemia, which frequently coexists.
- In the presence of magnesium deficiency PTH secretion is defective leading to the presence of, or worsening of hypocalcaemia which will not respond to treatment unless the magnesium deficiency is corrected. In magnesium depletion there is defective trans-membrane electrolyte transport. This can cause loss of intracellular potassium and of the renal tubule's ability to retain potassium. Treatment with potassium supplementation is often unsuccessful unless magnesium is replaced at the same time.

Causes of hypomagnesaemia

- gastrointestinal losses
  - vomiting
  - diarrhoea
  - losses from fistulae
  - malabsorption
- renal losses
  - chronic parenteral therapy
  - osmotic diuresis
- diabetes
- drugs
  - alcohol
  - loop diuretics
  - aminoglycosides
  - cisplatin
  - cyclosporin
  - amphotericin
- metabolic acidosis
- hypercalcaemia
- other causes
  - phosphate depletion
  - hungry bone syndrome

Treatment

Symptomatic magnesium deficiency, especially if associated with hypocalcaemia or hypokalaemia, requires parenteral treatment.

- Although the total deficit may be of the order of 150 mmol this should not be replaced immediately.
- Magnesium sulfate 50% solution contains ~2 mmol magnesium/mL. Although this can be given by i/m injection it is usually more comfortable and controlled to give it by i/v infusion. An initial 4–8 mmol should be given over 15 min followed by a slow infusion of 1 mmol/h. The rate of the infusion can be adjusted in the light of the response in plasma magnesium.
- In the presence of renal impairment plasma magnesium can rise quickly and so particular care must be undertaken if magnesium infusion is contemplated in the presence of renal failure.
- After repletion has been achieved intravenously, or in less severe cases, treatment can be continued orally.
- No available oral magnesium supplement is readily available in the UK. Compounds which have been used include the chloride, oxide, and glycerophosphate. In all these instances the dose is frequently limited by the purgative properties of magnesium salts. There is some evidence to suggest that the addition of calcitriol or alfacalcidol might improve magnesium absorption.

Chapter 80
Osteoporosis

Introduction

Although the term 'osteoporosis' refers to the reduction in the amount of bony tissue within the skeleton, this is generally associated with a loss of the structural integrity of the internal architecture of the bone. The combination of both these changes means that osteoporotic bone is at high risk of fracture, after even trivial injury. Although most fractures are related to bone mass to some extent the most common osteoporotic fractures are those of the wrist (Colles), hip, and compression fractures of vertebral bodies.

Underlying causes of osteoporosis

- gonadal failure
  - premature menopause (age <45)
  - hypogonadism in men, e.g. acquired and Kleinfelters syndrome
  - Turner's syndrome
  - oestrogen receptor defect
- conditions leading to amenorrhoea with low oestrogen (persisting >6 months)
  - hyperprolactinaemia
  - anorexia nervosa
  - athletic amenorrhoea
- endocrine disorders
  - Cushing's syndrome
  - GH deficiency
  - hyperparathyroidism
  - acromegaly with hypogonadism
  - hyperthyroidism
  - diabetes mellitus
- gastrointestinal disorders
  - malabsorption
  - postgastrectomy
  - coeliac disease
  - Crohn's disease
- liver disease
  - cholestasis
  - cirrhosis
- neoplastic disorders
  - multiple myeloma
  - systemic mastocytosis
- inflammatory conditions
  - rheumatoid arthritis
  - cystic fibrosis
- nutritional disorders
  - parenteral nutrition
  - lactose intolerance
- drugs
  - corticosteroids (>7.5 mg prednisolone equivalent per day for >6 months)
  - heparin (when given long term, particularly in pregnancy)
  - chemotherapy (primarily by gonadal damage)
  - gonadotrophin releasing hormone agonists
  - cyclosporin
  - anticonvulsants (long term)
- metabolic abnormalities
  - homocystinuria
  - hereditary disorders
  - osteogenesis imperfecta
  - Marfan's syndrome

Pathology

Osteoporosis may arise from a failure of the body to lay down sufficient bone during growth and maturation; an earlier than usual onset of bone loss following maturity; or an increased rate of that loss.

Peak bone mass

- mainly genetically determined
  - racial effects (bone mass higher in Afro-Caribbean and lower in Caucasians
  - family influence on the risk of osteoporosis – may account for 70% of variation
- also influenced by environmental factors:
  - exercise – particularly weight-bearing
  - nutrition – especially calcium
- exposure to oestrogen is also important
  - early menopause or late puberty (in males or females) is associated with increased risk of osteoporosis.

Early onset of loss

- early menopause
- conditions leading to bone loss, e.g. glucocorticoids.

Increased net loss

- ageing
  - vitamin D insufficiency
  - declining bone formation
  - declining renal function
- underlying disease states (see p. 585).

Lifestyle factors affecting bone mass

Increase

- weight-bearing exercise

Decrease

- smoking
- excessive alcohol
- nulliparity
- poor calcium nutrition

Table 80.1 WHO proposals for diagnosis of postmenopausal osteoporosis

T score	Fragility fracture	Diagnosis
≥ –1		Normal
<–1 but ≥–2.5		Low bone mass (osteopenia)
<–2.5	No	Osteoporosis
<–2.5	Yes	Established (severe) osteoporosis

Epidemiology

- The risk of osteoporotic fracture increases with age. Fracture rates in men are approximately one half those seen in women of the same age. A women aged 55 has approximately a 1/3 chance of sustaining an osteoporotic fracture in the rest of her life. The corresponding figure for a man is 1/12.
- Each year in women in the UK there are in excess of 25 000 vertebral fractures that come to clinical attention together with over 40 000 wrist fractures and 50 000 hip fractures. The latter are a particular health challenge as they invariably result in hospital admission. 1/5 of hip fracture victims will die within 6 months of the injury and only 50% will return to their previous level of independence. It has been estimated that the overall cost of osteoporotic fractures in the UK is £942million annually.

Investigations to exclude and underlying cause of osteoporosis

Useful in most patients

- full blood count
- ESR
- biochemical profile
- renal function
- liver function
- calcium
- thyroid function
- testosterone and LH (only in men)

Useful in specific instances

- oestradiol and FSH (in women where menopausal status not clear)
- serum and urine electrophoresis (if raised ESR or plasma globulin elevated)
- endomyseal antibodies (if any suggestion of coeliac disease)
- other investigations for specific diseases.

Low trauma fractures associated with osteoporosis*

- Colle's fracture
- vertebral
- hip
- proximal humerus
- rib
- pelvis

* These patients should undergo investigations and/or treatment for osteoporosis (Eastell *et al.*, *QJM* 2001, 94: 575–97).

Presentation

- Usually clinically silent until the onset of fracture.
- 2/3 of vertebral fractures do not come to clinical attention.
- Typical vertebral fracture:
  - sudden episode of well-localized pain
  - may or may not have been related to injury or exertion
  - may be radiation of the pain in a girdle distribution
  - pain may initially require bed rest but gradually subsides over the following 4–8 weeks: even after this time there may be residual pain at the fracture site
  - osteoporotic vertebral fractures only rarely lead to neurological impairment.
- Any evidence of spinal cord compression should prompt a search for malignancy or other underlying cause.
- Following vertebral fracture a patient may be left with persistent back pain, kyphosis or height loss.
- Although height loss and kyphosis are often thought of as being indicative of osteoporosis they are more frequently the result of degenerative disease. They cannot be the result of osteoporosis in the absence of vertebral fracture.
- Peripheral fractures are also more common in osteoporosis.
- If a bone breaks from a fall from less than standing height that represents a low trauma fracture which might indicate underlying osteoporosis.
- Osteoporosis does not cause generalized skeletal pain.

Major risk factors
[other than previous fragility fracture] include the following:

1 Untreated hypogonadism [premature menopause, 2° amenorrhoea, 1° hypogonadism in women; 1° or 2° hypogonadism in men]
2 Glucocorticoids [7.5mg per day prednisolone for 6 months or more]
3 Disease associated with increased prevalence of osteoporosis [eg gastrointestinal disease, chronic liver disease, hyperparathyroidism, hyperthyroidism]
4 Radiological osteopenia

Other risk factors in national and international guidelines include family history, low body weight, cigarette smoking, height loss or low bone mass as assessed by other techniques.

Lifestyle advice
> Adeqate nutrition especially with calcium and vitamin D
> Regular weight bearing exercise
> Avoidance of tobacco use and alcohol abuse

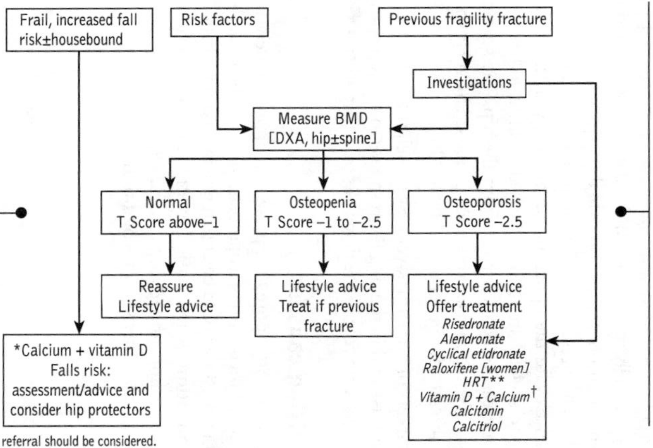

Previous fragility fracture
Defined as a fracture from standing height or less and includes prevalent vertebral deformity. A previous fragility fracture is a strong independent risk for further fracture and may be regarded as an indication for treatment without the need for BMD measurement when the clinical history is unequivocal

Investigations
> FBC, ESR
> Bone and liver function tests [Ca, P, alk phos, albumin, AST/γGT]
> Serum creatinine
> Serum TSH

If indicated
> Lateral thoracic and lumbar spine X-rays
> Serum paraproteins and urine Bence Jones protein
> Isotope bone scan
> Serum FSH if hormonal status unclear [women]
> Serum testosterone, LH and SHBG [men]

For men aged less than 65 years, specialist referral should be considered.
* Recommended daily dose 0.5–1 g and 800 IU respectively
** HRT: oestrogen in women, testosterone in men
† Vitamin D and calcium are generally regarded as adjuncts to treatment.
BMD: Bone mineral density
DXA: Dual energy x-ray absorptiometry
HRT: Hormone replacement therapy

Fig. 80.1 Algorithm for medical management of men and women aged over 45 years. Reproduced with kind permission.

Investigation

Establish the diagnosis

- Plain radiographs are useful for determining the presence of fracture. Apart from this, they are of little utility in the diagnosis of osteoporosis.
- *Bone densitometry* In order to identify the presence of osteoporosis it is important to actually measure the BMD. This is usually carried out at the hip and/or lumbar spine using dual energy x-ray absorptiometry (DXA). The presence of degenerative disease or arterial calcification can elevate the apparent bone density of the spine without adding to skeletal strength. Increased reliance is therefore being placed on measurements derived from the hip. The scheme for the diagnosis of osteoporosis which was proposed by WHO has generally been accepted for general use (Table 80.1).
- Biochemical markers of bone turnover may be helpful in the calculation of fracture risk and in judging the response to antiresorptive therapy but they have no role in the diagnosis of osteoporosis.

Exclude underlying causes

An underlying cause for osteoporosis is present in approximately 1/3 of women and over 1/2 men with osteoporosis. Many of the underlying causes (see table, p. 585) should be apparent from a careful history and physical examination. A few basic investigations are useful to exclude the more common underlying causes. Other investigations may be needed to exclude other specific conditions.

Table 80.2 Drug treatments available

Treatment		Effective dose	Spine BMD	Spine #	Hip BMD	Hip #
HRT	Oral	2 mg E2	++	?	+	↓[a]
		0.625 mg conjugated	++	↓	+	?
	Transdermal	50 μg daily				
SERMs	Raloxifene	60 mg daily	+	↓	+	–
Tibolone		1.25/2.5 mg	+ 2% at 2 yrs	?	+ 2% at 2 yrs	?
Bisphosphonates	Etidronate	400 mg for 14/90 days	+	–/↓	–	–
	Alendronate	10 mg daily/ 70 mg weekly	++	↓	+	↓
	Risedronate	5 mg	++	↓	+	↓
Calcium and vitamin D		1 g + 20 μg (800 IU)	+	–/↓	+	↓
Calcitonin	S/c or i/m		+	?	?	?
	Nasal	Not available in UK	+	↓	?	?
Calcitriol		0.25 μg 2x day	+	↓	?	?
Fluoride		Not available in UK	++	↓	+	?

[a] No RCT evidence.

Monitoring therapy

- Best by bone densitometry (maximum improvement in first year, minimal change thereafter)
- Minimum time interval 18 months, ideally 2 years
- Effective treatment leads to modest rise (~5% at spine)
- This may be replaced by biochemical markers as assays improve.

Treatment

Treatments should, whenever possible, be judged by their effect on fracture reduction. Although some treatments are specific to certain clinical situations there are also general measures that apply to all patients with osteoporosis.

In addition to treatments aimed at improving bone mass it must be remembered that fractures can be prevented in other ways. Thus it is prudent to try and minimize the risk of falling by adjusting the home environment and reviewing the need for medications such as hypnotics and antihypertensives. There is evidence that wearing hip-protecting pads reduces the risk of femoral neck fracture but these devices are not popular with patients and compliance is poor.

Lifestyle measures

- Stop smoking
- Moderate alcohol consumption
- Encourage weight-bearing exercise
  - impact exercise such as skipping or jumping increases bone mass
  - lower impact exercise, e.g. walking outdoors for 20 min 3× weekly may reduce fracture risk
- Encourage well balanced diet
- Ensure adequate calcium intake
- If necessary give supplements to achieve calcium intake of 1–1.5 g daily
- Over age 65, administration of 1 g calcium daily with 20 μg (800 IU) of vitamin D reduces the risk of non-vertebral fractures.

Corticosteroid-induced osteoporosis

Corticosteroid treatment is one of the major secondary causes of osteoporosis. Not all patients receiving steroid treatment do lose bone and it is not clear what determines this. There is some suggestion that patients on corticosteroids may have bones that are more fragile than would be suggested by the BMD. It is often suggested that such patient should be treated at a higher bone density than would be case for other causes of osteoporosis.

The National Osteoporosis Society have recently produced guidelines for the management of corticosteroid-induced osteoporosis.

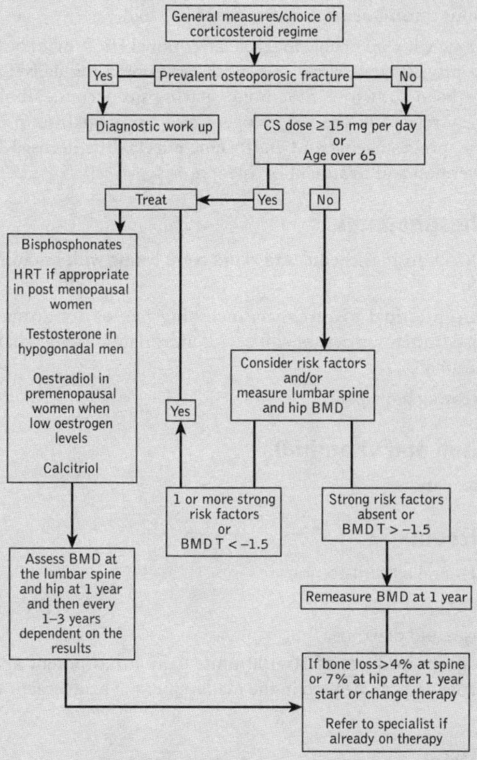

Fig. 80.2 Guidelines for the management of corticosteroid-induced osteoporosis guidelines, reproduced with permission of the National Osteoporosis Society. Reproduced with permission.

Complications of therapy

HRT

- Symptoms include menstrual bleeding, fluid retention, and mastalgia.
- Breast cancer incidence increased, and limits therapy to 10 years after age 50. The benefits are rapidly lost on cessation of therapy.
- Venous thromboembolism increased 2–3 fold.
- Women who are unable to take conventional HRT might be able to take progestogens alone (e.g. norethisterone 5 mg daily); several have been shown to have bone-sparing properties. Tibolone is closely related to the progestogens and has a mixture of oestrogenic, progestogenic and androgenic effects. It is licensed for the prevention and treatment of osteoporosis.

Bisphosphonates

- Difficult dosing schedules to avoid complexing with calcium in GI tract.
- gastrointestinal disturbance, including nausea (etidronate and risedronate), oesophagitis (alendronate), and diarrhoea (etidronate).
- increasing bone pain.

Calcium and vitamin D

- constipation

Calcitonin

- parenteral administration
- flushing
- nausea and diarrhoea

When given in doses of 50–100 units daily it has potent analgesic properties and can be used in the management of acute fracture pain.

Calcitriol

- risk of hypercalcaemia and needs regular (ideally 3 monthly) plasma calcium measurements

In men

See algorithm above (p. 591, Fig. 80.1).

- Secondary causes of osteoporosis are more common in men and need to be excluded in all men with osteoporotic fracture.
- Hypogonadal men show an improvement in bone mass on testosterone replacement this should be used as primary treatment in hypogonadal men. This treatment might benefit eugonadal osteoporotic men.
- Bisphosphonates benefit bone mass in men in a similar way to postmenopausal women.

In premenopausal women

- Osteoporosis in premenopausal women is rare but well recognized.
- It is important to exclude underlying causes of bone loss.
- Osteoporosis can very rarely occur in conjunction with pregnancy or lactation. This is frequently self limiting and usually requires little treatment other than calcium supplementation.
- In the absence of a pre-existing fracture, fracture risk is low. Frequently all that is needed is calcium supplementation and lifestyle advice until the menopause when more active therapy is needed to counteract menopausal bone loss.
- In other situations, particularly where fractures are present, most of the therapies that are used in postmenopausal women, with the exception of HRT, can be used.
- Some caution needs to be exercised over the use of bisphosphonates in younger people:
  - teratogenic
  - long skeletal retention time making their long-term safety paramount
  - in such patients it is often worth considering agents such as calcitriol or calcitonin and only using bisphosphonates if these fail.

an alternative strategy is to give no treatment unless there is an osteoporotic fracture if the BMD is stable over 2–4 years.

Fluoride

- gastritis
- lower limb pain
- ? increased peripheral fracture risk

Chapter 81
Paget's disease

Paget's disease is the result of greatly increased local bone turnover, which occurs particularly in the middle aged or elderly.

Pathology

- The primary abnormality in Paget's disease is gross overactivity of the osteoclasts resulting in greatly increased bone resorption. This secondarily results in increased osteoblastic activity. The new bone is laid down in a highly disorganized manner and leads to the characteristic Pagetic abnormality with irregular packets of woven bone being apparent on biopsy and disorganized internal architecture of the bone on plain radiographs.
- Paget's disease can affect any bone in the skeleton but is most frequently found in the pelvis, vertebral column, femur, skull and tibia. In most patients it affects several sites but in about 20% of cases a single bone is affected (monostotic disease). Typically, the disease will start in one end of a long bone and spread along the bone at a rate of about 1cm per year. Although it can spread within an affected bone it appears that the pattern of disease is fixed by the time of clinical presentation and it is exceedingly rare for new bones to become involved during the course of the disease.
- Paget's disease alters the mechanical properties of the bone. Thus, Pagetic bones are more likely to bend under normal physiological loads and liable to fracture. This can take the form of complete fractures which tend to be transverse rather than the more common spiral fractures of long bones. More frequently, fissure or incremental fractures are seen on the convex surface of bowed Pagetic bones. These may be painful in their own right but are also liable to proceed to complete fracture. Pagetic bones are also larger than their normal counterparts. This can lead to increased arthritis at adjacent joints and to pressure on nerves leading to neurological compression syndromes and, when it occurs in the skull base, sensorineural deafness.

Aetiology of Paget's disease

Unclear. There are two major theories:

- familial
  - some genetic associations, especially with 18q
  - these are not invariable
- viral
  - inclusion bodies similar to those seen in viral infections are present in pagetic osteoclasts
  - some workers have found paramyxoviral (measles or canine distemper) protein or nucleic acid in pagetic bone
  - others are not able to replicate this.

Epidemiology

Paget's disease is present in about 2% of the UK population over the age of 55. Its prevalence increases with age and it is more common in men than women. Only about 10% of affected patients will have symptomatic disease. It is most common in the UK or in migrants of British descent in North America and Australasia, but rare in Africa. Recent studies in the UK and New Zealand have suggested that the prevalence may be declining with time.

Clinical features

- 90% asymptomatic
- Most notable feature is pain. This is frequently multifactorial:
  - increased metabolic activity of the bone
  - changes in bone shape
  - fissure fractures
  - nerve compression
  - arthritis
- Pagetic bones tend to increase in size or to become bowed (16% cases): bowing can be so severe as to interfere with function
- Fractures (either complete or fissure) present in 10%

Investigation of Paget's disease

The diagnosis of Paget's disease is primarily radiological.

Radiological features of Paget's disease

- early disease – primarily lytic
  - V-shaped 'cutting cone' in long bones
  - osteoporosis circumscripta in skull
- combined phase (mixed lytic and sclerotic)
  - cortical thickening
  - loss of corticomedullary distinction
  - accentuated trabecular markings
- late phase – primarily sclerotic
  - thickening of long bones
  - increase in bone size
  - sclerosis

An isotope bone scan is frequently helpful is assessing the extent of skeletal involvement with Paget's disease. It is particularly important to identify Paget's disease in a weight-bearing bone, because of the risk of fracture. The uptake of tracer depends on the disease activity and isotope bone scans can also be used to assess the response to therapy.

In active disease plasma alkaline phosphatase activity is usually elevated. An exception to this is in monostotic disease when there may be insufficient bone involved to raise the enzyme levels above normal. Alkaline phosphatase activity responds to successful treatment. There is little advantage in using the more modern markers of bone turnover over the total alkaline phosphatase activity for the monitoring of Pagetic activity. A possible exception to this is in patients with liver disease where changes in bone alkaline phosphatase might be masked by the liver isoenzyme.

Complications

- Deafness present in up to 1/2 of cases of skull base Paget's
- Other neurological complications are rare. These can include:
  - compression of other cranial nerves with skull base disease
  - *spinal cord compression* most common with involvement of the thoracic spine and is thought to result as much from a vascular steal syndrome as from physical compression. It frequently responds to medical therapy without need for surgical decompression.
  - platybasia which can lead to an obstructive hydrocephalus that may require surgical drainage.
- Osteogenic sarcoma
  - very rare complication of Paget's disease
  - rarely amenable to treatment.
  - presents with increased pain/radiological evidence of tumour, and a mass
- Any increase of pain in a patient with Paget's disease should arouse suspicion of sarcomatous degeneration. A more common cause however, is resumption of activity of disease.

Pagetic sarcomas are most frequently found in humerus or femur but can affect any bone involved with Paget's disease.

Indications for treating Paget's disease

- pain
- neurological complications
- disease in weight-bearing bones
- prevention of long term complications
- young patients
- in preparation for surgery
- hypercalcaemia
- following fracture.

Treatment

Treatment with agents that decrease bone turnover reduces disease activity as indicated by bone turnover markers and isotope bone scans. There is evidence to suggest that such treatment leads to the deposition of histologically normal bone. Although such treatment has been shown to help pain there is little evidence that it benefits the other consequences of Paget's disease. In particular, the deafness of Paget's disease does not regress after treatment although its progression may be halted. Nonetheless it has become generally accepted to treat patients in the hope that future complications of the disease will be avoided. Typical indications for treatment of Paget's disease are listed in the table opposite.

The bisphosphonates have become the mainstay of treatment. Calcitonin and plicamycin are no longer used.

Goals of treatment

- Normalize bone turnover.
- Alkaline phosphatase in normal range.
- The more aggressive the initial therapy, the longer the disease remission.
- Minimize symptoms.
- Prevent long term complications.
- No actual evidence that treatment achieves this.

Monitoring therapy

- Plasma alkaline phosphatase every 6 months.
- Clinical assessment.

  Re-treat if symptoms recur with objective evidence of disease recurrence (alkaline phosphatase or positive isotope scan).

  If treating for asymptomatic disease re-treat if alkaline phosphatase increases 25% >nadir.

Table 81.1 Bisphosphonates licensed in the UK for Paget's disease

Drug	Dose	Duration of treatment	Side-effects
Etidronate	5 mg/kg per day orally in middle of 4 h fast (max 400 mg)	6months	Nausea Diarrhoea Bone pain Increased fracture Focal osteomalacia
Pamidronate	3 x 60 mg i/v infusion or 6 x 30 mg i/v infusion	Fortnightly interval Weekly interval	Influenza like symptoms Increased bone pain Iritis
Risedronate	30 mg orally, on rising and wait 30 min before breakfast	2 months	Increased bone pain Nausea
Tiludronate	400 mg daily orally in middle of 4 h fast	3 months	Nausea Diarrhoea Increased bone pain

Chapter 82
Inherited disorders of bone

Osteogenesis imperfecta

Osteogenesis imperfecta is an inherited form of osteoporosis in which there is a genetic defect in collagen production. Several different mutations are recognized and these produce different clinical pictures; these are generally separated into four different types (see table).

In addition to the osteoporosis and easy fracture there may also be abnormalities of the teeth (dentigenesis imperfecta), blue sclerae, and hearing loss.

Radiological fetures include:

- generalized osteopenia
- multiple fractures with deformity
- abnormal shape of long bones
- wormian bones in skull.

Recent studies have demonstrated that infusions of pamidronate lead to increased bone mass and reduced fracture incidence in affected children. Patients with milder disease might only be recognized in adulthood; it appears that oral bisphosphonates may be helpful in their management.

Prenatal diagnosis of severe types is possible from ultrasound, and genetic couselling should be offered to at-risk families.

Table 82.1 Classification of osteogenesis imperfecta

Type	Inheritance	Stature	Teeth	Sclerae	Hearing	Genetic defect
I	AD	Normal	Normal	Blue	Variable loss	Substitution for glycine in a1(I)
II	AD/AR	Lethal deformity				Rearrangement of COL1A1 and COL1A2
III	AD/AR	Progressive	Abnormal	Variable	Loss common	Frameshift mutation prevents deformity normal combination of procollagen a2(I)
IV	AD	Mild	Abnormal	Normal	Occasional loss	Point mutations in a2(I) or a1(I)

Part VII
Paediatric endocrinology

Chapter 83
Growth and stature

Growth

Regulation of growth

Normal human growth can be divided into three overlapping stages (the Karlberg model), each under the control of different factors.

- *Infancy* Growth is largely under nutritional regulation, and wide inter-individual variation in rates of growth is seen. Many infants show significant 'catch-up' or 'catch-down' in weight and length, and by 2 years length is much more predictive of final adult height than at birth.
- *Childhood* Growth is regulated by growth hormone (GH). Height velocity is conditional on height centile position and there is very little change in centile band on height (distance) charts.
- *Puberty* The combination of GH and sex hormones promotes bone maturation and a rapid growth acceleration or 'growth spurt'. In both sexes, oestrogen eventually causes epiphyseal fusion, resulting in the attainment of final height.

Sex differences

Adult heights differ between males and females by on average 13 cm. However, during childhood, onset of the pubertal growth spurt is earlier in females, who are therefore on average taller than males between the ages of 10 and 13 years.

Tempo

Within each sex there may also be marked inter-individual differences in *tempo* of growth (or rate of attainment of final height). Delay or advance of bone maturation is linked with timing of puberty and often runs in families, reflecting probable genetic factors. Comparison of *bone age* (estimated from a hand radiograph) with chronological age is therefore an important part of growth assessment.

Final height

Final height is estimated as the height reached when growth velocity slows to less than 2 cm/year and can be confirmed by finding epiphyseal fusion on hand radiograph +/– knee radiograph. Final height is largely genetically determined and a target height can be estimated in each individual from their parent's heights.

Assessment of growth

Measurement

- From birth to 2 years old, supine length is measured ideally using a measuring board (e.g. Harpenden Neonatometer). Two adults are usually needed to ensure that the child is lying straight and legs extended.
- From 2 years old, standing height is measured against a wall-mounted or free-standing stadiometer with the measurer applying moderate upwards neck traction and the child looking forward in the horizontal plane.
- To minimize error in the calculation of height velocity (cm/year), height measurements should be taken at least 6 months apart using the same equipment and ideally by the same person.
- Measurement of *sitting height* and comparison with *leg length* (*standing height – sitting height*) allows an estimate of body proportion.

Growth charts (Figs. 83.1 and 83.2)

Height and growth velocity should be compared to age and sex appropriate reference data by plotting values on standard growth charts (e.g. the UK 1990 Growth Reference, Child Growth Foundation, London, UK).

Mid-parental height (MPH)

MPH is an estimate of the child's genetic height potential and is calculated as

[(*mother's height* + *father's height*)/2] + 6.5 cm (for boys) or – 6.5 cm (for girls).

It can be used as a crude prediction of the child's expected final height, but there is a wide target range (MPH ± 10 cm) and it is more commonly used to assess whether the child's current height centile is consistent with genetic expectation.

Bone age

Skeletal maturation proceeds in an orderly manner from the first appearance of each epiphyseal centre to the fusion of the long bones. From chronological age 3–4 years, bone age may be quantified from radiographs of the left hand and wrist by comparison with standard photographs (e.g. Greulich and Pyle method) or by an individual bone scoring system (e.g. Tanner–Whitehouse method). The difference between bone age and chronological age is an estimation of tempo of growth and also timing of puberty,

Secular trends

Children's heights increased by >1 cm in England and by >2 cm in Scotland during the period from 1972 to 1994, and similar trends are seen in many other countries. Population growth references used should be appropriate to the population studied and may occasionally need to be updated.

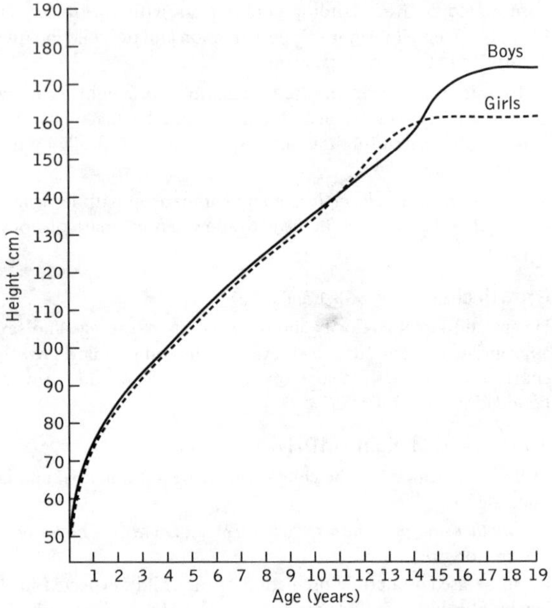

Fig. 83.1 Typical-individual height-attained curves for boys and girls (supine length to the ages of 2; integrated curves of Fig. 83.2).

which usually develops when bone age reaches around 10.5 years in girls and 11–11.5 years in boys, although the correlation between bone age and pubertal timing is approximate. Girls reach skeletal maturity at a bone age of 15 years and boys when bone age is 17 years. Thus, bone age allows an estimation of remaining growth potential and can be used to predict final adult height.

Final height prediction

Predictions of final height can be derived from information on current height, age, pubertal status and bone age using calculations described by Tanner and Whitehouse, or Bailey and Pinneau among others (see De Waal *et al.* 1996)

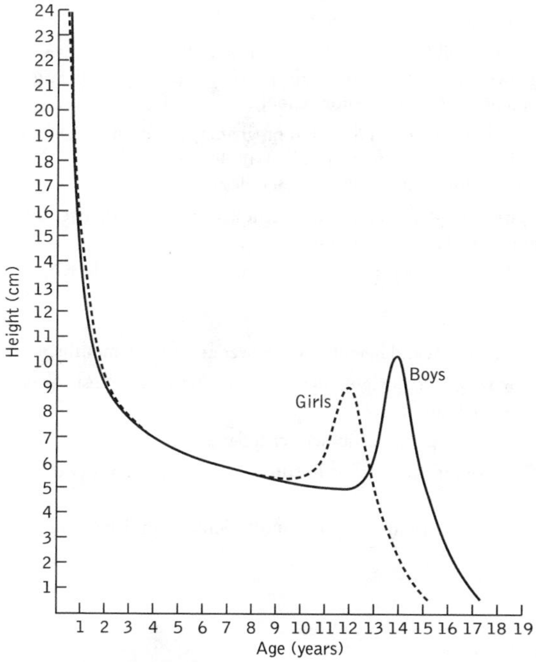

Fig. 83.2 Typical-individual velocity curves for supine length or height in boys and girls. These curves represent the velocity of the typical boy and girl at any given instant.

Short stature

Definition

Short stature is defined as height less than the 2nd centile for age and sex on an appropriate growth chart. However, abnormalities of growth may be present long before attained height falls below this level and may be detected much earlier by assessing growth velocity.

Assessment

History

- Who is concerned, child or parents?
- What are the parental heights?
- Birth weight and gestation?
- Has the child always been small, or does the history suggest recent growth failure? Try to obtain previous measurements (e.g. from parents, GP, health visitor, school).
- Ask about maternal illness in pregnancy, gestation at delivery, size at birth (weight/length/head circumference), childhood illnesses, medication, and developmental milestones.
- Systematic enquiry for headaches, visual disturbance, asthma, abdominal symptoms, and diet.
- Is there a family history of short stature or pubertal delay?

Examination

- Assess height and height velocity over at least 4–6 months.
- Low weight-for-height suggests a nutritional diagnosis or gastro-intestinal cause.
- Pubertal stage using Tanner's criteria.
- Observe for dysmorphic features, presence and severity of chronic disease.
- Measure parents' heights and calculate mid-parental height (MPH).

Causes of short stature

- familial short stature
- constitutional delay in growth and puberty
  - these first two together account for ~40% of cases
- GH deficiency (8%)
  - primary ('idiopathic')
  - secondary pituitary/hypothalamic malformation, brain tumours, cranial irradiation, psychosocial deprivation
- intrauterine growth retardation (7.5%)
- skeletal dysplasia (e.g. achondroplasia, hypochondroplasia)
- dysmorphic syndromes (e.g. Turner's syndrome, Noonan's syndrome, Down's syndrome)
- chronic illness (including hypothyroidism, coeliac disease, congenital heart disease, chronic renal failure, inflammatory bowel disease)
- endocrine disorders (hypothyroidism, hypoparathyroidism, Cushing's syndrome)
- malnutrition
- metabolic bone disease (e.g. nutritional or hypophosphataemic rickets)
- GH resistance (rare genetic mutations).

Investigations

- Laboratory tests include full blood count, ESR, electrolytes, thyroid function, calcium, phosphate, antigliadin and antiendomyseal antibodies, IGF-I and IGFBP-3 levels, karyotype (in girls), and urinalysis.
- These tests may also be clinically indicated: GH provocation testing (e.g. ITT), IGF-I generation test (for GH resistance, see p. 626), skeletal survey (for bony dysplasia), and anterior pituitary function.

Familial short stature

Although stature does not follow strict Mendelian laws of inheritance, it does relate to parental height and is probably a polygenic trait. It should be remembered that short parents may themselves have an unidentified dominantly inherited condition (e.g. hypochondroplasia).

Table 83.1 Comparison of GH provocation tests

	Insulin (i/v)	Clonidine (oral)	Glucagon (i/m)
Age	>10 years	5–10 years Unreliable in puberty and in adulthood	<5 years and in neonates
Advantages	Gold standard Also tests ACTH–cortisol axis	Simple and safe	Safe Also tests ACTH-cortisol axis
Disadvantages	Risk of severe hypoglycaemia but good safety record in experienced centres	Postural hypotension and somnolence	Nausea may last 3–4 h Great care because of late hypoglycaemia

Other agents (e.g. L-dopa or L-arginine) are less commonly used. Measurement of GH levels after exercise has poor sensitivity and specificity for detecting GH deficiency.

Constitutional delay of growth and puberty

Clinical features

- This condition often presents in adolescence but may also be recognized in earlier childhood. Although it is more prevalent in males, this may reflect a bias in level of concern.
- Characteristic features include short stature and delay in pubertal development by >2 standard deviations (SD) and/or bone age delay in otherwise healthy children. Short sitting height percentile compared to leg length is typical.
- There is often a family history of delayed puberty.
- Bone age delay may also develop in a number of other conditions, but in constitutional delay, bone age delay usually remains consistent over time and height velocity is normal for the bone age. Final height often does not reach target height.
- GH secretion is normal, although provocation tests should be primed by prior administration of exogenous sex hormones if bone age is >10 years.

Management

Often only reassurance is necessary. Treatment is sometimes indicated in adolescent boys who have difficulty coping with their short stature or delayed sexual maturation.

- Low-dose *oxandrolone* (2.5 mg/day for 3–12 months, oral) A synthetic derivative of testosterone which has significant growth-promoting but minimal virilizing actions. While high doses promote early epiphyseal fusion and may therefore reduce final height, low-dose therapy increases current growth but has no effect on final height. Growth velocity on treatment usually doubles but is only sustained if the boy has reached 4 mL testes volume by the end of the period of treatment. Therefore occasionally longer treatment durations have been tried (0.07–0.1 mg/kg per day).
- *Testosterone* (50–100 mg intramuscularly, monthly for 3–6 months) Usually limited to boys 14 years and over who have significant concern about delayed sexual development.

GH assessment

GH is normally secreted overnight in regular pulses (pulse frequency 180 min). Frequently sampled overnight GH profiles are costly and laborious and therefore standardized stimulation tests are more commonly useful. Peak GH <20 mU/L indicates GH deficiency (values >10 and <20 mU/L indicate partial GH deficiency). However, there can be large variation between different assay methods and exact cut-offs must be locally validated. In late pre-puberty there is a physiological blunting of GH secretion and when bone age is >10 years, sex steroid priming (testosterone 100 mg i/m in boys, oral stilboestrol 1 mg 2× daily for 2 days, or oral ethinylestradiol 20–50 μg 2× daily for 3 days in either sex) is necessary before GH testing.

A number of different agents may be used to stimulate GH secretion (Table 83.1). All tests should be performed in the morning following an overnight fast, and serial blood samples are collected over 90 min.

IGF-I generation test

Measurement of IGF-I levels before and following administration of GH (0.1 IU/kg per day) s/c for 3 days allows an assessment of GH sensitivity/resistance

Growth hormone deficiency

Primary GH deficiency

Primary GH deficiency is usually sporadic, but rarely it may be inherited as autosomal dominant, recessive or X-linked recessive and may be associated with other pituitary hormone deficiencies. It may represent a defect in homeobox genes (e.g. *Pit-1* (leading to GH, TSH and PRL deficiency), *HESX-1*) which control hypothalamic-pituitary development and in some cases may be associated with mid-line defects, such as optic nerve hypoplasia and corpus callosum defects (i.e. 'septo-optic dysplasia'). GH deficiency usually arises because of failure of release of GHRH from the hypothalamus.

Clinical features

- *Infancy* GH deficiency may present with hypoglycaemia. Coexisting ACTH, TSH, and gonadotrophin deficiencies may cause prolonged hyperbilirubinaemia and micropenis. Size may be normal as foetal and infancy growth are more dependent on nutrition and other growth factors than on GH.
- *Childhood* Typical features include slow growth velocity, short stature, decreased muscle mass and increased subcutaneous fat. Underdevelopment of the mid-facial bones, relative protrusion of the frontal bones because of mid-facial hypoplasia, delayed dental eruption and delayed closure of the anterior fontanel may be seen. These children have delayed bone age and delayed puberty.

Secondary GH deficiency

Brain tumours and cranial irradiation

Pituitary or hypothalamic tumours may impair GH secretion and deficiencies of other pituitary hormones may be be coexist. Cranial irradiation, used to treat intracranial tumours, facial tumours and acute leukaemia, may also cause GH deficiency. Risk of hypothalamic-pituitary damage is related to total dose administered, fractionation (single dose more toxic than divided), location of the irradiated tissue and age (younger children are more sensitive to radiation damage).

GH secretion is most sensitive to radiation damage, followed by gonadotrophins, TSH, and ACTH. Central precocious puberty may also occur and may mask GH deficiency by promoting growth but will compromise final height if untreated. At risk children should therefore be screened regularly by careful examination and multiple pituitary hormone testing.

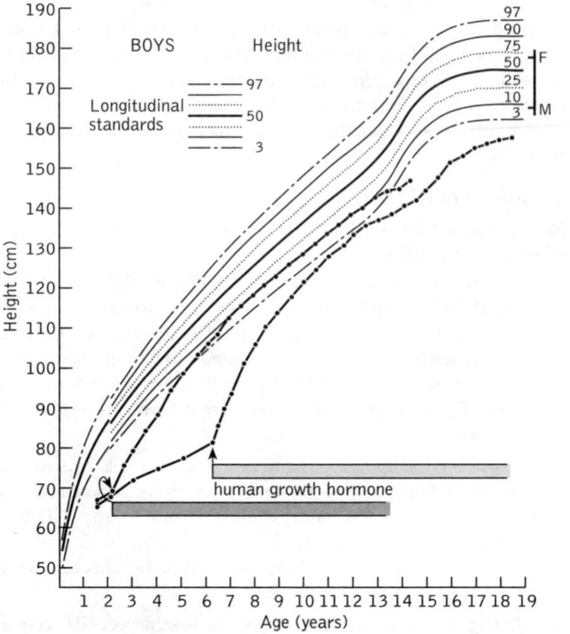

Fig. 83.3 Heights of two brothers with isolated growth-hormone deficiency treated with human growth hormone from ages 6;2 years and 2;1 years. Catch-up of older brother is partly by high velocity and partly by prolonged growth and is incomplete. Younger brother shows true complete catch-up. F and M, parents' height centiles; vertical thick line, range of expected heights for family. (With permission.)

Psychosocial deprivation

Severe psychosocial deprivation may cause reversible inhibition of GH secretion and growth failure, particularly in boys as a result of sexual abuse. GH secretion improves within 3 weeks of hospitalization or removal from the adverse environment and catch-up growth is often dramatic, although these children may continue to exhibit other features of emotional disturbance.

Treatment of GH deficiency (Fig. 83.3)

Recombinant human GH has been available since 1985 and is administered by daily s/c injection.

- *Dose* The replacement dose for childhood GH deficiency is 12–15 IU/m^2 per week (~0.5 IU/kg per week), which is higher than doses used in adulthood (0.07–0.18 IU/kg per week). Catch-up growth is optimized if GH is commenced early. Some recommend a higher dose during puberty, reflecting the normal elevation in GH levels at Tanner stage 3–4, however there is as yet little evidence for its efficacy.
- *Side-effects* Local lipoatrophy and benign intracranial hypertension occur rarely. Slipped upper femoral epiphises is associated with GH deficiency, and the incidence is similar before or after GH treatment. Other pituitary hormone deficiencies may be unmasked by GH therapy and thyroid function should be checked within 4–6 weeks of commencing therapy.
- *Retesting in adulthood* Once final height is achieved, GH secretion should be retested as up to 50% of subjects with GH deficiency in childhood subsequently have normal GH secretion in adulthood. Studies are in progress to establish if GH replacement should be continued in adulthood in order to maintain lean body mass, muscular strength, and bone density or whether treatment can be delayed until symptoms become evident.

GH resistance

GH resistance may arise because of primary GH receptor defects or secondary to malnutrition, liver disease, type 1 diabetes or circulating GH antibodies. *Laron syndrome* is a rare autosomal recessive condition caused by a genetic defect of the GH receptor. Affected individuals have extreme short stature, high levels of GH, low levels of IGF-I and impaired GH-induced IGF-I generation (p. 623). Treatment with exogenous IGF-I may be available on a trial basis.

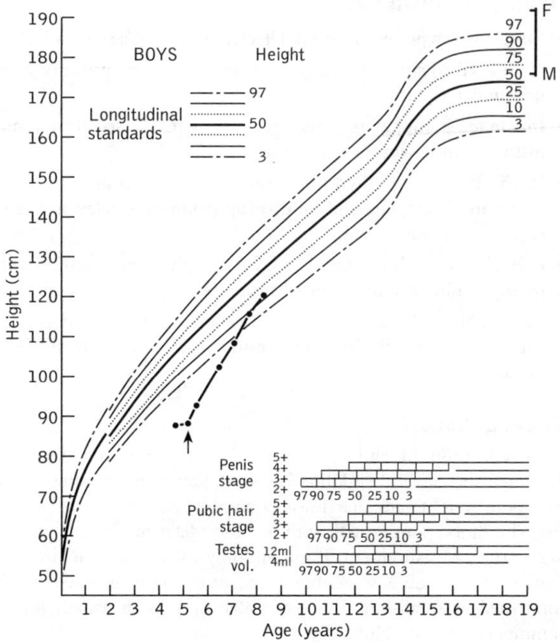

Fig. 83.5 Height of child with psychosocial short stature. Note catch-up on removal, marked by arrow, from parental home. (With permission.)

Hypothyroidism (Fig. 83.4)

- Congenital hypothyroidism is detected by neonatal screening.
- Hypothyroidism presenting in childhood is commonly autoimmune in origin.
- Incidence is higher in girls and those with personal or family history of other autoimmune disease.
- In childhood, hypothyroidism may present with growth failure alone and bone age is often disproportionately delayed. Rarely, early puberty may occur.
- Investigations show low T_4 and T_3, high TSH, positive antithyroglobulin, and microsomal antibodies.
- Replacement therapy with oral thyroxine (100 $\mu g/m^2$ per day titrated with thyroid function) results in catch-up growth unless diagnosis is late.

Coeliac disease

More common in children with other autoimmune disorders. Although the classical childhood presentation is an irritable toddler with poor weight gain, diarrhoea, abdominal pain and distension, in later childhood poor growth with bone age delay may be the presenting feature. Measurement of antiendomyseal and antigliadin antibodies are valuable screening tests, but diagnosis needs to be confirmed by small-bowel biopsy. Catch-up growth usually follows commencement of a gluten-free diet.

Skeletal dysplasias

- This heterogeneous group of mostly dominantly inherited disorders includes *achondroplasia* and *hypochondroplasia.*
- These children usually have severe disproportionate short stature and a positive or suspicious family history.
- Radiological assessment by skeletal survey often allows a specific diagnosis to be made.
- High dose GH therapy has been used in these disorders with some success, although surgical leg lengthening procedures after puberty may be an additional option.

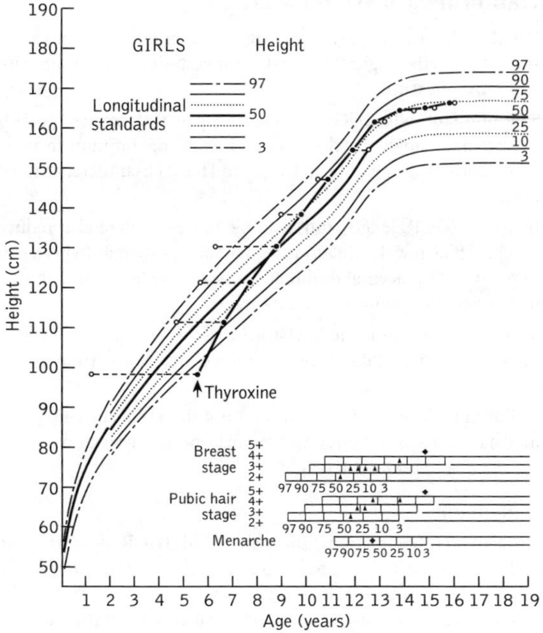

Fig. 83.4 Response of hypothyroid child treated with thyroxine. Solid circles, height for age; open circles, height for bone age. (With permission.)

Intrauterine growth retardation

- IUGR is defined as growth failure on serial antenatal ultrasound scans, but birth weight <3rd centile for gestational age is often used as a proxy measure.
- 85% of infants with IUGR show catch-up growth by age 3 years but 15% remain small. Catch-up growth is more common in infants with relative sparing of birth length and head circumference (>10th centile).
- In severe IUGR, length and head circumference are also reduced. Severe IUGR may be due to maternal factors such as hypertension in pregnancy, placental dysfunction, or a wide range of chromosomal or genetic conditions in the foetus.
- Silver–Russell syndrome is characterized by severe IUGR, lateral asymmetry, triangular facies, clinodactyly, and extremely poor infancy feeding and postnatal weight gain.
- Children with severe IUGR who do not undergo catch-up growth may have early onset puberty despite bone age delay and therefore achieve a very poor final height.

Management

The role of GH therapy in the short child with IUGR remains controversial. High-dose GH increases growth velocity and possibly final height, however in theory may exacerbate the intrinsic risk in these children to insulin resistance and type 2 diabetes in adulthood.

Turner's syndrome (see p. 391)

Turner's syndrome should always be considered in a girl who is short for her parental target and the classical dysmorphic features may be difficult to identify at younger ages. Karyotype usually confirms the diagnosis, although sufficient cells (>30) should be examined to exclude the possibility of mosaicism.

Clinical features

There may be a history of lymphoedema in the newborn period. Typically, growth velocity starts to decline from 3–5 years old and gonadal failure combined with a degree of skeletal dysplasia results in loss of the pubertal growth spurt. Mean final height is consistently 20 cm below the normal average within each population (143–146 cm in the UK). GH secretion is normal although IGF-I levels may be low. 10% progress through puberty spontaneously but only 1% develop ovulatory cycles.

Management

- High dose *GH therapy* increases final height, although individual responses are variable. GH therapy should probably be commenced around 5–7 years old when growth velocity tends to slow.
- The anabolic steroid *oxandralone* has been used in addition to GH to promote growth from the age of 9 years, but its effect on final height is yet unclear.
- Oral *oestrogen* is commenced between 12–14 years to promote secondary sexual development and pubertal growth. It should be started in low dose (ethinyloestradiol 1–2 μg/day), gradually increased with age. *Progesterone* should be added if breakthrough bleeding occurs or when oestrogen dose reaches 10 μg/day.

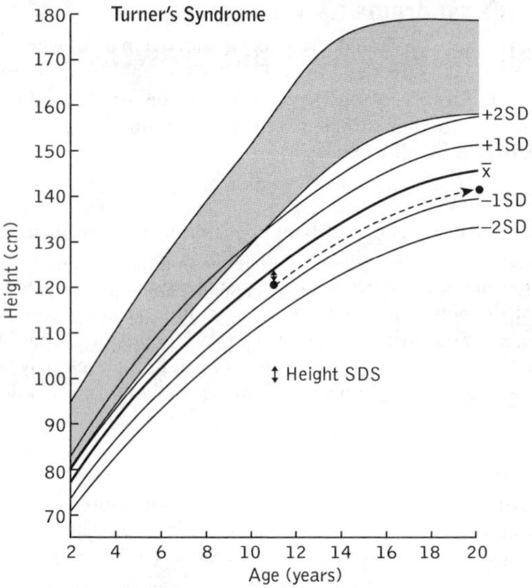

Fig. 83.6 Height SDS for chronological age extrapolated to final height. (With permission.)

Tall stature and rapid growth

Definition

Although statistically as many children have heights >2 SD above the mean as have>2 SD below the mean, referral for evaluation of tall stature is much less common than for short stature. Socially, for boys heights up to 200 cm are increasingly acceptable, whereas for many girls heights >180 cm may be unacceptable. However, tall stature and particularly accelerated growth rates may indicate an underlying hormonal disorder, such as precocious puberty. For causes, see p. 634.

Assessment

History

- Is tall stature long-standing or does the history suggest recent growth acceleration? Try to obtain previous measurements.
- Enquire about size at birth, infancy weight gain, and neurological development.
- Enquire about headaches, visual disturbance, and evidence of puberty.
- Is there a family history of tall stature or early puberty?

Examination

- Assess height and height velocity over at least 4–6 months.
- Pubertal stage?
- Dysmorphic features?
- Measure parents' heights and calculate MPH (p. 615).

Investigations

The following investigations may be clinically indicated:

- wrist radiograph for bone age
- sex hormone levels (testosterone, oestrogen, androstenedione, DHEAS), baseline and LHRH-stimulated LH and FSH levels
- karyotype
- serum IGF-I and IGFBP-3 levels
- oral glucose tolerance test – GH levels normally suppress to low or undetectable levels (<1 mu/L).

Causes of tall stature in childhood

Normal variants

- Familial tall stature.
- Early maturation (largely familial but also promoted by early childhood nutrition and obesity. Final height is not excessive as bone age is advanced).

Hormonal

- Precocious puberty (see p. 640).
- GH or GHRH excess ('pituitary gigantism') resulting from pituitary adenoma or ectopic adenomas is a very rare cause of tall stature (p. 215).
- Other hormonal excess, e.g. hyperthyroidism, hyperinsulinism, CAH.
- Rarely, oestrogen receptor or aromatase deficiencies delay puberty and epiphyseal fusion resulting in tall adult height.

Chromosomal abnormalities

- XXY (Klinefelter syndrome).
- XYY, XYYY (each 'extra Y' confers on average 13 cm additional height).

Other rare syndromes

- Overgrowth and dysmorphic features are seen in Marfan's syndrome, homocystinuria, Sotos syndrome, Beckwith–Wiedemann syndrome, and Weaver's syndrome.

Management of tall stature

After excluding abnormal pathology, often only reassurance and information on predicted final height is necessary. In younger children, early induction of puberty using low-dose sex steroids advances the pubertal growth spurt and promotes earlier epiphyseal fusion. In older children already in puberty, high-dose oestrogen therapy in girls, or testosterone in boys, have been used to induce rapid skeletal maturation. However, theoretical side-effects of high-dose oestrogen therapy include thromboembolic disease and oncogenic risk. Therefore other agents which inhibit central GH secretion (e.g. somatostatin analogues or anticholinergic agents) or block peripheral GH action are in trial.

Reference

De Waal WJ *et al.* Accuracy of final height prediction and effect of growth-reductive therapy in 362 constitutionally tall children. *Journal of Clinical Endocrinology and Metabolism* 1996; 81:1206–1216.

Chapter 84
Puberty

Normal puberty

Puberty is the sequence of physical and physiological changes occurring at adolescence culminating in full sexual maturity.

Age at onset

Average age at onset of puberty is earlier in girls (10–12 years) than in boys (12–13 years), but may vary widely and is influenced by a number of factors:

- *Historical* Age of menarche has decreased this century from 17 years in 1900 to 12.8 years today, presumably as a result of improved childhood nutrition and growth.
- *Genetic* Age at onset of puberty is partly familial.
- *Race* Afro-Caribbean girls tend to have earlier puberty than whites.
- *Weight gain* Earlier puberty is seen in girls who are overweight, whereas girls who engage in strenuous activity and are thin often have delayed puberty.

Triggers of puberty

- Adrenal androgens (DHEAS and androstenedione) rise 2 years before puberty starts ('adrenarche'). This usually causes no physical changes but occasionally results in early pubic hair and acne.
- Pulsatile secretion of LHRH from the hypothalamus at night is the first step in initiation of puberty. This results in pulsatile secretion of LH and FSH from the pituitary and the gonadotrophin response to LHRH administration reverses from the prepubertal FSH predominance to a higher response in LH levels.

Physical changes

The first indication of puberty is breast development in girls and increase in testicular size in boys. In each sex, puberty then progresses in an orderly or 'consonant' manner through distinct stages (see Table 84.1). Puberty rating by an experienced observer involves identification of pubertal stage; particularly breast development in girls and testicular volume (by comparison with an orchidometer) in boys.

Pubertal growth spurt

Increasing oestrogen levels in both boys and girls leads to increased GH secretion. Thus, peak height velocity occurs at puberty stage 2–3 in girls and is later in boys, at stage 3–4 (testicular volume 10–12 mL).

Table 84.1 The normal stages of puberty ('Tanner stages')

Boys			
Stage	Genitalia	Pubic hair	Other events
I	Prepubertal	Vellus not thicker than on abdomen	TV[a] <4 mL
II	Enlargement of testes and scrotum	Sparse long pigmented strands at base of penis	TV 4–8 mL Voice starts to change
III	Lengthening of penis	Darker, curlier and spreads over pubes	TV 8–10 mL Axillary hair
IV	Increase in penis length and breadth	Adult type hair but covering a smaller area	TV 10–15 mL Upper lip hair Peak height velocity
V	Adult shape and size	Spread to medial thighs (Stage 6: Spread up linea alba)	TV 15–25 mL. Facial hair spreads to cheeks Adult voice
Girls			
Stage	Breast	Pubic hair	Other events
I	Elevation of papilla only	Vellus not thicker than on abdomen	
II	Breast bud stage: elevation of breast and papilla	Sparse long pigmented strands along labia	Peak height velocity
III	Further elevation of breast and areola together	Darker, curlier and spreads over pubes	
IV	Areola forms a second mound on top of breast	Adult type hair but covering a smaller area	Menarche
V	Mature stage: areola recedes and only papilla projects	Spread to medial thighs (Stage 6: spread up linea alba)	

[a] TV, testicular volume: measured by size-comparison with a Prader orchidometer.
Adapted from Tanner JM (1962) *Growth at adolescence*, 2nd edn. Blackwell Scientific Publications, Oxford.

Precocious puberty

Definition

- Early onset of puberty is defined as <8 years in females and <9 years in males.
- Gonadotrophin dependent ('central' or 'true') precocious puberty is characterized by early breast development in girls or testicular enlargement in boys.
- Gonadotrophin independent puberty occurs due to abnormal peripheral sex hormone secretion, resulting in isolated development of certain secondary sexual characteristics, particularly virilization.

Assessment of precocious puberty

History

- Age when secondary sexual development first noted.
- What features are present and in what order did they appear? e.g. virilization (pubic, axillary or facial hair, acne, body odour), genital or breast enlargement, galactorrhoea, menarche, or cyclical mood changes?
- Is there evidence of recent growth acceleration?
- Family history of early puberty?
- Past history of adoption or early weight gain?

Examination

- Breast or genital and testicular size; degree of virilization (clitoromegaly in girls indicates abnormal androgen levels).
- Neurological examination, particularly visual field assessment and fundoscopy.
- Abdominal or testicular masses.
- Skin (?*café-au-lait* patches – McCune–Albright (p. 703), or NF-1).
- Assess height and height velocity over 4–6 months.

Investigations

The following investigations may be clinically indicated:

- wrist radiograph for bone age
- sex hormone levels (testosterone, oestrogen, androstenedione, DHEAS)
- LH and FSH levels (baseline and 20, 60 min post i/v LHRH)
- 17-OH progesterone levels (baseline and 30 and 60 min post i/v synacthen)
- tumour markers (αFP, βhCG)
- 24 h urine steroid profile
- abdominal ultrasound scan (adrenal glands; ovaries)
- MRI scan (cranial; adrenal glands)

Central precocious puberty

This is due to premature activation of pulsatile LHRH secretion from the hypothalamus and the normal progression in physical changes is maintained ('consonance'). As precocious puberty is defined as occurring younger than 2 SD before the average age, in a normal distribution 2.5% of children will have early onset puberty. In practice, in girls central precocious puberty is more likely to be idiopathic or familial, whereas boys have a greater risk of intracranial or other pathology.

Causes

- Idiopathic or familial.
- Intracranial tumours, hydrocephalus or other lesions.
- Post cranial irradiation or trauma.
- Hypothyroidism (elevated TRH stimulates FSH release)
- Gonadotrophin-secreting tumours (e.g. pituitary adenoma or hepatoblastoma) are rare.
- May also be triggered by long-standing elevation in sex hormones resulting from any peripheral source or biochemical defect (e.g. poorly or untreated CAH).

Treatment

Aims of treatment are:

- To avoid psychosocial problems for the child or family.
- To prevent reduced final height due to premature bone maturation and early epiphyseal fusion. A *final height prediction* is often necessary when considering the need for inhibition of puberty.

Pituitary LH and FSH secretion can be inhibited by maintaining constant high levels of LHRH, given by monthly i/m injection, e.g. *leuprorelin acetate* 3.5 mg i/m monthly. Treatment efficacy should be monitored regularly by ensuring that LH and FSH levels post i/v LHRH remain at low prepubertal levels. More often in girls than in boys the dose interval may need to be reduced to 3 weeks.

Non-gonadotrophin-dependent precocious puberty

At least two genetic syndromes have been identified, both resulting in abnormal activation of gonadotrophin receptors independent of normal ligand binding. Thus, in these conditions the gonads autonomously secrete sex hormones and levels of LH and FSH are suppressed by feedback inhibition.

McCune–Albright syndrome (see p. 703)

This is a sporadic condition due to a somatic activating mutation of the G protein a subunit which affects bones (polyostotic fibrous dysplasia), skin (*café-au-lait* spots) and potentially multiple endocrinopathies. A number of different hormone receptors share the same G-protein-coupled cyclic AMP second messenger system and hyperthyroidism or hyperparathyroidism may also be present.

All cells descended from the mutated embryonic cell-line are affected, while cells descended from non-mutated cells develop into normal tissues. Thus, the phenotype is highly variable in physical distribution and severity.

Testoxicosis

This is a rare familial condition resulting in precocious puberty only in boys due to an activating LH receptor mutation. Testes show only little increase in size and on biopsy Leydig cell hyperplasia is characteristic. Treatment is by use of androgen receptor blocking agents (cyproterone acetate).

Premature thelarche

Premature breast development in the absence of other signs of puberty may present at any age from infancy. Breast size may fluctuate and is often asymmetrical. The cause is unknown, although typically FSH levels (but not LH) are elevated and ovarian ultrasound may reveal a single large cyst. Bone maturation, growth rate, and final height are unaffected.

'Thelarche variant'

This is an intermediate condition between premature thelarche and central precocious puberty. The aetiology is unknown. These girls demonstrate increased height velocity and rate of bone maturation and ovarian ultrasound reveals a more multicystic appearance, as seen in true puberty. There is probably a whole spectrum of presentations between premature thelarche and true precocious puberty. Decision to treat should take into account height velocity and final height prediction.

'Premature adrenarche' and 'pubarche'

The normal onset of adrenal androgen secretion ('adrenarche') occurs 1–2 years before the onset of puberty. 'Premature' or 'exaggerated' adrenarche is thought to be due to increased androgen production or sensitivity and presents with mild features of virilization, such as onset of pubic hair ('pubarche') or acne, in the absence of other features of puberty. Note: clitoromegaly in girls suggests a more severe pathology with excessive androgen production (e.g. CAH or androgen secreting tumour).

Management

- The management of premature adrenarche usually only requires reassurance after exclusion of other causes.
- Symptomatic treatment may be indicated if adrenarche is pronounced and many of these girls may subsequently develop features of polycystic ovary disease. In these cases androgen receptor blocking agents may be useful, e.g. cyproterone acetate (Dianette is a preparation including ethinyloestradiol).

Peripheral sex hormone secretion

- Excessive peripheral androgen secretion may occur due to CAH, or androgen-secreting adrenal or gonadal tumours. These children usually have rapid growth, advanced bone age and moderate-to-severe virilization in the absence of testicular or breast development. (Note: a testicular tumour may cause asymmetrical enlargement).
- Peripheral oestrogen production from ovarian tumours are a rare cause of precocious breast development in girls.

Delayed puberty

Definition

Delayed puberty is defined as failure to progress into puberty by >2 SD later than the average, i.e. >14 years in girls and >16 years in boys. Clinically, boys are more likely to present with delayed puberty than girls. In addition, some children present with delay in progression from any pubertal stage for >2 years.

Psychological distress may be exacerbated by declining growth velocity relative to their peers. In the long term, severe delay may be a risk factor for decreased bone mineral density and osteoporosis.

Causes

General

- Constitutional delay of growth and puberty (this is the most common cause; see p. 622)
- Chronic childhood disease, malabsorption (e.g. coeliac disease, inflammatory bowel disease), or undernutrition.

Hypergonadotrophic hypogonadism (see pp. 382, 432)

Gonadal failure may be:

- congenital (e.g. Turner's syndrome in girls, Klinefelter's syndrome in boys)
- acquired (e.g. following chemotherapy, local radiotherapy, infection, torsion).

In these conditions basal and stimulated gonadotrophin levels are raised.

Gonadotrophin deficiency (see pp. 522, 571)

- Kallman syndrome (including anosmia)
- hypothalamic/pituitary lesions (tumours, post radiotherapy, dysplasia)
- rare inactivating mutations of genes encoding LH, FSH (or their receptors).

These conditions may also present in the newborn period with micropenis and undescended testes in boys.

Investigation

The following investigations may be clinically indicated:

- LH and FSH levels (basal and post iv LHRH stimulation)
- plasma oestrogen or testosterone levels.
- measurement of androgen levels before and after hCG therapy may be used to indicate presence of functional testicular tissue in boys
- karyotype
- pelvic ultrasound in girls to determine ovarian morphology
- ultrasound or MRI imaging in boys to detect an intra-abdominal testes.

It may be difficult to distinguish between constitutional delay and gonadotrophin deficiency, as gonadotrophin levels are low in both conditions. In these cases, induction of puberty may be indicated with regular assessment of testicular growth in boys (which is independent of testosterone therapy) followed by withdrawal of treatment and reassessment when final height is reached.

Management

Depending on the age and concern of the child and parents, exogenous sex steroids can be used to induce pubertal changes.

Treatment

Boys

Testosterone (by i/m injection) 50 mg 4–6 weekly, gradually increasing to 250 mg 4 weekly.

- Monitor penis enlargement, pubic hair, height velocity, and adult body habitus.
- Side-effects include severe acne and rarely priapism.
- Testicular size remains prepubertal unless spontaneous puberty occurs.

Girls

Oestrogen (oral). Start at low dose (*ethinyloestradiol* 2 μg daily) and gradually increase.

- Promotes breast development and adult body habitus.
- *Progesterone* (oral) should be added if breakthrough bleeding occurs or when oestrogen dose reaches 10 μg/day.

Chapter 85
Sexual differentiation

Normal sexual differentiation

Gonadal development

- In the male or female embryo, the bipotential gonad develops as a thickening of mesenchymal cells and coelomic epithelium around the primitive kidney. This *genital ridge* is then colonized by primordial germ cells which migrate from the yolk sac to form the *gonadal ridge*. In the absence of a Y chromosome, the gonad will develop into an ovary.
- In the presence of a normal Y chromosome, immature Sertoli cells, germs cells, and seminiferous tubules can be recognized by 7 weeks, and testis differentiation is complete by 9 weeks. The *SRY gene* is an essential 'sex determining region' on the Y chromosome which signals for testis differentiation.

Internal genitalia

- Embryonic *mullerian* structures form the uterus, fallopian tubes and upper 1/3 of the vagina.
- In males, *antimullerian hormone* is secreted by immature *Sertoli* cells in the testis by 6 weeks, and this causes regression of the mullerian structures. *Leydig* cells appear in the testis around day 60, and produce *testosterone* under placental hCG stimulation. Testosterone promotes growth and differentiation of the *wolffian ducts* to form the epididymis ,vas deferens, and seminal vesicles.

External genitalia

- In the absence of any androgen secretion, labia majora, labia minora, and clitoris develop from the embryonic genital swelling, genital fold, and genital tubercle respectively.
- Development of normal male external genitalia requires testosterone from the testis and this signal is amplified by conversion to *dihydrotestosterone* by the enzyme *5α-reductase*. In the presence of dihydrotestosterone, the genital tubercle elongates to form the corpora cavernosa and glans penis, the urethral fold forms the penile shaft, and the labioscrotal swelling forms the scrotum. This process commences around 9 weeks and is completed by 13 weeks. Testicular descent in males occurs in the later 2/3 of gestation under control of foetal LH and testosterone.

Assessment of ambiguous genitalia

Most cases of intersex/ambiguous genitalia present at birth. Involvement of an experienced paediatric endocrinologist and surgeon should be sought as early as possible.

History

- Any maternal medication during pregnancy?
- Are parents consanguineous or is there a family history of ambiguous genitalia?
- Is there a neonatal history of hypoglycaemia or prolonged jaundice?

Examination

- Assess clitoris/phallus size; degree of labial fusion; position of urethra/urogenital sinus (anterior or posterior).
- Are gonads palpable? (check along line of descent).
- Are there any signs indicating panhypopituitarism? (e.g. midline defects/hypoglycaemia/hypocortisolaemia/prolonged jaundice).
- Dysmorphic features of Turner's syndrome may be seen in XO/XY or XX/XY mosaicism.

Investigations

- Bloods for karyotype, electrolytes, blood glucose, 17-OH progesterone.
- Ultrasound of pelvis and labial folds (for mullerian structures and gonads).
- EUA, cystogram, and photographs.
- After 48 h old, when the neonatal hormonal surge has decreased, repeat bloods for 17-OH progesterone, cortisol, LH, FSH and androgen levels. Collect a 24 h urine sample to measure the steroid profile.

Specific tests

- Short synacthen test in a virilized XX (when CAH is suspected).
- 3-day HCG test in a undervirilized 'male' (testes present or 46,XY) examines stimulated gonadal production of androgens and may be diagnostic of biosynthesis defects or androgen insensitivity.
- LHRH test examines pituitary gonadotrophin secretion (this test is only informative in the neonatal period).
- Glucagon test examines cortisol and GH secretion.
- Androgen receptor function can be tested on cultured fibroblasts from a genital skin biopsy.
- DNA analysis for androgen receptor mutation and CAH mutations.

Ambiguous genitalia (see p. 484)

Male and female internal and external genitalia develop from common embryonic structures. In the absence of male differentiating signals, normal female genitalia develop. Genital ambiguity may therefore occur as a result of chromosomal abnormality, gonadal dysgenesis, biochemical defects of androgen synthesis, inappropriate exposure to external androgens or androgen receptor insensitivity.

Definitions

- *Male pseudohermaphrodite* An individual with 46,XY karyotype and male gonads but with ambiguous or female external genitalia.
- *Female pseudohermaphrodite* An individual with 46,XX karyotype and female gonads but with ambiguous or male external genitalia.
- *True hermaphrodite* An individual, irrespective of karyotype, who has both ovarian and testicular tissue. Internal genitalia may also be mixed and external genitalia may be male, female, or ambiguous

Female pseudohermaphrodite

Biochemical defects leading to androgen oversecretion

Congenital adrenal hyperplasia (CAH – 21-hydroxylase deficiency most commonly) is the most common cause of ambiguous genitalia in 46,XX (see p. 654)

Maternal hyperandrogenism

The female foetus may be virilized if maternal androgen levels exceed the capacity of placental aromatase to convert these to oestrogen. This may occur due to maternal disease (e.g. CAH, adrenal and ovarian tumours) or use of androgenic medication in pregnancy (e.g. stilboestrol).

Gonadal dysgenesis

- *46,XX* Normal male differentiation can occur if the *SRY* gene has been translocated onto an autosome.
- *45,XO* In Turner's syndrome mild dysmorphic features may be present, but infants with XO/XY mosaicism may present with ambiguous genitalia.

Male pseudohermaphrodite

Gonadal dysgenesis

- XY gonadal dysgenesis is caused by microdeletion of the *SRY* gene on the Y chromosome and results in a normal female phenotype.
- Other sex-determining genes are probably required as gonadal dysgenesis can occur in presence of the *SRY* gene. In addition, it is suggested that early testicular failure may result from torsion or infarction.

Biochemical defects of androgen synthesis

- Rare deficiencies of the enzymes *5α-reductase, 17-ketosteroid reductase* or *3ß-hydroxysteroid dehydrogenase* are autosomal recessively inherited and may result in variable degrees of undervirilization.

Androgen receptor insensitivity syndrome (see p. 486)

Defects of the androgen receptor gene on the X chromosome, or autosomal post-receptor signalling genes, may result in complete or partial androgen insensitivity.

- *Complete androgen insensitivity*, or *testicular feminization syndrome* Results in normal female external genitalia and usually only presents with testicular prolapse in childhood or primary amenorrhoea in adolescence.
- *Partial androgen insensitivity* The most common cause of XY pseudohermaphroditism. Presentation may vary from mild virilization to micropenis, hypospadias, undescended testes or only decreased spermatogenesis.

Gonadotrophin defects

- Gonadotrophin deficiency may occur in *hypopituitarism* or may be associated with anosmia (*Kallmann syndrome*). It usually presents with delayed puberty but is an occasional cause of micropenis and undescended testes.
- LH receptor gene defects are rare, and result in complete absence of virilization as the testes are unable to respond to placental hCG.

Antimullerian hormone deficiency or insensitivity

Testes are usually undescended and uterus and fallopian tubes present.

Management of ambiguous genitalia

In the newborn period, the infant should be monitored in hospital for:

- hypoglycaemia (until hypopituitarism is excluded)
- salt wasting (until CAH is excluded).

Explain to the parents that the infant appears to be healthy, but has a birth defect that interferes with determining gender. It is helpful to show the parents the physical findings as you explain this. Refer to the infant as 'your baby', although some parents prefer to use a non-gender-specific name (e.g. Charlie/Sam/Jo) rather than wait until gender has been assigned. Advise them to postpone the registration of birth until after further investigations, and discuss what they will say to relatives and friends.

Sex assignment

Decision on the sex of rearing should be based on the optimal expected outcome in terms of psychosexual and reproductive function. Parents therefore should be allowed discussion with an endocrinologist, a surgeon specializing in urogenital reconstruction, a psychologist/psychiatrist, and a social worker. Following the necessary investigations and discussions, early gender assignment optimizes the psychosexual outcome.

Further management

- If female sex is assigned, any testicular tissue should be removed.
- Reconstructive surgery may include clitoral reduction, gonadectomy, and vaginoplasty in girls, and phallus enlargement, hypospadias repair, and orchidopexy in boys. In both sexes multiple-stage procedures may be required.
- Topical or systemic *dihydrotestosterone* may enhance phallus size in male infants and a trial of therapy is sometimes useful before gender assignment.
- Hormone replacement therapy may also be required from puberty into adulthood.
- Continuing psychological support for the parents and children is very important.

True hermaphrodite (see p. 487)

This condition arises as a result of chromosomal mosaicism (46,XX/XY or 45,46,XO/XY).

Congenital adrenal hyperplasia

(see p. 364)

A number of autosomally inherited enzyme deficiencies result in cortisol deficiency, excess pituitary ACTH secretion, adrenal gland hyperplasia.

21-hydroxylase deficiency (>90%)

The most common cause of CAH results in cortisol and mineralocorticoid deficiency, while the build-up of precursor steroids is channelled towards excess adrenal androgen synthesis. Different gene defects result in different degrees of enzyme dysfunction and thus wide variation in phenotypes.

Clinical features

- Virilization of female foetuses may result in clitoromegaly and labial fusion at birth. 75% have sufficient mineralocorticoid deficiency to cause renal salt-wasting. Because males have normal genitalia at birth, they may present acutely ill in the neonatal period with vomiting, dehydration, collapse, hyponatraemia, and hyperkalaemia. Non-salt-wasting boys present with early genital enlargement and pubarche.
- If untreated or poorly treated, both sexes may develop pubic hair, acne, and rapid height velocity. However, advanced bone maturation and precocious puberty may result in very short final height.
- *'Non-classical CAH'* is due to milder 21-hydroxylase deficiency, and affected girls present in later childhood or adulthood with hirsuitism, acne, premature/exaggerated adrenarche, menstrual irregularities, and infertility.

11-β hydroxylase deficiency (~5%)

This enzyme, which converts 11-deoxycortisol to cortisol, is the final step in cortisol synthesis. In addition to excess adrenal androgens, the overproduced precursor corticosterone has mineralocorticoid activity. Thus, in contrast to salt wasting in 21-hydroxylase deficiency, these subjects may have hypernatraemia and hypokalaemia. Hypertension is rarely seen in infancy, but may develop during childhood and affects 50–60% of adults.

Specific investigations for CAH (see also investigation of ambiguous genitalia)

- *Plasma 17-OH progesterone* An elevated level indicates 21 hydroxylase deficiency, but it may be difficult to distinguish this from the physiological hormonal surge which occurs in the first 2 days of life. This test should therefore be repeated (together with 11-deoxycortisol) after 48 h of age.
- A 24 h urine steroid profile (also collected after 48 h of age) should confirm the diagnosis and allows detection of the rarer enzyme defects.
- Blood and urine collection after i/v synacthen stimulation is often required to discriminate between the different enzyme deficiencies.
- Plasma and urine electrolytes should be monitored daily over the first 2 weeks.
- Plasma renin level is also useful to confirm salt wasting.

Other rare enzyme deficiencies

- *3β-Hydroxysteroid dehydrogenase deficiency* Impairs cortisol, mineralocorticoid and androgen biosynthesis. Males have hypospadias and undescended testes, however excess DHEA, a weak androgen, may cause mild virilization in females.
- *17α-Hydrolxylase deficiency* Impairs cortisol, androgen, and oestrogen synthesis, but overproduction of mineralocorticoids leads to hypokalaemia and hypertension.
- *Cholesterol desmolase deficiency* ('lipoid adrenal hyperplasia') An extremely rare cause of cortisol, mineralocorticoid, and androgen deficiency.

Management

- *Hydrocortisone* (15 mg/m^2 per day orally in three divided doses) In addition to treating cortisol deficiency, this therapy suppresses ACTH and thereby limits excessive production of adrenal androgens. Occasionally higher doses are required to achieve adequate androgen suppression, however over-treatment may suppress growth.
- In salt losers, initial *i/v fluid resuscitation* (10–20 mL/kg normal saline) May be required to treat circulatory collapse. Long-term mineralocorticoid replacement (*fludrocortisone* 0.05–0.3 mg/day) may have incomplete efficacy, particularly in infancy, and *sodium chloride* supplements are also needed. Up to 10 mmol/kg per day may be needed in infancy.
- *Reconstructive surgery* (clitoral reduction, vaginoplasty) Often performed in infancy and further procedures may be required at preschool age and during puberty.

Monitoring of hormonal therapy

- *Height velocity and bone age* If hydrocortisone therapy is insufficient, growth rate will be above normal and bone age will be advanced. Conversely, if hydrocortisone therapy is excessive, growth is suppressed.
- *Cortisol* and *17-OHP* Blood levels should be assessed at least annually. Levels should be measured before and 2 h after each hydrocortisone dose during a 24 h period; these may be collected at home by the parents using 'spot' capillary blood samples.
- *Mineralocorticoid and sodium replacement* Should be monitored by measuring plasma electrolytes, renin and aldosterone levels, and by regular blood pressure assessments.

Genetic advice

The inheritance of CAH is autosomal recessive and parents should be informed of a 25% risk of recurrence in future offspring. If the mutation is identifiable on DNA analysis in the child and parents, chorionic villus sampling may allow prenatal diagnosis. Maternal *dexamethasone* therapy from around 5–6 weeks of pregnancy has been used to prevent virilization of the female foetus without significant maternal complications. However, there is a theoretical risk of adulthood hypertension and type 2 diabetes in the offspring, and this therapy is controversial.

Further reading

Brook CGD (ed.) *Clinical Paediatric Endocrinology*, 3rd edn. 1995. Blackwell Science, Oxford.

Hochberg Z (ed.) *Practical Algorithms in Pediatric Endocrinology*. 1998. Karger, Basel.

Hughes IA. *Handbook of Endocrine Investigations in Children*. 1989. John Wright & Sons, Bristol, UK

Wilkins L: In Kappy MS, Blizzard RM, Migeon CJ (ed.) *The Diagnosis and Treatment of Endocrine Disorders in Childhood and Adolescence*, 4th edn. 1994. Charles C Thomas, Springfield, Illinois.

Part VIII
Neuroendocrine tumours of the gastrointestinal tract

Chapter 86
The diffuse neuroendocrine system

Tumour distribution

Neuroendocrine cells are particularly prominent in the gastrointestinal tract and pancreas. Neuroendocrine tumours arising in these sites cause well-recognized clinical features according to the hormonal products produced (see Table 86.1).

Some rare functioning tumours of the diffuse neuroendocrine system produce ectopic hormones: for example, ACTH, growth hormone-releasing hormone (GHRH) and parathyroid hormoe (PTH) causing acromegaly, Cushing's syndrome, and hypercalcaemia respectively.

Table 86.1 Characteristics of the main neuroendocrine tumours of the gastrointestinal tract and pancreas

Site	Product	Syndrome
Pancreatic β cells	Insulin	Insulinoma (70% of pancreatic NE tumours)
Pancreatic α cells	Glucagon	Gluacagonoma
Pancreatic δ cells	Somatostatin	Somatostatinoma
Pancreatic G cells	Gastrin	Gastrinoma (20% of pancreatic NE tumours) Zollinger-Ellison
Pancreatic VIP cells	VIP	VIPoma
Stomach	Gastrin	Zollinger–Ellison
	Somatostatin	MEN-2
	ACTH	Cushing's
Small intestine	Serotonin, tachykinins	Carcinoid (also stomach, and pancreas)
	Gastrin	Zollinger-Ellison, MEN-1
	Somatostatin	MEN-2
	ACTH	Cushing's

Chapter 87
Carcinoid syndrome

Definition and classification

- The carcinoid syndrome results from neuroendocrine tumours with the ability to produce serotonin and tachykinins which cause typical symptoms of diarrhoea, flushing, bronchospasm, and right heart failure. The development of carcinoid syndrome is not invariable in patients with carcinoid tumours, and is commonest in patients with midgut metastatic tumours.
- Carcinoid tumours may be classified into foregut, midgut, and hindgut tumours on the basis of their anatomical location (Table 87.1).
- About 85% of carcinoid tumours develop in the gastrointestinal tract, 10% in the lung, and the rest in various organs such as the thymus, kidney, ovary, and prostate.

Epidemiology

- The annual incidence of carcinoid syndrome is of the order of 1/100 000 population, although some estimates are up to 8/100 000, as many may be indolent.
- Carcinoid tumours of the ileum present at a mean age of 50–60 years with equal frequency in males and females.

Table 87.1 Classification of carcinoid tumours

Origin	Organ	Hormones	Symptoms
Foregut	Thymus	CRH, ACTH,GHRH	Cushing's, acromegaly
	Lung	CRH, ACTH, GHRH	Cushing's, acromegaly
		Serotonin	Carcinoid syndrome
	Stomach	Histamine, gastrin	Flushing, ZE syndrome
	Duodenum	Gastrin, somatostatin	ZE, somatostatinoma
	Pancreas	ACTH, GHRH, PTH	Cushing's acromegaly, ↑Ca
Midgut	Ileum	Serotonin, kinins	Classical carcinoid
	Appendix	(Serotonin)	Not hormone related
Hindgut	Colon	PP, hCG	Not hormone related
	Rectum	Somatostatin	Not hormone related

Pathology

- Carcinoid tumours arise from neuroendocrine cells.
- They are characterized histologically by reaction to silver stains and neuroendocrine markers e.g. neuron-specific enolase, synaptophysin, and chromogranin.
- The tumours usually produce a variety of hormones and vasoactive substances. Serotonin is most commonly produced, synthesized from 5 hydroxytryptophan and metabolized by monoamine oxidase to 5-hydroxyindole acetic acid (5HIAA).
- Other substances that may be produced include – ACTH, GHRH, PTH, histamine, substance P, prostaglandins, kallikrein, and dopamine.
- Carcinoid tumours may be further classified on the basis of histological appearance into typical (well-differentiated) and atypical (cellular atypia and increased mitoses). Atypical carcinoids are more aggressive, more likely to metastasize (>50%) and are associated with a poorer survival.

Clinical presentation

See Table 87.2.

- The original description of the carcinoid syndrome includes flushing, diarrhoea, asthma, right heart valvular lesions, and pellagra-like skin lesions.
- In a published series of patients from Sweden with known gastrointestinal carcinoids, 84% presented with diarrhoea, 75% with flushing, and 44% with intestinal obstruction. During the course of the illness it was noted that 33% of the patients had carcinoid heart disease and 15% complained of symptoms of wheezing.
- The carcinoid flush may be precipitated by spicy food, hot drinks, alcohol, exercise, and postural changes. Surgery and infections may also provoke a severe attack leading to a carcinoid crisis.
- The cause of flushing is heterogeneous and results from the release of vasoactive substances such as 5-HT, tachykinins, kallekrein, and substance P. Longstanding carcinoid is often associated with a violacious flush and facial telangiectases whereas typical acute attacks are associated with a diffuse erythematous flush affecting the face and upper thorax. A bright red patchy flush is associated with gastric carcinoids with an excess of histamine release.
- Cardiac signs are invariably associated with right sided valvular lesions. The tricuspid and pulmonary valves are frequently retracted by a fibrotic process.
- Arthritis may occur in a small number of patients. Sclerotic bone metastases may be seen in patients with foregut tumours.
- Almost all patients with the carcinoid syndrome due to gastrointestinal tumours have metastases, usually in the liver. Some bronchial carcinoids may present with the classical features of the syndrome without evidence of metastases. Tumour size is an unreliable predictor of metastases.

Table 87.2 Clinical presentation of patients with carcinoid tumours

Symptoms due to carcinoid syndrome	Other distinct clinical syndromes
Diarrhoea	Zollinger–Ellison (gastrin mediated)
Flushing	Somatostatinoma (somatostatin)
Intestinal obstruction	Cushing's (CRH or ACTH)
Bronchospasm	Acromegaly (GHRH)
Pellagra	Bright red flushing (histamine)

Biochemical investigations

- Urinary 5-HIAA has a sensitivity for the diagnosis of carcinoid syndrome of about 70% and a specificity of 100% in patients with carcinoid syndrome. When analysing urinary 5-HIAA it is important to suggest a diet excluding bananas, avocado, pineapple, walnuts, chocolate, and coffee and also to avoid drugs such as salicylates, chlorpromazine, and L-dopa.
- The most sensitive marker for carcinoid syndrome is plasma chromogranin A, which has been found in 100% of patients, although the specificity is lower than for 5-HIAA since most tumours with neuroendocrine differentiation are associated with increased levels of plasma chromogranin A. This test is not widely available for clinical use.
- A plasma gut hormone profile may also be useful for the identification of tumour markers such as gastrin, pancreatic polypeptide, neuropeptide Y, and somatostatin.
- Liver biochemistry is an unreliable marker of liver involvement, and the alkaline phosphatase may remain in the normal range despite extensive metastatic disease.

Monitoring treatment

- Urinary 5HIAA can be useful to monitor therapy if these are elevated at diagnosis.
- CT/MRI can be useful to monitor tumour bulk.

Tumour localization

- Imaging with abdominal ultrasound, CT, and MRI is directed at detection of metastatic spread. On CT, hepatic carcinoid masses are usually multifocal showing enhancement after i/v contrast and frequently with low attenuation areas of necrosis. MRI is at least as sensitive as CT with lesions being iso-intense on T-1 weighted images but of high signal on T-2 weighted images.
- Radionucleotide scanning with indium-labelled octreotide provides very useful information about the localization of metastatic disease and frequently identifies previously unidentified extra-hepatic sites of disease. About 85% of carcinoid tumours have somatostatin receptors and the technique predicts which tumours are suitable for octreotide therapy.
- Radiolabelled ^{123}I-metaiodobenzylguanidine(MIBG) is also taken up by carcinoid tumours of varying degrees. It is not as sensitive as the octreotide scan but when positive indicates a possible use for ^{123}I-MIBG therapy.
- PET scanning has come into clinical use in some centres and uses a short-lived isotope precursor of serotonin synthesis (^{11}C-labelled 5-HTP) which is concentrated and taken up by carcinoid tumours.
- Angiography is a sensitive investigation but because it is invasive it is rarely indicated unless embolization is to be considered.

Carcinoid heart disease

- Occurs in two-thirds of patients with the carcinoid syndrome. Typically it affects patients with higher levels of urinary 5HIAA. Whether the mechamism is directly due to serotonin is currently not known.
- Pathologically the lesions are characterized by fibrous thickening of the endocardium in plaques.
- The right side of the heart is usually involved. Thickening and retraction of the tricuspid and pulmonary valve leaflets lead to tricuspid regurgitation in nearly all, and less commonly pulmonary regurgitation, tricuspid stenosis, and pulmonary stenosis. The left side is only involved in 10%.
- Valvular replacement leads to improvement, but surgery may be associated with significant morbidity and mortality.

Treatment

Surgical treatment

- In patients with local disease, surgery can be curative. Even in patients with bulky disease with liver and mesenteric metastases, surgery may still be of benefit by affording a more favourable response to medical treatment and in alleviating symptoms due to fibrosis and intestinal obstruction.
- Pulmonary carcinoids are usually treated with conservative resection, although more extensive surgery ± radiotherapy is recommended for atypical carcinoids. Small-bowel resection with resection of local affected mesentery is the treatment of choice for small-bowel carcinoids. Appendiceal carcinoid tumours <2 cm in diameter are treated with appendectomy; larger tumours are an indication for right hemicolectomy.
- Surgery may be helpful if there are one or two large hepatic metastases, and this may lead to a considerable improvement in symptoms.

Somatostatin analogues

- Octreotide (50–200 μg s/c 3x daily) and the more recently developed long-acting analogues reduce the level of biochemical tumour markers in the majority of patients and control symptoms in around 70% of patients. However, radiological evidence of tumour regression is rare. Patient resistance to octreotide occurs in many patients after a few years. The mechanism is unclear, and may be due to changes in receptor signalling.
- Patients are usually commenced on 50–100 μg 3× daily of s/c octreotide, and the dose increased as necessary. Many patients prefer to transfer to a long-acting form of somatostatin analogue. It is helpful to 'cover' the change-over with a couple of weeks of s/c octreotide. Patients may still occasionally need 'top-up' doses of s/c octreotide when established on lanreotide or long-acting octreotide.
- Octreotide is the most effective treatment for a carcinoid crisis and is given as an i/v infusion at a rate of 100 μg/h.

Hepatic embolization

Can be performed with gelfoam powder or with chemotherapy injected into the hepatic artery. These procedures are considered palliative and usually reserved for patients not responding to medical treatments. The duration of improvement may be short-lived, and side-effects occasionally include development of the hepatorenal syndrome. Liver transplantation may be considered in selected patients.

Radioactive isotope therapy

Treatment with indium-labelled-DTPA-octreotide and with ^{123}I-MIBG is currently undergoing clinical assessment.

External beam radiotherapy

May provide palliation in those with bone or central nervous system metastases.

Chemotherapy

The most promising combination of chemotherapy using streptozotocin and 5-flurouracil produces only short-lasting responses in 10–30% of patients with carcinoid tumours, in contrast to the 50–60% response rate of pancreatic neuroendocrine tumours. Cisplatin and etoposide may produce a useful response in patients with anaplastic tumours.

α-Interferon

There is a good biochemical response rate (about 45%) with clinical improvement of the symptoms of carcinoid syndrome in 70% of patients. Tumour shrinkage has also been described in 12% of patients. Recently a combination of α-interferon and octreotide has been shown to produce good biochemical response rates in patients previously resistant to either drug alone.

Pellagra

- Rarely pellagra may develop due to nicotinamide deficiency secondary to excessive tryptophan metabolism.
- Nicotinamide supplementation is therapeutic.

Perioperative management of carcinoid tumours

It is useful to give s/c octerotide during the immediate pre- and perioperative period, as surgery may be associated with release of various vasoactive neurotransmitters leading to hypotension and bronchospasm.

Prognosis

- Individual patients have been reported to live 20 or sometimes 30 years after the diagnosis of metastatic carcinoid tumour, but this should not be considered a benign disease. The 5 year survival rate when liver metastases are present is approximately 20–40%, with a median survival time being about 2 years.
- The median survival time has been shown to increase to up to 5–7 years following the use of more active and aggressive therapy.
- Somatostatin analogues and interferon therapy has improved not only the survival time but also the quality of life of patients.
- The prognosis is greatly influenced by the development of carcinoid heart disease, which is nowadays amenable to heart valve replacement.

Further reading

Kulke MH, Mayer RJ. Carcinoid tumours. *New England Journal of Medicine* 1999; 340: 858–868.

Chapter 88
Insulinomas

Definitions

- An insulinoma is a tumour of the endocrine pancreas that causes hypoglycaemia through its secretion of insulin.
- Unlike other endocrine tumours of the pancreas, where malignancy is common, insulinomas are usually benign and only about 15% have evidence of metastases.
- More than 80% are solitary but some are multiple, either simultaneously or consecutively, a situation likely to be associated with multiple endocrine neoplasia (MEN)-1 in approximately 10%.

Epidemiology

- The annual incidence of insulinoma is of the order of 1–2 new cases per million population.
- Insulinomas are found with equal frequency throughout the head, body, and tail of the pancreas.

Clinical presentation

- Symptoms of hypoglycaemia (see p. 741).
- Patients may give a history of relief of symptoms with food, and weight gain occurs in 30% of patients.
- Hypoglycaemia is defined as a blood glucose concentration of ≤2.5 mmol/L.

Biochemical investigations

(see Chapter 98, p. 742)

- The diagnosis of hypoglycaemia is best established by asking the patient to attend for a 15 h fasting glucose test on three separate occasions.
- In the rare cases where the fasting glucose fails to reveal hypoglycaemia, assay for blood glucose, insulin and C peptide following a period of 30 min exercise in a fasting patient will usually prove diagnostic.
- A 72 h inpatient fast is nowadays rarely necessary but could be considered if the outpatient tests prove negative but clinical suspicion remains high.

Tumour localization

See Table 88.1.

- Islet tumours are often small and may not be detected by any imaging technique. The available radiological investigations have a wide reported range of sensitivity which often depends on the equipment and operator.
- CT using spiral scanning to reduce respiratory artefact demonstrates enhancing lesions as small as 5 mm after i/v contrast with a sensitivity of approximately 50%.
- Endoscopic ultrasound which requires specialized equipment and expertise may identify tumours as small as 5 mm and has been reported to have a sensitivity of about 80%. The head of the pancreas is visualized with the probe in the duodenum, and the body and tail with it in the stomach.
- Intraoperative ultrasound using a high frequency transducer applied directly to the pancreas has a sensitivity of around 90%.
- The risk of multiple tumours makes a thorough examination of the whole pancreas essential at operation.

Table 88.1 Radiological localization of pancreatic insulinomas

Localization technique	Reported sensitivity (%)
Transabdominal ultrasound	30–61%
Endoscopic ultrasound	80%
Intraoperative ultrasound	90%
Computed tomography	42–78%
Magnetic resonance imaging	20–100%
Octreotide scanning	68–86%
Pancreatic arteriography	29–90%
Venous sampling	84%

Treatment

- The treatment of choice in all but elderly or debilitated patients is surgical removal. The perioperative mortality rates are less than 1% in the hands of a specialized pancreatic surgeon. The mortality is largely influenced by the incidence of acute pancreatitis and peritonitis. Postoperative hyperglycaemia may occur even following partial pancreatectomy.
- Medical treatment to control symptoms may be possible using a combination of diazoxide and octreotide (p. 744).

Prognosis

- Following removal of a solitary insulinoma, life expectancy is restored to normal.
- Malignant insulinomas, with metastases usually to the liver, have a natural history of years rather than months and symptoms may be controlled with medical therapy or specific antitumour therapy using streptozotocin and 5-fluorouuracil.

Chapter 89
Gastrinomas

Definitions

- Gastrin, synthesized in the G cells situated predominantly in the gastric antrum, is the principal gut hormone stimulating gastric acid secretion.
- The gastrinoma syndrome is due to the excessive release of gastrin by neuroendocrine tumours of the gastrointestinal tract and pancreas. <40% of tumours arise in the gastrointestinal tract.
- 90% of tumours causing the gastrinoma syndrome are sited in what has been termed the 'gastrinoma triangle'. This is bounded by the junction of the cystic and common bile ducts superiorly, the junction of the second and third parts of the duodenum inferiorly, and the junction of the neck and body of the pancreas medially.

Epidemiology

- Although gastrinomas are rare they represent the second most commonly diagnosed pancreatic islet cell tumour after insulinoma.
- The estimated prevalence is of the order of 1/million.

Clinical presentation

- Peptic ulcers that are multiple and refractory to standard medical treatment.
- A high prevalance of peptic ulcer complications including perforation, haemorrhage, and pyloric stenosis.
- Malabsorption and diarrhoea may be the main presenting complaint and is due to acid-related inactivation of enzymes and mucosal damage in the upper small bowel.
- There may be a history of familial endocrine disease, e.g. MEN-1 in up to 1/3 of patients.
- Approximately 60% have metastasized at the time of diagnosis and 1/3 of gastrinoma patients have MEN-1.

Biochemical investigations

- The diagnosis rests on finding an inappropriately elevated fasting plasma gastrin in the presence of increased gastric acid secretion (see Table 89.1).
- Patients should have antisecretory treatment stopped before the test (3 days for H2 blockers and 2 weeks for proton pump inhibitors) since these drugs are associated with hypergastrinaemia. Gastrin levels above 250 pmol/L are rare in patients taking proton pump inhibitors.
- A gut hormone profile may identify elevated plasma levels of pancreatic polypeptide or other gut hormones.
- The tumour localization techniques described for insulinomas are also relevant for gastrinomas (see Table 88.1, p. 676).
- Up to 40% of tumours are duodenal, many are very small and tumour localization can be a major clinical problem. They are frequently associated with local lymph node disease.
- Selective arterial angiography may be combined with a provocative test for gastrin release using a bolus of secretin for elusive small tumours.

Table 89.1 Causes of hypergastrinaemia

Low or normal gastric acid production	Elevated gastric acid production
H2 blockers	Gastrinoma
Proton pump inhibitors	G cell hyperplasia
Vagotomy	
Hypochlorhydria	
Short gut syndrome	
Renal failure	
Hypercalcaemia	

Treatment

- The treatment of choice is surgical tumour removal although this is usually only considered after the tumour has been identified pre-operatively.
- Operation is rarely justified in patients with known hepatic metastases, although some authors have claimed benefit from tumour debulking
- In patients where preoperative localization has failed to identify a tumour, the patient is often best maintained on medical therapy with CT scanning and arteriography repeated at intervals rather than recommending exploratory surgery.
- Octreotide does not appear to be more effective at relieving symptoms than H2 blockers or proton pump inhibitors and there is no data to support the view that octreotide alters the natural history of the tumours.
- In patients with MEN-1 syndrome, the usual policy is to operate when a well-defined tumour can be identified although it must be remembered that these patients are particularly prone to multiple small gastinomas in the duodenum.

Table 89.2 Treatment options for gastrinomas

Medical treatment	Surgery	Palliation
Proton pump inhibitors	Tumour resection	Chemotherapy
H2 blockers	Tumour debulking	Hepatic artery embolization
Octreotide	Liver transplant	

Chapter 90
Glucagonomas

Definitions

- Glucagonomas are neuroendocrine tumours that are usually located in the pancreas and produce the glucogonoma syndrome through the secretion of glucagon and other peptides derived from the preproglucagon gene.
- Over 70% of glucagonomas are malignant, but they are also very indolent tumours and the diagnosis following the appearance of the characteristic rash has often been overlooked for many years.

Epidemiology

- The annual incidence is estimated at 1/20 million.

Clinical presentation

See Table 90.1.

- The characteristic rash, necrolytic migratory erythema occurs in over 90% of cases and usually manifests initially as a well-demarcated area of erythema in the groin and migrating to the limbs, buttocks and perineum.
- Mucous membrane involvement is common, with stomatitis, glossitis, vaginitis, and urethritis being frequent features.
- Glucagon antagonizes the effects of insulin, particularly on liver glucose metabolism and glucose intolerance is a frequent association.
- Sustained gluconeogenesis also causes amino acid deficiency and results in protein catabolism which can be associated with unrelenting weight loss.
- Glucagon has a direct suppressive effect on the bone marrow resulting in a normochromic normocytic anaemia in almost all patients.

Table 90.1 Clinical features of the glucagonoma syndrome

Site	Clinical features
Skin	Necrolytic migratory erythema (90%)
Mucous membranes	Angular stomatitis
	Atrophic glossitis
	Vulvovaginitis
	Urethritis
Nails	Onycholysis
Scalp	Alopecia
Metabolism	Glucose intolerance (90%)
	Protein catabolism and weight loss
Haematological	Anaemia
	Venous thrombosis
Psychiatric	Depression
	Psychosis

Biochemical investigations

- The diagnosis is confirmed on finding raised plasma glucagon levels.
- A gut hormone profile may show elevated neuroendocrine markers such as pancreatic polypeptide.
- Impaired glucose tolerance and hypoaminoacidaemia may be present.

Tumour localization

- At the time of diagnosis >50% of glucagonomas will have metastasized and most primary tumours will be >3 cm in diameter.
- These tumours rarely present problems of radiological localization, and transabdominal ultrasound and CT scanning are usually adequate.
- Small benign tumours may require specific techniques for localization (see table on p. 676) with octreotide scanning probably being the best for evaluating the extent of metastatic disease.

Treatment

- Surgery is the only curative therapeutic option, but the potential for cure can be as low as 5%.
- In malignant disease, surgical cure can be achieved if the metastases are confined to the liver and the patient is considered for a liver transplant.
- Octreotide or long acting somatostatin analogues are now the treatment of first choice with excellent results achieved in treating the necrolytic migratory erythema. Octreotide is less effective at reversing the weight loss and has an inconsistent effect on diabetes control.
- Palliative chemotherapy using streptozotocin and 5-fluorouracil has been shown in 75% of patients to produce a 50% reduction in glucagon levels with remissions often lasting over a year.
- Hepatic artery embolization is often associated with a dramatic relief of symptoms with remissions of several months.

Chapter 91
VIPomas

Definitions

- In 1958, Verner and Morrison first described a syndrome consisting of refractory watery diarrhoea and hypokalaemia associated with a neuroendocrine tumours of the pancreas.
- The syndrome of watery diarrhoea, hypokalaemia, and achlorhydria (WDHA) is due to secretion of vasoactive intestinal polypeptide (VIP), and tumours that secrete VIP are known as VIPomas.

Clinical presentation

- The most prominent symptom in most patients is profuse watery diarrhoea which is secretory in nature and therefore rich in electrolytes.
- Other causes of secretory diarrhoea should be considered in the differential diagnosis (see box).
- The metabolic abnormalities which typify the VIPoma syndrome include hypercalcaemia which in some cases may be due to an associated MEN-1 syndrome (see box).

Differential diagnosis of secretory diarrhoea

- infection due to *Escherichia coli* or cholera toxins
- laxative abuse
- villous adenoma
- other gut neuroendocrine tumours such as carcinoid tumours and gastrinomas
- carcinoma of the lung
- medullary carcinoma of the thyroid
- systemic mastocytosis
- immunoglogulin A deficiency.

Clinical features of the VIPoma syndrome

- watery diarrhoea
- hypokalaemia
- achlorhydria
- metabolic acidosis
- hypercalcaemia
- hyperglycaemia
- hypomagnesaemia
- facial flushing

Biochemical investigations

- Elevated levels of plasma VIP are found in all patients with the VIPoma syndrome, although false positives may occur in dehydrated patients caused by diarrhoea due to other causes.
- A gut hormone profile may identify raised tumour markers such as pancreatic polypeptide and detection of the other causes of the watery diarrhoea syndrome such as those caused by gastrin and glucagon.
- Urinary catecholamine excretion should be investigated, especially in children in whom it is more common to find the tumours residing in the adrenal medulla.

Tumour localization

- The majority of tumours secreting VIP originate in the pancreas while others arise from the sympathetic chain.
- Primary VIPomas have very rarely been reported to have arisen from such varied sites as lung, oesophagus, small bowel, colon, and kidney.
- Most patients present with large tumours which can be easily identified by transabdominal ultrasound or CT although in others additional methods of tumour localization as previously described are required (see p. 676).

Treatment

- Surgery to remove the tumour is the treatment of first choice if technically possible. Surgical debulking may be of palliative benefit.
- Somatostatin analogues such as octreotide therapy produce good symptomatic relief of the diarrhoea in most patients and long-term use may result in tumour regression.
- Glucocorticoids in high dosage have also been found to produce good relief of symptoms.
- A trial of lithium may be warranted in resistant cases and may also be used in combination with octreotide.
- Chemotherapy using streptozotocin with 5-fluorouracil has resulted in response rates of >50%.
- Hepatic artery embolization can give temporary respite from severe diarrhoea.

Chapter 92
Somatostatinomas

Definitions

Somatostatinomas are very rare neuroendocrine tumours occurring both in the pancreas and in the duodenum and producing a characteristic clinical syndrome due to secretion of somatostatin.

Epidemiology

Since many somatostatinomas are not associated with a clinical syndrome the true incidence is unknown although the clinically relevant tumours have been estimated to occur with an incidence of 1/40 million.

Presenting features

See box.

- Glucose intolerance or frank diabetes mellitus may have been noted for many years prior to the diagnosis and retrospectively often represents the first clinical sign. It is probably due to the inhibitory effect of somatostatin on insulin secretion.
- A high incidence of gallstones has been described as has also been seen with long-term treatment with octreotide.
- Diarrhoea, steatorrhoea, and weight loss appear to be consistent clinical features and may be associated with the inhibition of the exocrine pancreas by somatostatin.
- Small duodenal somatostatin tumours may occur in association with neurofibromatosis type 1 (von Recklinghausen syndrome) (43%) and although these rarely cause the inhibitory clinical syndrome they present with obstructive biliary disease through local spread of the tumour.
- The clinical syndrome may be diagnosed late in the course of the disease when metastatic spread to local lymph nodes and liver is already apparent.
- Infrequently associated with MEN 1 (7%).

Clinical features of the somatostatinoma syndrome

- glucose intolerance/diabetes mellitus (95%)
- gallstones (68%)
- diarrhoea and steatorrhoea
- weight loss (25%)
- anaemia (14%)
- hypochlorhydria

Biochemical investigations

- Plasma somatostatin levels will be raised and may also be associated with raised levels of other neuroendocrine tumour markers including ACTH and calcitonin. Multisecretory activity is commoner wih pancreatic than duodenal somatostatinomas (33 vs 16%).

Tumour localization

- Transabdominal ultrasound and CT scanning may demonstrate the tumour since metastatic disease is often apparent at presentation. Additional methods of tumour localization as previously described may be required (see table on p. 676).

Treatment

- Surgery should be considered first line treatment if a cure appears feasible.
- Hepatic embolization could be considered and chemotherapy with streptozotocin and 5-fluorouracil can be used to control malignant disease.

Part IX
Inherited endocrine syndromes and multiple endocrine neoplasia

Chapter 93

McCune–Albright syndrome

Background

This is characterized by:

- polyostotic fibrous dysplasia
- *café-au-lait* pigmented skin lesions
- autonomous function of multiple endocrine glands.

Genetics

A sporadic condition involving a somatic mutation in the gene (*GNAS1*) that encodes the α chain of the stimulating G protein of adenyl cyclase (GSα mutation). This results in activation of adenyl cyclase and may be the molecular basis for the autonomous function of affected glands.

Features

- *Polyostotic fibrous dysplasia* Multiple expansile bony lesions which can cause fracture deformities and nerve entrapment develop before the age of 10. Radiographs of the femora and pelvis are most useful for screening.
- *Café-au-lait pigmentation* Characterized by an irregular border (cf. neurofibromatosis which have a smooth border), do not cross the mid line and tend to be ipsilateral to the bone lesions, occurring more frequently in the sacrum, buttocks, and lumbar spine.
- *Endocrinopathies* (See Table 93.1).
- Involvement of *other organs* (see Table 93.2).

Diagnosis is made with two of the above clinical triad. If indicated, genetic analysis of lesions may be made. Blood tests looking at the mutations of DNA may be available soon. Several different mutations in the *GNAS1* gene are described.

Table 93.1 Endocrinopathies in McCune-Albright syndrome

Condition	Presentation	Treatment
Precocious puberty	Frequent initial manifestation	Cyproterone acetate
	Typically aged 1–9	
	Low gonadotrophins	
	Adults fertile	
	Less frequent in boys	
Thyroid nodules	50% become toxic because of autonomous nodule function	Antithyroid drugs, surgery, radioiodine
	Nodules present in all	
GH-secreting pituitary tumours and prolactinomas	GH levels high – as patients with GH pituitary adenoma	Octreotide, surgery
	GH does not suppress with oral glucose	
	Tumours present in only 40% – others hyperplasia of somatotrophs	
	Prolactin elevated in 80%	
Cushing's syndrome	Adrenal hyperplasia or adenoma	Adrenalectomy
Hypophosphataemic rickets	Similarities to tumour-associated osteomalacia	Calcitriol, phosphate supplements
	↓Phosphate ↓ 1,25-Vit D, ↑AP; low PO_4 renal reabsorption; normal Ca, 25-OHD and PTH	
	Possibly related to circulating factor secreted by fibrous dysplasia lesions	

Treatment

- *Polyostotic fiibrous dysplasia* Surgery may be complicated by bleeding and radiotherapy has a limited effect.
- *Endocrinopathies* (see Table 93.1).
- *Prognosis* Most patients live beyond reproductive age. Bone deformities may reduce life expectancy. Sudden cardiac death is uncommon.

Table 93.2 Involvement of other organs

Hepatobiliary (common)	Neonatal jaundice, elevated transaminases, cholestasis
Cardiac (common)	Cardiomegaly, tachyarrthymia, sudden death (uncommon)
Gastrointestinal	Polyps, splenic hyperplasia (and thymus), pancreatitis
Central nervous system	Microcephaly, failure to thrive, developmental delay

Chapter 94
Neurofibromatosis

Definitions

- *Neurofibromatosis type I* (NF-1) (von Recklinghausens disease) Refers to multiple neurofibromas, *café-au-lait* spots, iris Lisch nodules, and other variable features including a low frequency of endocrine abnormalities.
- *Neurofibromatosis type II* (NF-2) Refers to bilateral acoustic neurofibromatosis. There are virtually no associated endocrine abnormalities.

NF-1

Genetics

The condition is autosomal dominant. The NF-1 gene locus is on chromosome 17; the gene product is neurofibromin which is a (GTP)-ase-activating protein. GTP is required for an active ras protein and wild-type neurofibromin promotes cleavage from GTP to GDP.

Features

- *Multiple neurofibromas* Cutaneous and subcutaneous lesions appear around puberty. Diffuse plexiformin neurofibromas (originating from larger nerve trunks), however, are congenital
- *Café-au-lait spots* Apparent shortly after birth.
- *Iris Lisch nodules* Became apparent after age 5.
- *Endocrine features* (see Table 94.1).
- *Variable features* (see Table 94.2).

Diagnosis

Should be apparent from aged 1. Currently only 70% of NF-1 mutations can be detected at the molecular level

Table 94.1 Endocrine features of NF-1

Puberty and pregnancy	Both are associated with a change in size of neurofibromas
Hypothalamus and pituitary	Optic gliomas (15% of NF-1 patients) impinge on adjacent tissues causing short stature, precocious or delayed puberty or the Russell diencepalic syndrome (hypothalamic syndrome, skin pallor and visual loss)
Phaeochromocytoma (0.5%)	Most commonly adrenal but extra adrenal at aortic bifurcation (organ of Zuckerkandl) may occur
Gut neuroendocrine tumours (1%)	Usually present as a pancreatic mass

Table 94.2 Variable features of NF-1

Optic pathway gliomas (15%)	Gliomas occur elsewhere, e.g. posterior fossa
Neurofibrosarcoma (6%)	Arise in diffuse plexiform neurofibromas. Usually present in 2nd or 3rd decades
Skeletal dysplasia	Sphenoid wing dysplasia (5%), scoliosis (5%), tibial pseudoarthrosis (1%), pectus excavatum, knee angulation deformities, ankle valgus and pes planus
Vascular dysplasia	Renovascular hypertension in 3%. Gastrointestinal and cerebral vascular systems may also be involved
Learning disabilities (60%)	
Seizures (5%)	
Short stature (6%)	
Macrocephaly (16%)	

NF-2

Genetics

The NF-2 gene is on chromosome 22q; the gene product is merlin (*mo*esin-*e*zrin-*r*adixin-*li*ke prote*in*) which is required for negative growth regulation.

Features

- This is a disorder of the CNS with cranial nerve and meningeal tumours. Cutaneous tumours occur, but the main clinical problem is CNS. Optic gliomas do not occur. Deafness is likely for all patients from bilateral acoustic tumours, which can be treated surgically or with the gamma knife.
- Ocular features include posterior subcapsular cataracts, retinal gliomas, pigmented retinopathy and gaze palsies.
- There are no specific endocrine features, but pregnancy may exacerbate meningiomas.

Chapter 95
Von Hippel–Lindau disease

Background

Characterized by:

- CNS and retinal haemangioblastomas
- renal cysts and carcinomas
- phaeochromocytomas
- occasionally pancreatic neuroendocrine tumours

Genetics

Autosomal dominant condition. The *VHL* gene is on chromosome 3 and is a tumour suppresser. Mutant VHL protein leads to VEGF expression in normoxia as well as hypoxia, thus enhancing the growth of these tumours which are often very vascular. VHL also interacts with the transcriptional factor elongin.

Table 95.1 Less common manifestations of Von Hippel-Lindau disease

Pancreas	Cysts
	Adenoma
Epididymis	Cystadenoma
CNS	Syringomyelia
	Meningioma
Liver	Adenoma
	Haemangioblastoma
	Cysts
Lung	Angioma
	Cysts
Spleen	Angioma

Features

- Estimated prevalence is 1/39 000. Average age of presentation 27 years. Nearly all patients will have manifestations by age 65.

Retinal angiomatosis

- This is the initial manifestation in 40% of patients. They are unusual before aged 10 but continue to develop through life. They tend to be peripheral in the retina appearing as red oval lesions. Bleeding and retinal detachment may occur.
- Treatment is with laser therapy.

Cerebellar and CNS haemangioblastoma

- 75% occur in the cerebellum and they are the initial presentation in 40%.
- Treatment is with surgery or radiotherapy.

Renal cysts and carcinoma

- Renal carcinoma is the commonest cause of death in VHL patients. They occur later than other VHL manifestations (at a mean age of 44). They tend to be multifocal and by aged 60 will occur in 70% of VHL patients. Cysts may be dysplastic.
- Diagnosis is by CT or MRI plus aspiration cytology
- Treatment is by surgery which may need to be repeated.

Phaeochromocytoma (see p. 329)

- These occur in up to 20% of VHL families and are bilateral in 40%. If VHL is diagnosed in a family regular surveillance should take place.
- Diagnosis is by CT or MRI, urine catecholamines, *meta*-iodo benylguanidine (MIBG) isotope scanning, and if necessary adrenal vein sampling which shows reversal of normal adrenaline to noradrenaline ratio.

Pancreatic tumours

- Treatment is with α- and β-blockade followed by adrenalectomy.
- 50% are malignant. Most of them are non-functioning but they may secrete VIP, insulin, glucagon, or calcitonin.

Table 95.2 Testing for Von Hippel-Lindau disease

Test	Age to start	Frequency
Palpation (renal and epidymal lesions)	5	Annual
Urinalysis	5	Annual
24 h urine catecholamines	5	Annual
Fundoscopy + fluorescein angiography	5	Annual
Brain MRI	10	3-yearly
Abdominal CT/MRI for kidney, adrenal, and pancreas	5	3-yearly

Table 95.3 Surveillance in Von Hippel-Lindau disease

	Affected	At risk
Annual	Examination	Examination
	Urinalysis	Urinalysis
	24 h urine catecholamines	24 h urine catecholamines
	Fundoscopy	Fundoscopy (aged 5–60)
Triennial	Brain MRI (to age 50, then 5-yearly)	Brain MRI (aged 5–40, then 5-yearly to age 60)
	Abdominal MRI	Abdominal MRI (aged 25–65)

Diagnosis

This is made by:

- two or more haemangioblastomas
- a haemangioblastoma and a visual manifestation
- one haemangioblastoma or visual manifestation and a family history of haemangioblastoma.

Screening

Genetic testing should be undertaken in affected families. This should ideally be performed at age 5 years. Certain mutations (substitution of an Arg by a Glu or a Try at codon 167) are associated with a high risk of phaeochromocytoma.

Chapter 96
Multiple endocrine neoplasia

MEN 1

Background

MEN-1 describes the association of the occurrences of tumours involving two or more endocrine glands:

- parathyroid hyperplasia
- pancreatic endocrine tumours
- pituitary adenomas.

Genetics

MEN-1 is an autosomal dominant condition with high penetrance. The gene on chromosome 11 q13 has recently been described. There is a germline mutation followed by a somatic deletion in the same region of the other chromosome, which allows tumour formation (Knudson's two-hit hypothesis). The gene product is menin, a pro-tooncogene. In contrast to MEN-2, a large number of different mutations can occur and a substantial proportion are sporadic.

Epidemiology

The prevalence of the condition has been estimated at 1/10 000.

Features

- *Parathyroid hyperplasia and adenoma* The usual presenting feature; occurs in nearly all cases.
- *Pancreatic endocrine tumours* Occur in 70% of patients presenting between age 15 and 50, if not screened. Different secreting types are seen (see Table 96.1). Diffuse pancreatic hyperplasia is usual, as are multiple adenomata. Multiple duodenal micro gastrinomas account for half of those seen in MEN-1.
- *Pituitary adenomas* Clinically apparent in 30%. Unlike the parathyroid and pancreas there is no pituitary hyperplasia. Different types occur (see Table 96.2).
- Other lesions (see Table 96.3).

Management

- *Parathyroid hyperplasia and adenoma* The timing of operation can be difficult if hypercalcaemia is mild. Operation is indicated for most patients and if there are complications. Usually total parathyroidectomy is performed with autotransplantation of one gland into the forearm and immediate replacement with calcitriol.
- *Pancreatic endocrine tumours* The surgical approach is controversial and an experienced surgeon is essential. For kindreds with aggressive disease, the pancreas and duodenum with adjacent lymph nodes should be removed. An alternative is enucleation of the palpable lesions and duodenal resection if indicated. Medical therapy can be used for gastrinomas (*omeprazole*) but medical therapy is less successful with insulinomas so a more aggressive surgical approach is important. For the treatment of metastatic disease see p. 677.
- *Pituitary adenomas* These are managed with surgery, drug treatment or radiotherapy (p. 211).

Table 96.1 Pancreatic tumours seen in MEN-1

Type	Frequency
Gastrinoma[a]	60%
Insulinoma[a]	30%
VIPoma	Rare
Glucagonoma	Rare
Ppoma	Rare
Non-functioning	Frequent

[a]These coexist in 10%.

Table 96.2 Pituitary tumours seen in MEN-1

Tumour	Frequency
Prolactinoma	60%
Acromegaly	30%
Non-functioning tumour	Rare
Cushing's disease	Rare

Table 96.3 Other lesions seen in MEN-1

Lesion	Frequency	Comments
Carcinoid tumours	10%	Foregut in origin
Lipomas	10%	Marker in affected individuals
Adrenal lesions	40%	Nodular hyperplasia; usually no endocrinopathy

Screening

See Tables 96.4, 96.5.

Because so many different mutations have been described, widespread genetic screening of probands and relatives is not currently feasible. First- and second-degree relatives of affected individuals should be screened biochemically. Screening allows the detection of malignant kindreds and lowers the age of detection of the syndrome by 20 years.

Table 96.4 Screening in MEN-1 (symptoms of hypercalcaemia and renal calculi, peptic ulcer, neuroglycopaenia, hyperprolactinaemia, acromegaly, hypopituitarism)

	Affected	At risk (aged 5–65)	Comments
Annual	Serum calcium	Serum calcium	90% identified by age 50
	Prolactin	Prolactin	
	Fasting gastrin	Fasting gastrin	Identifies lesions up to 3 years before radiological appearance
	+ gut hormone profile	+ gut hormone profile	
	+ test meal (for gastrin and PP)	+ test meal (for gastrin & PP)	
3-yearly	MRI pancreas		
5-yearly	MRI pituitary		

Table 96.5 Screening of patient families with isolated lesions

Parathyroid adenoma	MEN present in 15%. Screen if male, aged <50 years, hyperplasia
Pancreatic tumours	Screen all especially gastrinomas and insulinomas

Who should be screened for MEN-1?

- male patients with hyperparathyroidism <50 years old
- patients with two MEN-1 tumours
- first degree relations of patients with MEN-1.

Prognosis

Malignant pancreatic tumours are the major cause of mortality. Those in MEN-1 appear less malignant than sporadic malignant pancreatic tumours and carry a better prognosis, with a median survival of 15 vs 5 years (MEN-1 vs sporadic). This may reflect earlier diagnosis.

Further reading

Brandi ML *et al.* Guidelines for Diagnosis and Therapy of MEN Type 1 and Type 2. *Journal of Clinical Endocrinology and Metabolism* 2001; 86: 5658–5671.

MEN 2

Background

MEN-2 includes two forms plus familial medullary thyroid cancer:

- *MEN-2a* Familial medullary thyroid carcinoma in combination with phaeochromocytoma and parathyroid tumours.
- *MEN-2b* Familial medullary thyroid cancer associated with phaeochromocytoma, ganglioneuromatosis (mucosal), and marfanoid habitus.
- Familial medullary thyroid carcinoma may also occur in isolation.

Genetics

These are autosomal dominant conditions. The *MEN2* gene is on the long arm of chromosome 10 (10q 11.2). Mutations affect the protooncogene *ret*, which is a transmembrane receptor with an extracellular cysteine-rich domain and intracellular tyrosine kinase domain. Different germline mutations cause different familial syndromes (Fig. 96.1).

The c-*ret* protooncogene is also involved in the aetiology of papillary thyroid carcinoma and Hirschsprung's disease.

Table 96.6 Medullary thyroid carcinoma (MTC)

Variety	Incidence (%)	Age at onset
Sporadic	75	5th decade
Hereditary		
MEN-2a	17	3rd decade
Familial MTC	5	4th decade
MEN–2b	3	1st decade

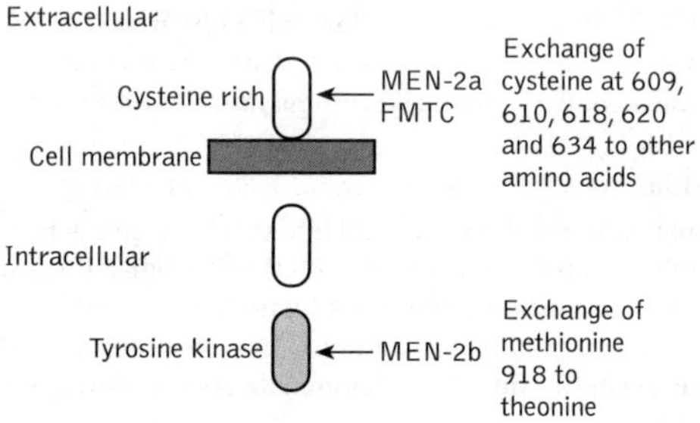

Fig. 96.1 Mutations in the ret protein in MEN-2a, 2b, and familary medullary thyroid cancer. Reproduced with kind permission of Blackwell Publishers.

Features

MEN-2a

- 30% of gene carriers never manifest clinically significant disease.
- *Medullary thyroid cancer (MTC)* Often the initial presentation. Phaeochromocytoma and parathyroid disease develop later. There may be a nodule diagnosable by FNAC, but the diagnosis may be made only on histology which shows the tumours often multifocal with C cell hyperplasia and stromal amyloid. Circulating calcitonin is elevated. With metastatic disease, diarrhoea is common (30%). Hypocalcaemia is not seen. Occasional tumours secrete ACTH, and MTC is a rare cause of ectopic ACTH secretion (Cushing's).
- *Phaeochromocytoma* Present later in 20–50% of affected individuals who may develop unilateral or bilateral (50%) tumours. They are multicentric, but malignancy is rare (0–8%). They must be ruled out before any surgery (e.g. on the thyroid).
- *Hyperparathyroidism* Occurs in 10–25% of affected individuals. Usually chief cell hyperplasia is found and hypercalcaemia is mild.
- *Cutaneous lichen amyloidosis* Seen in some affected patients. There is a pruritic and lichenoid lesion over the upper back, biopsy of which shows amyloid. It may present before MTC develops.

MEN-2b

- Many patients do not have a family history and the syndrome is due to a new mutation.
- There are mucosal neuromas on the distal tongue and conjunctiva, thickened lips, a marfanoid habitus (with slipped femoral epiphysis and pectus excavatum), and mucosal neuromas throughout the GI tract. MTC presents earlier and mucosal neuromas are pathognomonic.

Pentagastrin test

- 0.5 μg/kg i/v over 10 s
- calcitonin measured at 2 and 5 min
- *Side-effects* Nausea, flushing substernal tightness which resolves in 2–3 min
- a rise in calcitonin indicates MTC or C cell hyperplasia.
- elevated basal levels of calcitonin which do not rise on pentagastrin seen in children, pregnancy, with some tumours (e.g. carcinoids), pernicious anaemia, thyroiditis, and chronic renal failure.

Table 97.2 Screening in MEN–2; genetic testing from age 3

Affected	At risk (or no documented mutation)	Comments
Annual calcitonin ± pentagastrin test	Annual calcitonin + pentagastin test	MTC present in 90% by age 30
Urine catecholamines	Urine catecholamines (from age 6)	
Serum calcium	Serum calcium	
MRI adrenals (every 3 years)		

Management

Medullary thyroid cancer

The definitive treatment is adequate surgery by total thyroidectomy and careful lymph node dissection. Postoperative thyroxine is administered to all (0.125–0.15 mg/day). Tumour spread is usually local but may also be distant. Regularly postoperative calcitonin measurement is necessary to detect recurrence every 6–12 months. MRI, octreotide scanning, and venous catheterization help to localize recurrence, treatment of which is surgical because MTC responds poorly to radiotherapy and chemotherapy. Octreotide may help to control diarrhoea but it does not have an antitumour effect.

Phaeochromocytoma

Treatment should precede that of MTC. 1/3 of patients develop a second adrenal tumour after removal of the first (see p. 329).

Hyperparathyroidism

(see p. 672).

Screening

Most mutations (>80%) are detectable. In a family with a known mutation, those who are positive require regular biochemical screening. Genetic analysis should be made as soon as possible after age 3. In a family with no detectable mutation, all first- and second-degree relations should be screened biochemically.

Prognosis

The prognosis is variable and in some residual disease may be dormant over years. Overall the 10 year survival rate is 65%. Early surgery beneficially affects prognosis, which may be why patients with MEN-2a have a better prognosis. The prognosis for patients with MEN-2b is significantly worse than for MEN-2a (65 v. 80% 10 year survival).

Further reading

Brandi ML *et al.* Consensus guidelines for diagnosis and therapy of MEN type 1 and type 2. *Journal of Clinical Endocrinology and Metabolism* 2001; 86: 5658–5671.

Indications for thyroidectomy in genetically affected children

- positive pentagastrin test
- age >5–6 years.

Who should be screened for MEN-2?

- patient with MTC or one MEN-2 associated tumour if aged <30 years or two MEN-2 associated tumours if aged >30 years.
- muscosal neuromas or somatic features of MEN-2b
- individual with a first-degree relative with MEN-2

Chapter 97
Carney complex

Genetics

- Autosomal dominant
- Inactivating mutation of PRKARIA on 17q in approximately 40% families.

Clinical features

- Spotty skin pigmentation
- Myxomas
  - heart
  - skin
  - mucosal
- Endocrine tumours (commonest is PPNAD causing Cushing's)
- Psammomatous melanotic schwannoma (PMS)

Diagnostic criteria

- 2 of the clinical features or 1 feature and an affected first degree relative or inactivating mutation of PRKARIA gene

Further reading

Stratakis CA *et al.* Clinical and molecular features of the Carney complex. *Journal of Clinical Endocrinology and Metabolism* 2001; 86: 4041–4046.

Endocrine tumours

- Primary pigmented nodular adrenocortical disease (PPNAD)
- Large cell calcifying Sertoli cell tumour (LCCSCT)
- GH/PRL producing pituitary adenoma
- Thyroid adenoma
- Ovarian cysts

Part X
Miscellaneous endocrinology

Chapter 98
Hypoglycaemia

Definition

Plasma glucose of <2.5 mmol/L associated with symptoms of neuroglycopaenia.

Epidemiology

Uncommon cause of symptoms in adults apart from patients with diabetes treated with insulin or sulfonylureas.

Pathophysiology

Physiology of glucose control

Blood glucose concentrations in non-diabetic individuals are regulated mainly by relying on the ability of the liver to absorb glucose at times of glucose excess and to release it at other times, regulated by insulin, GH, cortisol, glucagon, and adrenalin.

- *Postprandial state* Hepatic glucose production is inhibited by both raised glucose and insulin concentrations.
- *Fasting state* Glucose falls with consequent fall in insulin secretion, stimulating hepatic efflux of glucose in the presence of cortisol, GH, and glucagon.
- The brain is completely dependent on circulating glucose for its energy demands, which are high and consist of up to 50% hepatic glucose output.

Mechanisms of hypoglycaemia

- Excessive/inappropriate action of insulin or IGF_1 – results in inhibition of hepatic glucose production despite adequate glycogen stores, while peripheral glucose uptake is enhanced.
- Impaired neuroendocrine response with inadequate counter-regulatory response (e.g. cortisol or GH) to insulin.
- Impairment of hepatic glucose production due to either structural damage or abnormal liver enzymes.

Causes of hypoglycaemia

Spontaneous hypoglycaemia

Divided into two categories:

- *Fasting hypoglycaemia* Occurring several (>5 h) hours after food, e.g. on waking or at night, or precipitated by prolonged fasting or exercise. It always indicates underlying disease.
- *Reactive/postprandial hyperglycaemia* 2–5 h after food.

Other causes

- *Insulinoma*
  - benign 85%, malignant 15%
  - occasionally part of MEN-1 (~10%)
- *Other tumours*
  - excessive IGF-2 secretion from large mesenchymal, e.g. fibrosarcoma, mesothelioma
  - hepatocellular carcinoma
  - adrenal carcinoma
- *Hormone deficiency*
  - Addison's disease
  - GH deficiency
  - isolated ACTH deficiency
  - hypopituitarism
- *β-cell hyperplasia* Very rare in adults
- *Autoimmune*
  - Antibodies to insulin (antibody-bound insulin dissociates leading to elevated free insulin). Commonest in Japanese patients. (Plasmapheresis and immunosuppression may be required if symptomatic despite frequent meals)
  - Insulin receptor activating antibodies (rare, commonest in middle aged women. May require treatment with plasmapheresis or immunosuppression)
- *Drug induced*
  - insulin
  - sulfonylureas
  - alcohol (impairs gluconeogenesis often associated with poor glycogen stores)
  - quinine causes hyperinsulinaemia
  - salicylates (?due to reduced hepatic glucose efflux)

(*cont.*)

Causes of hypoglycaemia *(continued)*

- *Organ failure*
  - acute liver failure
  - chronic renal failure
- *Infection*
  - septicaemia, e.g. gram negative or meningococcal; related to high metabolic requirements, reduced energy intake and possibly cytokines from the inflammatory process
  - malaria
- *Starvation*
  - anorexia nervosa
  - kwashiorkor
- *Inborn errors of metabolism*
  - glycogen storage disease
  - hereditary fructose intolerance
  - maple syrup disease
- *Postprandial*
  - Idiopathic – anxiety associated with autonomic but not neuroglycopaenic symptoms
  - Incipient diabetes mellitus – occasionally presents with postprandial hypoglycaemia, possibly related to disordered insulin secretion
  - Alcohol induced
  - Post-gastrectomy (late dumping) – due to rapid gastric emptying, with brisk glucose absorption resulting in greater than normal insulin release 1.5–3 h after food

Clinical features

- Hypoglycaemia should be considered as the cause of symptoms in any patient with a 'funny turn' or unexplained collapse or loss of consciousness.
- The aim of the history should be to differentiate fasting hypoglycaemia from postprandial or reactive hypoglycaemia.
- Responses to hypoglycaemia are sequential, with a deterioration in neuropsychological performance occurring at plasma glucose 3–3.5 mmol/L, subjective perception of hypoglycaemia at 2.7–2.9 mmol/L, and EEG changes at 2 mmol/L. Patients with recurrent hypoglycaemia may get symptoms at a lower glucose concentration, while patients with poorly controlled diabetes mellitus get symptoms at higher levels.
- *Adrenergic symptoms* Pallor, sweating, tremor, tachycardia.
- *Neuroglycopaenic symptoms* Poor concentration, double vision, irritability, perioral tingling, poor judgement, confusion and violent behaviour, changes in personality, focal neurological consequences, seizures and coma.
- The majority of symptoms of acute hypoglycaemia are adrenergic, but neuroglycopaenic symptoms occur with subacute and chronic hypoglycaemia

Investigation

- Glucose strip – unreliable for low glucose concentrations, but if level <4 mmol/L a laboratory glucose should be measured.
- Liver function tests
- Ethanol concentration
- Cortisol (± synacthen test)
- Fasting insulin, C-peptide, proinsulin, and glucose during hypoglycaemia (Table 98.1)

Inappropriately elevated insulin in presence of hypoglycaemia suggests insulinoma or self-administration of insulin or sulfonylurea

Presence of C-peptide indicates endogenous insulin release – either insulinoma or sulfonylurea. Insulinomas often associated with elevated pro-insulin : insulin ratio.

- Fasting 3-hydroxybutyrate (elevated in most causes of hypoglycaemia, but suppressed if insulin present e.g. insulinoma, self-administration of insulin or sulfonylureas).
- Consider IGF-I and II (IGF-II may be normal in non-islet cell hypoglycaemia (NICH), but this is in association with suppressed IGF-I and GH, usual IGF-II : IGF-I ratio 3 : 1, ratio >10 seen in NICH) (see p. 745).
- Chest radiograph– ? fibrosarcoma, mesothelioma.
- Consider insulin and insulin receptor antibodies.
- Consider assay for presence of sulfonylureas.

Further investigation of fasting hypoglycaemia

- *Glucose and insulin* After 15 h fast – glucose <2.5 mmol/L and insulin >5 mU/L is inappropriate.
- *Insulin suppression test*
  - *Rationale* Insulin administration to induce hypoglycaemia should suppress endogenous insulin secretion. C-peptide is secreted in equimolar concentrations to insulin, and therefore serves as a measure of endogenous insulin secretion.
  - *Method* Intravenous insulin administered 0.05–0.1 U/kg per hour over 2 h and measurements of plasma C-peptide and glucose made. Glucose <2.5 mmol/L in association with a C-peptide >150 pmol/L is inappropriate and suggests the presence of an insulinoma. The test should be terminated at this point. Results are more accurately interpreted using age-matched normative data as the decrease in C-peptide reduces with increasing age.
  - *Caution* Close continual observation is essential as hypoglycaemia may induce seizures or loss of consciousness, and require appropriate emergency treatment. Cortisol deficiency and hepatic dysfunction should be excluded before performing the test.
- *72 hour fast* Probably the most reliable test for hypoglycaemia, but rarely required (detected 98% patients with insulinoma, compared with 71% at 24 h). The patient should remain active. Plasma glucose, insulin, C-peptide and pro-insulin are measured 6 hourly and the test is terminated if the glucose < 2.5 mmol/L or after 72 h. 3-hydroxybutyrate should be measured at the end of the fast and its presence makes insulinoma unlikely.
- *Localization of tumour* (see p. 676) MRI or spiral CT are usually first line investigations

Table 98.1 Biochemical features of insulinoma and factitious hypoglycaemia

Plasma marker	Insulinoma	Sulfonylurea	Insulin injection
Glucose	↓	↓	↓
Insulin	↑	↑	↑
C-peptide	↑	↑	↓

Management

Acute hypoglycaemia

- *If unconscious* 25–50 mL 50% glucose intravenously into a large vein, followed by a saline flush as the high concentration of glucose is an irritant and may even lead to venous thrombosis.
- 1 mg glucagon i/m may be administered if there is no intravenous access. This increases hepatic glucose efflux, but the effect only lasts for 30 min, allowing other means of blood glucose elevation (e.g. oral), before the blood glucose falls again. It is:
  - ineffective with hepatic dysfunction and if there is glycogen depletion, e.g. ethanol-related hypoglycaemia
  - contraindicated in patients with insulinomas as it may induce further insulin secretion.
- Oral glucose (ideally food) should be administered as soon as the patient is alert and conscious.
- *Secondary cerebral oedema* May complicate hypoglycaemia, should be considered in cases of prolonged coma despite normalization of plasma glucose. Mannitol and or dexamethasone may be helpful.

Recurrent hypoglycaemia

If definitive treatment of the underlying condition is unsuccessful or impossible, symptoms may be alleviated by frequent (e.g. 4 hourly) small meals, including overnight. In some circumstances (e.g. incipient diabetes mellitus) an α-glucosidase inhibitor (e.g. acarbose) will delay disaccharide absorption and reduce symptoms.

Insulinoma

- Surgical excision should be performed in fit patients. Perioperative localization is often possible with palpation and intra-operative ultrasound.
- Failed surgery or unfit patients may be sucessfully treated using somatostatin analogues such as *octreotide* 100–200 μg 3× daily, although larger and more frequent doses may be necessary. *Diazoxide* (150–800 mg/day) may also be helpful. It inhibits insulin release by
  - stimulation of postassium channels and so preventing depolarization
  - stimulation of a receptors on pancreatic ß cells
  - inhibition of cAMP phosphodiesterase, enhancing glyogenolysis.

Insulinoma (see p. 674)

- *Incidence* 1–2/ million per year.
- *Epidemiology* F>M, 10% have MEN-1, 80% of MEN-1 have multiple tumours.
- *Pathology* 90% tumours <2 cm. Malignant tumours are larger.
- *Biochemistry* Inappropriately elevated insulin and C-peptide in presence of hypoglycaemia. Proinsulin levels are often disproportionately high because of increased release from tumour.

Non-islet cell hypoglycaemia

Excess IGF-II secretion from tumours such as fibrosarcomas and mesotheliomas is associated with hypoglycaemia associated with suppressed insulin, C-peptide, and IGF-I. The mechanism is related to an increase in tissue bioavailability. IGF-II is usually IGFBP bound, which maintains it within the circulation. Autonomous IGFBP-II secretion by tumours leads to suppression of GH secretion and therefore reduced IGF-I and IGFBPs. IGF-II may therefore remain 'free' in the circulation, with increased tissue bioavailability, leading both to suppression of IGF-I and GH and also to hypoglycaemia due to binding and stimulation of insulin receptors.

Definitive treatment is removal of the tumour. Therapy with GH replacement may allow increase in binding proteins and IGF-I and reversal of hypoglycaemia.

Malignant insulinomas

- Surgical debulking or embolization may provide some symptomatic relief.
- Somatostatin analogues and diazoxide can be helpful.
- Chemotherapy using streptozotocin with 5-flurouracil can lead to tumour shrinkage.

Further reading

Marks V, Teale JD. Investigation of hypoglycaemia. *Clinical Endocrinology* 1996; 44: 133–136.

Service FJ. Hypoglycaemia. *Endocrinology and Metabolism Clinics of North America* 1997; 26 (4): 937–952.

Chapter 99
Obesity

Definitions in terms of body mass index

- *healthy weight* BMI 18.5–24.9
- *overweight* BMI 25–29.9
- *obesity* BMI >30
- *extreme obesity* BMI >40.

Epidemiology

- Increasing prevalence of obesity (overweight) in the UK – 16% (45%) men and 18% (34%) women obese (overweight).
- Obesity is an important risk factor for life-threatening diseases such as ischaemic heart disease (quadrupled risk if BMI >29), hypertension, cerebrovascular disease, type 2 diabetes and cancers such as breast, ovary, endometrium, prostate, and bowel (see Fig. 99.1).
- Obesity is also a risk factor for various physical conditions such as osteoarthritis, varicose veins, obstructive sleep apnoea, operative complications.

Body mass index (BMI)

- *Body mass index* (BMI) = weight (kg)/[height/m]^2.
- *Waist/hip circumference* Waist is measured after overnight fast, halfway between the lower costal margin and the iliac crest. Hip circumference is measured over the widest part of the gluteal region. Reflects distribution of fat: >0.9 in women, >1.0 in men indicates central obesity (increased risk of type 2 diabetes mellitus, hypertension and ischaemic heart disease).
- *Waist circumference alone* (M >102 cm, F >88 cm) is associated with increased cardiovascular risk.

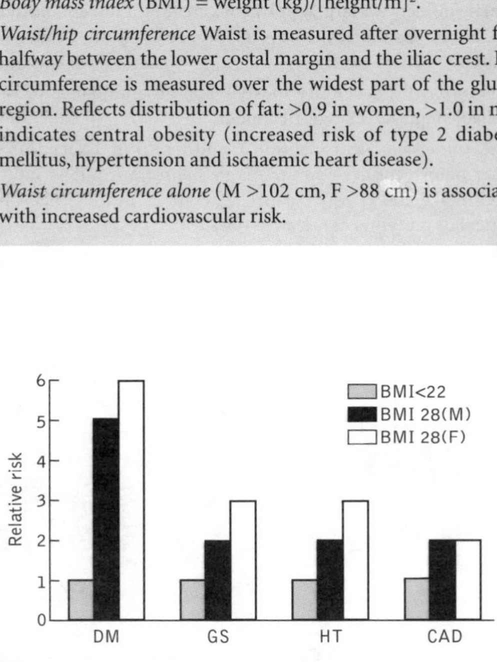

Fig. 99.1 Relationship between BMI and relative risk of complications. RR (relative risk) of type 2 diabetes mellitus (DM), gallstones (GS), hypertension (HT) and coronary artery disease (CAD) in males (M) and females (F) with elevated BMI.

Aetiopathogenesis of 'simple' obesity

- *Genetic factors* Estimates of heritability range from 20 to 40%. The genetic influence is largely polygenic, creating a susceptible individual. Single gene defects are very rare (e.g. leptin, Prader–Willi, Laurence–Moon–Biedl).
- *Environment* A sedentary lifestyle and an abundance of readily available high-fat, energy-rich foods.
- *Neuroendocrine* Neuropeptide Y and leptin in association with other neuropeptides and aminergic neurotransmitters modulate food intake and energy balance. Alterations in these neurotransmitters or receptors may lead to obesity.

Leptin

Encoded by *Lep* gene (chromosome 7q31.3); synthesized in and secreted from adipose tissue. Central effects in the hypothalamus result in decreased food intake and increased energy expenditure. Leptin has been shown to exert potent antiobesity effects in animals such as the *ob/ob* (leptin deficient) mouse, but its role in humans remains unclear. Most obese humans do not have abnormalities of the leptin gene. Plasma leptin is increased in obese humans, and obese humans appear to be leptin resistant. Reduced leptin transport to the brain has been suggested as a potential mechanism of leptin resistance in humans. It has been suggested that the primary role of leptin in the human may be to indicate sufficient fat stores for growth and reproduction. Rodents with abnormalities of leptin receptors (*db/db* mice or *fa/fa* rats) are also obese. There are no data suggesting that leptin receptor abnormalities are likely to play a major role in human obesity in the population.

Neuropeptide Y

NPY is synthesized in the arcuate nucleus of the hypothalamus, and transported axonally to the hypothalamic paraventricular nucleus. It is a potent appetite stimulant and reduces sympathetic output, so reducing energy expenditure. NPY concentrations are increased by insulin and glucocorticoids, and reduced by leptin and oestrogen. Genetic studies have not shown any association between the genes for NPY or its receptor in human obesity.

Evaluation of an obese patient

- Assess history of weight gain, previous treatment and weight loss, and family history.
- Document eating habits, and physical activity.
- Consider secondary causes:
  - hypothyroidism (measure TSH)
  - Cushing's syndrome (measure 24 h urinary free cortisol and consider dexamethasone suppression testing)
  - hypothalamic disorder (uncontrolled appetite – MRI)
- Consider rare genetic causes:
  - Prader–Willi (morbid obesity, with mental retardation, chromosome 15)
  - Lawrence–Moon–Biedl (obesity associated with polydactyly, mental retardation, retinitis pigmentosa)
- Assess coexistent risk factors for vascular disease (smoking, diabetes, family history)
- Consider co-existent conditions, e.g. polycystic ovary syndrome
- Assess presence of co-morbid conditions:
  - Osteoarthritis, obstructive sleep apnoea, psychological (low self esteem, depression).

Investigations

- fasting glucose
- lipid profile
- measurement of distribution of fat (waist circumference)
- ECG
- TSH

Metabolic syndrome (syndrome X)

This describes a clustering of metabolic risk factors – hyperinsulinaemia, impaired glucose tolerance or frank diabetes, increased VLDL, reduced HDL, hypertension, and central or visceral obesity. The syndrome is associated with marked increased risk of vascular disease. Data suggest that over 95% of centrally obese patients have at some risk factors, less than 50% of subcutaneously obese patients do.

Management

Aims

- to reduce consequences of obesity
- to reduce weight with realistic targets (0.5–1 kg/week), and maintain weight loss
- to reduce mortality
- to prevent childhood onset in other family members.

Diet

- Reduction of calorie intake to 600 kcal below estimated initial maintenance energy is a logical initial goal in any weight loss programme. A reduction in fat intake in particular can lead to a marked decrease in calorie intake – a diet containing <30% calories from fat is ideal.
- Very low calorie intake diets may sometimes be used in specialist centres.
- Diet alone does not usually maintain weight loss, and the majority of dieters regain weight within 3 years.

Exercise

- An exercise programme and behavioural modification improves the chances of maintaining weight loss. The aim should be for at least 20 min exercise 3–5 times/week.
- Regular exercise will also lead to a beneficial effect on other risk factors, with a reduction in blood pressure and improvement in lipid profile.
- Behavioural modification with support from groups or family is important.

Drug treatment

- Indicated for patients with obesity or overweight patients with significant comorbidity.
- The primary goal is to achieve 10% weight loss, and management should commence with 3 months of diet and lifestyle changes.
- Weight loss of <10% presenting weight and BMI >30 kg/m^2 are an indication for considering drug treatment.

Drugs acting on the gastrointestinal system

Pancreatic lipase inhibitors (orlistat)

Reduction in fat absorption, results in 25–35% dietary fat loss in faeces (<5% in placebo). It leads to an average weight loss of 10% in a year when used as part of a weight control programme and has been shown to be effective in patients with diabetes. It is administered 120 mg within an hour of every main meal (up to3× day). It is licensed for use for 2 years, and contraindicated in patients with malabsorption or cholestasis and in women who are breast-feeding. Side-effects include oily rectal discharge, fatty stool and faecal urgency, and the potential for deficiency of fat-soluble vitamins.

Centrally acting anti-obesity drugs

- Drugs acting on serotinergic pathways, e.g. *fenfluramine* and *dexfenfluramine*, have been withdrawn because of associations with valvular heart disease and pulmonary complications.
- *Phentermine* (15–30 mg daily) acts by suppressing appetite, due to sympathomimetic and stimulant activities. It should be used for 12 weeks only and has been associated rarely with pulmonary hypertension.
- *Sibutramine* (5–20 mg daily) acts centrally as a serotonin and noradrenaline reuptake inhibitor which leads to reduced food intake and increased satiety. Sibutramine once daily is effective as part of a weight reduction programme. Side-effects include nausea, insomnia, dry mouth, and in some individuals increased blood pressure and heart rate. It should therefore be used cautiously in those with hypertension or vascular disease.

Evaluation and continuation of treatment

Responders to drug therapy show evidence of 5% weight loss within 3 months of starting treatment. Lack of response at this time should lead to discontinuation of therapy.

Surgery

Gastroplasty or gastric bypass is an effective treatment, but usually reserved for failure of other modalities of treatment in those with morbid obesity and cardiovascular risk factors. It has been shown to be effective in reducing hypertension and development of type 2 diabetes mellitus.

Benefits of weight loss

Diabetes mellitus

- Weight loss of >5 kg halves the risk of developing type 2 diabetes.
- Weight loss of 5–10% in those with type 2 diabetes improves glycaemic control, sometimes allowing reduction or withdrawal of medication.
- Weight loss leads to a reduction in diabetes-related mortality.

Hypertension

- Every 1 kg fall in weight leads to a fall in BP of 1–2 mmHg.

Hyperlipidaemia

- Every 1 kg weight loss leads to a fall in LDL cholesterol of 0.02 mmol/L and TG of 0.015, while HDL rises by 0.009 mmol/L.

Obesity-related cancers

- Weight loss of 0.5–9 kg is associated with a 53% reduction in deaths.

Chapter 100
Endocrinology and ageing

Introduction

Endocrine dysfunction in the elderly can produce symptoms which are often attributed to the ageing process itself.

- increased levels of noradrenaline, ADH
- decreased levels of renin, aldosterone, GH, IGF-I, oestradiol (in women), testosterone (in men)
- electrolyte disturbances common
- impaired carbohydrate metabolism.

Thyroid disease

Thyroid disease is twice as common in the elderly as in younger patients (see Table 100.1).

- Concomitant disease and polypharmacy are common in the elderly and may alter the interpretation of results, e.g. corticosteroids and dopaminergic drugs may reduce the reported TSH values in hypothyroid patients.
- Concurrent non-thyroidal illness reduces free tri-iodothyronine (FT_3) and (less commonly) reduces free thyroxine (FT_4).

Hyperthyroidism

- 2% of elderly.
- Presentation is often atypical, often with few signs or symptoms.
- Commonly, symptoms are mainly in a single, vulnerable organ system, e.g. depression, lethargy, anxiety, confusion and agitation; muscle wasting and weakness; heart failure, arrhythmias, atrial fibrillation.
- A low TSH concentration is associated with an increased cardiovascular mortality and a threefold higher risk of atrial fibrillation in the next 10 years. 2–24% of elderly patients with atrial fibrillation are hyperthyroid and 9–35% of elderly patients with hyperthyroidism have atrial fibrillation.
- Treatment options are similar to those in younger patients
- Radioactive iodine is favoured because it is definitive and it avoids risks of surgery. Hypothyroidism is common after radioiodine therapy in elderly people.

Hypothyroidism

- 2–7% of elderly people.
- Male : female ratio increases with ageing.
- Commonest causes are previous surgery or radioiodine therapy and autoimmune thyroiditis.
- Only 25% present with classical symptoms of hypothyroidism.
- An insidious decline in health and mobility is more common than cold intolerance, hair loss or skin coarsening.
- The elderly are more susceptible to hypothyroid coma than younger people; it is rare.

- Hypothyroidism should be considered in elderly patients with increased CK or transaminases, decreased Na, macrocytic anaemia, or dyslipidaemia.
- Thyroid replacement therapy should be done cautiously as ischaemic heart disease may be unmasked or exacerbated, e.g. 12.5–25 μg/day of T_4 increased by 12–25 μg increments every 3–8 weeks until TSH is normalized.
- Total replacement T_4 dose is lower in the elderly than in younger patients (in younger patients approximately 1.6 μg/kg is required but older patients require 20–30% less).
- Compliance may be problematic. Supervised therapy or administration using a Dossett box may help. Alternatively, calculate the total weekly dose of thyroxine and give 70% of the total dose once a week or 50% of the total dose twice weekly.

Multinodular goitre

- Incidence increases with age (90% of women >70 years, 60% of men >80 years).
- Management similar to that of multinodular goitre in younger patients (see p. 57).

Thyroid cancer

- Total incidence rate for all thyroid cancers is unchanged but the relative frequencies are altered.
- Papillary carcinoma is more common in young and middle aged patients, but the prognosis is poorer in the elderly.
- Follicular carcinoma is more common with ageing.
- Anaplastic thyroid carcinoma occurs almost exclusively in patients >65 years. It presents with a rapidly growing hard mass which is often locally invasive and may be associated with metastatic lesions. The prognosis is poor.
- Sarcomas and primary thyroid lymphomas are more common in elderly patients.
- Overall evaluation and treatment is similar to that of younger patients but accurate preoperative histology is very important as tumours not treated surgically (e.g. anaplastic carcinoma and lymphoma) are relatively more common.

Table 100.1 Changes in thyroid-related investigations with ageing

TSH	No significant change; secretion remains pulsatile but loss of physiological nocturnal TSH rise is blunted
T_4	Unchanged overall (both secretion and clearance ↓)
T_3	10–50% decrease occurs at an earlier age in women than in men
rT_3	↑
Thyroid antibodies	Prevalence ↑ with age; significance uncertain(2% at age 25, 15–32% at age 75)
24 h radioactive iodine uptake	Unchanged

Adrenal function

The symptoms of deficiency or excess are often non-specific, and mimic common complaints of the elderly (such as falls or confusion) with normal adrenal function.

Table 100.2 Changes in adrenal-related investigations with ageing

Dynamic tests of adrenal function	Normal
Stress(physical, trauma, surgery)	Cortisol release prolonged and exaggerated
Dynamic tests of cortisol secretion in Alzheimer's disease (e.g. CRH test, dexamethasone suppression test)	Abnormal
CRH test in diabetes mellitus and hypertension	ACTH response prolonged and exaggerated

Growth hormone

- IGF-I falls with increasing age.
- GH pulse amplitude and duration decreased but pulse frequency unchanged.
- IGF-BP3 falls with age.
- Older patients with GH deficiency related to pituitary disease are easily differentiated from other subjects with an age-related decline in IGF-I.
- Treatment with GH leads to increased lean body mass and bone mineral density, and decreased adipose tissue, in elderly subjects.
- The role of GH in healthy older people or elderly people with acute catabolic states (e.g. burns, surgery) has yet to be defined.
- Currently GH treatment is indicated only in patients with pituitary disease and documented biochemical and clinical GH deficiency.

Gonadal function

- Free testosterone levels decrease slowly with age, but significant inter-individual variation. SHBG increases with age.
- Fat body mass increases more than lean body mass with age, and there is increased aromatization of androgens to oestrogens; the effects of this are unclear.
- Testicular weight, Leydig cell function, and FSH/LH response to GnRH stimulation all decrease with age.

Erectile dysfunction

- 50% of men over 60 have erectile dysfunction; 90% of these men have concurrent medical problems or are on medication potentially causing impotence.
- Aetiology often multifactorial (e.g. arteriopathy, neuropathy, diabetes, drugs).
- Evaluation similar to that of younger patients (p. 454).
- 30% of men over 75 develop erectile dysfunction after prostatectomy (cf. 7% of younger men after prostatectomy).

Testosterone therapy

- Few studies in elderly people.
- Profoundly low testosterone should prompt a search for causes of hypogonadism (p. 426) (but note that serious chronic disease in elderly people, especially with malnutrition and debilitation, may be associated with hypogonadism).
- Data point towards a positive effect on muscle mass and strength. No clear benefit to fertility, impotence or osteopenia.
- Risk of increased haematocrit, liver dysfunction (particularly if testosterone taken orally), increased prostatic size, and dyslipidaemia.

Fertility

- Spermatogenesis persists into old age.
- Ejaculate volume and sperm motility increase; morphologically abnormal sperm decrease, sperm count remains the same.
- In women, FSH/LH levels rise postmenopausally (see section on menopause, p. 399).
- Low FSH/LH may indicate hypopituitarism, although in elderlypeople this may be depressed by non-specific illness.

Fluid and electrolyte homeostasis

Renal function and homeostatic mechanisms of fluid balance decline with age. With ageing, there are also alterations in the function of several hormones:

- *ADH* Exaggerated response to hyperosmolar stimuli, blunted response to overnight dehydration
- *ANP* ↑
- *renin and aldosterone* ↓ basal and stimulated levels
- *creatinine clearance* ↓ by 8 mL min^{-1} $1.73m^{-2}$ per decade after age 30

Renal concentrating capacity and thirst perception are impaired in the presence of fluid deprivation and may be combined with an inability to ingest fluids because of the presence of a physical disability.

- In younger people, thirst is perceived at plasma osmolalities >292 mOsm/kg
- In older people, thirst is perceived at plasma osmolalities >296 mOsm/kg.

Combined with disease or drug therapy, elderly patients are at high risk of disturbances of fluid balance, often manifesting as hypo- or hypernatraemia.

Hyponatraemia

- 2–20% prevalence in elderly people
- often associated with medication (e.g. diuretics)
- commonest electrolyte disturbance in cancer
- symptoms include confusion, lethargy, coma, fits
- hyponatraemia often reflects an underlying condition and hence is a poor prognostic marker
- approach is similar to that of hyponatraemia in younger patients (p. 237).

Calcium metabolism

- Prevalence of primary hyperparathyroidism is 10/100 000 in women <40 years old, rising to 190/100 000 in women >65 years old.
- Half of all cases of primary hyperparathyroidism occur in women >60 years old.

- Elderly people are more prone to symptoms (weakness, fatigue, confusion) at relatively mild levels of hypercalcaemia (2.8–3.0 mmol/L).
- Other causes must be excluded.
- Management is similar to that described in p. 550.
- Surgery is not contraindicated by age alone.

Further reading

Grimley Evans J, Williams TF, Michel J-P, Beattie L (ed.) (2000) *Oxford Textbook of Geriatric Medicine.* Oxford University Press, Oxford.

Vermeulen A (ed.) (1997) *Ballière's Clinical Endocrinology and Metabolism: Endocrinology of Ageing* 11,2

Chapter 101
Endocrinology of critical illness

Endocrine dysfunction and AIDS

Thyroid

- *Infections* Rare; usually postmortem diagnoses. Thyroid function is usually euthyroid or sick euthyroid.
  - *Pneumocyctis carinii* pneumonia Thyroiditis associated with eu-, hypo-, hyperthyroidism.
  - *Mycobacterium aviium intracellulare* (MAI) Demonstrated at post-mortem only.
  - *Cryptococcus neoformans* Demonstrated at post-mortem only.
- *Neoplasm* Rare. Usually eu- or sick euthyroid.
  - *Kaposi's sarcoma (KS)* Hypothyroidism rarely reported due to infiltration.

Adrenal

- *Infection* Histologically common. Adrenal function usually maintained since 10% of residual adrenal tissue is adequate for normal function.
  - Cytomegalovirus (CMV), *Mycobacterium tuberculosis* (TB), *Cryptococcus*, toxoplasma, MAI, KS CMV adrenalitis is found on postmortem examination in 40–90% of patients dying of AIDS.
- *Neoplasm* Post-mortem finding of KS.
- *Drug induced*
  - *rifampicin* induces increased hepatic steroid metabolism. In subjects with already compromised adrenal reserve may precipitate an Addisonian crisis
  - *ketoconazole* inhibits cortisol synthesis
  - *megestrol acetate* possesses glucocorticoid activity, so abruptly stopping megestrol after long-term treatment may precipitate an adrenal crisis.

Gonads

- *Decreased libido and impotence* Common in men with AIDS. Half of such men have subnormal testosterone and about 40% have inappropriately normal or low gonadotrophins.
- *Infection* MAI, toxoplasma, CMV, TB reported for testes.
- *Neoplasm* Lymphoma and KS reported for testes.
- *Drug induced*

– *ketoconazole* inhibits steroidogenesis causing lowered testosterone levels
– *megestrol acetate* acts as a progestagen. May be used in combination with testosterone.

Pituitary

- *Anterior hypopituitarism* Very rare
- *Posterior pituitary dysfunction* causing diabetes indipidus (DI) Common
- *Infection* Toxoplasmosis, TB
- *Neoplasm* Cerebral lymphoma.

Wasting syndrome

Definition

The involuntary loss of more than 10% of baseline body weight in combination with diarrhoea, weakness, or fever.

Treatment

- *Nutritionally based strategies* Universally employed. Have limited effect on body weight if not combined with other strategies.
- *Appetite stimulants* Megestrol acetate is the most studied. It significantly increases caloric intake and weight compared to placebo.
- *Androgen therapy* Testosterone deficiency may contribute to the wasting syndrome in men and women with AIDS. *Testosterone* increases lean body mass in patients with wasting and hypogonadism. Patients gain on average 3.5 kg in lean body mass after 12 months of intramuscular testosterone (250 mg/3× weekly).
- *Growth hormone therapy* Patients with the wasting syndrome are probably resistant to the actions of GH, as suggested by high serum GH and low insulin-like growth factor (IGF)-I levels. The most likely cause for this is undernutrition. Studies of high dose GH (0.1 mg/kg per day s/c) have shown consistent improvements in lean body mass averaging 1.6–3 kg over 3 months.
- *Cytokine modulators* Thalidomide is a potent inhibitor of TNF. It increases body weight and reduces protein catabolism in patients with the wasting syndrome with median weight gains of 4 kg after 12 weeks of treatment at a dose of 100 mg 4× daily.

HIV-I protease-inhibitor associated lipodystrophy, hyperlipidaemia, and diabetes mellitus: 'lipodystrophy syndrome'

- Protease inhibitor therapy of HIV-1 infection may result in a syndrome of peripheral fat wasting, central obesity, hyperlipidaemia, and insulin resistance. There may be 'buffalo-hump' fat deposition.

Cancer

Chemotherapy and radiotherapy may have endocrine effects.

Anticancer chemotherapy

There are three types of anticancer chemotherapeutic agents:

- *Cytotoxics* These have no direct hormonal sequelae. Alkylating agents are more likely to induce permanent male sterility (without affecting potency) and in females they may induce premature menopause which may increase the liklihood of osteoporosis.
- *Immunomodulators Prednisolone* in excess causes Cushing's syndrome and acute withdrawal may precipitate adrenal insufficency. *Cyclophosphamide* in particular may cause early menopause. Thyroid dysfunction has been reported rarely with *tacrolimus* and *interferon-α and -ß* therapy.
- *Hormones*
  - *Progestogens* are used in breast cancer; of these, *megestrol acetate* has potent glucocorticoid activity and thus may cause Cushing's syndrome in excess or adrenal insufficiency if abruptly withdrawn.
  - *Aromatase inhibitors* such as *aminoglutethimide* may cause adrenal insufficiency and corticosteroid replacement is necessary.
  - *Trilostane*, which inhibits 3β-hydroxysteroid dehydrogenase, may also cause adrenal insufficiency.
  - *Gonadorelin analogues*, used for prostatic cancer and breast cancer, cause an initial increase in LH levels and then suppression and cause side-effects similar to orchidectomy in men and the menopause in women.
  - *Antiandrogens* used in prostatic cancer have predictable side-effects such as gynaecomastia, hot flushes, impotence, and impaired libido.

Radiotherapy

- Cranial radiotherapy whose field encompasses the hypothalamo–pituitary area may result in hypopituitarism (see p. 113).
- Head and neck irradiation may result in hypothyroidism and hypoparathyroidism.
- After 5 or more years of follow up, 50% of patients treated with radiotherapy only for laryngeal and pharyngeal carcinoma will develop hypothyroidism; combined surgery and radiotherapy results in roughly 90% of patients developing hypothyroidism. The rates for hypoparathyroidism were 88% and 90% respectively.
- Radiotherapy affects the testes dose-dependently. Fertility is affected much more than its androgen synthesizing capacity so that most men have normal testosterone levels unless given testicular doses >20–30 Gy.
- The effects of radiotherapy to both ovaries is amplified with age. Premature menopause may be elicited by doses >10 Gy.

Syndromes of ectopic hormone production

Definition

The elaboration into the systemic circulation, of a hormone or other biologically active molecule, by a neoplasm (benign or malignant) which has arisen from a tissue that does not normally produce that hormone or molecule and resulting in a clinically significant syndrome.

SIADH due to ectopic vasopressin production

Diagnosis

- The diagnosis of SIADH is made by finding an inappropriately concentrated urine in the face of a dilute plasma (<270 mmol) in the absence of hypovolaemia. Hyponatraemia is a *sine qua non.*
- The commonest tumour causing this syndrome is small cell carcinoma of the lung, so a chest radiograph is mandatory.
- These tumours have usually metastasized at presentation although palliative radiotherapy and chemotherapy are useful in improving quality of life.
- Other causes of SIADH must be excluded (see p. 243).

Management

- The initial management is fluid restriction with daily monitoring of the plasma sodium. We recommend 500 mL of oral fluid per day until the sodium is within the normal range (usually by day 3).Thereafter the fluid restriction can be relaxed depending on the plasma sodium. 1500–2000 mL/day is usual.
- For patients who cannot comply with fluid restriction, *demeclocycline* can be used to produce a nephrogenic diabetes insipidus to achieve a normal plasma sodium. Curative surgery will also cure the SIADH, as will chemotherapy in the 10% of small cell carcinomas that are cured in this way.

Table 101.1 Effects of ectopic hormones

Hormone	Clinical syndrome
ACTH	Cushing's syndrome
Vasopressin	Syndrome of inappropriate antidiuretic hormone
Parathyroid hormone rP	Hypercalcaemia
hCG	Gynaecomastia, loss of libido, hyperthyroidism
CRH	Cushing's syndrome
GHRH	Acromegaly
Erythropoietin	Polycythaemia
IGF-2	Hypoglycaemia

Table 101.2 Ectopic hormone production

Tumour	Ectopic hormone typically produced by tumour
Squamous cell lung carcinoma	PTHrP
Lung carcinoid	ACTH, vasopressin, CRH
Small cell lung carcinoma	Vasopressin, ACTH, CRH, GHRH
Medullary carcinoma of thyroid	Calcitonin, ACTH, CRH

Tumours most frequently associated with the ectopic ACTH syndrome

- Small cell carcinoma of the lung
- Carcinoid tumours of the bronchus
- Carcinoid tumours of the thymus
- Carcinoid tumours of the pancreas or gut
- Phaeochromocytoma or paraganglioma
- Medullary thyroid carcinoma

Cushing's syndrome due to ectopic ACTH and CRH production

Carcinoid tumours and ectopic hormone production

See p. 667

Hypercalcaemia of malignancy

NB. Primary hyperparathyroidism is relatively common and may therefore co-exist with malignancy.

Treatment

See p. 553.

Table 101.3 Hypercalcaemia: mechanisms and tumour types

Mechanism	Tumour type
Bony metastases	Breast carcinoma is the commonest cause
	No correlation between extent of bone secondaries and degree of hypercalcaemia
	PTHrP may co-exist
PTHrP secreting tumours	Squamous cell carcinoma of the lung is the commonest cause
	Squamous cell carcinoma of skin, oesophagus, and head and neck; lymphoma – hypercalcaemia is rare
	Adult T-cell lymphoma (HTLV-I associated) – hypercalcaemia is very common
Elevated vitamin D	Lymphoma (exclude sarcoidosis)
Stimulation of osteoclastic resorption by cytokines	Multiple myeloma, 'non-secretory myeloma'

Endocrinology in the critically ill

ACTH and cortisol

- Plasma cortisol increases rapidly after all forms of injury.
- After moderate to sever injuries, plasma cortisol start to fall after a day or two but only reach normal levels after a week.
- In patients with severe burns, plasma cortisol is elevated for at least 2 weeks.
- For uncomplicated surgery, plasma cortisol returns to normal after 4 days.
- Cortisol deficiency should be suspected in an acutely ill patient with a plasma cortisol of <600 nmol/L.

TSH and thyroid hormones

- TSH levels usually remain stable in acute injury. Total T_4 tends to fall but remains within the normal range.
- With prolonged illness the total T_4 tends to fall below the normal range. The fT_4 remains in the normal range.
- T_3 levels fall after injury and may remain suppressed for 2–3 weeks after a severe injury. The rT_3 level rises.
- In prolonged critical illness the thyroid function conforms to the 'sick euthyroid syndrome' (see p. 19).

Gonadotrophins and gonadal steroids

- In acute injury there is little disturbance in the hypothalamo–pituitary–gonadal axis.
- In prolonged illness there may be a fall in plasma testosterone in men which is not accompanied by a compensatory rise in gonadotrophins.

Hormone replacement and critical illness

There is no evidence that hormonal supplementation in the critically ill improves outcome.

Differential diagnosis of possible manifestations of endocrine disorders

Palpitations

- thyrotoxicosis
- phaeochromocytoma
- anxiety states
- cardiac arrhythmia
- caffeine excess

Sweating

- thyrotoxicosis
- phaeochromocytoma
- acromegaly
- chronic infection (e.g. TB)
- haematological malignancy (e.g. lymphoma)
- idiopathic

Obesity

- Cushing's syndrome
- hypothyroidism
- idiopathic

General malaise, tiredness

- hypo- or hyperthyroidism
- Addison's disease
- Cushing's syndrome
- diabetes mellitus
- chronic illness
- idiopathic including chronic fatigue syndrome

Flushing

- carcinoid
- primary gonadal failure
- mastocytosis
- medullary thyroid cancer
- drugs and alcohol
- idiopathic

Liver disease

Sex hormones – males

- Hypogonadism occurs in 70–80% of men with chronic liver disease. There is a combination of primary testicular failure and failure of hypothalamo–pituitary regulation.
- Alcohol acts independently to produce hypogonadism. There is a combination of primary testicular failure and failure of hypothalamo–pituitary regulation.
- The effects of elevated oestrogens result in increased loss of the male escutcheon, loss of body hair and redistribution of body fat, palmar erythema, spider naevi, and gynaecomastia.
- The increased conversion of testosterone and androstenedione to oestrone is attributed at least in part to portosystemic shunting. In addition, the large increase in SHBG concentration will increase the oestrogen/testosterone ratio as testosterone has a higher affinity for SHBG.
- Spironolactone may result in iatrogenic feminization by inhibiting testosterone synthesis by blocking 17-hydroxylase activity.
- There is no evidence that exogenous administration of androgens reverses hypogonadism in chronic liver disease.

Sex hormones – females

- Alcoholism increases the frequency of menstrual disturbances and spontaneous abortion but does not affect fertility.
- Liver dysfunction of whatever aetiology is associated with an early menopause.
- Alcohol rather than liver disease is the prime cause of hypogonadism. Non-alcoholic liver disease is only associated with hypogonadism in advanced liver failure when it is accompanied by encephalopathy and impaired GnRH secretion.
- Plasma testosterone and oestrone concentrations are usually normal, androstenedione concentration is increased and dehydroepiandrostenedione and dehydroepiandrostenedione sulfate levels are reduced.

Thyroid (Table 101.5)

- The liver synthesizes albumin, T_4-binding prealbumin (TBPA), and T_4-binding gobulin (TBG), all of which bind thyroid hormones covalently and reversibly.
- Thyroid function tests must be interpreted with caution in patients with liver disease. In acute liver disease, e.g. acute viral hepatitis, TBG levels are increased which increases the measured total circulating T_4 and T_3 levels. In chronic cirrhosis and chronic active hepatitis TBG may be decreased. In other chronic liver disease and in hepatomas, TBG is increased. The liver deiodinates T_4 to T_3 and this is impaired in liver disease. The T_4 is preferentially converted to rT_3 and there is an increase in the rT_3/t_3 ratio. Table 101.5 summarizes the changes in TFTs with liver disease. Free T_4 and T_3 assays are essential for the accurate interpretation of thyroid status in liver disease.

Adrenal hormones

- Patients who abuse alcohol may develop a clinical phenotype of Cushing's syndrome with moon facies, centripetal obesity, striae, and muscle wasting, and may have increased plasma cortisol concentrations. This is termed '*pseudo-Cushing's syndrome*'.
- Reversible (on abstention) adrenocorticorticoid hyperresponsiveness occurs in alcoholics. In liver disease cortisol metabolism may be impaired leading to elevated plasma cortisol levels, loss of diurnal cortisol variation, and failure to suppress with dexamethasone.

Table 101.4 Sex hormone changes in liver disease

Hormone	Level
Testosterone	↓
SHBG	↑
Oestrone	↑
Oestrodiol	↑→
LH	Inappropriately low/normal
FSH	Inappropriately low/normal
Prolactin	↑→

Renal disease

Calcitriol

There is impaired renal conversion of 25-hydroxyvitamin D_3 to 1,25 $(OH)_2D_3$ in end-stage renal failure (ESRF) leading to metabolic bone disease (see p. 571).

Parathyroid hormone and renal osteodystrophy

- Serum parathyroid hormone PTH secretion is stimulated by low serum calcium in ESRF. This is due to decreased renal phosphate clearance and impaired renal calcitriol secretion.
- As renal function declines, an elevated PTH and a decreased calcitriol can be detected with creatinine clearance of 50 mL/min. This rise in PTH is initially sufficient to maintain the serum calcium in the normal range.
- In ESRF patients are markedly hyperphosphataemic and hypoclacaemic. The degree of hyperparathyroidism progresses in line with the fall in renal function. Tertiary hyperparathyroidism occurs when PTH secretion becomes autonomous and hypercalcaemia will persist even after renal transplantation.
- Hyperparathyroid bone disease and osteomalacia are the main mechanisms behind the development of renal osteodystrophy, resulting in bone pain and deformity.

Treatment of renal osteodystrophy

- Maintainence of normal phosphate levels with phosphate binders (such as calcium carbonate) and the treatment of osteomalacia. The increased use of calcium carbonate has been suggested as the cause of the increased incidence of adynamic renal osteodystrophy, but intensive vitamin D therapy and peritoneal dialysis are probably also contributory.
- Alfacalcidol or calcitriol (which does not require renal 1α-hydroxylation) are effective in treating osteomalacia.
- Calcitriol at a dose of 1–2 μg/day is used for established renal osteodystrophy. Lower doses of calcitriol (0.25–0.5 μg/day) are used in early ESRF to prevent the development of renal osteodystrophy.
- Parathyroidectomy is advocated in bone disease uncontrolled by vitamin D therapy or the development of tertiary hyperparathyroidism.

Table 101.5 Thyroid function changes in liver disease

Hormone	Acute hepatitis	CAH/PBC	Cirrhosis
T_4	↑↓	↑	↓
fT_4	↑	→	↑
T_3	↓	↑	↓
fT_3	↓	↓	↓
rT_3	↑	→	↑→
TSH	↑	↑	↑→
TBG	↑	↓	↓

CAH: chronic active hepatitis
PBC: primary biliary cirrhosis

Prolactin

Hyperprolactinaemia is common in ESRF but is usually mild, i.e. <1000 mU/L. The cause is both increased secretion and decreased renal clearance.

Gonadal function

- Hypogonadism, clinical and biochemical, is common in ESRF.
- In men, there is impaired pulsatile release of LH, although basal LH levels are usually elevated due to impaired renal clearance. Serum FSH is usually normal or mildly elevated.
- In women, levels of oestrodiol, progesterone and FSH are reported to be within the normal range in the early follicular phase but fail to show the usual cyclical changes. Menstrual disturbance is common. Amenorrhoea, polymenorrhoea, and menorrhagia can also occur on dialysis. Infertitility is the rule and conception on dialysis is the exception.
- Sexual dysfunction is common in both sexes but has been better studied in men. 60% of men have some degree of impotence and examination yields 80% to have testicular atrophy and 14% to have gynaecomastaia.
- Treatment of hypogonadism in ESRF is suboptimal. Testosterone therapy is not associated with any clinical benefit in men.

Growth hormone and growth retardation

- Basal GH levels are normal but there is impaired secretion following an adequate hypoglycaemic stimulus in 40–70% of patients with ESRF.

- There is impaired growth in children, particularly during periods of greatest growth velocity and puberty is delayed. This combination leads to short stature. The improved growth velocity after renal transplantation is often too little too late in order to attain a normal stature.
- Recombinant human GH (rhGH) has been shown to be an effective treatment for growth retardation in children with stable chronic renal failure (CRF) and ESRF as well as after renal transplantation.

Thyroid

The 'sick euthyroid' finding is common in CRF (see p. 19).

Adrenal

- The adrenal axis is not impaired clinically by CRF.
- There is evidence of blunted cortisol response to hypoglycaemia but is not relevant clinically.
- Patients with amyloidosis are at risk of hypoadrenalism due to adrenal amyloid infiltration.

Chapter 102
Perioperative management of endocrine patients

Trans-sphenoidal surgery/craniotomy

Preoperative

- Confirm the following:
  - anterior and posterior pituitary function normal or on adequate replacement
  - short synacthen test (check at 0 and 30 min)
  - fT_4
  - LH, FSH, oestradiol or testosterone
  - prolactin
  - urea and electrolytes
  - group and save serum has been done
  - recent (<3 months) MRI pituitary
  - formal visual field perimetry and visual acuity assessment
- Record therapeutic options discussed with patient, including:
  - risks of surgery (e.g. CSF leakage, meningitis, bleeding, partial or total hypopituitarism including diabetes insipidus and potential effects on fertility, recurrent disease and visual deterioration)
  - need for lifelong follow up.
- Start antibiotic prophylaxis on the night before surgery (*flucloxacillin* 500 mg 4× day and *amoxycillin* 500 mg 3× day i/v or orally; if penicillin allergic, use *erythromycin* or *clindamycin*).
- Continue for 5 days after surgery, or longer if CSF leakage.
- If steroid deficient or if steroid reserve unknown or if patient has Cushing's disease (inadequate stress response), give *hydrocortisone* 20 mg orally with morning premedication.

Postoperative

- Consider steroid status:
  - Start i/m (not i/v) *hydrocortisone* (100 mg 4× day) postoperatively.
  - Convert to oral hydrocortisone (20 mg/10 mg/10 mg) when eating and drinking.
  - After nasal packs removed (following trans-sphenoidal surgery), stop steroids (usually <48 hours).
  - When steroids stopped, check 9 a.m. cortisol level next morning.

- Repeat 9 a.m. cortisol next day as well.
- In patients with Cushing's disease, 9 a.m. cortisol (×2) <50 nmol/L indicates cure; occasionally cortisol takes a few days to fall to undetectable levels.
- In patients without Cushing's disease:

9 a.m. cortisol level	Action
>550 nmol/L	Stay off steroids
400–550 nmol/L	Advise to start steroids if unwell (give patient supply of oral and parenteral hydrocortisone to take home with appropriate written advice)
<400 nmol/L	Start regular oral hydrocortisone (10 mg/5 mg/5 mg)

- If patient acutely unwell with postural BP drop when steroids stopped, check random cortisol and start steroids.

- Fluid balance – watch for diabetes insipidus:
  - Postoperatively, restrict to 2 L total fluid input (i/v and p/o).
  - Record fluid input/output assiduously.
  - If patient becomes polyuric (200 mL/h for >3 or more consecutive hours), then urgently check plasma U&Es, plasma and urine osmolalities and urinary sodium. While waiting for results allow free oral fluids; aim to replace the fluid deficit.
  - If diabetes insipidus confirmed by the results, give a single dose of *deamino-D-arginine vasopressin* (*DDAVP*) (1 μg s/c).
  - When fluid deficit has been replaced (usually orally), restart 2L fluid restriction (again include i/v and p/o routes).
  - If polyuria recurs, treat as before.
  - Regular U&Es, plasma and urine osmolalities required.
  - If polyuria continues to recur up to and after 96 h post operatively, consider regular DDAVP (intranasally if possible (not if a trans-sphenoidal approach is used), otherwise give DDAVP p/o or if no alternative, s/c).
  - Hyponatraemia 1 week after a trans-sphenoidal adenectomy may be due to SIADH or to cerebral salt wasting. Check urinary sodium and assess fluid status to differentiate between these diagnoses (cerebral salt wasting causes high urinary sodium and is associated with dehydration; SIADH has a low urinary sodium and not associated with dehydration).
- Check remainder of pituitary function between day 3 and day 5 postoperatively.
- Recheck visual field perimetry.

- Give information to patient including advice on driving and contact details for the Pituitary Foundation support group:
  - The Pituitary Foundation, 17/18 The Courtyard, Woodlands, Bradley Stoke, Bristol BS12 4NQ. Telephone: 01454 201612.

Thyroidectomy

Preoperative

- Ensure euthyroid. If surgery is required in the presence of hyperthyroidism, give *potassium iodide* (60 mg 3× day for 10 days); this reduces thyroid hormone release and probably decreases perioperative blood loss. Oral *propranolol* (30–120 mg 3× day) reduces clinical manifestations of thyrotoxicosis.
- Vocal cord function check by indirect laryngoscopy.
- Warn of postoperative risks, including recurrent laryngeal nerve damage (<1%), keloid scarring, haemorrhage, permanent hypoparathyroidism (<0.5%), hypothyroidism (10%).

Postoperative

- Risk of haemorrhage in first 24 h, particularly major haemorrhage deep to the strap muscles leading to airway compression. Watch for stridor, respiratory difficulties, and wound swelling. Drainage from wound drains is unhelpful. Treat by evacuating haematoma, consider intubation or tracheostomy. Clip removers and artery forceps should be kept to hand.
- Recurrent laryngeal nerve damage is permanent in <1% and transient in 2–4%. Patient's voice is often husky for about 3 weeks postoperatively and may be treated with lozenges and humidified air.
- Symptomatic unilateral damage can be treated by stabilization of the affected cord in adduction by submucosal *Teflon* injection under direct laryngoscopy.
- Bilateral damage leads to unopposed adductor action of the cricothyroid muscle which causes glottis closure and airway obstruction. Treatment involves reintubation, paralysis, *hydrocortisone* (100 mg 4× day i/m for oedema), extubation at 24 h – if that fails, a tracheostomy should be performed.
- If recurrent laryngeal nerve damage is persistent at 9 months, an attempt can be made to resuture the nerve.
- Monitor calcium. Hypoparathyroidism is usually evident within 7 days. See section on hypoparathyroism (p. 559) for treatment.
- Following total thyroidectomy for malignancy, the patient should be left off thyroxine to allow the TSH to rise for the postoperative radioiodine uptake scan (see p. 91).
- If total thyroidectomy is performed for hyperthyroidism, thyroxine 125 μg should be commenced. Check TSH in 6–8 weeks.

- Following partial thyroidectomy, transient biochemical hypothyroidism is common during the first 2 months and does not warrant treatment unless persistent.

Parathyroidectomy

Postoperative

- Risk of ↓ calcium, ↓ magnesium, ↓ uric acid, metabolic acidosis, and haematoma formation.
- Calcium begins to fall postoperatively after about 4–12 h; the nadir is reached by 24 h. Symptoms usually precede the fall in calcium.
- Hypocalcaemia is sometimes transient and can return to normal within 2–3 weeks.
- Initially check calcium, albumin, and magnesium at least daily.
- If patient becomes hypocalcaemic the differential diagnosis includes:
  - *Permanent hypoparathyroidism* Check PTH level after day 3; level will be undetectable (<1 pg/mL).
  - *'Hungry bone syndrome'* due to extensive skeletal remineralization (↓Mg, ↓PO_4, ↓Ca^{2+}).
  - *'Functional hypoparathyroidism'* Check PTH level after day 3; level will be detectable. Spontaneously improves over 3 days to 3 weeks. Can be caused by the suppression of the other parathyroid glands, parathyroid gland ischaemia or hypomagnesaemia.
- Hypocalcaemia:
  - Treat with 2.4 g of *oral calcium*/day with either *calcitriol* (1 μg daily, orally) or *1α-cholecalciferol* (1 μg daily, orally).
  - If severe (<1.6 mmol/L), give *calcium gluconate* (10%, 2–3 ampoules slow i/v) for cardioprotection; administer with ECG monitoring.
  - Follow this with an i/v infusion of *calcium gluconate* (15 mg/kg) over 4 h in 1 L of 0.9% saline.
  - Note: 10% calcium gluconate = 88 mg calcium. Therefore dose required is (1.7 × weight in kg) mL of 10% calcium gluconate. Infund over 4 hours.
  - If hypocalcaemia persists or recurs, try oral calcium supplementation and calcitriol.
  - Treat hypomagnesaemia with i/v *magnesium sulfate* (1–2 g, 10% solution over 6 h). Oral magnesium is poorly absorbed, and causes diarrhoea.
  - Try to wean off calcium supplementation and continue *calcitriol* or *1α-cholecalciferol*.

Phaeochromocytoma

Preoperative

- Ensure adequate α- and β-blockade.
- Start α-blockade before β-blockade (unopposed β-blockade can lead to marked vasoconstriction, ischaemic damage and hypertension).
  - *α-blockade* Start *phenoxybenzamine* (10 mg, orally, 4× day) – an irreversible a-blocker. Adequacy of dose can be assessed by monitoring the haematocrit and postural fall in blood pressure (reflects vasodilation). Start at least 1 week before surgery.
  - *β-blockade* Start *propanolol* (40–80 mg, orally, 3× day) at least 48 h after phenoxybenzamine begun.
- Control BP with α- and β-blockers. Add calcium channel blocker or ACE inhibitor if necessary. *α-methyltyrosine* (a false catecholamine precursor which inhibits tyrosine hydroxylase, the rate-limiting step for catecholamine synthesis) is rarely used to control BP.
- Give i/v *phenoxybenzamine* (0.5 mg/kg in 250 mL 5% dextrose over 2 h) for the 3 days prior to surgery.

Postoperative

- Watch for ↓BP: sudden withdrawal of catecholamines leads to marked arterial and venous dilatation. This is worsened by inadequate volume loading and should initially be treated with volume replacement rather than by pressor agents.
- If hypertension persists 2 weeks postoperatively, then residual tumour or metastases must be considered.
- If bilateral adrenalectomy performed, see below.

Bilateral adrenalectomy (see p. 297)

- Give *hydrocortisone* (100 mg, 4× day, i/m) postoperatively; this will provide adequate mineralocorticoid as well as glucocorticoid cover. Continue this for 2 days postoperatively. Monitor U&Es.
- From day 3, give *hydrocortisone* p/o (double usual replacement dose, e.g. 20 mg/10 mg/10 mg) and add *fludrocortisone* p/o (100 μg daily).

Chapter 103
Syndromes of hormone resistance

Definition

Reduced responsiveness of target organs to a particular hormone, usually secondary to a disorder of the receptor or distal signalling pathways, and leading to alterations in feedback loops and elevated circulating hormone levels.

Thyroid hormone resistance

See p. 47.

Androgen resistance

See p. 486.

Glucocorticoid resistance

- Diminished sensitivity to glucocorticoid leads to reduced glucocorticoid feedback on CRH and ACTH, leading to increased CRH, ACTH, and cortisol concentrations.
- The clinical features are not due to excess glucocorticoid as there is reduced peripheral tissue sensitivity. However, elevated ACTH leads to increased secretion of mineralocorticoid (e.g. deoxycorticosterone) and androgen (DHEA and DHEAS). This may lead to hypertension and hypokalaemia, hirsutism and acne in women, and sexual precocity in males.
- Glucocorticoid resistance may be differentiated from Cushing's syndrome as despite evidence of increased urinary cortisol, abnormal suppression with dexamethasone, and increased responsiveness to CRH, the diurnal rhythm of cortisol secretion persists, there are no clinical features of Cushing's syndrome, BMD is normal or increased, and there is a normal response to insulin induced hypoglycaemia.
- Low-dose *dexamethasone* treatment (2 mg/day) may efficiently suppress ACTH and androgen production.

ACTH resistance

- A rare autosomal recessive disorder where the adrenal cortex fails to respond to ACTH, in the presence of an otherwise normal gland. (Mineralocorticoid secretion is preserved under angiotensin II control.)
- The presenting clinical features include hypoglycaemia which is often neonatal, neonatal jaundice, increased skin pigmentation, and frequent infections.
- Occasionally, ACTH resistance is a component of the *triple A syndrome* of alacrima (absence of tears), achalasia of the cardia, and ACTH resistance.
- *Biochemical features* Undetectable or low 9 a.m. cortisol, with grossly elevated ACTH (often >1000 ng/mL), and normal renin, aldosterone and electrolytes, and impaired response to short synacthen test.

Mineralocorticoid resistance

Also known as type 1 pseudohypoaldosteronism, this is a rare inherited disorder which usually presents in children with failure to thrive, salt loss and dehydration.

- Biochemically there is evidence of high urinary sodium, despite hyponatraemia, hyperkalaemia, high plasma aldosterone and plasma renin activity.
- Diagnosis requires proof of unresponsiveness to mineralocorticoids.
- Treatment is with sodium supplementation. With time treatment can often be weaned, and salt wasting is unusual following childhood.
- *Biochemical features*
  - ↓serum sodium
  - ↑serum potassium
  - ↑urinary sodium
  - ↑plasma aldosterone
  - ↑plasma renin activity

Part XI
Diabetes

Chapter 104
Diabetes: classification and diagnosis

Background

Diabetes mellitus (DM) is characterized by an elevated blood glucose. The classification of diabetes has also recently been revised to give an idea of the underlying cause or defect. Currently 2–6% of the UK population have diabetes but only 1/2 to 2/3 are thought to be diagnosed. Worldwide 100 million people have diabetes and this will probably double by the year 2010.

Current classification of diabetes

Type 1 (5–25% of cases): pancreatic islet β cell deficiency

- autoimmune – associated with anti-glutamic acid decarboxylase (GAD), islet cell, and insulin antibodies
- idiopathic

Type 2 (75–95% of cases): defective insulin action or secretion

- insulin resistance
- insulin secretory defect

Others

- Genetic defects of β cell function
  - maturity onset diabetes of the young (MODY)
  - chromosome 20, HNF4α (MODY 1)
  - chromosome 7, glucokinase (MODY 2)
  - chromosome 12, HNF1α (MODY 3)
  - chromosome 13, IPF-1 (MODY 4)
  - mitochondrial DNA 3242 mutation
  - others
- Genetic defects of insulin action
  - type A insulin resistance
  - leprechaunism (type 2 diabetes, intrauterine growth retardation + dysmorphic features)
  - Rabson–Mendenhall syndrome (DM + pineal hyperplasia + acanthosis nigricans)
  - lipoatrophic diabetes
  - others
- Diseases of the exocrine pancreas
  - pancreatitis
  - trauma/surgery (pancreatectomy)
  - neoplasia
  - pancreatic destruction, e.g. cystic fibrosis, haemochromatosis
  - others

(*continued on page 801*)

Diagnosis

DM is a biochemical diagnosis. In 1985 the World Health Organization (WHO) revised its guidelines to give a diagnostic template based on a 75 g oral glucose tolerance test (OGTT) which remained the gold standard until it was futher revised in 2000. The venous plasma glucose levels for this are shown on p. 803. In 1997 the American Diabetes Association (ADA) suggested lowering the normal fasting plasma glucose level to <6.0 mmol/L and the diabetic level to >7.0 mmol/L. The aim of this was to reduce the need for an OGTT and the 2 h post glucose load measurement. A fasting glucose would therefore be the diagnostic test of choice and only pregnant women would expect to have a 2 h postprandial level checked. A diagnosis of diabetes would be made in any symptomatic person with a random blood glucose >11.1 mmol/L. Asymptomatic patients or those with intercurrent illness would still require a further abnormal result before a diagnosis of diabetes could be made.

Current classification of diabetes *(continued)*

- Endocrinopathies
  - Cushing's syndrome
  - acromegaly
  - phaeochromocytoma
  - glucagonoma
  - hyperthyroidism
  - somatostatinoma
  - others
- Drug or chemical induced
- Infections
  - congenital rubella or cytomegalovirus (CMV)
  - others
- Uncommon forms of immune-mediated diabetes
  - anti-insulin receptor antibodies
  - stiff man syndrome (type 1 diabetes, rigidity of muscles, painful spasms)
  - others
- Other genetic syndromes associated with diabetes
  - Down's syndrome
  - Klinefelter's syndrome
  - Lawrence–Moon–Biedl syndrome
  - myotonic dystrophy
  - Prader–Willi syndrome
  - Turner's syndrome
  - Wolfram's syndrome (or DIDMOAD – *d*iabetes *i*nsipidus, *DM*, *o*ptic *a*trophy + sensorineural *d*eafness)
  - others
- Gestational diabetes.

Classification

The first accepted classification of diabetes was drawn up by WHO and modified in 1985. The original classification suggested just two major groups and an 'others' group. These two main groups are:

- insulin dependent DM (IDDM) or type 1
- non-insulin dependent DM (NIDDM) or type 2

In 1997, at the same time as the ADA proposed a change to the diagnostic criteria, an alteration in the classification to include both clinical stage and aetiology was also suggested. The clinical staging is from normal glucose tolerance through impaired glucose tolerance (IGT) and/or impaired fasting hyperglycaemia (IFG) and on to frank DM, which is split into non-insulin requiring, insulin requiring for control, and insulin requiring for survival. The aetiological groups are shown in the list on p. 799. The suggestion is to remove the terms IDDM and NIDDM and to expand the type 1, type 2, and 'others' groups to give a better idea of underlying cause.

Table 104.1 WHO classification

		Venous plasma glucose (mmol/L)
Normal	Fasting	<6.0
	and	
	2 h post-prandial	<7.8
Diabetes	Fasting	>7.0
	or	
	2 h post-prandial	>11.1
IGT	Fasting	<7.0
	and	
	2 h post-prandial	7.8–11.1
IFG	Fasting	6.0–6.9

Table 104.2 Spectrum of diabetic disorders in Europe

Idiopathic type 2	50%
Predominant ß cell defect (type 1 like)	18%
Type 1	15%
Latent autoimmune diabetes in adults (late onset type 1, positive GAD antibodies)	10%
MODY	5%
Mitochondrial diabetes with deafness	1%
Insulin receptor defects	<1%

Adapted from Groop (1998).

Table 104.3 Differences between type 1 and type 2 diabetes

	Type 1 diabetes	Type 2 diabetes
Peak age of onset	12 years	60 years
UK prevalence	0.25%	5–7% (10% of those >65 years of age)
Aetiology	Autoimmune	Combination of insulin resistance, ß cell destruction and ß cell dysfunction
Initial presentation	Polyuria, polydypsia, and weight loss with ketoacidosis	Hyperglycaemic symptoms but often with complication of diabetes
Treatment	Diet and insulin from outset	Diet with or without oral hypoglycaemic agents or insulin

Genetics

Type 1 patients

The overall lifetime risk in a white population of developing type 1 diabetes is only 0.4%, but this rises to:

- 1–2% if your mother has it
- 3–6% if your father has it
- siblings have about a 6% risk
- monozygotic twins have a 36% concordance rate.

Islet cell antibodies are seen in 3% of Oxford schoolchildren but in 40% of monozygotic twins and 6% of siblings of type 1 patients. A genetic predisposition is therefore suggested, but this also highlights the importance of environmental triggers as not all those with antibodies go on to get diabetes. Genetic predisposition accounts for 1/3 of susceptibility to type 1 diabetes.

Although several different regions of the human genome are linked to the development of type 1 diabetes, the most common are the major histocompatibility complex (MHC) antigens/human leukocyte antigens (HLA). Over 90% of type 1 patients in this country have either HLA-DR3, DR4, or both. Certain variants of the DQβ1 or DQA1 gene result in the expression of susceptible alleles of DR3/DR4. Interestingly this association is not true in all races, notably the Japanese.

There are currently 10 distinct genetic areas (IDDM1–IDDM10) known to be linked to type 1 diabetes; some relate to MHC genes, others to the insulin gene region. MHC antigens commonly found in those with type 1 diabetes, and felt to predispose to it, are B15, B8, and DQ8. The DR2, DQ6, and DQ18 genes appear to be protective. Linkage studies have suggested type 1 susceptibility genes on chromosomes:

- 6q (also known as IDDM5)
- 11p (IDDM2)
- 11q (IDDM4)
- 15q (IDDM3).

These genetic variations may help to explain susceptibility, but their link to the increased levels of islet cell antibodies, anti-glutamic acid decarboxylase (GAD) antibodies, and anti-tyrosine phosphatase antibodies (anti-IA-2 antibodies) often seen soon after diagnosis is less clearly decided. These three antibodies, if all are present, give a non-diabetic individual an 88% chance of developing type 1 diabetes in the next 10 years.

Maturity onset diabetes of the young

MODY 1 (HNF4α)

- Accounts for <0.0001% of all type 2 patients and about 5% of cases of MODY.
- Usually presents in adolescence or early adulthood <25 years of age
- Can give severe hyperglycaemia with 20% needing insulin therapy and 40% oral agents
- Results in a high frequency of microvascular complications.
- Inherited as an autosomal dominant with a defect on chromosome 20q resulting in altered activity of the hepatic nuclear factor (HNF)4α gene which is a positive regulator of HNF1α. This is a transcription factor found in the liver and β cells of the pancreas where it acts as a transactivater of the insulin gene in rat models.

MODY 2 (glucokinase)

- Accounts for <0.2% of type 2 patients and 10% of cases of MODY.
- Presents in early childhood
- Gives only mild hyperglycaemia and therefore infrequent microvascular complications with 90% controlled on diet alone and insulin usually only needed when they become pregnant.
- Autosomally dominantly inherited with a defect in the glucokinase gene on chromosome 7 resulting in altered glucose sensing in the β cells of the pancreas and impaired hepatic production of glycogen.

MODY 3 (HNF1α)

- Affects 1–2% of type 2 patients and accounts for 70% of MODY patients.
- Presents in adolescence or early adulthood (peaks around 21 years of age).
- Causes severe hyperglycaemia and frequent microvascular complications; 1/3 require insulin therapy and 1/3 require oral agents.
- Linked to a mutation on chromosome 12q24 which directly alters HNF1α activity. How this causes type 2 diabetes is not fully understood.

Type 2 patients

In type 2 patients the concordance between monozygotic twins for diabetes is much higher (60–100%, versus 36% for type 1) but the rate amongst dizygotic twins is much less, suggesting a much stronger genetic element in its aetiology than for type 1 diabetes. Unlike type 1 patients, however, those with type 2 do not seem to have the same HLA-linked genes. In most families this appears to be polygenic, although the much less common maturity onset diabetes of the young (MODY) is autosomal dominant but only accounts for a few percent of all type 2 patients. MODY is currently split into four types, with type 4 accounting for 15% of cases and currently accounting for those that do not fit into types 1–3, although a chromosome 13 defect in the insulin promoter factor 1 gene may fall into this group.

Other recognized genetic subtypes of type 2 diabetes include *mitochondrial diabetes*, which effects 1–3% of type 2 patients and is maternally transmitted. It is associated with deafness and other neurological abnormalities. *Insulin resistance* is an important part of type 2 diabetes and rare genetic defects causing this are recognized. A 40% reduction in the biological effect of any given insulin molecule is suggested by clamp studies in type 2 patients, but these rarer genetic syndromes may result in a more severe picture.

References and further reading

Alberti KGMM, Zimmet PZ, for the WHO consultation. Definition, diagnosis and classification of DM and its complications. Part 1: Diagnosis and classification of DM. Provisional report of a WHO consultation. *Diabetic Medicine* 1998; 15: 539–553.

Alcolado JC, Thomas AW. Maternally inherited DM: the role of mitochondrial DNA defects. *Diabetic Medicine* 1995; 12(2):102–108.

Groop LC. Prediction and prevention of type 2 DM. *Topical Endocrinology* 1998;10: 13–16.

Hattersley AT. Maturity onset diabetes of the young (MODY). *Baillière's Clinical Paediatrics* 1996; 4(4): 663–680.

Robinson S, Kessling A. Diabetes secondary to genetic disorders. *Baillière's Clinical Endocrinology and Metabolism* 1992; 6: 867–898.

Chapter 105
General management and treatment

Background

After diagnosis all patients with diabetes need to see a dietitian and a diabetes nurse specialist and have a full medical assessment. The first priority is dietary advice, which should always take into account the patient's circumstances and culture and be individually tailored in order to be achievable.

Assessment of the newly diagnosed patient

History

- duration of symptoms, e.g. thirst, polyuria, weight loss
- possible secondary causes of diabetes, e.g. acromegaly
- family history
- presence of complication of diabetes
- risk factors for developing complications e.g. smoking, hypertension, hyperlipidaemia.

Examination

- body mass index (BMI)
- clues for secondary causes
- cardiovascular system (especially BP + peripheral pulses)
- signs of autonomic and peripheral neuropathy
- eyes – for retinopathy

Investigations

Initial investigations will be modified by the history and examination but as a minimum should include:

- blood tests for urea and electrolytes, liver and thyroid function, and a full lipid profile
- urine tests for ketones, macro- and (if negative) microalbuminuria
- an ECG in all type 2 patients.

Treatment

In type 1 patients, insulin therapy is mandatory along with dietary advice and standard diabetes education. The education of all newly diagnosed patients is intended to provide an incentive for good compliance. A full education package should include:

- an explanation as to what diabetes is and what it means to the patient
- aims of treatment, e.g. rationale of reducing complications and exact values to aim for

- types of treatment – not just drugs but also dietary advice and lifestyle modification such as increased physical activity, stopping smoking, and reducing alcohol intake
- self monitoring, e.g. both the method(s) of doing this, the reasons for doing it, and what to do with the results
- an idea of some chronic complications of diabetes and what to look out for, e.g. a chiropodist's input and review is advised, especially for type 2 patients
- advice regarding DVLA, insurance companies, and Diabetes U.K.

All type 2 patients should be considered for such an educational package. In most the next step is to try diet, exercise, and weight reduction (if obese, which most will be) before initiating drug therapy if control is not adequate. If this fails to improve control adequately after 3 months, consider oral therapy with *metformin* in the overweight and *sulfonylureas* in the lean.

After the initial assessment all patients should be put into a formal review system, whether by their GP or in a hospital diabetic clinic, for further education, maintenance of good control, and complication screening.

Dietary advice

In the overweight patient (e.g. BMI >25) a reduction in total intake to aid weight reduction is also required. A standard diabetic diet should aim to have

- <10% of its energy in the form of saturated fat (<8% if hyperlipidaemic)
- <30% from all fats
- 50–60% as carbohydrate which is mostly complex high fibre
- sugar limited to about 25 g/day
- sodium content <6 g/day in most people or <3 g/day if hypertensive.

Alcohol is a significant source of calories, and a reduction in the overweight or hypertriglyceridaemic patient is advisable.

Oral hypoglycaemic agents

Sulfonylureas

These agents are used as first line treatment in non-obese patients with type 2 diabetes.

- The first generation agents *chlorpropamide*, *tolbutamide*, and *tolazamide* are still used today.
- Second generation agents such as *glibenclamide*, *gliclazide*, and *glipizide* are now more commonly used.
- Third generation agents such as *glimepiride* have recently become available.

Mode of action

Sulfonylureas act by stimulating a receptor on the surface of β cells, closing a potassium channel and opening a calcium channel with subsequent insulin release. A doubling of glucose-stimulated insulin secretion can be expected with both first and second phase insulin secretion affected. This results in a 1–2% reduction in HbA1c long term.

Side-effects

These are hypoglycaemia and weight gain. In the UK Prospective Diabetes Study (UKPDS) the mean weight gain seen after 10 years of therapy was 2.3 kg while the incidence of major hypoglycaemic events was 0.4–0.6%/year. Occasional skin reactions, alterations in liver function tests, and minor gastrointestinal symptoms may be more important. Also avoid sulfonylureas in porphyria.

Biguanides

Metformin is first line therapy in the obese type 2 diabetic and is also used in some insulin-treated, insulin-resistant, overweight subjects to reduce insulin requirements. The UKPDS showed significantly better results from metformin for complications and mortality compared to other therapies in the overweight type 2 diabetic. Although a 1–2 kg weight loss is seen initially, UKPDS data suggests it does not significantly alter weight over a 10 year period.

Mode of action

Metformin works by decreasing hepatic gluconeogenesis and increasing muscle glucose uptake/metabolism, so increasing insulin sensitivity. With long term use a 0.8–2.0% reduction in HbA1c can be expected.

Table 105.1 Properties of sulfonylureas

Sulfonylurea	Length of action	Begins working within	Daily dose (mg)
Glibenclamide	16–24 h	2–4 h	2.5–15
Gliclazide	10–24 h	2–4 h	40–320
Glipizide	6–24 h	2–4 h	2.5–20
Chlorpropamide	24–72 h	2–4 h	100–500
Tolbutamide	6–10 h	2–4 h	100–1000
Glimepiride		2–4 h	1–6

Table 105.2 Biguanides and prandial glucose regulators

Drug	Length of action	Begins working within	Daily dose (mg)
Metformin	24–36 h	2.5 h	500–2000
Repaglinide	4–6 h	<1 h	0.5–16
Nateglinide	–	–	180–540

Side-effects/contraindications

Contraindicated in patients with renal (creatinine >140 nmol/L), hepatic, or cardiac impairment, or who consume significant alcohol. Gastrointestinal side-effects include nausea, epigastric discomfort, and diarrhoea and occur in up to 1/2 of patients in the first 1–2 weeks of treatment, but are usually transient. If the starting dose is low (e.g. 500 mg once daily) most people develop a tolerance to these and are able to take higher doses; <5% are totally intolerant. Rarely skin rashes and lactic acidosis occur. The latter, when seen, is usually in patients with hepatic, renal, or cardiac impairment. Using radiological contrast media with metformin is associated with an increased risk of lactic acidosis and therapy should be stopped for a few days before such investigations. Lactic acidosis occurs very infrequently e.g. 0.024–0.15 cases/1000 patient years in a Swedish study. *Phenformin* was used in the past but was withdrawn due to an increased risk of lactic acidosis. Although it is known to reduce folic acid and vitamin B_{12} absorption this is not usually a problem clinically with metformin.

Prandial glucose regulators

This new form of therapy can be used in type 2 patients who have inadequate control on diet or metformin. *Repaglinide* is a non-sulfonylurea oral hypoglycaemic agent which stimulates the secretion of insulin from pancreatic β cells. It works on separate parts of the β cell sulfonylurea receptor from the sulfonylureas. Its use results in an approximate 0.6–2% reduction in HbA1c levels. Its very short duration of action reduces the risk of hypoglycaemia compared to some sulfonylureas. It should not, however, be used in patients with renal or hepatic impairment and may result in hepatic dysfunction so periodic liver function test monitoring is required.

α-Glucosidase inhibitors

Used in type 2 patients who have inadequate control on diet or other oral agent alone. When taken with food acarbose reduces post prandial glucose peaks by inhibiting the digestive enzyme α-glucosidase which normally breaks carbohydrates into their monosaccharide components, thus retarding glucose uptake from the intestine and reducing postprandial glucose peaks. Some improvement in lipids has also been reported.

These undigested carbohydrates then pass into the large intestine where bacteria metabolize them, which may explain the common side-effects of postprandial fullness/bloating, abdominal pain, flatulence, and diarrhoea. Starting at 50 mg once daily and gradually increasing the dose at 2–3 weekly intervals improves tolerance to this therapy. Less commonly, jaundice and elevated hepatic transaminase levels can also be seen. In the UK PDS adding *acarbose* to other therapies resulted in a further 0.5% drop in HbA1c.

Table 105.3 Oral hypogylcaemic agents: summary

Class	Mechanism of action	Expected reduction in HbA1c (%)
Sulfonylureas	Stimulate pancreatic insulin secretion	1.5–2.5
Biguanides	Increases muscle glucose uptake and metabolism; decreases hepatic gluconeogenesis	0.8–2.0
Prandial glucose regulators	Stimulate pancreatic insulin secretion	0.5–1.9
α-Glucosidase inhibitors	Inhibits a digestive enzyme	0.4–0.7
Thiazolidinediones	Activate PPAR-γ receptor	0.6–1.5

Thiazolidinediones

This novel class of drugs act as insulin sensitizing agents by activating the peroxisome proliferator activated receptor (PPAR-γ) which stimulates gene transcription for glucose transporter molecules such as Glut 1. The first of this class was *troglitazone* which reduces insulin requirements by up to 30% and HbA1c by 1% either when used alone or in combination with other oral agents. This was withdrawn soon after its UK launch because of reports of hepatotoxicity but is still being used in other countries. Other agents such as *rosiglitazone* and *pioglitazone*, are now available in the UK. Their main side-effect is hepatotoxicity, and normal liver function before starting therapy with monthly liver function test (LFT) for the first year seems sensible.

Indications

Type 2 diabetes, oral combination with metformia or a sulfonylurea

Dose

- Rosiglitazone 4–8 mg/day
- Pioglitazone 15–30 mg/day

Side-effects

- Fluid retention
- Hepertotoxicity

Insulin

Insulin is required in all patients with type 1 diabetes, and some with type 2, for the preservation of life; in other type 2 patients it is needed to achieve better glycaemic/metabolic control or for the relief of hyperglycaemic symptoms. Most insulin is in a biosynthetic human form (from yeast or bacteria) at a standard concentration: U100 (100 units/mL). Some countries still supply U40 and U80 strengths, so care should be taken with patients from abroad. There is also a sizable minority of patients taking bovine or porcine insulins. Bovine insulin is extracted from cattle pancreas and is more antigenic than both human and porcine alternatives and so gives more lipohypertrophy and lipoatrophy.

Insulin can currently only be given by i/v or s/c routes, although inhaled formulations may soon be available. Standard insulins come as 10 mL vials for use with a 0.5 mL or 1.0 mL syringe or as 1.5 mL or 3.0 mL cartridges for use in pen devices. The insulin itself is unmodified/neutral or mixed with agents such as zinc to alter its onset of action, peak effect, and duration of action. Thre are >30 types of insulin preparation available, which should allow full 24 h cover for a wide variety of lifestyles.

The main problems with all insulin regimens are weight gain and hypoglycaemia. The later occurring overnight can be troublesome, especially as the patient may not know it has occurred and because of the counter-regulatory hormone response (the *Somogyi phenomenon*) just reacts to the hyperglycaemia the next morning by increasing their evening insulin. Occasional 3 a.m. blood glucose levels may help sort this out. Care with alcohol and adjustments of insulin and pre-bed snacks if nocturnal physical activity such as sex is on the cards will also reduce nocturnal hypos.

Types of insulin

Short acting (soluble/neutral) insulins

Unmodified or neutral insulins are short acting but are not identical. Human *actrapid* has an onset 30 min after injection with a peak onset at 2–4 h and a duration of up to 6–8 h; human *velosulin* has a similar onset and duration but an earlier peak effect. All the soluble formulations require a 20–30 min interval between injecting and eating to be effective.

Table 105.4 Suggested aims of treatment

Fasting blood glucose	<7 mmol/L
HbA1c	<7.2% (or <6.5% in those with significant complications)
Blood pressure	<140/80 mmHg
Body mass index	20–25 ideally
Home monitoring	Capillary blood glucose estimations fasting, pre-meal, 2 h postprandially and pre bed. These will need to be frequent enough to allow alterations in treatment and assessment of adequate control. Often adequate with 3x week in stable type 2 patients and daily in stable type 1 patients.

Table 105.5 Insulin: summary

Type of insulin	Examples	Peak activity (h)	Duration of action (h)
Insulin analogue	Humalog (insulin lispro)	0.5–1.5	<6
	Insulin Aspart (NovoRapid)		
Short acting	Human Actrapid	1–3	<8
	Humulin S		
Intermediate acting	Human Insulatard		
	Humulin I		
	Human Monotard		
	Humulin Zn	4–8	<24
Long acting	Human Ultratard	6–24	<36

Insulin analogues

Insulin *lispro* (Humalog) and Insulin *Aspart* (NovoRapid) have been modified to allow injecting and eating to occur simultaneously as they have a more rapid onset of action and earlier peak effect with peak blood insulin level approximately 1.5–2.5 times that from the same dose of standard neutral human insulin. The duration of action is also shorter at 5 h and this may cause problems if there are long gaps between meals.

A long-acting analogue (Insulin Glargine) is available in parts of Europe and the USA and will soon be available in the U.K.

Intermediate acting (isophane) insulins

Insulin action can be extended by addition of protamine or zinc to give an isophane insulin with an onset of action 1–2 h after injection, a peak at 4–6 h, and a duration of action of 8–14 h. Different preparations have slightly different profiles when looking at peak effect and maximal insulin concentrations as with soluble preparations.

Long acting insulins

Insulin to which only zinc is added such as human ultratard or Humulin Zn can have an even later onset of action of 4 h, peak at 6–18 h, and last up to 24–36 h.

Biphasic/mixed insulins

Combinations of soluble/neutral and isophane insulins are now extremely popular. The amount of soluble insulin present varies from 10 to 50%, 30% being the most popular. Depending on its monocomponents onset is normally at 30 min, peak effect 2–6 h, and duration 8–12 h. Insulin analogue biphasic preparations are also available with an onset, peak, and duration all slightly shorter than these.

Insulin regimes

Twice daily free mixing

Historically very popular with 2/3 isophane, 1/3 soluble, and 2/3 of both pre-breakfast and 1/3 pre-evening meal. The main problems are mixing them, and pre lunch hypos or hyperglycaemia. If on the same doses twice daily look out for pre-evening meal hyperglycaemia and increase the morning isophane dose to compensate for this, with a reduction in the morning soluble often needed to reduce pre-lunch hypoglycaemia.

Twice daily fixed mixture

Most commonly a 30% soluble/70% isophane mixture but, although this is not ideal for pre-lunch control or alterations in diet and exercise that are not preplanned, it is indicated in type 2 patients with poor control, those with significant osmotic symptoms and those in whom there is no room to increase oral agents. A suitable starting regimen is a 30/70 mixture with 2/3 pre-breakfast and 1/3 pre-evening meal. The exact doses tend to vary widely depending on insulin sensitivity but a reasonable starting regimen may be 10–15 units pre-breakfast and 5–10 units pre-evening meal.

Basal bolus regime

Soluble insulin or an insulin analogue given 3x day pre-meal with a pre-bed isophane; potentially has more flexibility with meal times, portions, and exercise than the previous regimens. The larger number of injections and the more frequent capillary blood glucose measurements needed makes it less popular with some patients.

If starting as the first type of insulin give three equal pre-meal doses and alter as required, e.g. 4–6 units is a reasonable starting dose, with 6–8 units of isophane pre-bed. If converting from a 2× day regimen reduce the total daily insulin dose by up to 10% and give 30–50% of the remainder as the bedtime isophane and split the rest evenly between the meals. Once the patient is on this regimen the evening isophane often needs to be increased to maintain adequate fasting sugars.

In patients on insulin analogues, and less often those on standard soluble insulins, a 2x daily isophane is occasionally needed especially if there is a long gap between lunch and the evening meal.

Continuous s/c insulin infusion (CSII)

Used in the USA but not commonly in the UK because of potential problems with pump failure, ketoacidosis, and cannula site infections. Soluble insulin is given continuously via a s/c cannula into the anterior abdomen.

Insulin and oral agent mixtures

In type 2 patients several combinations are occasionally used. The two most popular are bedtime insulin + daytime tablets, or more frequent insulin + metformin. In the first, oral agents continue during the day with a pre-bed isophane used to give acceptable fasting sugars pre-breakfast. Although often starting at 10 units/night, doses 5–6 times that are not infrequently needed. This regimen is complicated but is suitable if someone else such as a district nurse or relative gives the insulin. The second regimen adds up to 2 g/day of metformin to any standard insulin regimen to reduce insulin requirements and improve control without the problem of further weight gain often seen if the insulin is continually increased.

Further reading

Alberti KGMM, Gries FA *et al.* A desktop guide for the management of non-insulin dependent diabetes mellitus (NIDDM): an update. *Diabetic Medicine* 1994; 11: 899–909.

ADA position statement. Nutrition recommendations and principles for people with diabetes mellitus. *Diabetes Care* 1994; 17: 519–522.

Bailey CJ, Turner RC. Metformin. *New England Journal of Medicine* 1996; 334: 574–579.

Campbell IW. Efficacy and limitations of sulfonyureas and metformin. In: Bailey CJ, Flatt PR, eds. *New antidiabetic drugs.* Nishimura, Japan: Smith-Gordon, 1990: 33–51.

Diabetes and Nutrition Study Group of the European Association for the Study of Diabetes. Recommendations for the nutritional management of patients with diabetes mellitus. *Diabetes Nutrition and Metabolism* 1995; 8(3): 186–189.

Ratner RE. Rational insulin management of insulin-dependent diabetes. In Leslie RDG, Robbins DE, eds. *Diabetes: clinical science in practice.* Cambridge: Cambridge University Press, 1995:434–49.

UK Prospective Diabetes Study (UKPDS) Group. Intensive blood-glucose control with sulfonylureas or insulin compared with conventional treatment and risk of complications in patients with type 2 diabetes (UKPDS 33) *Lancet* 1998; 352: 837–853.

UK Prospective Diabetes Study (UKPDS) Group. Effect of intensive blood-glucose control with metformin on complications in overweight patients with type 2 diabetes (UKPDS 34) *Lancet* 1998; 352: 854–865.

Chapter 106

Diabetic eye disease

Epidemiology

Diabetic retinopathy remains the commonest cause of blindness in the working population of developed countries. Currently 2% of the UK diabetic population are thought to be registered blind, giving a person with diabetes a 10–20-fold increased risk of blindness. It is suggested that 84 000 of the 7.8 million diabetic North Americans will develop proliferative retinopathy each year and another 95 000 macular oedema.

The prevalence of diabetic retinopathy depends on the duration of diabetes, glycaemic control, blood pressure control and the racial mix of the group being examined, but about a 30% prevalence for a general diabetic population is often quoted.

In type 1 patients <2% have any lesions of diabetic retinopathy at diagnosis and only 8% have any features of it by 5 years (2% proliferative), but 87–98% have abnormalities 30 years later, 30% of these having had proliferative retinopathy. In type 2 patients 20–37% can be expected to have retinopathy at diagnosis and 15 years later 85% of those on insulin and 60% of those not taking will have abnormalities.

The 4 year incidence for proliferative retinopathy in a large North American epidemiological study was 10.5% in type 1 patients, 7.4% in older onset/type 2 patients taking insulin, and 2.3% in those not on insulin. In the UK currently maculopathy is a more common and therefore more significant sight-threatening complication of diabetes. It is suggested that 75% of those with maculopathy have type 2 diabetes and that there is a 4 year incidence of 10.4% in this group. Although type 2 patients are 10 times more likely to have maculopathy than type 1 patients, 14% of type 1 patients who become blind do so because of maculopathy.

Diabetic retinopathy, like many microvascular complications, is more common in the ethnic minorities than in Caucasians. It should also be remembered that cataracts are more common in people with diabetes and are actually the most common eye abnormality seen. These occur in up to 60% of 30–54 year olds. Other abnormalities to look for include vitreous changes such as asteroid hyalosis which occur in about 2% of patients. These are are small spheres or star-shaped opacities seen in the vitreous which appear to sparkle when illuminated under an examining light and do not normally affect vision.

Classification and features of diabetic retinopathy

- background retinopathy
  - microaneurysms
  - haemorrhages
  - hard exudates
- preproliferative retinopathy
  - soft exudates/cotton wool spots
  - intra-retinal abnormalities (IRMAs)
  - venous abnormalities (e.g. venous beading, looping, and reduplication)
- proliferative retinopathy
  - new vessels on the disc or within 1 disc diameter of it (NVD)
  - new vessels elsewhere (NVE)
  - rubeosis iridis (± neovascular glaucoma)
- maculopathy
  - haemorrhages and hard exudates in the macula area
  - reduced visual acuity with no abnormality seen

Clinical features and histological features

The classification of diabetic retinopathy is based on ophthalmoscopic examination but several other changes not seen macroscopically may explain some of these clinical findings.

One of the first histological changes seen is thickening of the capillary basement membrane and loss of the pericytes embedded in it. Both have been linked to hyperglycaemia in experimental models, with sorbitol accumulation and advanced glycation both having a role. In normal retinal capillaries there is a 1 : 1 relationship between endothelial cells and pericytes. Pericytes may control endothelial cell proliferation, maintain the structural integrity of capillaries, and regulate blood flow. Altering these roles, along with the increased blood viscosity, abnormal fibrinolytic activity, and reduced red cell deformity also seen in diabetes may lead to capillary occlusion, tissue hypoxia, and the stimulus for new vessel formation. Exactly how locally produced growth factors, altered protein kinase C, alterations in oxidative stress responses, and alterations in the autoregulation of retinal blood flow combine to cause this remains unclear but is avidly debated.

The natural progression is from background to preproliferative/premaculopathy then to proliferative retinopathy/maculopathy, and ultimately sight-threatening disease.

Background retinopathy

Capillary microaneurysms are the earliest feature seen clinically, as red 'dots'. Small intraretinal haemorrhages or 'blots' also occur, as can haemorrhage into the nerve fibre layer which are often more flame shaped. With increased capillary leakage hard exudates, which are lipid deposits, can also be seen.

Preproliferative retinopathy

A *cotton wool spot* is an infarct in the nerve fibre layer which alters axoplasmic transport in ganglion cell neurones giving an oedematous infarct seen as a pale/grey fuzzy edged lesion, which gives it its name. Intraretinal microvascular abnormalities (IRMAs) are tortuous dilated hypercellular capillaries in the retina which occur in response to retinal ischaemia. A further change seen is alternating dilatation and constriction of veins (venous beading) and other venous alterations such as duplication and loop formation. Overall there are large areas of capillary non-perfusion occurring in the absence of new vessels.

The Early Treatment of Diabetic Retinopathy Study (ETDRS) suggested that certain of these features matter and suggested a '4–2–1' rule:

- 4 quadrants of severe haemorrhages or microaneurysms
- 2 quadrants of IRMAs
- 1 quadrant with venous beading.

If you have one of these features there is a 15% risk of developing sight-threatening retinopathy within the next year; if two are present the risk rises to 45%.

Proliferative retinopathy

New vessels are formed from the retina and can grow along, into, or out from it. A scaffolding for fibrosis then forms. There are two forms of new vessels: those on the disc or within one disc diameter of the disc (NVD) and new vessels elsewhere (NVE). Both give no symptoms but cause the problems of advanced retinopathy such as haemorrhage, scar tissue formation, traction on the retina, and retinal detachment which actually results in loss of vision. That is why panretinal photocoagulation, which can result in the regression of these new vessels, is used when they are seen.

Diabetic maculopathy

Oedema in the macula area can distort central vision and reduce visual acuity. Any of the above changes can co-exist with maculopathy. The changes seen can be:

- oedematous (clinically it may just be difficult to focus on the macula with a hand-held ophthalmoscope)
- exudative (with haemorrhages, hard exudates, and circinate exudates)
- ischaemic (capillary loss occurs but clinically the macula may look normal on direct ophthalmoscopy but unperfused area will show up on fluorescein angiography)
- any combination of these.

A ring or circinate pattern of lipid deposits suggest a focal defect which may be treated with focal laser therapy, whereasa more diffuse problem may require more extensive treatment with a macula grid of laser.

Eye screening

As so many patients can expect to develop eye complications, some of these are sight threatening, and treatment can reduce this, a suitable screening programme is advisable. Patients with diabetes should undergo ophthalmic examination eyes at least once a year. A full examination should include the following.

Visual acuity

Use a standard Snellen chart for distance and check each eye separately. Let the patient wear their glasses for the test and if vision is worse than 6/9 also check with a pinhole as this will correct for any refractive (glasses) error. If it does not correct to 6/9 or better consider more careful review; some maculopathy changes cannot be seen easily with a hand-held ophthalmoscope and an ophthalmology review may be needed. Cataracts are a more likely cause, so look carefully at the red reflex. If vision gets worse with a pinhole, assume maculopathy is there until proven otherwise.

High blood glucose readings can give myopia (difficulty in distance vision) and low blood glucose hypermetropia (difficulty in reading), although this is not universal.

Eye examination

- Dilate the pupil before looking into the eye.
  - Use *tropicamide* 1% in most cases as it dilates the pupil adequately in 15–20 min and lasts only 2–3 h.
  - In those with a dark iris you may also need *phenylephrine* (2.5%) added soon after the tropicamide to give adequate views.
  - The main reasons not to dilate are closed angle glaucoma and recent eye surgery but, as such patients are usually under an eye clinic already, most people are suitable for dilatation.
  - 1% *pilocarpine* drops can be used (although not routinely) if acuity is >6/12 after dilatation. They may speed up reversal and allow driving sooner.
- Once the pupil is dilated, look at the red reflex to check for lens opacities. Examine the anterior chamber, as although rare, rubeosis iridis is important to pick up. The vitreous is examined before examining the retina. When examining the retina use the optic disc as a landmark, follow all four arcades of vessels out from it, examine the periphery, and at the end examine the macula as this can be uncomfortably bright through a dilated pupil and if done at the

start makes it difficult for anyone to keep their eye still enough to complete the examination adequately.

Retinal photographs

It is said that although consultant diabetologists are more accurate than GPs, they still miss some cases of retinopathy when compared to the gold standard of an ophthalmologist. One way to reduce the 'false negative' rate for a screening programme is to use retinal photography as well as ophthalmoscopy. Over 90% of people can have good quality photos performed. This is usually done with 35 mm slide film although digital images are now of sufficiently good quality, require a less intense flash, and avoid the delay of having to develop film. The photographs/images obtained should then be graded/assessed by a trained observer.

When to refer

The physician performing eye screening will need good links with an interested ophthalmologist. Referral will depend on local preferences, but consider the timing and need for referral discussed in the table below.

Reasons for and timing of referral to ophthalmologist

- immediate referral
  - proliferative retinopathy, as untreated NVD carries a 40% risk of blindness in <2 years and laser treatment reduces this
  - rubeosis iridis/neovascular glaucoma
  - vitreous haemorrhage
  - advanced retinopathy with fibrous tissue or retinal detachments
- early referral (<6 weeks)
  - preproliferative changes
  - maculopathy, both for non-proliferative retinopathy involving the macula or for any haemorrhages/hard exudates within 1 disc diameter of the fovea
  - fall of >2 lines on a Snellen chart (whatever fundoscopy shows)

routine referral

- cataracts
- non-proliferative retinopathy with large circinate exudates not threatening the macula/fovea

Treatment

Glycaemic control

There is good epidemiological evidence for an association between poor glycaemic control and worsening of retinopathy. The Diabetes Control and Complications Trial (DCCT) looked at intensive glycaemic control in type 1 patients over 6.5 years and showed a 76% reduction in the risk of initially developing retinopathy in the tight glycaemic group compared to the control group. The rate of progression of existing retinopathy was slowed by 54% and the risk of developing severe non-proliferative or proliferative retinopathy was reduced by 47%. The UKPDS looked at type 2 patients over a 9 year period and showed a 21% reduction in progression of retinopathy and a 29% reduction in the need for laser therapy. The long term benefits of improved glycaemic control are therefore clear.

However, the DCCT, the UKPDS, and several previous studies also showed an initial worsening of retinopathy in the first 2 years in the tight/improved glycaemic control groups, and all patients therefore need careful monitoring over this period. The long term benefits outweigh this initial risk.

Blood pressure control/therapy

There is good evidence for an association between both systolic and diastolic hypertension and retinopathy in type 1 patients, but the link may only be with systolic hypertension in type 2 patients. The UKPDS looked at blood pressure control in type 2 patients and showed that the treatment group, with a mean BP of 144/82 mmHg, when compared to the control group which had a mean of 154/87 mmHg, had a 35% reduction in the need for laser therapy. Adequate BP control, e.g. <140/80 in type 2 patients, is therefore advocated.

Using antiotensin converting enzyme inhibitors (ACEIs) as first line therapy is also suggested. Experimental evidence suggests these agents may have antiangiogenic effects by altering local growth factor levels as well as any benefit from reducing blood pressure. Studies using *enalapril* and *lisinopril* have both shown a reduction in the progression of retinopathy in type 1 patients.

Lipid control/therapy

Experimental evidence suggests oxidized low-density lipoprotein (LDL)-cholesterol may be cytotoxic for endothelial cells. Epidemiological data also suggests an association between higher LDL-cholesterol and worse diabetic retinopathy, especially maculopathy with exudates. A total cholesterol >7.0 mmol/L gives a fourfold greater risk of proliferative retinopathy than a total cholesterol <5.3 mmol/L. A worse outcome from laser therapy in those treated for maculopathy has also been seen if hyperlipidaemia is present. Aggressive lipid lowering is therefore advocated, especially in maculopathy.

Antiplatelet therapy

In view of the altered rheological properties of diabetic patients these agents have been tried, but the results are variable. No evidence that they make things worse has been shown, and some studies suggest *aspirin* and *ticlopidine* may slow the progression of retinopathy although the benefit was small.

Lifestyle advice

Although stopping smoking reduces macrovascular risk its effect on retinopathy is less clear. Alcohol consumption and physical activity also show no consistent effect.

Risk factors for developing/worsening of diabetic retinopathy

- duration of diabetes
- type of diabetes (proliferative disease is more common in type 1 and maculopathy in type 2)
- poor diabetic control
- hypertension
- diabetic nephropathy
- recent cataract surgery
- pregnancy
- alcohol (variable results which may be related to the type of alcohol involved, e.g. worse in Scotland than Italy)
- smoking (variable results but appears worse in young people with exudates and older women with proliferative disease)

Surgical treatment

Laser treatment

- Up to 1500–7000 separate burns, of 100–500 μm diameter, each taking about 0.1 s to apply, are needed for panretinal or 'scatter' laser photocoagulation. For oedematous/exudative maculopathy a macula grid may use only 100–200 burns of 100–200 μm diameter separated by 200–400 μm gaps, avoiding the fovea. The ETDRS (Early Treatment Diabetic Retinopathy Study) showed laser therapy was better than no treatment in all visual acuity subgroups, with a 24% blindness rate at 3 years in the non-treated eyes compared to a 12% rate in the treated group.
- Laser therapy is usually performed as 3–4 sessions of outpatient treatment on conscious patients. Topical local anaesthetic drops allow a contact lens to be placed on the cornea and are often all that is needed. In some patients, however, as this procedure may be slightly uncomfortable, a retro-orbital injection (performed through the inside of the lower eyelid) can be given to anaesthetize the eye.
- The laser energy is absorbed by the choroid and the pigment epithelium which lie below the neurosensory layer which also absorbs the energy/heat and is destroyed.
- In patients with severe proliferative retinopathy, pan-retinal photocoagulation reduces visual loss (i.e. an acuity >1/60 or worse) by over 80% while a macula grid reduces visual loss in maculopathy by over 50%.
- Laser treatment aims to prevent further visual loss, especially in maculopathy, not to restore vision, and the distinction must be emphasized to all patients requiring treatment. The benefits from laser therapy currently outweigh the risks, which include accidental burns to the fovea if the eye moves during therapy, a reduction in night vision and, in a small number, interference with visual field severe enough to effect the ability to drive.

Vitrectomy

If the vitreous contains scar tissue, haemorrhage, or any opacity, a vitrectomy to remove it may help restore vision and allows the chance for intraoperative laser treatment or a better view for postoperative laser therapy. It can also help reduce retinal traction and allows retinal reattachment to be performed. A success rate at restoring vision of 70% is seen but the risk of worsening vision, detaching the retina, or worsening lens opacities should also be consider.

Cataract extraction

This is a common procedure with a slightly higher complication rate than in the non-diabetic population. Approximately 15% of patients undergoing a cataract extraction can be expected to have diabetes. A large lens implant should be considered, especially if laser therapy is going to be needed subsequently. Worsening of maculopathy after cataract extraction is also a risk which needs careful monitoring.

Useful addresses

Action for Blind People, 14–16 Verney Road, London SE16 3DZ. Tel: 020 7732 8771

Partially Sighted Society, Queen's Road, Doncaster DN1 2NX. Tel: 01302 323132

Royal National Institute for the Blind, 224 Great Portland Street, London, W1N 6AA. Tel: 020 7388 1266

Further reading

British Multi-Centre Study Group. Photocoagulation for diabetic maculopathy. *Diabetes* 1983; 32: 1010–1016.

Early Treatment Diabetic Retinopathy Study Research Group. *Archives of Ophthalmology* 1985; 103: 1796–1806.

Chapter 107
Diabetic renal disease

Background

Diabetic nephropathy is now a major cause of premature death in patients with all types of diabetes. Approximately 1/6 patients entering most renal replacement programs in developed countries will now have diabetes, at least 50% having type 2 diabetes.

Definition

Diabetic nephropathy is defined as albuminuria (albumin excretion rate >300 mg/24 h, which equates to a 24 h urinary protein >0.5 g) and declining renal function in a patient with known diabetes who does not have a urinary tract infection, heart failure, or any other renal disease. This is usually associated with systemic hypertension, diabetic retinopathy, or neuropathy, and in the absence of these the diagnosis needs to be carefully evaluated.

Epidemiology

Microalbuminuria has a prevalence of 6–60% of patients with type 1 diabetes, after 5–15 years duration of diabetes. Diabetic nephropathy will occur in up to 35% of patients with type 1 diabetes, more commonly in men and in those diagnosed under 15 years of age with a peak incidence approaching 3%/year 16–20 years after onset of diabetes. Of those type 1 patients who develop proteinuria 2/3 will subsequently develop renal failure. In the UK 15% of all deaths in diabetic patients <50 years old are due to nephropathy.

In type 2 patients there are more obvious racial differences, with up to 25% of Caucasians and 50% of Asians expected to develop nephropathy giving a prevalence in a general clinic of 4–33%. The duration of diabetes before development of clinical nephropathy is also often shorter in type 2 than in type 1 patients. This may be due to an initial delay in diagnosis of type 2 diabetes.

Table 107.1 Definitions

Proteinuria	Urinary protein >0.5 g/24 h
Albuminuria	Urinary albumin excretion rate > 300 mg/24 h or >200 μg/min
Microalbuminuria	Urinary albumin excretion rate 30–300 mg/day or 20–200 μg/min

Making the diagnosis

A urine positive on dip testing for protein (i.e. >0.5 mg/L protein or >300 mg/L albumin) suggests diabetic nephropathy. A timed urine collection either overnight or over 24 h will confirm proteinuria or albuminuria, but other causes of proteinuria must be excluded before labelling this diabetic nephropathy. Proteinuria from non-diabetic renal disease occurs in up to 10% of type 1 and 30% of type 2 patients. Urinary tract infections, acute illness, heavy exercise, and cardiac failure are the most common causes to exclude. The absence of hypertension or diabetic retinopathy would also question the diagnosis, and confirmation from a renal biopsy may be required.

If the urine is standard dip test negative for albumin, microalbuminuria should be looked for. The implementation group for the St Vincent Declaration recommend that all patients with negative protein on conventional urinalysis are annually screened for microalbuminuria. A urinary albumin : creatinine ratio >2.5 mg/mmol in men and >3.5 mg/mmol in women or a positive urine dip test (urine albumin >20 μg) should be followed by a timed urine collection repeated three times with at least two abnormal.

Pathology

Although macroscopically there is an increase in kidney size, microscopically there is thickening of the glomerular basement membrane, expansion of glomerular supporting tissues (the mesangium) and fibrotic changes in both efferent and afferent arterioles. If localized this is termed *nodular glomerular sclerosis* (Kimmelsteil–Wilson nodules) and if more widespread, *diffuse glomerular sclerosis.*

The thickened basement membrane initially results in an alteration in its electrical charge but not in pore size, which allows increased passage of albumin into the glomerular ultrafiltrate seen clinically as microalbuminuria.

False positives for microalbuminuria

- exercise
- urinary tract infection
- menstruation
- semen.

Pathogenesis

Hyperglycaemia

As with all microvascular diabetic complications, hyperglycaemia has been implicated in the pathogenesis of diabetic nephropathy via metabolic alterations. The DCCT showed a reduction in the development of microalbuminuria in patients with better glycaemic control, which would support this. The UK PDS showed similar improvements. These metabolic alterations may be due to sorbitol accumulation from the polyol pathway, due to the accumulation of advanced glycation end-products (AGE) or to an as yet unknown mechanism.

AGE have been linked to the extracellular matrix accumulation known to occur in nephropathy. The use of aminoguanidine to block renal AGE accumulation and an associated slowing in the progression of albuminuria and mesangial expansion would support their role in the pathogenesis of nephropathy. The evidence for the polyol pathway's importance comes from aldose reductase inhibitor trials, the results of which are more variable. Ongoing studies (e.g. Action 1 and Action 2 for aminoguanidine) will examine whether any agents are useful clinically.

Haemodynamic alterations

Increased intraglomerular pressures can be associated with elevations in systemic blood pressure (85% of type 1 patients with nephropathy are hypertensive), increased vasoactive hormones (e.g. angiotensin-II, endothelin) or altered levels of specific growth factors (e.g. TGF-β, IGF-I, and VEGF). Hormonal and growth factor alterations have been suggested as important in the initial hyperfiltration phase seen in type 1 patients who progress to nephropathy, and a role for angiotensin-II in the accumulation of extracellular matrix has also been postulated. Whether these changes are secondary to or independent of hyperglycaemia is not certain.

Genetic predisposition

There is an increase in red blood cell sodium–lithium countertransport activity in nephropathic patients and their parents in some populations, and an increased incidence of hypertension in the relatives of diabetic patients with nephropathy. An association between nephropathy and polymorphisms of the ACE gene has also been noted.

Smoking

A consistent link between cigarette smoking and nephropathy has been known for some time, but an aetiological mechanism is not yet known.

Natural history

In 20–40% of type 1 diabetic patients there is initially a period of glomerular hyperfiltration. The first sign of nephropathy, however, is microalbuminuria, usually occurring 5–15 years after the onset of type 1 diabetes but possibly present at the time of diagnosis in type 2 diabetes. Associated with this is often the development of hypertension, a reduction in high-density lipoprotein (HDL)-cholesterol and an increase in LDL-cholesterol and triglycerides.

This progresses to the next stage of frank proteinuria or albuminuria, which has a peak incidence ~17 years after the diagnosis of type 1 diabetes. This is the start of overt nephropathy, as in both type 1 and type 2 patients an approximate 10 ml min^{-1} 1.73 m^{-2} reduction in glomerular filtration rate occurs each year once the albumin excretion rate has reached 300 mg/day, although in some patients the deterioration may be more rapid, and treatment may reduce it. Once serum creatinine concentration reaches 200 μmol/L, a fall of 1 ml/min per month in glomerular filtration rate is then expected. This leads to end-stage renal failure (ESRF) with uraemia and potentially death 7–10 years after onset of albuminuria. A plot of the reciprocal of creatinine against time demonstrates a relatively straight line showing the projected rate of deterioration.

Patients with diabetes and persistent proteinuria/albuminuria have a high mortality, due to cardiovascular disease in 40% of cases. Nephropathy carries a 20–100 times greater mortality than in age-matched diabetic patients without proteinuria.

Risk factors for development of microalbuminuria

- duration of diabetes
- poor long term glycaemic control
- hypertension
- dyslipidaemia
- hyperfiltration
- parents with renal disease.

Treatment

Treatment options for ESRF are either renal dialysis (haemodialysis or ambulatory peritoneal dialysis) or renal transplantation, but life expectancy with either is no better than with some common malignancies. Several other therapies can, however, delay the progression to this stage.

Blood pressure

Controlling hypertension reduces the progression to microalbuminuria and from this to albuminuria and subsequent progression to ESRF. Blood pressure should be reduced to <130/85 mmHg with avoidance of hypotension, although if proteinuria is >1 g/day a better target is <120/75 mmHg. Weight loss, alcohol restriction, and reduced salt intake help, but drugs are usually needed to achieve this.

Studies show benefits from β-blockers, frusemide, hydralazine, and calcium channel blockers, but the ACEIs are currently the preferred first line agent in both microalbuminuric and albuminuric patients as they also have an effect on kidney function independent of their hypotensive action. Several studies suggest, however, that more than one agent will be required to control BP adequately.

Large studies with several ACEIs have confirmed their benefit in hypertensive patients by delaying the progression of microalbuminuria to albuminuria and then to ESRF. There is no documented benefit in treating normotensive patients without microalbuminuria. *Captopril* (50 mg 2× day) for 2 years in type 1 patients with microalbuminuria reduced progression to albuminuria by 68%. *Enalapril* (10 mg daily) given to type 2 patients with microalbuminuria for 5 years reduced progression to albuminuria by 67%. When used for 4 years in type 1 patients with nephropathy, captopril (50 mg 2× day) reduced the risk of death, dialysis, and transplantation by 50% and slowed the reduction in creatinine clearance.

The EUCLID study looked at treating normotensive microalbuminuric type 1 patients. In this study *lisinopril* reduced the albumin excretion rate by nearly 20% compared to placebo but there was a 3 mmHg lower blood pressure in the treatment group. From this it is suggested that normotensive type 1 patients be treated with an ACEIs. An *enalapril* study in normotensive type 2 patients showed similar results.

Glycaemic control

Correction of hyperglycaemia can reverse glomerular basement membrane thickening and mesangial changes. Studies looking at progression to microalbuminuria and subsequent progression to frank albuminuria (e.g. the Steno 1 and II Studies, the KROC Study) also suggest a clinical benefit from improving glycaemic control. In the DCCT tight glycaemic control of type 1 patients was shown to reduce progression to microalbuminuria by 30% and subsequent progression to albuminuria by 54%. Not all trials confirm this (e.g. the Microalbuminuria Collaborative Study Group Trial and the UK PDS) and not all patients with good control in the above trials gained benefit.

Even so, the current treatment aim is to normalize or significantly reduce HbA1c (<7.2%) while avoiding any weight gain or hypoglycaemia associated with the increased used of both oral agents and insulin needed to do so.

Dietary protein restriction

High dietary protein can damage the kidney by increasing renal blood flow and intraglomerular pressures in experimental situations. For microalbuminuric type 1 patients reducing dietary animal protein intake in small studies appears to reduce both hyperfiltration and micralbuminuriam, and the benefit in more severe renal impairment is more evident. In type 2 patients the UK PDS showed an initial reduction in microalbuminuria with dietary modification which may in part be related to protein reduction. A dietary protein content <0.8 g/kg is suggested.

Lipid lowering

Although diabetic nephropathy is not shown to reduce the progression of microalbuminuria to albuminuria or renal failure, these patients have a significant dyslipidaemia and a high cardiovascular mortality and require careful lipid monitoring and aggressive treatment. The use of aspirin for similar reasons is also advisable.

Further reading

Ahmad J, Siddiqui MA, Ahmad H. Effective postponement of diabetic nephropathy in normotensive type 2 diabetic patients with microalbuminuria. *Diabetes Care* 1997; 20: 1576–1581.

Diabetes Control and Complications Trial Research Group. The effect of intensive treatment of diabetes on the development of microvascular complications of DM. *New England Journal of Medicine* 1993; 329: 304–309.

Diabetes Control and Complications Trial Research Group. Effect of intensive therapy on the development and progression of diabetic nephropathy in the DCCT. *Kidney International* 1995; 42: 1703–1720.

EUCLID Study Group. Randomized placebo-controlled trial of lisinopril in normotensive patients with insulin-dependent diabetes and normoalbuminuria or microalbuminuria. *Lancet* 1997; 349: 1787–1792.

Laffel LMB, McGill JB, Dans DJ on behalf of the North American Microalbuminuria Study Group. The beneficial effect of angiotensin converting enzyme inhibition with captopril on diabetic nephropathy in normotensive IDDM patients with microalbuminuria. *American Journal of Medicine* 1995; 99: 497–504.

Lewis EJ, Hunsicker LG, Bain RP, Rohde RD for the Collaborative Group. The effect of angiotensin converting enzyme inhibition on diabetic nephropathy. *New England Journal of Medicine* 1993; 329: 1456–1462.

Microalbuminuria Captopril Study Group. Captopril reduces the risk of nephropathy in IDDM patients with microalbuminuria. *Diabetologia* 1996; 39: 587–593.

Ravid M, Brosch D, Levi Z *et al.* Use of enalapril to attenuate decline in renal function in normotensive, normalbuminuric patients with type 2 DM. *Annals of Internal Medicine* 1998; 128: 982–988.

UK Prospective Diabetes Study Group. Intensive blood glucose control with sulphonylureas or insulin compared with conventional treatment and risk of complications in patients with type 2 diabetes (UKPDS 33). *Lancet* 1998; 352: 837–853.

UK Prospective Diabetes Study Group. Tight blood pressure control and risk of macrovascular and microvascular complications in type 2 diabetes: UKPDS 38. *BMJ* 1998; 317: 703–713.

UK Prospective Diabetes Study Group. Efficacy of atenolol and captopril in reducing risk of macrovascular and microvascular complications in type 2 diabetes: UKPDS 39. *BMJ* 1998; 317: 713–720.

Chapter 108

Diabetic neuropathy

Involvement of cranial, peripheral, and autonomic nerves may be found in patients with diabetes, and termed diabetic neuropathy; this usually suggests a diffuse, predominantly sensory peripheral neuropathy. The effects on nerve function can be both acute or chronic as well as being transient or permanent. The consequences of neuropathy include:

- neuropathic ulcers, usually on the feet
- Charcot arthropathy
- altered sensation (both pain and increased sensitivity to normal sensation)
- impotence (with autonomic neuropathy).

Pathology

Diabetic neuropathy is one of the microvascular complications of diabetes. Pathologically distal axonal loss occurs with focal demyelination and attempts at nerve regeneration. The vasa nervorum often shows basement membrane thickening, endothelial cell changes, and some occlusion of its lumen. This results in slowing of nerve conduction velocities or a complete loss of nerve function. Both metabolic and vascular changes have been implicated in its aetiology.

Classification of diabetic neuropathies

- sensory neuropathy
  - acute
  - chronic
- autonomic neuropathy
- mononeuropathy
  - entrapment neuropathy
  - external pressure palsies
  - spontaneous mononeuropathy
- proximal motor neuropathy (diabetic amyotrophy)

Pathogenesis

Hyperglycaemia is probably the underlying cause of the histological and functional changes. Several possible mechanisms have been suggested:

- Overloading of the normal pathways for glucose metabolism resulting in increased use of the polyol pathway which leads to increased levels of sorbitol and fructose and decreased levels of myoinositol and glutathione. This may result in more free radical damage and also lowers nitric oxide levels, so altering nerve blood flow. Experimental models using aldose reductase inhibitors which can improve some aspects of diabetic neuropathy add some weight to this theory.
- Possible accumulation of AGE (via non-enzymatic glycation) may also have a role to play, as could the hypercoagulable state and altered blood rheology known to occur in all patients with diabetes. Aminoguanidine, which blocks AGE formation, when used in animal studies can increased both nerve conduction velocities and nerve blood flow in diabetic subjects, strengthening the role of AGE accumulation in this process.
- In the more acute neuropathies, acute ischaemia of the nerves due to vascular abnormalities has been suggested as the cause but again the underlying reason why this should occur is still unclear. Insulin-induced 'neuritis' may occur when insulin therapy is started and blood glucose levels fall.
- Other potential aetiological factors include changes in local growth factor production and oxidative stress.

Further work is needed to clarify the exact role of each of the above mechanisms. In the meantime, studies showing improvements in neuropathy associated with good diabetic control strengthen the argument for the role of hyperglycaemia and offers us one treatment option while we await other therapies.

Peripheral sensorimotor neuropathy

Although hyperglycaemia can alter nerve function and often gives some sensory symptoms at diagnosis, correcting the hyperglycaemia can often resolve these. Chronic sensorimotor neuropathy, on the other hand, is the most common feature of peripheral nerve involvement seen in patients with diabetes. The exact prevalence of diabetic neuropathy varies in most studies because of the different definitions and examination techniques used. For example, sensitive nerve conduction studies can show up to 80% of patients have abnormal results. In more normal practice, however, 20–30% of unselected patients can be expected either to have symptomatic neuropathy or have abnormalities on examination which are clinically significant. But at least 50% of these patients are asymptomatic. This will increase with increasing duration of diabetes, so although 7–8% of type 2 patients may have abnormalities at diagnosis, 50% can be expected to have them 25 years later.

Features

- Usually insidious onset with numbness or paraesthesia, often found on screening rather than as a presenting problem.
- Starts in the toes and on the soles of the feet then spreads up to mid shin level, mostly in a symmetrical fashion. Less often it also involves the fingers and hands.
- Affects all sensory modalities and results in reduced vibration perception thresholds, pinprick, fine touch, and temperature sensations.
- Decreased vibration sensation and absent ankle reflexes are often the first features found. Another risk factor for ulceration is inability to feel a 10 g monofilament.
- Less often the skin is tender/sensitive to touch (hyperaesthesia) or frank pain can occur.
- Painful neuropathy affects up to 5% of a general clinic population. This pain may be sharp, stabbing or burning in nature, and at times very severe.
- There may also be some wasting of the intrinsic muscles of the foot with clawing of the toes.

Mononeuropathies

Peripheral mononeuropathies and cranial mononeuropathies are not uncommon. These may be spontaneous or may be due to entrapment or external pressure. Of the peripheral mononeuropathies median nerve involvement and carpal tunnel syndrome may be found in up to 10% of patients and require nerve conduction studies and then surgical decompression. Entrapment of the lateral cutaneous nerve of the thigh is also seen more commonly in those with diabetes, giving pain over the lateral aspect of the thigh. Common peroneal nerve involvement causing foot drop and tarsal tunnel syndrome are also recognized but less common.

Cranial mononeuropathies usually occur suddenly and have a good prognosis. Palsies of cranial nerves III and VI are the most common seen, but these are not a common problem in patients with diabetes. In the IIIrd nerve palsy sparing of the pupillary responses is usual. Spontaneous recover is slow over several months and no treatment apart from symptomatic help such as an eye patch is needed. Unlike entrapment neuropathies where decompression may help, no effective treatment is currently available in most of these cases with spontaneous mononeuropathies.

Proximal motor neuropathy (diabetic amyotrophy)

This is an uncommon but disturbing condition to have, mostly affecting men in their 50s with type 2 diabetes. It presents with severe pain and paraesthesia in the upper legs, and is felt as a deep aching pain which may be burning in nature and can keep patients awake at night, put them off eating, and result in marked cachexia. This, with proximal muscle weakness and wasting of the quadriceps in particular, can be very debilitating. The lumbar sacral plexus lower motor neurones are affected and improvement is usually spontaneous over 3–4 months. Before making this diagnosis, however, consider other causes such as malignancies and lumbar disc disease.

Oral antidiabetic agents may play a part in the aetiology of this problem and conversion to insulin therapy is advised, although the anorexia experienced when the pain is severe can make this difficult. Although recovery happens over a few months only 50% recover fully, but no other treatment is currently known to improve on this.

Examination

- Mandatory at diagnosis and at least yearly in all asymptomatic patients.
- Test vibration, fine touch (with a 10 g monofilament), and reflexes as a minimum. Using a neurothesiometer or biosthesiometer gives a more quantitative measure of vibration than a 128 Hz tuning fork. Inability to feel the vibrating head at >25 V in the toes is associated with a significant risk of neuropathic ulceration and should be considered a sign of 'at risk' feet.

Differential diagnoses

- uraemia
- vitamin B_{12} deficiency
- infections (e.g. HIV and leprosy)
- toxins (e.g. alcohol, lead, mercury)
- malignancy.

Treatment

- *For all patients* Review by a chiropodist and if indicated an orthotist to give education on foot care and suitable footwear is advised. If followed by regular chiropody review this can help prevent some problems developing.
- *Asymptomatic patients* No drugs are yet available, but aldose reductase inhibitors such as *tolrestat* are advocated for this indication by some.
- *Painful neuropathy* Initially try capsaicin 0.075% topically to the affected area, being careful to avoid normal skin because this chili pepper extract, which depletes sensory nerve terminals of substance P, can be uncomfortable when applied to normal skin. It can take several weeks to be effective and may induce tingling and so worsening of symptoms initially. In some patients simple analgesics such as *paracetamol* or opiates such as *tramadol* have been shown to help. In more severe cases tricyclic antidepressants are the first line treatment of choice with *imipramine* 20–100 mg at night being less sedative than *amitriptyline* 25–75 mg. Although newer agents such as *carbamazepine*, *phenytoin*, and *paroxetine* have less anticholinergic effects, they are also not as effective and are therefore used as second line, although recent data for *gabapentin* may buck this trend. If the pain is severe and like an electric shock, anticonvulsants such as *carbamazepine* and *phenytoin* may however be more effective.
- *Hyperaesthesia* Occlusive dressings such as Opsite may prove helpful. For more severe pain, oral agents are needed.

General treatments

Specific treatments for each form of neuropathy have been discussed above, but there is some evidence for more general therapies.

- Poor diabetic control appears to be associated with worsening neuropathy and improving glycaemic control is advocated in any patient, especially if neuropathy is present.
- The use of evening primrose oil in rats and preliminary human studies suggests this may improve some aspects of diabetic neuropathy. The mechanism by which this works is not certain but it does increase production of cyclo-oxygenase-mediated prostanoids such as prostacyclin which could act as a vasodilator and so improve nerve blood supply.
- Other more specific vasodilators have also been examined, with α blockers and ACEIs showing particularly useful results in experimental settings.
- Polyol pathway inhibition with aldose reductase inhibitors and non-enzymatic glycation inhibition with agents such as aminoguanidine are also being examined.
- An alternative approach is not to try to improve the underlying problem but to alter the body's response to it. Nerve growth factor (NGF) and IGF-I have been examined for their ability to cause nerve regeneration and growth, and NGF in particular looks potentially very interesting. Other such agents are also under investigation.

Autonomic neuropathy

The commonest effect of autonomic neuropathy is erectile dysfunction which affects 40% of men with diabetes. Only a small number develop the severe gastrointestinal and bladder dysfunction. The recent interest in *sildenafil* has highlighted this. Abnormal autonomic function tests can be expected in 20–40% of a general diabetic clinic population. The increased problems during surgery from cardiac involvement should be remembered.

Clinical features

- impotence
- postural hypotension (giving dizziness and syncope in up to 12%)
- resting tachycardia or fixed heart rate/loss of sinus arrhythmia (in up to 20%)
- gustatory sweating (sweating after tasting food)
- dysphagia with delayed gastric emptying, nausea/vomiting
- constipation/diarrhoea
- urinary retention/overflow incontinence
- anhidrosis (absent sweating on the feet is especially problematic as it increases the risk of ulceration)
- abnormal pupillary reflexes.

Assessment

At least annually check:

- lying and standing BP (measure systolic BP 2 min after standing; normal is <10 mmHg drop, > 30 mmHg is abnormal)
- pupillary responses to light.

Other less commonly performed tests to consider if the diagnosis is uncertain or in high risk patients include:

- *Loss of sinus arrhythmia* Measure inspiratory and expiratory heart rates after 5 s of each (<10 beats/min difference is abnormal, >15 is normal).
- *Loss of heart rate response to Valsalva manoeuvre* Look at the ratio of the shortest R-R interval during forced expiration against a closed glottis compared to the longest R-R interval after it (<1.2 is abnormal).
- *Blood pressure response to sustained hand grip* Diastolic blood pressure prior to the test is compared to diastolic blood pressure after

5 min of sustaining a grip equivalent to 30% of maximal grip. A diastolic BP rise >16 mmHg is normal, <10 mmHg is abnormal. A rolled up blood pressure cuff to achieve the required hand grip may be used.

- For *gastric symptoms* consider a radioisotope test meal to look for delayed gastric emptying.

Treatment

This is based on the specific symptom and is usually symptomatic only. In all patients improvement in diabetic control is advocated in case any of it is reversible, but this is not usually very helpful or effective.

Postural hypotension

- May be exacerbated by drugs such as diuretics, vasodilators, and tricyclic antidepressants.
- Mechanical measures such as sleeping with the head elevated and wearing support stockings may help.
- Ensure an adequate salt intake.
- *Fludrocortisone* 50 μg once daily initially and increased as required up to 400 μg may be helpful, but beware of hypertension or oedema.
- *Desmopressin* and *octreotide* have also been used.

Impotence (see p. 451)

Libido is not normally affected and pain is also unusual, so look for hypogonadism and Peyronie's if they are present. Autonomic neuropathy is the likely cause but many drugs, especially thiazides and β-blockers, can also cause it, as can alcohol, tobacco, cannabis, and stress. These should be assessed by direct questioning. Examination should include:

- genitalia and secondary sexual characteristics
- peripheral pulses (as vascular insufficiency may play a part)
- lower limb reflexes and vibration thresholds (to confirm that neuropathy is present).

Biochemical screening should at least include:

- prolactin
- testosterone
- gonadotrophins (LH/FSH).

Exacerbating factors such as alcohol and antihypertensive drugs should be modified. The main therapies are:

- *sildenafil* (start at 25–50 mg, increase to 100 mg if needed)

- intraurethral *alprostadil* (start at 125 μg, increase to 250 or 500 μg if needed)
- intracavernosal *alprostadil* (trial dose is 2.5 μg, treatment is 5–40 μg)
- vacuum devices.

None of these is ideal. Sildenafil, although an oral therapy, is effective in only 60% of those with diabetes and is contraindicated with severe heart disease and those on nitrates, which rules many out.

Gastroparesis

Delayed gastric emptying can cause recurrent hypoglycaemic episodes. Promotilic agents can also help. Treatment options:

- *cisapride* (10 mg pre-meals/3–4 × day) – now withdrawn in the UK
- *metoclopramide* (5–10 mg pre-meals/3 × day)
- *domperidone* (10–20 mg pre-meals)
- *erythromycin* (acts as a motilin agonist to increase gastric emptying but may make patients feel nauseated so of limited use)
- surgery (gastric drainage procedures should not be undertaken lightly).

Large bowel involvement

Constipation is treated with standard bulking and softening laxatives. The episodic diarrhoea is more troublesome, and treatment for this may include:

- *loperamide* (2 mg 4× day) or codeine phosphate (30 mg 4× day)
- antibiotics in case of bacterial overgrowth, such as *erythromycin* 250 mg 4× day for 7 days, or tetracycline 250 mg 2× day for 7 days
- other agents such as *clonidine* and *ondansetron* have also shown some benefit.

Neuropathic bladder

Sacral nerve involvement can cause bladder abnormalities with reduced sensations of bladder fullness and increased residual volume after micturition. Regular toileting initially may help but intermittent self-catheterization or a long-term catheter may be required.

Anhidrosis

Dry feet can cause cracks in the skin and act as a site for infection. Emollient creams may help prevent this.

Further reading

Boulton AJM, Gries FA, Jervell LA. Guidelines for the diagnosis and outpatient management of diabetic peripheral neuropathy. *Diabetic Medicine* 1998; 15(6): 508–514.

Chapter 109
Macrovascular disease

People with diabetes have a significantly greater risk of coronary heart disease, cerebrovascular disease, and peripheral vascular disease than the non-diabetic population. Most people with diabetes will die from one of these (75% of patients with Type 2).

Epidemiology

The exact prevalence and incidence of macrovascular disease and its outcomes will vary depending on the age, sex, and ethnic mix of the patients being assessed. In general cardiovascular disease accounts for 75% of deaths in type 2 patients and 35% in type 1 patients. Although the atheroma seen is histologically the same as in a non-diabetic population, it tends to be more diffuse and progresses more rapidly. It also occurs at an earlier age and affects both sexes equally: women therefore seem to lose their natural premenopausal advantage.

- Overall peripheral vascular disease occurs in up to 10% of patients and they have up to 15-fold greater risk of needing a non-traumatic amputation than the non-diabetic population.
- Thromboembolic cerebrovascular events occurs in up to 8%, which is a 2–4-fold increased risk compared to the non-diabetic population and accounts for 15% of deaths in type 2 patients.
- The risk of having a myocardial infarction is also increased 2–4 times. Women seem particularly at risk of cardiovascular disease compared to the non-diabetic population.

Patients with type 1 diabetes have half the rate of coronary heart disease, 1/3 the rate of cerebrovascular disease, and 2/3 the rate of peripheral vascular disease compared to type 2 patients, but their rate of all these is greater than that for the non-diabetic population. Men and women are equally affected, with the incidence rates for ischaemic heart disease about 6 times that of both cerebrovascular and peripheral vascular disease.

Secondary prevention

- stop smoking
- aspirin
- β-blockers
- lipid lowering drugs.

Pathogenesis

Atherosclerosis has a well known set of risk factors, such as smoking and family history, all of which still apply in a diabetic population. Some factors, however, are more common in those with diabetes and may also confer a greater risk to the diabetic population. These include:

- *Glycaemic control* In type 1 patients worsening hyperglycaemia is said to relate to the degree of disease present. In type 2 patients this association is less clear cut, although the UKPDS does suggest this is also the case as better glycaemic control was associated with a trend for fewer myocardial infarctions.
- *Hypertension* More common in both type 1 and type 2 patients and results in vascular endothelial injury so predisposing to atheroma formation. The UKPDS suggests blood pressure control is a more important individual risk factor than glycaemic control.
- *Hyperlipidaemia* Common: e.g. hyperinsulinaemia in insulin-resistant type 2 patients causes reduced HDL-cholesterol, elevated triglycerides (and VLDL), and smaller denser and therefore more atherogenic LDL-cholesterol.
- *Obesity* An independent risk factor, more common in type 2 patients. Central obesity in particular is more atherogenic.
- *Insulin resistance* or elevated circulating insulin/proinsulin-like molecule levels are known to increase the risk of atherosclerosis in both diabetic and non-diabetic populations. This may be linked to impaired endothelial function.
- *Altered coagulability* Circulating fibrinogen, platelet activator inhibitor (PAI)-1 and von Willebrand factor levels are increased and platelets are less deformable. This may be more prothrombotic, but the exact significance remains uncertain.

The UKPDS has shown the major risk factors for coronary heart disease in type 2 patients to be elevated LDL-cholesterol, decreased HDL-cholesterol, hypertension, hyperglycaemia, and smoking. Exactly why these risk factors are commonly seen/linked in the same patient, particularly type 2 diabetic patients, is uncertain. Several hypotheses have been put forward, but none as yet explains them all adequately. However, each suggests an element of genetic susceptibility mixed with environmental effects. A genetic predisposition to insulin resistance, for example, may combine with poor intrauterine nutrition to produce a low birthweight infant with a susceptibility to vascular disease and diabetes later in life. But other factors must be involved. as not all those who later develop diabetes and vascular disease were small at birth.

Lipid abnormalities found in patients with diabetes

Hyperlipidaemia in a patient with diabetes, at any level of cholesterol, is associated with a greater risk of macrovascular disease than in a non-diabetic population. Patients with diabetes may have altered activity of insulin-dependent enzymes such as lipoprotein lipase which results in delayed systemic clearance of certain lipids. This, combined with altered hepatic production of apoprotein-B containing lipoproteins, gives a more atherogenic profile.

Usual findings are of increased triglyceride containing lipoproteins, chylomicrons, and VLDL. Although more common in the insulin-resistant type 2 patients this can also be seen in type 1 patients as can a low HDL-cholesterol (HDL_2 especially). Other atherogenic changes include a tendency to develop small dense LDL cholesterol particles and a greater tendency to oxidative damage which renders them even more atherogenic. Lipoprotein (Lpa) levels are also often raised.

Even so, other common primary causes of hyperlipidaemia, such as familial hypercholesterolaemia or familial combined hyperlipidaemia, should not be missed. Screening for secondary causes of hyperlipidaemia such as hypothyroidism or drug induced (alcohol, thiazides, and β blockers in particular) is also strongly advised.

Management

In all patients the first treatment is dietary modification. In a patient who is actually following a good diabetic diet, however, there is often not much room for improvement.

Other standard advice should also be given:

- stop smoking (reduces risk of death by about 50% over a 15 year period)
- reduce weight if overweight/obese
- increase physical activity.

While the reductions in mortality, re-infarction, and stroke in the major lipid lowering trials such as the 4S study (Scandinavian Simvastatin Survival Study), CARE (Cholesterol and Recurrent Events Trial), LIPID (Long-term Intervention with Pravastatin in Ischaemic Disease), and WOSCOPS (West of Scotland Coronary Prevention Study) are all very impressive, the diabetic subgroups show as good if not better reductions although the numbers in each were relatively small. In 4S, for example, the simvastatin-treated diabetic subgroup (4.5% of those in the study) had a 23% rate of major coronary events

Table 109.1 Lipid reduction studies

	4S	WOSCOP	CARE	LIPID
Type of study	Secondary prevention of CHD	Primary prevention of CHD	Secondary prevention of CHD	Secondary prevention of CHD
Duration of study (years)	6	5	5	6
Number studied	4444	6595	4159	9014
Mean total cholesterol (mmol/L) (range)	6.8 (5.5–8.0)	7.0 (>6.5)	5.4 (<6.2)	(4.0–7.0)
Age range (years)	35–70	45–64	21–75	31–75
% men	81	100	86	83
% with diabetes	4.5	1	17	8.6
Treatment	Simvastatin 20–40 mg daily	Pravastatin 40 mg daily	Pravastatin 40 mg daily	Pravastatin 40 mg daily
Event reduction for major coronary events	34% for non-diabetics 55% for diabetics	31% overall	23% for non-diabetics 25% for diabetics	23% overall

compared to 45% in the diabetic placebo group, while the non-diabetic simvastatin group had 19% and the placebo non-diabetic group had 27%. On the basis of this it is suggested that if 100 patients with diabetes who have angina or are post myocardial infarction are treated with simvastatin for 6 years, 24 of the 46 expected coronary deaths and non-fatal myocardial infarctions can be prevented. Ongoing lipid lowering trials including larger numbers with diabetes such as CARDS (Collaborative Atorvastatin Diabetes Study) and ASPEN (Atorvastatin Study for the Prevention of Endpoints in Non-insulin dependent diabetes) will help to clarify this further.

Once the above lifestyle measures have been implemented, consider the need for drug therapy. The Sheffield tables, New Zealand tables or the Joint British Societies Coronary Risk Predicion Chart (see p. 927) should be used to determine risk in primary prevention. In a diabetic patient a total cholesterol : HDL-cholesterol ratio is preferable to using total cholesterol alone, especially in women. Also, while a 3% risk cut-off is advocated by many, the use of a 1.5–2% level in higher risk groups such as the diabetic population is not without support. Remember that a fit patient with diabetes has a similar risk when compared to a non- diabetic of the same age and sex who has also had a coronary event. In those with known coronary heart disease, cerebrovascular or peripheral vascular disease use the 1997 Standing Medical Advisory Committee guidelines for statins in secondary prevention. These suggest, following a trial of dietary modification:

- Treat a total cholesterol >4.8 mmol/L or an LDL-cholesterol >3.3 mmol/L using pharmacological agents such as statins.
- The treatment aim is a total cholesterol <4.5 and an LDL of <2.6 mmol/L.

Lower targets for each are advocated by many, especially for those patients post coronary artery bypass grafting or post angioplasty. Triglycerides should be brought <1.5 mmol/L, as above this atherogenic lipoprotein changes are said to occur.

In those with mixed hyperlipidaemia, consider a fibrate or a statin licenced for this indication. A fibrate will reduce triglycerides by 30–40% and LDL-cholesterol by 20% while a statin would reduce triglycerides slightly less (10–15%) and LDL-cholesterol slightly more (25–35%). Fibrates also alter the LDL-cholesterol to its less atherogenic form. The choice of agent must be tailored to the individual patient. For hypercholesterolaemia alone a statin is first choice, as in the non-diabetic patient, and in severely resistant patients combination therapy with statins, fibrates, and less often resins may be required.

Treatment aims for lipids

Primary prevention

- Treat if risk table analysis gives a >3% risk per year.

Secondary prevention

Following failure of diet treat:

- total cholesterol >4.8 mmol/L to <4.5 mmol/L (or <4.0 post CABG/angioplasty)
- LDL cholesterol >3.3 mmol/L to <2.6 mmol/L
- aim to have triglycerides <1.5 mmol/L.

Investigations

Take a full history and carefully examine the patient. In all patients then check:

- dip test urine for protein
- serum urea, electrolytes, and creatinine (and creatinine clearance if creatinine is raised)
- fasting lipids
- ECG (for left ventricular hypertrophy and signs of ischaemia).

Also consider:

- the need for a chest radiograph for signs of heart failure/cardiomegaly
- an echocardiogram
- cortisol + dexamethasone suppression test
- catecholamines
- renin/aldosterone.

Hypertension

Epidemiology

Hypertension is twice as common in the diabetic population as in the non-diabetic population, and standard ethnic differences in the prevalence of hypertension still hold true. It is known that hypertension worsens the severity of and increases the risk of developing both microvascular and macrovascular disease. Using a cut-off of >160/90 mmHg, hypertension occurs in:

- 10–30% of patients with type 1 diabetes
- 20–30% of microalbuminuric type 1 patients
- 80–90% of macroalbuminuric type 1 patients
- 30–50% of Caucasians with type 2 diabetes.

Using the UKPDS suggested target of 140/80, hypertension is even more common.

Pathogenesis

- *Type 1 patients* Hypertension is strongly associated with diabetic nephropathy and microalbuminuria and occurs at an earlier stage than that seen in many other causes of renal disease. This may inpart be linked to a genetic predisposition also giving increased activity in red blood cell sodium–lithium counter-transport activity which leads to increased peripheral vascular resistance. Insulin may also have a suppressive effect on renin release, so giving hyporeninaemic hypoaldosteronism.
- *Type 2 patients* Hypertension is associated with insulin resistance and hyperinsulinaemia; again, this may be genetically mediated. Hyperinsulinaemia can directly cause hypertension by increasing sympathetic nervous system activity, increasing proximal tubule sodium resorption, and stimulating vascular smooth muscle cell proliferation. Hyperglycaemia also has an antinatiuretic effect and with hyperinsulinaemia leading to hypokalaemia which results in both glucose and sodium reabsorption being increased all increases the potential for hypertension.

Management

Treatment aim

The current recommendation is for all patients with diabetes to have a blood pressure <140/80 mmHg. The hypertension study in the UKPDS highlights the benefits for type 2 patients of such a treatment

Management of acute myocardial infarction

Patients with diabetes are more likely to have a myocardial infarction and more likely to die from it than the non-diabetic population. This may be due to a greater likelihood of myocardial pump failure. Several studies highlight this:

Trial and outcome examined	Non-diabetic subgroup	Diabetic subgroup
ISSI-2		
Non-streptokinase 4 year mortality	27%	41%
GUSTO		
In-hospital mortality	6.2%	10.6%
GISSI-2		
Re-infarction rates	14%	30%

Up to 20–40% of patients admitted to hospital with a myocardial infarction will have hyperglycaemia, many of whom will not have previously diagnosed diabetes.

As in the non-diabetic population, streptokinase and aspirin have proven benefits. The previous contraindication for thrombolysis in those with proliferative diabetic retinopathy has been questioned by many. Tight glycaemic control (blood glucose 7–10 mmol/L) using i/v glucose and insulin for at least 24 h followed by s/c insulin, as used in the DIGAMI study, also has benefits. In this study, patients with an admission blood glucose >11.0 mmol/L who were treated with this regimen had a 7.5% absolute risk reduction in mortality at 1 year and an 11% risk reduction at 3.5 years compared to the control group (i.e. 33% mortality with treatment vs 44% in controls at 3.5 years). This equates to 1 life saved for every 9 treated with this regimen. The exact reason for this is unclear.

- It is suggested that all patients with a blood glucose >11 mmol/L benefit from such treatment whether previously known to have diabetes or not. Using an admission HbA1c to detect those with undiagnosed or stress-related hyperglycaemia can be useful, but should not result in withholding the acute treatment of this hyperglycaemia in such patients. It may, however, help to identify those who may be troubled by hypoglycaemia and may not therefore be suitable for s/c insulin or sulfonylureas in the intermediate or long term.
- Using ACEIs early after myocardial infarction gives a 0.5% absolute risk reduction in 30 day mortality and a 4–8% risk reduction over 15–50 months in a general population. Analysis of the diabetic subgroup in the GISSI-3 study showed a 30% reduction in 6 week mortality for the diabetics (8.7% vs 12.4%) compared to a 5% reduction for non-diabetics. In view of the greater proportion of diabetics with poor left ventricular function after myocardial infarction compared to the non-diabetic population, this difference is very important.

level on mortality, diabetes related end-points, and microvascular end-points. In this a 10/5 mmHg difference in blood pressure was associated with a 34% risk reduction in macrovascular end-points, a 37% risk reduction in microvascular end-points, and a 44% risk reduction in stroke. The recent Hypertension Optimum Treatment (HOT) study again suggests a target of <140/80 mmHg although in those who already have significant end-organ damage a lower target is advocated by some (<130/80).

Predisposing conditions

Other conditions which can cause both hypertension and hyperglycaemia should be considered, e.g. Cushing's syndrome, acromegaly, and phaeochromocytoma (see relevant sections).

End-organ damage

Look for evidence of end-organ damage (eyes, heart, kidneys, and peripheral vascular tree in particular).

Assessment of cardiac risk factors

Look for associated risk factors for coronary heart disease.

Treatment

General

Once this initial assessment is complete, modify other risk factors such as glycaemic control, smoking, and dyslipidaemia. Then look at:

- weight reduction if obese
- reduced salt intake (<6 g/day)
- reduced alcohol intake (<21 units/week in men,<14 in women)
- exercise (20–40 min of moderate exertion 3–5 times/week).

Pharmacological

After this, start drug therapy for the hypertension. Most agents currently available will drop systolic blood pressure by no more than 20 mmHg at most. Remember that in the UKPDS blood pressure study, 1/3 of those achieving the tight blood pressure targets we are now aiming for required three or more drugs to do so.

- In the presence of microalbuminuria or frank proteinuria, always consider an ACEI first line.
- In Afro-Caribbean diabetics a diuretic may also be needed to improve the efficacy of the ACEI as these and ß-blockers are less effective than calcium channel blockers and diuretics in these patients.
- Although many studies suggest the superiority of the ACEI the UKPDS did not confirm any difference between captopril and

atenolol, so if urinalysis is clear other agents such as loop or thiazide diuretics, β-blockers, and calcium channel blockers are also often used first line.

- These agents are again used second line but also consider angiotensin-II receptor blockers and α-blockers, both of which are probably under-used.
- Several agents, such as high dose thiazides and β-blockers, can, however, worsen diabetic control, mask hypoglycaemia, and exacerbate dyslipidaemia so tailor the drugs chosen to each patient.
- In those with angina a β-blocker has added benefits
- In those with peripheral vascular disease vasodilators such as the calcium channel blockers and α-blockers are beneficial.

The ongoing Antihypertensive and Lipid Lowering Treatment to Prevent Heart Attack Trial (ALLHAT), which includes a large diabetic cohort, should give further help when choosing which agent to start with.

Further reading

Hanssen L, Zanchetti A, Carruthers SG *et al.* Effects of intensive blood pressure lowering and low dose aspirin in patients with hypertension: principal results of the Hypertension Optimun Treatment (HOT) randomised trial. *Lancet* 1998; 351: 1755–1762.

Malmberg K for the DIGAMI (DM, Insulin Glucose Infusion in Acute Myocardial) study group. Prospective randomized study of intensive insulin treatment on long term survival after acute myocardial infarction in patients with DM. *BMJ* 1997; 314: 1512–1515.

Pyorala K, Pedersen TR, Kjekshus J *et al.* Cholesterol lowering with simvastatin improves prognosis of diabetic patients with coronary heart disease. *Diabetes Care* 1997; 20: 614–620.

UKPDS Group. Tight blood pressure control and risk of macrovascular and microvascular complications in type 2 diabetes: UKPDS 38. *BMJ* 1998; 317: 703–713.

UKPDS Group. Efficacy of atenolol and captopril in reducing the risk of macrovascular and microvascular complications in type 2 diabetes: UKPDS 39. *BMJ* 1998; 317: 713–720.

Zuanetti G *et al.* Effect of the ACE inhibitor lisinopril in diabetic patients with acute myocardial infarction. Data from GISSI-3 Study. *Circulation* 1997; 96: 4239–4245.

Chapter 110
Diabetic foot

Risk factors for foot ulcer development

Several features/factors are thought to predispose to ulcer formation, and awareness of these may highlight 'at risk' patients for education and other preventive strategies. These ulcers can occur anywhere on the foot, but the tips of claw/hammer toes and over the metatarsal heads are the most frequent sites. The risk factors/features include:

- *Peripheral neuropathy* (seen in up to 80% of diabetic patients with foot ulcers) reduces awareness of pain and trauma caused by footwear and foreign bodies in shoes. Look for reduced monofilament sensation (e.g. reduced to a 10 g monofilament) and reduced vibration perception thresholds (e.g. reduced sensation to a 128 Hz tuning fork for <10 s or >25 V with a biosthesiometer), suggesting at risk feet.
- *Autonomic neuropathy* leading to anhidrosis can dry out the skin and cause it to crack, so allowing a portal of entry for infection. These feet are often warm and dry with distended veins.
- *Motor neuropathy* can result in altered foot muscle tone, wasting of small muscles, raising of the medial longitudinal arch, and clawing of the toes which can put more pressure through the metatarsal heads and heels so predisposing to callus and ulcer formation. Electrophysiology can help examine this, but is too invasive for widespread routine use.
- *Peripheral vascular disease* (seen in up to 10% of patients) and *microvascular circulatory disease* leads to local ischaemia, increasing the potential for ulcer formation and can delay wound healing when ulceration occurs. Always examine peripheral pulses and consider doppler studies if abnormal. An ankle : brachial artery ratio of >1.1 suggests arterial disease.
- *Duration of diabetes* relates to the presence of the above factors but is often quoted as an independent risk factor, as is increasing age. But type 2 diabetes may be present and undiagnosed for some time.
- The presence of *other microvascular complications* such as nephropathy and retinopathy is also a risk factor for foot ulcer development.
- *Previous ulceration* is another important risk factor, and anyone with previous problems deserves very careful monitoring/follow up.

Table 110.1 Epidemiology of foot ulceration in the UK

Prevalence of foot ulceration	5–10%
Number of people with diabetes developing foot ulcers	14 000–42 000
Proportion of people with diabetes undergoing lower limb amputation	1%
Number of people with diabetes undergoing lower limb amputation per year	2000
Annual NHS expenditure on diabetes foot-related care	£13 million

Table 110.2 Clinical features of diabetic feet

Neuropathic feet	Ischaemic feet
Warm	Cold/cool
Dry skin	Atrophic/often hairless
Palpable foot pulses	No palpable foot pulses
No discomfort with ulcer	More often tender/painful
Callus present	Claudication/Rest pain
	Skin blanches on elevation and reddens on dependency

Table 110.3 Wagner's classification of diabetic foot lesions

Grade 0	High risk foot, no ulceration present
Grade 1	Superficial ulcer, not infected
Grade 2	Deep ulcer with or without cellulitis but no abscess or bone involvement
Grade 3	Deep ulcer with bone involvement or abscess formation
Grade 4	Localized gangrene (toe, forefoot, heel)
Grade 5	Gangrene of the whole foot

From Wagner (1983).

- *Lack of diabetes monitoring* and lack of previous examinations of the feet are also recognized risk factors.
- *Mechanical, chemical or thermal trauma/injury* are often the predisposing factor, and any profession or pastime that increases the risk of these is a risk factor.

Treatment

This is a multidisciplinary problem requiring collaboration between interested diabetologists, diabetes nurse specialists, chiropodists, orthotists, vascular surgeons, plastic surgeons, and occasionally orthopaedic surgeons. Treatment is aimed at several distinct areas, namely:

- at-risk feet with no current ulceration
- treating existing ulcers
- treating infected ulcers
- treating osteomyelitis
- treating vascular insufficiency.

At-risk feet with no current ulceration

When at-risk feet are identified in any patient with diabetes, standard advice should be given and this will need to be repeated/reinforced regularly. This advice would usually include:

- General advice on nail care, hygiene and care with footwear – often best from the chiropodist.
- Reinforce the need for regular daily examination of the feet by the patient or carer.
- Consider regular chiropody review as well as self-monitoring. Also reinforce the need for more urgent review if the patient discovers problems.
- Consider the need for modification of footwear or special footwear if there are abnormalities with foot posture or problems with pressure loading on certain parts of the foot. Padded socks can also reduce trauma. Advise the patient to examine shoes before putting them on, wear lace-ups or shoes with lots of room for the toes and avoid ill-fitting fashion shoes. In some people protective toecaps can prove very useful.
- Avoid walking barefoot.

At the moment no other therapy is advocated in this group of patients, but, as discussed in the neuropathy section, good diabetic control is important and other agents may be useful in the future such as aldose reductase inhibitors, inhibitors of non-enzymatic glycation, and various growth factors.

Existing ulcers

All ulcers should be considered deep and involving bone until proved otherwise. Also:

The Charcot foot

Epidemiology

This is a relatively rare complication of diabetes: an average district general hospital clinic will have 3–10 patients with this problem.

Pathogenesis

It is suggested that blood flow increases due to sympathetic nerve loss. This causes osteoclast activity and bone turnover to increase, so making the bones of the foot more susceptible to damage. Even minor trauma can therefore result in destructive changes in this susceptible bone.

Clinical features

The most likely site is the tarsal–metatarsal region or the metatarsophalangeal joints. Initially it gives a warm/hot, swollen, and often uncomfortable foot, which may be indistinguishable from cellulitis and gout. Peripheral pulses are invariably present and peripheral neuropathy is evident clinically.

Plain radiographs will be normal initially and later show fractures with osteolysis and joint reorganization with subluxation of the metatarsophalangeal joints and dislocation of the large joints of the foot. Isotope scans with technetium are abnormal from early on, but differentiation form infective or other inflammatory causes can be difficult. MRI scanning may prove more useful for this in the future as may ^{111}indium-labelled white cell studies if infection is suspected.

Eventually, in the untreated patient, two classic deformities are seen:

- a 'rocker bottom' deformity due to displacement and subluxation of the tarsus downwards
- medial convexity due to displacement of the talonavicular joint or tarsometatarsal dislocation.

Management

If diagnosed early, immobilization may help prevent joint destruction. Exactly how best to do this is not agreed but using a non-walking plaster cast or an Aircast type of boot is needed for at least 2–3 months while bone repair/remodelling is going on. Some advocate immobilization for anything up to a year. The recent use of bisphosphates to speed this up by reducing osteoclast activity is interesting and already under further evaluation.

- *Optimize diabetic control.*
- *Reduction of oedema* is important to aid healing.
- *Regular debridement* of callus and dead tissue/skin is important for both neuropathic and ischaemic ulcers. Debridement is usually best with a scalpel and forceps although chemical agents (such as *Varidase*, which contains streptokinase) can occasionally help. But, as these agents can also damage healthy tissue, use under careful supervision. More recently the use of sterile maggots has been shown to be effective. After debridement apply dressings but change these regularly. Be careful that tight dressings do not impair a poor circulation further and that thick dressings or quantities of sticky tape to hold them on do not cause their own skin trauma or pressure effects.
- *Infection control* Infection may be localized but any evidence of deeper infection or sinus formation raises the possibility of osteomyelitis. Systemic symptoms may be minimal as may pain/tenderness so be suspicious of more severe infection than you can see in everyone. The organisms may be ordinary skin commensals given a port of entry but send swabs for culture and think of *Staphylococcus aureus* or streptococci as likely organisms.

  If a sinus is present, probe it and if down to bone assume there is osteomyelitis. Culture anything you get out. Plain radiographs may show bone erosion or destruction with osteomyelitis; radioisotope scans using technetium can show increased uptake with both infection and Charcot arthropathy. The use of MRI scanning can be useful to differentiate in this situation.

  If infection is present use triple therapy with *flucloxacillin* (500 mg 4× daily), *ampicillin/amoxicillin* (500 mg 3× daily) and *metronidazole* (200 mg 3× daily) or consider using *amoxicillin/clavulanic acid* (250/125 mg 3× daily) or *ciprofloxacin* (500–750 mg 2× daily) and *clindamycin* (300–450 mg 2× daily) depending on the organisms grown and patient tolerability. This will need to be i/v/rectal initially if the infection is severe and for the deeper infections several months of therapy may be needed. If osteomyelitis is present consider using *ciprofloxacin* or *sodium fusidate* which have better bone penetration and again use for several months.

  In some patients this approach fails to control osteomyelitis adequately and resection/amputation is required, so regular liaison with an interested surgeon is imperative.
- *Reducing trauma* and *pressure relief* in neuropathic ulcers Padded socks can reduce sheer stress and trauma. Suitable shoes and insoles can help to relieve pressure to allow healing to occur as long as unnecessary walking is minimized. If this is not enough a pneumatic boot/Aircast boot or a total contact cast may be needed. These allow the patient to be mobile but take the weight away from

the ulcerated area or foot and put all the weight/pressure through to the calf instead. The involvement of both chiropodists and orthotists is therefore essential.

- *Revascularization* Always consider coexistent vascular disease in a neuropathic foot or predominantly ischaemic ulcers/feet. Vascular bypass grafting/reconstruction or angioplasty can give excellent results with a 70–95% limb salvage rate often quoted. The improved blood supply will also help healing of existing ulcers and may negate the need for amputation or allow the area requiring resection to be minimized. If vascular intervention is unsuccessful or not possible then amputation is required, preferably as a below-knee procedure to give a better mobilization potential postoperatively.

Further reading

Boulton AJM. Foot problems in patients with DM. Chapter 58 in Williams G, Pickup JC (ed.), *Textbook of Diabetes*, 2nd edn, 1997. Oxford: Blackwell Science.

Management of Diabetic Foot Disease. A National Clinical Guideline recommended for use in Scotland by the Scottish Intercollegiate Network (SIGN). 1997 (available from SIGN Secretariat, 9 Queen Street, Edinburgh, EH2 1JQ).

Wagner FW. Algorithms of diabetic foot care. In: Levin ME, O'Neil LW, eds. *The Diabetic Foot*, 2nd edn. St Louis: Mosby Yearbook, 1983: 291–302.

Chapter 111
Diabetes and pregnancy

Background

2–4/1000 women who become pregnant have previously known diabetes, and 2–3% of pregnant women have a diagnosis of gestational diabetes made during their pregnancy. In both cases there are risks both to the mother and the foetus, with an historical foetal abnormality rate of up to 30% or 12 times that of the background population often being quoted.

Risks

Foetal

With greater emphasis on improving glycaemic control, a 2.5–3-fold increased congenital malformation rate in mothers with previously known diabetes and a 1.8-fold increase in those without, compared to the non-diabetic population, is more realistic now. Cardiac, renal, and neural tube defects occur, particularly sacral agenesis. Hyperglycaemia in the first 8 weeks of foetal life, during organogenesis, is thought to be the underlying cause. This explains the lower rate in those with gestational diabetes which classically occurs later than this, but not completely. Alterations in oxygen free radicals, myosinositol, and arachidonic acid metabolism and alterations in zinc metabolism have also been implicated.

The most common problem seen in the infant is macrosomia (in 8–50%), which can result in birth trauma and an increased intervention rate. As well as causing obesity, foetal hyperinsulinaemia also accelerates skeletal maturation, delays pulmonary maturation, and causes increased growth of insulin-sensitive tissues giving hypertrophy of the liver and heart. These infants also have an increased risk of hypoglycaemia, seen transiently in up to 50%, and jaundice, with rates of 6–50% quoted, and up to 50% of these requiring phototherapy. Polycythaemia is also seen.

Maternal

Maternal problems include an increased risk of infection and of pre-eclampsia, which is 2–3 times as likely to occur as in a non-diabetic mother.

Inheritance of diabetes

If the background rate of diabetes is 0.15%, the infant of a diabetic mother has a 2% rate and the infant of a diabetic father has a 6% rate. Interestingly the risk of type 2 diabetes in the child of a type 2 mother is much higher at 15–30%, rising to 50–60% if both parents have type 2 diabetes.

Known diabetics and pregnancy

Most women with diabetes have normal deliveries and normal babies. In most instances these are women with type 1 diabetes, although in some ethnic groups type 2 patients may make up a sizable group. In both groups it is sensible to have pre-conception glycaemic control optimized, e.g. preferably an HbAlc <7.0% or in the non-diabetic range. The congenital malformation and spontaneous abortion rates are significantly higher when the HbA1c is elevated. Once the HbA1c is 4–6 standard deviations above the normal non-diabetic range there is a fourfold increased in the malformation rate; at over 6 standard deviations above normal, this rises to a 12-fold risk. In the type 2 patients converting from oral agents to insulin is important. If not possible prior to conception it should be done as soon as a woman is found to be pregnant. Oral agents are potentially teratogenic and because of their ability to cross the placenta can further stimulate foetal β cells.

Pre-conception management

Pre-conception and post-conception advice is similar to that given to non-diabetic women, namely stopping smoking, reducing alcohol intake, avoiding unpasteurized dairy products, and adding oral folate supplements (5 mg/day). Reviewing the need for any.potentially teratogenic drugs they may be taking (e.g. antihypertensive agents usually), and what they can be swapped to, is also advised.

Ideally all patients who have diabetes and are pregnant should be managed in a combined clinic with an interested obstetrician. Reviews are initially 2–4 weekly then 1–2 weekly in the last third of pregnancy.

Maintain good glycaemic control

This is not just because of the risk of ketoacidosis which occurs in <l% of diabetic pregnancies and is associated with foetal loss in 20% of episodes, but also because of macrosomia in the foetus and both an increased foetal mortality (up to 2.2% of births in diabetic mothers) and an increased intervention rate at delivery. Aim to keep the glucose and HbAlc in the non-diabetic range to try to reduce the morbidity and mortality associated with pregnancy and diabetes. It should be remembered, however, that even with perfect control there is a small but significant excess of major congenital malformations in these children and an unexplained risk of late stillbirths.

Monitoring during pregnancy

- Capillary blood glucose monitoring is performed at least 4 times/day.

Target glycaemic control

- fasting glucoses of <5 mmol/L
- postprandial glucoses of <7 mmol/L
- keep the HbA1c in the non-diabetic range.

Treatment regimen

A basal bolus regimen gives greatest flexibility and is commonly used to achieve this target. In type 1 patients insulin requirements often fall in the first trimester, increase slightly in the second and then continue to rise until about 36 weeks, falling back to pre-pregnancy levels after delivery. In type 1 women remember early pregnancy is a cause of falling insulin requirements and recurrent hypoglycaemia. It has been suggested up to 40% of women with type 1 diabetes will experience significant hypoglycaemic episodes when pregnant and that hypoglycaemic awareness may alter. Advice regarding care with driving and other potentially hazardous pursuits is therefore needed early in pregnancy, if not before conception. Type 2 women requiring insulin usually need 0.9 units/kg per day initially and 1.6 units/kg per day later in the pregnancy.

Monitoring of diabetic complications during pregnancy

Certain diabetic complications are known to worsen during pregnancy, and screening for nephropathy and retinopathy in particular is advised at least each trimester.

Foetal monitoring

Scanning of the foetus is performed at 10–12 weeks looking for congenital abnormalities and to confirm dates. Repeat scanning to check for excessive growth/macrosomia at 18–20 weeks, 28 weeks, 32 weeks, and 36 weeks, although the exact timing and frequency can vary between centres.

Management of delivery

At delivery, most units have set protocols but, in general, induction soon after 38 weeks gestation (or not later than expected delivery date) and the use of a continuous insulin infusion with a separate dextrose and potassium infusion to maintain stable blood glucose levels is advisable. This is important as maternal hyperglycaemia during delivery can be associated with neonatal hypoglycaemia and an adverse neurological outcome in the infant.

After delivery

Monitoring of the infant with capillary blood glucoses post delivery is also often performed. The increased potential for hypoglycaemia in the mother and the baby if breast-feeding also needs watching out for, and extra carbohydrate snacks for the mother are often needed along with a 20–25% reduction in pre-conception insulin requirements. One day's worth of breast milk contains about 50 g of carbohydrate. Oral hypoglycaemic agents should not be recommenced until after breast feeding has stopped.

Treatment regimen for labour/delivery

- If labour is induced, omit the previous evening's long acting insulin.
- Infuse 10% glucose at 75–125 mL/h (with 20 mmol potassium per 500 mL bag) .Infuse via a syringe driver 2–4 units/h of soluble insulin initially (usually made as 50 mL soluble insulin in 50 mL of 0.9% saline in a 50 mL syringe).
- Monitor capillary blood glucose levels hourly and adjust the infusion rate of the insulin to keep blood glucose levels in the 6–8 mmol/L range.
- Monitor fluid balance carefully (especially if oxytocin is also being given).
- Check serum sodium if labour lasts over 24 h (or 8 h with oxytocin)

After delivery

- Halve the i/v insulin infusion rate.
- Continue to monitor capillary blood glucose hourly for at least 4 h then 2–4 hourly until the mother is eating normally.
- Return to pre-pregnancy regimen when eating normally but be careful as insulin requirements can be low for the first 24 h.

Gestational diabetes

Epidemiology

Pregnancy potentially induces a state of insulin resistance with increases in the levels of growth hormone, progesterone, placental lactogen, and cortisol. This can therefore result in altered glucose handling. Impaired glucose tolerance during pregnancy occurs in up to 2–3% of pregnant women and may be associated with an increased risk of subsequent type 2 diabetes in 20–50% of patients. Worsening maternal insulin resistance and associated hyperglycaemia usually becomes evident from the second trimester onwards if it is going to occur.

As with women previously known to have diabetes, there is an association with worsening carbohydrate intolerance and a worse maternal and foetal outcome. Untreated gestational diabetes has been shown to have a perinatal mortality of 4.4–6.4% compared to 0.5–1.5% in a similar ethnic normoglycaemic population. Intensive insulin treatment has been shown to reduce such complications. This is the rationale for careful multidisciplinary care of these patients.

Treatment

Initial treatment is with dietary advice and in 10–30% insulin is also required. Insulin therapy should be considered if fasting blood glucoses are >6.0 mmol/L or post prandial levels are >8 mmol/L. Obesity is not uncommon and the importance of post-delivery dietary modification and weight reduction, to reduce the risk of future type 2 diabetes, should also be reinforced. The varying insulin requirements during pregnancy occur as in those with previously known diabetes, and most (but not all) will not need insulin treatment following delivery. Monitoring is with home capillary blood glucose measurements, daily if on diet alone and more frequently if on insulin therapy. The frequency needed depends on the results obtained with the aim to keep all readings <7.0 mmol/L. If diet alone fails, a basal bolus insulin regimen as used in the known diabetic is usually required. Decide on the total initial daily dose on the basis of the degree of hyperglycaemia present; 4–6 units per bolus is usual.

As with the previously known diabetic mother, the aim is to have a normal delivery , more often at 38 weeks to term depending on foetal growth. An oral glucose tolerance test 6 weeks after delivery is needed in all patients not requiring insulin post-delivery to confirm a return to normal glucose metabolism. A further reinforcement of diet and weight advice at this time is also usual practice. Whether these patients

Methods of screening

- Urine dip testing for glucose should be performed on every pregnant woman at every antenatal visit.
- If glycosuria is found a fasting glucose is performed and if >6.0 mmol/L a 75 g OGTT is needed.
- Routine screening at 28–32 weeks is also often performed,either with random blood glucoses or a fasting blood glucose and if a fasting level is >6.0 mmol/L or a postprandial level is >7.0 mmol/L an OGTT is required.
- The diagnostic criteria for diabetes are no different from those in the non- pregnant population. A diagnosis of gestational diabetes or gestational IGT is made if the fasting glucose is 6.0–7.8 mmol/L and/or the 2 h postprandial level is 9.0–11.0 mmol/L by the UK/St. Vincent definition. The WHO definition has a fasting level of 7.8 mmol/L and/or a 2 hour postprandial level of 7.8–11.1 mmol/L.

Table 111.1 Interpretation of the 75 g oral glucose tolerance test during pregnancy

	Plasma glucose (mmol/L)	
	Fasting	2 h proprandial level
Diabetes	>7.0	>11.0
Gestational IGT	6.0–7.8	9–11
Normal	<6.1	9

High risk groups

Most women are found on routine screening at about 30 weeks, but certain high risk groups should be screened earlier. These risk factors include:

- previous gestational diabetes
- a large baby in their last pregnancy, e.g. >4.0 kg at term
- a previous unexplained stillbirth/perinatal death
- maternal obesity
- family history of diabetes (first degree relatives)
- polyhydramnios.

should be followed up in view of their increased risk of diabetes is unclear at this time, but annual fasting blood glucose levels in asymptomatic women with a normal 6 week postpartum OGTT is often advised and more careful review is suggested in those with abnormal OGTTs.

Further reading

Dornhorst A, Chan SP. The elusive diagnosis of gestational diabetes. *Diabetic Medicine* 1998; 15: 7–10.

Garner P. Type 1 DM and pregnancy. *Lancet* 1995; 346: 157–161.

Girling JC, Dornhurst A. Pregnancy and diabetes mellitus. In Pickup J, Williams G (ed.) *Textbook of Diabetes,* 2nd edn, 72.1–34. Oxford: Blackwell Science, 1997.

Ilkova H. Screening for gestational diabetes. *Diabetes Reviews International* 1995; 3(3): 1–2.

Jardine Browne C *et al.* Pregnancy and neonatal care *Diabetic Medicine* 1996; 13: 843–853.

Contraception and diabetes

Oral contraceptives

The early combined oral contraceptive pills (OCP) impaired glucose tolerance and caused hyperinsulinism and so were not advised in patients with diabetes. The use of third-generation low-dose oestrogen-containing combined OCPs (e.g. 20 μg ethinyloestradiol) is safe in women <35 years of age. Third-generation OCPs are advised as they have a better risk profile for arterial disease and only occasionally increase insulin requirements.

As in the non-diabetic population, standard advice regarding the pill should be given and its avoidance in at-risk groups such as overweight smokers with a family history of thromboembolism and coronary heart disease is sensible. There is an increased risk of cerebral thromboembolism in type 1 patients, but the OCP dose not increase this.

In those with microvascular disease or coronary risk factors, the progesterone-only 'mini-pill' (POP) is safer than the combined OCP as it has no significant adverse effects on lipid metabolism, clotting, platelet aggregation, or fibrinolytic activity .It has been suggested that levonorgestrel- and norethisterone-containing POPs may reduce HDL2 cholesterol subfractions. The avoidance of POPs in those with established arterial disease is advised.

Barrier methods

The sheath and the diaphragm were historically the contraceptive method of choice in people with diabetes, and do not have the metabolic risks of the oral contraceptives described above. But, both are less effective forms of contraception with a failure rate of 0.7–3.6/00 couple years for the sheath and 2/100 couple years for the diaphragm, compared to nearly 0.2/100 women years with the combined OCP. In a population in which pregnancy carries significant risks, other forms of contraception are therefore now more often advocated.

Intrauterine contraceptive devices (IUD)

There is a concern that diabetes might make a pelvic infection associated with an IUD more severe and may render both copper containing and inert IUDs less effective, but not all studies have confirmed these worries. Nevertheless, if an IUD is used in a woman with diabetes a progestagen-releasing variety or a small copper device with regular use of spermicides are the current favourite options.

Hormone replacement therapy (HRT)

As with the OCP, diabetes itself is not a contraindication to the use of HRT. The oestrogens in HRT differ from those in the OCP and may actually reduce insulin resistance and also protect against coronary disease, although they may not actually reduce cardiovascular events in those with established coronary artery disease.

Chapter 112
Intercurrent events or disease

Surgery

Preoperative assessment

Careful preoperative assessment is essential because of an increased risk of death and complications such as fluid overload from coronary heart disease and diabetic nephropathy. Any preoperative assessment in a patient with known diabetes should therefore include:

- an adequate history of diabetic complications
- a full examination looking for evidence of peripheral vascular disease, peripheral neuropathy, and lying/standing blood pressures in case of autonomic neuropathy
- assessment of current and overall diabetic control using blood glucose measurements in all patients and glycated haemoglobin.
- general investigations should include serum urea + electrolytes/creatinine, full blood count, urine dip testing for protein, and an ECG (in anyone >45 years old).

Any further investigation will be based on problems found in the history or examination such as foot ulceration and potential osteomyelitis which may give a source for infection such as an MRSA.

Attempts should made to improve diabetic control, either on the ward or in a diabetic clinic, for any patient undergoing an elective procedure whose control is inadequate. An HbA1c <7.2% is considered good control, but an acceptable levels for most procedures would be <9%. Even with a good HbA1c level the preoperative glucose level (and if >11 mmol/L the urine ketones) should always be measured as the perioperative treatment is based on this and some stabilization before administration of an anaesthetic may be required, particularly in the emergency situation.

Perioperative management

Ideally patients with diabetes are best operated on in the morning at the start of the list.

Patients normally on diet alone should have their capillary blood glucose levels checked hourly and avoid i/v dextrose, and often need no other modification to their treatment. Patients taking oral agents should stop metformin preoperatively and miss their other agents on the morning of the procedure. If on chlorpropamide it should be missed the day before as well. Capillary blood glucose levels are again monitored regularly (1–2 hourly) and if >7.0 mmol/L start a dextrose + insulin regime as detailed below and aim to keep the glucose in the 7–11 mmol/L range.

Insulin regimens

Continuous i/v insulin infusion regimen/'sliding scale' insulin

50 units of soluble insulin in 50 mL 0.9% saline (giving 1 unit/mL) are placed in a 50 mL syringe and run through an automated syringe driver at a predetermined rate depending on regular capillary blood glucose measurements. Most units now have written guidelines for this type of regimen and each will need to be tailored to an individual patient, e.g. in insulin-resistant patients much larger amounts of insulin are needed. One such regimen is:

Blood glucose (mmol/L)	Insulin infusion rate (units/h or mL/h)
0–4.0	0.5 (+ recheck in 30 min)
4.1–7.0	1.0
7.1–11.0	2.0
11.1–17.0	4.0
>17.1	6.0–8.0 (+ review regimen)

I/v insulin regimens such as this should never be given without i/v fluids and potassium to avoid hypoglycaemia or hypokalaemia, e.g. start with 100 mL of 5% dextrose containing 5 mmol of potassium per hour. The postoperative rotating of dextrose and non-glucose containing i/v fluids can increase the risk of hypoglycaemia, especially if there is not careful monitoring of the blood glucose. Initially hourly capillary blood glucose levels are needed, moving to 2 hourly measurements postoperatively once stable results are obtained. An attempt at keeping the i/v dextrose infusion rate relatively constant makes this sort of regimen slightly safer. A preoperative potassium and daily repeat measurements are also required.

Postoperatively, once the patient has started eating adequately aim to revert back to a standard s/c insulin regimen with a premeal dose of insulin 30 min before food and the infusion stopping once this is working, i.e. when the food arrives. Patients previously on oral agents who require an i/v insulin regimen may have an increased insulin demand due to infection or the stress of the procedure and may require s/c insulin initially rather than just reverting to their preoperative oral agent(s), so be especially careful in this group.

The GIK regimen

Although not as popular as the above 'sliding scale' continuous regimen, this method does have the advantage of everything being given together so reducing the risk of insulin being given on its own. Into a 500 mL bag of 5% dextrose add 8 units of soluble

(*cont.*)

(*cont.*)

insulin and 5 mmol of potassium. Run this mixture at 100 mL/h and measure capillary blood glucoses hourly initially, aiming for levels of 7–11 mmol/L ideally and 5–15 mmol/L at worst. If >15 mmol/L, swap this infusion for one with 10 units of insulin but also check the serum potassium level to see if that also needs adjusting. If blood glucose is <5 mmol/L reduce the insulin to 6 units/500 mL of 5% dextrose. After each alteration recheck blood glucose levels after 1 h and adjust further if required. Once stable reduce the capillary blood glucose levels to 2 hourly. As with the other i/v regimen, convert to regular therapy once the patient is eating.

Certain situations may require further modification of this regimen, such as open heart surgery where the use of glucose-rich solutions and hypothermia can mean that higher doses of insulin are required initially.

In patients taking insulin undergoing a morning operation miss the morning insulin dose and start on a dextrose + insulin regimen as below. If on an afternoon list give half the normal morning dose of soluble insulin with a light breakfast and start the dextrose + insulin regimen at midday. Again aim to keep the blood glucose in the 7–11 mmol/L range.

Suitable insulin regimens

These come in two forms, the current favourite being a continuous i/v infusion adjusted on the basis of blood glucose measurements with a fixed dextrose infusion. The other is a single bag containing dextrose, insulin, and potassium known as the *Alberti regimen* or the *GIK (glucose insulin potassium) regimen* (opposite).

Skin/connective tissue/joint disease

Skin

Diabetes results in an increased occurrence of infections such as vaginal candida, candida balanitis, and *Staphylococcus aureus* folliculitis. Ulceration in the feet due to neuropathy and peripheral vascular disease should also be considered. Other skin features to look for include the following.

Conditions specific to diabetes

- pretibial diabetic dermopathy ('shin spots')
- diabetic bullae (bullosis diabeticorum, very rare tense blistering on feet/lower legs classically)
- diabetic thick skin (scleroderma of diabetes seen in 2.5% with type 2 diabetes)
- periungual telangectasia (venous capillary dilatation at the nail fold seen in up to 50% of people with diabetes).

Conditions seen more commonly in those with diabetes

- necrobiosis lipoidica
- vitiligo (seen in 2% with type 1 diabetes)
- granuloma annulare (though this association is not proven conclusively).

Conditions associated with the other biochemical features seen in diabetes

- acanthosis nigricans (with insulin resistance)
- eruptive xanthomata (with hypertriglyceridaemia).

The most common skin lesion in diabetes are shin spots or diabetic dermopathy. These occur more commonly in men than in women and affect up to 50% of people with diabetes. Their aetiology is uncertain. They present initially as red papules and progress to give well circumscribed atrophic areas, brownish in colour. Usually seen on the shins, they can also be found on the forearms and thighs. There is no effective treatment of these but they usually resolve spontaneously over 1–2 years.

Necrobiosis lipoidica is seen in 0.3–1% of people with diabetes, and 40–60% of those with necrobiosis also have diabetes. It is more common in women than in men. Classically seen on the shins, it has an atrophic centre with telangectasia around the edge of an oval or irregular lesion, although early lesions can be dull red plaques or papules. Treatment with topical or injectable steroids may help improve these lesions; skin grafting and cosmetic camouflage have also been used.

When looking at the skin do not forget to check injection sites for lipohypertrophy or lipoatrophy as these are often much more amenable to treatment or correction. In the past an insulin allergy rash was also commonly seen, but more recently a transient local reaction, thought to be an IgE-mediated reaction, is more often seen.

Connective tissue/joint disease

Diabetes is associated with an increased incidence of pseudogout and osteoarthritis, but the classical condition to consider is the 'stiff hand syndrome' or *diabetic cheiroarthropathy.* In this the skin thickens and tightens which, in association with sclerosis of the tendon sheaths, results in limited joint mobility in the hands and less commonly the feet. This reduced joint mobility gives an inability to place the palms of the hand flat together and make the 'prayer sign'. No specific treatment for this currently exists.

Chapter 113
Social and practical aspects

Current regulations for fitness to drive motor vehicles

Diabetes is said to influence the ability to drive safely because of hypoglycaemia or complications such as a reduction in vision acuity or fields. It carries a similar risk of accidents to epilepsy (e.g. relative risk of 1.23–1.24 compared to standard drivers). The Driver and Vehicle Licensing Agency (DVLA) Drivers Medical Unit produced a revised set of guidelines in February 1999, which are outlined below.

A group 1 licence is the standard motorcycle/motor car licence (e.g. categories A and B) which also allows you to drive a private minibus carrying up to 16 people (category D1) or a vehicle between 3.5 and 7.5 tonnes (category C1). A group 2 licence allows you to drive heavy goods vehicles (HGVs) and passenger carrying vehicles (PCVs), and all holders of these must inform the DVLA of their diabetes what ever their treatment.:

- Any patient with uncomplicated diabetes who is on *diet alone* does not need to inform the DVLA unless they live in Northern Ireland, they develop complications which will interfere with their ability to drive, or their therapy changes.
- Women who develop *gestational diabetes* need to inform the DVLA and must re-inform them 6 weeks after delivery if still on insulin. They must also stop driving while pregnant if their control is poor and automatically lose their group 2 licence until after delivery.
- *Insulin-treated patients* are required to inform the DVLA if they are on insulin therapy and will need to renew their licences every 1–3 years. They must demonstrate satisfactory control, recognize warning symptoms of hypoglycaemia, and have acceptable eyesight for a standard group 1 licence. New applicants for a driving licence or existing drivers starting on insulin do not automatically get a C1 + D1 licence. From 11/9/98 some previous licence holders, subject to annual review, can keep their class C1 vehicle licence for 3.5–7.5 tonne lorries, but not for D1. Since 1991 they were also barred from driving HGVs or PCVs. Drivers licensed before 1/4/91 who are on insulin are reassessed annually and may still do so.
- *Patients managed with tablets* need to inform the DVLA and can normally continue to hold both a group 1 (until 70 years old) and a group 2 licence, subject to a satisfactory medical. If vision deteriorates, hypoglycaemia is a problem, or they require insulin therapy this may alter.

Travel

Travel across time zones, exposure to unaccustomed exercise, and new infections make this an important area for both patient and doctor education. It is common sense to take more insulin than is needed for any time away, in case of an accidental loss or breakage. If new insulin supplies are needed, remember not all countries use only the U100 strength and tell the patient travelling abroad to look out for this, e.g 30 units or 0.3 mL of U100 strength insulin equates to 0.75 mL of the U40 form and 0.38 mL of U80. A letter stating the need to carry insulin, needles, and syringes/pen devices will also make Customs formalities slightly easier.

Patients with diabetes need the same immunizations and malaria prophylaxis as other travellers. In case they acquire an infection or illness while travelling, standard 'sick day rules' should be reinforced. These suggest that:

- Insulin therapy should never be stopped and may actually need to be increased, even when food intake is reduced.
- If the patient is unable to tolerate solid food, a liquid form of carbohydrate such as Lucozade or Dioralyte should be taken instead. A patient who is unable to tolerate adequate oral fluids should seek medical advice.
- If unwell monitor urine for ketones and if present seek medical advice.
- During any illness consider increasing the frequency of capillary glucose testing.

Travel and adjustments in therapy are usually more of a problem for insulin-treated patients as those on oral agents can adjust the timing of their tablets to the new time zone with less risk of significant deteriorations in control.

In the insulin-treated patient:

- On short flights where the differences in time zones is small no major insulin adjustments are needed, but make sure snacks and extra carbohydrate are packed with hand luggage as the timing, quality, and quantity of airline food is rather variable.
- On longer flights where time zones are crossed the adjustments needed will depend on their initial regimen and the direction of travel. If travelling east to west the day is longer and extra doses are needed; west to east gives a shorter day and so a reduction in therapy is required. With a basal bolus regimen take soluble insulin with each meal given and intermediate acting insulin given to fit in with the evening at the destination. In a twice daily mixed regimen give an extra dose of soluble when going east to west and miss the evening isophane when going west to east.

(*cont.*)

(*cont.*)

Exercise

Non-diabetic people initially breakdown muscle glycogen for 5–10 min, then use circulating glucose and non-esterified fatty acids. Hepatic glucose production increases, but free fatty acids are the main fuel used after 1–2 h of exercise and without some form of energy intake most people become hypoglycaemic after 2–3 h of strenuous exercise. Insulin sensitivity also decreases the day after severe exertion.

Type 1 diabetes

Insulin requirements are reduced during exercise. To reduce the risk of hypoglycaemia with acute exercise decrease the pre-exercise insulin dose, which would have its peak during the exercise, by 30–50%. If the exercise is due to last more than 2 h also take 20–40 g of extra carbohydrate before and hourly during exercise.

If the site of the insulin injection is the area being exercised absorption may be accelerated, especially if exercise is undertaken soon after the injection of an insulin analogue. So inject into an area that won't be exercised. With extreme exercise it may take several hours, if not until the next day, to fully replenish muscle glycogen stores and care is needed to avoid hypoglycaemia during this period.

Type 2 diabetes

Exercise increases peripheral glucose uptake and reduces endogenous insulin secretion. Physical training can increase insulin sensitivity which in type 2 patients can result in a reduction in HbA1c, blood pressure, weight, and a better lipid profile. Hypoglycaemia is not usually a problem unless the patient is taking sulfonylureas, so extra carbohydrate is not normally indicated. In those using these agents a reduction in dosage may however be advisable.

Complications from diabetes and driving

Loss of hypoglycaemic awareness will result in permanent loss of an HGV/PCV licence and a temporary loss of a standard licence until specialist reports can confirm that awareness has returned. Any doctor making this diagnosis must tell the patient they are legally obliged to inform the DVLA of this diagnosis. If the patient refuses to do so the medical adviser at the DVLA should be informed once the patient has been informed in writing of the intention to do so. Avoiding all hypoglycaemic episodes for at least a month will help to regain hypoglycaemic awareness in some patients. A patient who is unable to regain this awareness *must* stop driving.

In a patient with frequent hypoglycaemic episodes or with poor control it seems sensible to advise them not to drive until things are better, and the DVLA should be contacted. As part of their regular checks the DVLA asks a doctor to complete a Diabetes III form which asks if control of the diabetes is satisfactory/stable and how long this has been for. This should help to pick up many of these patients. If you say their control is poor or unstable, do not forget to tell the patient what you have done and arrange to see them to improve this problem as reports to that effect will be needed by the DVLA before their licence is renewed.

Visual requirements are that you can read a number plate with 79.4 mm high letters at 20.5 m with glasses/contact lenses if worn. This equates to a visual acuity of between 6/9 and 6/12 on a Snellen chart. Group 2 licence holders must have an acuity of 6/9 or better in their good eye and not worse than 6/12 in the bad, but will not be licenced if they have an uncorrected acuity worse than 3/60 in either eye. Visual field defects of any sort, especially if bilateral, result in loss of HGV/PCV licences and may affect a standard licence.

Other complications such as limb amputations can alter the ability to drive, but driving is still possible if the vehicle is suitably modified.

Useful addresses

DVLA (Driver and Vehicle Licensing Agency), Drivers Medical Unit, Longview Road, Morriston, Swansea SA99 1DA. Tel: 01792 783795. Fax: 01792 783687

Diabetes U.K, 10 Queen Anne Street, London W1M 0BD. Tel 020 7323 1531. BDA motor insurance quote line: 01903 262 900

Chapter 114
Emergencies in diabetes

Diabetic ketoacidosis

Diabetic ketoacidosis has a mortality of 2–5%. Many deaths occur due to delays in presentation and initiation of treatment, with a mortality rate of up to 50% in the elderly.

Diagnosis

This is usually based on a collection of biochemical abnormalities, namely:

- *hyperglycaemia* >11.1 mmol/L
- *acidosis* arterial pH <7.3, serum bicarbonate <15 mmol/L, base excess <–10
- *ketonuria* Some dip testing methods only check for acetoacetate and acetone but not β-hydroxybutyrate. Captopril can also give a false positive test for urinary acetone. Ketones may also interfere with some creatinine assays and give falsely high readings.

There is an uncommon condition of *euglycaemic ketoacidosis* (in 1–3% of cases at most) when ketones are produced early on in patients with a reduced carbohydrate intake. Blood glucose is <17 mmol/L, acidosis is marked, and dehydration is not usually severe. Treatment is to initiate oral carbohydrate intake and monitor the need for i/v insulin/fluids as in full-blown hyperglycaemic ketoacidosis.

Epidemiology

Diabetic ketoacidosis is common in type 1 patients, with 1 in 11 subjects in the European IDDM complications study (EURODIAB) reporting hospitalization for this over a 12 month period. The incidence is 5–8/1000 diabetic patients per year, usually type 1 patients but up to 25% of cases are patients with newly diagnosed/presenting diabetes some of whom subsequently obtain adequate control with oral agents or diet alone. In up to 50% of cases an infection is the precipitant and in 10–30% of cases it is their first presentation with diabetes.

Pathogenesis

Diabetic ketoacidosis occurs as a result of insulin deficiency and counterregulatory hormone excess. Insulin deficiency results in excess mobilization of free fatty acids from adipose tissue. This provides the substrate for ketone production from the liver. Ketones (β-hydroxybutyrate, acetoacetate, and acetone) are excreted by the kidneys and buffered in the blood initially, but once this system fails acidosis develops. Hyperglycaemia also occurs as the liver produces glucose from

Precipitants of diabetic ketoacidosis

infection	30–40%
non-compliance with treatment	25%
inappropriate alterations in insulin (i.e. errors by patient or doctor)	13%
newly diagnosed diabetes	10–20%
myocardial infarction	1%

lactate and alanine which are generated by muscle proteinolysis. The reduced peripheral glucose utilization associated with insulin deficiency exacerbates this.

Hyperglycaemia and ketonuria cause an osmotic diuresis and hypovolaemia with both intracellular and extracellular dehydration. Glomerular filtration is reduced and blood glucose levels therefore rise even further as do the levels of counterregulatory hormones such as glucagon. The metabolic acidosis due to ketone accumulation leads to widespread cell death which combined with hypovolaemia is fatal if untreated.

Clinical features

Polyuria, polydypsia, and weight loss are often seen. Muscle cramps, abdominal pain, and shortness of breath (air hunger or Kussmaul's breathing, with deep regular rapid breaths, suggesting acidosis) can also occur. Subsequent nausea and vomiting can worsen both the dehydration and electrolyte losses which often precede the onset of coma (occuring in about 10% of cases). Remember to consider other causes of coma and a raised blood glucose such as head injury, alcohol, and drug overdoses.

On examination the breath can smell of ketones (like nail varnish remover) with postural hypotension (exacerbated by peripheral vasodilatation due to acidosis) and hypothermia also frequently seen. Infection and trauma can precipitate this problem and should be carefully looked for, especially in the unconscious patient.

Hypovolaemia at presentation is usually at least 5 L with electrolyte losses of 300–700 mmol of sodium, 200–700 mmol of potassium, and 350–500 mmol of chloride accompanying this. The daily intake of both sodium and potassium is 60 mmol, so the severity of this is apparent.

Management

Having first assessed the need for immediate resuscitation, and commenced a 0.9% saline i/v infusion, take a history and examine the patient to look for obvious precipitants such as surgery, trauma, sites of infection, or myocardial infarction. Initial investigations will be modified by the history and examination and suggested site of infection but should at least include:

- blood for urea/electrolytes (note ketone/creatinine assay interaction)
- full blood count (a leukocytosis can occur without infection)
- arterial blood gases (P_aCO_2 will be low due to hyperventilation with a metabolic acidosis, check pH and bicarbonate)
- cultures of blood and urine
- chest radiograph and ECG

Initial treatment of ketoacidosis

I/v 0.9% saline

- 2 L in 2 h then 1 L over 2 h, 2 L in next 8 h and 4 L/day thereafter until blood glucose <11 mmol/L. Then convert to dextrose saline or 5% dextrose.
- If the patient is profoundly shocked (e.g. systolic BP <80 mmHg with severe dehydration or sepsis) or oliguric, this may need to be given more rapidly and colloids may also be needed. If elderly or there are signs of heart failure or cerebral oedema this may need to be given more slowly.

Potassium

Once the serum potassium is known the 0.9% saline has potassium added with the dose adjusted based on hourly serum potassium measurements until stable and measured 2–4 hourly over the next 12–24 h. Add:

- 40 mmol/L if K^+ <3.0 mmol/L
- 30 mmol/L if K^+ 3.0–4.0 mmol/L
- 20 mmol/L if K^+ 4.1–5.0 mmol/L
- 10 mmol/L if K^+ 5.1–6.0 mmol/L
- none if K^+ >6.0 mmol/L.

Insulin (via a continuous i/v infusion)

- 50 units of soluble insulin in 50 mL of 0.9% saline given at 6–8 units/hour to drop glucose by about 5 mmol/L per hour and adjusted to keep blood glucose 10–14 mmol/L until after ketoacidosis has cleared (usually need 3–6 units/hour).
- Alternatively use 50 units of insulin in 500 mL of 0.9% saline with added potassium infused at 80–100 mL/hour initially with a maintenance dose of 30–60 mL/hour once blood glucose is adequately controlled. I/m regimes should be avoided and used only as a last resort. Give 20 units of soluble insulin initially with 10 units hourly until blood glucose falls and then 20 units 6 hourly until control is achieved.

- in the older patient (>40 years) also include an ECG and cardiac enzymes, even if asymptomatic.

Replacement of fluids, electrolytes, and insulin is the mainstay of treatment, along with treating any precipitant, such as infection. To monitor this treatment central venous access and urinary catheterization are often necessary and a nasogastric tube may be useful, especially in the unconscious patient. In elderly people, those with a cardiac history, or those with autonomic neuropathy central venous access is imperative.

Monitoring

Once treatment has commenced, monitor fluid balance carefully and avoid fluid overload. Check capillary blood glucose hourly with serum potassium, sodium, and glucose 2 hourly and arterial blood gases 2–4 hourly depending on response. Reduce the frequency of tests once stabilized but check electrolytes at least daily for the first 72 h. Continuous ECG monitoring will aid the detection of hypo- and hyperkalaemia in the acute phase. Magnesium and phosphate levels should also be checked as these can occasionally require replacement therapy.

Additional therapies

- *I/v bicarbonate* is only rarely indicated as it can cause hypokalaemia and paradoxically worsen intracellular acidosis. If used, give only when the pH is <6.9 using 250 mL of 1.26% bicarbonate given over 30–60 min initially and monitor arterial blood gases to assess response, aiming for pH no greater than 7.1. This should probably only be used in an intensive care setting. Do not use 8.4% bicarbonate as its high sodium load can too rapidly alter electrolyte levels and precipitate pulmonary oedema as well as causing local tissue necrosis if it extravasates.
- In severe hypotension unresponsive to colloids and crystalloids inotropes may be required but agents such as *dopamine*, *dobutamine*, and *adrenaline* will all exacerbate insulin resistance necessitating a more aggressive sliding scale regime.
- *Heparin* in s/c prophylactic doses can be given in the unconscious or immobile patent.
- Cover with *i/v broad-spectrum antibiotics* should be used if no obvious precipitant is found and appropriate antibiotics if a site of infection is found.
- Cerebral oedema typically presents 8–24 h after starting i/v fluids with a declining conscious level and may have a mortality as high as 90%. If this occurs *dexamethasone* (12–16 mg/day) and *mannitol* (1–2 g/kg body weight) may be given.

Subsequent treatment

Once the blood glucose is stable in the 10–15 mmol/L range, the ketoacidosis has settled, and the patient is eating and drinking normally consider swapping on to a s/c insulin regime but overlap the i/v and the first s/c dose by 2 h. Stabilize on this therapy before discharge from hospital. Once the i/v potassium supplements have stopped, give oral supplements for at least 48 h with regular serum monitoring.

Patient education to determine the cause and so avoid a further occurrence, or for earlier presentation if it does occur, should also ideally be performed before discharge.

Hyperosmolar, non-ketotic hyperglycaemia

This is a more sinister complication than ketoacidosis with a mortality as high as 50% and is said to be found in 11–30% of adult hyperglycaemic emergencies. It affects an older population than ketoacidosis (middle aged or elderly), 2/3 of cases are in patients with previously undiagnosed diabetes, and its insidious onset can be mistaken for many other conditions including a stroke.

Diagnosis

This is again a biochemical diagnosis:

- *hyperglycaemia* (usually 30–70 mmol/L)
- serum osmolality *high* (> 350 mmol/kg)
- *no acidosis* arterial pH 7.35–7.45, serum bicarbonate >18 mmol/L, but remember lactic acidosis with infection or a myocardial infarction may alter this.
- *no ketonuria* + on urine dip testing can occur with starvation and vomiting.

Serum osmolality (in mosmol/kg) can be calculated if not available from the laboratory using the following equation:

osmolality = 2(sodium + potassium) + glucose + urea

Epidemiology

This occurs in an older age group of insulin-producing type 2 patients, a large proportion of whom will not previously be known to have diabetes. Ingestion of high-sugar-containing drinks, intercurrent infection, and myocardial infarction are all commonly seen as precipitants of this condition. Drugs such as glucocorticoids, cimetidine, phenytion, thiazide, and loop diuretics have all been implicated in the pathogenesis of this problem.

Pathogenesis

This occurs from a combination of insulin deficiency and counter-regulatory hormone excess with the insulin present stopping ketone production but in insufficient quantities to prevent worsening hyperglycaemia.

Clinical features

There is normally an insidious onset with several days of ill-health and profound dehydration at presentation (equivalent to a 9–10 L deficit).

Confusion is not uncommon, nor is coma (especially once serum osmolality >440) and occasionally fits occur. Gastroparesis and associated vomiting with gastric erosions and subsequent haematemesis can occur. These patients are also hypercoagulable, and venous thromboses and cerebrovascular events are important to exclude.

Management

Initial investigation and treatment is the same as for ketoacidosis with fluid, electrolyte and insulin replacement, although there are a few important exceptions as these are older patients:

- The fluid regime should be less rapid/vigorous. Central venous access for monitoring is more often required. e.g. 1 L of 0.9% saline over the first hour, 1 L 2 hourly for the next 2 h, then 1 L 4–6 hourly.
- If hypernatraemic (serum sodium >155 mmol/L) consider 0.45% saline, rather than 0.9% although this may increase the risk of cerebral oedema if serum sodium or osmolality is altered too rapidly as it has a mortality as high as 70%.
- Prophylactic s/c heparin should be considered, although recent evidence suggests more formal anticoagulation carries a high risk of upper gastrointestinal bleeding.
- A gentler insulin regime is needed with 3–6 units/h of soluble insulin i/v aiming to reduce the blood glucose by a maximum of 5 mmol/h to avoid precipitating cerebral oedema.
- A more aggressive use of i/v antibiotics is encouraged.

Subsequent treatment

Continue i/v fluids and insulin for at least 24 h after initial stabilization and then convert to maintenance therapy such as s/c insulin or oral hypoglycaemic agents. Patient education to avoid further episodes is also advisable.

Hypoglycaemia

This complication of the treatment of diabetes should be excluded in any unconscious or fitting patient. If prolonged it can result in death. Most insulin-treated patients can expect to experience hypoglycaemic episodes at some time, with up to 1/7 having a more severe episode each year and 3% suffering recurrent episodes. The 25% of people on long term insulin who lose their hypoglycaemic awareness are of particular concern. Nocturnal hypoglycaemic episodes with a hyperglycaemic response the next morning (due to increased counter-regulatory hormones – the Somogyi phenomenon), which tend to occur in younger insulin-treated patients, should not be forgotten and may only present with morning headaches or a drunken feeling.

Diagnosis

This is a biochemical diagnosis from a blood glucose <2.5 mmol/L but is often first picked up by the patient, their family, or their doctor from the clinical features below. Saving serum before treatment for blood glucose, insulin, and C-peptide levels will confirm the diagnosis and may help determine the cause.

Pathogenesis

Hypoglycaemia results from an imbalance between glucose supply, glucose utilization, and insulin levels resulting in more insulin than is needed at that time. A reduced glucose supply occurs when a meal or snack is missed, or as a late effect of alcohol. It can also be due to delayed gastric emptying with autonomic neuropathy or be associated with coeliac disease, Addison's disease, or an acute illness, such as gastroenteritis. Increased utilization occurs with exercise and high insulin levels mostly with sulfonylurea or exogenous insulin therapy. The net result of this imbalance is hypoglycaemia.

Human insulins have a slightly faster onset of action and a shorter duration of action than their animal predecessors, and a lot of patients report alterations in hypoglycaemic awareness when they switch from one to the other. Even so, no definite evidence of specific hypoglycaemic alterations due to human insulin itself have been reported.

Sulfonylurea therapy can cause hypoglycaemia due to β cell stimulation. This is most commonly seen from *glibenclamide*, especially in the elderly and those with reduced renal excreting ability, but can occur in anyone who takes this therapy and fasts, especially with longer acting agents such as *chlorpropamide*.

The biguanide *metformin* and the α-glucosidase inhibitor *acarbose* are unlikely to precipitate hypoglycaemia, but insulin-sensitizing

Signs and symptoms of hypoglycaemia

Autonomic

- sweating
- pallor
- anxiety
- nausea
- tremor
- shivering
- palpitations
- tachycardia

Neuroglycopaenia

- confusion
- tiredness
- lack of concentration
- headache
- dizziness
- altered speech
- incoordination
- drowsiness
- aggression
- coma

agents such as the ACEIs and newer agents such as the thiazolidinediones (e.g. *rosiglitazone*) may do so.

Clinical features

The features of hypoglycaemia can be divided into two main groups: autonomic symptoms and neuroglycopenic symptoms, as shown on p. 915. The autonomic symptoms usually occur first (when the blood glucose <3.6 mmol/L), but some drugs such as the non-selective β-blockers and alcohol may mask these with neuroglycopenia (at blood glucose <2.6 mmol/L) then causing confusion with no warning. Some patients lose these predominantly autonomic warning symptoms and are therefore at higher risk of injury.

Management

In the conscious patient, oral carbohydrate (20–30 g) is often sufficient to resolve the problem. This can be given as 5–6 dextrosol tablets or as a glass of milk or orange juice. Having raised the sugar rapidly then give something to maintain a normal blood glucose level such as two digestive biscuits. In the confused patient a buccal gel (e.g. hypostop, a 30% glucose gel) is an alternative although this should not be used in the unconscious patient as there is a risk of aspiration.

In the unconscious patient, once a blood sample has been taken for glucose estimation, treat with 25–50 mL of 50% dextrose i/v or 1 mg of i/m or deep s/c glucagon. Glucagon mobilizes glycogen from the liver and will not work if given repeatedly or in starved patients with no glycogen stores. In this situation or if prolonged treatment is needed, i/v glucose is better (50% initially then 10%).

Subsequent management

Having corrected the acute event determine why it happened and, if possible, alter treatment or lifestyle to stop it recurring. Extreme exercise may require an alteration in insulin doses for 24 h, and alcohol causes not only initial hyperglycaemia but also a degree of hypoglycaemia 3–6 h after ingestion, and may alter insulin requirements the next morning. Education to avoid precipitating hypoglycaemic episodes in these situations is advisable. Recurrent hypoglycaemic events may also herald a deterioration in renal or liver function and these should be excluded.

Further reading

Amiel SA, Tamborlane WV, Sherwin RS. Defective glucose counterregulation after strict glycaemic control of insulin-dependent DM. *New England Journal of Medicine* 1987; 316: 1376–1384.

Cranston ICP, Amiel SA. Hypoglycaemia. In: Leslie RDG, Robbins DC, ed. *Diabetes: Clinical Science and Practice.* Cambridge: Cambridge University Press, 1995: 375–391.

Frier B. Hypoglycaemia in DM. In Pickup J, Williams G, ed. *Textbook of Diabetes*, 2nd edn. Oxford: Blackwell Science, 1997.

Hepburn D, Deary IJ, Frier BM *et al.* Symptoms of acute insulin induced hypoglycaemia in humans with and without IDDM. *Diabetes Care* 1991; 14: 949–957.

Krentz AJ, Nattrass M. Acute metabolic complications of DM: diabetic ketoacidosis, hyperosmolar non-ketotic syndrome and lactic acidosis. In Pickup J, Williams G, ed. *Textbook of Diabetes*, 2nd edn. Oxford: Blackwell Science, 1997: 39.1–23.

Lebovitz HE. Diabetic ketoacidosis. *Lancet* 1995; 345: 767–772.

Part XII
Lipids and hyperlipidaemia

Chapter 115

Lipids and coronary heart disease

Physiology

The two main circulating lipids, triglycerides and cholesterol, are bound with phospholipid and lipoproteins to make them more water soluble for transportation throughout the body. The apoproteins on the surface of these soluble masses help the body to recognize each of the different transport complexes:

- *Chylomicrons* Contain 85% triglycerides and 4% cholesterol. Made in the mucosa of the small intestine, they are broken down in the liver and peripheral tissues by lipoprotein lipase. Initially they contain apoprotein B-48 (apo B-48) but also acquire apo E and apo C-II from circulating HDL. Following metabolism by lipoprotein lipase in capillary endothelial cells, which is activated by apo C-II, chylomicron remnants are then removed by specific apo B and apo E receptors in the liver.
- *Very low density lipoproteins (VLDL)* Contain 50% triglyceride, 15% cholesterol, and 18% phospholipid. They are the main carrier of triglycerides in circulation. Made with triglycerides synthesized in the liver, they also contain apo B-100 and apo E. VLDL are broken down by lipoprotein lipase in peripheral tissue to give IDL, or other remnants which are removed by the liver.
- *Intermediate density lipoproteins (IDL)* These VLDL remnants contain mostly cholesterol and phospholipid and are either removed by the liver or metabolized to form LDL.
- *Low density lipoproteins (LDL)* Contain 45% cholesterol, 10% triglycerides, and 20% phospholipid. LDL has apo B-100 in its surface and transports most of the cholesterol in circulation. The liver has specific LDL receptors to extract it from the circulation. Half of the body's circulating LDL is removed from the plasma each day, mostly by the liver. Small dense or oxidized LDL (usually only 15% of the LDL pool) is not so easily recognized by these receptors and a scavenger pathway in macrophages and liver sinusoidal endothelial cells removes these via an acetyl-LDL receptor. Accumulation of oxidized LDL in macrophages produces the foam cells seen in atheromatous plaques.
- *High density lipoproteins (HDL)* Made in the liver and gut contain 17% cholesterol, 4% triglycerides, and 24% phospholipid. HDL transports 20–50% of circulating cholesterol.

In practice, patients are managed by their levels of cholesterol (total, LDL, HDL) and triglycerides. Elevated total or LDL cholesterol with normal triglycerides is *hypercholesterolaemia*. Isolated elevation of

Lipid measurements

Measurements should not be taken during an acute illness or during periods of rapid weight loss as these artificially lower the results. This is particularly important from 24 h after a MI for up to 6 weeks (less if thrombolysed), as during this time the levels of total and LDL cholesterol may be falsely reduced.

Pregnancy or recent weight gain will increase lipid levels. Following rapid weight gain or weight loss, leave at least a month before reassessing lipid levels.

Full lipid profile

gives:

- total cholesterol
- HDL cholesterol
- LDL cholesterol
- triglycerides.

This needs to be a fasting sample, preferably after a 12 h overnight fast (water is allowed). If non-fasting, only total and HDL cholesterol measurements are accurate. Triglycerides rise postprandially and LDL is usually calculated with the formula below, so is inaccurate if not fasting. It is also invalid if triglycerides are over 4.5 mmol/L:

LDL (in mmol/l) = total cholesterol – HDL – 0.45(triglycerides)

The use of total cholesterol alone can be misleading as isolated HDL elevation can increase the value. Use of a total:HDL or an LDL : HDL ratio is preferred, especially in women and people with diabetes mellitus. Most risk calculation tables, such as the New Zealand tables, now use these ratios rather than total values alone.

Variations between assay method and different samples should not lead to more than a 3% variation, but more than one measurement should be used to decide on initial pharmacological intervention.

Conversion factors

American studies are often given in mg/dL rather than the SI units of mmol/L. A conversion of mmol/L × 38.8 gives mg/dL of cholesterol and mmol/L x 88.5 gives mg/dL of triglycerides.

triglyceride is *hypertriglyceridemia* and both together is *combined or mixed hyperlipidaemia.*

There is a direct linear relationship between hypercholesterolaemia and coronary heart disease (CHD). A man with a total cholesterol of 6.5 mmol/l has double the risk of CHD of a man with a total cholesterol of 5.2 mmol/l, and half the risk of a man with a cholesterol of 7.8 mmol/l. Intervention studies show that reductions in total and LDL cholesterol reduce coronary and cerebrovascular events as well as mortality.

HDL cholesterol has an inverse relationship with CHD, i.e. increased levels are beneficial. A low HDL cholesterol may be due to lack of physical exercise, obesity, or the presence of hypertriglyceridaemia, and occurs in smokers. Whether isolated hypertriglyceridaemia causes vascular disease is still debated.

Mixed hyperlipidaemia is clearly associated with CHD. The Helsinki Heart study showed a fourfold greater risk of cardiac events if the LDL : HDL ratio was >5.0 and the triglycerides >2.3 mmol/L compared to those with lower levels of triglyceride. Hypertriglyceridaemia is associated with a low HDL cholesterol as well as small dense LDL particles. The aim of keeping triglycerides <1.5 mmol/L is to indirectly increase the HDL cholesterol as well as for the small dense LDL to revert to the more benign, less dense LDL. Small dense LDL has a lower binding affinity for the LDL receptor, resulting in a longer half-life as well as greater susceptibility to oxidation.

Pathogenesis

Hyperlipidaemia is due to a combination of genetic factors and dietary intake, and as secondary to other conditions. It is a major risk factor for atherosclerosis.

- *Primary hyperlipidaemias* Usually genetically determined
- *Secondary hyperlipidaemias* Due to a combination of other diseases, drugs, and dietary anomalies.

Atherosclerosis

In atherosclerosis subintimal plaques start in medium-sized blood vessel walls when LDL cholesterol accumulates. A cholesterol-rich necrotic core surrounded by smooth muscle cells and fibrous tissue then develops. These plaques can calcify. If the surface of the plaques ulcerates, thrombosis occurs which can obliterate the lumen of a blood vessel.

Plaques may result from diffusion of elevated LDL cholesterol, a qualitative abnormality of LDL cholesterol, endothelial cell damage, or a combination of these. Endothelial cell damage may be due to:

- physical trauma, e.g. with hypertension
- toxins, e.g. tobacco or alcohol
- low grade infection or inflammation, e.g. chlamydia
- immune complex damage.

CHD/atherosclerosis risk factors

Male sex, increasing age and a positive family history are all linked with a greater risk for atherosclerosis, but they are beyond our control. Several modifiable risk factors are, however, recognized:

- *Cigarette smoking* >10 cigarettes/day increase the CHD odds ratio by 6.7-fold, while stopping smoking reduces risk of myocardial infarct (MI) by 50–70% within 5 years.
- *Hypertension* Increases the CHD odds ratio by 2.7-fold. Each 1 mmHg drop in diastolic blood pressure reduces the MI risk by 2–3%. But remember aspirin reduces MI risk by 33%.
- *Diabetes mellitus* (see p. 858).
- *Hyperlipidaemia* A 10% fall in total cholesterol results in a 25% decrease in CHD risk, and plaque regression with reducing lipids is well documented.
- *Other* Less strongly associated factors include type A personality, hyperuricaemia, lack of exercise/sedentary lifestyle, and obesity.

Assessment of CHD risk

Risk assessment tables for CHD are now available such as the Sheffield tables, the New Zealand tables, and the Joint British Societies Coronary Risk Prediction Chart. These calculate the likelihood of the patient's absolute risk of CHD over a period of years and/or the individual's relative risk assuming CHD is not present at this time. The data used for assessment include sex, age, blood pressure, presence of left ventricular hypertrophy, smoking, diabetes mellitus, and the measured values of total cholesterol, HDL cholesterol, or the ratio of total : HDL cholesterol. The tables give a prediction which is useful for estimating the need for treatment.

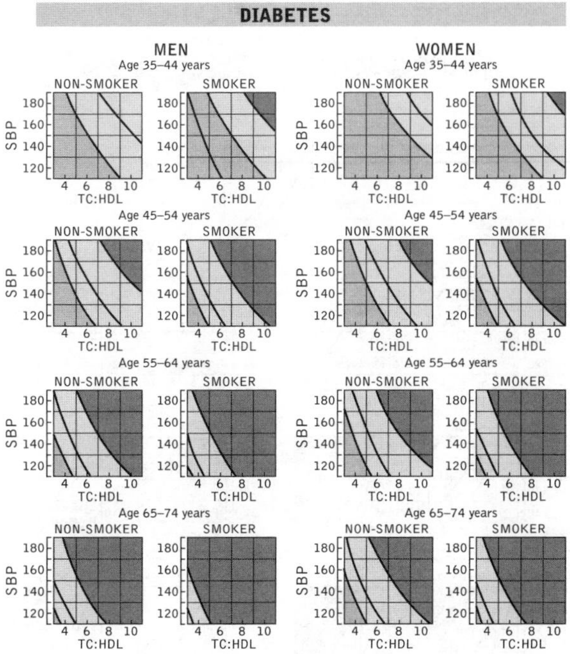

How to use the Coronary Risk Prediction Chart for Primary Prevention

These charts are for estimating coronary heart disease (CHD) risk (non fatal MI and coronary death) for individuals who have not developed symptomatic CHD or other major atherosclerotic disease.

The use of these charts is not appropriate for patients who have existing disease which already puts them at high risk. Such diseases are:

- CHD or other major atherosclerotic disease
- Familial hypercholesterolaemia or other inherited dyslipidaemia
- Established hypertension (systolic BP > 160 mmHg and/or diastolic BP > 100 mmHg) or associated target organ damage
- Diabetes mellitus with associated target organ damage
- Renal dysfunction

- To estimate an individuals absolute 10 year risk of developing CHD find the table for their gender, diabetes (yes/no), smoking status (smoker/non smoker) and age. Within this square define the level

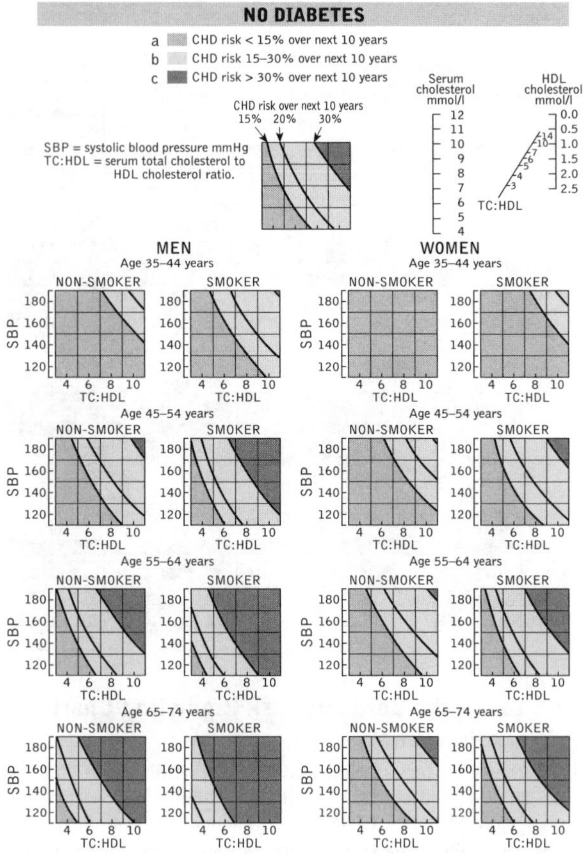

Fig. 115.1 Joint British Societies Coronary Risk Prediction Chart. Reproduced with permission.

of risk according to systolic blood pressure and the ratio of total cholesterol to HDL cholesterol. If there is no HDL cholesterol result then assume this is 1.0 mmol/l and then the lipid scale can be used for total cholesterol alone.

- High risk individuals are defined as those whose 10 year CHD risk exceeds 15% (equivalent to a *cardiovascular* risk of 20% over the same period). As a minimum those at highest risk (≥ 30% c) should be targeted and treated now, and as resources allow others with a risk of > 15% (b) should be progressively targeted.

- Smoking status should reflect lifetime exposure to tobacco and not simply tobacco use at the time of risk assessment.
- The initial blood pressure and the first random (non fasting) total cholesterol and HDL cholesterol can be used to estimate an individuals risk. However, the decision on using drug therapy should be based on repeat risk factor measurements over a period of time. The chart should not be used to estimate risk after treatment of hyperlipidaemia or blood pressure has been initiated.
- CHD risk is higher than indicated in the charts for
  - Those wih a family history of premature CHD (men <55 years and women <65 years) which increases the risk by a factor of approximately 1.5.
  - Those with raised triglyceride levels.
  - Those who are not diabetic but have impaired glucose tolerance.
  - Women with premature menopause.
  - As the person approaches the next age category. As risk increases exponentially with age the risk will be closer to the higher decennium for the last four years of each decade.
- In ethnic minorities the risk chart should be used with caution as it has not been validated in these populations.
- The estimates of CHD risk from the chart are based on groups of people and in managing an *individual* the physician also has to use clinical judgement in deciding how intensively to intervene on lifestyle and whether or not to use drug therapies.
- An individual can be shown on the chart the direction in which the risk of CHD can be reduced by changing smoking status, blood pressure or cholesterol.

Individuals at risk with hyperlipidaemia

- those with premature CHD (<55 years in men, <65 years in women)
- those with signs of other atherosclerotic disease (e.g. PVD, cerebrovascular disease)
- those with diabetes mellitus
- those with signs of insulin resistance such as acanthosis nigricans
- postmenopausal women not on HRT
- those with a high alcohol intake (women >14 units/week, men >21)
- those with a family history of hyperlipidaemia
- those with a family history of early CHD or other atherosclerotic disease
- those with known secondary causes of hyperlipidaemia (drugs and diseases as in p. 942).

Chapter 116
Primary hyperlipidaemias

Background

There are two distinct elements in the diagnosis of primary hyperlipidaemias: the *genotype* and the *phenotype.* At present the family history and the phenotypic findings in other family members are used as a surrogate for a genetic diagnosis. DNA-based technology currently employed in research may in the future become more clinically useful not just for initial diagnosis but also for family screening.

Polygenic hypercholesterolaemia

This is the most common cause of isolated hypercholesterolaemia. LDL clearance appears to be reduced by a variety of mechanisms, and the E4 allele of apo E is a common association. Patients do not have the characteristic xanthelasmata or extensor tendon deposits seen in familial hyperlipidaemia. It is usually diagnosed by primary screening programmes or when investigating some manifestation of atherosclerosis.

Familial hypercholesterolaemia

FH is an autosomal dominant disorder. Its gene frequency is 1 in 500 in western Europe and North America. In FH, hypercholesterolaemia is due to an increase in LDL cholesterol because of an LDL receptor mutation (on the short arm of chromosome 19) reducing the number of high affinity LDL receptors by up to 50%, so reducing LDL clearance. More than 300 mutations have so far been described. These can lead to several situations causing elevation of circulating LDL cholesterol by:

- not producing any LDL receptors
- failure of LDL receptors to move to the cell surface
- abnormal binding of the receptor to LDL
- inability to adequately internalize LDL for metabolism

Patients with FH have premature CHD (i.e. men <55 years old, women <65 years old) and must be treated vigorously as their standardized mortality ratio is at least nine times greater than normal.

Clinical characterization

- Total cholesterol >7.8 mmol/L (> 15 in homozygotes), LDL high from birth.
- Normal triglycerides.
- Clinical stigmata: xanthelasmic deposits around the eyes and on tendons (i.e. fingers, hands, elbow, knee, and the Achilles tendon). Tendon xanthoma is more specific for FH than arcus or xanthelasma. 7% of heterozygote FH (aged >19 years of age) have tendon xanthomas, although 75% of their parents exhibit this feature with separate studies suggesting 75% of homozygous men and 72% of women have tendon xanthomas.
- Early onset of a corneal arcus (in the 30–40 year age group).
- Achilles tendinitis may be the first clue to the presence of this condition in childhood.
- Homozygotes can have CHD presenting in childhood and certainly before the age of 30.
- Heterozygotes usually present after 30 years of age.
- A strong case can be made for FH where there may not be clinical stigmata but there is a strong family history and first degree relatives with early onset CHD, e.g. before 50 years of age.

It is estimated that more than half of heterozygous FH patients will die from CHD before reaching 60 years of age if left untreated and that

1 in 20 of those under 60 years old surviving an MI are FH heterozygotes. FH patients need to have their families investigated and the homozygous FH may need non-pharmacological therapies such as plasmapheresis or surgical procedures such as ileal bypass, portocaval shunts, or liver transplantation. These treatments are not readily available and, along with pharmacological treatments, may be superseded by gene therapy in the future.

Screening at present is by measurement of blood lipids and looking for clinical stigmata or signs. It should involve immediate family and can be done at any age. In newborn infants cord blood has been used to look at LDL cholesterol levels. Between the ages of 1 and 16 years heterozygotes will have a twofold higher cholesterol than unaffected siblings, so standard lipid profiles can be used. Over 16 years of age, use a full fasting lipid profile and clinical examination.

Familial defective apolipoprotein B-100

FDB is an autosomal dominant trait where a genetic defect of apo B-100 results in the delayed clearance of cholesterol. It is due to a single point mutation on apo B (e.g. Arg 3500→Gln). This condition affects 1/600 people. All lipids originating from the liver are bound to apo B-100. Two different mutations have also been described which result in increased levels of an LDL more prone to oxidation, causing delayed receptor pathway clearance of LDL which overloads the scavenger pathways so increasing circulating cholesterol levels.

The diagnosis is made on slowly rising cholesterol levels and DNA studies for the point mutation. The management is similar to that of FH. 2% of cases previously described as FH are estimated to be due to FDB. Protease inhibitors have been reported to exacerbate this condition which may present with eruptive xanthomata.

Familial hypertriglyceridaemia

This affects up to 1/300 people, often as an autosomal dominant trait with elevated VLDL levels, and is frequently accompanied by hypercholesterolaemia. Eruptive xanthomata (red and painful) and lipaemia retinalis can accompany massive triglyceridaemia, as can pancreatitis. Exacerbating factors include alcohol and drugs such as thiazide diuretics, glucocorticoids, and the oral contraceptive pill. Adherence to a low-fat, alcohol-free diet with weight reduction usually helps.

Rare genetic hypertriglyceridaemias

Two rare but important familial causes of gross hypertriglyceridaemia are *lipoprotein lipase deficiency* and *apolipoprotein C-II deficiency*. Both are autosomal recessive conditions which present in childhood and are characterized by the presence of hyperchylomicronaemia.

- *Lipoprotein lipase* the enzyme needed to metabolize chylomicrons; complete absence of this enzyme or production of an inactive form are both recognized defects. Usually people are heterozygous, but a much rarer and more severe homozygous form is also seen.
- *Apo C-II* Needed for the activation of lipoprotein lipase, and its deficiency results in hyperchylomicronaemia. Patients do not have premature CHD but can have recurrent abdominal pain due to pancreatitis.

Familial combined hyperlipidaemia

FCHL is a definite risk factor for CHD. It occurs in 1/250 people. Patients usually present around 10 years later than those with FH. The aetiology is not yet known. It is the most common type of inherited dyslipidaemia, estimated to cause 10% of cases of premature CHD. It has no unique clinical manifestations and the diagnosis is based on raised lipids (greater than 95th centile for age) and a family history of premature CHD in first degree relatives.

Familial dysbetalipoproteinaemia

Also known as *type III hyperlipidaemia* or *broad beta disease.* It is associated with early onset CHD. It is an uncommon disorder affecting 0.01–0.04% of people, giving elevated IDL and chylomicron remnants. A characteristic clinical feature is the presence of *palmar striae xanthoma. Tuberous xanthomata,* found over the tuberosities of the elbows and knees, may also be present. The xanthomata of this familial disease can also be found on pressure areas, e.g. heels. In this condition, there is accumulation of IDL. Apo E is a constituent lipoprotein of IDL which has three genetically determined isoforms resulting in the apo E phenotypes E_2, E_3 and E_4. E_3/E_3 occurs in 55% of people, E_2/E_2 occurs in 1%. E_2 has the lowest binding affinity to the apo E receptors and is therefore cleared from serum most slowly. Apo E_4 has the greatest affinity and is more rapidly cleared. Patients with familial dysbetalipoproteinaemia are phenotype E_2/E_2.

Rare familial mixed dyslipidaemias

These should be considered in any patient with unexplained neurology, organomegaly, or corneal opacities.

Two inborn metabolic disorders associated with atherosclerosis are:

- *Apolipoprotein A1-CIII deficiency* Should be suspected if hyperlipidaemia is corrected within 24 h of infusing 500 mL of normal fresh frozen plasma.

  Familial lecithin : cholesterol acyltransferase (LCAT) deficiency In this recessively inherited disorder an enzyme necessary for intravascular lipoprotein metabolism is deficient resulting in elevated cholesterol and triglycerides. Clinically corneal lipid deposits result in visual disturbances and renal deposits in glomerular damage, proteinuria, and often renal failure.

The following disorders are not linked to the occurrence of premature atheroma formation:

- *Tangier disease* (analphalipoproteinaemia or familial alphalipoprotein deficiency) In this autosomal recessive condition apo A-I, which is found on HDL, is deficient. HDL levels are low, as is cholesterol, while triglycerides are normal or high. Cholesterol accumulation gives enlarged orange-coloured tonsils, hepatosplenomegaly, polyneuropathy, and corneal opacities.
- *Fish eye disease* A rare disorder from northern Sweden with high VLDL levels, low HDL and a triglycerides-rich LDL. As well as hypertriglyceridaemia, dense corneal opacities occur giving visual impairment.
- *Abetalipoproteinaemia* Results in fat accumulation due to failure of apo B-100 production. Cholesterol levels are low with no LDL and VLDL in many cases which results in fat accumulation in the gut and nerves. Vitamin E injections may prevent some of the neurological abnormalities observed (ataxia, nystagmus, dysarthria, and motor + sensory neuropathies) but usually not the retinitis pigmentosa and acanthocytes which also feature.
- *Hypobetalipoproteinaemia* This autosomal dominantly inherited condition gives a total cholesterol of 1–4 mmol/L and can be associated with organomegaly and neurological changes in middle age due to fat deposition and abnormal red cell morphology. The homozygotic state is similar to abetalipoproteinaemia.
- *Hyperalphalipoproteinaemia* or HDL hyperlipoproteinaemia Results in mildly elevated HDL and total cholesterol; and may

be beneficial. No treatment is needed but don't forget this can also occur with exercise, exogenous oestrogen, phenytoin and phenobarbitone use, or from alcohol.

Chapter 117
Secondary hyperlipidaemias

Background

Secondary dyslipidaemias are relatively common, accounting for 10–20% of hyperlipidaemic adults. These can give a mixed hyperlipidaemia or a lone increase in cholesterol or triglycerides. There are multiple causes and treatment is based upon managing the primary disease before making a further decision on the raised lipids. Often more than one cause is apparent in secondary hyperlipidaemias.

Causes

Include those below and in Table 117.1.

- *Diet* Due to excessive consumption of saturated fats and carbohydrate. Anorexia nervosa can also cause hypercholesterolaemia as a strict low fat, low calorie diet results in reduced cholesterol and bile acid turnover so increased circulating levels.
- *Obesity* (see p. 741)
- *Diabetes mellitus* (see p. 862)
- *Hypothyroidism* Said to occur in 4% of those with hyperlipidaemia and in a compensated form in a further 10%. Usually resulting in hypercholesterolaemia with a total cholesterol of 9–20 mmol/L. It also worsens genetic dyslipidaemias due to decreased synthesis of hepatic LDL receptors.
- *Chronic renal disease* Decreasing creatinine clearance is accompanied by hypertriglyceridaemia and a reduction in HDL cholesterol. Proteinuria, as seen in the nephrotic syndrome, is associated with hypercholesterolaemia. Peritoneal dialysis may increase gut glucose load and worsen hypertriglyceridaemia. Remember cyclosporin increases LDL.
- *Liver disease* Especially with cholestasis which gives hypercholesterolamia with an abnormal LDL cholesterol. Primary biliary cirrhosis may elevate total cholesterol to >12 mmol/L. Severe hepatocellular damage may lower LDL cholesterol by decreasing production of its component parts and the enzymes which metabolize it.
- *Cushing's syndrome* Glucocorticoids increase VLDL production and give hypertriglyceridaemia. The associated weight gain and glucose intolerance can make this effect more pronounced.

Table 117.1 Potential causes of secondary hyperlipidaemia

Elevated LDL cholesterol	Elevated triglycerides	Reduced HDL cholesterol
Diet (high saturated fats, high calories, anorexia)	Diet (weight gain + excess alcohol)	Diet (some low fat diets)
Drugs (glucocorticoids, thiazide + loop diuretics, cyclosporine)	Drugs (glucocorticoids, ß-blockers, oestrogens, isotretinoin)	Drugs (anabolic steroids, tobacco, beta adrenergic blockers)
Hypothyroidism	Hypothyroidism	Type 2 diabetes
Nephrotic syndrome	Type 2 diabetes	Insulin resistance syndromes/ obesity
Chronic liver disease	Insulin resistance syndromes	Chronic renal failure
Cholestasis + biliary obstruction	Cushing's syndrome	
Pregnancy	Chronic renal failure	
	Peritoneal dialysis	
	Pregnancy	

- *Lipodystrophies* A very rare group of disorders, hallmark of which is regional, partial or generalized fat loss associated with hyperlipidaemia, especially unusually raised triglyceride. Also associated with glucose intolerance.
- *Glycogen storage diseases* Can have elevated lipids (triglyceride, cholesterol, and mixed hyperlipidaemia) quite commonly, but usually only in type I (Von Gierke's disease), type III (Forbes' disease), and type IV (Hers' disease).
- *Gout* Hypertriglyceridaemia occurs in about one-third of those with gout. Alcohol excess plays a part but it is not the sole cause.
- *Drugs* Medications commonly implicated are:
  - β-blockers, especially the non cardioselective ones
  - thiazide diuretics
  - exogenous oestrogens
  - anabolic steroids
  - glucocorticoids
  - isotretinoin
  - protease inhibitors (said to cause hyperlipidaemia in 50% after 10 months of treatment) (p. 770)
- *Excessive alcohol consumption* There is a J-shaped relationship between alcohol consumption and CHD. The ideal seems to be 2–3 units/day, maximum 14 units/week in women, 21 units/week in men.
- *Pregnancy* Cholesterol rises throughout pregnancy, mostly in the second trimester. Triglycerides also rise, but in the final trimester and mostly in those with underlying genetic abnormalities. Both return to normal by 6 weeks post partum.

Chapter 118

Management of dyslipidaemia

Background

The emphasis will depend on the cause of the hyperlipidaemia and is aimed at reducing cardiovascular, peripheral vascular, and cerebrovascular risk. There are now recommended target values when treating patients.

Primary and secondary prevention

It is universally accepted that tackling hypercholesterolaemia in secondary prevention works. We now have solid evidence to support this, especially in the context of CHD, where a 10% fall in total cholesterol is estimated to result in a 25% decrease in CHD risk. Fatty lesion regression has also been clearly demonstrated. The gain is within 2 years of lowering the cholesterol, whether by diet or a combination of diet and drugs.

Tackling cholesterol in primary prevention is controversial. There have been primary prevention trials which show benefit from lowering cholesterol. The financial burden of this has to be confronted. An approach to this is to use the available risk assessment tables (p. 927). An example would be to definitely treat if the risk of CHD is greater than 3% per annum after a trial of dietary intervention. It has been argued that we should aim to treat if the risk is 1.5% per annum, but presently the economic argument against this holds sway.

Specific interventions

Dietary advice

All patients should see a dietitian. Fats should constitute <30% of energy consumed and saturated fats must be <30% of the total fat content. Vegetable and marine mono- and polyunsaturated fats should be increased in the diet. Total dietary cholesterol should not exceed 300 mg per day. Foods advocated include fresh fruit and vegetables, which are important sources of antioxidants. Four months should be given to see if dietary manipulation will work. It is unusual to see more than a 25% fall in cholesterol from dietary measures.

Alcohol should be <14 units/week for a woman and < 21 units/week for a man.

Weight control

All overweight patients must be encouraged to lose weight. Weight reduction is closely attuned to dietary advice and physical exercise. Most weight is lost in the first 4 months of a regimen. A 10 kg weight loss in an obese subject can reduce LDL cholesterol by 7% and increases HDL cholesterol by 13%.

Physical activity

Physical activity, especially aerobic exercise, is recommended. This should involve becoming breathless and be performed for 30–40 min at least 3–5 times per week. Acute exercise will transiently change lipoprotein levels and increase lipoprotein lipase activity. These effects becomes more permanent with regular training. Triglyceride levels fall, HDL cholesterol levels rise, especially the HDL_2 subfraction with more vigorous exercise, and LDL cholesterol is less dense and atherogenic. The alteration seen is dose dependent with increasing exercise and a 20% alteration in each variable is achievable after 6 weeks.

Modification of other risk factors

Other risk factors such as hypertension, smoking, and diabetes mellitus must be addressed.

Drug therapy

Numerous agents can be used for both primary and secondary prevention in patients in whom diet has been ineffective.

HMG CoA reductase inhibitors (statins)

- *Indications* High LDL or VLDL ie. primary hypercholesterolaemia, heterozygous + homozygous FH, mixed hyperlipidaemia. These medications are not licensed for use in children and should be used with caution in women of childbearing age because of insufficient safety data in pregnancy and potential teratogenicity. The medication should be stopped for at least 3 months before pregnancy is planned. Women must be warned about pregnancy when on these drugs.
- *Mechanism of action* Competitive inhibition of 3-hydroxy-3-methylglutaryl coenzyme A (HMG CoA) which is the rate-limiting enzyme in cholesterol synthesis. Its activation increases hepatocyte LDL receptor numbers and reduces VLDL synthesis while enhancing its hepatic clearance.
- *Side-effects* Although these drugs are known to cause headaches, nausea, and some abdominal discomfort, the main concerns are a hepatitis-like picture and myositis. Liver function tests and creatine kinase should be measured before they are prescribed and used with caution in those with an excessive alcohol intake. It is recommended that the medications should be discontinued if the liver enzymes aspartate transaminase (AST) and/or alanine transaminase (ALT) show more than a 2–3-fold elevation above the upper limit of normal. Liver function tests should therefore be checked 3–4 monthly initially and at least annually in the long term. Myositis is rare and tends to occur when prescribed with other medications, e.g. cyclosporin, fibrates, or when renal impairment or untreated hypothyroidism are present. Clinically there is a picture of swollen tender muscles and creatine kinase being greater than 10 times the upper limit of normal. Rhabdomyolysis is even rarer, but led to the withdrawal of cerivastatin.
- *Interactions* All statins interact with *cyclosporin* and *nicotinic acid* and are used with caution with *fibrates. Warfarin* interacts with atorvastatin and simvastatin. *Erythromycin* interacts with atorvastatin, fluvastatin, pravastatin and simvastatin. *Digoxin* interacts with atorvastatin and simvastatin. *Rifampicin* interacts with fluvastatin and pravastatin. Atorvastatin may also interact with the *oral contraceptive pill, antacids* and some *antifungals.*

Table 118.1 Comparative lipid lowering profile of statins

Statin	% fall in LDL_c	% fall in triglycerides	% rise in HDL_c
Atorvastatin	38–54	13–32	3–7
Fluvastatin	17–34	8–12	3–6
Pravastatin	18–34	5–13	5–8
Simvastatin	28–48	12–38	8–12

- *Costs* In 1992 it was estimated that CHD prevention by a cholesterol lowering program using a statin calculated as cost per Quality Adjusted Life Year (QALY) was £400–£550 compared with hip replacement (£1100), coronary artery bypass surgery (£1300), breast screening (£5000), and hospital haemodialysis (£17 500). In the same year (1992) about £500 million was spent in the NHS for CHD, of which more than a half was for inpatient hospital care. In 1997 the Standing Medical Advisory Committee issued guidelines on the use of statins and, based on that advice, Warwickshire Health Authority calculated that it would cost them 20% of their drug budget, some £100 000 per practice, to implement. These costs do not include diagnostic tests as well as time to detect, counsel, and treat the patients. These costs are enormous and are very relevant in the context of limited NHS resources. There is no case against secondary prevention, but screening and primary prevention are economically still a very sensitive issue.

Fibrates

- *Indications* High VLDL, triglycerides, or IDL, i.e. mixed hyperlipidaemias which have not responded adequately to diet or other therapy. These medications are less effective than the statins at lowering cholesterol but better at increasing HDL cholesterol and more effective in lowering triglycerides. Reduce triglycerides by 20–60%, increase HDL by 15–30%, and reduce LDL by 5–25%.
- *Mechanism of action* Alter lipoprotein metabolism to reduce VLDL triglyceride synthesis by increasing lipoprotein lipase activity and LDL-receptor mediated LDL clearance while increasing HDL synthesis. The effect on LDL cholesterol may vary in isolated hypertriglyceridaemia to increase LDL cholesterol.
- *Side-effects* Occasionally cause nausea, anorexia, or diarrhoea and precipitate gallstones (mostly clofibrate). Also pruritus, rashes, hair loss, and impotence. They should not be used in patients with severe liver disease (AST >2–3 times upper limit of normal) and renal dysfunction (creatinine >150 μmol/L) as they are conjugated in the liver prior to excretion by the kidney. Myopathy, although rare, is the main concern, and the risk of this increases if used with statins.
- *Interactions* Use with caution in combination with *statins.* Can enhance the effects of *warfarin* and *antidiabetic agents* and is contraindicated in those on *Orlistat.*

Anion exchange resins (bile acid sequestrants)

- *Indications* High LDL, i.e. hypercholesterolaemia. Although the mainstay of lipid-lowering therapy in the past, these are now best

Table 118.2 Dosage of lipid-lowering drugs

Drug	Dose/day
Statins	
Atorvastatin	10–80 mg
Fluvastatin	20–40 mg
Pravastatin	10–40 mg
Simvastatin	10–80 mg
Fibrates	
Bezafibrate	400–600 mg
Ciprofibrate	100 mg
Clofibrate	50–65 kg, 1.5 g; >65 kg, 2 g
Fenofibrate	200–400 mg
Gemfibrozil	0.9–1.5 g
Anion-exchange resins	
Cholestyramine	12–36 g (in single dose or up to 4× day)
Colestipol hydrochloride	5 g 1–2× day (max 30 g/day)
Nicotinic acid group	
Acipimox	500–750 mg in divided doses
Nicotinic acid	300 mg–6 g in divided doses
Omega-3 fatty acids	
Maxepa	10 g

used as adjuncts when LDL has not fallen enough with a statin alone. They are also the only drugs licensed for use during pregnancy.

- *Mechanism of action* Bind to bile acids in the gut so reducing their enterohepatic circulation and increasing bile acid excretion. This increases hepatocyte cholesterol requirements which increases LDL receptor production so reducing circulating LDL levels. Under optimum conditions, LDL cholesterol can be reduced by 20–30%, triglycerides rise by 10–17%, and HDL increases by 3–5%.
- *Side-effects* These agents remain in the gut, so constipation, bloating, nausea, and abdominal discomfort are not uncommon. Constipation, found in 35–40% of those on these agents, can be helped with bulking laxatives. Less often a bleeding tendency due to vitamin K malabsorption can be seen. These agents can also exacerbate hypertriglyceridaemia but HDL cholesterol is often increased slightly. To reduce the side-effects start with low doses and build up gradually over the next 3–4 weeks while maintaining a good fluid intake.
- *Interactions* These agents can reduce the absorption of *warfarin*, *digoxin*, *β-blockers*, *pravastatin*, *cerivastatin*, *fluvastatin* and *hydrochlorothiazide*. Many other agents such as *simvastatin* have not been checked so to avoid any potential interaction advise patients to take all other drugs 1–3 h *before* or 4–6 h *after* the resin.

Nicotinic acid and acipimox

- *Indication* High LDL, VLDL, IDL, or triglycerides. Nicotinic acid is the most effective medication for increasing HDL-cholesterol. In practice, however, their use is limited by the side-effect profile, especially flushing.
- *Mechanism of action* Work by inhibiting lipolysis in adipocytes so altering fatty acid flux and reducing VLDL synthesis and HDL clearance. VLDL levels fall, as do triglycerides (by 20–50%) and LDL (by 5–25%) while HDL levels rise (by 10–50%).
- *Side-effects* Common, with 30% unable to tolerate these agents. Vasodilatation giving cutaneous/facial flushing occurs in most patients but tends to improve after 2–3 weeks of therapy or if given prostaglandin inhibitors such as aspirin in combination with it. Avoid taking with hot drinks as these increase its absorption and so worsen the flushing. Gastritis is also a common problem but the more severe hepatitis occurs in only 3%. Tachycardias, dry skin, and exacerbations of gout and precipitation of acanthosis nigricans and retinal oedema are also recognized side-effects. *Nicotinic acid* can adversely affect glucose control in diabetes mellitus. *Acipimox*, a nicotinic acid analogue, seems to be less problematic but is also less potent.
- *Interactions* Potentiate the effects of antihypertensive therapies.

Which drug to use when (for diet-resistant dyslipidaemias)

Elevated LDL cholesterol only

- first choice
  - statins
- second choice
  - bile acid sequestrants
  - nicotinic acid
  - fibrates

Combination therapy if the above fail to reduce LDL adequately includes:

- statin + bile acid sequestrant (can give 50% fall in LDL + 10–15% rise in HDL)
- statin + nicotinic acid (can give a 50% fall in LDL + 25–50% rise in HDL)
- nicotinic acid + bile acid sequestrants (can give 35% fall in LDL + 25–50% rise in HDL)
- statin + bile acid sequestrant + nicotinic acid (can give 66% fall in LDL + 25–50% rise in HDL)

Elevated triglycerides only

- first choice
  - fibrates
  - nicotinic acid
- second choice
  - omega-3 fatty acids

All three groups can occasionally be used together if one or two of the above groups are insufficient.

Mixed hyperlipidaemia

- first choice
  - fibrate
  - statin with mixed licence (atorvastatin or simvastatin)
  - nicotinic acid

As with elevated LDL alone, combination therapy may sometimes be useful with emphasis on avoiding side-effects and interactions as above.

Omega-3 fatty acids (e.g. Maxepa)

- *Indications* Severe hypertriglyceridaemia.
- *Mechanism of action* Inhibit the secretion of VLDL due to increased intracellular apo B-100 destruction. Normal patients see both a fall in VLDL and LDL but LDL may rise in the hypertriglyceridaemic individual.
- *Side-effects* As high doses are needed, this is a high calorie load and may increase obesity. More commonly gives nausea and belching.
- *Interactions* None significant.

Further reading

American Diabetes Association. Management of dyslipidaemia in adults with diabetes. *Diabetes Care* 1998; 21(1).

Downs JR, Clearfield M, Wies S *et al.* Primary prevention of acute coronary events with Iovastatin in men and women with average cholesterol levels: results of AFCAP/TexCAPS. Air Force/Texas Coronary Atherosclerosis Prevention Study. *JAMA* 1998; 299: 1615–1621.

Dyslipidaemia Advisory Group, on behalf of the Scientific Committee of the National Heart Foundation of New Zealand. 1996 National Heart Foundation guidelines for the assessment and management of dyslipidaemia. *New Zealand Medical Journal* 1996; 109: 224–232.

International Atherosclerosis Society. *Clinician's Manual on Hyperlipidaemia*, 4th edn. London: Science Press.

Joint British recommendations on prevention of CHD in clinical practice. *Heart* 1998; 80: Supplement 2.

Reckless, JPD. Economic issues in coronary heart disease prevention. *Current Opinion in Lipidology* 1996; 7: 356–362.

Royal College of General Practitioners. *Guidelines for the Management of Hyperlipidaemia in General Practice.* March 1992.

Sacks FM, Pfeffer MA, Moye LA *et al.* The effect of pravastatin on coronary events after myocardial infarction in patients with average cholesterol levels. *New England Journal of Medicine* 1996; 335: 1001–1009.

Scandinavian Simvastatin Survival Study Group. Randomized trial of cholesterol lowering in 4444 patients with CHD: the Scandinavian Simvastatin Survival Study. *Lancet* 1994; 334: 1383–1389.

Shepherd J, Cobbe SM, Ford I *et al.* West of Scotland Coronary Prevention Study Group. Prevention of CHD with pravastatin in men with hypercholesterolaemia. *New England Journal of Medicine* 1995;333: 1301–1307.

Aims of treatment

In general the aim in asymptomatic patients (primary prevention) should be to achieve:

- total cholesterol <5.2 mmol/L
- LDL cholesterol <3.4 mmol/L
- HDL cholesterol >1 mmol/L (total : HDL ratio <4.5)
- triglycerides <1.7 mmol/L

For patients with CHD or post MI (secondary prevention), the target should be:

- total cholesterol of 4–5 mmol/L
- LDL cholesterol <2.5 mmol/L
- triglycerides <1.5 mmol/L

In diabetes mellitus, patients with CHD or PVD, LDL cholesterol should be <2.6 mmol/L and in those without CHD or PVD, the LDL cholesterol should be <3.4 mmol/L.

If these optimal levels are not achievable, at least a 30% fall from pretreatment serum cholesterol concentration is acceptable.

Normal ranges

All values are for serum unless specified otherwise.

Serum	A serum sample is collected in a plain tube, left to permit clotting, then centrifuged and separated.
Plasma	A plasma specimen is collected in a tube containing EDTA or lithium heparin, centrifuged immediately, separated, and usually frozen.

Notes

[a] Lithium heparin tube cold spun immediately.

[b] Serum, cold spun, flash frozen.

[c] Fasting, trasylol tube, lithium heparin, cold spun and flash frozen.

[d] Acid-containing container.

Thyroid function

TSH 0.5–6 mU/L

Total T_4 70–140 nmol/L

Free T_4 9–25 pmol/L

Total T_3 1–3 nmol/L

Free T_3 3.4–7.2 pmol/L

Adrenal and gonadal function

Cortisol (9 a.m.)		280–700 nmol/L
Aldosterone	supine	100–500 pnmol/L
	erect	200–1000 pmol/L
Plasma renin activity	supine	1.1–2.7 pmol/ml/hr
	erect	2.8–4.5 pmol/ml/hr
DHEAS	women	4.9–9.4 μmol/L
	men	2.3–12 μmol/L
Androstenedione		3.8 nmol/L
17-hydroxyprogesterone	follicular	1–20 nmol/L
	luteal	1–20 nmol/L
Oestradiol	follicular	17–260 pmol/L
	mid-cycle	370–1470 pmol/L
	luteal	180–1100 pmol/L
	men	<220 pmol/L
Progesterone	follicular	<3 nmol/L
	luteal	16–77 nmol/L
	men	0–6 nmol/L
Testosterone	men	9–42 nmol/L
	women	1–2.5 nmol/L
Dihydrotestosterone	men	1–2.6 nmol/L
	women	0.3–0.03 nmol/L
Sex hormone binding globulin	women	22–126 nmol/L
	men	18–50 nmol/L

Pituitary hormones

Prolactin		<450 mU/L

Women

FSH	follicular	0.5–5 U/L
	mid-cycle	8–15 U/L
	luteal	2–8 U/L
	post-menopausal	>30 U/L
LH	follicular	3–12 U/L
	mid-cycle	20–80 U/L
	luteal	3–16 U/L
	post-menopausal	>30 U/L

Men

FSH	0.5–5 U/L	
LH	3–8 U/L	
Growth hormone (basal)	0–20 U/L	
IGF-1	20–40 y	9.5–45
	40–60 y	7.5–30
	>60 y	5–22.5
ACTH[a]	10–80 ng/L	

[a] Lithium heparin tube cold spun immediately.

Bone biochemistry

Parathyroid hormone[b]	1–6.1 pmol/L
25 hydroxycholecalciferol[b]	7–30 μg/L
1, 25 dihydroxycholecalciferol[b]	20–50 ng/L
Calcitonin[a]	<0.08 μg/L

[a] Lithium heparin tube cold spun immediately
[b] Serum, cold spun, flash frozen
[c] Fasting, trasylol tube, lithium heparin, cold spun and flash frozen

Plasma gastrointestinal and pancreatic hormones

Insulin (fasting)[c]	5 mU/L
C-peptide (fasting)	0.4 nmol/L
Gastrin[c]	0–40 pmol/L
Glucagon[c]	0–50 pmol/L
Vasoactive intestinal polypeptide (VIP)[c]	0–30 pmol/L
Somatostatin[c]	0–150 pmol/L
Chromogranin[c]	150 pmol/L

Tumour markers

βhCG	0–15 IU/L
Carcinoembryonic antigen (CEA)	0–15 μg/L
Prostate specific antigen (PSA)	0–4 μg/L
Alphafetoprotein	0–10 kU/L

Urinary collections

Urinary free cortisol	0–280 nmol/24 hr	
Urinary catecholamines[d]		0–0.2 μmol/24 hr
	adrenaline	0–1 μmol/24 hr
	noradrenaline	0–0.2 μmol/24 hr
	3-methoxytyramine	0–2 μmol/24 hr
	metadrenaline	0–2 μmol/24 hr
	normetadrenaline	0–3 μmol/24 hr
Urinary 5 hydroxyindoleacetic acid (5HIAA)[d]		
Urinary calcium	1.25–3.75 nmol/L	
Urinary phosphate	7.5–25 μmol/L	
Urinary potassium	20–60 mmol/L	
Urinary sodium	50–125 mmol/L	

Serum A serum sample is collected in a plain tube, left to permit clotting, then centrifuged and separated.

Plasma A plasma specimen is collected in a tube containing EDTA or lithium heparin, centrifuged immediately, separated, and usually frozen.

[d] Acid containing container

Urinary collections

Appendix: Patient support groups and other endocrine organizations

Useful addresses (UK)

Addison's Disease Self Help Group*

Androgen Insensitivity Syndrome Support Group
PO Box 269, Banbury, Oxfordshire
OX15 6YT

CAH Support Group*

Carcinoid Syndrome Support Group*

Conn's Syndrome*

Diabetes UK
10 Queen Anne Street, London, W1M 0BD

The Gender Trust*
PO Box 3192, Brighton, BN1 3WR

Child Growth Foundation*

Kleinfelter's Syndrome Association*

British Menopause Society*

National Osteoporosis Society
PO Box 10, Radstock, Bath, BA3 3YB

National Association for the Relief of Paget's Disease*

Polycystic Ovaries Research and Support Group*

Kallmann's Syndrome
The Pituitary Foundation, PO Box 44,
Bristol BS99 2UB

The Pituitary Foundation
PO Box 44, Bristol BS99 2UB

British Thyroid Foundation
PO Box 97, Weatherby, West Yorkshire,
LS23 6XD

Thyroid Eye Disease Association*

The Turner Syndrome Society*

* Contact Group via Society for Endocrinology, 17/18 The Courtyard, Woodlands, Bradley Stoke, Bristol BS32 4NQ.

Useful addresses overseas

American Diabetes Association
1701 North Beauregard Street,
Alexandria, VA 22311, USA

American Thyroid Association
Montefiore Medical Centre,
111 East 210th Street, Room 311, Bronx,
New York 10467, USA

Australian Pituitary Foundation
PO Box 4792, North Rocks, NSW 2450,
Australia

Australian Thyroid Association
PO Box 186, Westmead, NSW 2134,
Australia

Brain and Pituitary Foundation of America
1360, Ninth Avenue, Suite 210,
San Francisco, USA

The Endocrine Society
4350 East West Highway
Suite 500
Bethesda, Maryland 2084–4426
USA

European Federation of Endocrine Societies
Medizinische Poliklinik der Universitat Wurzburg
Klinische Forschergruppe
Rontgenring 11
D 97070 Wurzburg
Germany

National Osteoporosis Foundation
1150 17th Street NW, Suite 500,
Washington DC 20036, USA

Pituitary Tumour Network Association
16350 Ventura Boulevard, Encino, CA
91436, USA

The Pituitary Foundation
TMP 532. 333 Ceder Street, Newhaven,
CT 06510, USA

Thyroid Foundation of Canada
96, Mack Street, Kingston, Ontario,
Canada

Useful web sites

www.diabetes.org.uk Diabetes UK

www.diabetes.org American Diabetes Association

www.thyroid.org American Thyroid Association

www.nih.gov National Institutes of Health

www.pcosupport.org Polycystic Ovarian Syndrome Association

www.endocrinology.org Society for Endocrinology (UK)

www.euro-endo.org European Federation of Endocrine Societies

www.british-thyroid-association.org British Thyroid Association

www.endo-society.org/pubaffai/factsheet.htm The Endocrine Society

Index